DUDJOM LINGPA'S CHÖD

Dudjom Lingpa's Chöd:

An Ambrosia Ocean of Sublime Explanations

by Pema Lungtok Gyatso

and

The Profound Heart Essence of Saraha

SECOND EDITION

A Terma Revelation of
Heruka Dudjom Lingpa

Translated by
Lama Chönam & Sangye Khandro
Light of Berotsana Translation Group

Berotsana Publications
Ashland, Oregon

Berotsana Publications
P.O. Box 124
Ashland, OR 97520 USA
www.berotsana.org

ISBN-13: 978-0-9888645-2-8

Library of Congress Control Number: 2014941663

Publication Data:
Tripiṭaka. Sūtrapiṭaka. Tantra. Dudjom Lingpa's Chöd. English.
Padma-lung-rtogs rGya-mtsho, gLing-sprul, 1852-?
[Nye rgyud gcod kyi khrid yig gsal bar bkod pa legs bshad bDud rtsi'i rol mtsho zhes bya ba bzhugs so. English] A Clearly Compiled Commentary on the Close Lineage of Chöd entitled An Ambrosia Ocean of Sublime Explanations by Pema Lungtog Gyatso.
bDud 'joms gLing pa, 1835-1904
[Sa ra ha pa'i snying thig zab mo bzhugs so. English.] The Profound Heart Essence of Saraha, Second Edition, a Terma Revelation of Heruka Dudjom Lingpa
Translated by Lama Chönam and Sangye Khandro , Light of Berotsana
pages cm.
Includes bibliographical references and index.
ISBN-13: 978-0-9888645-2-8
I. Chönam, Lama, translator. II. Khandro, Sangye, translator. III. Title: Dudjom Lingpa's Chöd. IV. Padma-lung-rtogs rGya-mtsho. bDud rtsi'i rol mtsho zhes bya ba bzhugs so. English. V. An Ambrosia Ocean of Sublime Explanations.
VI. bDud 'joms gLing pa. Sa ra ha pa'i snying thig zab mo bzhugs so. English.
VII. The Profound Heart Essence of Saraha.

22 21 20 19 18 2 3 4 5

Cover design and art by Christopher Banigan.
Designed and typeset by Gopa & Ted2, Inc.

FSC MIX Paper from responsible sources FSC® C016245 Printed in Canada

Line drawing of Heruka Dudjom Lingpa by Christopher Banigan.

The translation of these two commentaries is dedicated
to the memory of our beloved master
Kyabje Dungsey Thinley Norbu Rinpoche.

Due to Rinpoche's profound kindness, wisdom, and guidance,
we have been able to serve the Dudjom lineage by bringing this terma
and its commentary into the English language.

Until all beings awaken their buddha nature,
may this wisdom continue to prevail!

Contents

Foreword by H.H. Katok Getse Mahāpaṇḍita

༄༅། །ན་མོ་གུ་རུ་མཉྫུ་ཤྲཱི་ཡེ། དེ་ལ་འདིར་ཉེ་བརྒྱུད་གཙོད་ཀྱི་ཁྲིད་ཡིག་གསལ་བར་བཀོད་པ་
ལེགས་བཤད་བདུད་རྩིའི་རོལ་མཚོ་ཞེས་བྱ་བ་གཞུང་བཟང་ཡིད་བཞིན་གྱི་ནོར་བུ་འདི་ལ།
མདོ་སྔགས་བཀའ་གཏེར་མ་ལུས་པའི་ཟབ་གནད་འདུས་པ་མཐའ་ཡས་རྒྱ་མཚོར་ཆུ་ཕྲན་བབས་
པ་བཞིན་ཡིན་ལ། དཔལ་མ་ཧཱ་གུ་རུ་ཧཱུྃ་ཛྲེ་གྲོ་ལོད་སྙིགས་དུས་ཀྱི་གདུལ་བྱའི་དཔལ་མགོན་དུ་
གཟུགས་སྐུར་བཞེངས་པ་སྤྲུལ་པའི་གཏེར་ཆེན་རིག་འཛིན་བདུད་འཇོམས་གླིང་པ་ལ། འཕགས་
ཡུལ་གྲུབ་བརྒྱའི་གཙུག་རྒྱན་གྲུབ་ཆེན་ས་ར་ཧ་པས་འོད་གསལ་དག་པའི་སྣང་ངོར་སྟོན་འཁོར་
དགོངས་པ་དབྱེར་མེད་ཀྱིས་བྱིན་རླབས་སྙན་བརྒྱུད་དུ་བསྩལ་བའི་སྐལ་ལྡན་ཚེ་གཅིག་གིས་འཇའ་
ལུས་ཆོས་སྐུར་གྲོལ་བའི་གདམས་པ། མཁའ་འགྲོའི་ཁ་རླངས་མ་ཡལ་ཉེ་བརྒྱུད་ཟབ་མོ་གཙོད་
ཀྱི་ཁྲིད་ཡིག་འདི་ལ། བློ་ཆོས་སུ་འགྲོ་བར་བྱེད་པ་ཐུན་མོང་བློ་ལྡོག་རྣམ་བཞིའི་ཁྲིད། ཆོས་
ལམ་དུ་འགྲོ་བར་བྱེད་པ་ཐུན་མིན་སྐྱབས་འགྲོ་སོགས་ནས་ཆོས་བདུན་གྱི་ཁྲིད། ལམ་གྱི་འཁྲུལ་
བ་ཞི་བར་བྱེད་པ་ཀ་དག་ཁྲེགས་ཆོད་ཁྱད་པར་གྱི་ཁྲིད། འཁྲུལ་སྣང་ཡེ་ཤེས་སུ་འཆར་བར་བྱེད་པ་
ཐོད་རྒལ་ཟླ་དྲུག་མ་ཟུར་དུ་བཞུགས་ལ། དེ་ལྟར་གདམས་ངག་ཚང་ལ་མ་ནོར་བ་འདི་གཞུང་བཞིན་
ཉམས་སུ་ལེན་ནུས་ན་ཚེ་འདིར་གྲོལ་བ་ཐོབ་པ་ནི། གཏེར་ཆེན་ཉིད་ཀྱི་སྐུ་རིང་ལ་འཇའ་ལུས་གྲུབ་
པ་བཅུ་ཕྲག་གཉིས་ལ་ཉེ་བ་དང་། འབྱུང་བ་བཞི་ལ་རང་དབང་ཐོབ་པ། དུག་གིས་མི་གནོད་པ་
སོགས་གྲུབ་པའི་རིག་འཛིན་བསམ་གྱིས་མི་ཁྱབ་པ་བྱུང་བ་དང་། དེ་ནས་རིམ་བཞིན་བརྒྱུད་པ་
གསུམ་ཡན་ཆད་ལ་འཇའ་ལུས་འགྲུབ་པ་ཟམ་མ་ཆད་པ་འབྱུང་བ་ནི། གཏེར་ཆེན་ཉིད་ཀྱི་ལུང་

བྱང་ལས། བརྒྱུད་པ་ཚིགས་གསུམ་ཚུན་ཆད་ལ༔ གདམས་པའི་ཟབ་རྒྱ་མ་ཆད་ན༔ འཇའ་ལུས་རིག་འཛིན་བརྒྱ་ཕྲག་འབྱུང༔ ཞེས་གསུངས་ཤིང་། དེ་ལྟར་གདམས་ངག་ཚང་ལ་མ་ནོར་བ། བརྒྱུད་ཐག་ཐུང་ཞིང་བྱིན་རླབས་ཀྱི་ཚན་ཁ་ཆེ་བའི་བདུད་གཅོད་ཟབ་མོ་འདི་ལ། རྒྱལ་སྲས་གཞན་ཕན་མཐའ་ཡས་ཀྱི་རྣམ་རོལ། ༧ཀུན་གཟིགས་སྐྱབས་མགོན་གླིང་སྤྲུལ་པདྨ་ལུང་རྟོགས་རྒྱ་མཚོ་ནི་གཏེར་ཆོས་ཡོངས་རྫོགས་ཀྱི་ཆོས་བདག་ཡིན་པ་མ་ཟད་གཏེར་ཆེན་ཉིད་ཀྱི་མདུན་ནས་དབང་ལུང་ཁྲིད་གསུམ་ལན་མང་དུ་གསན་ཡོད་པས་གཏེར་ཆེན་ཉིད་ཀྱིས་ཁོང་ལ་འགྲེལ་བ་ཞིག་འབྲི་དགོས་པའི་བཀའ་གནང་བ་དང་། ཡང་གཏེར་ཆེན་ཉིད་ཀྱི་ཐུགས་སྲས། ཡུལ་རེབ་ཀོང་གི་སྔགས་པ། ཕུར་ཐོགས་སྟོང་གི་གཙོ་བོ་རྗེ་རྡོ་རྗེ་རྣམ་རྒྱལ་སོགས་སློབ་ཆེན་དུ་མས་བསྐུལ་མ་གནང་བ་བཞིན། སྐྱབས་མགོན་གླིང་སྤྲུལ་པདྨ་ལུང་རྟོགས་རྒྱ་མཚོ་ནས་གཏེར་ཆེན་བླ་མའི་ཞལ་རྒྱུན་ལྟར་གབ་པ་མངོན་དུ་ཕྱུང་། སྦས་པ་གསལ་བར་བཀྲལ། སྡེབ་འཁྲུགས་དག་པར་མཛད་ནས་གསལ་བར་བཀོད་པ་ལ། གཏེར་གཞུང་རྩ་བའི་ཁོག་ཕུབ་ནས། བཀའ་གཏེར་དག་སྣང་ལས་བྱུང་བ་ཕ་རྒྱུད་ཐབས་ཀྱི་བརྒྱུད་པ། མ་རྒྱུད་ཤེས་རབ་ཀྱི་བརྒྱུད་པ། གཉིས་མེད་མཉམ་སྦྱོར་གྱི་བརྒྱུད་པ། རྟོགས་ལྡན་ཉམས་མྱོང་གི་བརྒྱུད་པའི་མན་ངག་རྣམས་ཀྱིས་ཟུར་རྒྱན་དེ་ལེགས་པར་བཤད་པའི་གཞུང་འདི་ནི་གཅོད་ཁྲིད་ཀུན་གྱི་རྒྱལ་པོ་ལྟ་བུ་ཡིན་པས། འདི་གཞུང་བཞིན་དུ་ཉམས་སུ་བླངས་ན་གསེར་འགྱུར་རྩི་ཡིས་ལྕགས་གསེར་དུ་བསྒྱུར་བ་བཞིན་ཉོན་མོངས་པའི་གཅོང་ནད་སེལ་བས་བདུད་རྩིའི་སྨན་མཆོག་ལྟ་བུ་དང་། ཐུན་མོངས་བློ་ལྡོག་རྣམ་བཞི་ནས་ཚོགས་གཉིས་ཟུང་འཇུག་སྣང་སྟོང་འགག་མེད་བསྐྱེད་རྫོགས་དབྱེར་མེད་རིག་སྟོང་མཐའ་བྲལ་རྫོགས་པ་ཆེན་པོའི་བར་དུ་གདམས་ངག་མ་ཚང་བ་མེད་པ་ཚིག་དོན་ཕུན་སུམ་ཚོགས་པས་རོལ་མཚོ་ཆེན་པོའི་ཀླུའི་བང་མཛོད་དུ་ནོར་བུས་གཏམས་པ་ལྟ་བུ། གཞུང་བཟང་འདི་འདྲ་དེང་སང་སྙེད་པར་དཀའ་བ་དང་། དར་ཁྱབ་ཆེན་པོ་མེད་པ་ལ་བརྟེན་ནས། ལྷག་བསམ་རབ་ཏུ་ཡངས་པ། དམ་པ་དུ་མའི་གདམས་ངག་ཡོད་པ། བློ་གྲོས་ཀྱི་རྩལ་དང་ལྡན་པ་བླ་མ་ཆོས་རྣམ་དང་། བོད་ཀྱི་སྐད་ཡིག་ལ་སྦྱང་བརྩོན་ལེགས་པར་མཛད་པ། དམ་པ་དུ་མའི་མདུན་ནས་མདོ་སྔགས་གཉིས་ཀྱི་ཚིག་དོན་ལ་སྒྲོ་འདོགས་ལེགས་པར་ཆོད་དེ་ནང་བསྟན་ལ་དད་འདུན་དང་ཕན་སེམས་ཆེ་བ། ཁྱད་པར་དུ་ཆོས་འདི་ལ་ལྷག་པར་མོས་པ། རྣམ་དཔྱོད་ཕུལ་དུ་ཕྱིན་པའི་ལོ་ཙཱ་བ་སངས་རྒྱས་མཁའ་འགྲོ་ཁོང་གཉིས་

ནས་གཞུང་བཟང་འདི་དབྱིན་ཡིག་ཏུ་བསྒྱུར་ཐུབ་པ་ལ་སྙིང་ནས་དགའ་སྤྲོ་དང་རྗེས་སུ་ཡི་རངས་ཡོད། མ་ཟད་དེང་སང་མ་རྟོགས་ལོག་རྟོགས་རང་བཟོ་སོགས་ཀྱིས་ལྷད་པ་སྤྲོལ་ངན་རྒྱུན་འབྱམས་སུ་གྱུར་བའི་སྙོག་མ་སངས་ཏེ་གཏེར་ཆེན་ཡབ་སྲས་ཀྱི་དུས་ལྟར་འཇའ་ལུས་རིག་འཛིན་གྲུབ་པའི་རྣལ་འབྱོར་ཕོ་མོས་ཕྱོགས་ཀུན་ཏུ་ཁྱབ་པས་སྨོན་འདུན་བཅས།།

།།ཀཿཐོག་དགེ་ཙྪེ་བཞི་པའི་མིང་འཛིན་པ་འགྱུར་མེད་བསྟན་པ་རྒྱལ་མཚན་ནས་བྲིས་པ་དགེ་བར་གྱུར་ཅིག ། སརྦ་མངྒ་ལཾ།། །།

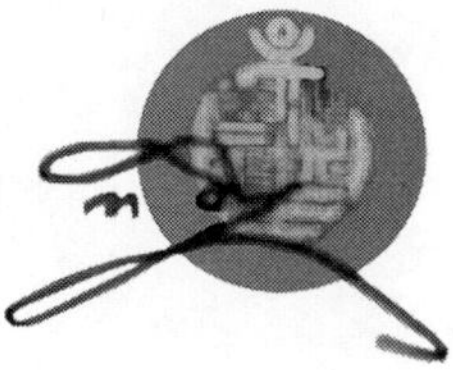

Foreword by H.H. Katok Getse Mahāpaṇḍita

Namo guru Mañjushrī ye!

THIS LUCID COMMENTARY on the close lineage of severance, or chöd, entitled *An Ambrosia Ocean of Sublime Explanations* by Pema Lungtok Gyatso[a] is a most excellent treatise that resembles a wish-fulfilling jewel or how all rivers converge with the ocean, in that it brings together the profound key points of the Sūtra, Mantra, and Terma traditions without exception. In these degenerate times, the Great Tertön, Vidyādhara Dudjom Lingpa[b]—an emanation of the glorious great guru Dorje Drolöd[c]—appeared to guide disciples. The crown ornament of the one-hundred mahāsiddhas of India was the great master Saraha,[d,1] who—through pure clear-light visionary awareness—bestowed the blessings of the aural lineage upon Dudjom Lingpa in the manner of the inseparable wisdom mind of teacher and retinue.

These are the sacred instructions that grant liberation to fortunate ones in a single lifetime by means of realizing the dharmakāya rainbow body. This profound **chöd commentary** of the **close lineage**[2] sustains the warmth of the ḍākinī's breath and includes teachings that inspire the mind to practice dharma, beginning with the common four thoughts that turn the mind. So that dharma will become the path, there are seven categories of instructions that include the uncommon cycles of refuge and so forth. So that confusion will be pacified on the path, the specific instructions on *ka dag trekchö*[e] are given. So that confused appearances will dawn as wisdom, there are also the additional instructions for the six-month *tögal*[f] practice that is part of the terma revelation. If this sacred transmission that is complete and unerring is practiced according to the teachings, then liberation will be brought about in a single lifetime.

During the life of the Tertön himself, there were close to twenty disciples who actually attained the rainbow body through mastery over the four elements.

[a] *skyabs rje gling sprul padma lung rtogs rgya mtshos*
[b] *bdud 'joms gling pa*
[c] *rdo rje gro lod*
[d] *sa ra ha*
[e] *ka dag khregs chod*; cutting through to original purity
[f] *thod rgal*; crossing over

Unscathed by poisons and the like, an inconceivable number of accomplished vidyādharas[a] were produced. Over the course of three generations, there have continued to be disciples who achieved the rainbow body as this was predicted by the Tertön himself:

> For three generations, if the continuity of these profound transmissions remains uninterrupted, there will be some one-hundred vidyādharas who will attain the rainbow body.

Thus, he spoke.

This profound method for the severance of the māras was composed by the incarnation of Gyalsey Zhenpen Tayey,[b] the omniscient Kyabje Lingtrul Pema Lungtok Gyatso, who was the dharma keeper for all terma revelations of Dudjom Lingpa. He received many empowerments, teachings, and transmissions from the Great Tertön directly and received permission to compose this commentary from the Tertön as well. In addition to that, many principal disciples requested that this commentary be written, including the heart disciple Dorje Namgyal[c] from Rekong who was principal among the thousands of *ngakpa*[d] lineage holders. Based upon the oral-transmission teachings of the Great Tertön himself, this commentary **illuminates** hidden meanings, clarifies obscure points, and **arranges** the order of presentation in a comprehensive way. The framework for this commentary is based upon the root terma, and that is adorned with the upadesha[e,3] of the father lineage of upāya,[f] the mother lineage of prajñā,[g] the nondual lineage of union, and the experiential lineage of the realized ones that are extracted from the teachings of the Buddha,[h] the termas, and pure visions. This **sublime explanation** is the king of all commentaries on the subject of severance. If practiced according to the text itself, then—like how alchemy can transform iron into gold—the chronic disease of the passions will be pacified. Hence, this is like a supreme **ambrosia** among medicine.

From the point of the four common thoughts that turn the mind through the stage of the union of the two accumulations, the harmonious joining of empty appearances, and inseparable generation and completion all the way to

[a] *rigdzin* (*rig 'dzin*); pure awareness holder
[b] *rgyal sras gzhan phan mtha' yas*; one of Paltrul Rinpoche's masters
[c] *rdo rje rnam rgyal*
[d] *sngags pa*; tantric lay practitioner
[e] *men ngak* (*man ngag*)
[f] *tab* (*thabs*); method
[g] *sherab* (*shes rab*); incisive knowledge
[h] Shākyamuni (*sha kya thub pa*)

the Great Perfection[a] itself, the sacred oral instructions involved here are lacking in nothing. Hence, the meaning of the style of presentation is rich like the jewel treasury of the nāgas found in the depth of the great **ocean**. These days, it is difficult to encounter a treatise of this caliber that, until now, has not been widely distributed.

I would like to thank the intelligent and well-intended Lama Chönam, who possesses many sacred lineage blessings, for undertaking the translation of this project into the English language. In addition, I offer heartfelt gratitude to the wise and exceptional lotsāwa Sangye Khandro, who has diligently studied the Tibetan language and become fluent. Having determined all doubts concerning the innermost meaning of Sūtra and Mantra in the presence of many sublime masters, she has great devotion toward the teachings of the Buddha and a pure intention to serve beings. In particular, she has exceptional devotion for this lineage of practice. I rejoice that, together, they have accomplished the task of translating this commentary into English.

Not only that, these days, teachings have become sullied by those who fail to realize the true meaning, have incorrect comprehension, or decide to include their own opinions and personal agenda. May this teaching cleanse those negative habits that actually bring ruin to the minds of beings. Just like during the time of the Great Tertön's life and legacy of heirs and disciples, I offer the prayer that, through these efforts, every direction may be filled with male and female practitioners who accomplish vidyādharahood and attain the rainbow body.

This was written by the one who holds the name
of the Fourth Getse of Katok.
May virtue prevail! May all be auspicious!

[a] Dzogchen (*rdzogs chen*); Atiyoga, Mahāsandhi.

Translators' Preface

> To the speech emanation of all the victorious ones' enlightened deeds, Dorje Drolöd, annihilator of all unruly misguided ones, who returned again to benefit beings in the degenerate times as the great glorious one, Heruka Dudjom Lingpa—with deep respect, we bow down.
>
> Until the passions of the mind are exhausted, the blessings of the holy dharma remain crucial. In that context, many scholars and mahāsiddhas have proclaimed this dharma to be especially timely; so disciples should take delight in this.

THE LOTUS BORN MASTER, Padmasambhava,[a] is inseparable with the Buddha, who is the guide of all gods and living beings. With compassion and blessings for beings in the degenerate times that surpass any other by virtue of expediency, this second buddha has once again expressed his kindness by intentionally manifesting to guide disciples as the Heruka Dudjom Lingpa. His self-occurring wisdom awareness welled forth from within to purify all conditioned phenomena in the nature of phenomena. In doing so, all phenomena appeared to him as divine wisdom males and females; and like one human to another, he exchanged profound truth in the form of conversation with the wisdom deities. As a great sovereign of the mahāsiddhas, to even hear a syllable of Dudjom Lingpa's sacred names will itself have the power to subdue the phenomena of human and nonhuman entities alike.

This genuine regent of Padmasambhava in modern times was born and lived in northeastern Tibet in the land of Golog from 1835 to 1904. Among the many treasures this Great Tertön revealed, he presented one of them called the *Sealed Secret Commentary*[b] to the famous Ju Mipham Rinpoche (1846-1912), who was and continues to be highly revered as a brilliant renaissance master whose scholarship and realization rocked the Tibetan Buddhist world at the turn of the twentieth century. When Mipham Rinpoche received this literary gift from Dudjom Lingpa, he responded to the Great Tertön directly with a letter

[a] *padma sam bha ba*
[b] *sang tri ka gya ma* (*gsang khrid bka' rgya ma*)

confirming his total confidence in the Tertön and his profound revelations. The letter he wrote in response reads as follows:

> To the lotus feet of the great manifest Tertön, regent of Padmasambhava, I present this letter with deep regard and devotion. That your wish-fulfilling rūpakāya, the result of countless kalpas of having generated the awakened mind, has manifested here to benefit the doctrine and beings is an expression of great kindness. Here, I am doing well and am presently engaged in a partial retreat.
>
> The reason for writing is to mention that, although these days there are many so-called treasure revealers in this land, I fail to feel a sense of faith or interest in them or their revelations; while at the same time I do not harbor wrong view toward them. After receiving and reviewing your revelation called the *Sealed Secret Commentary* just once, I found it to be extremely succinct; and although there are new dharma terms being used, I found yours to be extremely relevant and pithy. Thinking this must be vajra speech that will illuminate and revive our tradition of the clear-light secret vajra pinnacle Atiyoga, a strong feeling of devotion wells forth in my heart.
>
> These days, mentally fabricated philosophies are proclaimed and promoted as Mahāsandhi instructions. Since most Nyingmapas are content to repeat the words and terms of other traditions, I find it extremely refreshing and fortunate to view a text that upholds Padmasambhava's own tradition during such dire circumstances. I am truly pleased by this revelation and not just mouthing these words. In fact, I had hoped to have a chance to see your golden face and tell you this in person; however, the distance between us is so far that it seems impossible.
>
> I ask you to pray that all of my dharma aspirations may reach fruition. Due to the times, the doctrine of the Earlier Translation School is on the decline. Hence, I also pray that your lotus feet will remain firm for one-hundred kalpas and that your commitment will endure undiminished so that the doctrine of the great Secret Essence will permeate all directions until the end of time.
>
> From my heart, I pray that I and all of your followers may enjoy the celebration of these aspirations coming true!
>
> *Respectfully submitted and sent by Mipham Namgyal*
> *on the fifth day of the third month*
> *from the cave of Tiger's Lair, along with a long stainless white offering scarf*

This is but a single example among the many words of praise other great scholars and realized practitioners have extolled upon this Tertön.

The extensive commentary that forms the corpus of this text includes the root-terma chöd commentary that is one of Heruka Dudjom Lingpa's profound sacred instructions of the hearing lineage, transmitted to him from the Treasury Expanse of the Spacelike Dharmatā by the crown jewel of Indian mahāsiddhas, Saraha. Entitled *The Profound Heart Essence of Saraha*,[a] it appears in this volume as Part Two and includes both common and uncommon preliminary instructions, the three-kāya meditation-recitation practice, the pointing-out instructions for identifying the view associated with the four samayas of Mahāsandhi, the stages of generation and completion, the way of wandering through fear-invoking environments, the methods for identifying upheavals and for accumulating merit, such as the practice of the four feasts, and various other subjects that belong to the path of chöd.

Generally, in Tibet that which is referred to as chöd, meaning severance, is mentioned by many scholars to have originated from Ḍākinī Machig Labdrön.[b] Nevertheless, in India—the land of the āryas—Āryadeva's *Great Verses*,[c] Nāropā's *Secret Severance of Equal Taste*,[d] Guru Rinpoche's *Severance of Confusion*,[e] and Padampa Sangye's *Pacification-Severance*[f] were counted as four major texts relating to chöd and sources of this lineage. Whatever the case, the source of these teachings originates from the sublime speech of the fully enlightened Buddha, the *Sūtra of Transcendental Incisive Knowledge*.[g] This teaching combines both the profound instructions of ascertaining emptiness with the vast conduct of the bodhisattvas. Padampa Sangye met this doctrine early on before it passed through a long series of lineage holders. Although we cannot determine the exact time of his birth, according to several well-informed assertions, Padampa's last visit to Tibet occurred sometime during the Second Rabjung Year of the Water Snake, 1113. His coming from India to Tibet marked the first time the chöd lineage came to Tibet, and he brought with him both the maternal and paternal aspects of the lineage.

While in Tibet, Padampa transmitted both lineages; and it was during this time that Machig Labdrön came to receive the lineages as well. In general, the lineages increased and spread similar to the way in which the distant lineage of

[a] *sa ra ha pa'i nying tig zab mo* (*sa ra ha pa'i snying thig zab mo*); Dudjom Lingpa

[b] *ma gcig lab sgron*

[c] *arya dewa'i tsik su ched pa chenpo* (*arya de ba'i tshigs su bcad pa chen po*); Āryadeva (*arya de ba*)

[d] *ro nyom sang chöd* (*ro snyoms gsang gcod*); Nāropā (*na ro pa*)

[e] *trül chöd* (*'khrul gcod*); Padmasambhava

[f] *zhi chöd* (*zhi gcod*); Padampa Sangye (*pha dam pa sangs rgyas*)

[g] *sherab kyi pa rol tu chin pa'i do* (*shes rab kyi pha rol tu phyin pa'i mdo*); *prajñāpāramitāsūtra*

Kāma and the close lineage of Terma were disseminated over time. The historical information concerning the lineages is clearly described in the history section of Part One of this volume, so there is no need to mention this further here.

Following that, the famous female yoginī who extensively propagated this dharma in the Snow Land of Tibet was indeed Machig Labdrön. From the perspective of definitive truth, many learned masters have praised and respected her as the dharmakāya mother Yüm Chenmo;[a] from an inner perspective, Ārya Tārā;[b] and secretly, the actual dharmakāya ḍākinī. Born in 1031, she lived for 101 years. There is conflicting information concerning the exact time of her life, so that should be taken into consideration as well. Nevertheless, during the course of her lifetime, many scholars of all four traditions brought Buddhist teachings from India into Tibet for translation. During that time, she became one of the most important Tibetan female practitioners to internalize the profound meaning of truth through the practice of chöd. Due to her influence, the chöd lineage was greatly regarded, accepted, and successfully transmitted to practitioners from all walks of life, not just only in Tibet but to the borderlands as well, including Nepal and back into India.

The seeds that would sprout with the potential for realization were sown by this most amazing ḍākinī in human form. Due to her efforts, the profound dharma lineages of chöd became pivotal for the realization of countless practitioners to come. These are some of the reasons why she is considered to be among the first major female practitioners to significantly influence Buddhism as practiced in Tibet. Machig taught many scholars and practitioners from India and Nepal and was the first female Tibetan scholar to give dharma teachings back to the Indian and Nepalese masters of the day. She was most famous for her total abandonment of the eight worldly concerns by remaining in uncertain, fear-invoking environments for most of her life until she passed into parinirvāṇa.

Later, during Dudjom Lingpa's life, she appeared to him in visions, like a mother to her child, and showed great care and loving kindness while transmitting the entire lineage of chöd to him. Dudjom Lingpa also had actual visions of Padampa Sangye, who not only entrusted all lineages to him, but also illuminated all key points on the view of emptiness.

Dudjom Lingpa's root-terma chöd commentary, *Heart Essence of Saraha*, is the basis for the author Pema Lungtok Gyatso's extensive commentary with nearly every word of the terma embedded within it. This all-encompassing commentary is Part One of this book and is called *A Clearly Compiled Commentary on the Close Lineage of Chöd entitled An Ambrosia Ocean of Sublime Explanations*. Wangda'e Kyabgon, or Lingtrul Pema Lungtok Gyatso, was born in 1852

[a] *yum chen mo*; Great Mother

[b] Pakma Drolma (*'phags ma sgrol ma*)

in the Golog region of Tibet and was a nonsectarian scholar learned in the philosophical tenets of the schools of Buddhism in their entirety, including all subjects of knowledge. He was a great master of the lineage and a highly realized individual, as well as being the regent of the terma revelations of his father guru, Dudjom Lingpa.

The subject of this incomparable commentary is enhanced by the upadeshas of nonsectarian scholars that are included throughout in the form of quotations, including the upadesha of severance called the *Great Verses* by Āryadeva, which are based on the source of the second turning of the wheel concerning the profound meaning of emptiness, the Great Mother *Prajñāpāramitā* in three sections—extensive, middling, and concise. Although all four major Tibetan Buddhist schools practice the profound lineage of severance: in the pages of this commentary the subject is not only clearly illuminated, it is highly supported by the speech of the Buddha and great Indian and Tibetan scholars and realized masters. It is further polished by the upadesha instructions that emerge from the lineage of realized practitioners.

Given that the root cause that prevents spiritual attainment is self-cherishing based upon ignorance, this treatise gives the actual tools needed to directly uproot this cause. By reading and studying this text, the minds of fortunate followers will be inspired to establish true faith and certain devotion. Not only that, through these instructions and the practices that accompany them, there is no doubt that sincere practitioners will go on to gain the confidence needed to bring their minds to fruition.

The process of bringing this text into the English language has involved a number of karmic interdependencies. First of all, as the translators, we can say with complete confidence that we possess a strong karmic link with this lineage based upon aspirations and devotion and have spent many years translating literature that belongs to this lineage, as well as personally dedicating our lives to these practices. For many years, we were well aware that this extensive commentary needed to be brought into English, as do all of the termas and their ancillary sections that belong to the Dudjom Tröma cycle of practice. Kyabje Dudjom Rinpoche, Jigdral Yeshe Dorje,[a] himself said many times that the Tröma revelations were the dharma of this time.

We finally began translating this commentary into English due to the request of Getse Mahāpaṇḍita's reincarnation, Kyabje Getse Rinpoche from the Katok lineage. Getse Rinpoche spent several years teaching this commentary at Iron Knot Ranch in response to repeated requests for instruction on the Dudjom Tröma chöd cycle from Lama Shenpen Drolma and her sangha. During that time, there was no English translation of the text available. One of the sangha

[a] *'jigs 'bral ye shes rdo rje*

members present—profoundly inspired by Getse Rinpoche's teachings and with heartfelt aspirations—offered to sponsor the effort to bring the text into English. Lama Shenpen, herself a devoted disciple of this chöd lineage with the purest intentions to serve sentient beings and the doctrine, requested us to translate this text and offered the monetary support necessary to sustain that aspiration. Getse Rinpoche kindly conferred the entire reading transmission upon us, and afterward we began the translation in 2012. Over the nearly two years it has taken to complete this task, Getse Rinpoche has been available for consultation and support every step of the way.

The primary volume that we used for the translation of Pema Lungtok Gyatso's commentary was compiled by the Bhutanese Lama Kunzang Wangdu, otherwise known as Lopon Nikula. He published the entire Collected Works of Heruka Dudjom Lingpa, which includes this commentary as Volume WA #20, printed at the KMT Press in Phuentsholing, Bhutan. This version is referred to here in the endnotes by the code LN. We compared that text with two other versions, namely, the modern version that is in a western-style softcover book format published in 2007 by the Beijing Peoples' Publishing House and is referred to here as the modern version with the code BPPH and the third version that is the one Kyabje Getse Rinpoche had in his possession. That is a handwritten copy in *üchen* script with no information about its origin aside from mentioning in the colophon that it was commissioned by the Queen Mother of Bhutan, Püntsok Chödron. We refer to this as the older version with the code BQM.

Although the LN version is in a digital format printed on Tibetan rice paper and is clear, lovely to behold, and very light to work with, as we began our work we came to notice there were a significant number of errors and omissions; so we sought to find other versions for comparison. According to information found in the BPPH version, during the life of Heruka Dudjom Lingpa an original woodblock version of this commentary was commissioned to be carved. However, due to the tumultuous times, that xylographic copy was unfortunately destroyed. Nevertheless, given that several of the great Tertön's disciples possessed copies of the original woodblock print, those copies became the source through which the BPPH and other future versions would be based. A second source [for the BPPH] was a cursive[a] version that had been commissioned by Jigdral Yeshe Dorje while still residing in Tibet and written by his disciple Kushap Gyurmed. Unfortunately, Kyabje Dudjom Rinpoche was then compelled to escape the Cultural Revolution to become a refugee in India and Nepal. Eventually, this cursive version of the Collected Works was brought out to him by a devoted and fearless courier who risked his life to do so. Dudjom Rinpoche then

[a] *ümed* (*dbu med*)

produced more copies of this cursive version and sent one set of the Collected Works of Dudjom Lingpa back to the great Tertön's homeland, Tergar.[a] That is the same source that Lopon Nikula used for his Bhutanese publication as well. Both of these versions—the copies based on the original woodblock and the handwritten cursive—are faulted by a number of errors and omissions. During the course of our translation, we came to rely upon the BPPH version as the most accurate source since it mainly emphasizes the woodblock version. For instance, the section describing the narrative context as it pertains to the title was entirely omitted from the LN and BQM versions but included in the BPPH version. We have noted other omissions and discrepancies in the text itself as endnotes.

Generally, our teacher Lord Buddha Shākyamuni showed skill and compassion in every deed that he did. Hence, he gave many different instructions to meet the needs of the myriad minds of sentient beings according to their capacities, all of which are distinctions based on skillful means. The pith point of the meaning, however, leads to the same place. Those who lack renunciation toward saṃsāra and are plagued by the strong habit of fixation upon the true existence of phenomena chain themselves to the iron fence of self-fixation. Still, they may claim to be yogis and yoginīs. If that is the case, then at least they must recall the crucial points of this lineage of transmission if they wish to become authentic practitioners of chöd. Without that, even just the attempt to practice chöd can actually endanger the mind, causing one to separate from dharma altogether.

We urge caution in this way because the practices and methods set forth in the pages of this book force one to directly confront the ignorance of self-cherishing, or the twofold self of the person and phenomena that have been fixated upon and cherished from countless previous lifetimes. Through utilizing the upadesha of the lineage holders and strongly invoking their blessings, a superior practitioner must be armed with the realization of the fundamental nature of truth. A middling practitioner should have confidence in the generation- and completion-stage practices, and at least there should be irreversible faith in the root masters and the lineage. Not only that, there must be confidence in the master and lineage as the source of blessings. Without that, there is no other means through which to internalize these teachings. As the translators, we made the difficult decision to not designate this as a restricted text; so it is all the more important to mention these points from the onset so that readers will know what to expect.

The root terma, or Part Two, involves thirteen sections of practice. They should be engaged in a progressive manner under the watchful guidance and care of a qualified teacher. The liturgies that are not included in the root terma's

[a] *gter sgar*, or the Tertön's encampment

chöd commentary can be found in the Tröma Volume of the Collected Works of Kyabje Dudjom Rinpoche, Jigdral Yeshe Dorje.

Once making a pure connection with a lineage-holding teacher, one must then receive the empowerments, transmissions, and commentaries that are relevant to this direction of practice. That would include receiving either the extensive or concise Dudjom Tersar Tröma empowerment. One may then begin the preliminary practices that involve the usual five-hundred thousand accumulations. These accumulations involve one-hundred thousand prostrations along with the refuge-verse recitation, one-hundred thousand accumulations of the bodhichitta verses, and one-hundred thousand maṇḍala offerings along with the verses. The uncommon preliminaries in this cycle involve the trikāya visualization-meditation practice where one-hundred thousand accumulations are required for each of the three ḍākinīs—Tröma Nagmo,[a] Vajravarāhī,[b] and Samantabhadrī.[c] That is followed by the seven-day retreat for training in the practice of wandering in fear-invoking environments. Then, the guru-yoga practice involves accumulating one-hundred thousand for each syllable of the mantra, or at least one million recitations.

According to the perspective of ordinary individuals, this teaching may seem contradictory with their way of thinking and engaging in moral conduct. Nevertheless, given that this path represents the extremely profound key points of practice that bring swift results, this is not just only a teaching to receive but also a practice and lifestyle that—if taken to heart—can mature the mind and bring liberation from saṃsāric bondage, even in a single lifetime. The capacity to engage in the fearless, uncontrived conduct of a chöd practitioner is entirely dependent upon the strength of the view applied to meditation and then conduct. This must be preceded by significant purification of obscurations and accumulations of merit. Hence, the common and uncommon preliminary practices are strongly emphasized here.

Generally, all buddhas and bodhisattvas initially cultivate the bodhichitta to work for the welfare of others, and then they begin their journey. In the interim, while accumulating great waves of virtue, they do this for the welfare of all sentient beings. Finally, when attaining fully enlightened buddhahood, this occurs for the benefit of sentient beings. That is why, in this text, there is no teaching to be found that is not sealed with this level of bodhichitta commitment involving training to arouse equal love and compassion for all living beings.

[a] *khros ma nag mo*
[b] Dorje Pagmo (*rdo rje phag mo*)
[c] Kuntuzangmo (*kun tu bsang mo*)

We would like to express deep gratitude to the entire team that serves the Light of Berotsana Translation Group. This includes all of you who are fellow translators, friends, and benefactors, as you are the ones who inspire us and allow us the freedom to continue doing our work. We would like to acknowledge Kay Henry for her dedication to the project and editorial skills. Heartfelt thanks go to Katok Getse Mahāpaṇḍita, Dhanakosha Foundation, Lama Shenpen Drolma and her sangha at Iron Knot, an anonymous patron, Stephanie Lain, Gopa Campbell of Gopa&Ted2, Inc. for the beautiful typesetting, Shashi Reitz for her constant support, and so many others who have contributed to this effort along the way.

In the transliteration of Sanskrit terms, we have departed from the standard practice by replacing ś, ṣ, and c with sh, ṣh, and ch, respectively. Superscripted, lowercase letters of the alphabet refer the reader to footnotes where—upon first occurrence—we have given the Tibetan and, where known, Sanskrit equivalents. The numbering of these notes begins again with the first letter of the alphabet on each new page. We extend our gratitude to Professor Vesna A. Wallace, Dept. of Religious Studies, University of California, Santa Barbara, for assisting us with the Sanskrit terms; and we have used various other references for Sanskrit in text citations, including *Guide to the Nyingma Edition of the Derge Kangyur and Tengyur* edited by Tarthang Tülku and published by Dharma Publishing. We have included the complete Sanskrit title where possible even though the text may have mentioned only the concise title of the text. Superscripted Arabic numerals refer to endnotes that will be found following the translation. These notes are numbered consecutively. The words of the root terma that are embedded within the commentary are inserted as boldface type and for the most part appear in consecutive order with some exceptions.

Dedication Prayer:

Undeceiving interdependent appearances are the phenomena of indication; emptiness free from all assertions is the innate, original state. Through this sublime dharma that transcends the two extremes, may all living beings realize the evenness of saṃsāra and enlightenment.[4]

Here is the great chariot that transports fortunate ones to liberation. In order to offer them this seat so that their minds may rest at ease, many have contributed to this effort by offering their support—mentally, physically, and financially. We dedicate this virtue we have amassed together, both directly and indirectly, to the welfare of all beings.

By the power of this virtue, may this doctrine prevail throughout all directions. May the doctrine of the great treasure revealer Dudjom

Lingpa spread across the face of this earth, bringing liberation to countless beings in these degenerate times. May the lotus feet of the supreme lineage holders remain for one-hundred kalpas. May the four elements become balanced; and may disease, famine, war, strife, and dispute be pacified. Finally, may the precious buddha nature blossom simultaneously in the minds of all living beings!

Lama Chönam and Sangye Khandro
Tashi Chöling, Oregon
Spring 2014

Part One

From the Twentieth Volume of the Secret and Profound Terma Collections of the Great Incarnate Tertön Dudjom Lingpa:

A Clearly Compiled Commentary on the Close Lineage of Chöd

entitled

An Ambrosia Ocean of Sublime Explanations

by
Pema Lungtok Gyatso

Homage and Introduction

Om swasti!

Through exceedingly peaceful, supreme compassion, the inconceivable profound traditions for severing the māras[5] are illuminated according to the faculties of those to be tamed. May the teacher of gods and humans, Buddha Shākyamuni, be victorious.

The intrinsic nature of discerning self-awareness, free from thought or expression, is nondual with all phenomena. To the Great Mother,[6] perfection of prajñā of all the sugatas and their heirs without exception, I bow down.

Lord of the all-pervasive victors, whose gloriously golden, youthful body appears like clouds at sunrise, with hair that resembles the color of a sapphire jewel bound in a knot at the crown, beautified by a flower garland of mind-captivating serpents—through your oceanic branches of melodious speech, all beings are delivered to the state of exaltation. With omniscience that is completely profound, vast, and all-illuminating, sole tutelary deity, bodhisattva Mañjushrī,[a] please lovingly remain in the core of my heart until I awaken.

In nondual bliss-emptiness, the sixteen joys expand as the completely radiant and charmingly attractive connate Ḍākinī of Space. Known as Vajravarāhī, She of Ecstatic Wrath enacts wrathful enlightened activity expressing the rapturous passion of fury.

You, who aggressively devour dualistic concepts with your sharp, white, bared fangs are ornamented with fearsome accouterments and are completely surrounded by the wisdom fire of the kalpas. Your majestic body is like a mountain of sapphire. O Glorious Kroti Kali[b] [i.e., Tröma Nagmo], please grant protection.

[a] Jampal (*'jam dpal*)
[b] *kro ti ka li*

Mother of the enlightened activity of the victors of the three times, lovely White Tārā,[a] you are a treasure trove of longevity and wisdom. Ārya Tārā, as a sole source of refuge, with heartfelt longing I pray; please befriend me.

Delighting always in the ecstasy of the taste of exaltation, you unite all limitless phenomena in the connate basic space of supreme clear light. Magnetizing the minds of beings in the three planes with the demeanor of passion, O Kurukullā,[b] Goddess of Power, may you bestow supreme well-being as well.

The wisdom arrow with the confidence of unborn realization skillfully strikes the shell of dimmed awareness, becoming the uncontrived method of fearless conduct. I praise this protector who has achieved the final state of nondual accomplishment. Having discovered the vajrakāya of glorious immortality, your enlightened speech is a sacred treasure of oral instructions. With loving compassion that never wavers from meeting the needs of beings in these degenerate times, to the Lake-Born Master[c] of beings, I show my heartfelt devotion.

The female form is the intrinsic nature of the mudrā of exaltation, such as the sole mother Wisdom Ḍākinī Labdrön[d] and the like. Through upāya, prajñā, and the indivisibility of the two, I bow to the assembly of the chöd lineage-holders, who are both learned and fully accomplished.

From the great Treasury Expanse of the Spacelike Dharmatā,[e] the nondual teacher and retinue appear as two. Having mastered the oceanic wealth of termas that bring maturity and liberation, you—Dudjom Lingpa—are my ultimate refuge.

Moreover, in order to tame disciples like myself, through myriad deeds all buddhas reveal themselves as virtuous guides. To all sublime masters of unrivaled kindness, I bow down in reverence.

The Great Mother represents the unity of emptiness and compassion that fully unites with the vehicle of the great secret. Who among the wise would not be transfixed by the opportunity to practice on this excellent path that accomplishes the two purposes according to one's wishes?

[a] Drolkar (*sgrol dkar*)
[b] Rig Chedma (*rig byed ma*)
[c] Tso Kye Dorje (*mtsho skyes rdo rje*); Padmasambhava
[d] Machig Labdrön
[e] *chö nyid* (*chos nyid*); nature of phenomena

This tradition is derived from the blessings of the close lineage[7] as the most profound heart essence of the accomplished vidyādharas. Given that the warm vapor of the mother ḍākinī's breath has not dissipated, I take great delight in giving this explanation that describes the nondual lineages of Kāma and Terma.[8]

To expand upon this, in the upadesha on the prajñāpāramitā—known as the Indian version of chöd—compiled by the great master Bhramin Āryadeva,[a] it states:[9]

> Free from the expression of an essence or basis, the meaning of the non-dual prajñāpāramitā is without the limitation of conceptualization, such as eternalism or nihilism. In regard to that, whatever I am capable of will be explained for the benefit of beings.

Thus, the indivisible nature of subject-object constitutes the essential meaning of all collected works of the victorious ones. That refers to the root of the genuine nature, or the meaning of the nature as it is, free from basis or support. This is rendered evident through discerning self-awareness wisdom or with prajñā that realizes the profound fundamental nature in harmony with that, along with the practice of the great compassionate upāya of bodhichitta. Then, without separating from the practice of vast conduct, such as generosity and the like, one unites these and familiarizes with the deity-yoga practice of the close path of Secret Mantra Vajrayāna. By swiftly perfecting both accumulations, the great state that does not fall to either limitation of existence or quiescence will be reached.

The meaning that is well known as the prajñāpāramitā is free from the limitations of conceptually fixating upon existing or not, as well as the conceptual mind of cherishing a "self". The way of practicing this according to the exceptional upadesha instructions involves the sacred dharma of the profound chöd, or severance of the māras, through explanations and visualizations, including the branches that accompany this.

Compelled by the wish to benefit others according to my capacity, I have arranged this explanation in four sections: an explanation of the history of the teaching that is to be explained, an expression of the greatness of this teaching, the way to internalize the meaning of the teaching, and revealing the results of having accomplished this.

1 History of the Teaching

First, the history of this teaching is as follows. Among the myriad dharmas that comprise the enlightened speech of the fully enlightened victorious Buddha, the

[a] *bram je arya de ba*

precious class of Sūtra holds the supreme exalted meaning of the prajñāpāramitā, the main subject of this text.

The intent of this [prajñāpāramitā] is described in two ways: a direct explanation of the profound nature of emptiness and a concealed meaning concerning the vastness of conduct, or the stages of manifest realization. Among these two, the first transmission [i.e., emptiness] began with Buddha Shākyamuni, Ārya Mawa'i Sengei Mañjushrī,[a] and glorious Āryadeva and was then passed to Padampa Sangye. The second transmission [i.e., conduct] was also passed from the fully perfected Buddha to Ārya Maitreya,[b] Ārya Asaṅga,[c] Vasubandhu,[d] and Āryadeva, who passed this to Padampa Sangye. Padampa Sangye came to hold both of these transmissions, which he then transmitted to Kyotön Sonam Lama.[e] He [i.e., Sonam Lama] transmitted this to Machig Labdrön. This lineage became known as the paternal lineage of upāya.

The wisdom intent of the prajñāpāramitā that is in conjunction with Secret Mantra is the transmission of the mode of practice that came from the Great Dharmakāya Mother Prajñāpāramitā, Ārya Tārā, and Ḍākinī Sukha Siddhi,[f] who transmitted this to Machig Labdrön. This came to be known as the maternal lineage of prajñā. The way that these two transmissions [i.e., paternal and maternal] unite as one is from Machig, who transmitted both to her heirs. Her lineage became known as the nondual lineage of both upāya and prajñā.

Furthermore, there are many ways of recognizing these lineages by other designations, such as the lineage of Kāma, Terma, that of the heirs, and so forth. All of those are otherwise referred to as distant lineages. The close lineage comes from Machig herself, appearing according to the needs of disciples in whatever way is deemed necessary in the form of a human female. From the ultimate perspective, she herself is the great dharmakāya mother; and from the inner perspective she is Ārya Tārā. Secretly, she is the actual wisdom dharmakāya ḍākinī. Hence, it is taught that it is not necessary to search for another lineage that precedes her.

In addition, Secret Mantra is recognized to stem from the victorious Vajradhara,[g] passed to Ārya Tārā, and then to Machig. She [i.e., Machig] had many visions of wisdom deities and received countless empowerments, as well as transmissions. Machig compiled texts entitled *The Udumwara of Secret Mantra,*[h] *The*

[a] Jetsun Jampal Maseng (*rje btsun 'jam dpal smra seng*)
[b] Jampa (*byams pa*)
[c] Tokmed (*thogs med*)
[d] Yignyen (*dbyig gnyen*)
[e] *skyo ston bsod nams bla ma*
[f] *su kha siddhi*
[g] Dorje Chang (*rdo rje 'chang*)
[h] *sang ngak udumwara* (*gsang sngags u dum ba ra*); Machig Labdron

Heart Essence that Dispels the Darkness of Ignorance,[a] and others. It is mentioned that there exist many cycles on the subject of generation and completion stages of Secret Mantra that she composed. Her principal transmission for chöd is what has presently come to be known as the cycle of Machig's aural lineage.

Along similar lines, this wisdom ḍākinī Machig Labdrön was predicted and praised by our teacher [i.e., Buddha Shākyamuni] in the *Sūtra Class Discerning the Pure from the Impure,*[b] in the *Root Tantra of Mañjushrī,*[c] and other texts to be an emanation of the Great Mother. Here in the Snow Land of Tibet, it was also predicted in the aural lineage of Machig that she would be the one to propagate the essential meaning of the unborn nature.[10] Furthermore, the great victor Padmasambhava gave many similar predictions. Some great teachers claim that, prior to Machig Labdrön, there was no particular dharma designation called "chöd". That is why here in Tibet it has become necessary to accept that she was the founder of the transmissions for the profound and sacred dharma of severing the māras, or chöd. Machig herself said, "Just as the Buddha has predicted, during the time of the five degeneracies through the tradition of a yoginī such as me, it will be necessary to tame all inhabitants in the Snow Land of Tibet." Those were her words.

This transmission of chöd that originates with her has been practiced in an unbiased way by many practitioners of various lineages until the present day. This tradition [of Machig] has thereby become well known as the universal practice for chöd. Not only that, the precious Tertön[11] himself had visions of Machig, where he was actually blessed by her magical wisdom kāya and she directly transmitted the entire lineage of chöd to him. In addition, Padampa Sangye also appeared to him [i.e., the Tertön] and transmitted the genuine pith instructions on the view of emptiness. The essence of the practice of chöd involves knowing the view, so the manner of these traditions is ultimately held within this profound transmission.

On this occasion to the best of my ability, I intend to emphasize both earlier and later transmissions and hope to illuminate the unification of both Kāma and Terma traditions. To that end, I have included this brief background information.

Furthermore, throughout the Early, Later, and other Translation Schools, there are limitless upadesha instructions involving severance teachings from the Kāma, Terma, and pure-vision lineages. How could all of that possibly be described here? Specifically, this transmission is considered exalted among them due to our supreme guide, the Great Tertön King of Dharma himself. As the

[a] *tük chüd marig munsel* (*thugs bcud ma rig mun sel*); Machig Labdron

[b] *do de drang nyik ched pa* (*mdo sde drangs snyigs 'byed pa*)

[c] *jam pal tsa wa'i gyü* (*'jam dpal rtsa ba'i rgyud, mañjushrīmūlatantra*)

mind treasures of the vidyādhara Dudjom Dorje[a,12] that have originated **from the** cycle of **the Treasury Expanse of the Spacelike Dharmatā,**[13] these superb oral instructions belong to the close lineage. Especially in these degenerate times, as the heart essence of the victorious ones of the three times, this timely dharma has the capacity to bring limitless disciples to maturity and liberation.

To explain this profound upadesha transmitted through the glorious mahāsiddha Saraha, there is the explanation of the title's meaning, namely, the Treasury Expanse of the Spacelike Dharmatā, as follows. The enlightened mind of our venerable master, the great treasure revealer King of Dharma, is omniscient wisdom free from duality. That is what is meant by the Treasury Expanse of the Spacelike Dharmatā. The nature of dharmatā is the basis of all phenomena, and the phenomena of the universe and inhabitants are similar to space. Likewise, the entirety of phenomenal existence as saṃsāra and enlightenment abides within this great emptiness, the basic space of the ground. The uncontrived inherent nature of that is the **dharmatā.** This dharmatā nature is the way of abiding of the profound intrinsic nature of awareness, perfectly pure from the beginning as a nature that does not abide in any way since it is free from elaborations, like space. Profound, vast, and free from depth or limit, this transcends the domain of the intellectual mind. Separate from any subjective assertions, it remains the very nature of the totality of saṃsāra and enlightenment. As the all-creating force of existence and quiescence based on the aspect of the basis for this arising, it is **spacelike.**

Concerning this, having not become an empty vacuity like the ordinary sky, the phenomena of saṃsāra involve distinctions, such as aggregates, elements, and sense sources. The dharma phenomena of the path involve the nine vehicles,[b,14] and the dharma of the result involves the oceanic qualities of kāyas, wisdoms, and so forth. As the source of all symbolic references and oral instructions, this is the profound treasury of the expanse of phenomena. For instance, because this resembles a valued treasure, it is called a **treasury expanse.** Among treasures within a great king's treasury, there are outer and inner distinctions as well as the most cherished treasure among them all, the innermost treasury. Like that, this dharma includes the innermost category of dharma transmissions. Although there are numerous categories for this, here, this is as he [i.e., the Tertön] stated. **From** among them, the concealed section that is the most superb is known here as this precious inexhaustible ornamental wheel.

This dharma possesses two great secrets. The first is based on the fact that the buddha nature [i.e., essence of the tathāgatas] pervades both saṃsāra and enlightenment, and the basic nature of buddhas and sentient beings involves

[a] *bdud 'joms rdo rje*

[b] *tekpa gu* (*theg pa dgu*)

not a hair's worth of difference in regard to that point. Nevertheless, sentient beings are unaware of their own mind's nature and have become shrouded by ignorance to wander in the confusion of saṃsāra without end. Hence, without realizing or actualizing their innate buddha nature, that nature remains secret to them since it is obscured or concealed. This lack of recognition is called "the obscured **secret**".[a]

Second, concerning this profound secret meaning, if there are disciples with keen faculties who possess karma and fortune, then this should be entrusted to them accordingly and transmitted on a personal basis. Otherwise, for those with lesser faculty whose minds are not mature, who impose their own ideas, lack karmic fortune, and exaggerate, this profound secret meaning must not only not be discussed with them, it must not even be implied; and that includes even the wind that carries this teaching to their proximity. In the manner of being extremely hidden, this teaching is under strict restriction so that this secret meaning can be practiced appropriately and the blessings will not diminish. The swiftness of the signs of accomplishment and so forth are among the many reasons and special features that qualify this as the hidden secret.[b] Through this profound and uncommon path of the unsurpassed secret, all states of mental fear concerning the existent self are destroyed within the basic space of the dharmatā that transcends cause and result. Therefore, this is **Mantra**. Possessing the seven qualities of the vajralike nature,[15] through the strength of abiding in that nature, there is the potential to directly eradicate all concepts based upon materializing. Since nothing can return to penetrate or disturb this nature, it is ultimately indestructible without transference or change. That is the **vajra**.

This Secret Mantra Vajrayāna vehicle is the synthesis of all qualities that occur on the path. Having not adjusted to the alterations of saṃsāra and enlightenment, all that is positive and negative can be upheld by this; so it is called "a **vehicle**". Based on that, among all secret teachings, this is the quintessential secret; among the profound, this is the epitome; among the essence, it is the heart ambrosia; and among the ambrosial nectars, it is superb. It is like pure gold that is the essence of the earth; salt that is the essence of water; butter that is the essence of milk; and the quintessential heart essence of all vehicles brought into one. Like the crème de la crème, it is **the innermost essence**.

All apparent phenomena that are held as truly existent are materialized through grasping fixation, so that is **materializing fixation**. Due to that, one hopes for benefit by believing in positive thoughts that are like the divine and has trepidation toward negative thoughts that will bring harm by appearing as though demonic. These relentless phenomena of benefit, harm, hope, and fear

[a] *gab pa'i sangwa* (*gab pa'i gsang ba*)
[b] *bepa'i sangwa* (*sbas pa'i gsang ba*)

that include attachment and fixation are the agents that bind one to this restriction. Becoming overpowered by obstructing forces, such as the four māras and forces that lead one astray, there is the misery of unbearable suffering based on karma and passions brought on through these circumstances. Having to powerlessly endure the unceasing continuation of obstacles based on the deluded phenomena of saṃsāra, there is no chance to attain liberation on the path. All of this is due to ignorance rooted in both states of self-fixation.

This basis of deluded ignorance that is the firm root for the tree of self-fixated existence and the tight bondage with dualistic hope and fear is directly cut off through the sharp weapon of prajñā that realizes selflessness. Severance within the space of the evenness of the dharmatā that is baseless from the root is called "**severing hope and fear**".

As a result of this teaching on severance that is superbly profound and unrivaled in terms of its exalted nature among all other paths and vehicles, there is victory over all nonconducive directions; so it is the sole panacea. Like a potent medicine that cures everything, it is called "the mahāmudrā[a] severance". This upadesha teaching is capable of delivering buddhahood in a single lifetime without postponing the results. As the supreme methods for awakening, these are called "the **pith instructions**".

Not only that, in saṃsāra from time immemorial until now—through the root causes and contributing circumstances of strongly potent and deluded duality based upon ignorance—one has lost the potential to even glimpse the direction of the basic dharmakāya buddha nature's way of abiding through personal strength. Nevertheless, in dependence upon this profound path, one is able to genuinely realize the unlimited awareness of the ground that is Samantabhadra's[b] originally pure fundamental way of being. As the sharp and profound upadesha method that allows the nature to be directly encountered and nakedly realized as the empty awareness dharmakāya itself, this is **the upadesha for encountering the fundamental nature itself**.

Exceptional profound oral instructions such as these are not to be found anywhere in the three realms of existence. That is why this dharma is a heart bindu[16] more precious than the heart blood of he who is supreme among all mahāsiddhas and vidyādharas, the King of Archers, glorious Saraha. This revelation is the sealed command of the profound wisdom intent of one-hundred thousand vidyādharas and one-thousand masters of accomplishment, including all ḍākas and ḍākinīs. Similar to the purest blood of their hearts, it is thereby known as ***The Profound Heart Essence of Saraha***.

The meaning of saying "**entitled**" is what the title refers to, namely, excep-

[a] *chag gya chenpo* (*phyag rgya chen po*)

[b] Kuntuzangpo (*kun tu bzang po*)

tionally profound pith instructions such as these. There are three reasons for explaining the title in this way.[17] By merely hearing the title of the text, superior individuals will comprehend the entire content from beginning to end. The middling will, like how a soldier is recognized by his insignia, understand which vehicle the treatise belongs to, whether high or low; whereas the lesser individuals will, like labels on medicine jars, find it easy to identify and locate the treatise based on the title. It states in the *Descent to Laṅkā*[a] as follows:

> If labels were not designated, the entire world would be confusing. Therefore, the skillful protector [i.e., the Buddha] found designated names for all phenomena.

Thus, as taught, by merely knowing the meaning of a title, some are able to comprehend the entire content of the text. Hence, that is why the title has been explained.

The rendering of homage is as follows. The meaning of reference to "the glorious Orgyen" and others [of the root terma] is that, by the strength of the oceanic accumulation of both levels of merit, namely, conceptual and nonconceptual wisdom, the fully endowed circumstance of the spontaneously present glory of the resultant two aims occurs. That is the meaning of "**glorious**". By the strength of this glory, the innate, inconceivable massing of wisdom qualities actually emanates before the field of meritorious disciples.

The origin of this [emanation] comes from the western direction of India called the land of Orgyen [i.e., Oḍḍiyāna].[18] At the border of this northwest region lies the place called **Orgyen**. There in the lake called Dhanakosha, [the Lake-Born One] was born in the pollen heart of a lotus without relying upon the cause of a father or the circumstance of a mother. In the manner of instantaneous awareness, he arose like a rainbow kāya that self-occurred. As the great state of self-arising, he was born in this way as the **Lake-Born** One. This astonishing, unrivaled, most precious nirmāṇakāya appeared intentionally due the aspirations of disciples. Free from birth, death, and decrepitude, his indestructible vajralike kāya was manifest while abiding on the ground of an immortal vidyādhara. Through this magical rainbow body, he spontaneously and constantly accomplishes the welfare of beings everywhere.[19] Nevertheless, from the perspective of definitive truth, he is not different from the actual victorious Buddha Vajradhara, so that is the meaning of "**vajra**". This vidyādhara lord of the ḍākinīs, the ever-excellent Lake-Born Vajra is supreme among all Indian and Tibetan vidyādharas and masters. The crown jewel of the oceanic masters, the one who attained the eight common and supreme siddhis, and who achieved

[a] *lang kar shek pa* (*lang kar gshegs pa*), *laṅkāvatārasūtra*

mastery over the outer and inner five elements was the Lord of Masters, **Saraha, who** transcended the ocean of qualities, including powers and the rest.

To these two masters, the glorious vajralike Dudjom[a] calls out saying, "**Bless** the mind streams of my fortunate **lineage-holding disciples** including **all** males and females, with the power of your enlightened body, speech, mind, qualities, and activities like an inexhaustible ornamental wheel. Pray, bring their three gateways to maturity as the three vajras and liberate them. Never separate from them for an instant and **care for them** through your great loving compassion. Without allowing their minds to deviate on an incorrect path, by mingling their minds with holy dharma, grant them enthronement and mastery as **dharma rulers victorious over the three realms. Gaining freedom** from the miseries of ordinary saṃsāra, **may** they be able to transcend the realms of beings and become sublime guides held in highest esteem." So he spoke.

It is said:

> When composing a shāstra,[b,20] the homage is not without purpose as it inspires devotion for the teachers and their teaching.

So from that perspective, self and others accumulate merit and pacify obstacles; and the treatise is able to be fully completed. It states in the *Sūtra of Vast Manifestations*:[c]

> The one with merit will fulfill all goals.

And the *Sūtra of Manifold Buddhas*[d] states:

> Whoever expresses even a minor positive act toward the victorious guides of beings will traverse the higher states of rebirth to arrive at the state of awakening.

Thus as taught, that is the homage.

Now according to this text's narrative context: if I were to elaborate a bit further on the meaning taken from the profound terma text on chöd, it is as follows. The tantras tell us:

> If delineated, the teacher and so forth are explained as the five fully endowed gatherings.

[a] *bdud 'joms dpal gyi rdo rje*; Dudjom Lingpa
[b] *bstan bcos*
[c] *do gya cher rolpa* (*mdo rgya cher rol pa, lalitavistarasūtra*)
[d] *sangye mang ched kyi do* (*sangs rgyas mang byed kyis mdo*)

Thus as taught, among the five fully endowed circumstances, first is the fully endowed circumstance of the place. **Due to** fixation, when **the** aspects of appearances are involved **with self and objects**, there comes to be interdependency. When there is an inability to separate from that, there is **entanglement.**[a] Given that this [condition] has become extremely all-encompassing, it is termed "**great**". Where have these ordinary dualistic concepts, including all relative objective phenomena, originated? The answer is the clear-light basic space of the ground. When within that [basic space] everything **collapses** and dissolves with**in its own place**, the fundamental nature of **selflessness** as **the** ground **of** ultimate **truth is directly seen.** Then all conceptual fixations that obscure **effortless** wisdom will be directly or **immediately liberated**, and wisdom **will well forth** as the **secret space of** definitive truth. **In this** open, **vast expanse of the great-bliss *bhaga*** [i.e., vagina] **of Samantabhadrī's secret enlightened mind**, the syllable ***eh*** represents the emptiness of prajñā and the syllable ***wam*** represents the exaltation of upāya. The aspect of **the unification of *eh*** and ***wam* is illuminated as the maṇḍala** of teacher, retinue, and so forth. **This manifests as the sacred ground of the self-appearing** absolute **Akaniṣhṭha.**[b]

To synthesize this key point: when—through self-appearing, pure wisdom free of duality—whatever appears arises as all-pervasive purity, such as the teacher, retinue, and so forth, this reveals the meaning of the words in the terma that state "this is" [i.e., the place]. In the *Extensive Magical Manifestation*,[c] it states:

> Wisdom free from duality is the dwelling place of all tathāgatas.

So, this is as taught.

The fully endowed teacher is nondual with the glorious Vajradhara, while ultimately the **teacher and retinue** are undifferentiated. From the perspective of faith, the glorious **Saraha, King of** Total Mastery, **appears** in whatever **magical manifestations** are deemed necessary.

The fully endowed **retinue** is wisdom's **dynamic strength** of the teacher himself appearing as the retinue. **Initially**, the retinue appears as the **wisdom sun** [i.e., disciple **Yeshe Nyima**[d]] of upāya and the principal **moon of prajñā** [i.e., disciple **Sherab Dawa'i Wangpo**[e]].[21] These two aspects of the retinue, as the nature of upāya and prajñā, are referred to in other texts when the meaning is being indicated, such as the moon indicating upāya and the sun indicating prajñā.

[a] *chang pa* (*'phyang pa*)
[b] Ogmin (*'og min*); Above All pure land
[c] *gyutrül gye pa* (*sgyu 'phrul rgyas pa*)
[d] *ye shes nyi ma*
[e] *shes rab zla wa'i dbang po*

Nevertheless, here they are reversed in that the order of reference is designated as the sun and then the moon because this emphasizes that upāya is never separate from prajñā and prajñā never separate from upāya. Hence, both **were empowered to listen** with respect.

The fully endowed dharma is the quintessential treasury of wisdom's **expanse** as the fully manifest fundamental nature **of the dharmatā**. For example, even among treasures—similar to being given the most cherished wealth—**so that the gateway to** this quintessential **great treasure trove was opened**, the ultimate wisdom intent could then be clearly revealed to others in the expanse of this wisdom. Among the abundant riches within that treasury, this is sublime. Similar to how a precious wish-fulfilling jewel is the source of all needs and desires, here—as the source of all temporary and ultimate qualities—this is so extremely rare it is called "**precious**".

The profound meaning of this subject—absolute dharma or realization—is not only difficult to fathom, as the absolute nature it is **inexhaustible**. That which expresses this is the dharma of transmission. When all forthright scholars and wise ones hear this, it is an **ornament** of joy for their minds. Given that the strength of inconceivable compassion and aspirational prayers is unceasing because of transferring from one fortunate disciple to the next and enduring for as long as saṃsāra exists, it is referred to as a wheel. This defines the actual meaning of the so-**called** dharma **wheel** of transmission and realization.[22] The secret, obscure meaning is clearly illuminated through **these great concealed notes** "**given to me**, who is known as **Longdrol Dorje Migyur**."[a,23] That is reference to the Great Tertön himself who received this [from Saraha] in the manner of a father bestowing the most **cherished** portion of his **wealth** upon his only son.

Concerning this, the abandonment [of passions] occurs by liberating all confused dualistic concepts without exception in the expanse of awareness; and vajralike, wisdom realization is attained by remaining unaffected by the faults of negativities. This name [i.e., Longdrol Dorje Migyur] rightfully applies since these undiminishing qualities of abandonment and realization are unfading.

The fully endowed time means the place of self-appearing wisdom when the assembly of teacher and retinue unite, so **at that time** they united. This transmission is unlike some common shāstras that include words based on ordinary intellectual understanding. In the wisdom of self-occurring **clear light**, self-manifesting pure appearances concerning all knowable things are unlimited and evenly **all-encompassing. By the self-arising luminosity** of supreme prajñā, the darkness of delusion that fails to know the nature of great all-pervasiveness is dispelled. This is **free from** being accomplished through **effort-based activity**

[a] *klong grol rdo rje mi 'gyur*

and is the intrinsic nature of the five wisdoms that primordially abide within the ground.

When **the** inner **radiance of this light** of the five essential great elements, free from the adventitious stains of obscurations, outwardly emerges as kāyas and pure lands, this is inseparable with the depth of wisdom prāṇa.[a] This is due to the nature of all aspects of enlightened vajra speech arising as the mode of the expression of words.

There are many categories of transmissions that rival this; however, concerning **this**, given that the future recipients will be numberless, it cannot be said that "these are their names, numbers, and so forth." That is because this is **unidentifiable** in terms of nature or numbers. Here, based on vast **meritorious accumulations** of merit over many lifetimes and the accomplished strength of excellent **aspirations**, along with the continuity of extremely positive **karma**: when the time arrives for these root causes and contributing circumstances to **converge**, then **this** transmission **will be self-emergent for the** exceptional **disciples** with **fortune, whoever they may be**. They will then internalize this by partaking of this feast like their own portion of wealth.

According to the tradition of teaching the *Magical Manifestation Matrix Secret Essence Tantra*,[b,24] there came to be two distinctions concerning the retinue, namely, the teacher himself and his connate retinue that exist simultaneously and a later separate category for subsequent recipients. Likewise, here, there are also two [aspects of the retinue] as the original disciples mentioned who indicate the first [i.e., connate retinue] and then future disciples indicating the second category.

In the profound terma of vajra speech, the [Tröma] tögal commentary, it mentions:

> In the expanse of the space of great clear-light exaltation, the maṇḍala of the face of the great lord among one-hundred mahāsiddhas, Saraha, is witnessed. His nature is undifferentiated from the buddha nature—the dharmakāya of the ground.

Thus as it states here, the nature of the dharmakāya of the ground, the essence of the sugatas, arises as one's teacher. In previous times, the teacher of the presence of the ground arose in the aspect of a mahāsiddha. These [i.e., teacher and ground] have been differentiated due to our dualistic minds, while ultimately they remain inseparable.

[a] *lung* (*rlung*); winds

[b] *gyutrül sang wa'i nyingpo gyü* (*sgyu 'phrul gsang ba'i snying po rgyud, guhyagarbhatattvavinishcayamahātantra*), *Guhyagarbha Tantra*

In this case, their nature is oneness as the vast expanse of clear-light exaltation. Not only that, as commonly stated:

> All victorious ones are the same within the wisdom expanse . . .

Like that, the nature of all victors of the ten directions and four times is one with this.

In the tantra *Two Segments*,[a] it states:

> I am the teacher and also the dharma. I am the assembly, as well as the recipient.

As stated, the manifestation of the teacher becomes the retinue and the dharma. This is similar to previous times when Buddha Vajradhara taught the classes of the great secret tantras. That is something quite different from the common shāstras, where teachings are compiled by ordinary individuals who claim that the source is the tantras. The difference is as significant as heaven versus earth. Although from the relative point of view it can be said that this text is a shāstra: from the perspective of the genuine nature, it holds true that this is the enlightened speech of the victorious ones.

The teacher appearing as Saraha occurred as follows. The Great Tertön himself proclaimed that he was the reincarnation of Shāriputra,[b] who was—among the two main disciples—the supreme one of prajñā. Concerning that, some tantras explain that Shāripu was an incarnation of the bodhisattva Nivāraṇavişhkambhin.[c,25] Hence, he was a reincarnate shrāvaka, not just an ordinary individual on the path of Hīnayāna. According to the perspective of disciples, Shāriputra manifested as the daughter of a merchant in order to become the consort of Saraha based on the power of enlightened intent and pure aspiration.

It is stated in the tögal commentary:

> *Kye!* Perfected prajñā is Ārya Shāripu. By arising as the merchant's daughter, she will guide the chariot so that I may traverse the grounds and paths when delighting in the union of empty bliss. During the future times of five-hundred degeneracies: by gaining confidence with the awakened mind of bodhichitta, I will then become a sublime hidden yogin. O Great Hero, holding me as your disciple, grant me the power to tame fortunate ones. May all who make a connection through this chariot of transmissions of indivisible upāya and prajñā be deliv-

[a] *tag pa nyi pa* (*brtag pa gnyis pa*); condensed version of *hevajratantrarāja*
[b] *sha ri'i bu*
[c] Dribpa Namsel (*sgrib pa rnam sel*); Fully Dispelled Obscurations

> ered to the ground of the dharmakāya. May I be able to maintain the glorious enlightened activities of the Lotus-Born Buddha Lord of the Dance[26] and empty the realms of saṃsāra.

Thus, and as stated:

> Through the interdependent purity of these aspirations and prayers, these days when the time has arrived . . .

Hence, it is just as taught. Once again, the transmission given through verse is:[27]

> Within the limit of the interconnected hands of the garland of subject-object, the innate nature of upāya and prajñā united is impregnated in the womb of the mother and sealed in the expanse of empty bliss. The extent is subsumed or completely contained to be held as the king of the vase. Since the space of great emptiness is a great analogy for emptiness, this great state of openness will not be determined through the core of a reed of grass.

Thus, this meaning is as follows. It is necessary to understand that **subject and object**, like **interconnected hands**, refer to the same thing as the term "entanglement" that was mentioned earlier. This means the state of uninterrupted [suffering] that has continued from beginningless time until now, referred to as "a **garland**". Until remedial wisdom is generated, **the limit** or continuity of this will continue on into the future. This and all phenomena of saṃsāra and enlightenment without exception originate from the dynamic strength of the clear-light nature of mind, the essence of the sugatas.

The glorious Saraha tells us:

> The mind alone is the seed for everything. From it, both existence and quiescence emerge.

Thus, this is similar.

It also states in the *All-Creating Monarch*:[a]

> If there is the desire to definitively realize this meaning, then this should be analyzed, for instance, as though it were the sky. The meaning is that the nature of phenomena is unborn, indicated by the unceasing nature of mind.

[a] *kun ched gyalpo* (*kun byed rgyal po*)

So, it is like that.

This ultimate truth of the ground of basic space must be understood to be, for example, like space. The indication is evident through the appearances that emerge that are the dynamic strength of mind's unceasing nature. This means that [the nature] abides as the innate nature of the unborn dharmatā. Based on that, the analogy and its meaning are readily understood. Based on analogy, the way that is indicated occurs through the aspect of appearances that originate from the dynamic strength of the ground's presence. The ultimate basis for these appearances is proven to exist as the **innate nature** of the ground of basic space. If that were not the case, then these appearances would have no basis from which to arise. If there were no basis for appearances to arise from, there would be no appearances arising dependent upon that [basis]. The aspect of whatever occurs as appearances is unceasing, proving there is a basis from which the appearances arise. This is just as it states in the scriptures on valid cognition. Like fire constituting the cause for the resultant smoke, it is impossible for there to be an occurring result devoid of cause. Since smoke would not occur if there is no fire, it is proven that smoke indicates fire. The same reasoning applies here.

Furthermore, since the nature of the basic space of the ground is free from the elaboration of existing, it is then possible for all appearances of that dynamic strength to appear. If that were not the case, then [appearances] would not be possible.

The glorious protector Ārya Nāgārjuna[a] tells us:

> Whatever qualifies as the nature of emptiness is accepted to be that nature. Whatever does not qualify as the nature of emptiness, will not be acceptable as such.

Thus, the key point is summarized in that quotation. Holding this meaning in mind, it also says in the *Precious Treasury of the Dharmadhātu*:[b]

> The examples indicating bodhichitta are similar to the sky.

The quote continues:

> This means that the awakened mind of self-awareness is equal to space.

And:

[a] Pakpa Ludrub (*'phags pa klu sgrub*)
[b] *chöying rinpoche'i dzöd* (*chos dbyings rin po che'i mdzod*); Longchen Rabjam

> The indications are that anything can arise from dynamic strength.

Thus, it is taught. The meaning of this is synthesized as follows:

> The nature of self-emergent wisdom is devoid of direction. Through definitive analogies, meanings, and indications, this is revealed.

So, it is taught.

Why is the way of identifying this correlation through indication being explained here? Given that certainty can be gained based on the way appearances of the ground arise from the ground [and] by connecting that notion with this subject, it becomes easier to comprehend this subject. Otherwise, according to the root commentary to the *Treasury of the Dharmadhātu*, it states:

> Upon the clear surface of the ocean, constellations in the sky appear as reflections. When, aside from appearing, there is certainty that their nature has no true existence, likewise the transparency of the basis for the arising [of this reflection]—the ocean—is also understood.

Similarly, when it is understood that the mind arising from the space of awareness is inseparable with the intrinsic nature of its designated basis of arising and—except for appearing—never departs from the intrinsic nature of emptiness, then the genuine state of [the mind's] fundamental nature can be known as spatial awareness. Hence, this is taught in order to understand how to identify spacelike emptiness. It remains difficult to understand this if one does not fully comprehend the meaning of mind versus awareness according to the tradition of Mahāsandhi.

From the perspective of analogies, indications, and their meanings—these three—it is necessary to gain certainty with the nature of the basic space of the ground that is emptiness possessing all supreme aspects.[28] The exceptional status of this [emptiness] is illuminated in all unsurpassed Secret Mantra tantras that are based on unchanging, connately emergent exaltation.

In the *Vajra Magical Manifestation*,[a] it states:

> That which abides in the minds of sentient beings is the aspect of immaculate self-emergent wisdom, the indestructible bindu of exaltation that pervades everything like space. This is the intrinsic nature of nonabiding dharmakāya.

[a] *gyutrül dorje* (*sgyu 'phrul rdo rje*)

Thus, and in the *Two Segments*, we are told:

> Always being the intrinsic nature of bliss—even throughout the realms of the world, buddha will not be discovered elsewhere. This nature of mind is the fully perfected buddha. The buddha is not revealed as otherwise.

Thus, and in the *Commentary to the Vajra Essence*,[a] it states:

> From beginningless time, all sentient beings are buddha because they possess this inherent nature.

Thus, this is as taught.

That which is called "buddha" is explained as follows. According to the assertion of the Omniscient Longchenpa, among the two aspects of buddha—namely, the spontaneously present buddha of the ground and the fully manifest resultant buddha[29]—this [discussion] refers to the former. In this way, when the nature of this ground is actualized as **upāya and prajñā in unity** or indivisible **bliss-emptiness**, all dualistic appearances without exception are subsumed within that expanse. Sealed as though invisible, it is said that this is called "**the mother sealed in the expanse**". As the source of saṃsāra and enlightenment without exception, this is called "mother". Hence, when designated as such, the origin of this connects with the sūtras and tantras.

In the sūtra classifications of the Great Mother [i.e., Yüm Chenmo], the ultimate intent of expressing the term "Great Mother" is that this indicates emptiness. In the tantra *All-Creating Monarch,* it states:

> By realizing the essential meaning, the buddhas of the three times will emerge.

So, it is taught. This should be revealed by the term "Great Mother".

In the scriptures on unsurpassed Secret Mantra, it is similarly taught that the clear light of the ground is referred to as the mother clear light. In addition, Chang Kya Rolpa'i Dorje,[b] who was an incarnation of the glorious Lord of Secrets, Dropukpa,[c] said:

> These myriad dualistic [appearances] amount to the smiling expression of the Mother. These transitions between birth and death amount to

[a] *dorje nying drel* (*rdo rje snying 'grel*)
[b] *lcang skya rol pa'i rdo rje*
[c] *sgro phug pa*

> the false speech of the Mother. Mother, you are inexpressible, having never existed; yet anything can manifest [from you] in a state of mutual dependency. Through this alone, comprehension can occur.

The key points of this quote are in harmony with this presentation.

In this way, impure appearances that are rendered invisible are designated as **impregnated in the** way that, when a child is conceived within the mother's **womb**, it is invisible. From this perspective, there is a similarity. To say that the **extent** of the many aspects of pure appearances as one's dynamic strength are exhausted or **subsumed** without exception refers to the fact that everything is **completely contained** or entirely consumed within the space of this clear light. Hence, similar to the explanations just given, this is epitomized by the term "place". In this place, the aspect of appearances arises as teacher and retinue.

In the *Glorious Secret Essence*,[a] it states:

> The wisdom of the space of the nature, as it is, is the mudrā of upāya, the cause of everything.

Thus, and in the *Guru Magical Manifestation Matrix*,[b] it states:

> The empty nature of the nonexistent mind is devoid of class, color, and shape. Nothing whatsoever exists, while anything whatsoever can appear. Unborn myriad magical manifestations emerge, and even the various maṇḍalas of the victors amount to the great magical manifestation of the mind.

And so it is with this transmission.

In the prose of the root terma, the great-bliss *bhaga*, Samantabhadrī, is referred to as the mother sealed as the expanse of bliss-emptiness. One must understand that these refer to the same thing. Samantabhadrī is the empty nature of the basic space of exaltation. The term *bhaga* can also be interpreted as the blissful nature of this space of emptiness. Conversely, if the term *bhaga* is interpreted as "to conquer", it then means that the gathering of thoughts—including their objects—vanish in the manner of being sealed [as emptiness] and are thereby conquered. Know these references to be similar.

In the *Concise Commentary*,[c] it states:

[a] *pal sangwa'i nyingpo* (*dpal gsang ba'i snying po*)

[b] *lama gyutrül drawa* (*bla ma sgyu 'phrul drva ba*)

[c] *drel chung* (*'grel chung*), Piṇḍārtha (*pinda 'rtha*), *shrīguhyagarbhapiṇḍārthaṭīkā*; Vimalāmitra

> The outer and inner celestial palace is the inherent space of phenomena that expresses the characteristics of a supreme sacred place. Since this is subsumed within the *bhaga*, it is called "always excellent".[a]

Thus, this is similar. Calling this a supreme sacred place also indicates the likeness to a sacred place.

In the Mahāsandhi tantra *Dynamic Strength of the Lion*,[b] it states:

> Within the expanse of Samantabhadrī's *bhaga*, the five elements of the phenomenal existence of saṃsāra and enlightenment are subsumed.

Thus, as taught, to say "five elements" means that—at the time of impurity as mentioned just above, although necessary to acknowledge these as the coarse outer elements—when pure as outer appearances, these are the purest essence of light. That is why all of this is intrinsically interlinked with the point being proven here.

Given that pure appearances are fully subsumed in this way, the example of the **king of the vase** is referred **to as held** like this. Conversely, from the perspective of the meaning of the basic space of the ground, the aspects of kāyas and wisdoms without exception that abide within the ground are not outwardly visible, but rather spontaneously present. This is like the example of a candle placed inside a vase being called the "king of the vase". It can be understood that, here, one is being told to hold or sustain this like an excellent vase overflowing with precious jewels.

In *Praise to the Dharmadhātu*,[c] it states:

> Like a candle within a vase that cannot be seen from the outside, this basic space of phenomena cannot be seen in the light of saṃsāra. Once the vase is broken, just as everyone can then see [the candle]—when through vajra samādhi the obstructions are fully conquered, it is then that the light of this [basic space of phenomena] will be luminous throughout limitless space.

This is similar to that quote.

In the Mahāsandhi tantras, we are told:

[a] *kun tu zang* (*kun tu bzang*)

[b] *senge tsal dzok* (*seng ge rtsal rdzogs*)

[c] *chö ying töd pa* (*chos dbyings bstod pa, dharmadhātustava*); Nāgārjuna

> This also reveals the meaning of the term "ever-youthful vase kāya".[a]

Concerning this, to say "vase kāya" and "buddha nature" describes the same meaning since both are synonyms. In particular, to reveal the way they are indicated through analogy is that **the** vast **space of great emptiness** pervading everything **is a** suitable and praiseworthy **great analogy** to indicate the nature of the basic space of the ground **since that is** the **nature of emptiness** that possesses all supreme aspects.

To continue with the quotation from the *All-Creating Monarch* mentioned above:

> The skylike nature is indicated by the example of the sky.

And in the *Prajñāpāramitā* mother sūtra, it states:

> If one were to wonder what this means, then gaze into the sky.

Thus, this is similar. Otherwise, to just individually determine and refute the true existence of the person, pillar, vase, and the like based on biased conditional phenomena amounts to a limited notion of emptiness. That is like how **the great state of openness will not be determined** to be empty **through the core of a reed of grass.** Hence, an approach such as that is extremely limited in comparison to what is presented here.

Furthermore, the meaning of the previous three lines can also be interpreted by summing up what was just mentioned. To say "hold the king of the vase," or the consummate appearances of the ground, and the analogy "that is spacelike" are phrases that set forth the foundation for this commentary. In this way, these sacred instructions are as stated in the tantras:

> Transmitted through the continuity of wisdom, symbolic indication,
> and aural transmission . . .[30]

Thus, as taught, since this instruction combines all three lineages that then emerge as the single taste of the wisdom expanse of all the victors, that is the wisdom-mind lineage of the victors. The appearances of the aspects of signs and indications of teacher and retinue are the symbolic-indication lineage of the vidyādharas, and transmission through hearing as the expression of sounds and words is the aural lineage of exceptional individuals as well. This manner of

[a] *zhonnu büm ku* (*gzhon nu bum sku*)

instruction is in accord with what is being explained in the terma itself, as well as mainly setting forth a brief description of the narrative context.

In other words, if applied to the ground—just as the appearances of dreams themselves are subsumed within the expanse of the sleeping consciousness—within the expanse of this space of the ground, all phenomena of saṃsāra and enlightenment without exception are subsumed and abide all-pervasively. At the time of the path, when this fundamental nature is actualized through the power of meditation, dualistic concepts vanish and pure appearances emerge. At the time of the result, the manifestations of self-appearing wisdom as pure appearances will arise all-pervasively and separate from the stains of adventitious obstruction. Hence, in the manner of sealing and so forth, confused appearances will never reoccur. These terms hold great import since this meaning is applicable to any occasion of the ground, path, or result—these three.

In general, the essence of the practice of chöd is the view; and in that vein, these instructions on chöd belong to the exceptional upadesha class of the Mahāsandhi.[31] Since according to the view of this tradition it is necessary to precisely realize the ground and the manner in which the appearances of the ground arise, it is acceptable here to consider that this explanation is given in conjunction with the concise teachings of this tradition found in the root terma. I have tried my best to clarify this section by considering that, if this meaning can be clearly understood, the meaning described in the narrative context concerning the other instructions of this profound treasure, as well as similar explanations, will all be easily comprehended.

If explained in extensive detail, the meanings of *eh wam*, magical manifestation, and other such terms are described in conjunction with the narrative contexts that accompany all great secret tantras, such as the *Guhyasamāja*,[a] *Guhyagarbha*, and others. In those tantras, the descriptions are as vast as they are astonishing. In this context, since it is necessary to begin [this commentary] by explaining the preliminary practices, the descriptions given here are mainly geared toward leading beginners on the path. Given that [extensive explanations] may not suit their minds and for fear of becoming overly verbose, I have decided to say only this much.

> All characteristics of elaborations that appear as subject-object are sealed in the *bhaga* of Samantabhadrī—the basic space of inseparable bliss-emptiness.
> The magical manifestation of nondual *eh wam* appears as the ground's presence of the pure maṇḍala.
> The intrinsic nature of the self-appearing dharmakāya is the basic

[a] *sangwa dü pa* (*gsang ba 'dus pa*); Gathering of Secrets

space of the sky, and the rūpakāya teacher that appears to others as a rainbow is the fully endowed, single taste of the colorful luster of five lights.
This is the great ornament that beautifies the clear-light appearances of the ground.
From within the expanse of the space of the dharmatā's primordial omniscience and awareness, the great terma of wisdom prajñā wells forth.
This secret upadesha, itself a great secret treasure, is self-emergent as a naturally appearing celebration for the sake of self and all others.

Hence, these are the verses that summarize the section.[32]

2 Expression of the Greatness of This Teaching

Second, an expression of the greatness is as follows. In the *Gathering of Precious Qualities*,[a] it states:

> With the close placement of supreme joy, respect, and faith and by dispelling obstructions and passions, stains are transcended. Directly engaging the welfare of others is the tranquil pāramitā of prajñā. Those heroes who engage in this way must be similar to ferrymen.[33]

Thus as taught, through close placement with joy, there is pure [inspired] faith. "Respect" means emulating faith. The finest faith is fully-convinced faith. By dispelling passions, obstructions, and the associated habits, stains are transcended. This nonabiding state beyond sorrow is not just for self-gain, but rather to directly enact the welfare of all sentient beings. The cause for this is that, by training in love and compassion as well as the prajñā that realizes selflessness, the mind stream becomes tranquil and tame. It is necessary for those of good fortune to bravely engage these oral-instruction teachings of the pāramitā of prajñā with courage and practice diligently like a ferryman. If one wonders why, it is because this approach surpasses other traditions. The reason for this is also mentioned by the wisdom ḍākinī Machig:

> This transcendental transmission is the lineage of Shākyamuni, the companion of this is the bodhisattva Samantabhadra, and the dharma is the essence of the Mother.

[a] *yon ten rinpoche düd pa* (*yon tan rin po che sdud pa*, *prajñāpāramitāsañcayagāthā*); verse summary of the *Sūtra of Transcendental Incisive Knowledge*

Thus, as taught, from the perspective of expressing the precious instructions, this [teaching] is connected to the perfectly pure source of the lineage, as well as being adorned as its own exceptional lineage.

The source of this transmission is the *Sūtra of Transcendental Incisive Knowledge*, and the lineage also comes from the victor Shākyamuni as mentioned earlier. From the perspective of experiential practice with the subject itself, this follows in accord with the deeds of the bodhisattva Samantabhadra and involves training in bodhisattva conduct, such as generosity and the like. Uniting that with the prajñā that realizes the nature of emptiness as the meaning of the Mother, the last two stanzas [in the quote] point out the exceptional nature of this practice.

To elucidate, it states in the *Prayer for Excellent Conduct*:[a]

> The elder among all victorious ones, who holds the name of Samantabhadra . . .

Thus, as taught, among all bodhisattvas, he who is Ārya Samantabhadra is, for example, like the first-born son of a king, the noblest of all. In order to traverse the paths and lead others along, one must train in harmony with the example of his conduct. For instance, when traveling on a path in the worldly sense, a worthy traveling companion is said to be someone with harmonious conduct and intentions. It is acceptable to designate a bodhisattva such as that as "a companion" since it is taught that sangha are the companions to befriend and accompany while accomplishing the path. Given that prajñā that realizes the meaning of emptiness as selflessness is the principal practice of this path, this is the essence of the sacred dharma of the Mother. Hence, that is the meaning.

This proves that this is the sole path to traverse by all the victorious ones, as it states in the *Gathering of Precious Qualities*:

> All victors who reside throughout the ten directions, from the past and in the future, have taken this as their path of transcendence, not otherwise.

So, it is taught.

Since this [text] represents the stages of practice on emptiness that are explicit in the Sūtra tradition of the Great Mother, this [explanation] carries with it the full capacity to uproot the causes of existence. In addition, given that this connects with the practice of the vast hidden meaning: rather than entering the path

[a] *zangpo chöd pa'i mon lam gyi gyalpo* (*bzang po spyod pa'i smon lam gyi rgyal po, bhadracaryāpraṇidhānarāja*)

to personal liberation from saṃsāra or the cessation of peaceful tranquility, this brings the cessation of both limitations of existence and quiescence.

In the *Uttaratantra*,[a] we are told:

> Self-existence without exception is severed by prajñā. In order to liberate sentient beings from existence through compassion, quiescence is not the goal.

Hence, this is similar to that.

Not just in those ways, all stages of the sublime dharma to be accomplished are either directly or indirectly subsumed within this practice of chöd. This is why chöd is such an exceptional practice of the path of the great vehicle. The entire dharma revealed by the Buddha converges or is brought to the path of the great vehicle that accomplishes the state of omniscience. Hence, it is taught that everything will ultimately merge with this single vehicle.

From the *Chapter on Great Truth*,[b] it states:

> O Mañjushrī! Whenever I teach dharma to beings and whatever the subject may be, it is always like this: to attain the state of all-knowing wisdom, to be led to the state of awakening, to merge with the great vehicle, to establish omniscience itself, and to fully perfect the sole objective. That is why I make no distinctions concerning vehicles.

Thus, this is similar.

To explain this in a way that is easy to comprehend, this [chöd] is not just a method that considers the teachings given on the suffering of the lower realms and how to attain a higher rebirth that is free from that suffering. Here, by gradually cleansing the mind stream and entering the path of the great vehicle, the method for attaining the state of omniscience is then revealed. This [chöd] is an aspect of that [i.e., the great vehicle] given that it is a means through which to enter that path.

For example, if one hopes to ascend to the roof of a building: by stepping upon the first step of the staircase leading there, it is then certain that one will be directed toward the roof. Like that, by prostrating, offering, and cleansing negativities, obscurations, and so forth based on a field of merit, merit is thereby accumulated, which renders the mind stream functional. Then, this path must gradually be traversed. These are not just my own ideas, for Machig herself has said:

[a] *gyü lama* (*rgyud bla ma*); Maitreya

[b] *denpa chenpo'i le'u* (*bden pa chen po'i le'u*)

The meaning of the sacred dharma is complete within chöd.

So, it is taught.

In particular, the practice of chöd unites with the path of Secret Mantra; and specifically, the transmissions for meditation, or the key points of the view and meditation [within chöd], are based on the level of the supreme vehicle's great perfection. Hence, this is the unsurpassed path that brings the state of Vajradhara in a single lifetime. The way this occurs will be understood in more detail during the course of this explanation.

The greatness of these qualities is described by Machig, as told to her son Töd Nyon:[a]

> O Son, listen here! This tradition of mine called the "mahāmudrā of chöd" surpasses any dharma. This contains the sublime features of the uncommon meaning of the extremely profound crucial points. Unlike other shāstras, this is the transmission on the key points of upadesha, the essence of all doctrines, the pinnacle of all vehicles, as well as the supreme heart of Sūtra and Mantra combined as one. This is the doctrine that liberates the four māras in their place, the supreme method that directly abandons the five poisons, the ax that cuts the tree of self-fixation from the root, the army that actually reverses the battlefield of saṃsāra, the powerful strength that subjugates eighty-thousand hordes of obstructers, the supreme medicine that cures the four-hundred and four diseases, and the result that is not postponed for a future lifetime but rather brings enlightenment to maturity in this lifetime. These are the sublime features of this yoginī's precious dharma unrivaled by any other doctrine.

Thus, as she said, reference to "this is the pinnacle of all vehicles" and other phrases are similar to references found throughout Mahāsandhi literature. That this is a teaching bringing enlightenment in a single lifetime clearly indicates that this must be connected to not only Mantra in general, or unsurpassed Mantra, but in particular to the upadesha class of Mahāsandhi.

Furthermore, these days, most practitioners are attached to this life and overpowered by self-grasping, so they fixate upon their own bodies and endowments. Such practitioners will strive in methods to reverse harmful humans and nonhuman entities, such as reciting wrathful mantra recitation, implementing reversal substances, and the like, as well as vigilantly meditating upon the wheel of protection and the vajra fence in order to self-protect. Even those who teach

[a] *thod smyon*

and learn will still hold fast to this life's name, fame, and position of respect in the monasteries and will engage in many social distractions and responsibilities that are contrary to the sacred dharma teachings. These are all causes for increased wandering in saṃsāra and can also become the causes that lead to the lower realms.

Conversely, in this teaching, all demonic obstructing forces expelled by those who perform wrathful activity motivated by aggression are magnetized to come forward through the strength of great compassion. They are placed in one's retinue, and the stages of the visualization of giving of one's cherished body and wealth to them free from attachment are engaged. Hence, this constitutes the supreme practice of the path of the great vehicle.

In order to turn one's mind from attachment to saṃsāra by directly cutting through all fixations that focus on close friends and relatives, gradually one is able to sever attachment toward objective appearances in general. Staying alone in an empty, uninhabited valley, fixation toward the true existence of outer appearances is then severed. Without regard, being able to offer one's cherished body and life essence as sustenance to the gods-māras, eventually attachment to one's body and true existence will be naturally cut through. To remain in the wakeful awareness of the unborn nature of basic space when the unceasing natural force of that dynamic strength self-liberates grasping-fixation, then within that emptiness, inner fixation upon self and true existence will naturally be severed. To achieve the immutable ground of the awareness of inseparable space-awareness employs the exceptional methods of the view that are the uncommon practice.

Those powerful nonhumans, both form and formless, who always harbor negative intentions and engage in harmful deeds toward many sentient beings will once again throw themselves down to the limitless lower realms of existence. That is why to benefit even one formless elemental spirit brings greater benefit than benefiting one-hundred form beings. Here, through this level of practice that captures and holds them with the hook of compassion and gives them flesh and blood, their minds are temporarily subdued and tamed; while ultimately they are brought to the state of enlightenment. Hence, great waves of benefit will be accomplished for others.

If one were to compare benefiting countless ordinary beings to benefiting a person who ensures that others will realize the meaning of the prajñāpāramitā, the latter brings greater merit. The practitioner himself or herself becomes a supreme field for merit. Likewise, to compare hundreds of ordinary accumulations of merit to the merit accumulated through offering one's body, the latter is exalted. Staying at one's home or monastery accumulating virtue through body and speech for a hundred days compared to staying just seven days in a fear-invoking environment, making offerings of one's body is far more beneficial. To compare feeling a sense of loving kindness toward those who love and think kindly upon you with showing loving kindness to a single being who expresses hatred and aggression, the latter is far more beneficial as this accumulates vast amounts of merit.

In the case of self or others becoming afflicted by any kind of disease or demonic-force possession, a ritual fabricator lacking prajñā and in a deluded state of mind is oftentimes summoned to give predictions to the hypocritical recipient about how he or she has been overcome by māras. Believing this nonsense, some will even go on to kill many innocent animals to offer their blood and flesh to the māras with the hope to extend their own life by taking the lives of others. Likewise, by hoping to be free from illness, [such hypocrites] will kill healthy animals for sacrificial offering. Given that these tactics are in direct opposition to the law of cause and result, this amounts to the most perverted form of wrong view. In fact, these views are nothing short of those who are basic heretics and barbarians.

Conversely here, with no regard for personal gain and, not only that, from the perspective of love and compassion, the cherished body of flesh and blood is given through diligence in practice. Based on the depth of the view of selflessness and through visualization based on samādhi, this is the supreme ceremony for removing obstacles in this life. Hence, the superb qualities that ensue are boundless. These explanations have been given in harmony with the subject of this section and are the speech of Machig herself, extracted from the aural lineage and condensed into these crucial pith points.

These teachings captivated the minds of the Indian masters to such an extent that they invited Machig to come to India [from Tibet]; however, she declined to do so. The dharma was abundant in the Indian language and many [Indian] transmissions were brought into Tibet. Nevertheless, Machig herself mentioned:

> The propagation of dharma from Tibet to India has occurred only through me.

These words of hers have become well known. In particular, this dharma [i.e., chöd] is an exceptional teaching that is meant to tame all beings in the Snow Land of Tibet. Machig tells us:

> O Fortunate Child! During the degenerate times, the doctrine of the great Sage will spread as follows. In the northern direction where there are one-hundred million Jambudvīpas,[a,34] there will be one-hundred million lands of Tibet. In the land of Tibet, there will be one-hundred million manifestations of Avalokiteshvara[b] as King Songtsen

[a] Dzambuling (*'dzam bu'i gling*); Rose-Apple Continent

[b] Chenrezig (*spyan ras gzigs*)

> Gampo[a] who will come, according to the predictions of the Sage. I, too, will appear in one-hundred million forms; and for whoever is causing harm whether in form or formless ways, especially for those who are unruly and negative whose time has come to be tamed, I will reveal the sacred dharma of the māra-taming mahāmudrā chöd in order to accomplish the welfare of all beings regardless of whether they are negative or positive. Just as the Sage has made predictions for degenerate times, the beings that dwell in the Snow Land must be tamed through this yoginī's doctrine.

Just as she predicted, it came to pass. Since Tibet is the field for the supreme Ārya Avalokiteshvara to tame: as his actual emanation, dharma king Songtsen Gampo's deeds were enacted throughout Tibet through myriad enlightened deeds for the welfare of the Tibetans. The select portion of dharma that this king bestowed upon the Tibetan people was known as the "king's collected works". Stemming from that, there are many transmissions of chöd that came through Machig. In the past, in order to tame the Tibetans, Avalokiteshvara generated bodhichitta, and Ārya Tārā promised to support and assist him so that now we are witnessing the maturity of those historical aspirations. Machig told us:

> From the outer perspective, I am Māyādevī;[b] from the inner perspective, I am Ārya Tārā; and secretly, I am Vajravarāhī. According to basic space, I am the Great Mother. At the beginning of the Buddha's doctrine, I was Gaṅgādevī.[c] Following that, I was Ḍākinī Dewa'i Ngödrub;[d] and later, I was the Tibetan lady Yeshe Tsogyal.[e] Now, Fortunate Child, I am myself.

Thus, she proclaims herself to be the manifestation of Ārya Tārā.

Given that Avalokiteshvara is the deity of compassion, Machig has told us:

> Love, compassion, and the awakened mind—these three—are the life force of my teachings.

Thus, as she mentions, the place to tame and the specific karmic summons for the transmission of chöd—these two—were exceptionally congruent in their unity.

[a] *srong btsan sgam po*

[b] Lhamo Gyutrül (*lha mo sgyu'phrul*); Goddess of Magical Manifestation

[c] Ganga'i Lhamo (*gang ga'i lha mo*); Goddess of the River Gaṅgā

[d] *bde ba'i dngos grub*; Blissful Siddhi

[e] *ye shes mtsho rgyal*; Ocean of Wisdom

Based on that, even for someone as insignificant as myself, to be praised as a dharma keeper by both tertöns—the supreme guide, an emanation of the great dharma king, Tertön Dudjom Pema Lingpa Tsal,[a] whose collections [i.e., new treasures] are called the *Collections of the Dharma King*,[b] and the Great Tertön, Dudjom Lingpa, who revealed many profound dharma treasures such as the one being explained—causes me to consider my own karmic fortune extremely great. This is why it is with great pleasure that I undertake the task of composing clear explanations to accompany a profound terma such as this. These personal implications slipped out as a matter of course due to being overcome with sheer delight and are in no way intended to disgust the minds of the noble ones.

Not only that, during these times of the five degeneracies, the blessings of these dharma teachings are more exalted than others. The way of recognizing the time of the five *dregs* is based on the duration of the great Sage's doctrine. The degeneracy of the doctrine occurs during the second half of the final five-thousand years of the doctrine [in this world]. That is the time of the final five-hundred years. The degeneracy of sentient beings occurs when their bodies and vitality become negative and weak and they take interest in destructive, nonvirtuous ways.

The degeneracy of passions occurs when the passions of attachment, hatred, jealousy, and the like become extremely coarse. In terms of the degeneracy of life expectancy, when Machig came into the world, it was said to be sixty years. From then, the life span of beings will continue to decrease to only ten years. The degeneracy of time occurs when untimely rains, snows, floods, tsunamis, hurricanes, tornados, illness, famine, and war all occur at random, such as what we are presently witnessing. During the time of these degeneracies, the fields of disciples are to be tamed through this doctrine of chöd. After recognizing the five degeneracies in this way, Machig herself said:

> Alas, so this is what is referred to as the five degeneracies! Fortunate Ones! These days few individuals practice according to the precious dharma. However much dharma is known is supposed to serve as an antidote for the passions. Regardless of that, it seems that however much dharma is known is supporting and strengthening the passions. Present-day practitioners give rise to inflated pride and haughtiness, rendering them incapable of taming their own minds. Like stones in the river, their teachers will be unable to bring a hair's tip worth of benefit to them. When a savage tradition that encourages dispute and turmoil unites with savage individuals to be subjugated, the goal of the

[a] *pad ma gling pa rtsal*, aka Ling Ter
[b] *chö gyal ka büm* (*chos rgyal bka' 'bum*); Songtsen Gampo

> precious dharma will be lost from sight. This is not the fault of dharma but rather the individual. Since this is the time of the degeneracy of sentient beings that become like incorrigible savages and also since it is the end of the Buddha's doctrine in this world, the authentic teaching fades.
>
> Hence, these days it is difficult to tame the minds of sentient beings through authentic teachings of the doctrine. Even those who are extremely sophisticated and well-mannered must still grow old, become decrepit, and experience their strength declining to a position of humility. Likewise, those who are in the prime of their youth will also grow physically old, while their minds still remain sharp.
>
> All beings unable to be tamed through the perfectly awakened Buddha will still have an opportunity to be tamed by the bodhisattvas. For example, the shāstras that are newly composed by the bodhisattvas will bring swift benefit to sentient beings. The beings of the Snow Land of Tibet have the opportunity to be objects tamed by Lord Avalokiteshvara. My occasion to tame beings is this present time. Especially since the time has arrived for the sacred dharma that severs the māras through this dharma designated as chöd, there is the interdependence to tame all unruly sentient beings. So it is, Fortunate Children.

In addition, in the mind training of the Kadampa tradition,[a] it states:

> When the five *dregs* arrive, the path of the bodhisattvas will become predominant. This will be the essential ambrosia of upadesha.

So just as taught, due to harmful influences by humans and nonhumans alike, these days there are few circumstances that bring about well-being; so the circumstances for suffering run rampant. When negative circumstances run rampant and when oral instructions such as these are relied upon, the negative circumstances can help to increase experiential realization on the path. Hence, this is like ambrosia that serves as an antidote for turning all poisons into potent medicine.

In Paṇchen Rinpoche Lozang Chögyan's[b] *Hearing Lineage of Ganden Guru Yoga*,[c] it states:

[a] *bka' gdams pa'i blo sbyong*

[b] *pan chen rin po che blo bzang chos rgyan*; Fourth Panchen Lama

[c] *ganden nyen gyü la chöd* (*dge ldan snyan brgyud bla mcho,*; Paṇchen Rinpoche Lozang Chögyan

> When the universe and inhabitants are completely filled with the results of negative karma—although unwanted suffering will shower down like rain—by seeing this as the exhaustion of negative karmic accumulations, grant blessings to take these negative circumstances as the path.

Thus as mentioned, at the moment of departing for the pure lands, the lord of our family whose kindness is unequaled—known as rainbow-body Vajradhara[35]—repeatedly offered these aspiration prayers.

Having met with oral instructions such as these and if there is the fortune to fully perfect practice according to the authentic tradition, then there is no better way to fulfill the aspirations of the sublime ones. Especially concerning these profound instructions that are the heart essence of the supreme mahāsiddha Saraha and the quintessence of Secret Mantra Vajrayāna, the teachings that sever actual fixation upon hope and fear, and the upadesha that allow one to encounter one's fundamental nature, this lineage is close, the blessings are great, and the pith instructions have not been mistaken. So needless to say, this lineage carries the greatness of the general qualities of the authentic profound termas.

Specifically, through this dharma, until now there have been many individuals who have attained supreme qualities, such as actually witnessing the accomplishment of the radiant rainbow body and so forth. The vajra predictions proclaim that in the future many countless more will occur. Since these are undeceiving words describing the meaning of this subject, one must have strong confidence in them. At the end of this text in the section on the entrustment of the teachings, it states:

> In this way, the fortunate ones revealing the stages of this path of practice are nondual with me, who is a buddha. If buddhahood is not attained in this life, then I have deceived you who are the fortunate lineage holders. This unsurpassed, essential dharma of the great vehicle is more precious than one's own heart blood.

Thus, it is as taught.

The rivers of the distant lineage of the wisdom sovereign of ḍākinīs, Machig Labdrön's instructions, and the close lineage of the chakravartin of the siddhas, the heart essence of the glorious Danunpa,[a] converge here as a single stream of Kāma and Terma. As a single key point that holds the meaning of the wisdom intent for these practices, this [convergence] exceeds other lineages. All those with intelligence must come to know this.

Through the pleasing melodious voice of the Great Sage, the eighty-four

[a] *mda' bsnun pa*; the Archer, Saraha

thousand categories of dharma were transmitted as the three vehicles, according to the faculties of the disciples. The essence of them all is the *Sūtra of Transcendental Incisive Knowledge*, and the method through which to practice that wisdom intent is this superb dharma of profound upadesha that comes through both the wisdom ḍākinī who manifested as a human female and the wisdom embodiment of the Lord of Siddhas, Danunpa. This dharma is the great vehicle that brings a conclusion to the limitations of saṃsāra and nirvāṇa. Given that this path grants awakening in this lifetime, this is the object of countless words of praise—worthy of the reliance of all who are fortunate.

> When the ominous circumstance of overflowing, polluted lake waters occurs, the flood of these degenerate times will burst forth.
> Aside from these instructions, like extracting the essence of ambrosia, no other medicine will maintain the life essence of the path to liberation.

Thus, these are the verses that summarize the section.

3 The Way to Internalize the Meaning of the Teaching

This has two parts:
1 General explanation of the description
2 Specific explanation of how to practice

Third, the manner of incorporating this meaning into practice is twofold: a general explanation of the description and a specific explanation of how to practice.

3.1 General Explanation of the Description

This has two parts:
1 Revealing the enumerations of scriptures that describe chöd
2 Explanation of this subject being described—chöd

First, for the general description there are two: revealing the enumerations of scriptures that describe chöd and an explanation of this subject being described—chöd.

3.1.1 Revealing the Enumerations of Scriptures that Describe Chöd

This has two parts:
1 Scriptures of the Kāma
2 Commentaries explaining the Kāma

First, generally the scriptures describing chöd are common to both traditions of Buddha's speech [i.e., Kāma], as well as the shāstras.

3.1.1.1 Scriptures of the Kāma

Among them, first there are the extensive, medium, and concise sūtras on the Great Mother, as well as the *Jataka Tales*[a] found in the sūtras that recount how, historically, our teacher [i.e., the Buddha] was a bodhisattva who [altruistically] offered his body, kingdom, wife, and the rest. All of the above can be placed in this [first] category [i.e., Buddha's speech.]

3.1.1.2 Commentaries Explaining the Kāma

Second, concerning the shāstras, there are four: the blessed lineage of Buddha's speech, the shāstra lineage of commentaries, the tradition of aural upadesha, and the tradition of the extremely profound close lineage.

For the first, there are three cycles with explanations by Machig revealing them, such as the outer expanded, extensive explanations of Buddha's speech, the inner upadesha, and the secret determination through indication, as well as others. For the second, there are the dharma cycles on chöd, including the commentaries that originate from the realized masters of India and Tibet, such as Āryadeva and others. The third includes all instructions that clarify crucial points explained by scholars and realized masters concerning the aural lineage, and a fourth category includes all secret wisdom-mind termas from glorious Saraha's *Profound Heart Essence*.

Furthermore, all sādhanas that belong to the Kāma tradition, as well as the sādhanas of this profound terma tradition and others—such as Lord Ngawang Püntsok's[b] daily practice of the profound path,[c] Karma Chakmed's[d] compiled feast sādhana called *Garland of Jewels for the Accumulation of Merit*,[e] and other sādhanas that accomplish enlightened activity—belong to the scriptures on chöd.

[a] *kye rab* (*skyes rabs, jātakamālā*); *Garland of Rebirths*, Āryashūra
[b] *rje ngag dbang phun tshogs*
[c] *lam zab gyun gyi naljor* (*lam zab rgyun gyi rnal 'byor*)
[d] *karma chags med*
[e] *tsok ley rinchen trengwa* (*tshogs las rin chen phreng ba*); Karma Chakmed

3.1.2 Explanation of This Subject Being Described—Chöd

This has three parts:

1 Actual meaning
2 How chöd applies to the scriptures
3 Synthesis of the meaning of the key points

Second is an explanation of this subject—chöd—in three parts: the actual meaning, how chöd applies to the scriptures, and a synthesis of the meaning of the key points.

3.1.2.1 Actual Meaning

This has four parts:

1 Nature of chöd
2 Distinctions
3 Etymology
4 Extent

For the first, there are four: the nature of chöd, distinctions, etymology, and extent.

3.1.2.1.1 Nature of Chöd

First, the nature is as follows. In conjunction with the exceptional methods of these practices, the nature of chöd is established from the perspective of severing the nonconducive direction toward self by means of realizing the prajñā of selflessness. From another perspective, this is posited as practicing through upāya and prajñā, in whatever way, with the exceptional realization that severs the nonconducive obsession with self. The first is the tradition that solely emphasizes the realization of the view of selflessness as the nature of chöd, whereas the latter is the tradition of engaging great compassion and the like with the practice of chöd. There is no contradiction between them.

3.1.2.1.2 Distinctions

Second, the distinctions are as follows. If distinctions are taken from the perspective of the object to realize, then there is the chöd that realizes the identitylessness of the person, the chöd that realizes the identitylessness of phenomena, and the chöd that realizes the intrinsic nature of phenomena as evenness—these three.

If distinguished from the perspective of the subject—realizing this, then there are two: the realization that comes through a general comprehension of selflessness and the chöd that realizes this directly. If distinguished from the perspective of the types of realization, there are three: the upāya of chöd that sustains all the visualizations and so forth based on great compassion, the prajñā of chöd that realizes selflessness, as well as the combination of those two as the chöd practice that unites upāya and prajñā.

If divisions are based on an individual's continuum, there are two: chöd for an ordinary person's continuum and chöd for the continuum of an ārya.[a] To make divisions from the perspective of the objective to be to exorcised, there is the outer chöd of the fear-provoking environment, the inner chöd of illness and demonic-force possession, the secret chöd of whatever concepts arise, and the chöd of the nature as it is concerning the five and the three poisons—these four. Machig herself said:

> Listen! Concerning this chöd tradition of mine, there is a reason for the four distinctions of outer, inner, secret, and nature as it is. First, concerning the four objects of chöd, the outer object is the specific severing of dread toward a fear-provoking environment; the inner object is the severing of illness and demonic-force possession; the secret object is the severing of whatever concepts arise; and the nature as it is involves the objective of severing the five and three poisons.

So she said. Concerning this, dread and such that are associated with a fear-provoking place, perpetual fixation concerning harm involved with illness, demonic-force possession, and varieties of concepts and seduction by the poisons are all to be severed.

If divisions are based upon the way of severance, then outer chöd involves severing fixation upon the true existence of the outer objects; inner chöd severs fixation upon the true existence of the mind; and the union of the outer and inner involves the severance of cherishing both body and mind, as well as fixating upon them as truly existing. These are the three. Machig said:

> Outwardly sever the objective patterns of appearances; inwardly sever fixation of the grasping mind; and binding them, sever the fixation of both mind and body.

Thus, it is just as she taught. Hence, the way of positing the outer severance and the like resembles how outer and inner phenomena are devoid of true existence and thus designated as outer emptiness and so forth.

[a] *pakpa* (*'phags pa*); sublime one

If divisions are made from the perspective of the way of practicing, the three are to wander in frightening, isolated places and so forth as the outer chöd supported by the objects; to give one's aggregates as food for the gods and māras as the inner chöd supported by the aggregates; and to sever the subtle root of saṃsāra, which is the single point of fixation upon true existence severed from the base. These are genuine severance practices based on experience. It is said:

> Wandering in fear-provoking places is the outer chöd, giving one's aggregates as food is the inner chöd, and severing the sole objective is the genuine chöd.

Hence, Jetsun Milarepa[a] and many other realized, learned masters are in agreement with this.

If divisions are made based on the common and the uncommon, training in the visualization of transferring one's consciousness into basic space and then giving the body as an offering to the gods-māras is in harmony with the historical account of our teacher's [i.e., Buddha Shākyamuni] giving of his own flesh and blood to the yakṣhas[b] and so forth. Hence, this chöd accords with the common approach of the path of training according to Sūtra. Visualizing one's consciousness becoming the deity, such as Tröma, and then giving the body left behind as an offering by imagining that it becomes whatever is desired is severance connected to the uncommon path of Mantra; hence, these are the two. Other ways of enumerating the divisions are as mentioned in the *Excellent Golden Garland*:[c]

> Giving one's flesh and blood to the gods, nāgas, yakṣhas, elementals, pishācī,[d] kumbhāṇḍa,[e] and the like is outer chöd. Recognizing that the beings of the six classes have been one's parents, meditating on love and compassion, and generating supreme bodhichitta is this yogin's inner chöd. Meditating that demonic forces are the meditation deity and offering immaculate ambrosia, as well as requesting to receive the two siddhis, is this yogin's secret chöd. The root of saṃsāra is grasping to the self; so in order to sever this from the root, meditating upon the fundamental nature of emptiness is this yogin's chöd of the nature as it is. Engaging in these aspects of chöd is the wisdom intent of Lord Buddha and the upadesha of Atisha, as well as this yogin's practice.

[a] *rje btsun mi la ras pa*
[b] *gnod sbyin*; spirits
[c] *pül chung ser treng* (*phul byung gser phreng*)
[d] *sha za*; flesh-eating spirit
[e] *drül büm* (*grul bum*); carnivorous troll

So, it is as taught.

Chöd that is free from hope involves the cessation of the limitation of quiescence, namely, fixation on the true existence of the object of hope, such as the state of buddha and so forth. Chöd that is without trepidation involves the cessation of the limitation of existence, namely, fixation on the true existence of the object of trepidation, such as the hells and so forth. The chöd of awareness concerning the inner meaning is the ground of all, involving whatever concepts of the grasping mind that arise being allowed to rest at ease within their fundamental nature. Realizing that—aside from self-appearing wisdom—the three kāyas are not established elsewhere, attachment to true existence is severed. That is called the "chöd of ceasing fixation toward the resultant aim of attainment". Realizing that all conceptual circumstances that lead to saṃsāra are completely free from fixation with true existence is the chöd that terminates the root of the three objects to abandon [i.e., the three poisons].

By realizing that all nonconducive circumstances associated with the four māras are—aside from emerging from within the reaches of the magical manifestation of one's own mind—otherwise nonexistent is the chöd of liberating oneself from the four obstructing māras by means of ceasing fixation upon true existence. These are all distinctions. It is as Machig spoke:

> Being without expectation severs the hope for buddhahood; being without fear severs anxiety about the hells; being without conceptual fixation severs awareness from within. Given that wisdom is self-arising, the three kāyas are severed. Given that concepts are liberated from the root, the three realms are severed; given that the object to sever emerges from the mind, the four demons are severed.

And so it is.

3.1.2.1.3 Etymology

Third, the etymology is that, since through chöd incorrect concepts such as self-fixation and so forth are severed, there is the term "chöd", which means "to sever". This is also referred to as "the sacred dharma that severs the māras", as stated:

> The sacred dharma dispels all obstructions and aspects of suffering.

Thus as mentioned, practice such as this dispels all obstructions and suffering. Otherwise, "sacred" refers to the nature of the fully enlightened Buddha's doctrine. In addition, "sacred dharma" is referred to as such because this teaching involves what all sublime individuals bring to their practice, as mentioned in the sūtras:

> That which is called "self" is the demonic mind. You have become this.

So, it is like that.

Since this [self] obstructs the path to liberation, self-fixation that is labeled "demonic" is severed. Furthermore, this dharma is the antidote for severing the four māras, so it is called "severance of the māras". For example, medicine that cures a certain illness is referred to as the medicine for that illness. This is similar. Saying "the objective of chöd" applies to the explanatory text; and since this [text] is similar to the place where the meaning of chöd as the subject abides, it is the locale of chöd. This is like how the speech of Buddha called the piṭaka, or basket, is the place or container where many categories of words and their meanings are subsumed. If applied to the meaning of this subject, saying "chöd" implies the realization of the subject and saying "objective" implies the meaning of selflessness that must be understood. Any realization that severs self-fixation involves the mind that knows the meaning of selflessness. Hence, it is expressed in this way.

To synthesize to the key point, in order to realize selflessness and understand that this [chöd] is the realization of severing the object of self-fixation, these words summarize that point, making it easier to express. Revealing words that seem to be out of order is, for example, like how in the Sanskrit tradition some words are placed together at random to make new words. If applied to both the subject and the explanation: then for those who wish to be liberated, this is the object to engage with by means of hearing, contemplation, and meditation—these three. That is why this is explained in this way.

3.1.2.1.4 Extent

Fourth, the extent [of chöd] begins with entering the path and continues until the ground of buddhahood is attained. Although it is not faulted to assert that the realization of the prajñā that experiences contrived great compassion and the nature of emptiness is posited as chöd, the state of the sublime buddhas who have completely eliminated all obstructions and associated habits is genuine chöd.

Given that until now I have not seen an explanation in commentaries concerning this discussion of the nature, distinctions, and so forth [of chöd], I have taken the time to elaborate on this in order to make these points clear. Nevertheless, this commentary is based on practical application; so in order to discover the key points, I have not overemphasized elaborations through words. The intellectually inclined should not feel frustrated [with this brevity]. Whatever the case, it is taught that a shāstra of the Buddha's doctrine is not composed in order to emphasize debate.

3.1.2.2 How Chöd Applies to the Scriptures

Second, the way this applies to the scriptures is as follows. Given that the source of this is the *Prajñāpāramitā* as mentioned previously, it is necessary to apply these instructions to that. Machig has also said:

> When reading the extensive, intermediate, and concise *Prajñāpāramitā*, it must be understood that in the chapter concerning māras—beginning with the occasion of form until omniscience—wherever attachment is referenced is the activity of māras.

Thus, and the quote continues:

> Form is not white, yellow, red, blue, green, or violet.

And:

> Form is that which has come from nowhere and goes nowhere, dwelling nowhere.

And:

> The uniform nature of all phenomena is the prajñāpāramitā, the nature of evenness.

And so forth.

It is taught that by knowing the view of emptiness, the realization of chöd occurs; and this sets the four māras free in their own place. Even these words from the sūtras reveal the meaning of chöd in this way. Saying "from form until omniscience" means that, if phenomena are held to as true, that holding becomes the objective of chöd since it involves the function of the māras. Without having attachment and through prajñā that realizes the lack of true existence, there is what is called "severance". Saying "form is [not] white . . ." establishes the example by means of the fundamental nature of the objective to realize. Then by searching for the designated meaning of form and so forth, the innate nature of emptiness must be known. When saying "form is that which has come from nowhere" and so forth, "comes from" means that, since it is born from cause rather than being inherent, the cause is actually *without characteristics*. Saying "goes nowhere" means that the result naturally exists without creation. Hence, the result is *without aim*. Saying "dwelling nowhere" means that the nature of form itself is naturally nonexistent as the nature that is *empty*.[36] This reveals the actual nature, the fundamental way that the three gateways to liberation[a] abide. Realizing that all phenomena are the inherent prajñāpāramitā, the nature of evenness is the extent of the realization of chöd. Through this realization, there exists the potential to give one's body and so forth without the bondage that comes through cherishing and grasping. This reveals the way of practicing by giving the body and the like.

Furthermore, in other prajñāpāramitā sūtras, meanings and words are extremely elaborate and extensive. In the *Gathering of Precious Qualities*, the key points are synthesized and easy to comprehend; so likewise, this must be explained in that way. Machig has said:

> All dharma is complete within chöd. An individual who is a practitioner of chöd is able to relate to any circumstantial phenomena. Given that this [chöd] is outwardly in accord with the pāramitās: even if the extensive, intermediate, and concise [pāramitās] are not understood, at least one must look into the *Gathering of Precious Qualities*.
>
> Given that inwardly this is in accord with Secret Mantra: even if the many categories of the tantras are not known, the sādhana of Vajravarāhī must be maintained.

Thus, it is as she said.

In addition, in the *Gathering of Precious Qualities*, it states:

> Whoever hears that the teaching of the prajñāpāramitā is nonexistent and that the bodhisattvas and the bodhichitta are nonexistent—without confusion or trepidation—that bodhisattva is practicing the prajñā of the tathāgatas.

Thus, this reveals the nature of chöd since the four limitations do not exist with the objective to attain the supreme omniscient prajñāpāramitā. In order to attain that state, an individual bodhisattva who meditates upon the path is also nonexistent, and the path through which the bodhichitta awakens is itself nonexistent. When taught and heard in this way, to understand the meaning and concentrate upon this with prajñā will precisely determine this. Hence, certainty in the inseparability of emptiness and appearances will be discovered.

When phenomena are realized as magiclike, there is no delusion. Through

[a] *nam tar go süm* (*rnam thar sgo gsum*)

meditation, attaining mastery over the realization of the meaning of emptiness, there is no fear. That is the path bringing the attainment of the state of the tathāgatas, and that is said to be the practice of the prajñāpāramitā. This reveals how the result to attain, the path to attain it, and the individual attaining this are all naturally nonexistent.

Generally, it is necessary to sever fixation on the true existence of any phenomena. Especially while diligently engaged in practice on the path, it is not correct for an individual to think "I must practice this path in order to actualize this result" and focus with fixation on true existence. Hence, it is crucial to bring an end to fixation on true existence in any form.

Otherwise, it is acceptable to apply this to the ground, path, and result—these three. Concerning the ground, all phenomena in the mind stream of an individual are naturally nonexistent; and the nature of the path that brings this to fruition, including the result, is practiced without delusion. Another option would be when an individual realizes himself to be naturally nonexistent; that is the selflessness of the person. To realize that this path and its fruition are also naturally nonexistent is the prajñā that realizes the selflessness of phenomena. In this way, the prajñā realizing both aspects of selflessness is the essence of chöd.

When the treatise [on chöd] is applied with the teachings found in the *Seventy Meanings on Emptiness*,[a,37] it mentions that those four lines [from the *Gathering of Precious Qualities*] actually point out the oral instructions. That is extremely fitting since, when the meaning of the instructions is internalized, that is the practice of chöd. In addition, it states:

> Whoever knows there are no form, feeling, recognition, consciousness, and mind and that phenomena are the unborn nature of emptiness is practicing the supreme prajñāpāramitā.

Thus, and the quote continues:

> To completely know that all phenomena have no true, inherent existence is to practice the supreme prajñāpāramitā.

Thus, the five aggregates and all knowable things without exception are revealed to be empty and free of true existence.

All of these quotations point to the same meaning that the prajñā realizing emptiness amounts to the comprehension of chöd because this actually severs fixation upon true existence. This information is merely suggestive. Nevertheless, through understanding this treatise, the meaning of emptiness without excep-

[a] *tong nyid dün chu pa* (*stong nyid bdun cu pa, shūnyatāsaptati*); Nāgārjuna

tion is revealed. Therefore, it is unnecessary to try to make correlations by introducing information that is only partial.

With this level of realization, it is necessary to eliminate grasping the two extremes as it states:

> Whatever does not exist is called "nonexistent". When the immature think they understand this, they will say, "This exists." And if they don't, they will say, "It does not." In truth, both the existent and the nonexistent are aspects of the nonexistent. A bodhisattva who knows this is certain to renounce.

So, it is taught. The nonexistent is naturally independent of root causes and contributing circumstances. It is said that the immature will misinterpret this and fall to an extreme. The learned will, on the other hand, renounce existence by correctly knowing the way of abiding to be free from extremes.

For this, initially, it is necessary to analyze by cultivating discerning prajñā, as it states:

> When it is determined through prajñā that uncompounded and compounded positive and negative phenomena have not a particle's worth of existence: from a worldly point of view, that constitutes being the prajñāpāramitā.

So, it is taught. The extent of seeing the fundamental nature is to know that phenomena are naturally nonexistent and seen to be spacelike, as it states:

> Form is not perceivable, and feeling as well cannot be seen. Recognition is not perceivable, and the mind cannot be seen. Whoever cannot see the consciousness, mind, and mental events sees the true nature of phenomena as taught by the Tathāgata. Sentient beings use words to express themselves such as saying "I see the sky", yet the meaning of how the sky is actually seen must be carefully analyzed.

So, it is taught. Even those of us who engage by materializing are able to realize this if we try. It states:

> Just as the nihilist Parivrajaka[a] understood the nonexistent and how the aggregates will be completely destroyed, a bodhisattva who under-

[a] Kuntugyu (*kun tu rgyu*), or Zojang (*bzo sbyang*)

> stands phenomena in this way will not depend on nirvāṇa, but will abide with prajñā.

So, it is taught.

How does this occur? The heretic Parivrajaka correctly understood the nature of ultimate truth by realizing the meaning of nonexistent emptiness. Just as the nirvāṇa that destroys the contaminated aggregates is attained by knowing the fundamental nature of phenomena, it is said that—rather than remaining in the lesser state of nirvāṇa—the unsurpassed prajñā that knows the nature of all phenomena will be attained. By seeing this truth as magical, it is as stated:

> Whoever knows that the five aggregates are like a magical display will not consider the magic and the aggregates as independent. Having pacified the mind that recognizes many distinctions, the supreme prajñāpāramitā is internalized.

Thus, all phenomena subsumed within the five aggregates are taught to be the same as a magical display. It is necessary to combine this with the method of practice, as it states:

> Whoever practices with the aim to benefit others based on loving compassion will reach the state of awakening by training with this dhāraṇī.[38]

So it is, and the quote continues:

> The qualities of upāya are fully sustained through prajñā, so the supreme state of the Tathāgata's awakening will be swiftly reached.

So it is, and the quote continues:

> By fully sustaining this through supreme upāya and prajñā, the Tathāgata's state of awakening will be reached without decline.

And:

> The awakened state and the Tathāgata are free from differentiation. If the upāya to accomplish this is seized, a bodhisattva wishing to attain this will be internalizing the prajñāpāramitā.

Thus as taught, saying "the Tathāgata and the state of awakening are free from differentiation" can be understood here to mean that the nature of the objective to realize as the nature as it is and the process for realizing that, namely wisdom, are inseparable. Therefore, by not following the paths of the shrāvaka[a] or pratyekabuddha[b] who realize things based on circumstance, it is necessary to follow and train on the path of the Omniscient One.[c] To reach the state of a bodhisattva, the practice is as it states:

> Without training on the ground of a shrāvaka or that of a pratyeka: in order to attain the state of omniscience, train in the teachings of the Buddha.

So, it is as taught.

The main objective for taming through the doctrine of chöd is that the individual must be of the class of Mahāyāna and possess sharp faculties. Hence, one initially realizes emptiness and then cultivates compassion. It states:

> A bodhisattva who practices the prajñā of the victorious ones must know that the aggregates are originally empty and unborn. Without resting in quiescence, he will engage in compassion for the realms of beings.

Thus, so that this realization will dawn in the mind stream, it is necessary for all outer and inner conducive circumstances to be complete, as it states:

> Possessing a virtuous spiritual guide and the view of vipashyanā's true seeing[d]: when the mother of all victors is heard, there will be no fear.

Thus, and for that, it is necessary to abandon nonconducive negative friends, as it states:

> Whoever accompanies negative companions can be affected adversely by them like an unfired clay pot that will fall apart when placed with water.[39]

Thus, and to explain the distinctions, it states:

[a] *dra chompa* (*dgra bcom pa*); foe destroyer
[b] *rang sangye* (*rang sangs rgyas*); solitary realizer
[c] Shākyamuni Buddha
[d] *lhagtong* (*lhag mthong*)

> Once again, what is this prajñā, how is this realized, and who is the realizer? Saying "what is this?" means to realize that this phenomenon is empty.

Thus, it is taught. This means that, by thinking "what is this prajñā?" prajñā is the objective to realize; and thinking "who is the realizer?" means the one who realizes this. Saying "how is this realized?" means that, by severing fixation upon true existence, the objective will be known by the mind that knows this through realizing this and so forth. Through the many distinctions applied to all phenomena, the fixation upon the outer appearances and the inner mind as truly existing will be severed. This way of severing the outer and the inner was taught previously.

There are three ways to distinguish the realization of the selflessness of the person, as it states:

> Just as it is for oneself, so it is for all sentient beings. Just as it is for all sentient beings, all phenomena can be known like that. To be free from both concepts of being unborn or born is the practice of the supreme prajñāpāramitā.

Thus, this reveals the realization of twofold selflessness and the genuine truth of the unborn nature of emptiness. Based on the way things appear according to relative truth: once arising, all phenomena are realized to be the nature of evenness, as it states:

> Just as a chakravartin ruler always travels on the same route bringing the seven precious ones[40] and an army of retinue along that path: likewise, by practicing this path, one will proceed to the prajñāpāramitā of the victorious ones; and along this path, all qualities will emerge.

Thus, just as whatever path a chakravartin ruler travels the seven royal representatives and the four hordes of retinue accompany him, here this prajñā accompanies all qualities of the path. Saying "this originates from the supreme prajñāpāramitā" implicitly reveals that there are other enumerations of distinctions concerning this subject. The manner of practice is as it states:

> To enter the supreme vehicle of all victorious ones with great generosity, a broad mind, and tremendous strength is to don immense armor and tame the magical māras.

Thus, this reveals that even though the shrāvakas and pratyekas are able to express great generosity through material wealth, they remain unable to give up the body. Here, "generosity" emphasizes giving the body. Having "a broad mind" means not just only abandoning the faulted conduct of body and speech, but refers to the perfectly pure morality based on the intention to control attachment to the body and self-cherishing. "Tremendous strength" means to not shy away from the practices on the path of the great vehicle that are engaged for the welfare of others, but rather without trepidation to eagerly enter the supreme path of the great vehicle. "Donning armor" means to not mingle the mind with the lower pursuit of self-centered concerns and to sustain single-pointed concentration by never succumbing to distraction. Taming the māras is as it states:

> With a mind that is like the sky, the strength of the hordes of deceivers will have no bearing.

Thus, as it is taught, from the perspective of possessing prajñā that realizes the lack of inherent existence, the deception of the māras or the magic of the māras is tamed or subjugated through that prajñā. Hence, it is necessary to practice the six pāramitās. In particular, it states:

> The giving of one's head and limbs without reluctance, giving all of one's possessions without hesitation, and knowing and understanding the futility of all phenomena that lack true existence—if flesh can be given in this way with no regret, then needless to say material things can be forsaken. In that case, it is impossible for there to be avarice.

Thus, that is the way of offering the body, and it goes on to state:

> Taking interest in generosity that is constant and without hesitation . . .

Thus and:

> A bodhisattva with clear intelligence will think, "May I give this as a gift to all sentient beings that exist throughout the three realms," and then actually give to them with the dedication, "May this bring about the awakening of all beings." Once given, there is no materializing of the deed itself.

Thus and:

> There are no expectations concerning the result of that deed.

Thus, and:

> By giving whatever brings happiness to oneself without any expectation, one works day and night for the welfare of others. Just like how a mother cares for her only child, one abides faultlessly with that attitude alone.

Thus, through this, the manner of expressing generosity is clearly revealed.

As it states, however many sentient beings exist throughout the three realms, including all classes of guests, to say "forsaking all material things and giving to everyone" points out the meaning of the white and mixed feasts. In order to generate the attitude to actually express generosity with all material things, first one must train with this visualization and become familiar. In order to express generosity to all sentient beings, there is no choice but to express this through the many things that harmonize with their wishes.

It states in the sūtra *Palpoche*:[a]

> One transforms into the form of that which will please and fulfill his needs.

Thus, the way of offering the body and so forth is to visualize whatever is necessary to meet one's needs. This is the general tradition of the bodhisattva's expression of generosity.

For example, it states:

> If a magician creates an illusory crossroads where millions of people are being beheaded and the bodhichitta is generated based on whatever those being killed must be feeling—for the one who understands that all these beings are illusory, there will be no fear.

Thus, through this, one can know the way of fearlessness when confronted with the magical deception of the gods-māras while wandering in terrifying places. Concerning this, the way that the upheavals and exorcisms occur will be explained later.

The etymology of chöd is as it states:

> [Chöd] is asserted to be the severing of attachment so that all such clinging is fully exhausted.

[a] *palpoche'i do* (*phal po che'i mdo, buddhavataṃsakasūtra*); Sūtra of the Great Bounteousness of the Buddhas

Thus, this means severing attachment to self-fixation, as well as severing the source, which is the mind attached to the true existence of each aspect of phenomena—including all habitual associations—and bringing this process to exhaustion. This is referred to as "chöd". Furthermore, it states:

> Severing [the cherishing of oneself] is supreme among a gathering of many beings and severing the overwhelming negative views of sentient beings . . .

Thus, saying "supreme among a gathering of many beings" means that, from the perspective of cherishing others more than oneself, one engages in the welfare of others and becomes their guide and protector; so one must sever the fixation of cherishing oneself.

In addition, one must be able to sever all negative views that others have in their mind streams, so that is another reason for the term "severance". This term includes both aspects of upāya and prajñā. Not only that, this is referred to as "taming the magical deception of the māras". Saying "any fixation whatsoever" reveals the etymology of what is referred to as "severing the māras".

The extent of the ground is as it states:

> From the time of adding a single drop of water to a vase until the vase is full, just as the water gradually increases until it overflows—even though at first the ordinary mind is predominant, by gradually cultivating the bodhichitta the perfection of positive qualities will bring about the state of awakening.

Thus and:

> From the time the supreme bodhichitta is cultivated until the state of unsurpassed awakening occurs, one must bring this to mind each day and night. The learned will strive to accomplish this.

Thus, it is like that.

To say "first there is the ordinary mind" means—whether relative or genuine bodhichitta—given that the actual nature is initially not evident, this [bodhichitta] mind must be cultivated. This reveals the meaning of the metaphor of a single drop of water slowly accumulating [to an overflowing vase]. By beginning in this way, the cause of perfect awakening is initiated. This is not saying that bodhichitta is gained, but that rather it is cultivated. From that time onward, by diligently engaging on the path and sustaining that mind, the time of the initial ground occurs. By saying "until unsurpassed awakening occurs" and "by the perfection of positive qualities, awakening will occur" reveals the conclusion of the extent.

Through these quotations, one must understand that the meaning [of chöd] is being clarified. Just as it is necessary to clarify the meaning of the classes of the inner tantras of Secret Mantra through their individual explanatory tantras and given that the Great Mother is so profound and difficult to comprehend, it is necessary for the meaning itself to be elucidated through the upadesha of the great dharma regents. Based on that, the stages of the nature of emptiness have been revealed; whereas other subjects, for the most part, have been implicated. Hence, the meaning cannot be revealed more clearly than this.[41]

Well then, if some were to claim that this presentation is unacceptable because—when explaining the common meaning of this text—explanations concerning the paths of unification and seeing[a,42] should be applied with the higher path, I would have to reply as follows. Generally, the speech of the Victorious One characteristically includes the primordial nature of all subjects. Especially in terms of the prajñāpāramitā, this is considered the ultimate subject of the Buddha's speech. Just as there are many explanations that analyze the meaning of the tantras of unsurpassed Mantra, here as well [i.e. Sūtra]—whether it is the actual meaning or the hidden meaning, principal or secondary—there are many explicit and implicit ways to describe this.

If that were not the case and a single point or meaning was being taught, then—except for that overt meaning—other interpretations would be unacceptable. Scholars from India and Tibet have applied this teaching according to a beginner's practice; and in doing so, there is no objection to include whatever quotations are acceptable in order to support their individual explanations. If that were the only level to interpret [the prajñāpāramitā] and if explanations and advice that are given according to the mental capacities of those like myself were not given, then what would be the point to study or contemplate this subject at the present time? Chöd is the practice that corresponds to the meaning of the Great Mother; so with that in mind, needless to say, it is necessary to give explanations that describe this.

Hence, in the *Ornament of Clear Realization*,[b] it states:

> The prajñāpāramitā is correctly explained through the eight categories of phenomena.[43]

Thus, it is as taught.

Just as the meaning of the sūtras is elucidated by the shāstras: if this subject

[a] *tsok lam* (*tshogs lam, sambhāramārga*) and *jor lam* (*sbyor lam, prayogamārga*)
[b] *ngon tok gyen* (*mngon rtogs rgyan, abhisamayālaṃkāra*); Maitreya

[i.e., chöd] is combined with eight topics through the practice of chöd, the complete unification of all aspects will be brought about. The eight are the basis of the aggregates, elements, and sense sources; the way of the path of the three vehicles; and the nature of all knowable things without exception that must be definitively realized, the practice of the knowledge of the ground, knowledge of the path, and the state of omniscience—these three; along with fully perfected upāya and prajñā as the objective of the visualization. When, with that, the experience of meditative training definitively occurs, that is the peak of unification. Not confusing the order of the training is the final unification.

By training in this way: when all stages of the visualization are gradually able to be actualized in a relatively short period of time, that is instantaneous unification. Based on the intention to attain the resultant dharmakāya, it is necessary to meditate in order for the practice of that to be complete as well. Nevertheless, since these days a majority of chöd practitioners are uneducated on this subject, there is probably no point to elaborate further.[44]

3.1.2.3 Synthesis of the Meaning of the Key Points

Third, to reveal the key points in brief, it states in the *Commentary on Bodhichitta*:[a]

> The bodhichitta of all the buddhas is not obstructed by thoughts, such as self and aggregates, but rather asserted to always be the characteristic of emptiness. It is necessary to meditate through effort with this mind moistened by compassion.

Thus, one may wonder, "What is this so-called awakened mind that is the mind of all fully perfected buddhas and befits the sacred path revealed for the sake of others?" The absolute fundamental nature of phenomena is not obscured by concepts that fixate on the true existence of a self, aggregates, and consciousness. The wisdom that always realizes the meaning of the characteristic of emptiness or that abides in this way is the mind of absolute bodhichitta. This also includes the mind moistened with great compassion that aspires to awaken in order to benefit others. That [bodhichitta] mind that is relative bodhichitta is not established according to the way that the confused mind grasps it. It is taught that these [two aspects][45] are meditated upon as inseparable.

Here, the practice of absolute bodhichitta involves the determination through discerning wisdom that all phenomena do not exist in the nature of emptiness. In formal equipoise, that nature is sustained and all subsequent experiences of those

[a] *chang chüb sem drel* (*byang chub sems 'grel, bodhichittavivaraṇa*); Nāgārjuna

phenomena, without a single exception, are viewed to be magical or dreamlike. Not only that, it states in Āryadeva's treatise on chöd:

> Supreme among methods is the mingling of basic space and awareness.

Thus, like that, the sacred method that renders the fundamental nature evident is the exceptional feature of this doctrine, the upadesha of mingling space and awareness. Hence, directly encountering this genuine fundamental nature enhances this realization. Those with duller, limited faculties will determine the meaning of emptiness through analysis; whereas, those with sharp faculties will —like opening the gateway to space—simultaneously actualize the mingling of space and awareness through the indication of the method given at the time of empowerment.

Although there are these two categories, this actually represents the wisdom intent of the past scholars. The sūtras tell us:

> If the selflessness of phenomena is discerned, analyzing that discerning wisdom and meditating upon it is the cause for attaining the result of nirvāṇa. Whatever other causes there may be will not bring about this state of quiescence.

Thus, as taught, the Great Tertön Lord of Dharma himself said that, for beginners, he only emphasized the need to analyze and determine by contemplating the section [in the root terma text] called "searching for the basis of the mental label". Not only that, he earnestly encouraged training in the methods for cultivating relative bodhichitta. Based on that and in reliance upon the mind that fixates upon a self or cherishes a self as the main focus, there are the practices of generosity involving giving the body without fixated attachment. In doing so, the key points for the other pāramitā practices must also be complete. From the perspective of the stages for simultaneously offering to the higher objects and expressing generosity to the lower, even beginners such as us are then able to perfect great waves of merit. The way of doing this from the uncommon approach is to train in the visualizations that correspond to the four feasts.[46] In these ways, to become familiar with the union of upāya and prajñā through practicing relative and genuine bodhichitta is the way to engage in the practice of chöd.

In Āryadeva's treatise on chöd, it also states:

> If one fails to realize that the meaning of the nondual pāramitās is free from virtue, nonvirtue, acceptance, rejection, hope, fear, and limitations all together—even though one may accumulate compounded virtue, liberation will not occur in that life. Therefore, not even a particle

> of any compounded, uncompounded, positive, or negative phenomena ever exists. Nevertheless, without relying upon upāya, prajñā cannot be actualized. This is like how, without preparing a field, the harvest cannot be reaped.

Thus, it is taught. Chöd is the unmistaken path of the bodhisattvas, as it states in the *Gayagori Sūtra*:[a]

> If the path of the bodhisattvas were synthesized, what might that be? In brief, there are two: upāya and prajñā.

So, it is as taught. Furthermore, in the Madhyamaka's[b] *Jewel Garland*,[c] it states:

> When self or others aspire to attain unsurpassed awakening, the root of that will be the bodhichitta. Stable like the king of mountains, with compassion reaching all directions, this wisdom need not depend upon direction or limit.

Thus, within chöd, the key points of practice that are said to be the causes for the state of unsurpassed awakening are fully complete with the mind of bodhichitta, extremely firm and all-pervasive compassion for sentient beings limitless like space, along with the view that does not rely on the two extremes. This is stated in detail in the *Essence of the Middle Way*:[d]

> Without forsaking bodhichitta, perfectly engage in the fearless conduct of the Sage. The one who searches for such wisdom is engaged in Buddha's conduct.[47]

As this is in harmony with that, one must train accordingly. The way to not forsake the bodhichitta is as it states:

> That which is adorned with love, compassion, and great knowledge is the seed of buddha, the bodhichitta. Therefore, the learned will never forsake that.

[a] *ga' ya go ri do* (*ga' ya go ri mdo, āryagayāshīrṣhahāmamahāyānasūtra*)
[b] *üma* (*dbu ma*); Middle Way
[c] *rinchen treng wa* (*rin chen phreng ba, ratnāvalī*); Nāgārjuna
[d] *üma nyingpo* (*dbu ma snying po, madhyamakahṛdaya*); Bhāvaviveka

Thus with love, great compassion, and the vast knowledge of upāya, an abundance of virtue is cultivated, such as through the seven branches of prostration and so forth. Through the profound knowledge of prajñā that sustains itself, there is realization that all phenomena have no characteristics of true existence. Since the bodhichitta adorned with these qualities is the cause for awakening, it must never be forsaken. The manner of ensuring this is as stated:

> One with intelligence and courage, who can't bear the suffering of others and exerts in perfectly pure diligence with strength and intelligence, will view this ordinary world that lacks prajñā, determine to free himself or herself from this quagmire of saṃsāra, and work to transport beings to freedom.

Thus, with intelligence that can fully discern phenomena and the great courage of a stable mind unaffected by any māras or passions, one endures the suffering of others because the suffering of others is unbearable. Exerting stable diligence toward positive virtue and possessing the potential to accomplish the welfare of self and others, the wise will repeatedly analyze the nature of ordinary sentient beings that lack the phenomena of prajñā and will first perfect the self-purpose of awakening in order to traverse the murky quagmire of saṃsāra and accomplish the state of awakening. Then, it states:

> Those who strive to be liberated will, through prajñā, sever all bondage and, through compassion, will try to liberate those who suffer in the unbearable prison of saṃsāra. Bound by the handcuffs of desire and the like, without protection, beings are drunk from the carelessness of having fallen into the slumber of delusion, robbed by discursiveness that steals away all virtues. If those [who suffer in this way] are not liberated, what then could be the benefit of having any powers?

Thus, through the sharp weapon of prajñā, one must sever all bondage in the mind stream and determine to liberate others through compassion.

Those who lack protection at death and so forth will find themselves in the relentless prison of saṃsāra, bound by the handcuffs of the passions, such as desire. Having been careless through the three doors and mentally slothful as though intoxicated by liquor, they have fallen into the slumber of delusion where they harbor perverted desires and harmful thoughts like robbers. Any virtue accumulated by these sentient beings has been squandered. If these beings are not liberated, then what is the benefit of having any powers? Aside from liberation, nothing else will benefit them. Know that this reveals the way to fully accomplish the welfare of others.

Furthermore, it states:

> Previously, those who have been possessed by the demonic force of the passions will—like pouring salt water on an open wound—further aggravate their own illness of suffering. In order to benefit and repay the kindness of those who have been caring, respectful, and beneficial toward oneself, nothing is more meaningful than placing them in the state of quiescence.

Thus, the way of benefiting others is revealed as follows. Those who have previously been possessed by the harmful demonic forces of the passions are likened to the example of pouring salt water on an open wound. Already tormented by the illness of suffering, they—like one—continue to engage in various harmful deeds that perpetuate further suffering. In past lifetimes, those are the same beings that have shown one limitless kindness through love, compassion, respect, and benefit. In order to repay them, except for placing them on the state of quiescence, what else is there to be done? Thinking in this way, determine to place them there.

Then, the way of relying upon the fearless conduct of the buddhas and their heirs is as stated:

> In order to benefit beings by embracing the wondrous and stable bodhichitta, the practitioner whole-heartedly enters this perfectly correct path.

Thus this reveals the concise meaning.

In order to expand upon this, it states:

> This love is free from harm and brings benefit through compassion. By realizing the sacred dharma, there is never complacency or avarice concerning generosity through dharma.

Thus, through love, all sentient beings are placed in states of well-being; and the wish to protect them ensures there are no harmful thoughts. By compassionately wishing that others who suffer could be free from that and in order to benefit them, one exerts in the understanding of the tradition of the great vehicle throughout the day and night without ever becoming complacent. Giving the dharma to all sentient beings free from avarice means to possess the intent and action of benefiting others.

Furthermore, it states:

> With honesty, no arrogance, and a mind that observes itself—when thoughts about others' faults arise, there is immediate concern toward the emergence of one's own faults.

Thus, with honesty that is free from deception: having subdued the mind of prideful arrogance, viewing with the mind that sees the meaning of interdependency just as it is, and not having concepts concerning the faults of others, only one's own faults are emphasized. Having a sense of true concern toward even the most insignificant personal fault is the way to sustain the perfectly pure inner intention. It states:

> To turn from engaging in disputes and worldliness and to befriend worldly believers, such as the heretics called Flung Afar[48] and even toward those who lack qualities, one should always show respect by thinking that one day they will gain the enrichment of qualities.

Thus, this means to personally turn away from taking sides, entering into disputes, insulting others, and the like, including joining with ordinary people who are busy engaging in meaningless worldly activities that lack dharma, who have no authentic spiritual tradition, or claim there is no future life, such as the heretical views of the Flung Afar. Know that, if others seem to lack qualities, they still possess the buddha nature and that the day will come when their qualities will be conspicuous; so one must always have respect by outwardly engaging with appropriate manners.

From the perspective of intention and action and by not mistaking the stages of abandonment and acceptance, the actual way of engaging in conduct is as it states:

> Generosity that occurs through compassion works to pacify the rivers of suffering of all sentient beings so they will all aspire to attain the state of omniscience.

Thus, generosity is expressed with no expectation for a response or a result, driven only by compassionate altruism. Concerning this, if one wonders who this is directed toward, it is directed toward those born through the four ways[49] as form and formless beings in order to fully pacify their suffering.

What is the purpose? Generosity is expressed in the manner of aspiring to accomplish the state of complete omniscience. Since, here, generosity is mainly taught in this way, this is harmonious with the wisdom intent of the tradition of chöd. Non-Buddhist sages will rely on bathing, wear human-bone mālās, have ungroomed hair, wear leaves, animal skins, hold small pitchers for drinking, and sit on grass cushions to indicate their yogin status. They will eat fruits [and] roots and please their personal deities by relying upon fire ritual and hardships, such as staying alone in the forests. Such conduct is similar to this [i.e., chöd]. Morality and the like are explained, as it states:

> The stainless morality of bathing in water, wearing the human-bone mālā of patience, donning the dreadlocks of diligence, exerting in concentration and prajña . . .

Thus, the remaining five pāramitās and their supports accumulate additional virtue as stated:

> Completely opening the mind and eyes, learned in knowing the ways of the world, donning the clothing of modesty, and cinching the belt of a calm mind, draped in the animal skins of compassion, and holding the vessel of stainless faith, guarding the mind with the gateway of the faculties, seated on the grass cushion of stability . . .

Thus, by knowing the two truths, the mind and eyes are opened. This means knowing the ways of the world, such as understanding the meaning of the Buddhist shāstras, respectfully prostrating to the gurus, and maintaining harmony with friends and relatives; donning the clothing of modesty, such as the leaves of trees, [and] possessing a peaceful, calm demeanor that is harmonious like a cinched belt; owning the animal skin of compassion that aspires to benefit sentient beings; owning a pitcher of faith in the Buddha's doctrine; guarding the gateway of the faculties with mindfulness that does not forget the virtuous nature of dharma; being seated on the grass cushion of stability not affected by māras; and sitting in the manner of harmony with practice.

In reliance upon these, the way of utilizing the wealth of qualities is as stated:

> The highest joy of the great vehicle is to completely rely on the hardship of remaining in the forest. The three results of the joy of concentration are utilized by the practitioner of close mindfulness.

Thus, this brings both temporary and ultimate benefit, as well as the highest joy of clairvoyance and liberation.

In the forest of great fortitude, capable of enduring hardships for countless kalpas, the flower blossoms of the branches of the path of awakening adorned with never-diminishing fruit mature. Free from the wild animals of the passions and the gatherings of cannibals [and] by perfectly relying upon the beautiful ripening of boundless virtue, to partake of the resultant joy of concentration that possesses samādhi is the field of experience of the four states of close mindfulness.[50]

The way of relying upon the outer and inner gatherings of root causes is as it states:

> Reciting the vast and profound classes of Sūtra to subdue all negativity and relying upon the two truths in order to do so is repeated through the teaching on interdependent origination explained by the sunlike teacher.

Thus, by reading the vast and profound classes of Sūtra's Great Mother *Prajñāpāramitā* and reciting prayers, all negativity and obscurations will be subdued without exclusion. The manner of interdependent origination was taught in reliance upon both relative and absolute truth by the supreme sun of the three realms, the victorious perfected Buddha. The repetition of that speech was then revealed to others. It states:

> The scent of the accomplished flower of mantra pervades all directions and respectfully bows each day to the sun of the perfected Buddha. In the hearth of discernment, all nonvirtuous concepts are completely incinerated.

Thus, in the hearth of discernment that reverses desire toward various objects, the firewood of erroneous mental fabrications is burned without trace.

In a shāstra by Asaṅga,[a] it states:

> In order to attain unsurpassed awakening, the Sage's fearless conduct is engaged like this.

Thus, it is taught.

Then, searching for the nature as it is, it can be said that whoever has eyes of wisdom is the only one with eyesight. In order to have that, the intelligent must diligently pursue this wisdom. Thus, based on reasoning, the way of searching for the view of the nature as it is was taught extensively.

Given that the speech of the Indian scholars concerning the general nature of the Bodhisattva's intent and conduct is so profound and pleasing, overcome with joy I included some of that here in conjunction with the present meaning. In particular, given that conduct of those assuming to be chöd practitioners can

[a] *jüg du wa* (*mjug bsdu ba*)

be extremely crude, proper conduct in this context is all the more imperative. To that end I have included all quotations from the chapter on fearless conduct [from Āryadeva's treatise on chöd]. Machig herself has given many teachings on the import of refining the mode of conduct, for it is as Orgyen Rinpoche [i.e., Padmasambhava] said:

> Although my view is as lofty as the sky, I regard the law of cause and result as carefully as enumerating particles of sand.

Thus, it is taught.

According to the histories called the *Bazhed Chronicles*, or the *Assertions of Ba*:[a,51] when the abbot of Secret Mantra, Padmasambhava, was preparing to depart [from Tibet], the master taught the upadesha *Garland of the View*[b] to the king and the twenty-one disciples at the place called the Tamarisk Forest of Trakmar.[c,52]

He advised:

> O Great King! Concerning this upadesha of mine, the view is in harmony with the dharmakāya, yet conduct must be in harmony with that of the bodhisattvas. Do not lose the view to conduct; for if you do, then both virtue and nonvirtue will be forsaken. Falling into the direction of a nihilist, that direction will be irreparable. Conversely, if the view follows the direction of conduct: then bound by materializing, there will not be liberation. O Great King! With this Secret Mantra of mine, the view is primary. In the future, many will fall to the lower realms by not discovering the actual view that strikes the cord of the absolute meaning. Still knowing how to verbalize the view, many charlatans will come who separate view and conduct while attempting to accomplish the welfare of others. Nevertheless—although there are many so-called teachings that will circulate—having been corrupted by individuals, the blessings will decline and few will achieve realization.

Thus, when carefully examined through intelligence, the meaning of his speech must be taken to heart.

In addition, just as it is taught that the practice of chöd is applicable to any level of teaching: if applied to the stages of path for the three levels[53] according

[a] *ba zhed (sba bzhed)*; Ba Salnang (*sba gsal snang*)
[b] *ta wa'i treng wa* (*lta ba'i phreng ba*); Padmasambhava
[c] *trak mar öm bu tsal* (*brag dmar 'om bu'i tshal*)

to the tradition of the incomparable great Lord Atisha, it is as stated in the *Lamp of the Path of Enlightenment*:[a]

> Whoever engages in any method by pursuing the well-being of saṃsāra for personal benefit, that individual can be understood to be inferior.

Thus, it is as taught.

Because in order to practice chöd it is so important to sever attachment to this life: among the stages that are preliminaries to that, the path of inferior individuals involves the contemplations on the difficult-to-attain precious human rebirth, death, and impermanence. By seeing the suffering of the three lower realms [and] having trepidation toward that, one practices to accept and reject virtue and nonvirtue while engaging in the methods to attain only the happiness of higher rebirth. The quote continues:

> Turning one's back on the happiness of the world, the individual who abandons negative deeds and pursues the goal of personal tranquility is called "mediocre".

The path of the mediocre individual involves seeing that the happiness and abundance of existence is faulted. Hence, this individual will turn away from that by cultivating a sense of repulsion along with always rejecting any negative karmic accumulations, while striving to achieve personal happiness or tranquility for oneself alone. As mentioned, since chöd is a perfectly authentic path that leads to liberation: by considering that the entirety of saṃsāra is faulted due to being an existence that—by nature—brings suffering, a sense of uncontrived longing to attain liberation is born. That is the path of the mediocre individual.

The quote continues:

> Realizing that just as there is suffering in one's stream of mind, the wish to fully exhaust the suffering of all other beings is cultivated. That individual is the supreme.

Thus, realizing that suffering in one's own mind is unbearable: based on that experience, to have the wish that the suffering of all others, including their habits, be completed eliminated and that they be led to the state of fully enlightened buddhahood is said to be the [intent of a] supreme individual.

Machig said:

[a] *chang chüb lam dron* (*byang chub lam sgron, bodhipathapradīpā*); Atisha

> Since love, compassion, and bodhichitta—these three—are the life essence of my lineage . . .

As she taught, motivated by love and compassion, the main practice is to train in bodhichitta. The actual practice for the uncommon path of the great individual is connected to the path of Secret Mantra. Concerning the way of entering Secret Mantra: since this is similar to what is mentioned in the *Lamp of the Path of Enlightenment*, these stages of the three individuals at the time of the path are also complete here.

In addition, among Lord Chedkhawa's[a,54] tradition on the seven meanings, it is taught that the preliminaries reveal the basis for the support [i.e., category of individual]. The actual practice involving the training in the two aspects of bodhichitta, taking negative circumstances as the path of awakening, how to practice for the duration of one's life, the extent of the mind training, the samaya of the mind training, and the advice for the mind training are the seven categories. Among them, the first two categories combine the way of training with the two aspects of bodhichitta as preliminaries for this [chöd]. In order to bring negative circumstances to the path of awakening, it states in the *Seven-Point Mind Training*:[b]

> When the universe and inhabitants are filled with negativity, bring those negative circumstances to the path of awakening.

Thus, from the perspective of both the mind of bodhichitta and the application of accumulation and purification, the way of bringing this to the path is also complete here [in chöd]. Especially when wandering in fear-invoking places, one must induce upheavals that have not yet occurred, utilize those that have, and bring them to completion. In the [section on] mingling one's life with practice, it states:

> In brief, the essence of upadesha is that practice must be combined with the five strengths.

Thus, propulsion, familiarity, cause, remorse, and aspiration are the five strengths. Among them, the first, the strength of propulsion, means that from this time onward as long as one lives or until enlightenment is reached, one aspires to never be separate from this profound upadesha for training in both aspects of

[a] *rje 'chad kha ba*

[b] *lojong don dün ma* (*blo sbyong don bdun ma*); Atisha

bodhichitta—the practice of severing the māras. Thinking in this way is propelling strength.

Second, the strength of familiarity is that, just as the strength of propulsion occurred, that very practice is brought to mind again and again until familiarity is gained. Third, the strength of the positive cause is that, in order for this realization to be born in one's mind stream, as much merit as possible is accumulated. Fourth, the strength of remorse means to think repeatedly about the faults of cherishing oneself and so forth, including everything that is nonconducive on the path, all of which is viewed as faulted. Fifth, the strength of aspiration is that—whatever virtue is engaged—in order for this to develop into realization, it is dedicated and prayers of aspiration are offered.

The extent of this training is as stated:

> All phenomena are subsumed as a single wisdom intent.

Thus, given that the wisdom intent of all dharma of the greater and lesser vehicles can be gathered into the methods for taming self-fixation—here as well, if practice serves as the antidote for self-fixation, then that is the extent of the realization that is cultivated in the stream of mind.

The samaya of the mind training is as stated:

> Train in the three aspects of the general meaning.

Thus, the samayas of mind training that are taught and that must be practiced are to abandon the claim of being a practitioner of chöd who has an advanced view yet ignores the vows, to never lose even the most minor disciplines so that the commitments will not be forsaken, to abandon claiming to be a practitioner of fearless conduct and the foolishness of engaging in various careless deeds, [and to abandon] maintaining partial patience while being harmed by humans or nonhumans, yet getting angry otherwise, and so forth.

To explain the advice, it states:

> All practice boils down to one; all antidotes boil down to one.

Thus, whatever practice it is, one must understand that—as the practice of chöd—it must tame self-fixation. No matter what negative circumstances surface, whether illness or demonic-force possession, the antidote or suppression to reverse that occurs through chöd. Given that this becomes the support for chöd practice, extensive information concerning this can be found in the treatise on mind training.

Whatever the case may be, chöd is the essence of the mind training of the great vehicle. If one desires to become an appropriate chöd practitioner, then—among the principal teachings on mind training that exist in the whole of India and Tibet—in the least, all chöd practitioners should study and contemplate Shāntideva's *Bodhicharyāvatāra*[a] and keep this close to their hearts. Through this practice of chöd, itself the profound practice of the Great Mother, a practitioner must apply unwavering diligence throughout the day and night.

It states in the *Gathering of Precious Qualities*:

> A bodhisattva who makes a long-term connection with this [prajñāpāramitā] will be able to liberate gods, humans, and the three lower realms. Those wishing to show this path to others must strive both day and night in the practice of this prajñāpāramitā. If a man discovers a precious jewel that has never been heard of, he should be overjoyed. Yet if he loses it through carelessness in the next moment, since it is now lost he will constantly suffer the wish to acquire it again. Like that, having entered the path of the supreme bodhichitta—like finding a precious jewel—the practitioner must take care not to lose this prajñāpāramitā.

Thus, it is as taught.

This treatise on the supreme teachings of chöd and the meaning of this subject are the resultant state of empty clarity, an exceptionally sublime sprout. Unsullied by the dirt of incorrect view and conduct or chaff of faulted explanations, this teaching of chöd severs the bondage of self-fixation. Imbued with the meaning of the Great Mother like a sword on the path of upāya and prajñā, this resembles the weapon used for reversing the battle of existence.

For those heroic bodhisattvas, this is a fitting teaching to rely upon. Those who claim to have attained the supremely precious qualities of accomplishment yet whose outer conduct is reckless and attached to ordinary stones and earth[55] think that receiving respect from others and meaningless distractions are the core of this practice. Such self-proclaimed chödpas are nothing short of self-indulgent.

> The key point of training in the supremely pure transmission of the
> bodhichitta is to practice the meaning of the sacred dharma that
> severs the māras.
> This explanation given in conjunction with the source [i.e., prajñā-
> pāramitā] includes commentary not previously illuminated.

These are the verses that summarize the section.

[a] *chang chüb sempa'i chöd pa la jüg pa* (*byang chub sems dpa'i spyod pa la 'jug pa*); Shāntideva

3.2 Specific Explanation of How to Practice

This has three parts:

1 Cleansing the mind through the preliminary practices
2 How to cultivate realization through the main practice
3 Supplementary advice for training in the complete transmission of the entrustment

Second, the specific explanation for the manner of practice involves three: cleansing the mind through the preliminary practices, how to cultivate realization through the main practice, and the supplementary advice for training in the complete transmission of the entrustment.

3.2.1 Cleansing the Mind through the Preliminary Practices

This has two parts:

1 Common general preliminaries
2 Uncommon specific preliminaries

First, for cleansing the mind through the preliminaries, there are two: the common general preliminaries and the uncommon specific preliminaries.

3.2.1.1 Common General Preliminaries

This has four parts:

1 Supplicating the guru
2 Training in the four thoughts that turn the mind
3 Refuge and bodhichitta
4 Accumulating merit through the maṇḍala and seven-branch offerings

First, the common preliminaries involve four: supplicating the guru in order to render the mind suitable, training in the contemplation of the four thoughts that turn the mind, taking refuge and generating the bodhichitta, and accumulating merit through the maṇḍala and the seven-branch offerings.

3.2.1.1.1 Supplicating the Guru

First, supplicating the guru is as follows:

> *Kye!* Embodiment of all victorious ones and their heirs without exception, you bring the minds of the fortunate disciples to fruition. With the power to liberate saṃsāra in the expanse of enlightenment—Sovereign of All Families, Guru, know me!

Saying ***kye*** means to call out with intense longing as stated in the *Tantra of the Emergence of Chakrasaṃvara*:[a]

> The guru is the buddha, the guru is the dharma, and likewise the guru is the sangha.

Thus, the guru is the nature of the Triple Gem, which are the objects of refuge. It states in the *Root Tantra of Mañjushrī*:

> To benefit others, all buddhas who came in the past, will come, and are present now have and will take rebirth in human forms among human beings.

Thus, and in the *Hevajra*,[b] it states:

> In the future, I will assume the rupakāya of the spiritual master.

Thus and in the *Vajra Tent*,[c] it states:

> In the future, the one called Vajrasattva will abide in the form of the vajra master. In order to benefit sentient beings, he will appear in an ordinary body.

Thus, in order for the buddhas of the three times to tame beings, they will reveal themselves in the form of the guru, as taught. As the **embodiment of all victorious ones and their heirs without exception**, [the master] blesses and **brings the mind** streams **of** all **fortunate disciples to fruition** so that the qualities of the path are ready to blossom and obscurations able to be purified. **With the power to** fully abandon all karma and passions of **saṃsāra**, [the guru] has actualized the nature of **the** great **expanse of enlightenment**, where all obscurations are abandoned and sentient beings are placed in the state of **liberation. Sovereign of all families** and oceans of maṇḍalas, all-pervasive master of great kindness, **guru, know me!**

Thus, it states in the *Fifty Verses of Guru Devotion*:[d]

> Concerning the guru and the vajra holder, do not consider they are separate.

[a] *gyü dom jung* (*rgyud sdom 'byung, shrīmahāsaṃvarodayatantrarāja*)
[b] *kye dorje* (*kye rdo rje, hevajratantrarāja*)
[c] *dorje gur* (*rdo rje gur*); instruction tantra of the *Two Segments* (*tag nyi, brtag gnyis*)
[d] *lama nga chu pa* (*bla ma lnga bcu pa, gurupañchashikā*); Ashvaghoṣha

Thus as taught, considering that the guru and personal deity are inseparable, offer supplications that are as the great master and protector Tsongkhapa[a] taught:

> When hearing the teachings: if difficult to retain; when contemplating: if difficult to understand; and when meditating: if nothing develops in the mind stream—then the exceptional upadesha involves knowing that the time to rely upon the power of the field of refuge has arrived.

So, just as taught, relying upon the power of an exceptional field of refuge is an inspirational method for realization to arise in the mind. Supplication to the guru even surpasses that.

In the *Five Stages,*[b] it states:

> This self-emergent bhagavan is the sole personal deity; yet since the vajra master bestows upadesha, no one surpasses that.

Thus, Buddha Vajradhara is the sole embodiment of all families without exception, the self-emergent bhagavan, as well as the surpassing bhagavan. Yet, when it comes to the vajra master who fully bestows upadesha upon disciples, a vajra master such as that will even surpass him [i.e., Vajradhara]. In order for disciples to accumulate virtue through a field of merit, it is said that the guru is more exceptional than Buddha Vajradhara.

In the *Accomplishing Wisdom,*[c] it states:

> The guru is Vajradhara, so whoever sees both as inseparable will gather all siddhis and thereby receive them all.

Thus—as the embodiment of common and supreme siddhis—when great connate wisdom blossoms in the mind stream, enlightenment will be realized in that lifetime, as [the] living buddha Yang Gonpa Chenpo[d] said:

> Given that the guru is the nature of the Triple Gem, all meditation deities, and the buddhas of the three times—by supplicating to him or her, all qualities that exist within saṃsāra and enlightenment will be received without interruption. In this life, fervent regard for the guru is the profound method through which to attain buddhahood.

[a] *rje tsong kha pa*
[b] *rim nga* (*rim lnga, pañchakrama*); Nāgārjuna
[c] *yeshe drubpa* (*ye shes grub pa*)
[d] *rgyal ba yang dgon pa chen po*; Kadampa master, 1213-1258

If there is no fervent regard, then qualities will not arise in the mind, as the glorious Lord of Secrets [i.e., Vajrapāṇi] told mahāsiddha Vajra Karma:[a]

> O Vajra Karma, lacking fervent regard for the guru and then claiming to have had a vision of the deity or profound levels of experience and realization is nothing short of fabrication.

It is as taught. However much fervent regard arises indicates how many qualities will arise, as Jigten Sümgon[b] said:

> If fervent regard is outstanding, then meditation will be excellent. If mediocre, then meditation will be mediocre. If fervent regard is inferior, then meditation will be lesser. So, depending on how much faith develops, this indicates how the qualities of enlightenment will arise in the mind stream.

So, it is as taught. Concerning this, the great Sakya Paṇḍita[c] also said:

> Although one is unable to internalize the ocean of transmissions, to meditate upon the guru at the crown of one's head and see him or her with faith while supplicating until tears well forth is the prodigious meditation to seize the path of liberation.

Thus, it is as taught.

> Praying single-pointedly to the embodiment of all families who is the supremely kind root guru, is the method through which all qualities of realization will be born in the mind stream.
> This magic of upadesha is easy to accomplish and brings immense results.

Hence, these are the verses that summarize the section.

3.2.1.1.2 Training in the Four Thoughts that Turn the Mind

This has two parts:

1 Meaning of "turning the mind"

2 Individual contemplations

[a] *ley kyi dorje* (*las kyi rdo rje*)

[b] *'jig rten gsum mgon*; Protector of the World, Drigung Kagyü master

[c] Je Sakya Paṇchen (*rje sa skya pan chen*), 1182-1251

Second, for the way of contemplating the four thoughts that turn the mind, there are two: the way of considering what is meant by turning the mind and the way of considering the individual contemplations.

3.2.1.1.2.1 Meaning of "Turning the Mind"

First, what is meant by "turning the mind" is to turn the mind from the six places of rebirth in saṃsāra. What method turns the mind? The mind is turned through training in the transmissions of the four thoughts. How does this reversal occur? By considering the precious human rebirth so difficult to attain and the impermanence of life, one is turning away from fixation upon the phenomena of this life alone. By contemplating the undeceiving truth of karma and the faults of saṃsāra, one turns from the phenomena of the future life by striving after the mere happiness of taking higher rebirth as a human or deva. The extent of the reversal is that by only seeing saṃsāra as a faulted state, attachment is reversed; and the desire for liberation becomes so deliberate that, when the mind of renunciation is born, the mind has turned.

3.2.1.1.2.2 Individual Contemplations

This has four parts:

1 Attainment of the precious human rebirth
2 Impermanence
3 Suffering of saṃsāra
4 Law of cause and result

Second, the individual contemplations involve four: considering the difficult-to-attain human rebirth, impermanence of life, the suffering of saṃsāra, and the law of cause and result.

3.2.1.1.2.2.1 Attainment of the Precious Human Rebirth

This has three parts:

1 Nature of the freedoms and advantages
2 Manner in which acquiring them is so meaningful
3 Reasons why they are so difficult to acquire

First, the contemplation upon the difficult-to-attain human rebirth is:

> Attaining a precious human life with freedoms and advantages is born from the excellent causes and results of interdependent accumulations

> and prayers—difficult to acquire again and again, like the *udumwara* flower. May the state of perfect omniscience be swiftly achieved!

As the root verses state, given that at this time there is the opportunity to accomplish dharma, there is **freedom**; and because the conducive circumstances to accomplish this are present, there are **advantages**. Through that support, once **attaining a precious human rebirth with** these freedoms and endowments, one has surely relied upon the root causes of gathering vast virtuous **accumulations** combined with the contributing circumstances of perfectly pure aspiration **prayers**.

Hence, the result of being endowed with such outstanding qualities ensures that the **excellent causes and results** that are dependent upon perfectly pure **interdependent** karma will be **born**. Later, the fact that it will be **difficult to acquire** this opportunity **again and again** is **like** the rarity of **the *udumwara* flower** blooming, an event that occurs only when a supreme nirmāṇakāya buddha or chakravartin ruler has entered this world. Without that, there is nowhere that this flower will blossom. Without wasting this support, one should intend to strive to extract the essence of this opportunity by attaining the temporary and ultimate states of basic well-being and happiness and especially the **state of perfectly omniscient**, fully enlightened buddhahood. Thinking in this way, make the prayer, "In this lifetime **may this** state **be swiftly achieved!**"

Concerning this, there is three: an explanation of the nature of the freedoms and advantages, the manner in which acquiring them is so meaningful, and the way to consider the reasons why they are so difficult to acquire.

3.2.1.1.2.2.1.1 Nature of the Freedoms and Advantages

For the first, the nature of the freedoms and advantages are as stated in *Resting the Mind in Repose:*[a]

> To acquire a human body amounts to being just a human rebirth, a general human rebirth, or a precious human rebirth.

Thus, as taught, generally there are three divisions concerning human rebirth. [For the first] to acquire a human body but have no inclination toward virtue and to then only accumulate nonvirtue is likened to those who live at the edge of civilization as barbarians. That amounts to being just a human existence. Then, there is the general category that involves being unable to practice the sacred dharma in a qualified way, so that life is squandered by distractions and conduct.

[a] *sem nyid ngal so* (*sems nyid ngal gso*); Longchen Rabjam

That involves a mixture of both positive and negative karma. A precious human rebirth means using the opportunity to tame the mind through study, contemplation, and meditation and having the capacity to inspire others toward the direction of virtue. Even if that is not the case, there would be the tendency to abandon nonvirtue and only accomplish positive virtue.

Among these, the latter is emphasized here; and for that, there are two categories: the freedoms and the advantages. First, for the freedoms, they include the explicit freedoms and the implicit freedoms that are subsequent to that.

First, it is stated in the *Gathering of Precious Qualities*:

> Through perfectly pure morality, the eight states of nonfreedom endured by wanderers will be abandoned; and through that, freedom will always be discovered.

So, it is as taught. Freedom that is based on being exempt from the eight states of nonfreedom is as the *Advice from a Spiritual Friend*[a] states:

> Holding incorrect views; birth as an animal, preta,[b] or in the hells; without ever hearing the words of the Buddha and in a land with no dharma; as a barbarian; with faculties incomplete; or as a long-life god—in any of these states of rebirth, there are the eight faults of lacking freedom. To be exempt from these states means that freedom has been acquired, so one must strive to avoid these reversed states of rebirth.

Thus, it is taught, and furthermore:

> The hells, pretas, animals, and long-life gods, barbarians and those with wrong view, no presence of Buddha, and faculties impaired are the eight states of nonfreedom.

As it mentions, this includes taking rebirth in any of the three lower states, such as that of the hells, pretas, and animals. Saying "long-life gods" according to some textual sources includes the two types of gods: those without perception and those without form. Among these two, the latter is more commonly known. Nevertheless, among the god realms of the four places of concentration[56] in the place called Bṛhatphala that is far removed from civilization: at the moment rebirth is taken until death arrives, the movement of the conceptual mind and

[a] *she tring* (*bshes spring, suhṛllekha*); Nāgārjuna
[b] *yidak* (*yi dvags*); deprived spirit

its thought formations are arrested; and the god remains in that state for many eons of time.

In the [terma] commentary, it also tells us:

> All long-life gods are distracted and constantly intoxicated by the sensual enjoyments that they experience, so the intention to enter dharma never occurs to them.

As taught, it also states in the *Words that Describe the Eight States of Nonfreedom*:[a]

> Just as it is taught that gods of the desire realm are always distracted by passion-based activities, those desire-realm gods also have very long lives.

From the *Accounts from the Gaṇachakra*,[b] it says:

> How can it be possible for those with distracted minds to find happiness? With no control over the mind for even an instant, how can they abide in a state without distraction?

Thus, it is as taught. When the mind is constantly distracted, dharma will not be accomplished since there is departure from the contentment of a restful mind. Having the freedom of not taking rebirth as a borderland barbarian where no dharma exists or with incorrect views—such as not believing in life after death, cause and result, or the Triple Gem; or rebirth in a place where Buddha has never come so the Buddha and his teachings are nonexistent; being disadvantaged with mental faculties impaired or handicapped as a mute—there is the freedom and opportunity to accomplish the dharma.

Second, for the corresponding subsequent freedoms, Omniscient Longchenpa asserts that, although one may not be directly born in these eight states of nonfreedom, it is necessary to not be overcome by the nonfreedom of momentary [obstacles] and limiting conditions that take freedom away.

In the *Precious Wish-Fulfilling Treasury*,[c] it states:

> Overcome by the tumultuous five poisons, being delusional, possessed by māras, being slothful, overflowing with negative karmic ripening, manipulated by others, wanting protection from fear, [and] being an

[a] *mi khom pa gyed kyi tam* (*mi khom pa brgyad kyi gtam, aṣhṭākṣhaṇakathā*); Ashvaghoṣha
[b] *tsok kyi tam* (*tshogs kyi gtam, saṃbhāraparikathā*)
[c] *yid zhin rinpoche'i dzöd* (*yid bzhin rin po che'i mdzod*); Longchen Rabjam

> artificial practitioner are all temporary conditions that contribute to the eight states of nonfreedom. These are misguided states since they render an individual unsuitable for the path to liberation.

So, as taught. In this case, given that the five passions are extremely coarse, the mind is constantly disturbed; it falls under the influence of negative companions, bringing on delusion. Being overcome by māras means to mistake the view and conduct and become involved with an incorrect path. Being slothful means to not show even the slightest interest or effort toward the spiritual path. Even if one tries, due to extreme negativity or illness, qualities will not develop. This is called "overflowing with negative karmic ripening". Being a servant or slave of others means to have no personal freedom; and wanting to be protected from fear of māras and harm-doers, as well as obsessing over this life's sustenance, means—although having entered the dharma—due to previous negative habits, going against the dharma. Being an artificial practitioner means to pretend to know dharma when that is not the case and to just pursue material gain and respect from others. These eight conditions will occur randomly and present obstacles to the accomplishment of dharma, so they are referred to as the limiting conditions of nonfreedom. Although a human rebirth has been acquired, it falls short of becoming a suitable vessel for dharma and the path that leads to liberation. Hence, by wasting that life's opportunity, the next rebirth is rendered unqualified.[57]

The quote continues:

> Those with strong grasping will have manners that are extremely negative, be unafraid of saṃsāra, lack any faith, engage with nonvirtue, show no interest in dharma, and have degenerate vows and samaya. Those are the eight states of nonfreedom that separate one from the path. Distancing one from the dharma, the torch of liberation is gradually extinguished.

Thus, this refers to being bound by strong fixation and attachment to this life's wealth, family members, and the like and having a basic human nature that is so distasteful that there is absolutely no potential to make spiritual progress. With no sense of fear or even slight trepidation toward the suffering of this life and the faults of saṃsāra—although having heard of the qualities of the Triple Gem and virtuous spiritual guides—one lacks any faith whatsoever. Engaging only in nonvirtue through body, speech, and mind; having no inspiration toward the holy dharma much like the reaction a dog has when grass is placed before him; allowing the prātimokṣha and bodhisattva vows to degenerate; and entering the door of Secret Mantra and then opposing the root guru and vajra family members so that samaya is allowed to decline are the eight states of nonfreedom that separate one from the path to liberation. Distancing one from the sacred dharma, the torch of liberation is then extinguished. That explains the quotation.

Secondly, the ten advantages are as follows: birth as a human, in a central land, with faculties complete, without reversed karma, with faith in the objects of refuge, at a time when the Buddha has come and the dharma is taught, the presence of the doctrine, as well as the presence of followers and loving, compassionate guides. Thus, taking rebirth as a human being means having the capacity to speak and understand the meaning of words. Concerning being born in a central land according to geography, this refers to the place that represents the heart of enlightenment where all buddhas of this excellent kalpa have and will enlighten, namely, Bodhgayā, India.[a] From that as the center, to the east there is a *mikhari*,[b] or the Sugar Cane Forest. To the south is a great river called Deva with abundant grassy reeds; to the west are two towns of ṛṣhis called Kawa and Nyewa'i Kawa;[c,58] and to the north is an *ishera*,[d] which means grassy hill. It is taught in the Vinaya[e] teachings that anything between these landmarks is referred to "the central land", whereas anything outside of them is considered to be a borderland.

To explain this from the perspective of the dharma as described by Ārya Asaṅga, saying "center" refers to wherever there are the four aspects of the retinue, namely, a male and female fully ordained bhikṣhu-bhikṣhuni and a male and female lay Buddhist upāsaka-upāsikā.[f] Any place other than where these four reside is considered to be a borderland. Even here in Tibet, given that of the principal of the four members of the retinue, the male bhikṣhu exists and the sacred dharma has been propagated, [Tibet] can also be considered a central land.

"Having complete faculties" refers to the visual consciousness and the rest. "Not having reversed karma" means having no intentional engagement with the weightiest karmas, such as the five heinous nonvirtues, and never forcing others to commit them. This is indicative. Yet according to the instructions of the masters: if whatever activity is engaged in is only for the sake of this life, in truth that is considered to be reversed karma. No matter what work one engages in, if it is solely for this life's gain, it said in the oral instructions of the masters that that is considered to be reversed karma. In the [terma] commentary, it states that

[a] Dorje Den (*rdo rje gdan*); Vajrāsana

[b] *mi kha ri*

[c] *ka ba* and *nye ba'i ka ba*; Pillar and Proximate Pillar

[d] *i she ra*

[e] *dül wa lung* (*'dul ba lung*), *vinayapiṭaka*

[f] *genyen* and *genyenma* (*dge bsnyen* and *dge bsnyen ma*); male and female lay practitioners

reversed karma refers to all those males and females and their associates who are not following the dharma. Actually, this is really pointing out that karma has turned toward a negative direction or become reversed. Having faith in the Buddha's doctrine that is suitable and worthy of feeling devotion toward [is the fifth]. When these five are complete in one's stream of mind as the conducive aspects for accomplishing dharma, they are personal advantages.

That the perfected Buddha came into this world, the dharma was revealed for the welfare of the objects to tame by turning the wheel of dharma, the doctrine has not declined but endures, there are followers, there is the opportunity to encounter loving and compassionate spiritual guides who are concerned about the welfare of others, as well as patrons of the dharma, are the five that afford the conducive circumstances for accomplishing the dharma. Since these five are circumstantial and act as conditional aspects for dharma practice, they are referred to as "circumstantial advantages". In these ways, the qualities of the ten advantages are present.

3.2.1.1.2.2.1.2 Manner in which Acquiring Them Is So Meaningful

Second, the way of contemplating how significant it is to acquire these is as follows. In dependence upon the body as a support, the way one gains the potential to fulfill both temporary and ultimate aims is as it states in the *Bodhicharyāvatāra*:

> This human life so difficult to acquire, once an individual attains something so meaningful . . .

So, it is. In dependence upon this if one strives to practice dharma correctly, then—like boarding a great vessel—there is the potential to cross over this ocean of suffering. The quote continues:

> By relying upon the vessel of a human body, one will traverse the great ocean of suffering. Given that this vessel will be difficult to acquire again, deluded ones must not sleep at such a crucial time.

So, it is as taught. Even temporarily, this is extremely significant as we are told in *Resting the Mind in Repose*:

> Here, as momentous as having seen the Buddha, hearing the dharma, and accomplishing it, this is significant for this life and the resultant future lifetimes since they too will depend upon this body of freedoms and advantages. Meditate repeatedly in a state of great joy.

Thus, having met and witnessed the guide Lord Buddha and the gurus who are the virtuous spiritual companions, hearing the dharma from them, and practicing that meaning, there is the potential for accomplishment—meaning there is the potential for this to make a significant impact in that life. Later, having strived in the causes for happiness, those results will mature to bring well-being. That the ultimate state of buddhahood can be accomplished is as the quote continues:

> Principal among human beings in the world, including gods, all protectors surrounded by hearers, solitary realizers, and heirs—although having attained the state of deathless ambrosia—by acquiring a precious supreme human rebirth, the freedoms and advantages are praised by saying "this body surpasses even that of the gods".

Thus, this refers to having the potential to attain the state of a buddha surrounded by a host of bodhisattvas, shrāvakas, and pratyekas.

This becomes an exceptional support for the path of the great vehicle, as the *Letter to a Disciple*[a] states:

> As the support for the path of the tathāgatas that guide all beings on their way, just what is this human body with its exceptional mental capacity? A path such as this will not be discovered even by gods, nāgas, asuras,[b] garuḍas, vidyādharas, *kinnaras*[c,59] or a Mahoraga python.[d,60]

So, in order to traverse to the state of the tathāgatas, this is the vessel that supports the entirety of bodhisattva conduct, such as generosity and the rest. With this support, there exists the strength of mind to swiftly transport all sentient beings without exception to the state of buddhahood by oneself alone. An exceptional support such as this human body that can give rise to the path of bodhichitta is said to be otherwise nonexistent even among the bodies of gods, nāgas, and the rest.

In *Resting the Mind in Repose*, it states:

> The wisdom ground that sees the truth of the nonconceptual state is, among gods and humans, easy to discover through the support of a

[a] *lob tring* (*slob spring*); Chandragomin
[b] *lhama yin* (*lha ma yin*); titans or demigods
[c] *mi'am chi* (*mi'am ci, drumakinnararāja*)
[d] *to che* (*lto'phye, uragādhipatiḥ*)

> human body. Since this truth is the essence of the excellent path of the vajra vehicle as well: by attaining a human rebirth, such results will be easily accomplished.

Thus, through the support of a human rebirth, it is even easy to directly realize the truth of nonconceptual wisdom. In the past, there have been some desire-realm gods who have done so based on their strong habit of having previously cleansed on the path with a human body as a support. Although [that rebirth] may be an acceptable vessel through which to see the true nature, it is still impossible to initially attain the path of an ārya while in the support of a higher god-realm form.

As mainly described earlier, the desire-realm gods exist in a state of nonfreedom. Hence, humans are superior when it comes to a support that will accomplish the path. In the *Tantra of the Emergence of Chakrasaṃvara*, it states:

> The inhabitants of the three continents may fully enjoy great wealth, yet with no other consideration they also have no intelligence so are unable to determine the difference between futility and the alternatives.

Thus, and the quote continues:

> Humans of Jambudvīpa are born through karma, so that place is known to be dependent upon karma.

Thus, but other continents are places dependent upon wealth. Since Uttarakuru[a] is in particular a place dependent upon negative fruition, it is an unsuitable environment to support the prātimokṣha vows and the seeing of truth. Compared to the inhabitants of Jambudvīpa, the inhabitants on other continents lack virtue and intelligence and are hence dull-minded and without discerning prajñā that specifically identifies meanings. On the other hand, the inhabitants of Jambudvīpa who are born through previous karmic deeds have great powers in their lives to accumulate karma, which is why that continent is based on karmic interdependency. Compared to other continents, this support is superior; so when it comes time for the gods to die, they often pray to be reborn in the human realm. This [human rebirth] is especially extolled as the support for the vehicle of Secret Mantra Vajrayāna.

In the tantras, it states:

[a] Draminyen (*sgra mi snyan*); Ominous Sound

> If humans strive to practice this superb king of Secret Mantra with diligence in their lifetimes, it will be accomplished—needless to mention, other siddhis.

Thus, it is as taught.

Concerning that, Ārya Pawo[a] has said:

> When a support such as this is obtained, it produces the seeds that transcend saṃsāra. The supreme seed of glorious awakening even surpasses a wish-fulfilling gem. Since all humans have this stream of qualities, who would let this go to waste?

Thus, it is as taught. This human body produces the seeds of liberation that transcend saṃsāra and generate the causes for the glory of awakening and the qualities of perfect enlightenment. Since this is so significant as a support from which unceasing qualities emerge in this life, extract the essence without allowing this to be wasted.

3.2.1.1.2.2.1.3 Reasons Why They Are So Difficult to Acquire

Third, the explanation concerning the reasons they [i.e., the freedoms and advantages] are so difficult to acquire has three: from the perspective of cause, from the perspective of analogy, and from the perspective of nature.

First, in the *Entering the Middle Way*,[b] it states:

> The cause of higher rebirth is not other than morality.

So, it is necessary to guard at least one category of vows in order to obtain rebirth based on the well-being of the higher states of gods and humans. Especially, to obtain the support of a precious human rebirth, it is as stated by the Bhagavan in the sūtras:

> Whoever expresses generosity will have great abundance. Whoever maintains the morality of vows will take rebirth in the higher realms.

Thus, he taught. In the *Jewel Garland*, it states:

> Through generosity, there will be abundance; and through morality, there will be happiness.

[a] *slob dpon dpa' bo*

[b] *üma la jüg pa* (*dbu ma la 'jug pa, madhyamakāvatāra*); Chandrakīrti

Thus, as mentioned, although it is necessary to guard pure morality as the basis, it is rare to actually encounter someone who strives in expressing generosity and the other pāramitās while supported with pure aspirations as the contributing, connecting force. It is also difficult for those who dwell in the three lower realms to even consider giving rise to virtuous thoughts. Gods are distracted by samādhi and the pleasures of desire; and even among humans, the places where dharma flourishes compared to where it does not are hard to find. Even if rebirth is taken in a place where dharma flourishes, it is unusual to encounter anyone who is practicing dharma in a qualified way. Among humans, it is exceedingly uncommon to encounter someone who is actively accumulating the causes for a human rebirth, such as keeping pure morality. In the *Four-Hundred Stanzas*,[a] it states:

> Most humans take hold of a less-than-sacred direction; and as a result, most ordinary individuals are certain to take rebirth in the lower realms.

Thus, most ordinary humans are actively pursuing a negative karmic direction that is less than sacred, accumulating the causes for the lower realms. Even now if we were to examine this, ordinary folks are busy taking lives, stealing, lying, and tricking others, engaged only in nonvirtuous activities. Even those who pride themselves on being followers of the victors are engaged in conduct that is contradictory to what they promised to uphold. Utilizing offerings given for the dead and the living, no matter the individual, they are only trying to pursue happiness for this life alone. Having attachment and aversion toward family versus enemies, they persist in nonvirtuous deeds. Especially, when examining any of one's own intentions and actions: since most everything leads to nonvirtue and the law of cause and result is inevitable, there is no choice but to take lower rebirth in the end. In these cases, human rebirth is no longer an option.

In the *Bodhicharyāvatāra*, it states:

> Through this conduct of mine, not even a human body will be acquired. If a human life is not attained, then there will only be negativity and no virtue. When the time arrives for a fortunate one to accumulate virtue: if he does not do so and once he is deluded by the suffering of lower realms, what can be then done? If he does not engage in virtue and only accumulates the opposite, for one-hundred eons of time not even the sound of a higher rebirth's happiness will be heard.

Thus, and the quote continues:

[a] *üma zhi gya pa* (*dbu ma bzhi brgya pa, catuḥshataka*); Āryadeva

> Even accumulating nonvirtue for an instant can lead one to the lowest hell realm for an eon. Having accumulated karma like this in saṃsāra from beginningless time, need it be mentioned that rebirth in the higher realms is not an option?

Thus, if virtue is not accumulated at present: once lower rebirth is taken—since there will be perpetual delusion and suffering—there will be no method to obtain higher states of happiness. Concerning disrespecting a bodhisattva, abandoning the dharma, and so forth: even at the moment such thoughts may occur, that nonvirtue can send one to the hells for an eon. Since that is the case and considering all the unpurified nonvirtue accumulated in one's mind stream from beginningless time, one will be flung to the lower realms where the happiness of higher realms will be obsolete.

Second are the difficulties given from the standpoint of analogy. It states in Nāgārjuna's *Advice from a Spiritual Friend*:

> The odds of taking rebirth as a human compared to an animal are as slight as the chances that a sea tortoise would surface with its head through a yoke that is bobbing randomly on the ocean's surface. Hence, humans with dignity will take care to reap the fruition of their life through dharma practice.

Thus, and from the *Transmission on Perfectly Correct Truth*,[a] it states:

> O Bhikṣhus! For example, when this great earth becomes a vast ocean—like a yoke tossed around on its surface by the wind—a blind tortoise comes up every one-hundred years to catch a breath. What do you think, bhikṣhus? Is it likely that the tortoise will surface with its neck through the yoke? They replied, "O Bhagavan, no it is not." The Bhagavan continued, "Bhikṣhus! Just like that analogy, this precious human rebirth is extremely difficult to obtain."

This is similarly stated in the sūtra called *Gathering of Flowers*,[b] as well as in the sūtra of *Ānanda Entering the Womb*:[c,61]

> For example, if a four-fingerbreadth length needle is standing upright and one tosses a handful of mustard seeds over it, the chances of a single

[a] *yang dag par den pa'i lung* (*yang dag par ldan pa'i lung*)
[b] *metog tsok kyi do* (*me tog tshogs kyi mdo*)
[c] *gawo ngal jüg gi do* (*dga' bo mngal 'jug gi mdo, garbhāvakrāntisūtra*)

> seed entering the eye of the needle are next to impossible. Obtaining a human rebirth is like that. To toss a handful of beans at a glass wall, the chances that a single bean will stick to that wall are similar to the likes of acquiring a single precious human rebirth. As these analogies point out, a precious human rebirth is truly rare and difficult to acquire.

Third is the difficulty of acquiring this [human rebirth] from the perspective of nature. Compared to the divergent classes of the lower realms, this precious human rebirth is difficult to obtain. In the sūtras, it states:

> The number of beings who find [a precious human rebirth] are likened to the amount [of beings] that would fit on the wheel of a chariot, compared to those in the hell realms being like the numbers of dust particles on the vast earth. The numbers of pretas are like snowflakes in a blizzard, whereas animals in comparison are like the numbers of grains in a beer barrel.

So, it is taught. It also states in the *Vinaya*:[a,62]

> From the history of both of Ānanda's nephews, it says that—once leaving the lower realms—the numbers of beings who return there again are equal to the particles of dust on the vast earth. The numbers of beings who leave there and then take higher rebirth are as many as the dust particles on the fingertips of the enlightened Buddha. Once transferring from higher realms of gods and humans, the number of beings who then take rebirth in the lower realms are like the dust particles on every inch of the earth without exception. Once transferring from either of those places, the number of beings who are reborn in the higher realms again is likened to the dust at the tip of Buddha's finger.

So, it states. Concerning that which we can actually see, there are many more animals than there are human beings; and among animals, the lowest states include birds that outnumber many other species. More so, there are insects that outnumber the rest. For example, in the summertime on a pile of horse manure or in a puddle of water, the numbers of insects are countless. In comparison, human rebirth is difficult to obtain. Padampa [Sangye] said:

> Generally, when just looking at the forms of sentient beings, it seems almost impossible to attain the precious human body. Especially when

[a] *lung zhi* (*lung gzhi, caturāgama*)

> seeing the forms of the pretas, it seems incredible that a precious human rebirth could be obtained.

Thus, it is as taught. Comparing the parallel classes of beings in the higher realms, humans are rarer than others. Among humans, those who meet the dharma are even less; and among them, those who practice in a qualified way are even fewer. For instance, among the millions of people who reside in the most populated cities in China, it is rare to find someone who has a human body that is being used to practice dharma according to the teachings. Not only that, it is rare to find those who engage in virtue versus nonvirtue and are actually interested in doing so. Hence, a precious human body is truly difficult to acquire. Therefore, having acquired a support that is so challenging to obtain, it is completely unacceptable to then use this for accumulating negative karma.

In *Advice from a Spiritual Friend*, it states:

> Whoever uses a golden vessel studded with gems to store filthy substances is senseless. Worse than that, whoever has obtained a human rebirth and uses it to accumulate negative karma is extremely senseless.

Thus, and in the *Bodhicharyāvatāra*, it states:

> Having found freedom such as this: if I do not familiarize with virtue, then there is nothing more deceptive or misguided than that.

Thus, it is as taught. So then, when everything is conducive and there is freedom at hand, it is necessary to work hard to attain rebirth in higher realms and avoid falling to the lower realms once again. In *Entering the Middle Way*, it states:

> When there is freedom and circumstances are conducive: if one does not take hold of that, then once having fallen into the ravine of circumstantial influences, in the future who will get this chance again?

Thus, now at this time if nothing is done to prevent falling into the ravine of the lower realms: later once one falls and is under the influence of circumstances, at that time it is unlikely someone will come along to lead you out of there to the higher realms.

Whenever the great spiritual master Geshe Chan Ngawa[a] was about to enter meditation, he would recite these verses and then enter meditation. If we too can bring the meaning of this to our minds, we will come to know something

[a] *dge bshes spyan snga ba*; Kadampa master, 1038-1103

of great import. It is for that reason that the glorious incomparable Lord Atisha has said:

> The fully endowed precious human rebirth is very difficult to acquire. Since it will be so in the future, make this opportunity meaningful through diligent practice.

Thus as taught, being diligent in practice, one must render this human rebirth meaningful.

It also states in the *Sūtra of the Ten Wheels of Kṣhitigarbha*:[a]

> With this state of leisure where eight states of nonfreedom have been abandoned and the torch of dharma burns: through the conduct of the great individual, the result should be attained.

Thus, in order to skillfully extract the essence of this precious rebirth while it is possessed and the torch of sacred dharma is present, one must strive to practice the path of the great vehicle and cultivate diligence toward that. In the terma commentary, it states:

> Since the present human body replete with eighteen freedoms and endowments is the result of previously accumulated excellent virtue, consider that—if this is not made meaningful now—once this previous result of virtue is exhausted, there will not be another opportunity to obtain happiness after that. Thinking in this way, make certain that the three doors engage in virtue.

Thus, it is as taught.

> As the support that possesses the qualities of the precious freedoms and advantages, this body is highly praised as more exalted than that of a divine being.
> And finding this is more meaningful than discovering a wish-fulfilling jewel.
> Thus extract the essence in this life since in the future it will be difficult to acquire again.

Thus, these verses summarize the section.

[a] *sa nying khor lo chupa* (*sa snying 'khor lo bcu pa*); a section of the *Sūtra of Kṣhitigarbha*

3.2.1.1.2.2.2 Impermanence

This has three parts:

1. The way that the external universe of the world is impermanent
2. The way that one's own life is impermanent and how death will occur
3. Other explanations concerning the ways of impermanence

Second is the contemplation upon death and impermanence.

> The external universe, this world, is impermanent and subject to destruction, creation, and endurance. The inner inhabitants, sentient beings, are subject to birth and death like the comings and goings in a marketplace. The days, months, and years—time itself—are like dancers' gyrations. O Guru, bless me to recall death and impermanence!

Thus, **the external universe of the world is impermanent**, given that in the end **it is subject to destruction.** In the beginning, it comes into **creation**; and in the interim, the way it **endures** remains fluctuating and unstable. **Inner inhabitants, sentient beings,** are impermanent as they are gradually **subject to birth and** eventual **death**, like how all the people in a **marketplace come and go.** Furthermore, **days, months, years, and time itself** are momentarily changing, like how **dancers** change costumes and assume myriad postures and **gyrations** in their dance. In this way, all compounded things are impermanent; and especially one's own life is impermanent, as each moment it moves toward its own demise. Nevertheless, until now having assumed that one will not die, this life has been spent in meaningless ways. Now, by knowing **impermanence** and the characteristics **of death**, one supplicates to the **guru to be blessed to recall** this.

For this, there are three: the way that the external universe of the world is impermanent, namely, through formation, endurance, obliteration, and vacuity; especially, the way that one's own life is impermanent and how death will occur; and other explanations concerning the way of impermanence.

3.2.1.1.2.2.2.1 The Way That the External Universe of the World Is Impermanent

For the first, in *Resting the Mind in Repose*, it states:

> The universe and inhabitants are impermanent. Through the formation and obliteration of existence—when the seven fires, the single flood, and the great tumultuous winds occur—the four jeweled mountains encircled by oceans and continents will also become impermanent.

> Since it is inevitable that all of this will become space, dharma must be practiced from the core of the heart.

Thus as taught, by contemplating how the universe and inhabitants of this world came into existence, will endure, will self-destruct, and become void, first the way formation occurred is as mentioned in the Abhidharma:

> At first formation occurred through the winds that permeated existence to the depths of the hells.

Thus, when the realms of this universe initially ceased to exist, there was only empty space for an indefinite period of time. From that, by the force of karma, the initial winds arose, becoming a maṇḍala of mobile energy. From then until a single sentient being was reborn in the hell realms, that duration of time became known as the eon of formation.

Concerning that, if the initial universe ceased to exist due to fire, then everything that extends all the way up to the first god realm of concentration would have ceased. Therefore, [first] the wind for the basis of Brahmakāyika[a] occurred. If obliteration occurred through water, then everything all the way up through the second level of the gods would have ceased to exist. Hence, the wind for the basis of the gods of Ābhāsvara[b] occurred. If obliteration occurred by wind, then everything up through the third realm of concentration would have ceased to exist; and the wind for the basis of the gods of Shubhakṛtsna[c] would occur. This is the way formation occurred, but the maṇḍala of wind that forms the basis of this world did not occur initially.

Among universe and inhabitants, the stages of the universe's formation are first. The realms that are not connected to physical earth come to exist in ascending order, and those that are connected occur from the bottom up. During the time of obliteration, it is said that our universe will be the last to cease to exist; and when formation occurs it [i.e., our universe] will be first. If the world that existed prior to this were to cease to exist due to fire, then first Brahmakāyika would have occurred. Gradually, the lower realms of concentration and the celestial palaces of the desire realms[63] such as that of the Paranirmitashavartin[d] all the way to Yāma[e] would come into existence. Given those realms are not connected to the physical earth, they occur in that way.

[a] *tsang ri* (*tshangs ris*); Province of Brahmā
[b] *ödsal* (*'od gsal*); Clear Light
[c] *gegyey* (*dge rgyas*); Abundant Virtue
[d] *zhentrül wangched* (*gzhan 'phrul dbang byed*); Mastery over Others' Creations
[e] *tab dral* (*thab bral*); Strifeless

All realms up through Trayatriṃsha[a] are connected to the earth, so they must come into existence after the universe is established. Gradually, below that, by the movement of wind accumulating for an extended period of time, the lower basis of this world becomes a wind maṇḍala that is vastly immense, many leagues in depth and breadth. The name of this wind is called Jampo.[b] The shape is spherical, pale blue in color, and unable to be destroyed even by a vajra.[64]

From that, by the power of sentient beings' karma, clouds filled with the essence of gold amass in the sky. From them, drops of rain descend that are the size of a chariot's wheel, accumulating for an extended period of time. Upon the wind maṇḍala, a vast maṇḍala of water converges. That is then relentlessly pounded by the wind from all four directions, so that most of it becomes bodies of water, while the remaining turns into the golden earth that rests upon that. Concerning the maṇḍala of wind, since it is the single basis for the trichiliocosm,[c] it is immense. The water and the golden earth become the basis for each of the four continents and are far less significant in size.

Then, from the massing clouds in the sky that contain the essence of various elements or seeds, bountiful rain descends and a great ocean coalesces upon the maṇḍala of the earth. The four directions are stirred by the wind that scatters and gathers the strongest elements. That causes millions of mountains to emerge upon the golden earth including Mt. Meru. Once again, through the wind that scatters and gathers the middling elements encircling and pounding the ring of mountains, millions of rings of seven golden mountains emerge around that perimeter. Then, through the sporadic pounding of the wind that scatters and gathers the inferior elements, the four continents, including the ring of mountains, come into existence. Given that these four continents simultaneously occur, this describes how the universe comes into creation.

As for the way the inner inhabitants are created, if the obliteration [of sentient beings] occurs through fire, then the life span, merit, and karma of the gods of Ābhāsvara at the second realm of concentration will be obliterated and they will meet with death. Rebirth then takes place in the celestial palace of the first realm of concentration, and the first to be born there has a large body and the notion of being the creator of that world. He is known as the ancestor of that world, the great Brahmā, who is principal. Those who are subsequently born are smaller in size; and since they think they were born based upon Brahmā's wish, they become members of his retinue. Gradually, the gods of the concentration

[a] *süm chu tsa süm pa* (*sum cu rtsa gsum pa*); Heaven of the Thirty-Three

[b] *'jam po*; Gentle Wind

[c] *tong süm gyi tong chenpo* (*stong gsum gyi stong chen po, trisahasramahāsahasra*); one billion worlds

realms such as Paranirmitashavartin up to the four classes of the great kings, who are the desire-realm gods, come into existence.

Following that, the humans of the northern continent Uttarakuru, the western Aparagodanīya,[a] and the eastern Pūrvavideha[b] come into existence. Aside from the northern continent of Uttarakuru, the humans residing on the other three realms will gradually accumulate an abundance of nonvirtue in stages of lesser, middling, and great.

Hence, in that order the beings of the preta, animal, and hell realms come into existence. The lowest among all hell realms is called Avīchī.[c] When a sentient being is first reborn there, that is when the eon of creation ends and the eon of endurance begins. Although the second and third realms of concentration have come into existence [prior to this], the way rebirth occurs is [initially] in the lower realms of concentration, such as Shubhakṛtsna, as well as the fourth.

When the universe comes into existence, it takes one intermediate eon; and when living beings come into existence, nineteen intermediate eons take place—totaling twenty. Within that context, to describe [how the inhabitants first came into] our southern continent of Jambudvīpa, when the gods of Ābhāsvara died, they were then reborn here during the period of time called the first eon. At that time, there were no phenomenal distinctions, such as sun, moon, constellations, seasons, years, months, days, nights, minutes, seconds, split seconds, males, females, feces, urine, houses, castes, skin colors, and shapes since all humans were just known to be living beings. Humans born during this first eon had miraculous powers with complete faculties; and since these qualities were concurrent with the major and minor marks and signs, they were beautiful to behold, vibrant in color, their bodies projected light, and their supernatural powers allowed them to fly through space. They did not depend upon material sustenance and instead consumed the joy of concentration. Their life spans were boundless as well.

When this world came into existence, the waters were gathered and perpetually pounded by the winds such that they were completely churned. That, combined with the general collective karma of sentient beings, caused the essence of the earth to resemble boiled honey the color of fresh butter. This essence pervaded the surface of the earth. When a single sentient being's habit to partake of material sustenance awakened, that being ate the essence of the earth by scooping it up with the fingertips to taste and consume. When others saw this, they followed suit by eating and experiencing the taste. Since the food they were consuming was coarse, they then lost the [subtle] capacity to miraculously pass

[a] Balangchöd (*ba lang spyod*); Bountiful Cow

[b] Lüpakpo (*lus 'phags po*); Elevated Body Height

[c] Narmed (*mnar med*); Naraka or Avīchī; Hell of Ultimate Torment

through space. Compared to before, their bodies became heavy and irregular; and the vibrancy of light vanished. Eventually, everything turned dark.

All of them then gathered and began to lament such that the sun, moon, constellations, seasons, and so forth naturally began to appear. The sun and the moon then became predominate over all four continents. From that time onward, all the beings ate an abundance of food; and their bodies grew dull and heavy. In contrast, those who ate less had excellent coloring with multi-colored vibrancy. The ones who were still vibrant in this way became prideful and proclaimed their superiority over the others, insulting them and causing them to become jealous. That brought on the fault of disrespect that then caused their vibrancy to disappear.

Once again, they gathered to lament; and by the force of sentient beings' collective karma, the essence of earth issued a similar scent that covered the face of the earth. The earth's color turned red like a *karnikara*[a,65] flower prevailing everywhere. By tasting that [earth], they preceded through the same stages as before until they began disparaging one another, which led to the eventual diminishing of everything.

They lamented again; and by the force of karma, a garden of seedlings emerged upon the great earth that were golden like the saffron flower,[b,66] pervading everywhere. They began consuming the flowers, and that caused all of their faults up through disrespect of one another to sequentially occur until all of their redeeming qualities once again disappeared. Again, they mourned; and through the power of karma, upon the vast face of the earth grew unplanted, perfectly formed, superlative rice without husks the size of four fingerwidths. The quality was such that, if sown in the morning, it would be ready to harvest by evening; and if sown in the evening, it would be ready by morning. The earth was so completely and consistently covered by this grain that there was never any trace of its harvest. Given that this food was coarse, the roughage from digestion turned into feces. In order for that to be eliminated, the different organs of the male and female bodies were formed. By associating with one another, the previous habit of fornication awakened in a single human. Turning into sexual desire that humans engaged in, desire developed and intercourse ensued. When the others witnessed this, they shouted out, "Stupid! What unacceptable behavior that is to engage in the presence of others. Such blatant disrespect!" Saying that, they scattered dirt upon the fornicators and scorned them profusely. Due to that, the perpetrators built a grass hut so that the others could not see, and that became the first abode.

Whenever these inhabitants wanted to eat the supreme rice, it was always

[a] *dong ka* (*dong ka*)
[b] *ka dam yu ka* (*ka dam yu ka*)

available to them. Eventually, one lazy individual took the breakfast portion after having just taken dinner in order to have that for the next morning. Seeing that, the others began to follow suit. Then, they all began to accumulate food in advance for two, three, seven, fifteen days, or even an entire month. With that, the rice began to develop a husk and was then required to plant in order for it to grow.

That was followed by the inhabitants becoming divisive and bickering over the ownership of the fields. The land was divided into parcels, so they then began stealing from one another. This was the starting point for the nonvirtue of stealing. At that time, they convened to discuss the situation; and among them, they appointed one person as their leader whose personality was noble and honest. They were then required to give one-sixth portion of their harvest to the leader as a tax. The leader dealt with conflicts in an honest way, so everyone grew to respect him; and he became known as the King Sammitīyas[a] and was the first known king of humankind.

The abode of the king became known thereafter as the king's palace. Those with less desire who renounced the comfort of living in abodes resided in isolated forests and became known as the ṛṣhis. Those who never stole or [engaged other nonvirtues] became known as the nobility, and those who stole from others were labeled the ordinary caste and the untouchables. This is how the various caste systems originated. The first king Sammitīyas and his son Öd Dzey, and, gradually, Gewa, Gechog, and Sojang Pak[b] became the first five kings of the original eon of time. Then came the five chakravartin universal monarchs: Māndhātā, Caru, Upacaru, Carumata, and Upacarumata,[c] who had sovereignty over the four continents. The monarchs that succeeded them had sovereignty over only a single continent.

Gradually, this became the ancestral heritage of the Shākyas, who were initially the Gautama clan of Zhungten.[d] His son was Senge Dram;[e] his son, King Shuddodhana;[f] whose son was the youthful bodhisattva Siddhārtha.[g] Beginning with Sammitīyas until Siddhārtha is the time of the royal lineage that included

[a] *gyalpo mang pö kurwa* (*rgyal po mang pos bkur ba*); Benevolent

[b] *'od mdzes, dge ba, dge mchog,* and *gso sbyang 'phags*; Beautiful Light, Virtue, Supreme Virtue, and Exalted Restoration

[c] Nga Ley Nu, Dzepa, Nye Dze, Dzeden, and Nye Dzeden (*nga las nu*, *mdzes pa*, *nye mdzes*, *mdzes ldan*, and *nye mdzes ldan*); Nurse From Me, Handsome One, Very Handsome One, Attractive One, and Very Attractive One

[d] *gzhung bstan*; King Firm Bow

[e] *senge'i 'gram*; King Lion's Jaw

[f] Zey Tsangma (*zas gtsang ma*)

[g] Don Tamched Drub (*don thams cad grub*); Accomplisher of Goals; Buddha Shākyamuni

some 973,531 kings who ruled [in India]. The royal lineage was discontinued from the time of Rāhula.[a]

As for the eon of endurance, it is taught:

> From the [beginning of] the intermediate eon down to the ten-year life expectancy, there is generation and dissolution for forty-thousand and eighteen eons. Once generation begins, the life expectancy increases up to eighty thousand [years]. In this way, the world comes into existence and endures for twenty intermediate eons.

Thus, it is taught. If one were to wonder whether the intermediate eon is part of the general eon of endurance, the answer is as follows. Once the life expectancy for the humans of Jambudvīpa reaches infinity, it then decreases to only ten years. That constitutes the first intermediate eon. Many scholars have also mentioned that this [life expectancy] gradually diminishes [from being fathomless] to eighty-thousand years. This is also referred to as "the long decline of time", during which time four of the one-thousand buddhas of this excellent age would have already entered this world.

When the life expectancy was forty-thousand years, Buddha Krakucchanda[b] came into the world; at thirty thousand, Buddha Kanakamuni[c] came; at twenty thousand, Buddha Kāshyapa[d] came; and at one-hundred years, our teacher came into this world. The information that describes human life expectancy in this world subsequent to this eon of endurance is not so clear. In the *Yogāchārabhūmi*,[e] it states that, after four types of humans come into existence, thieves will begin to lie out of fear of punishment, hence marking the beginning of false speech. Thereafter, it seems fairly certain that humans began to accumulate exceptionally negative karma. The origins for rebirth in the lowest hell realms began according to what was just described. If that had not been the case, there would have been no reason to be reborn in such dire straits.

Then again, in other intermediate eons, the dual process of [the life expectancy] increasing up to eighty thousand and decreasing down to ten [years] is counted as a single cycle. Eighteen of these cycles are referred to as "the eighteen intermediate cycles"[f] [in our kalpa]. During the first of these [eighteen] when the life expectancy increases to eighty thousand [years], the perfected Buddha

[a] Dra Chen Dzin (*sgra gcan 'dzin*); Buddha's son
[b] Khorwa Jik (*'khor ba 'jigs*); Conqueror of Cyclic Existence
[c] Serthub (*gser thub*); Golden Sage
[d] Ödtrung (*'od srung*); Guardian of Light
[e] *sa de* (*sa sde*), *yogāchārabhūmishāstra*; Asaṅga
[f] *khugpa cho gyed* (*khug pa bco brgyad*)

Maitreya[67] will enter the world. From then onward, with the exception of one, the remaining [buddhas of the one thousand] will all appear during the eighteen intermediate cycles. After the final descent to ten years and the expectancy increases back to eighty thousand, that is referred to as a "long upward eon"; and it is during that cycle the final buddha of the one thousand to come in the excellent eon, Möpa Tayey,[a,68] will appear.

Concerning this, although the individual cycles of the long downward decline, the long upward decline, and the eighteen intermediate are listed separately, the duration of the timing is equal because—during the individual long decline or growth—the time duration is deliberate compared to the eighteen intermediate cycles; [hence, they even out].

One may wonder what a ten-year life expectancy is like. In the Abhidharma, it states:

> Then, due to the path of karmic residue, life is as short as ten years. That eon is spent with weapons, illness, and famine.

So it is.

Overwhelmed by nonvirtue, life expectancy, vitality, and population, the life span gradually regresses to become extremely limited, such as ten years in duration. During that time, a girl of only five years will be sent off to marry. The ideal garments that inhabitants will wear will be robes made from hair; the select food will be millet;[b] and the best of ornaments will be weapons. Except for the bitter taste, all five flavors—such as butter, sesame, honey, molasses, and salt—will be obsolete. That intermediate eon will reach a conclusion through the onset of the eons of weapons, war, and famine.

During the eon of weapons, intentions will be crude to the point where extreme ill will based on hatred will arise toward everything the inhabitants encounter. Whatever they pick up will turn into a deterrent, and they will attempt to take the lives of one another. All of them will take immediate rebirth in the hells when they die. During the eon of disease, due to nonvirtuous accumulations, nonhuman spirits will become disturbed and inflict incurable diseases that take the lives of most humans. They too will then be reborn in the hell realms. During the eon of famine, gods will cause widespread drought by stopping the rain. The few grains remaining will be stored in small containers, and the broth that they drink will be made from dried bones. These humans will be known as the Rügong Karpo.[c] There will also be those who meticulously pick

[a] *mos pa mtha' yas*; Boundless Devotion

[b] *ko tra pa*

[c] *rus gong dkar po*; White Bone Ones

up each grain, place it in water, stir, and then drink that. They will be known as the Turmey Tsowa.[a]

The eon of weapons will endure for only seven days; the eon of disease, seven months; and the eon of famine, seven years and seven months. The cause for liberation from those intermediate eons is to take the vow to abstain from killing[69] for at least one day and to offer medicine and food to the sangha. This is mentioned in the sūtra called *Heap of Castles*.[b]

During this time, the inhabitants on two of the continents[70] will have stronger ill will, paler complexions, and cowardice and will endure hunger and thirst. The approach of such events will never occur on the continent Uttarakuru.

During the eon of obliteration, it is as stated in the Abhidharma:

> During the eon of obliteration, the universe—including the existence of hell—will be exhausted.

Thus, it is taught.

In the eon of obliteration beginning with the exhaustion of the hells, the universe gradually degenerates until it fully concludes. Prior to that, inhabitants are obliterated in the following way. Since there will no longer be any beings taking rebirth anew in the hells, the hells will empty. The karma for beings to be born in the lowest hells will be exhausted, so rebirth will then be taken in higher realms. Those who still have residual karma will take rebirth in other realms in the world. Similarly, those who remain in the seven hot hells, the eight cold hells, all pretas who were abiding in the hells, and the animals living in the oceans will vanish in the same way as previously explained. The animals that live with gods and humans in the desire realms will become extinct along with the inhabitants of those realms.

The way human beings become obsolete following the exhaustion of the preta realms is as follows. In Jambudvīpa, by the power of the dharmatā, the samādhi of concentration will arise in the mind of a single human. This will be referred to as the bliss and joy arising from isolation that brings quiescence. Hearing about this, others will cultivate the samādhi of the first level of concentration. Once the second level of concentration is reached, humans will become extinct. Inhabitants of the eastern Pūrvavideha and western Aparagodanīya will become extinct in the same way. Due to the obstructions of karma ripening, those residing on the northern Uttarakuru will be unable to realize the samādhi of concentration and will take rebirth as desire-realm gods. The six classes of desire gods will be

[a] *thur mas 'tsho ba*; Survivors with a Single Grain

[b] *khang bu tsekpa* (*khang bu brtsegs pa, kuṭāgarasūtra*)

emptied in the same way just explained once the samādhi of the first level of concentration is cultivated in their minds.

The way that the inhabitants on the first level of concentration are exhausted is as follows. Through the power of the dharmatā, a god from the first level of concentration will attain the samādhi of the second level. He will then proclaim, "The joy and bliss gained through this samādhi brings quiescence." When others hear this, they, too, will be able to attain the state of the second level of samādhi. By the generation of the second level of samādhi, their realm will be emptied.

If obliterated through fire, by that force alone, the inhabitants will be emptied [from the realm]. If obliterated through water, the [inhabitants] of the second realm will develop the third realm's level of samādhi and take rebirth there. If obliterated through winds, then the inhabitants of the third will develop the samādhi of the fourth and take rebirth there. Whatever the case, the time it takes for the inhabitants of the universe to become exhausted will be nineteen intermediate eons.

Following that, the way the universe is emptied is as the Abhidharma explains:

> Through fire, water, and wind, the phases of obliteration are threefold. The three concentrations, such as the second, third, and so forth—according to order—occur based on the limitations of their own characteristics. Since the fourth is [devoid of this], it is immovable.

Thus, it is taught. In the world of living beings, everything is emptied with no trace of life left behind, all the way to the first realm of concentration. The sky becomes cloudless and the sun four times more intense than before. Vegetation and forests completely evaporate.

Likewise, with the coming of the second [i.e., sun or fire], all streams and ponds evaporate; with the third, the four great rivers dry up;[71] with the fourth, great lakes, such as Lake Manasarovar,[72] evaporate; and fifth, the oceans completely vanish. Sixth, the entire earth, including the ever-enduring Mt. Meru, begins to spew smoke; and seventh, everything becomes a single blazing flame of fire. Through the tongue of that fire, the first realms of concentration turn into flames; and the celestial palace of the first realm is incinerated. Then the flames perish, and everything becomes empty like space.

The obliteration through water occurs in the realm of Ābhāsvara, where from the gathering of clouds a great torrential rain descends. Like salt dissolving in water, everything disintegrates. The obliteration through wind is universal since, if the karmic wind is able to destroy Mt. Meru, [it is] needless to mention what remains.

Concerning this, there are some who claim that, through winds, everything will vaporize like the sensation experienced by a person suffering from an imbalance of wind. Hence, when there is obliteration through fire, water, and wind—

these three—according to order, the concentration realms are emptied from the first through the third. It should be understood that the reason the fourth concentration realm is not obliterated through fire, water, and wind is due to the fact that this is the peak of the concentration realms. Additionally, obliteration occurs like this because the mental analysis that is present in the first realm of concentration is concurrent with fire. In the second [realm], there is joy that is concurrent with water; and in the third, breathing that is concurrent with wind. For the fourth concentration realm, there is no cause for the external obliteration of the universe; so based on that contributing circumstance, that realm remains immovable.

Well then, does that mean the fourth realm is static? No, it, too, is impermanent because the celestial palace, including the sentient beings of this fourth realm, will all be eradicated. The stages of how that obliteration occurs are mentioned in the Abhidharma:

> Seven times through fire and with a single great flood—although obliterated seven times through water—following the seven series of seven through fire, in the end, obliteration will occur through wind.

Thus, as taught, the universe is initially obliterated by fire. This occurs seven times over through the process of growth and obliteration, when finally there is destruction by a great flood. During the seven series of seven obliterations through fire, there is eradication through a single great flood each time. Following this, once again obliteration occurs through seven series of fires followed by wind. All together, the obliteration through fire occurs fifty-six times; through water, seven times; and through wind, just once. In summation, obliteration involves sixty-four stages.

In the commentary, it mentions that the obliteration by fire occurs forty-nine times. That total does not count the final obliteration through fire that occurs after the flood. Many scholars also give this same explanation. This explanation concerning the way existence came about, endures, and so forth is well known according to the tradition of the Abhidharma.

The great Omniscient One[a] said in his *Wish-Fulfilling Treasury* that clarifications given there have been drawn from the *Supreme Wish-Fulfilling Tantra*[b] with commentary by Vimālā[c] called *Pearl Garland*.[d] The account given here has some differences; however, there is no contradiction. This is similar to

[a] Longchen Rabjam, Longchenpa (*klong chen rab 'byams*)
[b] *yid zhin chog gi gyü* (*yid bzhin mchog gi rgyud*)
[c] Vimālāmitra (*bi ma la mi tra*)
[d] *mu tig treng drel* (*mu tig phreng 'grel*); Vimālāmitra

how there are discrepancies concerning this in the *Yogāchārabhūmi* versus the Abhidharma. If one wishes to know more about this subject, one should read the auto-commentary called *White Lotus*.[a,73]

In these ways, it takes one intermediate eon for the universe to be obliterated; and for both universe and inhabitants, it takes twenty intermediate eons. Having completely dissolved, there comes to be emptiness like the vacuity of space that then endures for another twenty intermediate eons. The entire process of these four—formation, endurance, obliteration, and vacuity—total eighty intermediate eons when combined. That duration is referred to as a great eon. In the Abhidharma, it states:

> Formation and the obliteration of that, vacuity, and endurance are equal since eighty [intermediate eons] are a great eon.

Thus, it is as taught. In these ways one must consider how the outer universe of the world systems is impermanent. The inner inhabitants who are the living beings have infinite life expectancies during the first eon, but that gradually declines all the way down to ten years as their endowments and vitality decrease. One must especially consider how since this universe that appears to be so solid and firm will be completely obliterated, needless to mention the inner inhabitants. In the *Advice from a Spiritual Friend*, it states:

> The earth, Mt. Meru, and the oceans are incinerated by seven blazing suns, and even the ashes of those who are embodied are not spared. Needless to say, what will become of the fragile human bodies?

Thus, as stated, even all forms will vanish in the end without trace, including Mt. Meru. Since that is the case, surely the extremely fragile and vulnerable human body is at risk.

3.2.1.1.2.2.2.2 The Way That One's Own Life Is Impermanent and How Death Will Occur

This has three parts:

1 Contemplating the certainty of death
2 The uncertainty of when
3 At death—except for dharma—how nothing will be of benefit

[a] *pedma karpo* (*padma dkar po*); Longchen Rabjam

Second, in particular, the way that life is impermanent is described threefold: contemplating the certainty of death, the uncertainty of when, and at death—except for the dharma—how nothing whatsoever will be of benefit.

3.2.1.1.2.2.2.2.1 Contemplating the Certainty of Death

First, the certainty of death is as stated in the *Wish-Fulfilling Treasury*:

> Since life is uncertain and the time of death unknown: knowing that death is certain, recall this from one's heart.

Thus, as taught, the reason this is so is that, when Yamā[a] arrives, there is no circumstance whatsoever that can reverse the arrival. Inasmuch as life cannot be extended,[74] the process of its decrease remains uninterrupted. Even during life, although death is inevitable, there is still not much time to practice dharma.

For the first, it states in the *Chapter on Impermanence*:[b,75]

> When the time arrives, whoever is a buddha, pratyeka, or even a shrāvaka must also abandon their bodies, so needless to mention the bodies of ordinary individuals.

Thus, no matter what rebirth is taken, there will be death. In the *Chapter on Impermanence*, it continues:

> Wherever one resides, there is no place on this earth where there will be exemption from death—not in space, nor in the depths of the oceans, not even in the center of the mountains.

Thus, regardless of location, death will arrive. The quote continues:

> Regarding the events of the past and what will come in the future, whatever they may be: when the time comes to drop the body, everyone must transmigrate. Since those phenomena will then come to an end, those with wisdom must bear this in mind. Having met the dharma, that is what must be put into practice.

[a] Chi Dag (*'chi bdag*) or Shinjezheshed (*gshin rje zhes gshed*); Lord of Death

[b] *mi tag pa'i tsom* (*mi rtag pa'i tshoms*); section within the *Udānavarga* compiled by Dharmatrāta

Thus, since all of those who came before and those who are to come must discard their bodies and transmigrate to another world, the wise must conclude that everything [about this world] is impermanent and will be obliterated. Accepting the sacred dharma, they should then engage in virtuous activity as just mentioned.

Death is also certain in terms of there being no difference concerning the fact that life is overcome by death for all beings, whether they have already died or have yet to. Even the fully perfected buddhas who have come before have passed into nirvāṇa in order to inspire disciples fixated upon permanence to practice the dharma. Likewise, if one does not think carefully and accepts how history recounts the stories of countless high and low individuals—such as scholars, practitioners, kings, ministers, bodhisattvas, and ordinary individuals of China and Tibet—although it may seem as though they are still living among us, not a single one of them remains.

By carefully considering this, none of them exist anywhere, having departed long before. Even concerning one's own immediate associates—such as khenpos, spiritual teachers, parents, dharma brothers and sisters, relatives, friends, enemies, and those whom one feels neutral toward, including every single associate—each one of them will surely depart from this world. Since there is no way that anyone can reverse impermanence and death, the certainty of death must be carefully deliberated.

Second, life cannot be extended; but the process of its decrease remains uninterrupted as stated in *Resting the Mind in Repose*:

> This life cannot be extended and is always on the decline.

Thus, and in the *Bodhicharyāvatāra*, it states:

> This life is always on the decline without interruption throughout the day and night. Even while declining since it cannot be extended, why then would someone like me not have to die?

Furthermore, if food supplies and other necessities that are not going to be used for a while are stored for several days or months, they will remain intact without deteriorating. One can also add additional supplies from elsewhere, and those supplies will then increase. When it comes to one's own life however, it is not like that. Not remaining static for even a moment, life is forever on the decline and will eventually self-exhaust. Since that is the case, nothing else can be introduced to prevent this from happening. Hence, why would someone like me, including others, not have to die?

These days, it is next to impossible to still be alive at ninety.[76] Not only that, like a pond without a water source, there is no way for [life] to increase. After a few months or perhaps years, it will simply evaporate. In addition, even if someone lives into their sixties, twenty-one thousand breaths are expended in the course of a day. A month extends that by thirty days and a year by twelve months. Twelve years are referred to as a full cycle; and once five full cycles have expired, the extent of life is more or less complete. These are the ways one must reflect upon the certainty of death.

Third, death is inevitable. Even during life, there is no time to practice dharma, as it states in the *Speech Bringing an End to the Four Incorrect Views*:[a]

> From today onward, even the longest human life expectancy will not exceed one-hundred years. During that time, from childhood until old age, life is spent without fully accomplishing one's purpose. Due to sleep, illness, and the rest, there is no opportunity for practice; so the true goal is completely squandered. For a human enjoying a state of well-being, just how much leisure time do they actually have?

For humans living when the life expectancy range is more or less one-hundred years, no matter what, it is unlikely their life will exceed that duration. Assuming that to be the case, then consider the fact that the first ten years are spent in childhood when the mind and body are still developing; so dharma practice does not occur. Later on, if the individual reaches eighty years, then the final twenty years of their life will be in a state of old age that will prevent them from practicing. Half of the one-hundred years would have been spent sleeping, and the rest of the time is filled with illness, strife, and so forth so that there ends up being virtually no time at all for dharma practice. Although the wish to accomplish dharma may have been there, these are the ways in which that wish remains unfulfilled.

From the perspective of well-being and the capacity to practice: once one is reborn as this kind of human being, it is taught that one should not depend upon having extra time to practice dharma. Understanding that—even if life is long—during childhood, dharma cannot be comprehended. While in adolescence, there will be no interest; and once old, there will be no potential. During the time in between, half of that is spent in sleep while the rest is spent in distractions, such as eating, drinking, and the like.

If the time actually spent on dharma were added up after all is said and done, it would amount to about five or six years at the most. Thinking in this way, one must come to grips with the statement that death is certain and there is no leisure

[a] *chin chi log zhi gog pa'i tam* (*phyin ci log bzhi 'gog pa'i gtam, caturviparyayaparihārakathā*); Mātṛceṭa

for dharma. In doing so, the determination to practice dharma without delay will surely occur. In the *Resting the Mind in Repose*, it states:

> Without remaining for long, death is inevitable so dharma practice must be embraced immediately!

Thus, it is as taught.

3.2.1.1.2.2.2.2.2 The Uncertainty of When

Second, contemplating the uncertainty of death is as stated in the *Wish-Fulfilling Treasury*:

> Merchants in a marketplace, a plantain tree at the river banks, the sound of thunder, clouds in the sky, the lives of living beings, and the pace of the sun and moon are impermanent and always in flux. Know that death is swiftly approaching.

So, it is unknown as to when travelling merchants will depart or when the plantain tree that grows from the river bank will perish. Likewise, the sound of thunder, the sudden vanishing of clouds, and the death of beings such as animals are all a mystery. Regardless of summer and winter, the pace of the sun and moon is extremely swift. Like these examples, death is swiftly approaching; and when it will descend upon one always remains a mystery.

Based on that, the life expectancy of those of us who occupy Jambudvīpa is uncertain; and there are many circumstances that can cause our death, yet few that will sustain life. Since the human body is delicate like a bubble on water, the time of death remains uncertain.

First, the uncertainty of life expectancy for inhabitants of Jambudvīpa is as follows. Although generally there are descriptions about the life expectancy of all sentient beings in the three realms, in Uttarakuru this is definitive; whereas in other worlds, the individual life expectancies are unable to be determined. Even among those, the inhabitants of Jambudvīpa are as the Abhidharma tells us:

> Here [i.e., Jambudvīpa], life expectancy is uncertain since at first it is boundless and later declines to only ten years.

Thus, previously the life span was boundless until eventually this declined so that the longest life was only ten years of age. That difference indicates extreme uncertainty. Even now, it is ambiguous as to who will die first—the youth, the elder, or the person in the prime of life. In the past, countless people younger than oneself have died, so it is obvious that the notion that those who are older will die first is unreliable. In the *Chapter on Impermanence*, it states:

> Between the next day and the next life, which will be first is indeterminate. Hence, don't just prepare for the next day; make preparations for the next life.

Thus, between the next day and the next life—since it is uncertain as to which will come first—in the face of such ambiguity, one must not prepare for the next day but rather make preparations for the next life. Consider carefully that there is no guarantee that one will not die on this very day.

Second, although there are many circumstances causing death, there are few that sustain life as stated in *Resting the Mind in Repose*:

> There are many circumstances for death and few for life.

Thus, given that the circumstances for death are many and there are few for life, the *Jewel Garland* also tells us:

> The circumstances for death are many, but for life they are limited. Given that everyone is bound to die, the dharma must always be practiced.

Thus, the many circumstances for death include varieties of illness, harm imposed by demonic-force possession from human and nonhuman forces, and so forth. The circumstances for life are limited in comparison; and even if one thinks something is a circumstance for sustaining life, in truth there is nothing that does not eventually turn into a cause for death. In order to avoid death, one searches for food, drink, medicine, a place to live, and companionship; yet the food and drink may become disagreeable, the medicine can be incorrect, the house can collapse, the close friends can deceive you, and so forth—all becoming more causes that contribute to death. Aside from becoming a circumstance for death, nothing noticeable actually supports life.

Third, that the body is delicate like a bubble on water is as follows. Since this body is so delicate, it is easily injured without even contracting a significant illness or the onset of harm. Even being poked by a thorn can cause an infection that may turn viral and take one's life. For this, the outer circumstances—such as earth, water, fire, wind, dangerous ravines, and the like—bring on fear that comes from inanimate objects. Due to one's karma—even if life is long—enemies, humans, and nonhuman demonic forces can interrupt this so that one is unable to live out [a full] life. This harm is imposed through animate objects.

The inner circumstances include harm imposed through illness from imbalances with wind, bile, phlegm,[77] and so forth that make it easy for this body to perish. In the *Advice from a Spiritual Friend*, it states:

> In this life, there are so many ways to be harmed; so life is even more fleeting than a water bubble in a windstorm. The capacities to inhale and exhale, or even wake up, are themselves a great marvel.

Thus, since there are so many harmful factors confronting the life of a human being, life is even more fleeting than a water bubble in a windstorm. Breathing in as well as out—and even having the chance to wake up in the morning without having died—is itself a great marvel. It also states in the *Jewel Garland*:

> Abiding in the circumstance of death is like a candle placed in the midst of a windstorm.

Thus, it is as taught. It is also taught that, among the ways to meditate on impermanence, meditating on the uncertainty of the time of death is extremely potent. Therefore, since the time of death is uncertain, it is necessary to practice dharma as soon as possible. In *Resting the Mind in Repose*, it states:

> Life is short, so it is sensible to reduce future plans and from today onward put effort toward dharma practice.

Thus, it is as taught.

3.2.1.1.2.2.2.2.3 At Death—Except for Dharma—How Nothing Will Be of Benefit

Third, except for dharma, nothing else is beneficial at the time of death as stated in the *Wish-Fulfilling Treasury*:

> When one dies, the environment, belongings, relatives, one's prowess, and all supports will become annulled without exception. Hence, the sacred dharma must be put into practice.

Thus, it is said all of that becomes annulled; and from the perspective of support, none of that will be of any benefit. Once death arrives, family members will be of no benefit; wealth and material things will be of no benefit; and one's body will have no purpose. One must think in this way. First, in the *Bodhicharyāvatāra*, it states:

> Once one is captured by the messengers of Yamā, how can family and friends be of benefit? When merit alone is taken as the refuge, I have even failed to rely upon that.

Thus, as mentioned: at death, merit alone will be of benefit by granting refuge. Otherwise, friends, relatives, fame, power, and the like—no matter what they may be—will be to no avail. Not only that, if one dies with attachment to any of that, one will fail to transcend the suffering of the lower realms. It is taught that, if family and friends show intense suffering [at one's death], then the deceased will suffer even more in the bardo. Therefore, think to yourself, "What is the benefit of attachment to family members?"

Second, contemplating how material things are of no benefit at death is as follows. At death, even if wealth comparable to the glory of a chakravartin ruler is possessed, one still lacks the power to take even a trace of it along. Moreover, if one has attachment or fixation toward this, it becomes the cause of inexhaustible suffering.

Third, that the body brings no benefit is as follows. Not just only that wealth, but this fleshly body born from the mother's womb that has been coexisting with oneself must be left behind, while the consciousness—like extracting a hair from butter[78]—transfers to the next lifetime; so it is of no benefit. Therefore, since nothing else is of benefit except for the dharma, one must only practice the holy dharma.

3.2.1.1.2.2.2.3 Other Explanations Concerning the Ways of Impermanence

Third, other categories of impermanence are as follows. In the *Sūtra Requested by King Bimbisāra*,[a,79] it states:

> Alas! Compounded phenomena are not everlasting. By virtue of the nature, these ebb and flow. If there is birth, then there will be death; if there is meeting, there will be parting; and if there is increase, there will be deprivation. Although there may be vitality during youth, this will be deprived by poor health; life expectancy as well will be robbed by death. Through attachment, suffering increases; yet through repulsion [toward saṃsāra], there can be liberation.

Thus, in the Vinaya, it states:

[a] *zük chan nying pö zhü pa'i do* (*gzugs can snying pos zhus pa'i mdo*, *bimbisārapratyudgamana-nāma-mahāyānasūtra*)

> In the end, all accumulations will reach a state of exhaustion; all states of fame and elevation will plummet; and the end result of all encounters will be separation.

Thus, it is as taught. The way that all of this is impermanent is as stated in the *Sūtra of Advice to the King*:[a]

> For example, if the four mountains supporting the four directions that are absolutely firm, stable, essential, indestructible, flawless, and majestic so that they seem to reach into the heavens suddenly collapse and everything around them including the earth, trees, branches, leaves, living beings, and elementals turn into dust, it would not be easy to escape from this catastrophe or to reverse it through any powers such as wealth, substances, mantra, or potions.
>
> Great King! Just like that, when the four great states of fear arrive, it will not be easy to quickly escape or reverse that through the powers of wealth, substances, mantra, medicine, and the like. What are the four? They are aging, illness, decrepitude, and death.
>
> Great King! Aging is that which will bring an end to youthfulness; illness brings an end to good health; decrepitude destroys everything that is flourishing; and death steals away life itself. From these, even if one is swift, there can be no escape or reversal through power, wealth, substances, or mantra; nor can this be cured with medicines.

Saying that "the iron mountains in the four directions are solid, firm, and essential" means they are not hollow. "Flawless" means they have no cracks or openings. "Being majestic" means that every aspect is dense and magnificent. Mentioning "trees" refers to large, older trees with many branches. The "elementals" are a category of beings. The "four mountains existing in four directions and then collapsing" indicates that old age and so forth—these four—will destroy youth. Hence, one should consider the meaning through the analogy.

It also states in the *Sūtra of Vast Manifestations*:

> The three realms of existence are impermanent like autumn clouds. The birth and death of beings resemble the gyrations of a dance. The duration of the life expectancy of living beings is like a flash of lightning or a cascading waterfall that swiftly plunges downward.

[a] *gyalpo la dam pa'i do* (*rgyal po la gdams pa'i mdo, rājāvavadaka*)

Thus, one should consider that the birth and death of beings is, for example, like when performers dance and change masks, indicating taking various future rebirths. Just as [with dance], the many expressions that are demonstrated indicate how living beings must go through constant transitions.

In the *Chapter on Impermanence*, it states:

> Many beings that can be seen in the morning are gone by evening and may never be seen again. Although many beings can be seen in the evening, by morning some of them may never be seen again.

Thus, that which was apparent this morning, by evening, will have vanished from sight and vice versa. The quote tells us:

> When, among many men and women, the youngest dies, what is the point in still believing they should have lived the longest and saying, "Oh, this person was too young to die!" Some die while still in the womb; likewise, some die at birth; some die when they first begin to crawl and others when they are already walking. Some die old, and some die young. Humans who are youthful gradually grow older like fruit ripening on the vine that will eventually drop off.

Thus, it is as taught. For the most part, what was said here is easy to understand; however saying "gradually" means they will eventually die. For example, consider a tree laden with ripe fruit and how the fruit will not stay on the tree for long but will inevitably fall to the ground. All of these explanations just given correspond with the aspect of coarse impermanence. It states in the Madhyamaka's *Four-Hundred Stanzas*:

> Anyone who says "I am alive" can claim to be alive in that moment; but after that, this may no longer be the case. The person who fails to know this will have a hard time knowing himself.

Thus, regardless of who it is, saying "I am alive" holds true only for the length of that moment, not otherwise. For example, the mind transfers from one object to the next by instantaneously pursuing the flow of thoughts that arise and subside. For instance, when swiftly reciting the sound of syllables and so forth, the timing of each syllable's sound and the aspect of each syllable remain distinct. The mind that is concentrating upon this is itself distinct, and that is why the mind is established as instantaneous in that moment.

To expand on this, saying "it is instantaneous" implies the shortest possible duration of time. For example, when a healthy person snaps their fingers, that moment can be divided into sixty-four micro-moments that would indicate a split second. That is why the instant the consciousness arises and subsides is referred to as "instantaneous". Just as the mind is momentary, all compounded phenomena are fleeting and instantaneous. Especially when it comes to life, life is instantaneous; so all living beings are only momentarily alive and otherwise not. Furthermore, the quote continues:

> Just as the flow of a river can be seen incorrectly and is said to be permanent . . .

As taught, for example, although a river flows swiftly, those with dull minds will think that yesterday's water is still apparent today. Confused by the continuity of rushing water that has no past or future, it is then incorrectly considered to be a single flow; while the instantaneous moments of change go unnoticed. Like that, in this world, it is rare to find those who understand their own nature, which is why the notion of life being permanent is a general incorrect assumption.

Concerning this, for the duration of merely placing one foot after the other—speaking a single word and having an instantaneous thought—life becomes reduced, and one gets closer to the feet of Yamā. Life does not cease for a single moment; and since that is the case, this life's nature is instantaneous. In fact, when it comes to life, there is no way to reconcile the erroneous notion that the life span will be lengthy. Except for being immediate, there is no life that exists beyond that; and aside from being designated by the mind, life has no true, inherent existence.

In the *Bodhicharyāvatāra*, we are told:

> Like the experience of a dream, all things that have been experienced in any way at all amount to just memories.

Thus, as taught, until now, no matter how much one's life has passed by, it is now just a memory as though nothing existed, like a dream experience. If one thinks about it, today's experiences will be just like that by this time tomorrow. In the future, once time is used up, everything will become just like that. Thinking that everything lacks true existence like a dream, rather than being complacent and accepting things as permanent and real with attachment, one must accomplish virtue. In the terma commentary, it states:

> From birth until the present—if one analyzes the duration of life expectancy—rather than being long, it is instantaneous. Thinking of this as dreamlike and not really true leaves no leisure time to rest so that virtue will be accomplished. Hence, meditate on steadfast renunciation and repulsion.

Thus, it is taught. All of this demonstrates the way of meditating on the subtle aspect of impermanence. Knowing that life has no true existence, like a dream, the cultivation of repulsion is an exceptional feature of this [chöd] commentary.

Scholars who followed the previous master Chagsorwa[a] practiced this as follows. Generally, the coarse aspect of impermanence is considered compounded, so obliteration of this would be definitive. With that consideration, there is no freedom but to die. These are the two [aspects of impermanence], as well as the subtle aspect of impermanence, which is that each instant is transient, like the examples of a cascading waterfall or a shepherd driving animals from behind.

Considering that sudden impermanence involves upheavals with elements, gods, and both, as well as death that is brought on due to circumstances associated with food, clothing, and dwelling places, they practiced by contemplating these three aspects [i.e., coarse, subtle, and sudden impermanence]. Our master, Shedrüb Tenpa'i Nyima Rinpoche,[b,80] whose sacred name is hard to casually repeat, advised that as years, months, days, and time in general progress, the inevitability of death is the aspect of coarse, outer impermanence. Through instantaneous time, the exhaustion of the life span is inner, subtle impermanence. Since while ingesting food it is possible to suddenly die, that sudden onset of death requires one to think that any meal could possibly be one's last.

When donning clothes, think this may be the last time to wear clothes; when having conversations with others, think this could be the last exchange you will have with them; and so forth. The application of this to every activity as a mind training is meditation upon impermanence with intense concentration. These are the three to practice. The key point of all aspects of impermanence is subtle transiency, so it is extremely important to contemplate the understated aspect. This is the advice that was given repeatedly.

Furthermore, the eight aspects of untimely death are as follows: patients who fail to rely upon healing ceremonies, receive incorrect medicine such as the wrong prescription, are punished through law, whose vitality has been stolen by human and nonhuman spirits, have been harmed by the elements such as fire, harmed through unruly vicious animals, fall from high places, and are harmed through zombies and curses. These categories were explained in the sūtra *Exceptional Extensive Prayers Made by Seven Previous Tathāgatas*.[c]

In other teachings, it also states:

[a] *phyag sor ba*

[b] *bshad sgrub bstan pa'i nyi ma rin po che*

[c] *de war shek pa dün gyi ngon gyi monlam gyi khyed par gyey pa'i do* (*bde bar gshegs pa bdun gyi sngon gyi smon lam gyi khyad par rgyas pa'i mdo, āryasaptatathāgatapūrvapraṇidhānavishe ṣha vistāranāmamahāyānasūtra*)

> Sleeping with an elderly woman or man, taking medicine without being ill, sleeping in an old house, going alone to a place haunted by elementals, not listening to the doctor's advice, entering a war zone, trying to win a losing battle, sleeping in a frightening environment full of demonic forces and obstructers while lacking potential . . .

These are all explained to be circumstances that bring on untimely death. In addition, to cross a river without a life support, drink poison, and so forth are described. It is also mentioned in the *Four-Hundred Stanzas* how contemplating death and impermanence amounts to an exceptional aspect of reasoning:

> In order to die, there would have had to be birth; those who are overpowered by negative karma will not think that they are living, but rather that they are dying.

Thus, as taught, this means that, without birth, there will be no death; and by the power of karma and passions, once there is birth, it is certain there will be death. Therefore, at present, we think that once we are born, we are alive; and in order to be alive, it appears as though there was birth. Actually, it is not like that. From the beginning, in order to die, we had to be born.

The Buddha taught, "Due to the circumstance of birth, there is aging and death." In the interim, there is aging, illness, and so forth so that one is overpowered by this and lacks even a moment of personal freedom. Aging and so forth are like the executioner of birth. Together, they drag one into the presence of Yamā without letting up for a single moment since the nature is to continue going forward without reprieve. Hence, this is like how, if the object to kill is beheaded, the result of such an action can only lead to death. Due to these causes and contributing circumstances, an individual can see things from a perspective that will only prepare them for death, not for life. One should not deceive oneself due to the wish to keep living. Commenting upon that, the Abhidharma tells us:

> O Hero of Men! Wherever a womb has been entered in the world: from the moment of the first night onward, each day after without delay that person approaches the presence of Yamā.

Thus, saying "hero" indicates that the object of entrustment is similar in status to a king. From the first night of entering the womb onward, each moment of every day one is swiftly approaching the presence of Yamā. It is taught that none can delay this process.

To illustrate the stages of what was just explained through metaphors, this process resembles a king's messenger under strict orders, a gypsy lady riding a camel, or the procuring of an executioner. For example, if a messenger is commanded by a ruthless, heartless king to deliver a message with strict orders to return, the actions of the messenger will be just as ordered, not otherwise. Similarly, the activity of birth solely occurs so there can be the process of death, not otherwise. Each moment of life moves one closer to death.

Then, for example, if a gypsy lady suddenly thinks she must return home and hurriedly jumps on a reclining camel just outside the threshold, the camel will think she is a skillful rider, stand up, and depart. The camel must then go wherever the lady directs him. Like that, all states of birth lead to death and are thus taken over by other [circumstances] that depend upon death. When one person attempts to kill another, they may hire an executioner; yet if the executioner is unable to do the job, he may turn sides and kill the procurer. Like that, birth does not have the potential to ensure life, so it will inevitably turn on itself to become the activity of death, not otherwise. Life is like the person who hired a killer and who was then killed himself. One must think in these ways.

The way to understand the meaning of these passages [is as follows]. First, in order for there to be death, there is birth; and that will then have to lead to death, like the example of the messenger. Although there is birth in order to die, if there were freedom, it would be acceptable to rest for a while; but there is no freedom to do so. There is no freedom, since the nature of [this life] does not depend upon oneself alone. If there were a method through which to reverse the external circumstances, that would be one thing; but that, too, is not the case. Although that is not the case, perhaps it would be possible to engage and prepare activities that sustain life and possibly delay death through the creation of hindrances. That, too, is also not the case. Since those options are unrealistic, one must decide that there is no choice but to die quickly. That is why the *Four-Hundred Stanzas* states:

> Like your previous death, time has passed by; that is how it is now and how it will be. It will never be acceptable to say that the process of death is going to be pleasant.

As it states, although we think that we are enjoying our present life, it is not really the case. Previously, just as we have proceeded to our death, now we are proceeding again; and in the future, we will continue to do the same thing. While traversing to our death, there will be no rest, not even for an instant. It is never going to be acceptable to assume that this life will always be pleasant, so one must develop a sense of heartfelt trepidation toward death.

The great teacher Geshe Putowa[a,81] has said that this meditation upon impermanence is the head of dharma practice, whereas the [explanations given concerning] the Sanskrit title and the homage are not.[82] Just as he said, this meditation on impermanence is the beginning point for dharma practice. Even our teacher [i.e., Shākyamuni] lay down upon a bed beneath two *sal* trees[b] in Kushinagara, India during his final miraculous deed; and removing his upper garment, said, "O Bhikṣhus, to view the kāya of the Tathāgata is difficult to come by, so look upon the Tathāgata. O Bhikṣhus, remain silent for a while. Just like this, the nature of all compounded things is to disintegrate. These will be the last words the Tathāgata speaks."

Thus, his final words were advice upon meditating on impermanence, and that was the last testament left for us to consider. The dharma king Tertön himself [i.e., Dudjom Lingpa] always emphasized impermanence while teaching, so for these reasons I have taken the time to explain this subject here in more detail. In the chöd commentary [i.e., root terma verses], it states:

> Without these key points then no matter what aspect of dharma is incorporated with effort and commitment, it will not be fully established and will end up like summer frost, mist on the mountains, or lightning flashing in the darkness.

Even the victors and their heirs of the three times initially relied upon this and then entered the path. From there, they arrived at the great citadel of liberation. If [we] do the same, there is no doubt we, too, will arrive there. Hence, it is necessary to consider that this transmission [on impermanence] is principal among all.

> The universe and inhabitants without exception are by nature destructible.
> This life is impermanent like a flashing bolt of lightning.
> In an instant without ever pausing, one arrives in front of Yamā, so abandon this negative mind that grasps to permanence as though it were poison.

Thus, these are the verses that summarize this section.

3.2.1.1.2.2.3 Suffering of Saṃsāra

This has two parts:

1 All realms of saṃsāra do not transcend the three types of suffering
2 Contemplating the individual suffering of the six classes

[a] *dge bshes pu to ba*
[b] *shing sa' la*

Third, the contemplation upon the suffering of saṃsāra is as follows:

> In this dungeon of unbearable misery, hopelessly pathetic, not a moment exists to experience happiness; further-increasing, limitless accumulations of karma continue to intensify. O Guru, grant liberation from this ocean of saṃsāra!

Thus, as taught, in this domicile of cyclic existence, impelled by the power of karma, rebirth is on-going. Once one falls into the three lower realms, suffering is truly **unbearable**. Having entered **the dungeon of** intense **misery** so difficult to bear: if rebirth occurs in the hell realms, **not a moment exists to experience** any kind of well-being or **happiness**. The body and mind become **hopelessly pathetic**. No matter what realm rebirth occurs in, there is no chance for permanent happiness. Given that, previously, the **accumulations of** positive and negative **karma** have been **limitless**: without purification through an antidote, those potentials **continue to intensify** in the stream of mind. Along with that, fresh karma is being accumulated and added to this storehouse, **further increasing** it. Hence, it is challenging to break free from **this ocean of saṃsāra**. By precisely seeing these faults, one supplicates the **guru**, who is like a sea captain, to **grant liberation.**

For this [topic], there are two: the way all realms of saṃsāra do not transcend the three types of suffering and contemplating the individual suffering of the six classes.

3.2.1.1.2.2.3.1 All Realms of Saṃsāra Do Not Transcend the Three Types of Suffering

For the first, it states in the *Treasury of Precious Qualities*:[a]

> Whether higher or lower realms within the six classes, there is no domicile in saṃsāra exempt from the suffering of suffering, the suffering of change, and pervasive compounded suffering.

So, it is. Wherever one is born, whether higher or lower realms, there will be the suffering of suffering, the suffering of change, and pervasive compounded suffering.[83] These three sufferings cannot be transcended. Among them, the first is the suffering of suffering as follows. When a feeling arises in the mind that will generate intense suffering within both mind and body, even an ordinary person

[a] *yon ten rinpoche'i dzod* (*yon tan rin po che'i mdzod*); Jigmed Lingpa

identifies this as misery and hopes to eliminate it, such as the pain of an illness. All tainted feelings based on suffering and the objective phenomena concurrent with them are similar to the suffering in the minds of hell beings, who perceive particular objective appearances, such as the molten ground, weapons, unpleasant sounds, and the like. This degree of suffering endured by all beings belongs to the category [of the suffering of suffering]. In the sūtras, it states:

> The sensation of suffering occurs when it arises, as well as while it endures.

Thus, this reveals the suffering of suffering. Concerning this, the nature is solely that of suffering since that is the predominate experience from the time it begins, endures, and in the interim until the conclusion. Among the three aspects of suffering, this is the vilest since—compared to the other two—the misery here is far worse. That is why this type of suffering received its name. For instance, that which is especially negative is referred to as "the worst of the worst". The term [i.e., suffering of suffering] is explained in a way easy to understand given that, before the initial suffering concludes, the subsequent suffering begins; and that then overcomes the first. Understand that this [term] is coined to indicate this intensity.

Second, the suffering of change is as follows. At present, ordinary individuals do not see that the happiness derived through the pleasurable things that they are partaking of with mental attachment is a form of suffering. Instead, they assume that it is pleasurable [because it is temporary]. Nevertheless, that situation will inevitably become impermanent, as well as becoming the catalyst for suffering. Although it seems that enjoying pleasurable experiences with loved ones is a state of happiness, the time will come when one must separate from them; so that will turn into the cause for painful sorrow. The sūtras tell us:

> The sensation of happiness begins by being blissful; and while enduring, it continues to be so. When it changes, it then turns into sorrow.

Thus, it is as taught. The definition of [change] can thus be understood through this. The sensation of tainted happiness and the mind and its objective appearances that are concurrent with that are also in this category.

For example, let's take the mind that experiences happiness on the level of the higher god realms and the appearances of the abundance of the gods and so forth. When happiness first occurs, although seemingly pleasurable, in truth the force of suffering is only temporarily arrested; so the pain of that experience is reduced, and the sensation of misery decreasing occurs. The discomfort then seems insignificant given that the shortcomings are temporarily not identified.

Hence, it seems to appear to be its opposite. Since the previous suffering has shifted or concluded, the mind of happiness comes to the fore while, nevertheless, the nature of that is not true happiness. That is why, once this happiness occurs and reaches fruition it will then appear as suffering.

For example, after walking a great distance and feeling exhausted, sitting down to relax brings pleasure to the mind in that moment. That experience occurs because the previous pain or exhaustion has come to an end and is now arising as pleasure. Although that is the case: by virtue of its nature, this is not true happiness. If one continues to sit down or stay in one place for too long, then—just like before—some form of displeasure will arise from that. No matter what causes the discomfort, that sensation will indicate how suffering will increase.

If the nature of the sensation was really a state of happiness, then while walking, sitting, sleeping, eating, drinking, sunning, or relaxing in the shade—no matter how much time is spent on these activities—that would indicate the increase in the sensation of pleasure that was felt when they were begun. That, however, is not the case. If these activities occur for too long, then they will only generate their opposite. This is mentioned in the sūtra *Ānanda Entering the Womb*:

> O Gawo! Know that whether walking, sitting, standing, or sleeping—during all such activities—individual suffering will ensue. If a contemplative examines the nature of these individual activities, then by spending the entire day walking—rather than standing, sitting, or sleeping—then the activity of walking will turn into suffering. Just by walking, the individual sufferings of either being too extreme, harsh, unbearable, and unpleasant will all come to pass. Hence, walking cannot be recognized as a source for happiness.

Thus, it is taught. The same teachings apply to the other three modes of conduct.[84]

> O Gawo! Nevertheless, in order to bring an end to the continuity of suffering that occurs through these modes of conduct, there will be the recognition of happiness when the other, new forms of suffering emerge. Although this occurs, Gawo, know that is merely an aspect of suffering. If it ends, it is only suffering that is ending; and when it endures, the reaction of suffering itself will occur. When that ends, the reaction will also end.

Thus, by applying this way of thinking to the modes of going, walking, sleeping, sitting, and so forth, [the import of suffering] will be clearly revealed. At the moment that tainted feelings of happiness occur—since they are by nature suffering—when it occurs, it is like that; and when it concludes, it is solely that nature.

When the feeling of tainted happiness occurs, in the second instant, its nature has already become the nature of another form of suffering. When that is over, in the next instant its nature becomes the nature of yet another form of suffering, just as it was taught. Reference to it being happiness when it first occurs and, here, saying that—when it occurs—it is only going to produce suffering are actually not contradictory. The reason is because, initially, when first experienced, the circumstances of that suffering are manifesting as happiness.

To synthesize the key points: although an experience may initially arise as pleasant, after some time goes by and the full impact becomes evident, that original experience will reverse itself. Then, when it is recognized as suffering, that proves how the nature of the experience is actually unpleasant. In the *Four-Hundred Stanzas*, it states:

> Just as the increasing experience of happiness will reverse itself, likewise the suffering that then increases will be irreversible.

So, the onset of tainted happiness will endure for a while but will eventually revert to suffering, no matter what degree of happiness it was. Conversely, when suffering is recognized and tainted suffering increases: although it may reverse itself, it is still not going to just turn into happiness. As mentioned, the tainted sensation of happiness is actually the nature of suffering; so when that increases, the fact that it is unhappiness becomes evident. For instance, when the sensation of tainted suffering increases, there is no way for that to become the experience of happiness. Hence, this indirectly reveals the meaning being presented.

If one recognizes the unreliability of a friend, due to that suspicion the danger of deception is not as threatening as it would have been. If from the beginning one fails to recognize there is any problem or places complete trust in that person [and] if that person is deceptive with ulterior motives, one's life could even be placed in jeopardy. Hence, it is always important to be extremely cautious and prudent. Likewise, more than the suffering of suffering, this aspect [of suffering] is deceptive and cause for anxiety.

Not only that, if one knows how to take the suffering of suffering as the path, it is as stated in the *Bodhicharyāvatāra*:

> Furthermore, the quality of suffering is that, through it, arrogance will be dispelled and compassion for fellow wanderers will arise. Negativity will be purified, and joy will be taken toward virtue.

Thus, it is as taught. In one way, [the suffering of suffering] involves qualities, whereas the latter [i.e., of change] does not. [For the suffering of change], based on the arising of attachment, craving, and so forth, feelings of arrogance and the like will not necessarily be eliminated; negativities will, in fact, proliferate, bringing on an onslaught of inexhaustible suffering.

Third, all-pervasive compounded suffering is as follows:

> The Bhagavan taught that, in brief, the five perpetually fixated aggregates[85] are the basis of suffering.

Thus, and he also said:

> O Bhikṣhus! This [suffering] is momentary.

As taught, this includes the tainted aggregates of the perpetual cause and the subtle way they self-destruct through momentary transience. Here, reference to "tainted" or *zagchey* in Tibetan is that the syllable *zag* means passion and *chey*[a] means the one possessing that. The "perpetual cause" refers to yearning desire. At the time of death, by thinking that one will separate from the body, the fear of losing the body and the attachment that ensues involve desire based on self-attachment.

Otherwise, if one thinks that another body as a support will be obtained and then once again the purpose of existence will be perpetuated, that is the yearning just mentioned. Hence, these two are causes for accomplishing the aggregates of the subsequent life. The first is due to craving and the subsequent due to grasping. The aggregates that arise from these two are termed "the aggregates of the perpetual cause".

For example, fire that originates from grass and wood is called "the grass and wood fire". Furthermore, concerning the tainted aggregates, the seven perpetual causes of the tainted aggregates and the aggregates that arise from desire are called "aggregates of perpetual causes". Given that aggregates arise from these two, it is expressed in this way. For instance, it is similar to how a tree that produces flowers and one that produces fruit are given different names, such as flower tree and fruit tree. This reference to all-pervasive compounded suffering is connected to the seeds of karma and the negative weakness of the passions. It also seems that these [passions] pervade the aggregates. Otherwise, the tainted aggregates that are not limited completely pervade all realms of existence. Hence, they are all-pervasive. That this process is actually compounded by karma and passions, or

[a] *zag* and *bcas*

generated by them, makes this compounded. In the *Compendium of Logic*,[a] it states:

> Due to falling under the power of root causes, there will be suffering.

Thus, it is as taught. Having fallen under the power of the root causes and contributing circumstances of karma and the passions, this amounts to suffering, as it states:

> All states of freedom amount to happiness, whereas all states of non-freedom amount to suffering.

So, this universal truth is similar. Furthermore, in reliance upon having acquired these aggregates of the perpetual cause, passions arise; and through that, karma is accumulated. This leads to all suffering of subsequent rebirths. Hence, this is a vessel [i.e., the body] that holds suffering. If the aggregates did not exist, then that which relies upon them—namely, the sufferings of illness, old, age and the like—would have no source from which to arise. Therefore, these aggregates that exist at present are the basis for all suffering and are interconnected with the seeds for the suffering of suffering that rely upon the formation of them.

Therefore, this [third suffering] is the vessel for the suffering of suffering; and through it [i.e., the third], there is the connection to the seeds of the suffering of change. It is also the conduit for the suffering of change; and through it, all compounded suffering of being overcome by the preceding karma and passions is present as compounded suffering. Due to that, the moment that these perpetual aggregates are obtained, they appear as compounded suffering. Being characteristic of compounded suffering and based on that, the aggregates of the perpetual cause are referred to as "suffering".

In the *Compendium of Logic*, it states:

> A wanderer suffering in saṃsāra is synonymous with the aggregates.

Given that [the aggregates] are under the power of karma and passions, there is suffering. A wanderer is one who constantly transmigrates throughout the classes and places of saṃsāra. This is said to be like the aggregates of the tainted perpetual cause, and this actually reveals that which is all-pervasively compounded. In the sūtras, it also states:

> Whatever is impermanent brings suffering.

[a] *tsed ma nam drel* (*tshad ma rnam 'grel, pramāṇavārttika*); Dharmakīrti

Thus, the impermanent aspect of these aggregates is also compounded suffering.

In the *Four-Hundred Stanzas*, it states:

> With impermanence comes certain detriment; whenever there is detriment, there can be no happiness. Hence, that is what transience brings.

Thus, whenever there is an impermanent, tainted material substance, this will involve some kind of detriment. The mind is unreliable and based on change, so it is not at all trustworthy. The mind's nature produces many unwanted scenarios—for instance, this present body that is impermanent and instantaneously changing gradually loses its strength as it declines into decrepitude. Given that these are the characteristics, [the body] is faulted and subject to detriment. Likewise, wherever there is impairment, there can never be happiness because whatever is even slightly transitory will bring about unhappiness. Because suffering is characteristic of detriment, it resembles having fallen into a pool of salt. Just like falling into a pool of salt and becoming saturated with that, all tainted things that are impermanent are saturated by suffering; and likewise, all compounded things that are tainted are solely characteristic of suffering. Furthermore, due to being brought about by both karma and passions, one is unable to come up with anything that approaches the direction of virtue; so the body and mind become dysfunctional and powerless. This is also the aspect of compounded suffering. Moreover, there is nothing mentioned here that cannot be included within the domain of the tainted aggregates.

Those who lack training will assume that the term "aggregate" refers only to our physical body, but that is not the case. It is necessary to know that all five aggregates are inclusive in the term. Within the five aggregates, there are no compounded phenomena that are not included; and since all defilements are included in the contaminated aggregates, the neutral sensation of being tainted and the mind and its objects that are concurrent with that are the all-pervasive suffering of karmic formations.

Whatever the case, this arises through its own causes, karma, and passions; and the nature is characteristic of suffering. This [suffering] is the objective that the sublime ones are repulsed by; and the learned ones have said that, once this becomes a conclusive circumstance for accumulating causes that lead to saṃsāra, it amounts to compounded suffering. In these ways, although these faults of compounded suffering are difficult for an ordinary individual to clearly identify, the āryas see them precisely as they are. In the sūtras, it states:

> If a strand of hair is on one's palm, this will go unnoticed. If it goes into one's eye, it causes discomfort and damage. Just like that, ordinary individuals are unable to see compounded suffering, like a strand of

> hair on their palm; whereas for the āryas, it is like having a hair in their eye, granting them a feeling of strong repugnance.

Thus, this is clearly illuminated through the analogies. The āryas' experience is like having a hair in one's eye so that, through this discomfort, faults are definitively known and even discomfort ensues. Through that, there is repugnance; and the mind becomes extremely weary, as taught. Saying "extremely" means that—more than the preceding two types of suffering—this [suffering] brings about a strong sense of weariness because the first two types of suffering do not pervade all phenomena, are not always present, and are easier to identify in terms of shortcomings.

As previously mentioned, there will be no separation from this form of pervasive suffering until one is liberated from saṃsāra. Hence, the shortcomings are greater and difficult to identify by ordinary individuals. Until these tainted aggregates have been abandoned even though the other two sufferings are present, they are not necessarily evident during every occasion. However, once encountering certain circumstances, they will then suddenly emerge. Hence, this [third suffering] is the basis for the other two types of suffering. The ability to recognize the shortcomings of the first two sufferings is present among spiritual practitioners of other religions, yet just identifying the faults of these two does not bring a sense of absolute comprehension concerning saṃsāra's pitfalls. For instance, if a great burden is being carried, however long this must be borne will determine the amount of discomfort. Likewise, until separate from this [suffering], there is no opportunity for comfort, happiness, or freedom from suffering.

Hence, the Bhagavan said, "Recognize suffering." That is the main point to understand. In this way, by understanding the nature of these three types of suffering, one will come to know what the Bhagavan meant when he said, "All sensations are based on suffering." Since all sensations that are tainted are revealed as suffering through this, the experiences that arise based on the passions—such as attachment and all sensations mingled with that—are by nature tainted. Those who dwell in the desire realm have all three types of suffering, whereas most gods of the form realm—except for the suffering of suffering—experience the other two. Those up to the fourth realm of concentration experience all-pervasive compounded suffering. In this way, the entirety of saṃsāra does not transcend any of these sufferings.

> Perfecting the gatherings for countless eons, when the Buddha fully awakened, the very first and final advice he spoke was that suffering must be known.
>
> He said that all tainted phenomena without exception are the nature of suffering.

He also gave this advice in the enumerations of the four seals[86] of
his utterance.
Hence, correctly knowing how to comprehend this is the heart
of our doctrine's tenets.
Not knowing this and claiming to be a Buddhist is as misleading
as the resonance of an echo.

Thus, these are the verses that summarize the section.

3.2.1.1.2.2.3.2 Contemplating the Individual Suffering of the Six Classes

This has two parts:

1 Contemplation on the suffering of the three lower realms
2 Contemplation on the suffering of the three higher realms

Second, for the sufferings of the individual realms, there are two parts: the contemplation on the suffering of the three lower realms and the contemplation on the suffering of the three higher realms.

3.2.1.1.2.2.3.2.1 Contemplation on the Suffering of the Three Lower Realms

This has three parts:

1 Suffering of the hells
2 Suffering of the pretas
3 Suffering of the animals

First, for the suffering of the three lower realms, there are three: the suffering of the hells, the suffering of the pretas, and the suffering of the animals.

3.2.1.1.2.2.3.2.1.1 Suffering of the Hells

This has three parts:

1 Suffering of the hot hells
2 Suffering of the cold hells
3 Suffering of the proximate hells

First, for the suffering of the hells, there are three: contemplating the suffering of the hot hells, the cold hells, and the proximate hells.

3.2.1.1.2.2.3.2.1.1.1 Suffering of the Hot Hells

First, for the hot hells, there are the great hot hells and the two proximate hells surrounding them.

First, the eight hot hells are known as Reviving, Black Line, Crushing, Screaming, Intense Screaming, Heat, Intense Heat, and Avīchī.[a] None of the hell realms exist beneath the other three continents, whereas thirty-two thousand leagues [i.e., *yojanas*] below Jambudvīpa's Bodhgayā is the locale of the Reviving hell. Every four-thousand leagues beneath that, the remaining seven hot hell realms are located in descending order. Generally, the basis for all eight hot hells is molten fire, and the surroundings are an inferno fence of flaming red iron. Flames engulf the environment from above and below, and [the inhabitants] are located within the massing fire.

First, concerning the Reviving hell, the sentient beings located there gather upon a blazing ground of molten fire holding weapons that occur through the power of their karmic accumulations, such as clubs, axes, arrows, wheels, and the like. Beating one another, their bodies split into hundreds and thousands of pieces; and they lose consciousness while falling to the ground. After that, they hear a sound from the sky saying "you are all now revived"; and with that, they come back to life and, just like before, begin to beat one another to once again repeat the experience of boundless torment.

Second, for the Black Line hell, those reborn there are captured by the denizens of the gates who then draw four, eight, sixteen, and many other black lines with hot pokers on the inhabitants' bodies; and wherever the lines are drawn, they then slice through that with their weapons. Third, in the Crushing hell, the denizens gather the inhabitants into a single group and then pile their bodies together and press them between iron mountains shaped like the heads of goats, sheep, tigers, lions, and others. This causes blood to ooze from their orifices. Once again, they are bunched together and smashed inside of a great iron mortar so that their entrails ooze out. They are then revived and smashed by a great iron boulder that drops upon them, torturing them relentlessly. Fourth is the Screaming hell. Here, all the inhabitants are running around searching for a place to rest and eventually come upon a house made of iron. Gradually, they enter; and once getting past the door, it closes on them, and they are trapped. Fire blazes from all directions, incinerating them, and they think, "Now there is no place to escape!" and cry out repeatedly.

Fifth is the Intense Screaming hell, which is similar to the preceding. Once arriving inside a double-walled iron building, they enter the inner chambers and

[a] *yang sö, tig nag, ngü jom, ngu bod, ngu bod chenpo, tsa wa, rab tu tsa wa*, and *narmed* (*yang sos, thig nag, bsngus 'joms, ngu 'bod, ngu 'bod chenpo, tsha ba, rab tu tsha ba*, and *mnar med*)

think, "Even if we can escape from here, we will never escape the outer walls," so that even more than before they are doubly tormented and wail repeatedly. Sixth is the hell of Heat, where the denizens place the inhabitants in huge, hot, metal cauldrons that are miles in width. There they are cooked alive, after which they are impaled on fiery iron stakes from the anus up through the head, and the flames shoot out from all of their orifices, such as the mouth, eyes, ears, nostrils, and every single pore. Afterward, they are thrown onto the molten ground either face up or down and are pounded and tortured by blazing metal hammers. Seventh is the hell of Intense Heat, where the inhabitants are impaled on the central prong of long steel tridents from the anus to the head and up to the two shoulders with the right and left side prongs. Fire shoots out from all of their orifices, such as the mouth and so forth. Their bodies are wrapped in fiery hot sheets of metal and placed in metal cauldrons that are even larger than before. There, they are boiled with various materials that cause the bones and flesh to detach. Then, they are dropped upside down into another blazing vessel and continue to boil there while attempting to escape at the top, bottom, and sides. Their flesh and blood disintegrate, and they turn into skeletons. They are then taken out and placed on the molten ground and impaled through the mouth with blazing molten hammers while lava is poured over them as they suffer unbearably. Finally, they are placed on the molten ground and smashed like before.

Eighth is the Avīchī hell that begins in the east, where the ground turns into blazing fire that stretches for hundreds of miles. The power of this raging fire engulfs the inhabitants gradually, incinerating their flesh, bones, and the like, charring them down to the marrow. Their bodies become like candlewicks, while the flames overwhelm their bodies. The same thing occurs for the remaining three directions. Then, the fire that has emerged from all four directions turns into a single blaze, and the suffering that ensues is uninterrupted as they scream out in pain. Aside from knowing that they are still alive, all of the inhabitants become indistinguishable with the fire.

Once again, they are painfully roasted on iron grates with fire embers and sparks popping like roasting barley. They are then forced to climb up and down great molten iron mountains, while their tongues are pulled out from their mouths and stretched out on the molten ground and [bodies] pegged down like flayed cow skin that is stretched so taunt that not a crease can be seen. Otherwise, they are also flayed with their backs upon the burning ground, and their mouths are forced open with iron tongs, while blazing hammers are shoved into their mouths. Molten copper is poured into their mouths so that their mouths and throats are burned, as well as the entrails that surface below them. The pain described here is merely an overview of what this is like, because there are countless such scenarios that take place there.

The *Thorough Exegesis*[a] refers to this:

> The fires of this world, sandalwood forests, the end of existence, and the hells—according to order—are seven times hotter than the preceding. Likewise, the suffering increases sevenfold.

Thus, more than the heat from an ordinary fire of this world, the heat from a sandalwood forest fire is seven times more intense. Likewise, the fire and heat at the end of existence is seven times more intense than that. Beyond that, the heat in the Reviving hell is seven times more intense; in the Black Line, seven times more intense; and so forth as the subsequent hells, as well as their sufferings, increase by seven in descending order. As taught in many great treatises, the duration of time for experiencing this suffering is compared to the human life expectancy and the god realms. However, to make this easier to comprehend if the time is determined based on human years, one trillion sixty-two billion years equals the time spent in the Reviving hell, which has the shortest time span among the eight hot hells. It is taught that the time duration for the remaining hells is double that.

The extent of those enumerations is that one-hundred million is one billion, and ten billion becomes one great billion. Ten of the great billions become one-hundred billion. According to counting one-hundred million years, the duration of life in the Reviving hell is said to endure for six-hundred billion years, sixty billion, twenty billion, or down to one or two billion [human years].

Likewise, for Black Line, [the duration] is ten trillion years, one trillion years, nine-hundred billion years, and then sixty billion human years. For the Crushing hell, it is one quadrillion, three trillion, six-hundred billion, and then eighty billion human years. For the Screaming hell, it is ten quadrillion, twenty trillion, nine trillion, four-hundred billion, and then forty billion human years. For Intense Screaming, it is six quadrillion, six-hundred trillion, thirty trillion, five-hundred billion, and two-billion eight-hundred million human years. For the hell of Heat, it is fifty quadrillion, three-hundred trillion, eighty trillion, four trillion, three-hundred billion, and sixty billion human years. In the two lowest hells, the human-year equivalents are numberless. So for Intense Heat, it is one half of an intermediate eon; and for Avīchī, it is an entire intermediate eon.

Concerning this, it states in the *Advice from a Spiritual Friend*:

> Unbearable suffering such as this must be endured for millions of years. Until nonvirtuous accumulations are exhausted, the inhabitants will not pass from these lifetimes.

[a] *nam shed rigpa* (*rnam bshad rig pa, vyākhyāyukti*)

Thus, saying "millions of years" is a generalization, since the timing is impossible to determine. Although endured indefinitely, until the potential for the karma to experience this suffering is exhausted, it will be necessary for the inhabitants to endure these experiences.

Second, the surrounding hells are as follows. Each one of the eight hot hells has four walls with four gateways. Surrounded by iron fences on the exterior, each fence as well has a gateway in the respective direction. At each of the gates, four additional hell realms exist called Fire Pit, Putrid Swamp, Forest of Weapons, and River Impossible to Cross[a]—totaling sixteen [i.e., four at each gate]. When those who are reborn in the hot hells are about to be released, they search for a place outside to rest. While doing so, that is when they encounter these surrounding hells, and the suffering begins again. Some inhabitants who do not take rebirth in the actual hot hells will find themselves reborn here.

First, the fire pit known as Crazed by Fire[b] has a surface composed of ashes within which are blazing hot cinders. When stepped upon, the inhabitant sinks down to the knees into the middle of fire that renders the flesh, blood, and skin into oblivion. Once again, the foot is pulled out and the flesh and skin are restored, and the process repeats itself.

Second, once departing from there, the next [destination] is the Putrid Swamp, an extremely foul swamp that the inhabitant sinks into up to their head. Inside this swamp, there are insects with sharp beaks called Iron Beaks. Their beaks are long and pointed like thorns, and with them they pierce through the inhabitant's skin, flesh, bones, and tendons down to the marrow that they suck up.

Once departing from that place, the next is the third, Forest of Weapons, where there is a road of sharp razors. By the power of their latent karma, here the sentient beings experience that they are walking on extremely sharp razors that cut and slice their feet when they step down; and when they lift their feet back up, they are instantly restored. Once departing from there, they encounter a forest with trees made of razorlike leaves. Here, the inhabitants see attractive looking trees that they rush over to. Once arriving there, from the leaves of the trees, swords shower down upon them that slice through all of their limbs. They then faint, and ferocious dogs arrive to bite and consume them. Once departing from there, they arrive at the mountainous forest of iron *shalmali* trees.[c] There, the forest and mountains have extremely sharp thorns, and ferocious dogs chase them into the heart of this environment. Upon arrival, all thorns point downward, which shoot out to cut through their bodies. When they arrive at the top of the mountains, crows with iron beaks called Sharp-Beaked Ones land upon their

[a] *mema mur gyi ob, ro ngak kyi dam, tson cha'i nak tsal,* and *chu lung rab med* (*me ma mur gyi 'obs, ro myags kyi 'dam, mtshon cha'i nags tshal,* and *chu klung rabs med*)

[b] *me nyon pa* (*me smyon pa*)

[c] *shalmali tsal* (*shal ma li'i tshal*)

heads and shoulders to the right and left and begin to pick out their eyeballs. Upon descending back down, all the thorns turn upward and shoot into their bodies, cutting them into pieces. Furthermore, all those who committed sexual misconduct in previous lives are reborn there. Enticed by the environment, their previous lovers call out to them from the peak of the mountains. Attempting to climb up and reach them, the thorns turn back upon them to pierce them profusely. Once arriving at the peak, there are females or males trying to hold and caress them with bodies like blazing iron so rough that they feel like the sharp edge of a saw. After that, they burst into flames.

Again, they are restored and, once again, see their lovers calling out to them from below; as they attempt to reach them, the thorns turn upward to pierce them. Arriving at the base, then the process repeats itself; so they experience suffering in this way according to their previous sexual deeds. These three environments can be counted as one since they are similar in terms of being tortured by weapons.

Fourth, once escaping from there, beings encounter the River Impossible to Cross. The earth surrounding it is covered by molten lava. Once entering [the river], their body sinks down into it, and the flesh and bones are incinerated. At the banks of the river, the messengers of hell are waiting and blocking the way while holding clubs, hooks, and lassos. They capture the inhabitants by these weapons and place them face up upon the molten ground. They inquire, "What do you want?" Unable to see or know what is going on, the inhabitants will nevertheless reply that they are hungry and thirsty. At that moment the messengers stick red hot pokers in their mouths and pour in molten copper. Although it is taught that the life expectancy for both neighboring hells—namely, the proximate and the single-day hell—is uncertain, until the strength of karmic accumulations for experiencing this suffering is exhausted, they must remain and endure this.

3.2.1.1.2.2.3.2.1.1.2 Suffering of the Cold Hells

Second, the cold hell realms are Blisters, Burst Blisters, Lamentation, Groans, Chattering Teeth, Utpalalike Cracks, Lotuslike Cracks, and Great Lotuslike Cracks.[a] The locale of these eight hells is ten-thousand leagues beyond the hot hells. From that point some thirty-two thousand leagues under that is the hell of Blisters, and the remaining seven are two-thousand leagues lower than that in

[a] *chu bur chan, chu bur dolwa, ah chu zerwa, kyi hud zerwa, so tam tam pa, utpala tar gey pa, pema tar gey pa, pema tar cher gey pa,* and *pema chenpo tar gey pa* (*chu bur can, chu bur rdol ba, a chu zer ba, kyi hud zer ba, so tham tham pa, ut pa la ltar gas pa, pad ma ltar gas pa, pad ma ltar cher gas pa,* and *pad ma chen po ltar gas pa*)

descending order. It is taught that the hell of Blisters and the Reviving hell are actually equal in level. The hell of Burst Blisters and Black Line are equal as well. The remaining hells are also equal according to order. In addition, it is said that there are four-thousand leagues between each [kind of hell].

Here, it is explained that there are only two-thousand leagues between each of the cold hells. If one were to wonder how they are then on an equal level, the hot hells are located at the pit of deep narrow gorges, whereas the cold hells are upon the peaks of the highest mountains. Some scholars assert that the additional two-thousand leagues are included in the height of the mountains versus the gorges. Generally, the cold hells are surrounded by snow peaks, and the land is submerged by glacial snow and ice. The skies are dark and engulfed by snow blizzards that are excruciatingly intense.

First, in the hell of Blisters, the body is tormented by blizzards that rage in the four directions so that blisters emerge all over the body, while the inhabitants huddle. Second, the Burst Blisters hell is colder than that, so the blisters burst and the body becomes covered with blood and pus. Third, the hell of Lamentation is even colder than that, and the suffering increases so that the inhabitants scream out in pain. Fourth, the hell of Groans is even colder; and given that the suffering increases, the lamentations turn into moans and groans. Fifth, the hell of Chattering Teeth is even colder; and with the suffering increasing, the inhabitants are unable to speak or moan as the jaw is locked by frigidity. Sixth, the Utpalalike Cracks hell is even colder, such that all cracks on the body split open and turn blue in color. Due to the frigid winds, five cracks evolve into six. For the seventh Lotuslike Cracks, since this is even more frigid, the blue-colored skin falls off the body, exposing raw flesh as this falls into ten or more pieces. For the eighth Great Lotuslike Cracks, it is even colder than the rest. The skin falls off, and the flesh is even redder than before as it opens up into hundreds of parts that completely split apart; and the inhabitants suffer as their skeletons are fully exposed. The life expectancy of these hell realms is also not short as stated in the Abhidharma:

> The life expectancy of the hell of Blisters is equal to the time it would take if every one-hundred years a single sesame seed were removed from a large vessel filled with seeds until that vessel became emptied. The life expectancy in the remaining realms is twenty times longer than that equation.

Thus, the analogy of a large vessel containing sesame seeds is based on the great measurement system of ancient India where such a vessel can hold some eighty loads of sesame seeds, much like a storehouse. If a single seed were taken from that every one-hundred years and once the seeds were all gone, the time it took for that to occur would indicate the life expectancy for the hell of Blisters. Twenty times that is the expectancy for the Burst Blisters, and likewise twenty times more for the remaining hells in descending order.

3.2.1.1.2.2.3.2.1.1.3 Suffering of the Proximate Hells

Third, the neighboring hells exist in proximity to both the hot and cold hell realms and are found within the human realms as well. It is taught that they occur near to the ocean shores. Hence, the locales and sufferings are indeterminate as stated in *Resting the Mind in Repose*:

> The locale of the proximate hells is indeterminate as they occur within mountains, forests, the sky, between crags, in fire, water, and the rest. The inhabitants abide there in small groups, in clusters, and sometimes alone where they are tormented by the individual sufferings that are endured. Hence, these are referred to as proximate locales.

Thus, as taught, in indeterminate places such as mountains, crags, water, fire, space, and so forth, inhabitants of the proximate hells abide at the shores of the oceans and between walls and pillars in a diversity of shapes. Taking rebirth there is due to throwing or eliminating one's bodily excrement on the walls or pillars of temples, as well as inappropriately using general materials that belong to the sangha community, such as their staffs used for begging.[87] Furthermore, it is taught that there are many other minor hell realms where some take rebirth with so-called extra flesh and are so obese that it appears that they have no limbs. Due to tremendous hunger, they devour their own flesh. There are also hell realms referred to as Pestle, Burned Log, and Trunk or Stem. The suffering endured is varied, depending upon the individual supports.

Previously, during the life of our teacher, Buddha Shākyamuni, one village butcher vowed to abstain from killing during the night but, nevertheless, took rebirth in the neighboring hell realms. At night, he experienced a state of enjoyment with four beautiful women offering him delicious food and drink in a lovely palace. In the daytime, that palace turned into an iron-hot inferno, and the four women became four ferocious dogs trying to devouring him. Another story involves a prostitute who never engaged in sexual misconduct during the daytime but, at night, did. Hence, taking rebirth in hell, she also experienced pleasure during the day but endured suffering all night long. These are some of the scenes [the ārya] Shroṇakoṭikarṇa[a] saw as he gazed out at the ocean shores.[88]

In the Vinaya, it states:

[a] Dro Zhin Kye Nawa Cheywa (*gro bzhin skyes rna ba bye ba*)

> In the daytime taking the lives of others, while at night adorned with the qualities of morality—through these actions, both excellent results and sins are experienced.

Thus, and the quote continues:

> At night attached to her lovers, while remaining moral in the day—through these actions, both excellent results as well as those based upon sin are experienced.

Thus, this concurs with how the inhabitants of the neighboring hells explained their situation to Shroṇakoṭikarṇa.

By means of numbers, there are some inhabitants who stay alone, as well as different numbers of them within groups. There is an account of some five-hundred monks who were staying together in a pleasing temple; and when they would gather for the noon meal at the ringing of the gong, suddenly the temple became a burning iron jail and their begging bowls turned into various weapons. They would then begin to fight among each other. Once the afternoon meal was complete, everything would revert back to the pleasant experience it was prior to that. It is taught that was the karmic result of an incident that occurred during the time of Buddha Kāshyapa. Many bhikṣhus were sustaining morality, but one day when they came together for the noon meal, they began to argue with one another, striking each other with their begging bowls.

In addition, in this hell realm the inhabitants will think that the entrance-ways, pillars, stoves, or ropes are their own bodies; and when they open doors, make fire on the stove, and so forth, they are tormented by suffering that is always diverse and uncertain. Therefore, there is no certainty in terms of locale, suffering, or life expectancy, hence the reason these realms are referred to as proximate or ephemeral by nature.

The causes for rebirth in these hell realms occur very easily, and even every day many such accumulations for this will occur. There are unfathomable accumulations that have occurred but have yet to ripen, which is why it is unacceptable to just relax in the face of this. One must feel a sense of trepidation toward these possibilities. Our present attitude is that there is a great distance between ourselves and these hell realms, but in fact the difference is as near as one round of breath. This is similarly mentioned in the *Bodhicharyāvatāra*:

> Having accumulated the karma for hell rebirth, how can one just sit there and relax?

Thus, and in the *Advice from a Spiritual Friend*:

> By the mere cessation of a sinner's breath, the time between that person and the hell realms is indicated. Having heard about the inconceivable suffering: if there is still no fear of this, that person must have a heart as hard as a diamond. If whoever sees the images, hears the accounts, recalls them, reads about them, and replicates them feels trepidation rising from within, needless to say how unbearable the actual ripening results will be.

Thus, all sinners who must certainly experience the suffering of the hells based on their karmic accumulations will at the moment their breathing stops immediately experience the suffering of the hell realms. When we hear about the inconceivable suffering of these hell realms: if fear still fails to arise within us, then our hearts must be as hard as a diamond. If not, then how is it that someone would not feel fear?

These are the main points of this explanation. Hence, one must feel trepidation for the following reasons. To see images of what the hells look like, to listen to accounts of how they are, to recall what that would be like, to read books that discuss them, to create replicas of the environment, and so forth—when fear arises, there is no need to mention what it would be like if the suffering of the hell realms were actually ripening upon oneself as the unbearable karmic result. And, so it is.

3.2.1.1.2.2.3.2.1.2 Suffering of the Pretas

Second, to contemplate the suffering of the pretas, there are three categories: those who abide in groups, those who are scattered about, and those who move through space.

For the first, the locale of these pretas is as follows. Some five-hundred leagues below this continent of Jambudvīpa is a kingdom within which is a city known as Kapilavastu.[a,89] In that place, not even a morsel of desirable substances exists, such as grass, water, and trees. The environment resembles a vast, red hot copper vessel blazing with redness. There, the principal residing preta is the dharma king Yamā surrounded by thirty-six varieties of pretas, as mentioned in the *Sūtra on Close Placement of Mindfulness*.[b] All of these pretas are hungry and thirsty, with dried up bodies that are dark in color and resemble burnt-out tree stumps. Their faces are blanketed with hair, and their mouths are extremely desiccated such that they are always trying to lick their lips.

[a] *ser kya ney* (*ser skya'i gnas*); Pale Yellow

[b] *do de drenpa nyer zhag* (*mdo sde dran pa nyer bzhag, saddharmānusmṛtyupasthāna*)

Those with external obscurations are tormented by hunger and thirst. They rush to rivers, lakes, and ponds and, once arriving there, encounter various beings averting them, holding swords as well as short and long spears. [Even if they can get there], the water they are seeing turns into pus and blood, rendering it unsuitable to drink.

Those with inner obscurations suffer from hunger and thirst as follows. Their mouths, throats, and limbs are very small and narrow, whereas their bellies are huge in comparison. Even though no one else is preventing them from finding food and drink, they are unable to partake of anything.

Those with perverted obscurations are affected through food and drink as follows. Whatever these pretas called "pretas with garlands of fire" ingest turns into fire and incinerates them. Here, there are also pretas called "partakers of filth", who partake of despicable things, like eating feces and utilizing extremely unclean things with raunchy smells. Others cut off their own flesh and eat it since they are incapable of partaking of any other proper food and drink. In the *Precious Wish-fulfilling Treasury*, it states:

> The outwardly obscured pretas see enjoyments, yet [are unable to utilize them]. The inwardly obscured ones' internal organs blaze on fire. The commonly obscured ones are always obsessed with food and drink, so twelve years later even the name of water will not be heard by them. All the while, it appears that others are harming them and preventing them from acquiring what they want.

Thus, it is taught. Furthermore, there are the specific obscured ones who have many other living beings eating off of their bodies. Tumors grow on them; and when they burst, they eat the contents of the tumors. There are myriad other varieties [of suffering] as well.

Second, the pretas who are scattered about emerge from the others and belong to the class of those who move through space. They partake of flesh in charnel grounds and so forth. They also exist in waters, deserts, at the shores of the oceans, and in a variety of ways. It states in the Vinaya:

> When one employs harsh speech, aggression, stinginess, and the incapacity to express generosity, rebirth in the world of pretas occurs.

Thus, and:

> When healthy and intoxicated by pleasures, as well as youth and wealth, unable to give even slightly to others, rebirth in the world of pretas will occur.

Hence, this quote is similar to the stories that the pretas told Shroṇakoṭikarṇa while he was wandering at the ocean shores. Saying *jungpa*[a] [i.e., an ancient term] means having avarice or being incapable of expressing generosity toward others. The term *gyag pa*[b] means to be without illness and so forth, so one feels a sense of self-empowerment or pride. Being intoxicated by arrogance is to possess pride.

In the *Autobiography of a Female Preta*,[c] it states:

> I gave birth to five boys at night and five boys in the daytime. Although I ate them all, I still do not feel satisfied.

Thus, there is also the category of [pretas] who eat their own offspring.

Third, the pretas that move through space are as follows. In *Resting the Mind in Repose*, it states:

> The pretas that move through space belong to the class of māras, rākṣhas, yakṣhas, *tsen*, and *gyalpo*.[d] Based on miraculous karmic abilities, they wander everywhere without obstruction, bringing about myriad modes of harm, sending illness, stealing vitality, obstructing life, and the like. Hence, they send harm and illness to others and are obsessed with fear since their minds are always confused. Most of the time, they are hungry and thirsty, and some of them are repeatedly tormented by the same illness or weapon that took their lives in the past as though it were occurring all over again. Some of the nonhuman species are always in motion, not remaining still for a moment. Although they magically wander, they think that the narrow passageways are guarded by others. It is taught that many types of undetermined suffering occur to them.

The extent of the pretas' lives is as the Abhidharma states:

> For pretas, one [human] month is a single day, multiplied by five hundred.

Thus, it is as taught. For the pretas who live in groups on and below the earth, one human month equals a day; and they will live for some five hundred of their own years. For the other types of pretas, life expectancy remains indeterminate.

[a] *'jung pa*
[b] *rgyag pa*
[c] *yi dak mo'i tok jöd* (*yi dvags mo'i rtogs brjod*)
[d] *dre, nödchin, sinpo, tsen*, and *gyalpo* (*'dre, gnod sbyin, srin po, btsan*, and *rgyal po*)

3.2.1.1.2.2.3.2.1.3 Suffering of the Animals

Third, for contemplating the suffering of animals, there are three: animals that abide in the depths, random animals, and the class of nāgas. First, it states in *Resting the Mind in Repose*:

> Animals abiding in the depths are as vast as the four treasures of water.[90] Each consuming the other, their suffering is boundless. In the depths of the dark ocean, they are fearful and constantly suffer from heat, cold, thirst, hunger, and preying upon one another.

Thus, as taught, from the four directions of Lake Manasarovar, four great rivers emerge. Within them, there are fish, *makaras*,[a,91] and so forth that devour one another, causing on-going torment. For those that abide in the oceans between the four continents[92] up to the water line on Mt. Meru, there is no appearance of the sun; and it is so dark they are unable to see in front of themselves. The sizes and colors of their bodies are diverse, and they are so abundant that they appear like piles of grain or piles of fermented beer grain. The larger devour the small without masticating, and they suffer by being incapable of moving at all. The smaller also feed off their predators from the inside out.

In addition, the levels of beings that reside within the great oceans involve two that are in the upper region and one that dwells in the lower depths. The [locale] for the first begins some twenty-thousand leagues from the [ocean's] surface; and between the lower two, there are twenty-five thousand leagues each in descending order. On the first level, there are two classes of makaras that belong to the category of fish. The size of their bodies is some seven-hundred leagues in length. They are capable of swallowing five-hundred merchants, including their ships.

Below that, the next level involves two classes of makaras that are called "fish swallowers" since they are able to guzzle down even the previously mentioned makara from the class of fish. Their bodies are twice as large as the first [class], some one-thousand four-hundred leagues in length. At the bottom of the ocean dwell the makaras called fish swallowers, who swallow the previously mentioned makaras. The bodies of these creatures are larger than the preceding, some two-thousand eight-hundred leagues in length. They are surrounded by many smaller creatures that they suppress and render dysfunctional.

These makaras always have their mouths gaping; and within them, many living beings nest. Occasionally when they close their mouths, all those creatures die, causing the ocean around them to turn red from their blood. Some

[a] *ma ka ra*

smaller fish with great strength will pierce through the makaras' bodies some two leagues, causing the makaras to experience intense pain and misery. Hence, these animals suffer inconceivably from the fear of heat, cold, thirst, and hunger as well as the constant scenario of being devoured by one another.

Second, random animals are as the quote continues:

> Random animals in the human realm include birds, animals, and so forth. They harm one another and are hunted by others. Horses, cattle, camels, donkeys, and many others suffer infinitely through being beaten and manipulated. Their lives are lost in order to give up their flesh, skins, and bones. The characteristic of this suffering is that there is no end in sight.

Thus, as taught, those who are scattered and dwell in the human realm are not the same as the pretas previously mentioned. These birds and wild animals are tormented and slain by the weapons of hunters and captured by traps and nets. The horses and cattle have their noses pierced and are castrated and forced to become beasts of burden. They are ridden and used for labor, such as plowing fields. Their blood is let and drunk and their fur forcefully ripped from the skin, while they are beaten with iron rods, clubs, and the like. Goats and sheep are killed for their meat, while wild animals are slaughtered for their skins. Elephants are murdered for their tusks, and some barbarians will even flay their skin while the animal is still alive. In order to extract substances such as mercury,[93] some animals are placed in large iron vessels and cooked down.

According to the customs of some non-Buddhists, many animals are sacrificed alive[94] by burning them to death, as well as offering their flesh and blood. The many ways that they suffer can be directly witnessed by us in our present lives.

Third, the suffering of the classes of nāgas is as the quote continues:

> The happiness and suffering of many nāgas is divided between day and night. Their happiness and suffering changes from morning to night, and some of them experience being caught in a rainstorm of hot sand. Others suffer separation between companions. Most of them are deluded and fear the garuḍa's wrath. They endure many kinds of torment.

Thus, as taught, although nāgas experience sporadic happiness in the morning, afternoon, and evening, at other times that becomes the torment of heat, cold, hunger, and thirst. Hence, their experiences of happiness and suffering are divided. Some of them experience being caught in rainstorms of hot sand, while others are expelled from their ranks and rejected. They then suffer horrendously from loneliness. Generally, all of them suffer from delusion and fear of garuḍas.

In this world of Jambudvīpa at the banks of Lake Manasarovar, there is a forest of *shalmali* trees where four classes of garuḍas reside. Garuḍas that are born from eggs will eat nāgas who are likewise born from eggs. The [garuḍas] born from the womb eat both womb- and egg-born nāgas. Those born from heat and moisture partake of nāgas born from all three—eggs, womb, and heat and moisture. Those born miraculously eat all four types of nāgas.

Furthermore, in the *Advice from a Spiritual Friend*, it tells us:

> The superior nāgas have many heads that indicate the degree of their suffering.

Thus, however many heads the superior kings of nāgas have indicates the degree of suffering and torment to be experienced. Furthermore, among the classes of nāgas, there are varieties of suffering, including anxiety toward the power of dhāraṇī's.[95]

The extent of their lives is as the Abhidharma states:

> The longest life expectancy for an animal is an eon of time.

Thus, the king of nāgas, Takṣhaka,[a] and others are able to live for an intermediate kalpa. A short life is to live from morning to evening, and the least would be for only a moment. Therefore, there is no determined life expectancy. Since the descriptions concerning the infallible law of cause and result are undeceiving, it is certain that all of us will fall into these lower realms. Even now, we are unable to bear a spark of fire or the coldness of the winter air striking our bodies, including feeling hungry and thirsty for a single day. We should bring to mind the thought, "If I were born in the hells or lower realms, how could I bear this?" Contemplating this on a daily basis and giving up these causes, one must accomplish the causes for taking rebirth in the higher realms while one has the support of this human life.

Ārya Nāgārjuna has said:

> If brought to mind today, one must recall the extreme heat and cold of the hells, the hunger and thirst of the pretas, and how their bodies become parched and dehydrated without food or drink. One must recall the suffering of the animals that occurs based on delusion and

[a] Jogpo (*'jog po*); a mythological nāga king

> abandon all such causes, while producing all causes for virtue and happiness. When the difficult to acquire in this world—the precious human body—is found, one must know how to think carefully and completely sever the causes for lower rebirth.

Thus, one should contemplate and observe the suffering of the hot and cold hells, the hunger and thirst of the pitiful pretas who are parched from deprivation, and the animals overcome by delusion, including those that are scattered about and dwelling in the depths of the seas. Having abandoned all these causes and once this human body has been acquired, the causes for rebirth in the higher realms must be produced. Hence, it is taught that one must be extremely careful concerning the full abandonment of the causes for the nonvirtuous states of the lower realms.

3.2.1.1.2.2.3.2.2 Contemplation on the Suffering of the Three Higher Realms

This has three parts:

1 Suffering of humans
2 Suffering of asuras
3 Suffering of devas

Second, contemplating the suffering of the realms of well-being [i.e., the higher realms] has three: the suffering of humans, the suffering of asuras, and the suffering of devas.

3.2.1.1.2.2.3.2.2.1 Suffering of Humans

First, the suffering of humans is as stated in the *Wish-Fulfilling Treasury*:

> Humans lack the opportunity for true well-being and are besieged by the misery of birth, old age, sickness, and death, including separation from loved ones, the inability to satisfy desire, and having to experience the unwanted. There are many hardships based on heat and cold when their needs are not met. The way some [humans] repay kindness is to harm others. Loved ones turn against one another, and meaningless jealousy abounds. Humans also indulge in pointless criticism and exaggeration.

Thus, as taught, among these the suffering of birth is as mentioned in the *Letter to a Disciple*:

> Squeezed and pressed within the unclean environment of the womb, tight and densely dark, the infant will remain encased in a womb that resembles the hells and must endure and suffer in the fetal posture.

Thus, if born from a mother's womb, to say that is "extremely uncomfortable and unclean" means that, within the womb, it is tight and narrow; and the fetus is pressed against organs and unclean substances. Crouched over and crowded, the fetus is tormented by this suffering in the following ways. Below the mother's stomach and upon the intestines, facing toward the spine, the fetus resides in the midst of unclean odors and substances for thirty-eight weeks. During the first week, the oval shape of the embryo is, for example, like frothy broth that emerges from cooked rice or the skin of creamy yogurt. By the second week, there is a bluish karmic wind called "permeating everything" that causes the embryo to take on an oblong shape resembling dried yogurt or frozen butter.[96]

By the third week, due to the wind called "treasure opening", the embryo becomes lumpy or fleshy, shaped like a metal scepter or a squirming earthworm. By the fourth week, the wind called "vast opening" causes the fetus to become spherical and solid like a mortar.[97] By the fifth week, the wind called "total conversion" causes the limbs to form; and the indications of the two shoulders, two thighs, and the head arise. By the sixth week, the wind called "vastness" causes the indication of the forearms and lower legs to form. By the seventh week, the wind called "swirling" causes the indications of the two hands, ankles, and feet—these four—to form. By the eighth week, the wind called "reversal and transformation" causes twenty indications to occur, such as the initial signs of the ten fingers and toes. Thereafter, each week will bring about a complete transformation so that, by the thirty-fifth week, the limbs of the fetus in the womb will be fully developed.

While abiding within the womb: when the mother eats or drinks something hot, the fetus will have the sensation of being dropped into a fire pit. If she partakes of something cold, it will be as though placed upon an ice block. When she jumps or runs, there will be the sensation of falling down a narrow gorge causing intense anxiety to arise. These are the reasons why it was previously mentioned that being in the mother's womb is like being in the hells. By the thirty-sixth week, the fetus will feel a sense of dislike for the womb; so by the thirty-seventh week, the fully developed infant will have a sense that the womb is unclean, foul-smelling, dark, and dungy. At the thirty-eighth week, by the strength of the wind called "gathering the extremities", the body of the child will rotate within the womb so the head will point downward with eyes closed. This is the wind that places the child in position for birth.

In this way, once two-hundred and sixty-six days have passed, the wind called "downward opening" will emerge; and through this karmic wind, the womb-bound child will be pushed out through the birth canal. Given that the cervix is extremely narrow, when the child tries to pass through this, it will feel as though it is being skinned alive or stung by hornets. The torment is extremely intense during the process of birth. Once born, although placed upon a soft blanket, for a while the child will feel as though he or she was placed upon a thorny bush. Although touched with hands or cloth, it will be as though being sliced by a knife. The initial roughness is unbearable to the touch and causes unpleasant sensations.

The suffering of old age is as stated in the *Sūtra of Vast Manifestations*:

> Through aging, a once-attractive body becomes unattractive; through aging, the charisma of presence and strength are stolen. Through aging, well-being is taken away and replaced by humiliation. Through aging, one is led toward death; and vitality as well is lost.

Thus, as taught, the body's posture bends like a bow, and the hair turns white like a tinder flower.[a] The forehead and entire body become wrinkled like a cutting board. Previously, when there was youth, the hair was dark, the body stood erect, [and] the skin was smooth and taunt. That same body changes so dramatically through the process of aging that it is as though it dies when, in fact, there is still life.

The Lord Supreme Ruler, Kalzang Gyatso,[b] said:

> A youthful body's flesh and blood is steeped with vitality. Every day, month, and year, that strength decreases; so wherever one observes, both body and mind gradually decline. Although still alive, the human body undergoes dramatic transformations. How sad it is to observe this.

Thus, while still alive in the same body, it will appear as though the body has been swapped. Until Yamā is encountered, the life expectancy will gradually decrease by days, months, and years, resembling the waning moon. Knowing this, the mind is saddened. The body's strength is lost so, when standing up, it feels like a tree trunk being uprooted. When sitting down, it feels like a rope snapping on a hanging bag of dirt that suddenly drops to the ground. When walking, steps are unsteady; and when speaking, speech is jumbled and hard to hear. When the organs decline, the eyes cannot see clearly; and when memory declines, things

[a] *tra wa'i metog* (*spra ba'i me tog*); flower from *Aeschynomene grandiflora*
[b] *skal bzang rgya mtsho*; the 7th Dalai Lama, 1708-1757

are easily forgotten. When the strength to utilize objects declines, it becomes hard to digest food and beverage. Furthermore, one will no longer be able to use or enjoy the desirable things that were once appreciated. Once life is practically depleted, death approaches.

Third, the suffering of illness is as stated in the *Letter to a Disciple*:

> For example, at the end of winter when the winds and snow are strong, the state of the grasses and trees and the vigor of the forest and medicinal herbs are depleted. Like that, through illness, vitality is spent; and the strength of the organs and bodily functions wanes.

Thus, as taught, when the warmth and coolness of the body become imbalanced, many types of pain and discomfort ensue. Becoming fragile, body weight is lost and the skin dries out, making it hard to even move around. When the body's elements become imbalanced, the mind suffers from depression, as days and nights seem to last forever. One is cautioned about foods that were once pleasing and enjoyable that will now be the source of further poor health and must be withheld against one's consent. Conversely, undesirable things, such as medicines, surgery, moxabustion, and the like will have to be endured whether one likes it or not. If certain diseases are not cured, then they lead to death; so the suffering endured will be intense.

Fourth, the suffering of death is as stated in the *Sūtra of Vast Manifestations*:

> The prospect of facing death, transference, as well as the process of future lives, and permanently leaving behind that which is cherished the most—never returning and never to be met again—is similar to a leaf that has dropped from a tree or the continuity of a flowing river . . .

Thus, first there is death and then transmigration, followed by the intermediate state of becoming. When there is the volition of connecting with the future lives, one must then separate from that which is cherished the most. Once dying, that person will never return or be met again.

For example, once a leaf falls from a tree, it cannot be placed back on the tree to once again grow. This also resembles a strongly flowing river that will not reverse its course. When the illness that brings about death arrives, no matter how many methods are applied, that illness will only escalate until the doctors give up and the divinations become irrelevant. Relatives full of sadness will surround the dying person making preparations for their passing, such as who will perform the last rites and deposit the body at the burial ground.[98] The dying person's vitality will be lost, the mouth will dry up, the lips will stick to the face, the nose will collapse, and the eyes will sink into the sockets. Breathing will turn into panting. The dying person will feel a sense of strong regret concerning previous misdeeds; and in a state of attachment toward family members, entourage, wealth, and material things, they will endure the suffering of permanent separation. These miseries are complicated and unbearable, not the least of which is leaving behind the cherished body itself.

Humans have an abundance of enemies and threats so that, once encountering an enemy, life can be cut short and all of one's possessions stolen or robbed. Furthermore, both humans and nonhumans impose various types of harm. Separating from one's close loved ones leaves the mind tormented by the pain of separation, while the speech laments in sorrow. There may even be physical attempts to harm one's own body by pounding on it, starving it, and the like. Not only that, if a close relative moves far away, then by recalling and longing for their company, one will mull over their good qualities; and all three doors will experience misery.

Furthermore, humans suffer from a lack of necessities, such as water and land, unwanted illness and demonic-force possession that can suddenly occur, including the inability to acquire crucial necessities, such as housing, and coveted wealth, fame, and the like. A human will exhaust himself through these various activities. There is constant disappointment among one another, such as the thought that someone is helping but only to find out they are harming. Even if one is in a position of power, such as that of a lama or a leader, the followers and others may fail to listen and turn against one another in the end. Otherwise, those who are jealous will say negative things, never expressing any good qualities. For no reason, one will be blamed through false claims; and even if one has qualities, rather than those being expressed, one will be disparaged. There are many sorts of suffering that totally disturb the body and mind, such as feeling jealously toward others who have qualities that one does not possess. In these ways, misery ensues.

Furthermore, in the *Accounts from the Gaṇachakra*, it states:

> The suffering of the lower realms exists even among human beings, without exception. The pain of their suffering can be equal to the hells. Some humans are so poor that they are comparable to the yamās of the world[a] [i.e., pretas], while some even suffer like animals since those who are powerful torture and suppress the underdog—not just occasionally but consistently like a flowing river. Some humans suffer from extreme poverty, while others from dissatisfaction. The suffering of endlessly searching for success is relentless, while everyone feels a sense of competitiveness to the point of even taking one another's lives.

[a] *shinje jigten* (*gshin rje'i 'jig rten*)

Thus, as taught, for the most part this quote is easily understood; however, saying "yamās of the world" is cryptic and refers to pretas. The harm they impose is unceasing like a flowing river. Some [humans] have extreme poverty, others dissatisfaction, and the suffering of constantly wishing to achieve the highest degree of success. Everyone is preying off the other and willing to kill. In addition, there is an abundance of suffering that depends upon each individual's status in life, whether high or low.

In the *Four-Hundred Stanzas*, it states:

> Those of higher status will suffer mentally, and those of lower will suffer physically. These two degrees of suffering undermine this world day in and out.

Thus, mental suffering occurs due to having excess responsibilities like that of a king. Physical suffering mainly occurs to ordinary individuals who are poor and subservient to others, and so forth.

> Among the higher realms, the human realm is considered principal;
> yet since there exists diverse suffering such as this, who then would not feel a sense of repulsion toward this existence?
> Alas! Thinking this is a place of well-being and happiness is so deluded! If the Tathāgata's own younger brother, Ānanda, suffered in this way, then who is there that can be content in this world?
> Through these teachings, confidence is gained in the truth of Buddha's speech.

Thus, these are the verses that summarize the section.

3.2.1.1.2.2.3.2.2.2 Suffering of Asuras

Second, contemplating the suffering of the asuras is as follows. Generally, the asuras have five classes as stated in the *Wish-Fulfilling Treasury*:

> Asuras exist in five classes: the glorious longevity devas, the powerful yakṣhas, the unruly māras, the butchering rākṣhas, and the savage class of nāgas. In addition, their bodies and life expectancies are uncertain and diverse.

Thus, the class of glorious longevity asuras have glory and excellent fortune that is equal to the devas of the thirty-third level, such as the god Vemachitra[a] and

[a] Takzangri (*thags bzang ris*); Excellent Woven Patterns

others. The powerful yakṣhas' wealth and abundance is great, as well as their powers and miraculous abilities that are equal to the four classes of kings. The class of unruly māras is inclined toward negativity, and the butchering rākṣhas harm sentient beings similar to the capacity of pretas that move through space. The class of savage nāgas takes sides, and their bodies and abundance fluctuates between joy and sorrow. They belong to the category of "dense ones" and are, therefore, referred to as "the class of deluded animals". This later class is counted among the class of asuras. It is taught that they are a combination of the class of devas and animals, and their bodies and life expectancies are uncertain.

The suffering that these classes endure is as stated in the *Wish-Fulfilling Treasury*:

> All asuras suffer from anger, fighting, and unwanted situations that ripen upon them, including their death. Given that their suffering is so diverse, they have no true happiness.

Thus, all asuras fight with the gods on the thirty-third level since their minds are full of angry aggression. They also bicker among one another. The suffering they endure through jealousy is like a cutting wind and their anger like a raging fire. Not being able to fulfill their wishes, unwanted circumstances ripening upon them and death are among the boundless miseries they endure. In the *Advice from a Spiritual Friend*, it tells us:

> The asuras will characteristically endure great suffering based on their anger toward the glory of the devas. Even though they have intelligence, they are obscured by the defilements of sentient beings and fail to see the truth.[99]

Thus, all asuras characteristically are overcome by pride and cannot stand the fact that devas have such glory and wealth. Possessing the defilements of sentient beings or fully ripened impediments, their aggregates are a product of fully ripened obscurations. Given that previous karma will fully mature: until they are free from this, the capacity to see the truth and achieve the mind of concentration will be obscured.

The manner through which these asuras fight is as follows. The root cause for their turmoil is that—among the inhabitants of Jambudvīpa—when an abundance of merit is accumulated, this increases the devas' good fortune; and that makes the asuras jealous. Devas will look at the daughters of the asuras, making them more envious. Because asuras are attached to the ambrosia of the devas: when they see the devas' wish-fulfilling trees adorned with their flowers and fruits, they become aggravated. The asuras think, "Since the glorious fruits and flowers that emerge from the wish-fulfilling trees belong to the devas, we should cut down the useless trunk that grows from our realm." It is said that their constant bickering originates from any of these reasons.

The locale [of the asuras] is within the hollow, lower part of Mt. Meru that is submerged in water. There are four locations there; the first is at the point where the water level and the mountain meet. Directly inside of that some twenty-thousand leagues below is the first level [of the asuras] and the city called Ödan.[a] The [king] is called Drachan,[b] Son of the Lioness. Then, some twenty-thousand leagues below is the second level and the city called Kartreng.[c] The king is called Gültreng.[d] Twenty-thousand leagues below that is the city called Zabpa[e] and the king called Metog.[f] Twenty-thousand leagues below that is the fourth-level city called Serdan[g] and the king of asuras called Vemachitra. When they fight with devas, sometimes all four kings join together, such as Vemachitra; and other times only the upper-level kings will fight. They wear strong armor made of lapis lazuli and crystal and wield swords, spears, bows, arrows, and other weapons.

The four branches of their military forces[100] emerge at the level of the water. Among the five guardians of Indra,[h] first they wage war with the eight classes of nāgas, such as the king of the nāgas, Gawo, and Nyer Gawo[i] who are inclined toward virtue. After that, they wage war with the nonvirtuous king of the nāgas, Rabjom,[j] the haughty black Huluka, Great Huluka,[k] and others who are asuras. If victorious, then the asuras will be forced into retreat; and if not, then the second guardians of Indra who reside on the first level of Mt. Meru will emerge. The leader of the first level is the yakṣha called Zhong Tok;[l] the second is Treng Tok;[m] the third is Tak Nyö;[n] and for the fourth, the four great kings and their retinues.[o]

During the battle with those who are lower, most of the asuras are reversed. If the higher asuras alone emerge and their attempt to defeat the devas is unsuccessful, they will then call upon Vemachitra to assist them. Vemachitra then becomes infuriated and pounds his foot upon the golden ground, and the great

[a] *'od ldan*; Possessing Light
[b] *sgra can*; Magnificent Roar
[c] *skar phreng*; Garland of Stars
[d] *'gul phreng*; Garland Necklace
[e] *zab pa*; Deep
[f] *me tog*; Flower
[g] *gser ldan*; Golden
[h] *chöd jin* (*mchod sbyin*)
[i] *dga' bo* and *nyer dga' bo*; Joy and Close Joy
[j] *rab 'joms*; Complete Subjugator
[k] *nag po 'gyings pa hu lu ka* and *hu lu ka chen po*
[l] *gzhong thogs*; Tray Holder
[m] *phreng thogs*; Garland Holder
[n] *rtag myos*; Always Intoxicated
[o] Dhṛtarāṣṭra, Virūḍhaka, Virūpākṣa, and Vaishravaṇa

earth including Mt. Meru begins to quake. The throne of Indra will also shake, and [Vemachitra] will then arrive to fight along with his entire army. When, through clairvoyance, Indra analyzes what caused this earthquake, he comes to know that a war will ensue; and it is taught that he, too, will then depart to wage war on the asuras.

Occasionally, if the guardians of the devas are unable to turn these asuras back, then the four great kings will go to the thirty-third level of the devas and say," O Great Indra, please look here. We five guardians have been unable to reverse the forces of the asuras. Now they have arrived at the terraces of Mt. Meru." [After they] say this, Indra then orders all devas on the thirty-three levels to fight. They all gather at Dün Sa Zang[a] in the presence of Indra, and he commands them, "All gods who only have a short time left to live and are preparing for death should stay back. Everyone else must enthusiastically join forces." Saying that, he then departs for the northern land of Gawa'i Tsal.[b] Through his miraculous powers, he observes the support for his vision[101] in that garden, at which time he is able to know the indications of their victory. The devas then journey to the forest called Tsub Gyur Gyi Tsal;[c,102] and while they are swimming in the pond, their anger returns, and once again the wish to wage war is aroused.

Then at the eastern garden of Go Cha Tsal,[d] they don sturdy armor made from a variety of jewels. Indra rides upon the central head of the enemy-defeating elephant Rabten[e] with thirty-three heads, flanked by the other thirty-two close leaders riding on the other heads. Wielding their armor and weapons, they wage war at the southern side of Mt. Meru. It is taught that whoever is defeated will continue to fight; and after three defeats, the battle will be over. Due to their merit, the bodies of the devas are seven times taller than the asuras; and they subdue all the asuras by throwing their weapons, such as vajras, wheels, arrows, and wooden pestles, as well as mountains from the face of the sun and the moon. The asuras fight with them and try to destroy them by throwing weapons, such as vajras, large arrows, swords, and mountains. When they [i.e., the asuras] throw the mountains, Indra's vajra causes the mountains to crumble.

Furthermore, all the weapons and body parts fall into the ocean, which turns red from the blood of the slain. When the asuras gaze at the reflections that appear in the lake called Kun Nang[f] at the city of Kar Treng, they can see images

[a] *'dun sa bzang*; Excellent Assembly Ground
[b] *dga' ba'i tshal*; Joyful Garden
[c] *rtsub 'gyur gyi tshal*; Thicket of Roughness
[d] *go cha'i tsal* (*go cha'i tshal*); Armor
[e] *rab brtan*
[f] *kun snang*; All-Illuminating

of the battles. It is taught that, even before the armies return home, their suffering begins because they can see who among their loved ones have lost their lives.

In war, if the devas' heads or waists are severed, they will die; but if other limbs or body parts are harmed or severed, they will be instantly restored. The asuras on the other hand are like humans and will die if any of their main organs have been damaged. While they fight, the earth quakes and the great mountains are reduced to particles of dust, while the skies of Jambudvīpa become filled with dust clouds. The glare from the weapons is blinding, and the sounds are overwhelmingly loud. It is mentioned in the *Sūtra on Close Placement of Mindfulness* that because Rāhula is an animal and cannot bear the strength of the sun and moon's glare, he covers them with his hands. In this way the sun and moon are eclipsed by Rāhula. At that time if the asuras are victorious, then they will chase the devas into the city Tana Düg.[a,103] If the devas are the winners, then the asuras will be chased all the way to the first lake [among the seven].[104]

Lha'i Ngawoche[b] [i.e., Indra] then states, "May all devas be victorious! May all asuras be defeated! May the animals be driven away! May there be joy!" Once this sound is heard, all asuras return to their own abodes. The asuras then run back onto the basis of the golden earth in the hollow part of Mt. Meru. Driven by the power of the devas, once they enter the golden city, the gate is closed behind them. Even the windows will no longer open, and it is taught they must remain imprisoned there for seven days' time.

The devas who fight with asuras are those located all the way up to the thirty-third level. Beyond that, beginning with the level called Yāma, it is not necessary for devas to fight with asuras.

3.2.1.1.2.2.3.2.2.3 Suffering of Devas

Third, contemplating the suffering of the devas is as stated in the *Wish-Fulfilling Treasury*:

> The suffering of all devas is as infinite as the oceans as they fall from grace, die, and so forth.

Thus, as taught, among the two—the suffering of the desire-realm devas and those of the higher realms—first, the suffering of falling from grace and dying is as follows.

It states in *Advice from a Spiritual Friend*:

[a] *ta na düg* (*lta na sdug* or *blta na sdug*); Pleasant to Behold

[b] *lha'i rnga bo che*; Great Drum of the Gods

> Even in the higher realms, due to having been immersed in ecstasy, the suffering of falling from that grace is even greater. Thinking in that way, the learned will not be attached to the exhaustible [happiness] of the higher realms.

Thus, the happiness that comes from the wealth and abundance utilized by the devas of desire is such that, when they see the signs of their demise, the suffering that follows actually surpasses the happiness they are leaving behind. Contemplating that, it is taught that those who are noble and wise should not be attached to the meaningless happiness that comes from exhaustible desires.

It is taught that the signs of death include five that are distant and five that are close. First, the *Advice from a Spiritual Friend* tells us:

> The body's coloring turns offensive, the cushion becomes uncomfortable, the flower garlands wither, clothing begins to stink, and the bodies get crusty from perspiration that never before existed. Such are the five signs of death for the higher realms.

As taught, when devas approach death, the luster of their bodies declines, and they become unattractive. They are no longer comfortable on their cushions and don't want to sit there. The garlands of flowers that adorn them wither, their clothing begins to smell, and their bodies take on an odor from sweat that was previously unknown. These signs indicate death approaching for those in the higher realms.

The close signs of death include the lessening of the bodies' light, bathing water that is no longer able to cleanse them, unpleasant sounds emerging from their clothing and ornaments, the need to blink their eyes, and attachment to a single place. In particular, [the devas] are known as "those of three occasions" since they know where they were born, by which cause, and where they will be reborn. If they are going to be reborn in the lower realms, then for five deva days they will experience intense suffering as though they had already taken rebirth there. The shortest deva day is fifty human years, so that duration would equal two-hundred fifty human years. Among sentient beings, hell beings suffer the most; however, the mental suffering of a deva at death surpasses even that. In the *Sūtra on Close Placement of Mindfulness*, it states:

> When devas fall from grace, intense suffering ensues that surpasses even the suffering of the hell beings by sixteen times.

Thus, as taught, when the signs of death arrive and a god is dying, the other gods will place a branch from the flowering trees upon his or her heart and say, "O

Brother [or Sister] Deva! May your transition at death bring you to an excellent rebirth in the realm of humans in Jambudvīpa. Once there, may the plow of your faith prepare the field of your merit." Like a worm being placed in hot sand, the dying deva will cry out, "O! All the various carriages, all the gently flowing streams and lakes—O how sad to separate from the cherished gods!" Lamenting like this, he will faint.

Thus, the meaning of these words of sorrow is that, in the deva realms, there are various carriages, gently flowing streams, and lakes; and cherished gods abound. By recalling all of this, they call out saying, "I am falling from the deva realm;" and their misery is great. Furthermore, the suffering of falling to the lower realms means that, although death arrives, no additional virtue remains in their storehouse so that they will fall into the three lower realms.

The suffering of losing their dignity is that all devas who possess great amounts of merit will experience the highest degree of desirable qualities. When devas whose merit is lower than that witness this, they lose their poise and dignity and are overcome with shame. Thereafter, they remain overwhelmed by misery.

The "suffering of killing by being cut open" means that, when they fight with the asuras, their limbs are cut off and they are even slain. The "suffering of being expelled" means that all devas who are courageous fighters will exile the weaker, powerless devas from their own abodes. The "suffering of distraction" is as stated in *Accounts from the Gaṇachakra*:

> All devas who enjoy desirables lack the mind of happiness. As attachment to desire gradually grows, its inner fire burns. How can those whose minds are so distracted ever know happiness? The mind does not remain undistracted for even an instant, since its nature is to be distracted and disturbed, never becoming peaceful. Like wind igniting fire, the fire will spread throughout the trees.

Second, the suffering of the higher realms refers to the form and formless devas who do not suffer in the ways mentioned. Nevertheless, since they have passions, there are obscurations; and they lack freedom over death or life. Hence, they too suffer from having to fall from grace and be reborn in lower places. The *Accounts from the Gaṇachakra* continues:

> Whoever belongs to the form or formless [deva realms] will be free from suffering. Those with the bliss of samādhi will be able to remain stable for eons of time without moving. Yet, since they are not fully liberated, they will eventually fall from that position. Although it seems they have transcended the waves of suffering and the misery of lower realms, this is short-lived. Like a bird flying in the sky or like an arrow

> shot with the strength of a child, the inevitability of landing or falling lower is certain. Like a butter lamp that burns until eventually burning out, all-pervasive suffering will prevail; and disadvantage will ensue.

Thus, as taught, for the most part, this quotation is easy to comprehend; however, "once again falling from grace" means to again fall into the lower realms. No matter how hard they try to rest in samādhi, they are unable to sustain this forever, like a bird that must eventually land. Having no control over death or life is like the metaphor of a lit butter lamp that is bound to extinguish. All-pervasive suffering will bring disadvantage upon them.

In the *Clarification of Transmissions*,[a] it states:

> In the filth of feces, there is no sweet smell; in the realms of saṃsāra, there is no happiness; in the pit of a fire, there is no coolness; and throughout existence, there exists no true joy at all.

Thus, as taught, bringing to mind the fact that in the realms of saṃsāra there is no permanent happiness and not even the slightest opportunity for true joy, it becomes crucial to cultivate heartfelt repulsion. This is stated in the terma commentary:

> Hence, those who enter the dharma and train their minds in these ways will be able to establish irreversible stability. Those who do not train in this way, although entering the dharma, will be like boulders rolling down a ravine. It will be easy for such individuals to revert back [to saṃsāra] given that their minds are unstable and undependable. This is the only inspiring force behind all dharma instruction, so it is a key point to always cultivate intense disdain [toward saṃsāra] through this alone.

Thus, it is as taught.

> The suffering of the three realms is unbearable; and even in the higher realms, there is no opportunity for true happiness.
> Knowing this key point, rather than hoping to remain in these realms of saṃsāra, one should cultivate the wish to be set free.

Thus, these are the verses that summarize the section.

[a] *lung rnam ched* (*lung rnam 'byed, vinayavibhaṅga*)

3.2.1.1.2.2.4 Law of Cause and Result

This has three parts:
1 General contemplation on cause and result
2 Specific contemplation
3 Way of confessing and vow to abstain from nonvirtue

Fourth, contemplating the law of cause and effect is as follows:

> The ripening of the results of positive and negative karma are undeceiving. The perpetually fixated mind habituated to joy and sorrow is the subjective agent engaging with causes and their results. O Guru, undeceiving Permanent Protector, know me!

Thus, **the ripening of the results of positive and negative karma are undeceiving** because the **habits** or seeds for that karma depend upon the mind, and the resultant states of **joy and sorrow** will be undeniably experienced. This is why the principal agent for all of this is the mind. **The perpetually fixated mind is the subjective agent who** accumulates **causes and** experiences **results.** Therefore, in order for the mind to gain mastery and the potential to know how to accept and reject virtue versus nonvirtue, one must **supplicate** the **guru** [**undeceiving permanent protector**].

For this, there are three: the general contemplation on cause and result, the specific contemplation, and the way of confessing and vow to abstain from nonvirtuous accumulations.

3.2.1.1.2.2.4.1 General Contemplation on Cause and Result

The first involves four: the manner of certainty, proliferation, abstinence and thereby not encountering, and the undeniable results of engaging.

First, whether an ordinary individual or an ārya: when it comes to the experience of happiness, even a hell-realm being must experience pleasure in dependence upon the circumstance of a cool breeze. Any pleasurable experience that occurs is due to previously accumulated virtue rather than being the result of nonvirtuous deeds. Suffering as well is due to previously accumulated nonvirtuous karma, including any misery that may arise in the mind stream of even an ārya on down to all kinds of moods experienced by beings. Suffering overall is not the result of the karma of virtuous deeds. In the *Jewel Garland*, it states:

> All suffering emerges from nonvirtue and so do all the lower realms. From virtue come all higher states of happiness, along with well-being in future lifetimes.

Thus, it is as taught.

Second, the mode of proliferation is that even insignificant virtuous karmic accumulations can bring extremely significant positive results. Insignificant nonvirtuous karmic accumulations can also produce extremely significant misery. Hence, the inner playing out of causes and results is dissimilar to how cause and result may appear externally. In the *Chapter on Impermanence*, it states:

> Although a nonvirtuous accumulation may seem insignificant: once passing from that life, the insignificant cause can produce great fear and the source of evil as though poison had been ingested. Although an accumulation may seem irrelevant, it can lead to great bliss in the next life, bringing about great purpose like varieties of ripening fruit.

Thus, and in the *Treasury of Precious Qualities*:

> Even the *ashota*[a] tree produced from a mustard-seed-sized seed can give rise to branches as long as a league in the course of a year. Nevertheless, the image of the proliferation of positive and negative karma still cannot be compared to that.

So, as mentioned in the Vinaya scriptures: even if the cause is merely the size of a mustard seed, in the course of a single year, the branches can grow to be as long as a league. Comparatively, the power of the proliferating results of positive and negative karma are in excess of that.

Third, karma that has not been accumulated and will, therefore, not be encountered refers to the fact that those results will be experienced no matter what the karma accumulated was, either virtuous or not. The need to experience unaccumulated karma is something that will never occur.

Fourth, if karma has been accumulated, then the result of that will never be wasted. No matter what kind of karma has occurred, virtuous or otherwise—if it is not destroyed by another circumstance—then even though it may take a very long time, eventually it will mature without being wasted. In the sūtras, it states:

> O Bhikṣhus! All accumulated karma is not going to ripen on the external ground of this earth. Likewise, this will not mature in the external elements of water, fire, and wind. Whatever the karma is, whether positive or negative, this will only mature upon this heap of aggregates, elements, and sense sources. All karmic accumulations of embodied beings will not be wasted even if it takes one-hundred eons. When the

[a] *a sho ta*

> time for these collections [of karma] to ripen arrives, that is when the results will mature.

Thus, as taught, this explains that whatever karma is accumulated by those who are embodied—unless eliminated by an antidote—even if it takes as long as one-hundred eons, that karma will not be wasted. When root causes and contributing circumstances join and the time arrives, whether good or bad, the results will ripen accordingly.

The way karma that has not been accumulated does not need to be encountered and, if it is accumulated, the way it is not wasted is also mentioned in the *Sublime Praise*:[a]

> Heretical sages claim that whatever karma they have accumulated, whether positive or negative, can be transferred to another like receiving a gift. You [i.e., the Buddha] have said that accumulated [karma] is never wasted and, if not, that it need not be encountered.

Thus, these claims that come from the heretical tradition of the Vedic sages state that the results of positive and negative accumulations that exist in the mind can be transferred to another's mind stream as though a gift were being given. The Buddha said that was not the case. A similar quote comes from the *King of Samādhi*:[b]

> Once accumulated, contrary to thinking, this will not be felt; karma accumulated by others will not be taken upon oneself.

Thus, saying "will not be felt" refers to not being experienced.

3.2.1.1.2.2.4.2 Specific Contemplation

This has two parts:

1. Description of karma and its results
2. Brief discussion about the importance of karmic distinctions

Second, for the specific contemplation, there are two: a description of karma and its results and a brief discussion about the importance of karmic distinctions.

[a] *khyed par pak töd* (*khyad par 'phags bstod, visheṣhastava*); Udbhaṭasiddhasvāmin
[b] *ting dzin gyalpo do* (*ting 'dzin rgyal po mdo, samādhirājasūtra*)

3.2.1.1.2.2.4.2.1 Description of Karma and Its Results

This has two parts:
1 Description of nonvirtuous causes and results
2 Description of virtuous causes and results

For the first, there are two: a description of nonvirtuous causes and results and virtuous causes and results.

3.2.1.1.2.2.4.2.1.1 Description of Nonvirtuous Causes and Results

This has two parts:
1 Recognizing karma of the ten nonvirtues
2 Explanation of the results

First, there are two: recognizing karma based on the path of the ten nonvirtues and an explanation of the results.

3.2.1.1.2.2.4.2.1.1.1 Recognizing Karma of the Ten Nonvirtues

First, in the Abhidharma, it states:

> From that, to synthesize the point, whether virtue or nonvirtue, it is said that there are ten paths for karma.

Thus, among the many varieties of virtuous and nonvirtuous karma, to synthesize the most potent, it is taught that there are ten. The ten nonvirtues are three of the body: killing, stealing, and sexual misconduct; four of speech: lying, slander, harsh speech, and gossip; three of the mind: craving, ill-will, and wrong view.

First, for killing, the Abhidharma continues:

> Killing means to intentionally and unmistakably take the life of another.

Thus, as taught, for this to occur, there are four factors: the basis, intention, action, and final result. The "basis" means another sentient being; the "intention" means recognition, motivation, and passion. Among those, recognition will be either deluded or not. For those who enter the military with the general notion that they will kill the enemy if encountered: then when they do kill, whether they recognize that object as being correct or not is irrelevant; so the distinction concerning confusion is irrelevant as well.

Otherwise, if one has the intention to kill, let's say, Devadatta[a,105] but ends up killing Indra[106] by mistake, the objective was confused; so a complete nonvirtue will not be accumulated. The intention is the wish to kill, and the passion to want to do so will come from any of the three poisons. This applies to the remaining nonvirtues.

The actual action means that—with weapons, poisons, mantric formulas, and the like—the outcome will be the same whether the deed is performed by oneself or whether someone else has been employed to do so. If someone else is discussing a plot to kill someone and one gets involved with that, then whenever the killing takes place—even though one did not directly take the life—the consequences are the same as asking someone else to do this for you. The final result means that the object to be killed dies before oneself. If the killer dies before the object or if they die together, then the complete nonvirtue is not accumulated. This is the way the defeat of killing is understood.

Second, stealing is as the quote continues:

> Stealing the wealth of others through overpowering or embezzling...

Thus, as taught, the basis involves any substance possessed by others rather than oneself. The intention is to recognize the motive that, based on any of the three poisons, there is the aspiration to take that object for oneself. The activity is to then steal it by directly overcoming through force or to covertly embezzle it. Whether directly stolen or acquiring someone other than oneself to do the deed, the results will be congruent. The final result occurs when one feels satisfied that the object has been acquired.

Third, for sexual misconduct the quote continues:

> There are four categories of sexual misconduct based on the desire to enter into a sexual relationship with an unsuitable partner.

Thus, as taught, an unsuitable sexual relationship means to engage in intercourse with an inappropriate, unacceptable partner. Committing sexual misconduct based on desire for someone depends upon whether that individual is an unsuitable male or female; belongs to another; is one's parent, offspring, a minor, or any relative as proximate as seven generations; is a vow holder such as a nun; involves intercourse in other orifices aside from the vagina, such as the mouth, anus, between the thighs, with the hands, or at inappropriate places such as inside temples, in front of any of the three supports,[107] parents, the ordained,

[a] Lhajin (*lhas sbyin*)

or in a gathering of others; or during daytime, inappropriate times such as a mother's final trimester during pregnancy, during menstruation, just after giving birth, while mourning, or during spiritual fasting practices. During any of these situations, even if the act occurs with a spouse, it is considered to be sexual misconduct.

The intention involves the three [poisons] as mentioned before; the activity is to enthusiastically engage in the deed; and the final result occurs when both organs unite, consummating the actual deed.

Fourth, speaking falsely is as the quote continues:

> Lying means using clear words and information to alter another person's mind and through visual, audial, or mental cognition—these three—including whatever is experienced, giving calculated explanations whether or not they are seen, heard, known, or felt.

As taught, the basis refers to what was seen, heard, cognized, and conceptualized. The opposite of that means having not seen and so forth; so for both of these, there are eight considerations. Concerning that, "seeing" means that which is visually experienced; likewise, hearing the audible and cognizing mentally includes comprehension through the olfactory, tactile, and gustatory consciousnesses [included as one]—totaling four. The opposite is to not see and so forth. Speaking to an individual who comprehends the meaning of words with the three intentions as mentioned before and with the intention of having seen something but claiming the opposite by saying something was not seen when it was or, likewise, claiming there was or was not physical contact with the intention to mislead and alter the other person's understanding are all deeds of lying. This may occur through speech or body language, such as demonstrating something through physical signs, so that the final result occurs when the other person assumes this to be true. It is taught that, if the other person fails to comprehend this [i.e., the lie], it then falls into the category of gossip.

Fifth, slander is as the quote continues:

> Slander occurs in order to cause a schism between persons involving the mind, using words based on passions.

Thus, as taught, this involves the threefold intention as mentioned before, whether individuals are harmonious or not, and must be motivated by the wish to cause a schism between those who are harmonious with the hope that they will remain permanently estranged. The activity involves using slanderous words whether true or false. Once spoken, the final result is that this is comprehended by another person regardless of whether the intended action actually comes to pass or not.

Sixth, harsh speech is as the quote continues:

> Harsh speech implies that which is unpleasant to hear.

Thus, as taught, the basis is a hostile mind directed toward another person who appears offensive. The intention is similar to the other [nonvirtues] but includes the use of harsh, nasty words. The activity includes saying anything whether true or false that criticizes the conduct, morality, or status of another person. The final result is when that object comprehends this.

Seventh is gossip as the quote continues:

> A passionate person will gossip, increasing the passions in the minds of others who listen to them. This kind of speech resembles flattery, lyrics in an opera, or ill-intended tales.[108]

Thus, unlike the preceding three, for the basis, gossip is simply pointless. The intention involves the three [passions] like before and clear comprehension of the subject being expressed. The activity involves any meaningless words that arise in the mind of someone filled with emotions. Some teachers assert that saying "passions in others will increase" refers to the fact that gossip stirs up many other shortcomings. Hence, this fits into its own category.

Previously, some masters have said that among the nonvirtues of speech such as lying, gossip resembles the flattering speech of a fake monk, a lustful song, a performer who gossips in the lyrics of an opera in order to entice others, and the ill-intended tales found in writings by heretics that are based on attachment. Likewise, [gossip] includes constantly complaining, as well as engaging in distractive chatter by placing effort toward the use of idle speech. The final result has already been mentioned.

Eighth, craving is as the quote continues:

> Craving means that, through perversion, there is attachment to the wealth of others.

Thus, as taught, the basis involves wealth and abundance. The intention means that, from any of the three poisons, the basis is identified through the motivation that aims to acquire that for oneself. The activity occurs by obsessively hoping to acquire the wealth or abundance of another person and, through attachment to that wealth, doing whatever it takes through inappropriate means such as stealing or robbing to satisfy the desire. The final result occurs when there is the wish to personally acquire the wanted things.

In order for craving to be complete, five factors are necessary as follows: a strong desire toward personal wealth and abundance, obsession toward the accumulation of further wealth and abundance, a desirous mind that notes the details and hopes to experience the wealth and superior possessions of others, a coveting mind that must acquire whatever good things others possess for oneself, and dwelling in a state of mind that is unable to feel a sense of shame or awareness of negativity because of being overwhelmed by craving.

Ninth is ill will, as the quote continues:

> Ill will means having aversion toward sentient beings.

Thus, as taught, the basis involves anyone that there is a sense of aversion toward. The intention is to identify [this person] and, motivated by any of the three poisons, to harbor the wish to harm them by even physically beating and so forth. Hoping that this object would either be killed, imprisoned, or that their wealth would diminish and such thoughts, the activity involves obsessively wishing harm upon them. The final result involves the decision to cause harm.

For this, the five factors are also necessary: an aggressive mind that fixates and concretizes the causes for bringing harm, a mind that cannot tolerate not harming others, a mind that constantly relives any inappropriate circumstances and holds grudges based on rage, a coveting mind that wishes to kill or beat, and a mind that is controlled by shamelessness and an inability to recognize faults.

Tenth, wrong view is as the quote continues:

> Wrong view considers the view of virtue and nonvirtue to be nonexistent.

Thus, the basis is the existence of virtue and nonvirtue. The intention is to disparage what that means [i.e., virtue versus nonvirtue]. Considering one's side to be right, there is the desire to disparage and belittle with any of the three passions. The activity involves placing mental effort toward that goal, and the final result involves that determination.

Among the ten nonvirtues, wrong view amounts to nihilism. For that, there are four: disparaging the root cause [for virtue versus nonvirtue] by claiming there are no positive or negative deeds, disparaging the result by claiming there is no maturity, disparaging the fact that there are previous and future lifetimes by saying they do not exist, and actually disparaging arhats by claiming that they do not exist.

Concerning this, there are also the five factors, namely, mental delusion that cannot comprehend the way things actually exist; a mind that enjoys negativity and cruelty; a mind that obsessively holds to incorrect reasoning concerning the nature of things; a neutral mind that disparages positive deeds, generosity, or offerings; and a mind that is overwhelmed by wrong view, shamelessness, and not knowing the results of negative deeds. These are the five. If these five are incomplete, then [wrong view] will not occur.

The weightiest negative karmic results are as stated in the *Advice from a Spiritual Friend*:

> The karma of being constantly obsessed and lacking any antidote or emphasis on positive qualities—these nonvirtues and virtues involve five important factors.

Thus, the term "constantly" refers to always engaging, meaning the specific activity. "Obsessive behavior" refers to the intensity of the motivation as the specific intention. Whether virtue or nonvirtue, disbelieving that either one has the opposite is the specific factor of lacking any antidote. Benefiting or harming one's parents or those who teach the dharma is the specific basis. Benefiting or harming the guru and Triple Gem and so forth is the specific basis of emphasizing qualities. Given that the results from these factors are definitively significant, they are referred to as "important".

Furthermore, the way the weighty nature of the path of these ten karmas affects the seven of body and speech is that the first [i.e., killing] is the weightiest and the subsequent nonvirtues' weight gradually decreases in comparison. Concerning the three of the mind, the final one [i.e., wrong view] is the weightiest, whereas the preceding are lighter. In addition, there is the consideration of activities that occur based on the strength of the passions, believing that to be qualified, rejoicing in the final act, holding this in the mind for an extended period of time, and the involvement of benevolent objects such as parents and so forth.

3.2.1.1.2.2.4.2.1.1.2 Explanation of the Results

Second, the result of [karma] is fourfold: the ripening result, the result in accord with the cause, the conditioning result, and the proliferating result. First, the ripening result is as stated in *Resting the Mind in Repose*:

> The weakest ripening result of the ten nonvirtues is rebirth as an animal, the middling is as a preta, and the weightiest is the suffering of the hells.

Thus, "weightiest" means karma accumulated through the strength of the three poisons so rebirth is taken in the hells. "Middling" indicates the pretas, and the "weakest" means as an animal. In *Sūtra on Close Placement of Mindfulness*, it states:

> The weakest of the ripening karmas is to take rebirth as an animal, the middling is as a preta, and the weightiest is rebirth in the hells.

Thus, it is as taught.

For the second, there are two: the result that is in accord with the cause and the experience in accord with the cause.

First, it states in *Resting the Mind in Repose*:

> Among the two that are in accord with the cause, it is taught that whatever is done brings the result of rebirth that is in accord with that and action that is similar to that cause.

Thus, in this life whatever nonvirtue has been accumulated, such as killing, carries over to the subsequent life; and that individual will delight in those same tendencies and actions. In the *One-Hundred Verses on Karma*,[a] it states:

> Those who engage and familiarize with nonvirtue will in the future life take rebirth that relies on nonvirtue, engages with nonvirtue, and pursues further nonvirtue.

Thus, it is as taught.

Second, the experience in accord with the cause is as the *One-Hundred Verses* continues:

> One day—even if rebirth is taken as a deva or a human—because of having previously taken others' lives, that person will suffer a short life with many illnesses. Having stolen, such individuals will be preoccupied with acquiring things that will become their adversary. Those who have committed sexual misconduct will, in their future life, have an unpleasant marriage and lose their spouse to others. Those who have told lies will be disparaged by many and deceived by others. Those who have slandered will have negative and unharmonious associates. Having spoken harshly, in the next life speech will be offensive and a source for unrest and turmoil. Having gossiped, in the next life, words will lack value and others will fail to trust or listen to one's speech. Through craving, there will be great desire that cannot be fulfilled. Through ill will, one will have no interest to be of benefit to others, and all actions will become a source of harm. Having wrong view, views will be negative and full of pretense.

[a] *ley gyapa* (*las brgya pa, karmashatakusūtra*)

Thus, as taught, most of this quotation is relatively easy to comprehend. However, saying "become their adversary" means to be in accord with the enemy, and saying "lose their spouse to others" means—whether male or female—their spouse will commit sexual misconduct by being with another partner. Saying "disparaged by many" means others will disparage that person, and saying "unrest and turmoil" means whatever they say will be offensive to others and become cause for turmoil. Saying "words will lack value" means others will not believe what is said. And saying "fail to trust or listen to one's speech" means that, whatever is said, others will have little or no confidence and speech will leave no impact, so eventually others will lose confidence. Saying "no interest to be of benefit to others" and "all actions will become a source of harm" means that there will be no way to benefit others and that rebirth will, in fact, only bring harm to others.

Third, that the dominant result[a] matures as the environment is stated in *Resting the Mind in Repose*:

> Having taken lives, the environment [of one's rebirth] will lack splendor; [and] the medicinal trees, harvests, flowers, water, and the like will lack potential and be tough to digest, even posing a threat to health. Having stolen, fruits and crops will not mature, and rebirth will be taken in lands where droughts weaken the environment and where hailstorms and famine are commonplace.
>
> Having committed sexual misconduct, rebirth will be in loathsome, filthy, foul-smelling, murky mires and around displeasing steep ravines. Having told lies, there will be disharmony and fear in the environment where one is born; the economy will be unstable; and others will be deceptive. Having slandered, rebirth will occur in environments that are hard to move around in, rough terrains, parched places like deserts, with drought-ridden canyons that are disagreeable in many ways.
>
> Having used harsh speech, one will be reborn in an environment where fallen trees and standing trunks abound, as well as thorny underbrush, dust, filth, and crops that are poisonous and coarse, including salt flats. Having gossiped, rebirth will occur in places where crops bear no harvest and seasons are reversed, the inhabitants are transitory, and the places uninhabited. Through craving, rebirth will occur in places where there are few harvestable crops, an abundance of husks, and where seasons and weather were once excellent but have since undergone change. Through ill will, rebirth will occur in places where fruits and harvests are hot and bitter to the taste. There will be many difficult circumstances and upheavals with rulers, dictators, thieves, wild creatures, and snakes.

[a] *dag po'i dre bu* (*bdag po'i 'bras bu*)

> Through wrong view, the environment of rebirth will lack natural resources, such as precious metals and gems, and there will be few fruits of harvest. There will be a lack of support or protection as well.

As taught, saying that "the environment will lack splendor" means that the land will lack richness. "Unstable abundance" refers to having unstable wealth. "Places with steep ravines" refers to deep valleys or unattractive basins. "Salt flats" means land completely covered and permeated with salt. "Reversal of the seasons" means that summer becomes winter and vice versa, so the natural timing is disturbed.

Fourth, the result of human effort [that produces a proliferating effect][a] is as the quote continues:

> The proliferating effect of nonvirtue produced through human effort means that whatever has been accumulated will proliferate and turn into suffering.[109]

With karma such as that, if there is no remedial antidote, this will continue to increase as mentioned in the *Sūtra on Close Placement of Mindfulness*:

> A deluded individual who accumulates negativity will continue to increase upon their negative karma so that it turns into great suffering.

Thus, saying "a deluded individual" means not knowing the result of cause and effect so not relying upon remorseful confession.

3.2.1.1.2.2.4.2.1.2 Description of Virtuous Causes and Results

Second, concerning the result of positive virtue, there are two: the path of karma and the result. First, there are the ten virtues, such as abandoning killing and the rest. This is having a virtuous mind that identifies the faults of killing coupled with the perfectly pure commitment to abstain from this, as well as the physical karma of the resultant state of abstinence. The same applies with stealing and sexual misconduct. This sequence also relates to the four of the speech and the three of the mind, with the distinction being how this applies to the karma of speech and the karma of the mind.

The basis, intention, activity, and final result are to be applied like before. For example, by abandoning the karmic path of killing: then from the perspective of recognizing this free from attachment, aggression, or delusion—these

[a] *kye bu ched pa'i dre bu* (*skyes bu byed pa'i 'bras bu*)

three—the basis would be a living being, the intention would be to not kill, the activity would be to maintain the vow not to kill, and the final result, the state of perfectly pure abstinence. The other [virtues] are to be understood accordingly.

Second, for the result [of virtue], there are four as before. First, the fully ripening result is that, through the gradual ripening of the lesser, middling, and greater virtuous deeds, rebirth as a human, desire-realm god, or a god in the two higher states progressively occurs.

The result in accord with the cause is, in that rebirth, there will be disdain for killing; and the benefits of a long and healthy life will be enjoyed. The dominant result is to take rebirth in a prosperous land where food and drink are nutritious and medicines potent. The proliferating result means that virtue continues to increase, and the results are the reverse of the nonvirtues. This applies to the remaining virtues.

3.2.1.1.2.2.4.2.2 Brief Discussion About the Importance of Karmic Distinctions

Second, to briefly explain the divisions of karma—from the perspective of the potential being greater or less, there are two: the certain experience of the results of karma and the uncertain experience. The Abhidharma explains:

> Strong passions and those that are extreme, the field of qualities and continuity, whatever has occurred, such as killing parents, will be definitive.

Thus, the definitive experience of the karmic result occurs when, from the perspective of intention, nonvirtue is accumulated through intense passion and virtue is accumulated through strong faith. Otherwise, although the passions and strong faith may not be intense, the continuous accumulation of virtue is from the perspective of the actual deed. When motivation is not strong and there is a lack of continuity, still benefit and harm will be directed toward the field of qualities such as the Triple Gem and others. This includes deeds such as karma accumulated through killing one's parents.

Although the intention may be that a deed will accumulate merit, if that turns into a heinous crime, the degree of karma becomes based on the strength of the object. In this way, whether virtuous or nonvirtuous karma: since it is certain that the results will be experienced, this is called "the experience of karma that is certain". Aside from that [category], other accumulations of karma that are less weighty are indeterminate.

Another category of the experience of karma that is certain involves karma that occurs, is accumulated, and brought to completion. Karma that occurs but is not accumulated brings an uncertain resultant experience. The difference between that and karma that is accumulated would be karma that occurs in dreams, unknowingly, unintentionally, based on forgetfulness, with remorse, and so forth. Although the preparation and final result are complete, the actual activity still remains incomplete.

For example, if the desire to kill someone is present along with the thought of taking pleasure in committing that deed, then—although those two factors are both complete—if the actual act of killing does not occur, the karma is still accumulated although it did not actually occur. When the preparation, actual deed, and final result—all three—are complete, it is the completion of karma that both occurs and is accumulated. Because personal desire is lacking, if one ends up killing against one's wishes, that is karma that occurs but is not accumulated. Although the ill intent arises, if it is instantly overcome by the antidote as well as having no motivation to kill and no preparation to do so, then—like walking and killing bugs underfoot inadvertently—it is said that this karma is incomplete by means of both action and accumulation.

In brief, if karma occurs with pleasure, then both the action and accumulation are complete. If karmic accumulation occurs against one's will, then although having happened, the accumulation remains incomplete. Although wanting to do something, if one is unable to do so, then the accumulation occurs even though the karma did not actually occur. Hence, when it comes to nonvirtue, one should take care to initially disengage the mind. Even if karma is accumulated through intention, one should not involve the body and speech. If perhaps both action and accumulation are complete, then if one immediately feels remorse and confesses, that karma will not be accumulated and instead will fall into the category of the experience of uncertain karma. Hence, one must train in these ways.

Otherwise—according to the wisdom intent of the sūtras and shāstras—by dreaming that one kills a human being and upon awakening to think "that was a good dream", to rejoice that this deed occurred actually implicates it to become both the completion of the deed and the accumulation. The way to understand these terms is that the meaning of "accumulation" is from the perspective of the motivation that intends to do something. Saying "the action or deed" means from the perspective of engaging in the preparation.

In short, both the completion of karma occurring, including the accumulation, and karma accumulated without the action are the certain experience of karma; whereas karma occurring without accumulation is the uncertain experience of karma. Furthermore, the experience of karma that occurs in the future life can be applied to any of the five heinous nonvirtues. The five heinous crimes as taught in the Abhidharma are to kill one's father, mother, or an arhat; to slander the sangha; and with a harmful intent, to draw the blood of a buddha. Four of them are straightforward; however, mentioning slandering the sangha refers to causing a schism in the sangha involving as many as two groups of four who are affected by one's words.

Concerning that, this means the perpetrator is attempting to divide the sangha into two separate groups based upon belief or disbelief in the Buddha's teachings. The perpetrator would hold beliefs that are contrary to the Buddha and try to convince one faction to join his position that is at odds with the other side. Those who fail to follow suit are considered contrary since they still follow the Buddha's teaching.

For example, previously during the lifetime of the Buddha, the one named Devadatta tried to compete with the Buddha. As stated in the Vinaya: "... [not partaking of] milk, meat, and salt, clothes, and abiding in isolation ..." Thus, just as the vows were given, [according to Devadatta] his followers were required to give up milk, meat, and salt, as well as wearing clothes that were manufactured, and required to abide in temples even while in the cities. These were the five basic modes of conduct or training. Kokalika, Khandadracha, Gyatsochin,[a] and others were ordered to hold these vows. Other sangha members took the direction of the Buddha's teachings, so there came to be a schism among the sangha. According to the doctrine of our buddha, there is no one who accumulated heinous nonvirtue through slander quite like Devadatta.[110] If this kind of schism occurs, then one must suffer in the lowest hell realm for an intermediate kalpa.

As for the remaining heinous crimes, although it is certain that rebirth will occur in the lower hell realms, it is still uncertain as to whether that rebirth will solely occur in the lowest hell of all. Even these days, if one causes a schism in the sangha, the negative repercussions are extremely weighty; yet the weight of such deeds would not even qualify as a schism when compared to that occurring among the close inner circle of Buddha's actual disciples.

In the commentary to the *Guhyasamāja Tantra* called *Illuminating Lamp*,[b] it states:

> The five heinous crimes are, along with the three types of killing, the rejection of the precious dharma, and the destruction of an image of the Buddha.

Thus, saying "rejection of the precious dharma" means to claim that the perfectly pure speech of the Buddha is not authentic. This is mentioned in the sūtra *King of Samādhi*:

[a] *ko ka li ka, khan da dra bya,* and *rgya mtsho byin*

[b] *drel pa dron sal* (*'grel pa sgron gsal, pradīpodyotananāmaṭīkā*); Chandrakīrti

> To compare destroying every stūpa that exists in Jambudvīpa to the rejection of the Buddha's sūtras, the sin for the latter is surpassing. To compare the killing of as many arhats as there are grains of sand at the banks of the river Gaṅgā to the rejection of the Buddha's sūtras, the sins of the latter are surpassing.

Thus, it is as taught. The *Uttaratantra* states:

> Whoever relies upon negative companions that harbor negative thoughts toward the Buddha, compared to those who engage in horrific actions, such as slaying parents or arhats and causing a schism among the sangha community: even in those latter cases, if the dharmatā nature is brought to mind, it is still possible to be liberated from such sins. Yet for those whose minds harbor aggressive hatred toward dharma, how can there ever be freedom?

Thus, the riveting faults derived from this negative karma are mentioned throughout the sūtras and the shāstras. Saying "causing a schism among the sangha community" means to divide the sangha. Saying "considering the dharmatā nature" means to have remorse for negative karmic accumulations and to bring the meaning of dharma to mind as taught by the victorious ones. If so, then there will be confession coupled with the vow not to repeat such deeds, hence bringing about purification.

The five proximate negativities that are close to the five heinous crimes are as follows. Committing sexual misconduct with one's own parents who are arhats; killing a definitively abiding bodhisattva who has accumulated merit over three countless eons and is bound to accomplish the excellent signs and marks so as to certainly awaken after one-hundred eons;[111] killing an ārya who is not a foe destroyer; stealing the wealth of the sangha that is offered; and destroying the supports of enlightened body, speech, and mind with a negative mind are the five. These five are called proximate heinous crimes because they are similar to the order of the five [principal] heinous, which are to kill one's mother, father, or arhat, create a schism in the sangha, and with a negative mind to draw the blood of a tathāgata. Through these negativities, there can only be rebirth in the hells. Nevertheless, even though the aspects of these [five] are similar to the five heinous crimes, there is a difference in terms of the weightiness of the ripening effect.

Concerning this, saying "stealing or embezzling offerings that belong to the sangha" means to take or embezzle any foodstuff that is intended for the sangha to eat. By doing so, the effect is to fall into the lowest hells. As for other material things that belong to the sangha: it is taught that, if stolen, the perpetrator will take rebirth in the hell realms of great darkness that encircle the lowest hell.

Generally, concerning that which is designated for the Triple Gem: even if a small article is stolen, the ripening effects become significant. In particular, when it comes to articles that are meant for the buddhas and bodhisattvas: if they are replaced and offered back, then purification is possible. Conversely, if the possessions of the sangha are stolen: then until the ripening effect is experienced, there will be no purification due to the weightiness. Hence, it is taught that great care should be taken.

Furthermore, from the perspective of the object and intention: whether the karma is potent virtue or nonvirtue, three levels of karma are involved. They are the karma that is immediately experienced in one's present life, the karma that is certain to be experienced in the life that follows such as the heinous crimes, and the karma that will eventually be experienced sometime after three successive lifetimes. In addition, from the perspective of ripening, there is karma based on merit that propels one into happy states of existence within the desire realm, the karma that lacks merit and propels one into the lower realms, and the unmoving karma that propels one into the higher realms.

Also, through the basis, intention, activity, and final result, the nonvirtue that is accumulated based on nonvirtue will bring extremely negative results. Given this always ripens as unwholesome karma, it is also referred to as karma that is totally unwholesome. From the basis on through to the final result, the accumulation of virtue that involves the virtue of the three realms ripens as that which is good, so it is wholesome virtue. It, too, is referred to as being totally wholesome. Karma that involves both is twofold, based on the intention being negative with activity that is positive, similar to the ṛṣhi Sem Ngen.[a] He offered a banquet to the sangha that resulted in his rebirth in the nāga realm due to his negative intention based on a perverted prayer that they all be reborn in a place where there was not even any grass. Hence, he himself was reborn in such a place.

Although this kind of karma is positive by nature, the aspect of the ripening result becomes negative. The result of both positive and negative karma depends upon a positive or negative mental attitude. Furthermore, similar [mixed] karma is accumulated by giving rise to aggressive hatred in order to take a life and then expressing generosity in order to be able to carry that out. There can be many other examples for this. There is also the example of Dedpon Nyingje Chenpö[b] who killed Mi Nag Düng Tüng Chen.[c] His action [of killing] was unwholesome,

[a] *sems ngan*; Negative Mind

[b] *ded dpon snying rje chen pos*; Captain of Great Compassion

[c] *mi nag mdung thung can*; Criminal with a Short Spear, or Dark-Robed One

whereas his intention was pure. The nature of this karma is negative, whereas the aspect of the result is positive.

Virtuous karma that is motivated by great compassion or bodhichitta is considered to be immaculate virtuous karma since it does not propel one into existence but rather becomes the cause for perfect awakening. Unlike that, other virtuous karma brings rebirth in existence, so it is contaminated virtuous karma. The virtue that sustains the prajñā of realizing the meaning of selflessness is the cause for attaining liberation, so it is concurrent with liberation. These are three further distinctions. In *Resting the Mind in Repose*, it states:

> Concurrent with liberation and so forth is the immaculate cause.

In the Madhyamaka's *Jewel Garland*, it states:

> Compassion as the essence of emptiness is the only way to attain awakening.

Thus, and so forth, this is the mode of immaculate [virtue], and the opposite is revealed as contaminated virtue. Hence, the way to recognize the karma of immaculate virtue is explained according to the commentary itself.

Explanations presented here concerning immaculate karma are different from those found in other important texts. Nevertheless, there is no contradiction as this description is a unique upadesha concurrent with this meaning, and it is acceptable from the perspective of the distinctions concerning the law of cause and result and the activity of acceptance and rejection. Generally, there are many distinctions concerning karma; however, here—aside from the distinctions concerning the ripening of wholesome virtuous karma that are found in the commentary—other descriptions have not been included.

From the onset, the descriptions concerning karmic cause and result need to be known. The great, unrivaled, glorious master Atisha said that, just because the descriptions of karmic cause and result are extremely subtle, it is unacceptable to take that for granted. By initially examining one's motivation, it is necessary to engage in the process of acceptance and rejection with tremendous care. When the mind is negative due to being overcome by the three poisons, nonvirtue ensues. The reverse of that is virtue, as it states in the Madhyamaka's *Jewel Garland*:

> When karma is generated by the three—desire, anger, and delusion—there is nonvirtue. On the other hand, karma generated without attachment, aggression, or delusion will bring virtue.

Hence, it is as taught. For example, if the root of a plant is poisonous, then the sprout and the stem will follow suit. If the root is medicinal, then the sprout and such will be likewise. Accordingly, engaging in karma by acceptance and rejection through the activities of the three doors is to engage in virtuous dharma that liberates lower rebirth and brings the attainment of higher states. The quote continues:

> Abandoning nonvirtue in a heartfelt way through body, speech, and mind and always engaging with virtue are referred to as the three aspects of dharma. Through such dharma, there will be liberation from the hells, preta realm, and animal realm; and the happiness, glory, and success of humans or gods will be acquired.

So, it is as taught. Those who ignore karmic results by claiming to have a higher view concerning emptiness will state that karmic cause and result amounts to the doctrine of a lesser pursuit, and that only the definitive truth need be realized. Such an approach is extremely vile.

In the words of the Lord of the Victors, Longchenpa:

> Those who ignore or belittle karmic cause and result are followers of the nihilist heretics. Those who base their confidence only upon the view of emptiness will plunge lower and lower toward the extreme view of nihilism. Those who catapult into this negative direction will never find freedom from the lower states of existence and will be far removed from the higher realms. They say that doctrines emphasizing conventional meanings such as cause and result, compassion, and meritorious accumulations will not bring buddhahood, whereas the uncontrived definitive meaning that resembles the sky is what the great yogis must meditate upon. Among nihilistic views, that is the epitome; and among lower paths, that is the lowest of all. How amazing to claim that, by blocking the cause, a result can be accomplished.

Thus, it is as taught. The Tibetan term *lo*[112] indicates something being extremely unacceptable. Blocking the cause and expecting to gain a result without accomplishing anything is extremely laughable and ludicrous; hence, it is as stated in the *King of Samādhi*:

> Suppose the moon and stars were to fall from the sky, the mountains and buildings collapse, or even if the element sky were to assume a different aspect, still, the words that you [i.e., the Buddha] have spoken will be never become false.

Thus, as taught, since the teachings that have been spoken by our teacher are undeceiving, just as he taught, one must believe in the law of karmic cause and result.

3.2.1.1.2.2.4.3 Way of Confessing and Vow to Abstain from Nonvirtue

Third, the way of confessing and taking the vow to abstain from nonvirtuous karma is as follows. In the *Bodhicharyāvatāra*, it states:

> Since suffering is due to nonvirtue, that alone should be pondered both day and night with the thought, "How can I set myself free from this?"

Thus, as taught, knowing that suffering arises based on nonvirtuous karma, both day and night one must ponder the methods that will liberate this process. Through the four remedial powers, one must confess and diligently vow to abstain from [negativity].

Concerning this, it mentions in the *Sūtra that Reveals the Four Dharmas*:[a]

> O Maitreya! If the great bodhisattvas possess the four dharmas, then even any accumulation of nonvirtue will be suppressed through the splendor [of the four]. What are the four? They are to feel remorse concerning negative deeds, application of the antidote, the power of reversing negativity, and the power of the support. Remorse for negative deeds means feeling a sense of constant regret toward nonvirtuous deeds. The application of the antidote means that, although nonvirtuous karma has been accumulated, virtuous karma is applied with tremendous fortitude. The power that reverses negativity means that, by purely taking the vow, one accomplishes a stable commitment. The power of the support is to take refuge in the buddha, dharma, and sangha and to never allow the bodhichitta to be lost.
>
> O Maitreya! In reliance upon these powers, negativity will no longer have the strength to suppress [virtue]. If great bodhisattvas possess these four dharmas, all accumulated negativity will be fully suppressed.

Thus, as taught, the power of remorse is the cultivation of intense remorse toward previously accumulated negativity similar to having ingested poison. The fact that, at present, there is a lack of strong remorse is due to not considering the results of negativity. The method of remorse involves constantly thinking that

[a] *chö zhi ten pa'i do* (*chos bzhi bstan pa'i mdo, caturdharmanirdesha*)

one must experience the undeniable results of great suffering that ensue from even seemingly insignificant accumulations of nonvirtue.

In the *Vase of Instructions*,[a] it states:

> If one were to partake of poison, just what do you think would be the outcome?

Like that, if three people ingested poison together and if one died, one became sick, and the other was about to fall ill, what would be the level of regret in that last person's mind? That is the level of regret we need to give rise to. By ingesting poison, the worst thing that could happen is to lose one's life; but when it comes to nonvirtue, one will fall into lower realms in the future life to experience infinite types of suffering. That is why the repercussions that arise from accumulating nonvirtue surpass those of ingesting poison. Hence, this first power is crucial; for if cultivated, the remaining powers will occur as a matter of course.

Accomplishing any virtue as the remedial force for nonvirtue is the power of the application of the antidote; and for this, there are six categories as mentioned in the *Collections of Advice*[b] as taught by Shāntideva:

> Rely upon the profound sūtras, aspire toward realizing emptiness, recite mantras, rely upon images of kāyas, make offerings, and rely upon the names of [the buddhas].

The first involves reading the words found in the classes of Sūtra, such as the prajñāpāramitā and so forth, memorizing the content, and reciting the scriptures, as well as internalizing both words and their meanings. Second, "aspiring toward realizing emptiness" means meditating upon the meaning of selflessness. Third, "relying upon mantra recitation" means reciting key mantras, such as the one-hundred syllable mantra, as well as the mantra of Buddha Akṣhobhya,[c] the dhāraṇīs of the stainless Ushnika Vijayi,[d] and the like. If one recites the one-hundred syllables of the tathāgatas according to sādhana practice, this is an extremely powerful way to purify negative karma. Especially by meditating upon glorious Vajrasattva above the crown of one's head, the one-hundred syllable mantra is then to be recited.

[a] *be'u büm* (*be'u bum*); teachings on the Khadampa tradition's *Stages of the Path* composed by Dolpa Sherab Gyatso

[b] *lab tü* (*bslab btus, shikṣāsamuccaya*); Shāntideva

[c] Mitrukpa (*mi 'khrugs pa*); buddha of the Vajra Family and eastern direction

[d] *tsüg tor* (*gtsug tor*); Crown Protuberance

In the *Essential Ornament*,[a] it states:

> The sole kāya of all the buddhas, Vajrasattva, is perfectly brought to mind abiding at the center of a white lotus and moon, adorned with vajra and bell. According to the sādhana for the one-hundred syllable mantra, to recite this twenty-one times daily ensures that all downfalls will be transformed through the blessings. It is said that negativity will no longer increase. This must even be practiced in between sessions. If one-hundred thousand recitations occur, perfect purification will be assured.

Thus, the *Stainless Confession Tantra*[b] explains that if recited twenty-one times each day the increase of negativity will discontinue; if recited one-hundred thousand times, all downfalls will be purified from the root; if one-hundred and eight times daily, then the downfalls and broken commitments of that very day will be purified.

Furthermore, in the *Tantra Revealing the Nature*,[c] it states:

> By reciting the one-hundred syllable mantra, the downfalls associated with the five heinous crimes, abandonment of dharma, and loss of morality will not only be purified, supreme siddhis will be attained. Just as it is taught that peaceful, extensive, magnetizing, and wrathful enlightened deeds will be accomplished, the benefits that occur will be exceedingly great.

Saying "to recite according to the sādhana" means to practice according to upadesha or sādhana that indicates the manner of recitation. Just as the manner of meditating and reciting Vajrasattva is mentioned within the ten sections of our preliminary practices, it is sufficient to meditate that Vajrasattva is upon one's crown with the mantric syllables arranged in his heart while maintaining the visualization of the descent and purification through ambrosia. Although not included in this commentary, it is excellent to insert this practice by extracting it from other sources.

Through this recitation, the way negativity and obstructions are eradicated is as stated in the *Dialogue with Subāhu*:[d]

[a] *nyingpo gyen* (*snying po rgyan*)
[b] *drimed shak gyü* (*dri med bshags rgyud*)
[c] *de nyid nangwa'i gyü* (*de nyid snang ba'i rgyud*)
[d] *püng zang gi zhü pa'i do* (*dpung bzang gis zhus pa'i mdo, subāhuparipṛcchānāmatantra*)

> Just as the flames of a forest fire in early spring will fully incinerate everything, including all obscurity of underbrush—with firelike recitation and morality like the wind that ignites it, the flames of great diligence will fully incinerate negativity. Just as, when the sun's rays strike the peaks of a snowy range, the brilliance is overwhelming and the snow begins to melt—by the penetration of the mantra's sun rays of morality, no matter how much negativity there may be, it will all be exhausted. Just as how a candle fully illuminates darkness—the darkness of negative accumulation over many lifetimes is swiftly dispelled by the candle of mantra recitation.

Thus, it is as taught. Concerning this, until there are indications of purification, one must continue the recitation. Indications of success are said to be dreams that one is vomiting foul food, drinking yogurt, milk, and so forth; vomiting; witnessing the rising of the sun and the moon; flying through space; the body or clothing catching on fire; the ability to defeat a buffalo or a black-robed person; seeing ordained male and female practitioners; climbing a sandalwood or fruit-bearing tree; seeing a tree that produces white fluid; mounting an elephant or a magnificent horse; ascending a high mountain or a lion throne; entering a celestial palace; or listening to dharma instructions.

Concerning these indications, if such dreams occur while one is engaged in this purification of negativity, then they are not just random dreams but actual indications of purification. The primary signs are if passions begin to decrease and faith and confidence in the guru, Triple Gem, and dharma increases so that the mind becomes more inclined toward dharma. These signs are authentic. Otherwise, it is said that there can be the danger of deception through dreams and so forth; while, nevertheless, it is said that magical manifestations are abundant.

Fourth, "reliance upon images" means, rather than pursuing fame and fortune for this life, one creates images out of devotion. Fifth, "reliance upon offerings" means to make varieties of offerings to the buddhas and to their stūpas. Sixth, "relying upon names" means to hear the names of the buddhas and great bodhisattvas just as found in the sūtra called *Three Heaps*[a] that is well known for confession of downfalls by reciting the names of the thirty tathāgatas, the names of the Medicine Buddha and seven tathāgatas, and in particular, the names of the peaceful and wrathful deities.

Generally, due to the great strength of these recitations, not only will all negative downfalls be purified, in particular all faults associated with broken samaya of Secret Mantra will be repaired. If the recitation is extensive, then one may use the section on prostrations found within the *Stainless Confession Tantra.*

[a] *püng po süm pa'i do* (*phung po gsum pa mdo, āryatriskandhakanāmamahāyānasūtra*)

Otherwise, it is acceptable to recite the verses that read, "Perfectly pure phenomena are spontaneously present from the beginning" and so forth as taken from the concise confession of the peaceful and wrathful. The blessings for this are extremely abundant. Even though in the sūtra of the *Three Heaps* the key points of the four remedial powers are complete, learned ones have said that it is best to recite the words of confession taken from the *Sūtra of Sacred Golden Light*.[a,113]

Thinking that—even at the cost of life itself—this negativity must never be repeated is the perfectly correct vow that amounts to the power of reversal from negativity. Even if one is unable to keep this vow: by thinking to keep it for the duration of a month or for a certain number of days, one must single-pointedly pray to be able to purely maintain the vows. Thinking "if only I could keep this vow" brings this to mind repeatedly so that the habit for the mind to sustain that direction will be formed. Trying one's best is necessary. Nevertheless, if the first power is present, then the mind's commitment to keep the vow will occur as a matter of course.

According to the speech of fully qualified scholars, the power of the support is to go for refuge and cultivate bodhichitta. In this way, through the first power, any increase of negativity is arrested and the resultant experience in accord with the cause[b] is purified. Through the second power, the negativity is completely uprooted, purifying the fully ripening result. Through the third power, the continuity of negativity will be interrupted; and the result of the cause in accord with activity[c] will be purified. Through the fourth power, given that negativity is now weakened, the result itself will be purified.

Concerning all of this, although the victorious ones have taught myriad ways to purify negativity, the consummation of all antidotes occurs through the four remedial powers. The way to practice this is mentioned in the selected writings of the great Tsongkhapa, and it is convenient to practice according to that. Hence, having remorseful regret such as this means that, no matter how strong the previous negative obscurations have been, in the future they will all become perfectly purified. It states in the *Advice from a Spiritual Friend*:

> Whoever has been careless in the past will become conscientious in the future. Like the moon free of clouds, that individual will become magnificent like Ānanda, Aṅgulimāla, Ajātashatru, and Shaṅkara.[d,114]

[a] *ser öd dam pa'i do* (*gser 'od dam pa'i mdo, āryasuvarṇaprabhāsottamasūtrendrarājanāmamahāyānasūtra*)

[b] *nyong wa gyu tün* (*myong ba rgyu mthun*)

[c] *ched pa gyu tün* (*byed pa rgyu mthun*)

[d] Kungawo, Sortreng, Tongden, and Deched (*kun dga' bo*, *sor phreng*, *mthong ldan*, and *bde byed*)

Thus, it is as taught.

Whoever has been carelessly overpowered by passions in the past—if shown by a spiritual guide the path of what to accept and reject—will later become conscientious and majestic like the moon free from clouds. Take the examples of the desirous Ānanda, the story of the youth Aṅgulimāla also known as Sor Mo'i Trengwa[a] who murdered one less than one-thousand individuals, the story of Ajātashatru otherwise known as Makyedra who killed his own father, the dharma king, and also Shaṅkara who committed the heinous crime of killing his own mother. Each of them later developed strong faith toward the Buddha; and by perfectly accomplishing his teachings, they were able to be set free from the result of their afflictions.

Knowing this, it is crucial to carefully incorporate how to accept and reject the law of karmic cause and result. In the [root terma] commentary, it states:

> These unerring instructions are revealed through the upadesha of Sūtra and Tantra concerning all aspects of accepting and rejecting the positive and negative aspects of karmic causes and results. Hence, this is the great chariot that leads to the citadel of the state of liberation.

Thus, it is as taught.

> For the result of positive and negative karma, happiness and suffering matures without denial.
> By applying what to accept and reject unerringly, such methods are the most sublime and beneficial for this and all future lifetimes.

Thus, these are the verses that summarize the section.

3.2.1.1.3 Refuge and Bodhichitta

This has two parts:

1 Refuge
2 Bodhichitta

Third is going for refuge and generating bodhichitta.

[a] Mi Düng War (*mi gdung bar*); Ancestor of the Humans; aka Sor Mo'i Trengwa (*sor mo'i phreng ba*); One with a Garland of Thumbs

3.2.1.1.3.1 Refuge

This has two parts:

1 General commentary on common refuge
2 Uncommon explanation on how to maintain the visualization

Among these two, refuge and bodhichitta, first [refuge] begins with:

> *Phet!*[a] To the primordial ground pure from the beginning, free from direction, Samantabhadrī; the intrinsic nature, pure within itself, Khachödma; and all-pervasive compassion evenly pervading as the kāya of the Wrathful Mother, Tröma—I go for refuge to actualize the consummate expanse of this wisdom mind.

As taught, according to the tradition of the supreme vehicle of Mahāsandhi, in the tantra *Reverberation of Sound*,[b] it states:

> The original ground abides as the triune wisdoms of the nature, intrinsic nature, and compassion.

Hence, "original ground" means the nature is empty, the intrinsic nature is lucid, and compassion is all-pervasive. Such is the nature itself of the triune wisdoms. This is also mentioned in the tantra *Self-Arising Awareness*:[c]

> The nature of this basic space is empty, the intrinsic nature is natural luminosity, and compassion is that which abides as the essence of awareness. Such is the basis for the arising of all enlightened qualities.

Thus, as taught, because the basic space of the ground free from all limitations of elaborations abides as the nature of emptiness, the nature is empty. That intrinsic nature is spontaneously present within the ground as the nature of kāyas and wisdoms. Given this is intrinsically luminous and unceasing, that is the lucid wisdom of the intrinsic nature. All-pervasive compassion abides as the essence of this awareness—indivisible appearances and emptiness. Although not appearing outwardly, this is designated as the aspect of the basis for the arising of all enlightened qualities. These aspects are, therefore, referred to as the three kāyas that abide within the ground as spontaneous presence.

[a] *phat*; pronounced "*pet*" or "*po'i*"
[b] *dra tal gyur* (*sgra thal 'gyur*)
[c] *rigpa rang shar* (*rig pa rang shar*)

In the *Precious Treasury of the Fundamental Nature*,[a] we are told:

> The self-awareness of the ground resembles a crystal orb. The empty aspect of that is the intrinsic nature of the dharmakāya, self-radiant luminosity is the sambhogakāya, and the basis of arising as an unceasing gateway is the nirmāṇakāya. Hence, in the ground of basic space, the three kāyas remain spontaneously present.

So, it is; and in the auto-commentary, it states:

> Empty awareness resembling a crystal is the dharmakāya, and the aspect of the five-colored light of lucid awareness is the sambhogakāya. The crystal's capacity to radiate externally but without doing so—remaining as the unceasing gateway for that arising—is the nirmāṇakāya. The three kāyas of the ground represent a single nature that is illuminated here through analogy.

In the *All-Creating Monarch*, it states:

> The trikāya essence of all the victorious ones is my intrinsic nature established as the uncontrived dharmakāya. My nature, uncreated, is the sambhogakāya; and my compassion is the manifest nirmāṇakāya—these three. This does not reveal a result that has been acquired elsewhere.

Thus, as taught, this is revealed through the term "creator" based on the aspect of being the basis for the origin of the entirety of saṃsāra and enlightenment. The self-appearing teacher of Tantra who represents the perfectly pure nature of the awakened mind as self-originating, clear-light wisdom is the Vajradhara of conventional meaning. Given that this awakened mind is the genuine Vajradhara, knowing that and saying "my" [in the quote] are crucial vajra words.

Concerning this, the distinctions based on three, such as the nature being empty and so forth, are as follows. That the intrinsic nature is uncontrived is based on primordially abiding as emptiness. Likewise, this reveals in a threefold way that the nature is uncontrived and luminous, as well as being the basis for the arising of manifest compassion. In addition, this does not reveal a result that has been acquired elsewhere, nor does it indicate how this abides primordially without effort. Based on that, here "intrinsic nature" represents emptiness, whereas "nature" corresponds to lucidity.

[a] *ney lük rinpoche'i dzöd* (*gnas lugs rin po che'i mdzod*); Longchen Rabjam

Generally, it is taught that the term "intrinsic nature" refers to emptiness and the term "nature" refers to the aspect of appearances. Nevertheless, throughout the tantras of Mahāsandhi, "emptiness" refers to the nature, whereas "lucidity" refers to the intrinsic nature. These two presentations are not contradictory, for it states in the auto-commentary of the *Precious Treasury of the Fundamental Nature*:

> The intrinsic nature as emptiness and the nature of lucidity are distinguished based upon the innate way of abiding and the essence of that. When the nature is empty and the intrinsic nature is lucid, that is distinguished based upon basic space and the empty essence of basic space. Ultimately, emptiness is the dharmakāya, lucidity is the sambhogakāya, and the manner of their arising as nirmāṇakāya remains the same.

Thus, it is taught. When mentioning "essence", one must understand that that corresponds to what reveals the qualities of the aspect of appearances that abide in an obscured manner as inconspicuous resultant qualities. Hence, here that which is referred to as being innate and basic space have the same meaning since the qualities of the essence that are inseparable with this basic space are called "qualities," or basic space.

Conversely, the appearances of that basic space are its essence, like ambrosia; for without these appearances, basic space alone would amount to skin that has no inner content. In that way, no qualities of the paths and results would ever be able to emerge. While arising from that ground, all pure and impure appearances still abide as the intrinsic nature of the trikāya. This is referred to as the trikāya's dynamic strength of the ground's presence. In the *Precious Treasury of the Fundamental Nature*, it states:

> Arising from that, even when the ground's presence emerges, the pure trikāyas are the self-appearing victors; and the impure appearances of the universe and inhabitants are empty by nature, lucid, and varied—these three. This is the manifestation of the dharmakāya, sambhogakāya, and the nirmāṇakāya—these three. The dynamic strength of this manifestation is the trikāya's appearance of the ground. Self-appearing spontaneous presence is not discovered elsewhere.

Hence, the pure trikāyas arising as the self-appearing wisdom of the victors themselves are the dharmakāya, the five families of the sambhogakāya, and the various manifestations of the nirmāṇakāya. Even the impure are inseparable emptiness and appearances; and through root causes and contributing circumstances, the various manifestations arise. This is posited as the trikāya, such as the nature being empty and so forth. Since everything is the self-radiance of the triune wisdoms of the ground, this shows how—except for externally appearing—nothing exists otherwise. From the three aspects of the ground, such as the nature being empty, purity gradually emerges.

The way of appearing as the three resultant kāyas is as follows. Given that the intrinsic nature of the ground is pure by virtue of its original empty nature, free as well from all temporary stains, this appears as the perfectly pure dharmakāya. This ultimately abides as the evenness of the inseparable nature of emptiness and awareness. From the perspective of conceptual designations, to abide as innate empty basic space like the sky is the kāya of the dharmatā or the kāya of the nature as it is. Inseparable with that, the wisdom aspect of this appearance is lucid and nonconceptual as wisdom dharmakāya. It states in the *All-Illuminating*:[a,115]

> In the space of inseparable dharmatā and dharmakāya, the radiance of wisdom is self-arising, self-appearing, and naturally lucid—lucidity and so forth that unceasingly appear. This nonconceptual clarity is wisdom dharmakāya.

Thus, as taught, the kāya of the dharmatā is its own fundamental nature that transcends all distinctions based upon relative elaborations. Aside from being indivisible like the sky, this nature is not established otherwise. Self-arising, there is no dependence upon effort. Self-occurring, appearances are free from stain as the radiance of naturally lucid wisdom and so forth. Hence, from this kāya of the dharmatā: although the nature seems to be differentiated, that is not the case. Abiding as self-radiance that is a mere unceasing lucidity, the nature of lucid wisdom is free from being nonconceptual and thereby referred to as "wisdom dharmakāya". From this lucid intrinsic nature, the sambhogakāya appears with the oceanic qualities of the major and minor marks in the following way. The quote continues:

> To itself, the primordial buddha self-appears as the sambhogakāya.

Thus, as taught, through qualities that are intrinsically self-lucid and self-appearing, the natural radiance manifests as the sambhogakāya. Saying "the primordial buddha" means that the basis for phenomena is intrinsic lucidity that exists primordially. From the wisdom of all-pervasive compassion, the various nirmāṇakāya manifestations emerge to tame in whatever ways are deemed necessary, as the quote continues:

> The compassionate nirmāṇakāya is free from the two limitations.

[a] *kun sal* (*kun gsal*)

Thus, from the dynamic strength of compassion, the appearance of the nirmāṇakāya is free from the two limitations. This too is the inseparable nature of appearances and emptiness, so it is free from the two limitations of eternalism and nihilism, while not abiding in either of the two limitations of existence or quiescence. That is because, if the nirmāṇakāya does not enact the welfare of others, then the continuity of benefiting others would cease and that would not be different from falling to the limitation of quiescence.

The *All-Creating Monarch* addresses this point:

> I, the All-Creating Monarch, am the nature of the three kāyas, abiding within nonconceptual evenness; the nature of the unelaborate dharmakāya. Miraculous birth that emerges from this intrinsic nature is the sambhogakāya that fulfills all desires. Compassion that enacts the welfare of those to tame in whatever way necessary is the nature of the nirmāṇakāya.

So, it is taught. Saying "I, the All-Creating Monarch, am the nature of the three kāyas" means that, from the perspective of appearances, this is nonconceptual freedom from duality. From the perspective of emptiness, to abide as the intrinsic nature of evenness is the nature of the unelaborate dharmakāya. This nature itself is the source for the emergence of the intrinsically lucid appearances of sambhogakāya that are ultimately unborn. Nevertheless, according to the relative way of emergence, this appears as though magical. Hence, the pure lands of the five families of the tathāgatas and all fully endowed qualities of the desirables, such as the teacher, retinue, and dharma, are the intrinsic nature that emerges as the sambhogakāya. Just as the compassionate nirmāṇakāya appears according to the perceptions of others, the limitless enactment of deeds for the welfare of those to be tamed is the nirmāṇakāya. That is how it is.

In this way, the practice of refuge involves precisely realizing the intrinsic nature of the trikāyas of the ground through prajñā and resting in that evenness with samādhi and single-pointed focus. Knowing the immediacy of self-awareness as the nature of the three kāyas is the tradition of the uncommon great secret. The *Treasury of Precious Qualities* states:

> The immediacy of knowing the nature of one's mind is resultant refuge.
> That is the exceptional feature of the vajra vehicles.

So, it is. The nature of one's mind realized as the innate trikāya wisdom is said to be the refuge of the tradition of resultant Vajrayāna. Therefore, it also states in the chöd called *Ḍākinīs' Laughter*:[a]

[a] *khandro'i ged gyang* (*mkha' 'gro'i bgad rgyangs*)

> This uncontrived self-occurring awareness is not seen as the nature of the objects of refuge. Due to that, those who have sunk into the ocean of suffering will go for refuge in the deities of the trikāya.

Thus, this refers to this nature as well. Not only that, all aspects of impure appearances of the ground are this self-radiance as well; so this phenomenal existence must be known to be the manifestation of the spontaneously present, primordially pure trikāyas. In the *Precious Treasury of the Fundamental Nature*, it refers to this:

> The spontaneously present trikāyas of all phenomena of saṃsāra and enlightenment are to be realized as the nature of the awakened mind [i.e., bodhichitta].

So, it is. This too arises as the play of enlightened body, speech, and mind as the *Treasury of the Dharmadhātu* tells us:

> All physical forms of the outer world and inner beings that appear are the ornaments of basic space arising as the manifestation of kāyas. All sounds that are heard, whatever they may be without exception, are the ornaments of basic space arising as the wheel of enlightened speech. Even inconceivable thought formations, movement, proliferations—as well as the nonconceptual—are ornaments of basic space arising as the wheel of enlightened mind.

It states in the auto-commentary *Treasury of Transmissions*:[a,116]

> All appearances within this awareness that involve the universe and inhabitants of phenomenal existence are dreamlike in their self-appearing and self-arising, like the nature of a water moon. All these reflections are the maṇḍala, or manifestation, of the kāyas of self-occurring wisdom. All sounds are the maṇḍala of enlightened speech, and all thoughts are merely arising as the great maṇḍala of enlightened mind's manifest nonconceptual ocean of wisdom.

Thus, just as taught, from the intrinsic nature of the trikāya space of the ground, the aspect of appearances, sound, and awareness arises. Ultimately, since this is the thoroughly pure manifestation of enlightened body, speech, and mind, that is the ornament. For instance, when a rainbow appears in the sky, this becomes

[a] *lung gi ter dzöd* (*lung gi gter mdzod*); Longchen Rabjam

an ornament [of the sky]. Even saying "wheel" means that this completely arises as that manifestation to the point of overcoming everything.

Concerning this, there are many supportive quotations not included here that exist throughout the tantras, such as the *All-Creating Monarch* and others, including upadeshas such as master Garab Dorje's introduction to *Encountering the Three Kāyas*.[a] Given that this meaning is such a profoundly secret key point, those details will not be included at this time. Through this key point about the perfection of the trikāya manifestations, all phenomena are known to be the pure play of enlightened body, speech, and mind.

In the *Treasury of the Dharmadhātu*, it states:

> There are no phenomena that are not perfected as the ornament of the three kāyas, so everything arises as the manifestation of enlightened body, speech, and mind.

So, it is as taught. If this key point is known, then—according to Mahāsandhi's own tradition—even during trekchö, phenomenal existence arises as pure; and during the generation stage, the practice of deity yoga is perfected.

These verses of refuge taken from the terma text indirectly reveal the way of visualizing the field of refuge that will be mentioned later on. Concerning this, whatever appears as the play of enlightened body, speech, and mind—the three vajra states—is pure self-radiance. This can only be ascertained through fervent regard while visualized in the aspect of the deities and field of refuge.

> Incapable of misleading others through the twisted words of jaded intellectuals, even though these designated sounds may not fill the mountains and valleys:
>
> By the arising of phenomenal existence as the play of purity, the children of the accomplished meditators of the Earlier School take great delight in this.

Thus, I composed this.[117]

Gaining certainty concerning these points, the next section is as follows. First,[118] by reciting *phet*, generally the reason the syllable *phet* is prominent throughout all recitations of chöd is as Machig points out:

> My spiritual tradition is comparable with the meaning of *phet*. *Pha* indicates the meaning of the pāramitās, and *tra* indicates the meaning of unsurpassed Secret Mantra. *Phet* is the combination of these two wrathful syllables; and by the mere recitation of the sound, lim-

[a] *ku süng tük tred* (*sku gsung thugs phrad*); introduction by Garab Dorje

itless qualities will emerge. Reciting *phet* allows the ability to inwardly suppress the head of self-fixation and outwardly pacify all illness and demonic-force possession. My spiritual tradition of the Mahāmudrā, this chöd, is outwardly the meaning of the pāramitās of Sūtra and inwardly the tantras of unsurpassed Secret Mantra. To combine these two and practice is known as the Mahāmudrā. Hence, this is similar to the sound of the syllable *phet*.

So, it is as taught.

Not only that, *pha* is the nature of upāya, and *tra* is the nature of prajñā; so this is the exceptional mantra that combines method and wisdom. Through secret mantras, awareness mantras, and retention mantras, there is nothing that does not reveal the meaning of upāya and prajñā; yet the pith of secret mantra is synthesized in *phet*. The reason is as the tantra *Vajra Pinnacle*[a] states:

> What is the meaning of the syllable *phet*? It is taught that this subjugates harmful entities and suffering and magnetizes exaltation. *Phet* indicates subjugation, such as towns and the like.

Harm-inflicting entities and the suffering of existence are all subjugated [through *phet*]. All states of peaceful ecstasy without exception are magnetized, and this sound also destroys all negativity, such as the stains of obstruction and the like. Reference to "towns and the like" means to destroy all kinds of negativity, including the causes and conditions. It is taught that [the recitation of *phet*] involves many qualities like this. Given that this destroys all harmful entities, it mentions above that this is a wrathful syllable.

In addition Machig has said:

> When the sound of *phet* resonates, there are various ways to interpret it; yet it serves as a reminder for visualizations.

So, it is. Given that this meaning is so vast and profound, a variety of points are revealed since [*phet*] serves as the reminder for all visualizations. On this occasion, [*phet*] is recited in order to remind one about the visualization for the field of refuge and so forth.

To expand upon that, at the time of the ground, these two syllables represent empty appearance; and at the time of the path, upāya and prajñā. At the result, they indicate the two kāyas. Even while visualizing the field of refuge and the like, this never departs from the intrinsic nature of empty appearances and so forth. Especially since *pha* indicates the method of appearances, in this case it

[a] *dorje tsemo* (*rdo rje rtse mo*)

indicates intrinsic clarity; *tra* indicates the prajñā of emptiness, so the nature is empty. When they are combined as *phet*, the dynamic strength of their indivisibility is shown to be all-pervasive compassion. This reveals the meaning of all refuge verses without a single exception.

The primordial original **ground** is the essence of the tathāgatas free from all limitations of elaboration. Given that this intrinsic nature is unsullied by faults, stains or habits, and the like, it is **pure from the beginning.** This uncontrived, self-occurring fundamental nature is unbound by the restrictions of duality. Abiding in the manner of all-pervasive great emptiness, this is **free from direction.** This empty wisdom nature is precisely realized to be the dharmakāya itself as **Samantabhadrī.** That self-radiance is itself the unobstructed aspect of **the intrinsic nature** of lucid appearances. Being unceasing, the confusion of appearances that is **pure within itself** is cleansed or purified within the **intrinsic** mode of being. This is the perfectly pure manifestation of the authentic rupakāya, the sambhogakāya **Khachödma.**[119]

The wisdom of **all-pervasive compassion** is the basis for the arising of both saṃsāra and enlightenment based on the distinctions of pure versus impure and awareness versus lack of awareness. Here, the dynamic strength of nonconceptual great compassion **evenly pervading** all beings to be tamed arises in the **kāya** of the nirmāṇakāya **Wrathful Mother, Tröma** Nagmo. To wisdom ḍākinīs such as this who embody the three kāyas, one **goes for refuge** by generating heartfelt faith and devotion. Hence, this is the general way of taking refuge.

In the *All-Creating Monarch*, it states:

> All facets of phenomenal existence, whatever they may be, constitute the three uncontrived aspects of nature, intrinsic nature, and compassion. This reveals who I am, the nature as it is of the three kāyas.

Thus, it is as taught. The nature is empty, the intrinsic nature is lucid, and the intrinsic nature of all-pervasive compassion is the way of abiding in the absolute **wisdom mind** of the three kāyas, or the nature as it is. All phenomena of the ground and the ground's presence are this **consummate expanse** without exception. Knowing this, then the fundamental nature can be **actualized** as discerning self-awareness. That is refuge in the genuine fundamental nature.

In the *Dynamic Strength of the Lion*, it states:

> The consummate, even pervasion is the supreme meaning of the essence.

So, it is taught. By actualizing the wisdom intent of the three kāyas in this way: within the even pervasion of that nature, the consummate synthesis of everything is the essence of the meaning, or the very supreme. If explained as such, it is appropriate to apply this understanding to the meaning of refuge on this occasion.

In addition, the meaning of these verses can be applied to any teachings concerning the ground and the result. Our guide, the Great Tertön himself, Lord of Dharma, taught that this is the uncommon way to explain this. Through the teaching just mentioned, a mere direction of this tradition can be understood. If one wants further clarification, it is necessary to receive explanations for several crucial secret points concerning the philosophy of Mahāsandhi.

Now is not the time for such explanations because this teaching is intended to emphasize the preliminaries. The recipients of teachings on the preliminary practices are accustomed to [more basic] instructions such as this; and since they are mainly beginners, if I were to explain [Mahāsandhi tantras] at this time, it would not be suited to their mind streams. Not only that, there is the danger of inappropriately revealing secret teachings, so I have decided not to elaborate beyond what is described here. Those who teach this subject should also be cautious about the sacred seal involved with those categories of [Mahāsandhi] teachings. It is advisable to give explanations according to the general direction of the sūtras.

For this, there are two: a general commentary on common refuge and an uncommon explanation on how to maintain the visualization of this terma.

3.2.1.1.3.1.1 General Commentary on Common Refuge

For the first, there are five: the cause for refuge that relies upon an object; the object of refuge that is reliant upon that; the degree of the commitment involved with taking refuge; the way of taking refuge; and having done so, the stages of training.

For the first, the great Tsongkhapa has said:

> Once dead, there is no guarantee that rebirth will not be taken in lower realms. However, it is certain that the Triple Gem will grant protection from that fear. Hence, refuge must be relied upon and the appropriate training maintained.

Since it is uncertain that one will not take rebirth in lower realms, protection comes from none other than the Triple Gem. By going for refuge with heartfelt devotion, one must then train in the disciplines of that system. Initially, for that, it is necessary to establish the cause for refuge. It is imperative that one feel a sense of repulsion and fear toward something, while believing that it is only the Triple Gem that has the potential to grant protection from that fear.

This is mentioned in the *Resting the Mind in Repose*:

> Those of lesser capacity have fear toward the lower realms. Those with middling capacity have fear toward existence; and the great ones, who see the suffering of saṃsāra, including all of its aspects, cannot bear the fact that others must endure such suffering. They are basically afraid of resting in a peaceful state of complacency or quiescence without actively engaging in some way.

So, it is like that.

Those of lesser faculty will feel fear toward the suffering of the three lower realms; the middling that belong to the class of the shrāvakas and the pratyekas will see the suffering of the six classes in existence and feel trepidation. The great ones will be unable to bear the torment of saṃsāra's suffering; and by especially witnessing the torment that others are enduring right now, they will be unable to bear that without acting. Hence, they are incapable of abandoning others and bringing only themselves out of saṃsāra to the single direction of peaceful complacency.

To expand on this, the lesser ones desire to personally attain the state of higher rebirth, such as that of a god or human being. The middling wish to personally attain the state of liberation, while the great ones take refuge based on the wish to attain fully perfected buddhahood for the welfare of others. Our refuge must be motivated like the great ones.

In the *Treasury of Precious Qualities*, it states:

> With fear, faith, and compassion—these three—thinking of others' welfare is the intention of the great ones. Through that, by recalling the Triple Gem, one goes for refuge.

Hence, it is as taught.

Second, the objects of refuge are as stated in the *Seventy Verses of Refuge*:[a]

> The buddha, dharma, and sangha are the protectors for all those wishing to be liberated.

Just as taught, undeceiving protection for those who wish to be liberated is found only with the Triple Gem. This reason is stated in the *Treasury of Precious Qualities*:

> The essence of the path and protection is the sacred dharma. The dharma originated from the Buddha, and those companions who prac-

[a] *kyab dro dün chu pa* (*skyabs 'gro bdun cu pa, trisharaṇasaptati*); Chandrakīrti

> tice this or who are the support for the training are the sangha. These [three] are called the Triple Gem and are the objects of refuge.

So, this is the path that leads to the state of liberation and omniscience. Due to that, its nature protects from the fear of existence and quiescence. Actual protection is based on the sacred dharma that was taught by the fully perfected Buddha Shākyamuni, the revealer of refuge. The companions who practice dharma are the followers of the Buddha, who train in the characteristics of the dharma or who bring into their mind stream the qualities of accomplishment. The sangha are those who take that as their support.

The Triple Gem are, thereby, the supreme objects of refuge. For example, if one must pass through a dangerous, frightening environment in order to reach safety, ideally there must be an undeniable passageway as well as a guide who shows the way. Once one embarks, it is also crucial to be accompanied by a reliable companion. Once these circumstances coincide, it will be possible to reach the destination, otherwise not. Therefore, our teacher has said:

> I will show all of you the path that brings an end to this agonizing existence. The Tathāgata is the teacher, but you yourselves must walk the path.

Since the sacred dharma is the actual path, Buddha said that path must be internalized. The reason that they [i.e., the Triple Gem] are worthy objects of refuge is that this Buddha freed himself from all states of fear and thereby became skilled in the means for delivering others from their fear. He possessed loving kindness toward everyone based on impartially engaging with great compassion. He is a worthy object of refuge because he enacted the welfare of everyone equally, regardless of consequence, and without expectation.

If there is no freedom from fear, then like a drowning person unable to save another, there will be no potential to protect others from that fear. Even though there may be the capacity to be set free from fear: without skillful means, there will be no benefit to the rest of us. This [refuge] is not like that. Even if there is always the skillful means to tame the objects to be tamed: if loving kindness is lacking, then the capacity to grant protection will remain uncertain. Since [the Buddha[120]] possesses great compassion for all living beings, like a mother loves her only child, protection is certain. If this [protection] depended upon deriving benefit from others, this would mean that we would be unable to derive benefit from Buddha; and it is possible that some beings would be exempt from protection because they had never been benefited before. This is not like that. Generally, whoever possesses these four exceptional qualities[121] is worthy of granting refuge to beings; yet it is only the Buddha who possesses [this potential]. Given that non-Buddhist gods such as Maheshvara, Brahmā, and others lack this potential, the Buddha remains the sole permanent source of refuge. That is why the dharma that he taught and the sangha who practice this are also worthy objects of refuge.

It states in the sūtra *Praise for the Worthy*:[a]

> Outwardly, endowed with all divergent strengths, you are fully accomplished. Since we immature do not possess such inner strength, we shall continue to suffer.

So, as mentioned, since the objects of refuge are capable of protecting objects to be tamed and guiding them on the path, that is why both outer and inner divergent causes and strengths must be complete. The strengths, or the outer divergent causes of bringing disciples to the path, were fully accomplished [by Buddha] during the time of practicing for three incalculable eons to become a conqueror. Although [he] fully accomplished this, nevertheless, the inner strengths that are the divergent causes of faith, confidence, supplication, and the like remained incomplete. Hence, immature ordinary individuals like me and others, who have from beginningless time until now failed to achieve this state, are compelled to experience the suffering of saṃsāra. The suffering experienced until now has not been the fault of the object of refuge but rather one's own. For oneself, it is only necessary to have single-pointed trust, generate faith, and follow the teacher; but even that has not been possible. That is why, to gain certainty with the qualities just mentioned, if one is able to single-pointedly trust, then it is impossible to not be protected—hence, the need for developing heartfelt determination.

Third, the degree of commitment involved with taking refuge is as Ārya Asaṅga taught in his treatise that teaches on the four categories, namely, knowing the qualities, knowing the differences, promising, and not speaking with others. The first is to take refuge by recalling the qualities of the Triple Gem. The qualities of buddha involve enlightened body, speech, mind, and enlightened activities—these four. The qualities of enlightened body are as stated in *Praise of the Minor Marks*:[b]

> Your body adorned by the minor marks is beautiful like ambrosia for the eyes, resembling constellations that adorn a stainless autumn sky.

So, it is as taught. The other points above are easy to comprehend, but the meaning of "ambrosia to the eyes" is that—upon seeing [this body of buddha]—the potential to cultivate joyful bliss develops. For example, even our teacher, the

[a] *ngak ö ngak töd* (*bsngags 'os bsngags bstod*)
[b] *pe ched la töd pa* (*dpe byad la bstod pa*)

supreme nirmāṇakāya, appeared in the enlightened body of a tathāgata, pure like solid gold and radiant with dazzling light rays that exceeded the brilliance of billions of suns. His stainless face was even brighter than billions of moons; his body pervasive like the span of the king of trees, the Nyadrodha;[a] his hair coil clear like the pure light of a stainless jewel; eyes as brilliant as a lotus flower and the blue *utpala*; his crown aperture so magnificent that even Brahmā dare not gaze upon it. He was adorned with the thirty-two major and eighty excellent minor marks, so one could not gaze enough upon his body, which appeared in harmony with everything that encountered it. To merely see [the Buddha's body] would bring purpose and meaning.

Qualities such as this are exclusive to those who are buddha, for not even the bodhisattvas below the tenth level possess them. Thinking [of the qualities] in this way inspires faith and the longing to actually encounter this; and by knowing that to recall these qualities of the Buddha great merit is amassed, one must meditate upon this until rapturous joy wells forth.

The qualities of enlightened speech are as stated in the *Chapter on the One Truth*:[b]

> If all sentient beings questioned you simultaneously, in a single instant you would know what they were saying; and through your melodious speech, you would answer each one individually with a single utterance. Hence, among guides in this world, you are the only one whose speech is as melodious as Brahmā. In order to eliminate the suffering of gods and humans, you turned the wheel of dharma.

Thus, the qualities of these words of the Buddha are explained as follows. According to however many sentient beings there are in the realms of the world, all the questions they may have would be based on multiple reasons concerning their individual desires. If all of these questions were simultaneously posed to the Bhagavan, he would instantly know and have an answer to each one of them. Through the single flow of his melodious response, he would respond to each one of them; and each would understand this according to their own language.

Based on that, understand that the Guide, the Bhagavan, possesses the melodious speech of Brahmā that is unrivaled among objects to be tamed in this world. His speech as well will eliminate all suffering of living beings, including gods and humans. In these ways, the wheel of dharma was turned according to the capacities of each individual. Since the enlightened speech of Buddha possesses the sixty branches of melodious speech: although teaching dharma through the

[a] *nya gro dha*; banyan, or Indian fig tree

[b] *denpa chig po'i le'u do* (*bden pa gcig po'i le'u mdo, satyakaparivarasūtra*)

Sanskrit language, each disciple could understand his speech according to their own language, needs, and capacities. One must recall these qualities, including the potential to fully dispel all doubts in an instant.

The qualities of enlightened mind involve two: qualities of omniscience and of loving kindness. For the first, it states in *Praise for the Worthy*:

> Through your wisdom alone, all knowable things are pervaded. Except for you, others [only] assume that knowable things are exalted.

So, only through the wisdom of buddha that pervades all knowable things, the nature is directly and simultaneously seen. This subjective wisdom is more exalted than objective knowable things. Except for the buddhas, when all other trainees have direct realization, they will no longer see relative truth. When they see relative truth, they will no longer have direct realization. In this way, [the Buddha] taught that, among both the mind and knowable things, knowable things are surpassing. Since all knowable things are not obscure in [buddhas'] omniscience—like placing a fresh *kyurura*[a] herb in the hand[122]—the buddhas precisely see the faculties and intentions of the objects to be tamed and are thereby skilled in the means for taming them.

The qualities of loving kindness are as stated in the *Praise called One-Hundred and Fifty Verses*:[b]

> All living beings are equally bound by their passions. In order to release them from those passions, you have been bound by compassion for a long time.

So, just as all living beings are helplessly bound by their passions, the Sage is likewise bound by great compassion. Thinking about the way of generating compassion, [the Buddha] is free from partiality, such as having no bias if someone on his right is massaging him with sandalwood oil while someone on his left is striking him with an axe. Thinking that it is only a buddha who would have developed the quality of loving compassion to this level, faith is generated.

For enlightened activities, it also states in the previous text:

> You taught that passions must be destroyed, and you revealed the deceptions of the māras. You told us about the inexhaustible nature of saṃsāra and also revealed the direction of fearlessness. Compassionate One with the intent to benefit others, you have brought goodness to

[a] *skyu ru ra, Emblic myrobalan*

[b] *gya nga chu* (*brgya lnga bcu, shatapañchāshatkanāmastotra*); Ashvaghoṣha

> all sentient beings. There is nothing to be found that you have not done for them.
>
> So, having explained to disciples the cause of suffering being the need to annihilate the passions: by abandoning that, you also warned them about the way the māras of saṃsāra use deception in order to trick. You spoke of the inexhaustible suffering and the characteristics of saṃsāra. You also revealed the method for abandoning this to be the cause for the direction of fearlessness, namely, liberation.

While engaged in this practice of acceptance and rejection, the compassionate Bhagavan intending to benefit others said that—if the time arrives to accomplish the welfare of sentient beings—then until that deed is done, you must do whatever it takes to accomplish that. Otherwise, what is the point?

It is as stated in *Praise for the Worthy*:

> You have never failed to fulfill your commitment to liberate all beings.
> How can there be such fully endowed circumstances and opportunities existing in other worlds where you have never been?

So, given that Buddha Shākyamuni does not exclude anyone who is suffering, anyone who is liberated from suffering is also affected by the strength of Buddha's blessings. For those who have not had the opportunity to have these fully endowed circumstances, whatever well-being comes their way is due to the strength of Buddha's blessings.

When temporarily not afflicted by suffering such as illness, that, too, is the blessing of Buddha's strength. Furthermore, Buddha benefits others in ways that are permanently pervasive and effortlessly spontaneous. The timing for this will endure as long as saṃsāra exists. The benefit will reach out to pervade all sentient beings; and when it does, there will be no need at all to apply any effort. This Buddha who has exhausted all faults and perfected all qualities has done so by internalizing dharma. Those who practice in the same way are the sangha who internalize sacred dharma so as to purify all faults and accomplish all qualities. The sangha are those who are not distracted from this practice and take refuge by precisely knowing the qualities of the Triple Gem.

Second, understanding the differences involves knowing the difference between the Triple Gem to be that sangha are those who accomplish the path, dharma is that which is accomplished, and buddha is the result of the accomplishment. Third, the commitment is to take refuge by knowing that the Buddha is the teacher, the sacred dharma is the actual object of refuge, and the sangha are considered the companions for accomplishing refuge. Fourth, not speaking about this to others means to know the acceptable and unacceptable aspects concerning Buddhist versus non-Buddhist teachers, their teaching, and their followers and to thereby only take refuge in the Triple Gem—not those who are in discord with this.

Fifth, the way of going for refuge will be explained here according to the upadesha of the previous lineage masters, as well as the Vajrayāna tradition. Omniscient Jigmed Lingpa has said:

> I go for refuge in the actual Triple Gem; the sugatas of the Three Roots; the enlightened mind as the intrinsic nature of the channels, winds, and bindus; and in the maṇḍala of the nature, intrinsic nature, and compassion until supreme enlightenment is achieved.[123]

Thus, the nature of the Triple Gem as the objects of refuge is that these are the sugatas of the Three Roots. The clear-light bodhichitta supported by the intrinsic nature of channels, winds, and bindus is the maṇḍala of the nature, intrinsic nature, and compassion.[124] Hence, refuge is taken in that intrinsic nature. Based on that, the manner of taking refuge in the Triple Gem is also stated in the *Treasury of Precious Qualities*:

> Refuge is taken in the Buddha as the teacher, the dharma as the path, and the sangha as the companions.

As taught, if applied to the oral instructions of the guru, then the fully perfected Buddha is the one who has revealed the path to us. One must think, "I must have confidence in the teachings on cause and effect that are the Buddha's speech; the sacred dharma is my actual path; and by relying upon the three trainings of the surpassing path, I will not oppose this by sullying it even with the subtlest of stains. The ārya sangha are my friends who assist in the accomplishment of the path, so I must become inspired by training in their example of conduct and never separate from them." Thus, it is said that one must make this kind of firm commitment. It is especially vital to go for refuge by aspiring to blend these three objects with one's stream of mind.

In the *Sūtra Requested by Ugra*:[a]

> By going for refuge in the Buddha, one hopes to attain the state of buddha. By going for refuge in the dharma, one aspires to realize the dharma; and by going for refuge in the sangha, there is the wish to

[a] *drag shül chen gyi zhü pa'i do* (*drag shul can gyis zhus pa'i mdo*, *ugraparipṛcchāsūtra*)

achieve the state of the ārya sangha. Taking refuge in the Triple Gem as such is called "taking outer refuge".

Jetsun Milarepa said:

> The Buddha, dharma and sangha—these three—are the outer objects of refuge. I am fully satisfied and fulfilled to take refuge in them. Hence, you too must follow suit.

So, as taught, given that this follows the tradition of the pāramitās, it is expressed in that way.

Omniscient Jigmed Lingpa said:

> According to the tradition of the common vehicles, Buddha is the teacher, the dharma the actual refuge, and the sangha are the companions through which to accomplish the path. Hence, refuge is taken with this in mind.

So, it is as taught.

The way of taking refuge in the Three Roots is to think that the guru who shows kindness in three ways is the embodiment of the Triple Gem, and that, likewise, the meditation deities and ḍākinīs are inseparable with the guru. Then, taking refuge by practicing and reciting single-pointedly is known to be the inner mode of refuge. Milarepa said:

> The guru, deities, and ḍākinīs are the three inner sources of refuge.

So, it is as taught. To expand upon this, since this is the way of taking refuge according to the general tradition of inner Secret Mantra Vajrayāna, it is as the Omniscient Jigmed Lingpa said:

> The general tradition of the uncommon vehicle is to offer the three doors to one's guru, to rely upon the meditation deity, and to take the ḍākinīs as companions while going for refuge.

Thus, that is what he taught concerning how to go for refuge. Saying "offer to the guru" is an exceptional key point concerning the way to rely upon the guru. Saying "rely upon the meditation deity" is to think that one's three doors and the enlightened body, speech, and mind of the yidam are inseparable. Saying "take the ḍākinīs as the companions" means to take companions that generate wisdom exaltation.

The way of taking refuge in the channels, winds, and bindus is to go for refuge in the pure channels, wisdom winds, and awakened mind—these three. The reason is that, by relying upon the channels, winds, and fluids, the great connate wisdom of bliss and emptiness will be precisely cultivated within the mind stream. This is also called "the secret mode of refuge". Jetsun Milarepa said:

> The channels, winds, and bindus—these three—are the secret objects of refuge.

Thus, it is as taught. Given that this is the tradition of taking refuge according to the secret, unsurpassed vajra essence, it is as he has taught. Omniscient Jigmed Lingpa said:

> According to the exceptional tradition of the supreme vajra essence vehicle, the channels support the nirmāṇakāya, the winds cleanse the sambhogakāya, and the bindus are pure as the dharmakāya. Such is the swift path for taking refuge.

So, it is as taught.

In addition, in one's vajra body, there are the abiding channels, mobile winds, and array of the bodhichitta fluids—these three. Through their function while impure, they manifest as three doors; and at the time of purity, as the accomplishment of three kāyas. There are the coarse channels, winds, and bindus and the nature of them, or the innate clear-light channels, winds, and bindus—these three. The pure nature of the innate channels is the nirmāṇakāya, the pure winds are the sambhogakāya, and the pure bindus mature as the wisdom of exaltation—the swift path of method for accomplishing the dharmakāya. This is how the mind stream will rely upon these constituents.

The way of taking refuge in the nature, intrinsic nature, and compassion is refuge according to the tradition of the quintessential Mahāsandhi. This refuge is as explained previously; and as Omniscient Jigmed Lingpa said:

> This is absolute, undeceiving, fundamental vajra refuge. The wisdom that abides in the enlightened mind stream of all objects of refuge is empty by nature, intrinsically lucid, and all-pervasively compassionate—these three—and determined as the inseparability to be accomplished in the mind stream.

So, it is taught. Saying "determined" means to decide, or to abide without wavering from that. If one trains in the inner and secret modes of this, then that is actual refuge according to the Vajrayāna teaching. Based on that, to take refuge in the Buddha as the teacher, the vidyādharas as the sangha, and the gathering of ḍākas and ḍākinīs as the companions, the general key points are complete.

3.2.1.1.3.1.2 Uncommon Explanation on How to Maintain the Visualization

Then for the actual practice, it is necessary to visualize the field of refuge. Although many variations found in the different chöd liturgies exist, the visualization that is in harmony with one's aspirations is the one to practice.

Generally, in the space in front appears the great dharmakāya mother surrounded by a host of buddhas and bodhisattvas in the ten directions. Like massing clouds, it is sufficient to consider that they fill the upper regions of space. It is best if these objects of refuge can be perfectly visualized since this is connected to the tradition of Secret Mantra. Even if the visualization is unclear, that is not problematic for as it states in the *Heap of Jewels Sūtra*:[a]

> For whoever believes in the victors and in their presence, they [i.e., the victors] will abide to always confer blessings and liberate them from all negativities.

So, since it is as taught, by thinking that the victors and their heirs are undoubtedly residing in the space in front, they will surely be present there. All of the buddhas have unobstructed omniscience as though all knowable things were witnessed as clearly as viewing a *kyurura* sprig in the palm of the hand. With the power of the qualities of perfect omniscience, they will unobstructedly know when they are being supplicated to through devotion.

With qualities of great compassion for all sentient beings like a mother for her only child, they will never knowingly forsake anyone. Although this omniscient compassion is there: if there were no potential to arrive before us without impediment, then they would not do so. However, for as long as it takes a champion to stretch out his arm or a single mental instant, they will arrive wherever necessary since their miraculous abilities are unobstructed. Hence, there is the potential to instantly arrive anywhere. Since enlightened activities are never postponed, there is no possibility for arriving in a timely manner sometimes and other times too late.

It is not the case that they will arrive before those who are important but not those who are lesser since there is no partiality toward any sentient beings based on attachment and aversion. All beings are seen as equal. Even if one were to think that they appear to those with karmic fortune but not to someone like

[a] *kon chog tsek pa* (*dkon mchog brtsegs pa, ratnakūṭasūtra*)

oneself who is overwhelmed by passions and an abundance of negativities and faults, [that is incorrect]. For example, one may wonder, "If a mother has many children and one of them falls ill, is her compassion for the sick one greater or less?" Like that, the victors and their heirs have surpassing compassion for beings whose negativities, obstructions, and faults are greater.

If one imagines that at this moment there are many others who are supplicating so it is possible that the victors will come to them and not to oneself and even if countless beings were supplicating simultaneously, countless emanations would surely arrive to remain before each supplicant. This is also mentioned in the *Uttaratantra*:

> The elements of the disciples and the methods through which to tame them are activities that tame based upon their faculties. Departing for wherever they abide and at any time, the buddhas will always be spontaneously engaged.

So, as taught, the buddhas directly see the various aspirations and elements of those objects to be tamed. They also see the appropriate ways through which to tame them. According to the faculties of the objects to be tamed, the buddhas have the potential to lead them to higher states of happiness and liberation. [The buddhas] will depart for and arrive wherever the objects abide and without postponing the timing. The fully enlightened buddhas will always spontaneously engage since all effort-based actions have been pacified.

Not only that, this is mentioned in the *Prayer for Excellent Conduct*:

> Upon a single particle, all buddhas abide—as numberless as there are particles—in the midst of the bodhisattvas, who are their heirs.

Thus, as taught, however many fully enlightened buddhas may exist—because their kāyas are free from being coarse or concrete and are the nature of wisdom—wherever enlightened mind pervades, enlightened body and speech also pervade. So upon a single particle, one must believe that countless buddhas and bodhisattvas abide as numberless as there are particles.

Initially, when all buddhas cultivate the bodhichitta, they do so for all of us sentient beings; and in the interim by accumulating merit over three countless eons, this is also done for the welfare of beings. Finally, upon awakening and gaining spontaneously present enlightened deeds, this too is revealed for the welfare of others. Since there is no other goal besides benefiting sentient beings, we must feel assured that the buddhas and bodhisattvas are present before us.

In short, among all buddhas, there is not a single one who does not look upon us without compassion or is unable to protect us. Hence, with such potential, it is impossible for them to abandon us. That is why, if we have doubt and are lacking faith, any shortcomings are our own. All buddhas' power to protect us is certain, so one must believe in this from the depth of the heart.

Then, imagine an assembly surrounding oneself that includes one's parents, enemies, and gods-māras, with all sentient beings as well. Consider they are all single-pointedly going for refuge with faith and devotion. To expand upon this, according to the tradition of chöd, the principal objects to go for refuge and to cultivate bodhichitta toward are eight groups of sentient beings. They include enemies with aversion toward oneself, harm-doing obstructing forces, circumstances that are brought on by obstacle creators, karmic demonic forces, bodily demonic forces, and obstructing demonic forces of the fear-invoking places—totaling six types of demonic forces. The remaining two are one's parents.

[For the first,] those who beat and strike oneself, steal possessions, threaten, slander, and the like, who have bad intentions, such as humans, are the enemies who harbor aversion toward oneself. [Second,] those who display magical feats, such as causing one to see visions and unusual phenomena, who stir up fear and terror causing one's hair to stand on end are the formless gods-māras included here as taught. Those demonic forces that bring illness and negativity to one's body and mind and steal one's life force and wealth, bringing torment and despair, are harm-doing demonic forces.

Concerning one's body, life essence, authentic presence, reputation, merit, ability to accomplish liberation, and so forth—both temporarily and ultimately—no matter what activities are engaged in, whether great or small, all those who attempt to thwart this and create obstacles are the circumstances brought about by obstacle creators. Connate dimmed awareness or self-fixation on the so-called "me", or whatever name is applied, grants no opportunity for liberation and is the root of all negativity. From that, confused habits emerge; and due to the strength and solidification of that, the classes of demonic forces who have been engaged only in the negative deeds of distracting one's mind from beginningless lifetimes until now have originated. That is called "the māra that accompanies oneself" referred to here as the karmic demonic force. Once one's bardo consciousness called a "gandharva[a]" enters the mother's womb, until the entire body develops, and while the flesh, bones, and skin self-mutate at death: during this entire process, one thinks, "I am the owner of this corporeal form made of flesh and blood." This unruly nonhuman entity is the demonic force of the body.

The outer appearances of the universe are the combination of the five elements comprising the array of realms in this world, such as the four continents and Mt. Meru. Each individual country, their mountains, valleys, forests,

[a] *driza* (*dri za*); smell eater

charnel grounds, rivers, oceans, and temples, stūpas, including dwelling places, and generally those who abide there who bring both well-being and harm and specifically the keepers of those lands—the gods-māras—are all referred to as the demonic forces of the place. The three inner demonic forces, along with the outer, total six. Those who have given this life's body and who have shown great kindness are one's parents, totaling eight. Those are the principal ones, and all living beings equal to space are included with them. With no source of hope or refuge aside from the Triple Gem, one prays, "You are all-knowing! Whether happy, sad, high, or low, no matter what circumstance, obstacle, or demonic force may hinder us, Triple Gem, know and look upon us!" Think like that; and without mouthing words, but from the bottom of the heart, generate intense longing and devotion.

Imagine that oneself, one's patrons, gods, māras, harm-doers, parents, and the beings of the six classes are placed under the protection of the Triple Gem, and that all of them are filled with respect. They bring their palms together in prayer and recite the refuge verses in unison. The six harmful ones, such as the enemies with hatred toward oneself, this life's parents, and all beings [recite], "From today onward, we take refuge in the guru, refuge in the buddha, refuge in the dharma, sangha, assembly of meditation deities, and the gathering of ḍākinīs and dharmapālas. Please grant us great blessings!" Recite these verses some one-hundred and one times or at least twenty-one times to accomplish this.

Then, think that the Triple Gem speak to you, saying, "Child of the Family! Having abandoned all negative karmic accumulations through constant faith and devotion, we shall protect and assist you." Then multitudes of light rays emerge from their enlightened bodies, speech, and minds to penetrate the three doors of self and all others. All negativities and obstructions accumulated through the three doors are purified, and one's body becomes clear like crystal. Within that state, the objects of refuge, oneself, and the gods-māras—these three—as well as the nature of refuge, become nonconceptual emptiness; and one rests in evenness. The objects of refuge, the ones taking refuge, and the nature of refuge—these three—are the nonconceptual dharmakāya nature of mind, unborn absolute truth. *Phet phet phet!*[125] Thus, visualize accordingly.

Fifth, the vows are twofold: the training for taking uncommon refuge in the Triple Gem and the uncommon advice for all three. First, it states in the *Certainty of the Three Vows*:[a]

> The three common and uncommon refuge vows are to cultivate respect for the individual categories of not searching for another source of refuge, harming any sentient being, or accompanying heretics.

[a] *dom süm nam ngey* (*sdom gsum rnam nges*); Ngari Panchen Pema Wangyal

Concerning this, there are the two categories of what to accept and reject. The vows concerning what to reject are that, by taking refuge in the buddha, dharma, and sangha, the individual trainings are described in that order. One must not take refuge by having expectation toward another object of refuge, such as a worldly god. One must abandon harming sentient beings and not accompany heretics. It states in the *Sūtra of Final Nirvāṇa*:[a]

> One who takes refuge in the Triple Gem is a perfectly pure upāsaka. They must never take refuge in another god. Having taken refuge in the sacred dharma, they must be free from harmful thoughts toward others. Having gone for refuge to the sangha, they must not accompany any heretics.

So, it is.

The vows to accept are as follows. Concerning the supports of Buddha's kāya, this includes even a broken image; the supports of dharma include a single syllable; and for the sangha, even someone who dresses like the ordained, including wearing a mere patch of saffron-colored clothing, must all be recognized as the actual Triple Gem and appropriate respect rendered. Also, [it states]:

> Even at the cost of one's life or for any other reason, the Triple Gem must never be abandoned; no matter how important the purpose, never search for a method other than this; do not break the continuity of the timely requirements; go for refuge for oneself as well as others while paying homage to the buddhas in whatever direction one goes.

Thus, and the five are that by saying "at the cost of one's life or for any other reason" means in order to receive a large gift, a high position of authority, and the like, to not abandon the Triple Gem for any such reasons. No matter how important the reason may be, aside from trusting the Triple Gem, do not search for another worldly method. By always recalling their qualities, never miss any timely requirements. Recognizing these benefits, when one goes for refuge, others will be brought to the path. One must pay homage to the images of the buddha in whatever direction one goes.

Secondly, the stages of visualization from the terma itself are as follows. Imagine that this **array of self-appearances instantly transforms into** the self-arising **pure land of the Khachöd Dewachen.**[b] The luminous ground is the color of lapis lazuli, vast and open. Pervading like limitless space itself, it is smooth and free

[a] *nyang dey kyi do* (*myang 'das kyi mdo*, *āryamahāparinirvāṇasūtra*)
[b] *mkha' spyod bde ba chen*; Space Activity of Exaltation

from any coarseness and even like the surface of a mirror. Beautiful to behold like the soft palm of a youth, at the moment of contact bliss ensues.

The lovely ornaments of the sky include billowing, colorful rainbow canopies filled with light molecules and silken parasols, as well as victorious banners and pennants. The ornaments of intermittent space include many ḍākas and ḍākinīs dancing and offering clouds of various substances, while showers of flowers rain down. The ornaments of the earth include being completely covered by many lotus flowers of different colors that, when pressed upon the ground, bounce back. Meadows and hills abound with medicinal flowers wafting with sweet fragrances that permeate like mist. Whatever is desired can be fulfilled in this place that is abundant with wish-granting trees, cleansing water springs, great oceans of ambrosia, golden sand, turquoise ponds with jewels piled upon the riverbanks, and so forth. All of the arrangements that make up a pure land are **perfectly complete** without exception.

In the center of this, in the space in front of where **self and all sentient beings** abide, **upon a lotus, sun, moon, and corpse seat, inseparable with the root guru, appears the** nirmāṇakāya **sole mother, Tröma Nagmo. She holds a** curved **vajra blade in her right hand and a skull filled with blood in the left. Her two legs are** in the **dancing** posture **upon a corpse** seat; **her mouth is gaping, tongue rolling, and** fangs bared. Her **three eyes are bulging. Her orange hair stands on end to touch the peak of existence,** while **a squealing black pig's head juts from her crown. Her breasts are voluptuous and lotus mature.** On her forehead, there is a piled smear of charnel-ground ash, on her cheeks a smear of menstrual blood, and on her chin a smear of fat. Those are the three smears.

Her upper body is adorned with a fresh elephant skin, the lower a leopard-skin skirt, her waist wrapped by a freshly flayed human skin. These are the three types of clothing that **she wears.** Her crown is adorned with dry skulls, and she wears a long necklace made from fifty fresh skulls. Her ankles and wrists have skull ornaments, and she sports a necklace of whitish-colored serpents of the kingly caste. Her earrings are made of snakes from the royal caste, while her diadem is composed of Bhramin-caste serpents. The bracelets adorning her arms and legs are made of common-caste green serpents, and her belt is made of black serpents from the untouchable caste. These are the ornaments composed of the five castes of serpents. Hence together, these are the two types of ornaments that are worn [i.e., skull and serpent], comprising **the eight charnel-ground ornaments.**

Standing in an expanse of wisdom fire and shimmering orbs of light, above her crown is the embodiment of all sambhogakāya gurus as red Vajravarāhī. She holds a curved vajra blade and a skull, while she **playfully** delights in the **dancing** posture and rests **amid an expanse of blazing wisdom fire. Above her crown appears the nature of the entire maṇḍala of all dharmakāya gurus appearing as the blue-black Samantabhadrī. She is naked and seated in the**

full-lotus posture upon a lotus and moon seat. Her two **hands are** united **in the mudrā of empty evenness, parallel to her heart. Envision that she abides within a radiant expanse of blue-black light molecules.**

Imagine that surrounding them are **the sublime masters of** all **nine lineages,** such as the wisdom-mind lineage and the rest. They **are facing** self and others **and gazing with great loving kindness and compassion.** Think, "They are the epitome of the objects of refuge." By reciting the verses *yeshe ka dag* and so forth mentioned before as much as possible, recall the meaning and **go for refuge.** As previously mentioned, trust this from one's heart.

From the [terma] commentary:

> **From this moment onward, until the heart of enlightenment is realized, I take refuge in you, supplicate you, bow down to you, rely upon you, place all hope in you, and offer my three doors. In all situations whether high, low, happy, sad, good, or bad, you are all-knowing. Grant blessings that my three doors may become the three vajras.**

Thus, it is taught. By thinking in this way, **completely offer oneself.**

Then, from all objects of refuge, rays of light radiate as mentioned before. Finally, all objects of refuge melt into light and dissolve into oneself. One's three doors and the enlightened bodies, speech, and minds of the objects of refuge become inseparable. Self and others, including phenomenal existence, are purified within the clear-light nature of emptiness.

Once again, like a rainbow arising in the sky, self-nature arises as the embodiment of the three-kāya ḍākinīs. By training in whatever appears as only pure, one delights in all food and drink as wisdom substances. Hence, train in the yoga of conduct as the path.

Although not the actual oral-instruction lineage—given that this is the uncommon refuge of the Vajrayāna tradition—if practiced accordingly, this becomes identical to the tradition of general Secret Mantra, the exceptional way of taking resultant refuge as the path. Therefore, I find this to be an important **key point.** Generally, while practicing chöd, refuge is extremely crucial for daily practice, for dispelling obstacles, and for enhancing realization. The unrivaled master Gyaltangpa[a,126] has said:

> Some say that during chöd practice, refuge need not be taken. Why would that be the case? They answer, if there is refuge, then upheavals

[a] *rgyal thang pa*

will not occur. For myself, I departed for the cave of Drog Pon[a] to practice chöd and abstained from taking refuge. During that time, I did not have a single upheaval. Then by generating faith and devotion in the Triple Gem, I took refuge; following which boundless upheavals occurred, and I was able to sever all of them in their own place.

Then someone came to visit me, and I mentioned to him that by not taking refuge I had not a single upheaval but by taking refuge the upheavals were abundant. I asked him, "What does that mean?" He replied, "Whoever has the potential to practice dharma, to engage in virtue, and to take refuge will have upheavals that the māras cannot bear or ignore. Those who are unable to take refuge are not worthy of being distracted by the māras' upheavals." That is what he told me.

If one supplicates the Triple Gem according to their wishes, there will certainly be accomplishment. For myself since then, when upheavals do not occur, I always emphasize refuge; and when unable to sever them, I also emphasize refuge. [Refuge] is the source for all qualities to emerge according to one's wishes.

So, it is as taught.

Whoever takes refuge in the undeceiving source that is the unsurpassed source of protection, the sacred Triple Gem, and relies upon this protection with single-pointed faith will come to know the source of all positive qualities.

Hence, these are the verses that summarize the section.

3.2.1.1.3.2 Bodhichitta

This has two parts:
1 The way of understanding the meaning of bodhichitta
2 The way of training in bodhichitta

Second, the cultivation of the bodhichitta is as follows:

Phet! I promise to liberate all beings from the ocean of existence. All sacred supreme objects of refuge, bear witness. Through my training to

[a] *grog phon*

> cultivate the bodhichitta, may I attain the glorious potential to empty the depths of saṃsāra.

As taught, saying ***phet*** serves as a reminder for the visualizations and to cultivate the awakened mind. The awakened mind is cultivated with the **promise to liberate all** limitless **beings** as vast as space **from the** great **ocean of** cyclic **existence.** Requesting **all the supreme** victors and their heirs, who are the **sacred objects of refuge,** to **bear witness:** if refuge and bodhichitta are practiced simultaneously, then the previously mentioned field of refuge serves as the witness for the cultivation of bodhichitta. The way to accomplish this is to think, "**Through my training to cultivate** aspirational **bodhichitta** followed by practical bodhichitta, I will accomplish the conduct of the victors and their heirs. By vowing to accomplish the state of fully enlightened buddhahood, one must maintain all the vows and trainings. By placing all beings of the three realms in the state of unsurpassed perfect buddhahood, make the prayer, "**May I attain the glorious potential to empty the depths of saṃsāra.**"

For this, there are two: the way of understanding the meaning of bodhichitta and the way of training in bodhichitta.

3.2.1.1.3.2.1 Way of Understanding the Meaning of Bodhichitta

For the first, the *Ornament of Clear Realization* describes this:

> Cultivating bodhichitta is for the benefit of others and involves the wish to attain the state of fully perfected buddhahood.

So, bodhichitta means focusing on the welfare of sentient beings with the wisdom and sincerity to attain the state of fully perfected buddhahood.

To expand on that, there are two implications. First is the implication that one is intending to place all sentient beings in the transcendent state of nonabiding, fully enlightened buddhahood, free from all obscurations. Hence, to think in this way is to pursue the purpose of others or to intend to benefit others through compassion. Then, thinking, "I too must accomplish all aspects of the unsurpassed state of omniscience," one pursues the goal of enlightenment or the intention to attain perfect awakening through prajñā. It is taught that these two are required.

Concerning the tradition of chöd, as mentioned before, there are eight principal objects to cultivate bodhichitta toward. Especially, one should take as the objects of compassion the harm-doing spirits and demonic forces. In the *Gathering of Precious Qualities*, it states:

> Even when dreaming, if the sentient beings who dwell in the three lower realms are witnessed, then at that moment one should pray to sever the continuity of their negativity.

Thus, and the quote continues:

> A bodhisattva who connects with this for a long time will be able to liberate gods and humans and the beings of the three lower realms.

So, it is as taught. By familiarizing with how the bodhisattvas cultivate loving kindness and compassion for the sentient beings of the lower realms, even in dreams such actions are made possible.

Reference to all spirits and demonic forces refers mainly to the classes of pretas and animals. From beginningless time, there has been a connection with them as one's parents and loved ones. Saying "gods, humans, and beings of the lower realms" refers to the beings of the six classes in general and especially to the eight objects for cultivating compassion [in chöd practice]. Those who dwell in the lower realms are mainly the spirits and demonic forces as revealed by the quote. The reason for this is that those spirits and demonic forces are generally afflicted by passions and specifically by harmful thoughts and hatred such that their negative karmic accumulations mature as various types of tormented behavior.

The result concurrent with the cause is that they are always obsessed with harmful thoughts toward others and pursue them only in order to consume their flesh and blood. Hence, in their future rebirths, they will again be born in the lower realms, such as the hells, where they will accumulate negativity unceasingly without refuge or protection. It is, therefore, necessary to tame them through maintaining only love and compassion toward them. These are the reasons why they are the primary objects of compassion.

In the *Four-Hundred Stanzas*, it states:

> Toward an ailing child, a mother will feel a particular sense of heartfelt concern. Likewise, the bodhisattvas will have surpassing loving kindness toward those who are the lowly ones.

Thus, it is taught that all bodhisattvas feel surpassing loving kindness toward those beings that are disadvantaged and tormented by suffering.

To elaborate upon this, there are two divisions: aspirational and practical [bodhichitta]. In *Resting the Mind in Repose*, it states:

> Cultivating the bodhichitta is based on the wish that immeasurable beings may attain the state of perfectly pure buddhahood. That involves

> both the aspiration and the practical application, namely, the aspiring mind and the application of corresponding deeds. This is like the wish to embark and the actual journey itself.

So, by recognizing the general characteristics for cultivating the bodhichitta, there are the two distinctions of the aspiration and the practical application. From the perspective of the intention, the wish to attain perfected buddhahood for the welfare of others is the aspirational mind. Through application, based on complete engagement, the bodhichitta that actually engages in conduct is the practical intention. This is indicated through both the wish to embark and the actual journey itself. That is relative bodhichitta.

Absolute bodhichitta is the pure dharmatā nature of phenomena like space, the wisdom that directly realizes the nature of emptiness. In the sūtra *Cultivating the Bodhichitta according to the Mahāyāna*,[a] it states:

> The bodhisattva Kāshyapa requested, "O Bhagavan! How is the bodhichitta cultivated?" The Buddha responded, "All spacelike phenomena have no characteristics, yet are perfectly pure as primordial clear light. That is called 'bodhichitta'. In harmony with that, to cultivate the precious state of mind that has never before been cultivated is referred to as 'arousing bodhichitta'."

Thus, it is as taught.

To directly realize this, becoming familiar with the meaning of emptiness from the onset is the practice of chöd. As previously described, emptiness is inclusive within the training of these two states of bodhichitta.

3.2.1.1.3.2.2 Way of Training in Bodhichitta

This has four parts:

1. From the perspective of the seven upadeshas based on cause and result
2. From the perspective of the four immeasurable qualities
3. By exchanging self for others
4. Through the activity of sending and receiving virtue and negativity

Second, the way of training the mind has four parts: training from the perspective of the seven upadeshas based on cause and result, training from the perspec-

[a] *chang chub tu sem kyed pa tekpa chenpo'i do* (*byang chub tu sems bskyed pa theg pa chen po'i mdo*)

tive of the four immeasurable qualities,[127] training by exchanging self for others, and through the activity of sending and receiving virtue and negativity.

3.2.1.1.3.2.2.1 From the Perspective of the Seven Upadeshas Based on Cause and Result

First, the perspective of the upadesha is according to the intent of the pāramitā tradition. The *Gathering of Precious Qualities* states:

> In this vehicle of the Buddha, there are those who aspire toward renunciation and those who recognize all beings to be equal as one's parents. Tame them through the mind of benefit and love.

Thus, it is as taught. Saying "in this vehicle of the Buddha" indicates the cultivation of bodhichitta, and saying "recognize all beings to be equal" indicates the way of initially establishing the mind of equanimity. Saying "recognize all beings as one's parents" indicates recognizing them as parents, recalling their kindness, and then wishing to repay that as the three [steps]. These three come about by making these distinctions concerning knowing how to cultivate this recognition. Saying "the mind of benefit" indicates compassion and saying "the mind of love" indicates love. Saying to "tame them" indicates that the taming involves actually engaging in this practice and taking on the full responsibility for doing so.

Likewise, it states in the *Intermediate Mother*:[a]

> One must see beings with an attitude of equanimity.

The quote continues:

> One must see beings with an attitude of love; one must see all sentient beings with an attitude of wishing to benefit them; and in the presence of all sentient beings, one must recognize them to be one's mother.

So, it is as taught. For this, there is the cultivation of striving to benefit others and striving to achieve the state of enlightenment.

First, the necessity to initially set forth the basis for striving to benefit others is like the example of how it is uncomfortable to place a bed on an uneven surface. If the mind of attachment and aversion toward sentient beings is not dealt with,

[a] *yüm bar ma* (*yum bar ma, pañchaviṃshatisāhasrikāprajñapāramitā*); intermediate-length *Prajñāpāramitā*

then there will be no potential to recognize living beings as having been one's mother and so forth. In order to initiate accomplishing the mind of equanimity and to make this easier, bring to mind a neutral person who is neither enemy nor relative. Then induce conceptual attachment or aversion toward that person; and if attachment is dominant, think, "For many lifetimes this person has been my enemy and has harmed me incessantly, so there is no reason to have attachment now." If aversion is dominant, think, "For many lifetimes this person has been my relative and has brought me great benefit, so there is no reason to feel hatred." Hence, this will arrest the concepts of attachment or aversion and, in doing so, allow the mind to remain in a state of equality.

Then, imagine a cherished one and induce attachment toward them, thinking, "Although this person benefits me now, in previous lifetimes he or she has been my enemy; and because of having inflicted harm upon me, just hearing his name incites unbearable terror." There were many times that such feelings occurred, and it is uncertain as to whether this will continue in the future; so arrest the mind of attachment by deciding it is baseless.

Then, imagine an enemy, thinking, "Even though this person is harming me now, in countless lifetimes he has been my cherished loved one who has brought me benefit. In fact, without this person, I was unable to live for even a moment; and likewise without me he would have suffered unbearably." There were many times that such feelings occurred, and it is uncertain as to whether this will occur in the future; so there is no reason to feel aversion. In this way, these preconceptions are arrested.

Then, by imagining both relative and enemy, arrest attachment and aversion by thinking as just described. Like before, consider all sentient beings and the concepts of attachment and aversion will be arrested. Follow this with the practice of cultivating the attitude of equanimity.

Given that it is necessary to establish a warm, positive feeling toward all living beings, there are three ways to do so. [First,] recognizing they have been one's mother is as follows. Bringing one's mother of this life to mind, not only has she been your mother for this life but also in many previous lives. It is taught that Buddha's mother of that life had been his mother in many previous lives. It is also explained to be the same situation for everyone else. This is the undeniable speech of the Buddha.

Given that saṃsāra is beginningless, so are lifetimes. Based on that, in saṃsāra it cannot be said there is a particular rebirth that has never been taken or a certain place that has never been visited. In the womb of each and every living being, we have been reborn countless times; so that is why one can decide that this life's mother has been a mother to you many countless times. Then, meditate in this same way by gradually thinking of your father, relatives, friends, those who are neutral including enemies, and finally all sentient beings.

[Second,] recalling their kindness is as follows. Imagine your mother and how she held you in her womb for ten months ignoring her own comfort, hunger, thirst, and so forth. Everything she did was for the welfare or protection of her child. Giving you a body and mind endowed with a precious human rebirth was her first act of kindness. Then after giving birth, she placed you on a soft surface, lovingly cuddled, and gazed upon her baby with compassion. She welcomed you into the world with a joyful smile and gently spoke to you by calling out your name. She warmed you next to her body and gave you her succulent milk, feeding you from her own tongue, and wiping away your mucous. She cleaned your bottom with her bare hands and protected you from the fear of fire, flood, ravines, and the like. She would prefer her own illness over your getting sick and would die in place of you if need be. These are her intermediate acts of kindness.

Once you became an adolescent, she taught you whatever she knew concerning how to eat, behave, and the like without concern for herself. If necessary, she was even willing to ignore her own accumulations of negativity, suffering, slander, and all hardships as she worked to sustain you by acquiring money to supply you with food and clothing. When you were hungry and thirsty, she gave you food and drink; and when you were cold, clothes; and when needy, money, without holding back. These were the later acts of her kindness.

In short, whatever she knew and whatever she was capable of doing was for your benefit to bring you happiness. She always protected you from harm and strife. Thinking about these acts, this kindness is not only limited to just this life but extends to whenever she has been your mother. Meditate that her kindness has been extremely great. Then, bring your father and the others to mind in successive order and recall how, whenever he has been your father, his care for you was like this.

[Third,] repaying this kindness is as follows. Imagine your mother and that this dear mother who has shown great kindness has become disturbed by the demonic force of the passions and lacks the foresight to even see the path that leads to happier states of rebirth or liberation. Blinded, she has no teacher leading her to higher realms of enlightenment. Every moment she is tormented by her negative ways. Generally, she is wandering in saṃsāra; and in particular, she will wander through the lower realms. Lost in the prison of the three types of suffering, of course she will expect her child to save her for, if not, who else would it be? If this responsibility does not fall on your shoulders, then where will it fall? That is why one simply must take care of her.

Even though benefiting her through food, drink, monetary assistance, and so forth is a way of accumulating merit—given that this mother herself has previously attained the state of a Brahmā and a chakravartin monarch—no matter how much she enjoyed the status and wealth of those material things, there was no stability, which is why she has become who she is now. No matter how abundant her contaminated happiness may have been, the danger is that these limited states of happiness will become the cause for further suffering, like rubbing salt on a boil. Only helping her to increase saṃsāra's happiness is not so meaningful, which is why you must think, "I must lead her to the state of fully enlightened buddhahood." Consider this until you are deeply affected and then apply this to your father and the others as before.

Next, for the actual cultivation of the mind that strives to benefit beings, there are three stages, beginning with the meditation upon love. Imagine your own mother to be actually suffering from poverty and other such difficulties. If that is not effective, then by bringing your mother into consideration: know that she is subject to the suffering of change and compounded suffering, and due to that she is presently tormented by all aspects of the suffering of suffering. Needless to mention taintless happiness, she does not even have a chance for ordinary exhaustible happiness.

At present, she occasionally thinks she is happy, yet—like sprinkling cool water upon an open boil—that glimpse of happiness is short-lived as once again it brings on more misery. Hence, her experiences never really depart from the suffering of change. Thinking, "There is never any everlasting happiness," consider how limited her happiness really is. Think, "If only my dear mother could truly find contentment. May she find happiness. I must make sure that she does." Repeat this many times. Then, mentally imagine that you send her various states of well-being and gradually apply the same way of thinking to your father and others as before.

The meditation on compassion is to imagine that your dear mother is actually suffering. Once again, consider that this has come about due to her having produced the causes to be tormented at present. Then think, "If only my dear mother could be free from her sorrow. May she be free from it. I must make sure that she is," and repeat this many times until you mentally receive her suffering. After this, meditate on your father and gradually the others.

The exceptional attitude involves imagining your mother in front of you and thinking about how much she suffers and how limited her happiness is. Then make the wish, "I must ensure that she is free from misery and placed in a state of true contentment." Commit yourself to this. Repeat this verbally many times, and then apply this same attitude to your father and gradually the others like before.

Second is the cultivation of the mind that aspires to attain awakening as follows. One should think, "A commitment such as this [i.e., liberating all beings] cannot be kept as long as I remain in my present state; but if I attain fully perfected buddhahood, then I can accomplish this. This must be attained. Not only that, even in order to help myself, the state of buddhahood must be attained." Contemplate this.

To expand upon this, each light ray that emanates from the Buddha's kāya has the capacity to lead countless beings to liberation. Even with each branch of enlightened melodious speech, the answers that fulfill each being are heard. From the all-engaging enlightened mind of omniscience and unbiased loving kindness, enlightened deeds are spontaneously accomplished; and even in a single instant, the purpose of all sentient beings can be inconceivably fulfilled. Hence, from the perspective of recalling the qualities of enlightened body, speech, and mind with inspired faith and an intensely motivated aspiration, think, "I must attain the state of fully perfected buddhahood for the purpose of all sentient beings. May this occur! I will do whatever it takes to achieve this." Thinking in this way, recite the words.

This training with these seven upadeshas[128] is found in the great teaching lineage of Atisha and has been included here according to the speech of many authentic scholars.

3.2.1.1.3.2.2.2 From the Perspective of the Four Immeasurable Qualities

Second, training **from the perspective of the four immeasurable qualities** is as follows. Although there is nothing not included in what was just presented, as a side note to that, it states in the *Sūtra Requested by Maitreya*:[a]

> O Maitreya! The aspiration for the welfare of others involves great love, compassion, joy, and great equanimity.

So it is, and Atisha said:

> Those who wish to enter the dharma door of the great vehicle, pacify their misery [such as heat], and dispel all darkness will find it worthwhile to try to arouse the bodhichitta that is like the sun and the moon—if need be, for an eon.
>
> So, by initially training to wholly cultivate this, make it stable just like a mountain. Those who wish to prepare for this development must practice the four immeasurable qualities, such as love; and through effort and by meditating extensively, abandoning attachment and jealousy, they must give rise to this by practicing a fully qualified ritual.

[a] *jam pey zhü pa'i do* (*byams pas zhus pa'i mdo, āryamaitreyaparipṛcchānāmamahāyānasūtra*)

So, it is as taught. Similarly, this is clearly taught by the great Longchenpa as mentioned in *Resting the Mind in Repose*:

> Beginners will first meditate upon equanimity. Once that is established, they will then meditate upon the remaining three.

So, it is as taught. First, based on equanimity, establishing the mind of equality is also emphasized here. By bringing to mind the objective field of all sentient beings, the way to meditate is as the quote states:

> The objective field includes all sentient beings. Examine the mind as follows. At present, you harbor attachment toward your father, mother, and relatives and hatred toward adversaries. O Mind, you are detrimental!

So, it is as taught. When initially examining the mind, think to yourself, "This attitude of attachment to parents and loved ones of this life and aversion toward others who are adversaries is extremely intolerable." Bring shame upon yourself. Then, so as to establish an equal mind [the quote continues]:

> Although they are enemies, since wandering through beginningless lifetimes, they have been parents, relatives, and so forth who have helped me in many ways. To repay this kindness, will you still harbor harmful thoughts toward them?

Thus, from previous lifetimes the relationship between enemies and oneself must be taken into consideration as though recalling the past. Think, "From beginningless time while wandering in saṃsāra, these enemies have been my parents and relatives countless times over and have brought me great benefit as well. These adversaries have been my mother, and I have been their son [or daughter]. At that time, like this life's mother, they cared for me with immeasurable kindness. When I grew up and became a householder, I abandoned these mothers and forgot about their kindness. I have even beaten them, failed to quench their thirst or ease their hunger, so that finally these mothers even died of famine. Now that karma returns to face me."

Occasionally, imagine that an enemy takes rebirth as a wealthy person. Think that you are poverty stricken and have been separated from your parents since youth. This wealthy man adopts you as his own child and sustains you with food and clothing, raising you, and showing you tremendous kindness. Then, one day once you grow up and come of age, you turn on him and try to harm him in various ways. You steal his wealth and other horrible things. Is this the way to repay kindness through harmful thoughts and actions really satisfactory? Consider this repeatedly. Whenever an enemy or adversary comes to mind, remind yourself that previously this person has brought you nothing but benefit; so what is the point in harboring a harmful attitude toward him now? How shameless! Meditate on this until you almost gain a sense of attraction to this same individual.

Then, think to yourself, "Even my relative has been an enemy and harmed me [in the past]. At present, we are sharing this suffering, so how can I now respond in a beneficial way? In previous lives, I have been this relative's mother and brought him benefit; but now in this lifetime, he repays my kindness with harm." These considerations apply to the way of thinking about enemies.

Then, reverse that and consider they are merely cloaked as relatives but are the very culprits that caused you to engage in attachment and aversion by trying to benefit them, hence acquiring an abundance of nonvirtue. Think that you are amassing inconceivable causes for suffering all over again. Meditate in this way until you feel disturbed by just recalling these relatives. Based on this logic, it is taught that, although there is no reason to have attachment toward enemies or aversion toward relatives, this will serve as an antidote for previous habits of attachment and hatred.

Then, bring to mind someone neutral who you have not specifically benefited or harmed and who does not induce feelings of strong attachment or aversion in you. The quote [from *Resting in the Mind in Repose*] continues:

> Toward a neutral one, friend, or enemy, benefit or harm is uncertain; so it is unnecessary to feel attachment or aversion toward them.

So, even neutral ones have from time to time been beneficial friends and other times harmful adversaries. Attachment or aversion is unnecessary to feel, so allow the mind to be equal; and in the future, do not give rise to attachment or aversion again. When one is unequipped with this training: based on any insignificant reason, attachment or aversion will surface. The order for meditating upon this is as the quote continues:

> First, toward all those who are relatives, attachment is to be abandoned as though they were neutral. Then abandon aversion for enemies as though they were neutral and remain without partiality. In order to be free from delusion even toward the neutral, have the intention to dispel the passions of all beings at once. Meditate like this without clinging.

So, it is as taught. Saying "delusion" indicates that, from the perspective of dullness, one will not accomplish the purpose of neutral ones by having attachment toward those who have not shown either benefit or harm. That means that, although having a loving mind of equality, it is not mixed with clinging or attachment. The quote continues:

> Everyone has the same wish to acquire happiness and rid themselves of suffering. Nevertheless, unknowingly, they engage the causes for suffering. Alas! May all passions of the pitiful wanderers, including their habits, be pacified through the attitude of equality. Even though they are tormented by intense attachment and hatred: in the impartial mind of equality, may they be free from attachment and aversion.

Thus, by thinking of this meaning and reciting the words, practice as follows. It states:

> Thinking in this way, meditate upon one, then two, three, and finally all inhabitants of the country. Then consider the continent, the four continents, the single universe, doubled, tripled, and the entire universe.

So, it is as taught. The extent of becoming familiar with this meditation is as the quote continues:

> The extent of accomplishment is to achieve a mind of equality concerning self, others, enemies, and relatives.

So, it is as taught.

Afterward, the objects of equality become nonconceptual, and everything that is merely the mind itself becomes like space. Within this empty, unborn absolute truth, rest free from elaboration. After meditating as described before, the objects of equality and so forth—including all phenomena—are the magical manifestations of mind. Rest within absolute emptiness as the spacelike nature of mind. That is nonconceptual equanimity as the unity of upāya and prajñā.

After this, the meditation on love is as follows. The quote continues:

> Having attained the mind of equanimity toward all beings in this way, like wishing that your mother will always meet with happiness, hold this attitude toward all living beings. The objective field of love includes all sentient beings. Make the wish that they will come to know the temporary happiness of gods and humans and the ultimate bliss of awakening. With this intention, meditate from one to all beings until all beings in the limitless directions have been included.

So, it is as taught. Although it is necessary to include all sentient beings while meditating in this way, first train by considering your own mother. Imagine your mother is born in the lower realms, such as the hells, deprived of both temporary and ultimate states of happiness. In another direction, imagine the array of the pure lands, such as Sukhāvatī.[a] Without necessarily focusing only on suffering, mainly imagine her lack of contentment. Do this by thinking that there [in the lower realms] the array of the place as a pure land is nonexistent, the qualities of the body are not endowed, clothing as well is nothing like in the pure land, and states of well-being, happiness, and so forth are also nonexistent. Apply this to every aspect. Thinking how intolerable this is, proclaim, "If only [all beings] could be endowed with true happiness. May it come to be! I must make sure it does." Repeatedly meditate upon this from the depth of your heart.

The stages of meditation are that, by starting with a single sentient being, then just like before, continue until all limitless living beings are included. The extent of this development in the mind stream is as the quote continues:

> The signs involve having loving thoughts for all beings that even surpass the way a mother loves her only child.

So, it is as taught and the quote continues:

> Afterward, allow everything to just rest in equanimity. This is called "great nonconceptual love", the indication of the unity of love and emptiness.

Thus, as taught, rest within the nature of emptiness.

Then, the meditation on compassion is as follows. The quote continues:

> Having meditated on love that permeates all living beings, then like the unbearable feeling of knowing your parents are suffering, give rise to compassion by thinking of the suffering of all beings.
>
> To expand upon that, think, "All supremely kind parents have been accumulating negative karma due to me. Tormented by the karmic results of heat, cold, thirst, hunger, beating, and killing, they are sunk in the turbulent rivers of birth, old age, sickness, and death. So pitiful are the ways that they must suffer. They have no mind of quiescence that hopes to be free from that, and there is no virtuous spiritual guide

[a] Dewachen (*bde ba can*); western field of Akaniṣhṭha, Exaltation

> to show them the correct path. Alas! Have compassion for those who wander endlessly in saṃsāra. Having seen this for myself, how can it be ignored? May my body, endowments, and virtue amassed throughout the three times instantly free all living beings from their suffering!" Consider this from the depth of your heart.

So, it is as taught.

To elaborate on this, think that your mother takes rebirth in lower realms, such as the hells. Then consider that, because of you, she has accumulated an abundance of negative karma and is now suffering from heat, cold, hunger, thirst, and the like. Think that she is sunk in the tumultuous river of birth, old age, sickness, and death and how futile it is that she must struggle and endure so many forms of suffering. Bring these many aspects of her suffering to mind one by one. Think, "She has no wish to aspire toward freedom from this; she is without a spiritual guide and still must wander in saṃsāra limitlessly. How pitiful! How can I abandon her under such circumstances?"

Cultivate an intense loving attitude toward her that is based upon feeling her unbearable misery. Think, "By the power of whatever virtue I have accumulated through my body and expressed through my wealth throughout the three times, may this free her from all suffering! I must ensure that she is free from this suffering!" And pray from the depth of your heart. Although this repeats what was already mentioned, this was not explicitly described during the teaching on cultivating love. To think that, through the force of your happiness and virtue, [all beings] receive this brings the best result. Although the order is not delineated here, the way of practicing is similar to what was mentioned before.

The extent of cultivating this in the mind stream is as follows. The quote continues:

> It is taught that the indications occur when the misery of beings becomes unbearable.

Thus, the misery of all sentient beings becomes extremely unbearable. The quote continues:

> Afterward, rest in nonconceptual compassion. The indication is when emptiness and compassion unite.

So, as taught, by resting in emptiness, the unity of emptiness and compassion is as mentioned before.

Then, the meditation on joy is as follows. The quote continues:

> Hence, with an attitude moistened by compassion, meditate with joy toward all beings and their individual states of happiness. Toward those beings that have contentment, all of whom have been your mother, think, "Without having to rely upon me in order to find happiness, each have discovered happiness for themselves. That is supreme. From now onward until awakening is attained, may they never be separate from this joy and contentment." Think in this way and consider each and every one of them.

Thus, it is as taught. Now think that your mother is reborn in the pure lands, and imagine that she has total happiness, such as a perfect environment, she wears exquisite clothing, and the like. Think, "How wonderful that she has acquired such happiness on her own without any help from me. From now until enlightenment, may she never be separate from happiness and well-being such as this!" Hence, consider this from your heart. The stages of meditation are to begin with one person and gradually include all living beings.

The extent of having developed this in the stream of mind is as stated:

> The sign is to be without jealousy and always feeling a sense of joy.

So, it is as taught. This means to have joy from your heart without even the slightest feeling of jealousy whenever noticing the enjoyment and happiness of others. It states:

> Afterward, nonconceptual concentration is the nature of joy, while tranquil happiness is spontaneously present within body, speech, and mind.

Thus, by cultivating the single-pointed concentration of resting within nonconceptual emptiness and abiding in evenness, the tranquil joy of having pacified the coarse passions, such as jealousy and the like, is spontaneously present in your body, speech, and mind. In addition, this may occur without having to engage in any effort.

Concerning this, Master Yeshe Nyingpo[a] has said:

> Equanimity is the ground made perfectly even, where the flower beds of love are planted, shaded by the [trees] of compassion, and watered with unsullied joy.

[a] *slob dpon ye shes snying po*

Thus, equanimity like the earth is the basis of everything. From that, love is like flowers planted everywhere. Compassion is like shade, and their connectivity includes the clean water of joy that is unsullied by negative intentions. It is said that by sprinkling everything with this [joy], then no deterioration will occur.

In this way, repeatedly familiarizing with the four immeasurable qualities, the perfectly pure surpassing intention will develop. That will then indicate that bodhichitta has been born in the mind stream. Although this way of training the mind in the four immeasurable qualities is commonly known as "the way to arouse bodhichitta through the four immeasurables", I have never seen an extensive explanation of precisely how to do that as detailed as this. Hence, all of the important points drawn from the root text *Resting the Mind in Repose* have been included here. During the degenerate times, the great bodhisattva Lord Jigmed Chökyi Wangpo [i.e., Paltrul Rinpoche][a] gave this oral transmission to my tutor of great kindness, Zhechen Rinpoche [i.e., Zhechen Gyaltsab],[b] who then in turn gave me all of the key upadesha instructions that are synthesized and included here.

> The ambrosial essence of the tutor's oral transmission has filled the
> vase of my mind.
> Through this and in order to benefit beings, I make this offering as a
> celebratory banquet of benefit for others.

Thus, these are the verses that summarize this section.

3.2.1.1.3.2.2.3 By Exchanging Self for Others

Third, cultivating the bodhichitta by exchanging self for others is as follows. In the *Palpoche*'s description of Manibhadra's[c,129] life, we are told:

> The suffering of beings makes me wish that it would transfer to me.
> May my body afford great comfort to all living beings.

Thus, these great masters have taught that this [quote] reveals the meaning at hand. To expand upon it, exchanging the status of cherishing both self and others is what is meant by "cherishing others more than oneself". Otherwise, transferring the suffering of others to oneself is a way of abandoning self-cherishing, and being of great comfort for all living beings means to become a vessel of happiness

[a] *dpal sprul 'jigs med chos kyi dbang po*
[b] *zhe chen rgyal tshab rin po che*
[c] Norzang (*nor bzang*)

that is applied to the practice of cherishing others. These can be explained individually as stated in the *Gathering of Precious Qualities*:

> By giving one's happiness to others without any expectation, work for the welfare of other beings throughout the day and night.

Thus, the way of giving one's happiness to others is to abandon self-concern, to apply effort toward benefiting other living beings, and to engage the exceptional way of doing so. At present, self-cherishing and obsession with self-purpose spans throughout the day and night, even while dreaming. Just like that, here that way of thinking is applied to others as the way of cherishing them. This practice was taught and emphasized by the great bodhisattva Shāntideva, so that is the meaning synthesized here.

Initially, it is necessary to meditate upon the equality of self and others. The way to do so is to equally establish both self and others in happiness and to dispel all suffering. Both self and others equally experience the objects of happiness and sorrow because these experiences are equally based on the mind as the subject wishing to have the experience. Even the suffering of others that is harmful and meant to be dispelled is not at all different from one's own suffering. The happiness of others is beneficial and meant to be acquired and that, too, is not different from one's own. Not only that, any other beings who are worthy objects for dispelling suffering and establishing happiness are always similar to oneself. Both self and others are equal in that everyone desires happiness and does not wish to suffer.

One may think, "This is dissimilar because there are countless other sentient beings that cannot possibly be protected in the same way that I alone protect myself. The suffering of others will also not really harm me." [The answer is] for example, even though there are many distinctions of the body parts such as arms, legs, and so forth, it is acceptable to claim these as one's body. Even though there are many sentient beings, it is acceptable to hold them all as a single object for establishing happiness and discarding harm. Even though one's suffering will not harm others because of fixating upon it as one's own, it becomes personally unbearable. Likewise, although the suffering of others will not harm oneself: if others are cherished like oneself, then the palpable understanding that their suffering is not different from one's own suffering will occur to the mind. Even saying "self and others" is just a mental designation and has never existed from the perspective of the object.

This view of exchanging self for others is the basis for all benefit and happiness; and since it is the tool for cultivating the cherishing of others more than self, it is a worthy exercise. No matter what kind of incorrect or contradictory thoughts may develop, those can be reversed through fully qualified logic. With that in mind, when cultivating the mind of exchanging self for others, it is as stated in the *Bodhicharyāvatāra*:

> Whoever holds the wish to swiftly protect self and all others should exchange self for others. Embrace this sacred, secret conduct.

Thus, given that this does not fit into the minds of practitioners of the lower vehicles, it must be kept secret. Possessing supreme qualities, knowing how to meditate upon exchanging self for others, and cherishing them more than self is a sacred, secret instruction. Cherishing oneself is the source of all defeat, and cherishing others is the source of all fully endowed qualities. One may think, "I am incapable of truly cultivating the thought of exchanging self for others." Nevertheless, through familiarizing with the process, this becomes viable.

In the *Bodhicharyāvatāra*, it states:

> By the strength of becoming familiar in this way—even though there is anxiety that occurs from merely hearing the name of an unwanted circumstance—if there is no exchange of self for others, one will not be content.

And:

> Concerning this body of mine, to give of it to another is no longer a hardship.

So, it is as taught. For example, just like the anxiety that wells up when the name of an enemy is heard—if later that relationship changes and this enemy becomes a close friend—when separated from them, the anxiety of unhappiness will occur. In these ways, all fluctuating feelings are merely based on the familiarity of the mind.

To expound on this, exchanging positions with another is not that difficult. If there is familiarity with treating self like others and others like self, then the mental capacity to do so will occur. Perhaps one may wonder, "Well, the body of another is not my own; so no matter how much I become familiar with that, how can another's body be seen as my own?" Even your own body has been created by the drops of blood and semen of parents who are other than yourself and has come about as the aspect of their bodies. Self-fixation has arisen by the power of having become familiar with it. Like that—toward others' bodies—if one becomes familiar and cherishes them like one's own, then this [exchange] will develop.

The *Bodhicharyāvatāra* continues:

> Just like having fixated upon the blood and semen of others to be one's own, likewise one must become familiar with others.

So, it is as taught. Becoming familiar with this and afterward by seeing this potential, one becomes inspired to meditate upon exchanging self for others. Concerning these stages of meditation referred to as exchanging self for others, by thinking, "This other person is me, their eyes are mine," and so forth is not the way to train.

This mind training involves two aspects, namely, exchanging the position of cherishing self and the mind of forsaking others. That means to cherish others like you do yourself and to then disown yourself like the way you have forsaken others. In this way, it is then taught to exchange your happiness with the suffering of others. By viewing self-cherishing as the enemy and abandoning the efforts applied to establishing personal happiness and by viewing cherishing others as a quality and doing away with the intention to forsake the suffering of others, one mainly tries to apply effort toward dispelling this suffering. In short, this practice is based on not caring about personal happiness and is engaged in order to dispel others' suffering.

There are two afflictions that may be detrimental to this mind training. When the support for the happiness and sorrow of both self and others is held to as individually existing, like solidly holding to the colors yellow versus blue, one will then rely on the joy and sorrow that emerge as based on being "mine"; so it must then be accepted or rejected. When this relates to others, by thinking "this is theirs," it is then neglected. The antidote for this is to recognize that, ultimately, self and others are not individually established. By observing each other, the thought of others arises for oneself and the thought of oneself arises for others. This is like the example of how the mountains on this side and the ones on the facing side view each other from their own perspective. This is not like deciding something is blue in color so that only the thought of blue will arise and not some other color.

In order to remove the obstacle of thinking that the suffering of others has no bearing upon oneself and so doing nothing to remedy it is as follows. To dispel the suffering of aging, there is no point to try to accumulate wealth while you are young because the suffering of aging does not affect the time of youth. Like that, this holds true for past and future lives, this year, the next, this month, the next, today, tomorrow, morning and evening, and so forth, which are all similar. Similarly, the pain in the feet will not be alleviated by the hands because they are different. If perhaps one were to think youth and aging are a single flow and hands and legs are a single unit so that is different from the notion of self and other, again it states in the *Bodhicharyāvatāra*:

> Saying "a single flow and a unit" is faulty, like naming a mālā and an army . . .

Thus, saying "flow" means appearing as a continuity, for example, something that indicates continuity, like naming a rosary of beads. This term does not apply to the individual beads. Once removing the beads one by one, the name "rosary" will no longer apply. Likewise, concerning the term "unit", this refers to a group or, for example, the military, which is not the term for each individual soldier; yet since the term does not exist independently of that, it is referred to as "faulty". Similarly, saying "continuity" refers to many consecutive instances of past and future. Also, for the term "unit" this implies many aspects gathering together. Otherwise, there is nothing existing of its own accord or by virtue of its own individual capacity.

It is necessary to apply the self of the self and the self of another to the meaning of the terms "continuity" and "unit". Except for merely asserting the reliance of self and other, by virtue of their nature, they do not exist. Having become familiar with self-cherishing from beginningless time: when suffering overcomes oneself, it is unbearable. If one were to become familiar with this manner of self-cherishing but direct this toward others rather than self, then their suffering would also become personally unbearable.

To expand upon this, by abandoning the pitfalls involved with exchanging self for others, the actual way of meditating is as follows. Thinking about the specific qualities of cherishing others and the faults of cherishing oneself, the mind [of self-cherishing] must be arrested as stated in the *Bodhicharyāvatāra*:

> However much happiness exists in the world, all of it comes from wishing happiness for others. However much suffering occurs in the world, all of that comes from hoping for personal happiness.

So, all temporary and ultimate states of happiness that come about in the world come from wishing that others will be happy and cherishing them accordingly. From the perspective of cherishing them, by saving their lives, this brings longevity; expressing generosity brings abundance; respecting them as higher than oneself elevates one's own states of rebirth; expressing their qualities, others will speak about one in many positive ways; and so forth. In short, even the ability to wear some warm clothing at present, eat and drink good food, all the way through the higher states of well-being and wealth experienced by gods and humans up to the state of fully enlightened buddhahood—all come about due to this.

Likewise, whatever degree of physical and mental suffering that exists in the world comes from cherishing oneself and hoping for personal happiness. Due to self-cherishing and the power of attachment, one engages in many types of nonvirtue in order to require happiness in dependence upon the desired object. Then, concerning whatever might interrupt that process, such as if the mind of aversion develops, then nonvirtue will continue to be accumulated. Hoping for personal happiness and in order to attain that, the lives of others are taken, resulting in the shortening of life. By physically harming others, illnesses occur; by stealing their wealth, poverty occurs; and likewise much negative karma is accumulated through ill will, craving, and the like. In brief, even hearing the slightest displeasing speech is due to the power of self-cherishing. The suffering of saṃsāra in general and especially the unbearable misery experienced in the lower realms all occur solely due to this.

What is the reason for explaining all of this? Ordinary, immature people like us are obsessed with cherishing only ourselves and pursuing self-gain. In doing so, we fail to accomplish our goal and, not only that, are tormented by the overwhelming pain of saṃsāra. At present, there is almost no hope of reversing what we have done. While on the path of training, the sage Buddha Shākyamuni cherished only others and was able to accomplish that sole aim. He achieved the two aims in an effortless, spontaneous way. This can be understood by examining the distinctions.

Therefore, by only cherishing oneself, various unwanted situations have been brought about from beginningless time until now. By wishing for personal gain, self-purpose has become predominate; and by engaging with incorrect methods, one has been distracted in that direction for countless eons while never accomplishing those self-oriented goals, let alone that of others. Not only that, one has endured nothing short of an abundance of misery.

By exchanging the wish to accomplish personal aims for that of others: when one then actually does accomplish their aims and once swift awakening occurs, there is no doubt that the twofold aim of self and others[130] will be spontaneously fulfilled in a completely all-encompassing way. Not engaging like this, time is squandered with meaningless, insignificant hardships. Hence, by understanding this situation, think again and again with effort and mindfulness that, if the principal enemy of self-cherishing is no longer a concern, then it will not develop; but if it is a concern, then it must be cut off! Becoming familiar, make sure that, if it is not occurring, it does not develop and does not continue if it is.

Likewise, by thinking again and again about the qualities of cherishing others, take heartfelt joy in that. Think to yourself, "May cherishing others that has not developed be cultivated as much as possible; and if it is present, then may it continue to increase. As much as possible, I must cultivate the mind that cares for others, loves them, and holds a positive attitude toward them."

Just like the previous attitude that was directed toward oneself, achieving ease in this way and gaining certainty through the strength of personal experience concerning the faults versus qualities of these two: once able to exchange their status, then other sentient beings will be cherished just like oneself. It is then that, when you see sentient beings tormented by suffering and lacking well-being—just like right now how you want to be free from suffering and enjoy personal happiness—one will then feel even more love and compassion toward them. Pure intentions will naturally surface as a matter of course. This can be logically proven. Gradually, even the cultivation of the bodhichitta will become perfectly qualified and authentic.

Hence, know that this way of thinking is the unsurpassed upadesha for training in the cultivation of bodhichitta. It is an extremely important key point for arousing bodhichitta by gradually familiarizing with the practice of love and compassion. Without this, the cultivation of bodhichitta will not be developed merely through rhetoric. Atisha has told us:

> What is the benefit if a bodhisattva who does not know how to train in love and compassion? Well then, what should be done? From the beginning, they must progressively engage in the training.

So, it is as taught. Saying "what is the benefit" is a satirical expression that indicates displeasure. Saying "what should be done" indicates that the way to resolve this must be engaged.

3.2.1.1.3.2.2.4 Through the Activity of Sending and Receiving Virtue and Negativity

Fourth, the practice of sending and receiving virtue and nonvirtue is as follows. The *Seven-Point Mind Training* states:

> Practice both sending and receiving interchangeably.

So, it is and the quote goes on:

> These two must take the breath as their mount.

So, just as it is taught, here it also states that, initially, one begins by meditating upon this present life's mother. Clearly imagining her and recalling her kindness, feel a sense of compassion for the many experiences of suffering that she has endured in saṃsāra. Think, "Now I must dispel her torment and bring her benefit by repaying her kindness. What will really be of benefit? Happiness will bring her actual benefit, and the causes for that are based upon virtue that brings indirect benefit."

So, imagine all of one's happiness and virtue in the aspect of white light exhaled out through the right nostril with the breath as its mount. This enters into the left nostril of your mother in front of you. Think that your happiness and virtue fills her entire being from the crown to the soles, and that her body and mind are overcome by happiness and virtue. Once again, remind yourself that it is suffering that actually harms your mother. The cause for that is nonvirtue that indirectly harms her. Therefore, while inhaling through your nostrils, along with that imagine that all suffering and negativity of your mother emerges from your mother's right nostril in the aspect of dark-colored light, led by breath. This enters through one's left nostril and settles into the center of the heart as a heap of darkness. Feel that your mother is freed from all suffering. Continue to rotate and train in this practice repeatedly. Follow this by gradually training to include your father and others.

For the daily practice, imagine that you are surrounded by all sentient beings of the six classes, who are gathered in human form, tormented by their suffering in a pitiful state. Think that your happiness and virtue is sent to them along with your breath like before. Once again, receive their negativity and misery just like before. In your heart, the self-cherishing attitude abides in the aspect of a scorpion, and all of their suffering then strikes it. Like a feather incinerated by fire, think that the scorpion is completely removed.

In the *Seven-Point Mind Training*, it states:

> In order to inspire the mind to practice this, recite these verses during all activities.

So, just as taught, the verses are as stated in the *Jewel Garland*:

> May all of their negativities ripen upon me, and may all of my happiness ripen upon them without exception.

So, it is as taught. This is also mentioned in the Gelukpa sādhana for guru yoga called *Inseparable Bliss-Emptiness*:[a]

> Venerable Protector, guru of great compassion, may all of the suffering, negativity, and obscurations of motherly sentient beings ripen upon me right now without a single exception. By sending my happiness and virtue to others, grant blessings that they may possess that very happiness.

Thus, recite this. In the text just quoted, it literally states "therefore, venerable guru . . ." Here, I have made a slight adjustment to the wording so that it reads

[a] *lama chöd pa'i cho ga de tong yer med ma* (*bla ma mchod pa'i cho ga bde stong 'byer med ma*)

["venerable protector"].[131] That is because this was extracted from the middle of a sentence.

Likewise, it states in the *Prayer for Supreme Love*:[a]

> From the peak of existence to the lowest of hells, throughout all countless realms, including all gatherings of gods and asuras with great bellies, may they know happiness and may I receive their suffering.

So, it is and from the *Aspiration for Supreme Conduct*:[b]

> The suffering of sentient beings in the hells, animals, and the messengers of death, those in human places including gods, asuras, and the rest, the limitless heaps of suffering endured by all beings—may all of this descend upon me, and may they find everlasting happiness.

Thus, this is mentioned in many authentic scriptures. Machig has also said:

> Not recognizing the kindness of motherly sentient beings, they have been considered as enemies and relatives. Due to the power of negative karma, these mothers have experienced the unending suffering of saṃsāra. May I take on all of their suffering. If only all of my happiness and virtue could become theirs. In order to establish all of these mothers in happiness until saṃsāra is emptied, may all of their sorrow and the causes of sorrow and negativity ripen upon me. If only they could enjoy perfect happiness. How joyful! By giving my body, wealth, merit, and prosperity, including all accumulations of virtue throughout the three times, to motherly sentient beings—without pursuing even an instant's worth of personal gain, such as peace and well-being—and by engaging in the purpose of living beings without any concern even for one's life, may all these motherly sentient beings know only happiness and the causes for happiness.

So, it is and the quote continues:

> In order to accomplish the welfare of all beings in general and particularly those who are harm-doers, whatever occurs to me—be it illness, sorrow, negative circumstances, enemies, or demonic-force possession—without backing down, I am happy if all of their misery can

[a] *jampa chog jin gyi mon lam* (*byams pa mchog sbyin gyi smon lam*)
[b] *chog gi chöd pa'i mon lam* (*mchog gi spyod pa'i smon lam*)

> ripen upon me and I can receive it. It is necessary to give rise to the uncommon mind that feels a great sense of joy if beings are freed from suffering and able to abide in an exceptional state of well-being.

Hence, familiarize with this repeatedly.

The practice of sending and receiving is as follows. Sending happiness out to others while wishing happiness for sentient beings is love. Receiving their suffering and wishing them to be free from suffering is great compassion. In this way, the practice is complete.

This is in harmony with the level of a beginner's mind and is also the upadesha concerning the exchange of self for others. When reaching higher levels on the grounds, one can then place others in happiness; there will be no fear toward the sudden onset of personal suffering; and never backing down when sending them one's body, wealth, and so forth are all exceptional methods that are put into practice. This also constitutes being the practice of the six pāramitās because sending happiness and virtue amounts to generosity; receiving negativity and suffering, to patience; when doing so, guarding from self-cherishing and personal interests is discipline; taking joy in these deeds is diligence; single-pointedly concentrating upon this is concentration; and precisely knowing how to engage in this practice is prajñā.

Therefore, this is also referenced in the commentary, where it is clearly elucidated as a sacred instruction of chöd and includes the manner of visualization as follows.

> **In addition, there are the two phases of practice for sending and receiving. First, wishing that all of the unbearably painful misery and habits experienced by beings that are in this ocean of saṃsāra may ripen upon oneself and that self alone would have to experience this, imagine all beings are freed from their misery at that very moment. Think that the result of one's happiness and virtue is received by all sentient beings and that they come to possess supreme well-being.**
>
> **Second, with each exhalation of breath think, that all causes and results of one's happiness and virtue are equally distributed along with one's breath to all beings, dissolving into them. Exhale the breath. While inhaling, imagine that the suffering, negativity, and obscurations of all sentient beings dissolve into oneself and that frees them from all suffering. Train the mind in this way.**

So, it is as taught.

In previous times, the great spiritual guide Geshe Chedkhawa taught this practice of sending and receiving to many lepers, and there came to be many cases where their illnesses were cured. This became famous as Chedkhawa's special teaching for curing leprosy. This method is exalted because many illnesses, such as leprosy, phlegm imbalance, and the rest, have come about due to previous negative karmic accumulations and cannot be cured by rituals or traditional medicines. Moreover, here, I have explained this repeatedly without reprise because the benefits are stated in the text *Jewel Garland* that has been quoted above and which goes on to explain:

> If the merit accumulated through this expression could be given a form: then since that would surpass even the number of grains of sand on the banks of the river Gaṅgā, the universe itself would be too small to contain it. This was spoken by the Bhagavan and can be proven logically as well. The mind that wishes to benefit countless living beings will [accumulate merit] that is similar to that.

So, as taught, just as the meaning of the last three lines states, the inconceivable benefits of this practice are proven through quotations and logic alike. In these ways, there is [benefit], which is why the Bhagavan taught this. Illuminating logic proves there is such [benefit] since the number of living beings is limitless and the wish to benefit all of them, as well as the merit accumulated in doing so, will be concurrent with their numbers. This explains the meaning.

Among the many ways to cultivate the bodhichitta, the seven stages of the upadesha based on cause and result are well known according to the wisdom intent of the prajñāpāramitā sūtras. In fact, chöd originates with the prajñāpāramitā sūtras as already mentioned. Even the four immeasurable qualities are as the *Intermediate Mother* states:

> O Rabjor! Great bodhisattvas must meditate upon great love, compassion, joy, and great equanimity.

So, as taught, this is also mentioned in Machig's teachings where she explains the mind training from this perspective. Even in the [terma] commentary where this subject comes up, that presentation and exchanging self for others are special methods for training the mind. Given that is the case, either by synthesizing those three key points or any of the above, one must apply effort to correctly train in this. The *Gathering of Precious Qualities* states:

> Without a sprout, there is no way for the trunk of a tree to have emerged in this world. How then could the leaves, flowers, and fruits come about? Without the bodhichitta, there is no way for a victorious

> one to be present in this world. How then could the resultant states of Indra, Brahmā, and the shrāvakas come about?

So, just as the analogies state, if there is no bodhichitta, there is no state of perfected buddhahood. If that is lacking, then there will be no guide to illuminate the path of karma and virtue. Then, like how the analogy of Indra and Brahmā represents the higher states of existence and the shrāvakas represent the state of the blissful prosperity of nirvāṇa, all of that would not come about. Just as a vessel is gradually filled beginning with the first drop of water, even the mind of a beginner will become the cause of the unsurpassed state of enlightenment. Even if the root of virtue seems insignificant and is sealed with this intention, that, too, becomes the cause for the state of enlightenment. The *Bodhicharyāvatāra* states:

> Other ordinary virtues are like a plantain tree; once the fruit matures, there will be no further fruition. The fruit tree of the bodhichitta, on the other hand, always produces fruit and will continue to do so without conclusion.

Thus, the result of virtue not sealed by bodhichitta is like the fruit produced by the plantain tree having a conclusion. Virtue sealed by the bodhichitta, on the other hand, will be like the continual fruition of a fruit tree nourished by the four elements that has no conclusion. The great master Atisha spoke on this:

> Having destroyed all lower realms and achieved liberation from all obscurations, to that which bestows the state of perfected buddhahood—the bodhichitta—I bow down.

Thus, as mentioned these verses are always quoted in the oral lineage of the Kadampas, as Geshe Nyug-rumpa,[a] has also said:

> If one is able to cultivate the mind of awakening, he himself accumulates merit, purifies his obscurations, and dispels his obstacles; for without this, even though meditating upon the channels, winds, essential fluids, deities, and emptiness as well—aside from familiarizing with one's desires—not even a partial accomplishment will come about.

[a] *dge bshes snyug rum pa*

Hence, without this then, for example, concerning the state of perfect awakening that one hopes to accomplish, forget about taking a single step in that direction; not even a partial step will occur.

The Omniscient Longchenpa has also said:

> The root of all phenomena of this world and beyond, the heart of all paths, the guide for all sentient beings, as well as the mount that swiftly leads to the unsurpassed celestial dwelling place, is the exceptional intention of the bodhichitta. Therefore, train to generate this.

So, it is as taught. In the *Sūtra Requested by Maitreya*, it states:

> O Bodhisattva! If you were to possess a single doctrine that empties all lower realms, that swiftly allows one to reach the state of fully perfected buddhahood, and without allowing this to fall into the hands of negative friends, what would that one doctrine be?
>
> It is as follows—the exceptional intention, the fully endowed mind of awakening. Maitreya! If you possess this doctrine, the lower realms will be emptied; and without falling into the hands of negative friends, you will ever so swiftly attain the state of unsurpassed perfected buddhahood.

Thus, and in the sūtra *Piṭaka of the Bodhisattvas*,[a] it states:

> O Shāripu! If a great bodhisattva were to possess a single doctrine that would contain all of the teachings of the Buddha and other limitless teachings, what would that single doctrine be? It is as follows: the fully endowed intention of the bodhichitta. Shāripu! If a great bodhisattva possesses this single doctrine, then he or she will be holding all teachings of the Buddha, including boundless others.

So, it is as taught. This practice alone will suffice; and since it is the swift path to awakening, it states in the sūtra *Piṭaka of the Bodhisattvas*:

> Those who wish to swiftly attain the state of unsurpassed perfect awakening must train in the exceptional intention of the bodhichitta.

Thus, it is taught. In the sūtra *Arranged as a Stalk*,[b] it states:

[a] *chang chub sem pa'i de nöd kyi do* (*byang chub sems dpa'i sde snod kyi mdo, bodhisattvapiṭaka*)
[b] *dong po köd pa'i do* (*sdong po bkod pa'i mdo, gaṇḍavyūhasūtra*)

> Child of the Family! If one possesses the cultivation of supreme bodhichitta, his or her physical activities and thoughts will be beneficial. Always accumulating virtue, everything will be in that vein.

So, it is taught, and the qualities are limitless.

In order to enter the gateway of Secret Mantra, empowerment must be received; yet it is certainly necessary to have cultivated the bodhichitta as well. It mentions this in *Vajrapāṇi's Empowerment Conferral Tantra*:[a]

> This extremely vast maṇḍala of the great dhāraṇī mantras of the greatest of bodhisattvas is profound, fathomless, and most secret among the esoteric. Unsuitable to be shown to negative beings, you, Vajrapāṇi, have revealed the very rare. Given this has never been heard before, who then are the beings this should be taught to?
>
> Vajrapāṇi replied, "O Mañjushrī! For those who have engaged by meditating upon bodhichitta: once accomplishing bodhichitta then, Mañjushrī, through this conduct of the bodhisattvas, may they then engage with Secret Mantra to enter the maṇḍala of the dhāraṇī mantras by receiving the empowerments of great wisdom. Those who have not completed their cultivation of the bodhichitta must not enter. They must not even be allowed to witness the maṇḍala or be shown the mudrās or mantras.

So, it is as taught. By thinking about what this means, the great Atisha conferred empowerment upon Geshe Sangpuwey.[b] Atisha spoke on this:

> What is the point of an empowerment that is not in harmony with an intention based upon love, compassion, and the awakened mind? Sangpuwey, don't be so busy.

So, it is as taught. On the path of Secret Mantra, the receiving of spiritual attainment also depends on this. In the *Unwavering Realization*,[c] it states:

> By relying upon the bodhichitta, it is taught the siddhis of secret mantra will be attained. Otherwise, all rituals that accomplish mantra will be without result.

[a] *lagna dorje wang kur wa'i gyü* (*lag na rdo rje dbang bskur ba'i rgyud, vajrapāṇyabhiṣhekamahātantra*)

[b] *dge bshes gsang phu bas*

[c] *mi yo wa'i tok pa* (*mi gyo ba'i rtogs pa*)

So, it is; and in the tantra *Vajra Pinnacle*, it states:

> For many hundreds of eons, no matter how hard one tries: among the four categories of individuals in this world, those who do not cultivate bodhichitta are filled with doubt, do not practice according to the teachings, and lack faith; although they practice, they will have no attainments.

So, as it mentions, being without the bodhichitta, not following according to the teachers' speech, and so forth, those who are in any of these four categories will not receive attainment.

In brief, the *Sūtra Requested by Palchin*[a] sums this up:

> If the merit of the bodhichitta were put to form, even the sky would not be large enough to contain it.

So, it is as taught. The benefits are immeasurable. The reason for this is also mentioned in the commentary on the *Four-Hundred Stanzas*:

> It explains here that, if the merit of a single bodhisattva were to be given a form, it would pervade all sentient beings who are themselves limitless. The Buddha's omniscience is also limitless, and the full dedication of that is also limitless.

Thus, and our teacher [i.e., Lord Buddha] also mentioned this in detail as stated in the *Sūtra Requested by Subāhu*:[b]

> O Bodhisattva! If you wonder how to fully perfect the pāramitā of diligence, then Subāhu, in order to do that the bodhisattvas have perfectly trained in this way. In each of the ten directions, there exist limitless realms of this world. In each of the realms of those worlds, beings are limitless. Although those beings are limitless, as such there are no limitations whatsoever. In order to benefit those limitless beings, then one must don the armor [of diligence]. In order for those limitless sentient beings to have happiness, the armor that is worn involves having a limitless perspective concerning benefiting those beings. Concerning that limitless perspective that hopes to bring infinite happiness to those

[a] *pal chin gyi zhü pa'i do* (*dpal byin gyis zhus pa'i mdo*)
[b] *lag zang kyi zhü pa'i do* (*lag bzang kyis zhus pa'i mdo, subāhuparipṛcchāsūtra*)

> beings, will the root of that infinite virtue become selfless or will it transfer to another frame of mind?
>
> Even while sleeping, throughout the day and night, the momentary mind is instantaneously increasing and expanding until fully perfected. Generating a limitless root of virtue with this momentary mind of each instant and perfecting the boundless heap of the bodhisattvas' meritorious accumulations, to then realize the state of awakening will not be difficult. Given that is the case, for oneself to amass infinite roots of ever-increasing virtue with this momentary mind in each instant means one will then perfectly see the infinite root of virtue increasing and expanding. With that as the basis, it will not be difficult to discover the state of fully perfected awakening. While perfectly seeing this and in order to attain the state of perfected awakening, think, "Hence, this diligence must never diminish even at the cost of life."

So, it is and the quote continues:

> Subāhu! Furthermore, the bodhisattvas perfectly train in this way. Whoever hopes to remove the suffering of limitless sentient beings, including the instantaneous connections of the momentary mind, will amass infinite roots of virtue with the instants of the momentary mind; and this will be ever-increasing. When the limitless root of virtue expands as such, think, "It goes without saying that whoever accomplishes this will wish to remove the suffering of infinite beings that dwell in limitless realms for countless eons through fathomless accumulations of merit."

Thus, as it is taught, by cultivating the bodhichitta in this way, infinite beings are brought benefit; and limitless happiness is established. This quotation reveals through logic that, since beings are placed in the state of the limitless qualities of fully perfected buddhahood, the root of virtue and boundless masses of merit are fully perfected every single moment.

Hence, my sublime master and tutor, whose name is difficult to even verbalize without an important reason, Do-ngak Chökyi Gyaltsen,[a,132] has said:

> That which is praised by the venerable victors and their heirs is the great pillar of the path of the supreme vehicle, the quintessence of all

[a] *mdo sngags chos kyi rgyal mtshan*

> dharma, the bodhichitta. Thus, heart son of mine, you must familiarize with this in the core of your mind.

From his loving kindness, he gave me this personal advice. I have already explained that this is the essential practice of the path of chöd.

> Wishing to attain perfected awakening for the welfare of others, these qualities of the bodhichitta are limitless.
> The methods that develop this in the mind stream without pretext must be held as the crux among practices.

These are the verses that summarize this section.[133]

3.2.1.1.4 Accumulating Merit through the Maṇḍala and Seven-Branch Offerings

This has two parts:

1 Offering the maṇḍala
2 Practicing the seven-branch prayer

Fourth, the accumulation of merit from the perspective of the maṇḍala and seven-branch offering prayer[a] has two sections: offering the maṇḍala and practicing the seven-branch prayer.

3.2.1.1.4.1 Offering the Maṇḍala

This has three parts:

1 Outer maṇḍala
2 Inner maṇḍala
3 Secret maṇḍala

For the first, the root verses state:

> *Phet!* The outer maṇḍala is the external arrangement of the all-pervasive trichiliocosm, the inner glory is the perfectly complete arrangement of one's body, and the self-appearing, spontaneously present array is the secret maṇḍala. In order to amass the accumulation of the two levels of merit, these offerings are made to the victorious ones.

[a] *yen lag dün pa* (*yan lag bdun pa, saptāṅga*)

Thus, it is taught.

While reciting these verses, the visualization is as follows. With the field of refuge envisioned as explained before, the method for offering the maṇḍala is to contemplate the outer, inner, and secret maṇḍalas.[134]

Saying ***phet***, one visualizes the field of refuge and so forth. **The outer maṇḍala is the outer arrangement of the all-pervasive trichiliocosm** universe. Considering that **the perfectly complete arrangement of one's body** is the four continents including Mt. Meru, they are offered. **The inner glory and** abundance is the inner maṇḍala offering. Imagining this and offering it to **the self-appearing, spontaneously present array** of the mind's nature **is the secret maṇḍala.** Here [for the secret], the term "maṇḍala" is interpreted as the support. **In order** for self and others **to amass** vast **accumulations of the two levels of merit, these** maṇḍalas **are offered to the victorious ones** and their heirs. So, it is.

For this, there are three: **the outer** maṇḍala, the **inner** maṇḍala, **and** the **secret maṇḍala.**

3.2.1.1.4.1.1 Outer Maṇḍala

First, it is as stated in the sūtras and tantras, such as the *Sūtra of Sacred Golden Light*:

> Whenever I became a chakravartin monarch, this was due to my having offered in the past to the victorious ones jewels that fill the oceans, earth, and the four continents.

Thus, as taught, even the Bhagavan himself said that in previous times he made offerings to the tathāgatas in this way. The tantras state:

> To the pure lands of the buddhas, the realms of the trichiliocosm without exception adorned with the desirable qualities are offered to perfect the wisdom of the buddhas.

So, it is as taught.

The principal source for all details concerning the enumerations of heaps for maṇḍala offerings is found in the eighth chapter of the root *Guhyasamāja Tantra*:

> This field filled with the seven royal signs is offered daily by the wise that possess prajñā in order to receive spiritual attainment.

Thus, as taught, it is asserted by scholars that this is the source; and even in the shāstra *Fifty Verses of Guru Devotion*, we are told:

> With supreme faith in the maṇḍala and during the three times, with palms pressed together holding a flower . . .

Thus, first a maṇḍala of heaped flowers is offered to the guru during three times, and then prostrations and service are offered as the quote states.

The quotation taken from the *Gathering of Precious Qualities* also mentions "this field". This is not referring to individual directions. Similar to our teacher, who was a supreme nirmāṇakāya emanation, there is a field to be tamed by just a single supreme nirmāṇakāya, although simultaneously sending a billion manifestations. This field would include the four continents, sun, moon, Mt. Meru, the desire gods' realms, and so forth.

The fifteen heaps that are described in the quote include the excellent dwelling place on the pinnacle of Mt. Meru, the four continents surrounding, the eight subcontinents, and the sun and moon as a pair. Saying "the seven royal signs" refers to the seven precious royal signs, as well as what the commentary for that called the *Illuminating Lamp* describes as "seven precious gems." They are ruby, sapphire, lapis, emerald, diamond, pearl, and coral.

This also reveals the great treasure vase as the source of all desirable abundance, including the categories of precious gems such as these. Including [the vase], with the preceding seven, this totals eight. It is taught that this twenty-three heaped maṇḍala tradition was embraced by many mahāsiddhas, such as Paṇḍita Nāropā, Master Abhekara[a,135] and others, including sublime Tibetan scholars and accomplished practitioners. Those individuals who are skilled in the accumulation of merit and who wish to accomplish the siddhi of mahāmudrā through the guru's upadesha are upholders of prajñā. By filling this field [of refuge] in this way, it is taught that one must offer this three times to the guru, who embodies the buddhas. Along with that, Drogon Chögyal Pakpa[b] added eight categories of offerings presented by Lāsyā[c] and so forth. The concise way of offering is to just recite "the foundation of the earth is adorned with . . ."[d] and so forth while making seven heaps. These are the three ways.

The way of practicing these offerings is as stated in the *Sūtra of Maṇḍala Offering*:[e]

[a] *pan chen na' ro pa* and *slob dpon a bhya ka ra*
[b] *'gro mgon chos rgyal 'phags pa*; a founder of the Sakya lineage
[c] Gegpama (*sgeg pa ma*); She of Beauty
[d] *sa zhi pö chü* (*sa gzhi spos chus*)
[e] *kyil khor gyi do* (*dkyil 'khor gyi mdo*)

> Generosity is to use the feces and urine from a cow; discipline is to smooth the surface; patience is to remove the insects or bugs; diligence is to fully engage this activity; concentration is the mind that focuses even for a moment; and prajñā is the clear designs.

So, it is as taught. It is taught that smoothing the surface with the five substances from the cow is the practice of generosity. The five substances are mentioned in kriyāyoga's *Excellent Attainment*:[a,136]

> The milk from a sorrel-colored cow, yogurt, butter, urine, and feces . . .

So, just as taught, these substances are used in many ways, such as sprinkling them upon the maṇḍala and so forth. The way of using them involves knowing two traditions: that of the Indian scholars and the assertions of some Tibetan masters.

For the first, the master Buddhaguhya[b] has said:

> First, no matter what the maṇḍala's dimensions are, that surface is covered by butter. The feces will turn into twenty substances; and upon that, the milk and yogurt are applied. The first [application] is three times more than the butter. First to squeeze the feces, place this in water; and then using muslin, drain the water through a strainer. Leave it like this between two to three days. Then by rotating, apply the substances gradually for seven days without missing two consecutive days.

Thus, that surface is covered by butter as the basis for the substances. The other four substances are the authentic combinations to apply. Gradually smoothing them on that surface is the basis or ground for the maṇḍala. Although the way of boiling [i.e., heating this] is not generally discussed, it states in *Victorious over the Enemy*:[c]

> By boiling this in a clean vessel, toss all clear water out along with the unclean substances. What remains is meant to be used.

So, by boiling, toss out the clear water and the sullied; the remaining is meant to be applied in whatever way is called for.

Second, the tradition of Tibetan scholars is as follows. It states:

[a] *cha gyü lek drub* (*bya rgyud legs grub*)
[b] Sangye Sangwa (*sangs rgyas gsang ba*)
[c] *dra ley nam gyal* (*dgra las rnam rgyal*)

> The Victorious One has said that, from a cow that grazes in a remote and clean environment, the five substances [to utilize] are this cow's butter, milk, yogurt, feces, and urine. If the grass a cow has grazed upon has been cut, treated, and so forth or rendered unclean from ingesting various substances, then the five substances from such a cow are not considered acceptable. That is why the need for cleanliness is mentioned here. When needed, it is difficult to find these substances; so the ritual for accomplishing pills is explained.
>
> Collect feces before it drops on the ground, dry it in the sun, and powder it in the shade. Then, mix the urine with this and dry it again. Repeating this three times, then the butter, yogurt, and milk are mixed in. Shape the pills the size of small bird eggs and dry them in the shade. This is the upadesha of the masters.

Thus, as taught, saying "ritual" means the method, and saying " powder" refers to grinding down. It is not enough to only locate such a cow; the color of the animal needs to be a pale yellow, or sorrel will suffice. The first-born calf is usually called "the first born", and it is said that is the recommended cow to acquire.

With substances such as this, the base of the maṇḍala is then polished; the perfect manner of polishing [is] morality. Removing any living creature from the base, such as any insect, is patience. To apply effort toward that is diligence. To focus the mind single-pointedly upon this as a continuity of moments is concentration. Clearly knowing how to draw or arrange this is prajñā.

The materials for the maṇḍala are at best precious jewels; middling, bronze or bell metal; and the least, stones or wood. Nevertheless, it is acceptable to use whatever is available. It states in *Master Kampala's Maṇḍala Ritual:*[a]

> With the basis of the maṇḍala made of pure sand and dung, remove the living creatures and create an excellent clay foundation.

Thus, it is acceptable to use clay for the maṇḍala base.

Therefore, the cause for accumulating personal merit is based upon whatever excellent abundance is amassed according to one's wealth. If there is nothing, then even earth and stones are appropriate. The size is not fixed and does not depend upon the quality of the material. It is said that, as long as the size is not smaller than a cubit, this will suffice as a method through which exceptional realization arises in the mind stream.

[a] *lobpon kam pa ley dzad pa'i mandala gyi cho ga* (*slob dpon kam pa las mdzad pa'i man da la gyi cho ga, maṇḍalavidhi*); Ratnākarashānti

Whatever the case may be, the surface of the maṇḍala must be smooth, even, and pleasing to behold. That is extremely important. The materials used for the heaps should be made of precious substances, medicines, herbal essences, and various grains. If those are unable to be acquired, it is said to still be acceptable to use whatever is available such as earth, stones, wood, and the like. The field of accumulation is as previously mentioned. Here, it is as stated in the terma commentary:

> **The outer maṇḍala is the outer vessel of the universe, including Mt. Meru, the four continents, as well as the subcontinents, and one-hundred million realms among which are the realms of the gods. Without considering that even as much as an atom's worth belongs to oneself, bring this to mind and present the offering.**

So, it is as taught. Saying "there is nothing that does not belong to oneself" means that all of these phenomena actually originate from the universal concurrent merit of sentient beings. Based on that notion, one owns a share of this; or one could say that, whether this belongs to oneself or not, it is merely a designation. Thinking and holding to the notion that this does belong to oneself is said to be acceptable. Saying "a billion" refers to the trichiliocosm. In terms of that, the enumerations of heaps are not clearly mentioned; but according to what is well known these days, the thirty-seven heaped maṇḍala offering is accepted according to contemporary oral tradition. Hence, through that, all else is subsumed. Here, this is explained according to that.

If possible, hold some flower petals [or substances for the heaps] between the thumb and forefinger of the right hand and extend the remaining fingers. Then sprinkle scented water and the cleansing cow substances over the surface in a clockwise direction. Recite *om benzar bhumi ah hung*. *Om* means to give supreme [siddhi and] abundance and to hold the jewel that is the source of all desires like a wish-fulfilling jewel. Here as well, it is acceptable to say that [*om*] functions to induce all desirable objects, such as the fully endowed glory of the outer universe. Whatever the case, as the exceptional syllable that gathers the blessings of all the victors' enlightened bodies, speech, and minds, this syllable leads all secret mantras; and that is also the case here.

Benzar bhumi means vajra ground. A vajra is invincible and indestructible, revealing the fact that the ground is solid and stable. Think that upon this ground are the sequentially arranged elements and upon them rests the extremely vast and powerful golden foundation of the earth. Saying *om benzar re khe ah hung*, *om* is the lead syllable meaning enlightened body, and the mantra ends with *ah* and *hung*, the seed syllables of enlightened speech and mind. Hence, these [syllables] bring blessings to increase the potency of this mantra. Saying *benzar re khe* means vajra patterns, and the vajra's meaning was explained above. Saying "patterns" means similar to that which is drawn, like the iron fence that fully surrounds the four continents. While reciting this mantra then, use the ring finger and scented water to make a circle at the perimeter of the maṇḍala base. When saying "in the center that is fully surrounded by the outer fence," think there is the golden foundation and the surrounding iron fence. Meditate that at the basis of all of this upon a wind maṇḍala is a single iron fence surrounding. By saying "*hung* in the center," place the flower held with the fingers of the right hand in the center of the maṇḍala and think that obstructions are removed.

According to another tradition, it is said that this [*hung*] is the seed syllable that generates Mt. Meru. Whatever the case, in the center Mt. Meru appears square-shaped and composed of four precious gems: silver in the east, lapis in the south, ruby in the west, and gold in the north. The total height is some one-hundred sixty thousand leagues, with the base penetrating eighty-thousand leagues into the depths of the ocean and eighty thousand above. Among the four gradual levels, the innermost is the highest. The ring of golden mountains surrounds the dimensions of this, with seven oceans interspersed between them. At the pinnacle of Mt. Meru are the thirty-three realms of the gods, and in their midst is the victorious celestial palace blazing with light like one-thousand suns. Surrounding this are wish-granting trees of the gods, as well as pools for bathing. There are jeweled palaces, divine ambrosia, divine brocade clothing, and precious mālās inconceivable to witness. There are boundless offering substances everywhere, such as the great drum of the gods that resounds the beat of the dharma. At the four levels are the four classes of great kings, including the Karoṭapāṇi yakṣhas[a,137] and the rest. Think that the king of the nāgas with great wealth abides in the oceans and upon the golden mountains.

Saying *shar lu pak po*,[b] place a heap in the east. From the perspective of Jambudvīpa, this continent abides to the east of the mountain. Given that the inhabitants of this continent have bodies twice as high as those who dwell in Jambudvīpa, the continent is literally called Elevated Body Height. The shape is like a half moon, and the level side faces the mountain. The earth and space are completely white in color, and the inhabitants have lovely forms with gentle hearts. Possessing vast abundance, they live in an environment filled with precious jewels.

When saying *lo dzam bu ling*,[c] place another heap to the south. On this continent, when the fruits from the tree named *tri shi* or *dzambu* fall into the waters, the sound of *dzambu* can be heard. Hence, that is the source of the name for

[a] *nödjin lagna zhong tok* (*gnod sbyin lag na gzhong thogs*)

[b] *shar lus 'phags po*; eastern Pūrvavideha, Elevated Body Height

[c] *lho 'dzam bu gling*; southern Jambudvīpa, Rose-Apple Continent

this continent Dzambuling, or Jambudvīpa in Sanskrit. Shaped like a triangular chariot box, the shortest side faces Mt. Meru. The earth and sky are blue, and in the midst of this is the indestructible vajra seat that will endure even if the eon self-destructs. To the east is Wu Tai Shan,[a] sacred place of Ārya Mañjushrī; to the south, the place of Ārya Avalokiteshvara, Mt. Tali;[b] to the west, the land of Oḍḍiyāna, the Land of the Ḍākinīs;[c] and to the north is Shambhala,[d] the seat of the Rigden dharma rulers, and so forth. Many such sacred grounds exist there. Imagine they are all filled with varieties of offering substances.

Saying *nub ba lang chöd,*[e] place a heap to the west. Here, cattle and wish-fulfilling jewels are utilized, and the continent is spherical. The sky and earth are red, and everything present is full of immeasurable abundance. Saying *chang dra mi nyen,*[f] place a heap in the northern direction. Since seven days before these inhabitants die they hear a previously unheard displeasing sound, the name of the continent came to be. The shape is square, and the earth and sky are golden. All inhabitants have lovely forms that illuminate light. Their abundance is equal to that of the gods, and the environment is filled to capacity with exceptionally wonderful offering substances.

According to the perspective of our continent Jambudvīpa, Pūrvavideha is to the east. Saying "east" is according to where the sun and moon arise; and depending upon that, the other directions are established. When the sun and moon encircle Mt. Meru, the mountain is in the center. In dependence upon that, there are no distinctions of east and so forth; so aside from that, these distinctions cannot be established at all. As the sun and moon encircle Mt. Meru in a clockwise direction and since the sun and moon rise and set above each continent, the direction they arise from is the east. Hence, the iron fence is in the southern direction, the sun and moon set in the west, and Mt. Meru is in the north. For example, from the perspective of Pūrvavideha, Uttarakuru is to the east; to the south is Pūrvavideha; to the west is Dzambuling; to the north is Aparagodanīya. The others follow suit.

To the right and left are the eight continents with shapes, abundance, and physical forms slightly less than the principal continents. Among them when saying "Pūrvavideha and the subcontinents,"[g] place slightly smaller heaps to the right and left of the eastern heap while thinking this represents the two subcon-

[a] Gyanag Riwo Tse-nga (*rgya nag ri bo rtse lnga*); the five-peaked mountain in China

[b] *ri bo ta li*

[c] Orgyan Khandro Ling (*o rgyan mkha' 'gro'i gling*)

[d] *sham bha la*

[e] *nub ba glang spyod*; western Aparagodanīya, Bountiful Cow

[f] *byang sgra mi snyan*; northern Uttarakuru, Ominous Sound

[g] *lu* and *lu pak* (*lus dang lus 'phags*)

tinents. Saying "Jambudvīpa and the subcontinents,"[a] place heaps to the right and left of the southern heap. Saying "Aparagodanīya and the subcontinents,"[b] place heaps to the right and left of the western heap. Saying "Uttarakuru and the subcontinents,"[c] place heaps to the right and left of the northern heap. Think that each continent is flanked by two subcontinents.

Then, the stage of placing heaps inside the four great continents begins with saying "precious mountain,"[d] and a heap is placed at the center of the eastern continent. That is mainly composed of an abundant variety of precious jewels, such as ruby, sapphire, lapis lazuli, emerald, diamond, pearl, and coral. Imagine there are extremely vast and abundant mountains of jewels. In addition, it is said that the jeweled mountains are broad and lofty with varieties of jewels emerging from them.

Saying "wish-granting tree,"[e] place a heap at the center of the southern continent. The principal abundance there is the wish-granting tree, extremely grand with roots made of gold, trunk of silver, branches of lapis, leaves of crystal, petals of gems, and red pearls for flowers. The fruits are the essence of diamonds. As a tree composed of the seven royal precious signs, this is the source of all desires and fully endowed abundance.

Saying "wish granting cow,"[f] place a heap at the center of the western continent. The main abundance there is the cow of plenty with horns made of diamonds, hooves of sapphire, and tail similar to a wish-granting tree. The hump and dewlap of the cow are well executed, and the color is golden brown. The form is perfect and pleasing to behold. Whatever is wished for, such as milk and so forth, unceasingly issues forth.

Saying "crops without harvest,"[g] place a heap at the center of the northern continent. The primary abundance here is the crops that need not be harvested, such as rice the size of four fingerwidths per grain growing everywhere. The grains are without husk and, if harvested in the morning, by evening mature once again; if harvested in the evening, are mature by the morning. Think that the color and taste are also exquisite. Then, at the inner face of each continent's principal locale as well as in the four cardinal directions, heaps are gradually placed as follows.

Saying "precious wheel"[h] and so forth while reciting these eight lines, think that the precious-wheel heap is [first] placed in the intermittent space of the

[a] *nga yab* and *nga yab zhen* (*rnga yab dang rnga yab gzhan*)
[b] *yo den* and *lam chog dro* (*gyo ldan dang lam mchog 'gro*)
[c] *dra mi nyen* and *dra mi nyen gyi da* (*sgra mi snyan dang sgra mi snyan gyi zla*)
[d] *rinpoche riwo* (*rin po che'i ri bo*)
[e] *pag sam gyi shing* (*dpag bsam gyi shing*)
[f] *död jo'i ba* (*'dod 'jo'i ba*)
[g] *ma mö pa'i lo tog* (*ma rmos pa'i lo tog*)
[h] *khorlo rinpoche* (*'khor lo rin po che*)

inner face of the precious mountain. This precious wheel is uncreated by others. By the power of the chakravartin monarch's merit, it is composed of the purest refined gold found in Jambudvīpa. With one-thousand spokes, the wheel spans some five-hundred leagues. The magnificence and qualities [of the wheel] rival the power of a second sun of this world. In terms of these qualities, they include elevating into the sky and traversing the distance of one-hundred thousand leagues in a single day. By the strength of the precious wheel, the elephant, horse, carriage, and foot soldier appear in the pathway of the sky as the four aspects of the monarch's cavalry.

In addition to that, the qualities include the ability to traverse to wherever one hopes to arrive, such as at the four continents and the divine dwelling places of the four great kings and so forth. Other qualities include that the chakravartin ruler can make it possible to hear that which was unable to be heard before. Even if there were no intention to express generosity or dedication: at the moment of seeing their king, the ministers and subjects are helpless but to express this. Such are the five qualities that are possessed.

Saying "precious jewel,"[a] in the intermittent space in front of the wish-granting tree is a precious jewel made of lapis lazuli with the capacity to illuminate darkness for as far as eight leagues. In the daytime, the qualities of the light dispel the torment of heat. Those suffering from thirst will be satisfied through the emergence of the eight qualities of pure water that issue forth from the jewel. Other qualities include fulfilling most every wish of the king. Light of various colors emerges from the eight facets of the jewel indicating the eight qualities that the jewel possesses, namely, the capacity to cure contagious diseases among beings as far as one-hundred leagues away; causing beings to rest in equanimity and have all of their needs fulfilled; ensuring there will be no drought or flooding brought on by disturbances in the atmosphere; ensuring relief for those tormented by the result of their nonvirtue, such as the threat of mental disturbances or negative physical locations such as deep, dark ravines; causing fruit-bearing trees to grow; causing springs of pure water to emerge, as well as ponds and gardens that are delightful to behold; ensuring animal rebirth will not be taken and that animals will be unable to impose harm; and ensuring protection from untimely death.

In the intermittent space in front of the cow of plenty is the precious queen, lovely to behold with a form that carries the scent of sandalwood and incense. Her sweet breath smells like the fragrance of the *utpala* flower. Like the ocean bird *kalantaka*,[b] whoever touches her experiences ecstasy. Those who reside in her place will have all suffering of hunger and thirst dispelled. Having abandoned the five faults of a woman—namely, pining for another lover, avarice,

[a] *norbu rinpoche* (*nor bu rin po che*)
[b] *ka lanta ka*

attachment to unacceptable things, taking pleasure in unacceptable things, and wishing to take the life of one's partner[138]—the five qualities she possesses are in harmony with the king's wishes. She bears many children, inspires harmony by caring for other females like her own mother and sister, increases the qualities of the kingdom, elevates the kingdom's status, and has no jealousy toward her husband or other females. Along with those, the precious female never gossips or wastes words, never holds wrong view, and even without a partner is not distracted by sensory stimuli such as sound, smell, taste, and touch. Think that this queen possesses these eight qualities.

In intermittent space in front of the place where crops grow without harvest is the precious minister. Think that he possesses qualities such as endowments that are extremely grand, including a variety of jewels like diamonds, emeralds, precious stones, and so forth that fill all directions. The riches never vanish, and he himself never deceives anyone or harms them in any way. He acts like a father to all subjects, so the mere sight of him brings joy and satisfaction to all.

In the intermittent region of southeastern space is the precious elephant complete with four legs, trunk, genitals, and tail as the seven limbs. His color is white like a snow mountain, and he possesses the strength of one-thousand ordinary elephants. At the moment other elephants catch his scent, they are unable to relax in his presence. He can fight in three places including water, land, and space and has the strength to circle Jambudvīpa three times in a single day. He is clairvoyant and can even be led by just a strand of string. Especially when mounted by the king, he knows where to go without command according to the king's wishes. He does not disturb the body of the rider nor harm any other living creatures as he walks. He is majestic in demeanor and does not incite fear in children, while always listening to whatever is commanded. He is victorious over the enemies at battle. Consider that these are the qualities that he possesses.

In the space between the south and the west is the precious horse, white like the night lily flower *kumudta*.[a] With a unicorn jewel of the gods, the horse sports boundless ornaments, such as the saddle and horse blanket that are adorned with many auspicious designs. The color, constitution, and size of the horse are perfect; and if commanded by the king to circle the world three times, this horse can do so in a single day's time without tiring. His body is healthy, flawless, and majestic. He does not disturb the rider's body and possesses every single pleasing quality that comes to mind.

In the space between the west and the north is the precious general. He never harms other living beings and has rejected all conduct that is not conducive with dharma. He is skilled in all worldly activities, and his body and mind are never weary of accomplishing perfectly correct deeds. He knows whatever the king

[a] *ku mud ta*

needs or thinks without it needing to be expressed; and without hesitation, his forces enter the direction of the enemies of the doctrine and beings in order to destroy them. He is skilled with mastery over establishing encampments and virtually all activities associated with war and retreat. Think that he possesses all qualities necessary to engage the king's activities.

Although the number of seven royal signs is not counted in the same way [each time]: when counting the precious householder as one of them, the precious general would then not be counted. The sūtras state:

> Both minister and general are counted as one, and the householder is either counted elsewhere or separately. In either case, the precious minister is counted separately. The precious minister has an excellent form with great strength that is capable of making the best decisions on any occasion. He has love and admiration for his master [i.e., the king] and is naturally stable like a trustworthy captain.

Thus, it is as taught; and among these [two] here, it is as stated in the *Actual Revelation Sūtra*:[a]

> This patient precious householder is the called the precious minister.

So, as mentioned, these two are counted as one. The tradition that counts the minister as separate is as stated in the *Wish-Granting Tree*:[b]

> Then, the precious seven led by the householder and minister also include the wheel, horse, jewel, elephant, and queen.

Thus, this presentation is in agreement with that.

In order for the chakravartin monarch to control one, two, three, or four continents, he uses a wheel made of iron, copper, silver, and gold, respectively. In order to use the first two, war with others is not necessary. Gradually, the weapons are crafted, followed by training in how to use them, at which time the precious general is then required. Even the final two wheels are not needed, as there is mastery over the enemy. This is why on this occasion it is said the wheel is of the final type, golden.

Given that it is acceptable to then make an offering of this level of chakravartin monarch who has mastery over the four continents, why then is the precious general still mentioned here as well? The answer is that, during this time

[a] *ngon chung gi do* (*mngon byung gi mdo*)
[b] *pag sam tri shing* (*dpag bsam 'khri shing*); Kshemendra

of extreme strife and degeneration, there are many pointless enemies threatening those who practice pure dharma. Hence, as a method to protect them from harm, the precious general is also offered. This information comes from the oral instructions of authentic scholars since, when the interdependent connection is made to be victorious over all nonconducive directions, this is then a crucial point of the wisdom intent.

In the intermittent space to the northeast is the great treasure vase made of solid gold. With a broad belly, long neck, curved spout, shallow bottom, and a scepter made of a sprig from a wish-granting tree with abundantly healthy branches, leaves, and fruit, the vase is adorned with boundless varieties of precious jewels. The neck is bound with superior silk from the god realm. The vase is filled to capacity with treasures of desirable substances. Think that it possesses qualities that are a source of all wishes based on the needs and desires of every living being.

Then, between those heaps in the eight [principal] and intermediate directions, the next series of heaps are gradually placed as follows. Say "Lāsyā" and so forth while reciting the next eight lines. In the intermittent space at the inner face of the precious wheel, think that the White Beauty [i.e., Lāsyā] with two hands and wrathful-fist mudrās appears. Holding five-pronged vajras with each hand to the right and left of her waist, she assumes a proud manner. Her head is poised with a slight bow to the left.

In the intermittent space at the inner face of the precious jewel is the golden Mālā[a] with two hands, holding a precious vajra mālā with wrathful-fist mudrās hoisted up level to her shoulders in the manner of conferring empowerment to all objects of offerings. In the intermittent space at the inner face of the precious queen is Gītā,[b] light red with two hands, stroking a golden *vina*[c] marked with vajras. She is in the guise of singing so melodiously that the resonance of sound mesmerizes the minds of others.

In the intermittent space at the inner face of the precious minister is Nartī.[d] Her body has a variety of colors, such as her face and both legs being white, her neck and upper body a pale red, her waist and both arms pale blue, and her thighs pale yellow. The rest of the body is blue. Of her two hands, the right holds a three-pronged vajra held up to her crown, while the left is held at her waist. She appears in the guise of various dancing postures.

In the intermittent space at the inner face of the precious elephant is Puṣhpā.[e]

[a] Trengwama (*phreng ba ma*); She of Garlands
[b] Lüma (*glu ma*); She of Song
[c] *piwang* (*pi wang*); guitar, stringed instrument
[d] Garma (*gar ma*); She of Dance
[e] Metogma (*me tog ma*); She of Flowers

Golden in color, her left hand holds a flower vessel marked with vajras, and the right scatters showers of flowers. In the intermittent space at the inner face of the precious horse is Dhūpā,[a] white in color. Her right hand holds an incense urn marked with vajras that satisfies all objects of offering, while her left holds wrathful fists in a threatening manner. In the intermittent space at the inner face of the precious general is Ālokā,[b] pale red in color. She holds a torch with the vajra fist in her right hand to her left shoulder in the manner of offering. Her left hand is in the mudrā of dance.

In the intermittent space at the inner face of the great treasure vase is Gandhā.[c] Green, in her left hand she holds a conch marked with vajras and filled with water to her heart, and in the right hand parallel with her shoulder she sprinkles scented water as an offering. All of these goddesses are not just singular, but rather one should think that they fill all regions of space.

Then, place the heaps sequentially at the inner face of the four directional goddesses. Saying "sun"[d] and so forth, recite the four lines; and while doing so, imagine that in the intermittent space at the inner face of Lāsyā a spherical sun maṇḍala made of fire crystal appears. The length is fifty-one leagues; and through the light rays that radiate, all light and dense states of darkness throughout the four continents are fully dispelled. Upon that appears a golden fence the height of one-half league. It has jeweled staircases, sloping roofs, and diverse divine beauties performing song, dance, and instrumentation. Think that the universe and inhabitants are endowed with these exceptional aspects.

In the intermittent space at the inner face of Gītā is a spherical moon maṇḍala made of water crystal, fifty leagues in diameter. Through the radiant coolness of its light, the dense darkness of the four continents is dispelled. Upon that is a silver, half-league-length fence encircling. It has jeweled staircases, sloping roofs, and male and female gods playing instruments, with song and dance. Think that the universe and inhabitants are fully endowed with these exceptional aspects.

In general, wherever the light of the sun pervades, the moonlight will not be evident; however, here, one must think that the light of both sun and moon pervade the entire universe [simultaneously]. Although one is required to imagine that the sun and moon appear close to Mt. Meru, in reality this is not the case; while at the same time, this poses no contradiction.

In the intermittent space at the inner face of Mālā is a white parasol made of divine silken brocade. The handle is composed of precious jewels, and the one-thousand spokes are crafted with the purest refined gold to be found in this

[a] Dügpöma (*bdug spos ma*); She of Incense
[b] Nangsalma (*snang gsal ma*); She of Light
[c] Drichabma (*dri chab ma*); She of Perfume
[d] *nyi ma*

world. The sapphire crest is extremely beautiful, and the parasol is studded with an array of gems and garlands of hanging pearls. Think that the qualities are magnificently attractive.

In the intermittent space at the inner face of Nartī is the grand victory banner that is victorious over all nonconducive directions. Its handle is straight yet pliant and studded with jewels. At the peak is a half-moon crest adorned with a precious vajra. The banner is made of three interwoven brocades from the finest divine materials replete with hanging garlands. There are tiny golden bells that peal with the breeze, emitting a lovely sound. The parasol is marked with various exotic animals, such as the sea monster makara, the fish *pükye*,[a,139] the eight-legged lion, and so forth. When the edges of the silken brocades are marked with exotic animals, that is referred to as a victory banner. If that marking is not there, then it is referred to as a banner. It is said that in both cases [i.e., with markings and without] when there are the three interwoven brocades, that reference is comparable to the modern-day hanging pennants.

Saying "gods and humans"[b] and so forth, place a significant heap in the center to indicate the fully endowed glory and abundance of whatever exists as the desirable qualities of gods and humans. Think that nothing is left incomplete, and everything is pleasing and clean as an inconceivable array of offerings like massing cloud formations. Think that you offer your body, wealth, and all virtue accumulated throughout the three times—comparable to the clouds of Samantabhadra's offerings—so that all regions of space are utterly filled to capacity.

There are two choices for the eastern direction's location: based on it being in front of oneself or being offered to an object. Actually, the one making the offering is in Jambudvīpa, so it seems it should be acceptable to consider the south to be facing the practitioner. Most practitioners use the eastern direction, as that faces toward the object of offering. Concerning this, first completely visualize Mt. Meru, including the four continents, the sun, moon, and so forth. Once familiar with that, increase that tenfold, then one hundredfold, one thousandfold, until the offering expands out to become the trichiliocosm universe. This is expanded upon in the Abhidharma:

> One thousand of the four continents, sun and moon, Mt. Meru, the desire realms of the gods, and the world systems of Brahmā are asserted to be the first chiliocosm of one thousand. When that thousandfold universe becomes another thousandfold universe, this is called "the intermediate realm of the world". Another thousandfold of that is the trichiliocosm.

[a] *spu skyes*
[b] *lha* and *mi* (*lha dang mi*)

So, it is as taught. To count the four continents, sun and moon, Mt. Meru and the six desire-god realms all the way up to the realm of Brahmā as one universe and to increase that one-thousand times over is the first thousandfold universe. This first universe counted as one, when increased one-thousand times over, is the second thousandfold universe called "the intermediate realm of the world". That intermediate realm of the world is counted as one; and when that increases yet another one-thousand times, this becomes the three thousandfold universe. To count everything beginning with the four continents all the way to Brahmā is one billion [universes].

According to the uncommon Mahāyāna tradition, as mentioned in *Vajrapāṇi's Empowerment Conferral Tantra* and the sūtra *Palpoche*:

> To count these trichilicosms as one comes to one-hundred million, recognized as the all-pervasive ocean [of phenomena]. Then one billion of that is called the initial continuum of the all-pervasive ocean; one billion of that is the intermediate continuum of the all-pervasive ocean; and one billion of that is the third continuum of the all-pervasive ocean. Otherwise, it is asserted that this is the pure land of the all-pervasive ocean adorned with a foundation and its flower essences, said to be a single nirmāṇakāya field to be tamed. Hence, by thinking the entire array of the pure land is fully complete, the offerings are made.

To expand on this—although there are many impure realms—without considering the impure aspect, it is important to make offerings by visualizing that the universe and inhabitants possess all fully endowed qualities similar to the pure lands. It states:

> By visualizing the field of buddha, this offering is made to place all beings in this perfectly pure state and so forth.

So, it is as taught. In the future, this becomes the cause for accomplishing the sublime pure lands where one's enlightenment will occur and is also the process of training in pure-land awareness. It states in *Benefits of the Maṇḍala*:[a]

> Once attaining buddhahood, the realms are completely pure.

Thus, it is as taught. Furthermore, at the conclusion of the verse that applies to the six pāramitās mentioned above, it states:

[a] *mandal gyi pen yon* (*mandal gyi phan yon*)

> Through this maṇḍala of the Sage, the six pāramitās will be attained. The body will become golden, free from all illness, attractive, and luminous like the moon; and rebirth will occur among the higher gods and humans. Endowed with wealth and gold, rebirth will be taken in the class of royalty.

Thus, it is taught. Since all conduct of the bodhisattvas can be synthesized into the practice of the six pāramitās, this [maṇḍala] practice allows the six pāramitās to be brought to completion, as well as becoming the training that swiftly traverses the grounds by practicing the consummation of the crucial points of bodhisattva conduct.

That the body becomes the color of gold and has no illness means that, temporarily, the state of higher rebirth as a god or human will be attained. Furthermore, each time the maṇḍala is offered, whatever size it may be, however many particles that exist below that offering all the way down to the base of the golden foundation are said to indicate the number of times one will attain the state of a chakravartin monarch. In *Master Kampala's Maṇḍala Ritual*, it states:

> The benefits of making this offering are that the ten pāramitās will be fully perfected, the two obscurations will be cleansed, and merit perfected; the samādhi maṇḍala will become clear, so the natural maṇḍala can be seen.

Thus, it is as taught. By cleansing obscurations and perfecting merit, this ultimately leads to the cause for attaining the state of buddhahood. Clarifying the meditation of the samādhi maṇḍala and seeing the maṇḍala of self-appearances will bring maturity with the generation stage of Secret Mantra. Until the realization of the completion stage is stabilized [and] if in the interim one fails to offer the maṇḍala due to disregard, that will result in the occurrence of extreme negative downfalls, such as taking the lives of ḍākinīs and so forth. The quote from the *Maṇḍala Ritual* continues:

> By not performing this [maṇḍala], the faults are that, until stability in the completion stage is attained and if maṇḍala practice is put aside, negative karma such as taking the lives of ḍākinīs will be accumulated. Hence, one must respect this.

So, it is just as mentioned.

Those who uphold Mantra commitments must offer maṇḍala to their guru during the three times of the day, such as early morning, afternoon, and evening. If they fail to do so, then it is said they will breach their samaya. Based on the information from the perspective of these verses: by clarifying the visualizations and by practicing this each day, the doorway leading to downfalls will be averted. That is why this is so important.

3.2.1.1.4.1.2 Inner Maṇḍala

Second, the inner maṇḍala is as follows. Take, for example, Paṇḍit Nāropā who relied upon his master Tilopā[a] for twelve years. After undergoing many hardships, he was taken to a drought-ridden valley where he asked his master how anyone could make maṇḍala offerings in such a place. Then thinking that he would make an offering of the maṇḍala, Nāropā looked around everywhere for water. Finding nothing, he sat there. Tilopā then asked him if his body had dried up as well. Then Nāropā drew blood from his body and sprinkled the earth in front with the blood. Taking some flesh from his ears and other places, he placed that as heaps for the maṇḍala. When Nāropā was offering the maṇḍala, Tilopā smacked him on the forehead with his shoe. Nāropā fainted and the following words were heard in the sky:

> By close fixation upon the so-called "me" and "mine", all immature beings experience this ground of confusion. Through the maṇḍala ritual that pleases the guru, without any hesitation I will offer myself.

Thus, these words were heard. At the moment that he came to, Nāropā expressed his experience in the following way:

> The aspect of the maṇḍala that includes the earth, the mountains, the sun, moon, and the like is not the supreme maṇḍala offering. The maṇḍala of the body is the unsurpassed offering, so there is no offering comparable to this.

Thus, he spoke. Having given rise to wisdom exaltation and exceptional levels of realization, he proclaimed that the words of the tantras and their meanings were lucid in his mind.

Even in the classes of the pāramitā sūtras, it mentions that, when the bodhisattva Tagtu Ngü[b] was trying to discover the meaning of the prajñāpāramitā while in the presence of the great bodhisattva Chöpag,[c] he offered his own

[a] *ti lo pa*
[b] *rtag tu ngus*; Always Crying
[c] *chos 'phag*; Sublime Dharma

body's blood by sprinkling it on the ground in front as the maṇḍala offering. In oral lineage teachings, I heard that was the time he composed the well-known maṇḍala verse "the foundation of the earth is adorned [i.e., *sa zhi pü chö*]." Nevertheless, whether that is correct or not still needs to be analyzed. Whatever the case, the sublime masters of the past actually did offer their own bodies as maṇḍala offerings in these ways. Although these days our mental capacity is not equal to theirs: by visualizing according to their example, the offering of the body as the maṇḍala remains extremely important as well as being the main emphasis in this tradition of chöd. The terma commentary also states:

> **Then, imagining that the maṇḍala of one's body is complete, present that as the offering. The skin is the golden foundation of the earth; the spine the king of mountains, Mt. Meru; the right arm is the eastern continent Pūrvavideha, Lüpakpo; the right leg, the southern continent, Jambudvīpa, Dzambuling; the left leg is the western continent Aparagodnīya, Balangchöd; and the left arm is the northern continent Uttarakuru, Draminyen. The fingers and toes are the subcontinents and their islands.**
>
> **The ribs are the ring of mountains; the body fat, the golden mountain; the intestines are the great turbulent oceans. The kidneys are the supreme steed; the liver, the wish-granting cow; the spleen, the great plateau of Ahmo Lika'i. The diaphragm is the dwelling place of the gods, the lungs are the wish-granting trees, and the heart is the treasure vase. The chakras are the offering goddesses who hold the eight auspicious emblems, and the seven royal signs are the glorious qualities of gods and humans. The blood and yellow fluids are the rivers and rainfall, the neck is the crystal stūpa, and the throat is the unceasing water source of the Gaṅgā. The head is the palace of perfect victory; the teeth, the uncultivated crops. The nose is Rāhula, and the eyes are the sun and moon. The ears are the formless realms, and the brain is the nectar of the gods. The pores are the wealth and endowments of gods, nāgas, and humans perfectly complete. Imagining and offering this is the inner maṇḍala offering.**

So, it is as taught. Other body parts are easy to identify as follows. The fingers, toes, and their joints are said to be the subcontinents and secondary continents. Among the [four] continents, there are the eight largest subcontinents; and along with them are many islands surrounding as the sūtras tell us. Saying "the Ahmo Lika'i plateau, the wish-granting tree, and the dwelling places of the gods" indicates that, at the peak of Mt. Meru in the thirty-third god realm, there is the city Tana Düg. In its center is the palace of the gods called Nampar Gyal[a] and surrounding that to the east is a garden called Shingta Natsok Tsal;[b] to the south is Tsub Gyur Gyi Tsal; to the west is the garden called Drepa'i Tsal;[c] to the north is Gawa'i Tsal. These are the four gardens. In order, these gardens have pools that are diverse, jagged, pleasurable, and that bring joy. Outside of these gardens in the four directions are, in order, the various excellent grounds, rough grounds, mixed pleasure grounds, and joyful grounds—these four.

To the perimeter of the city in the east is the wish-granting tree called Yongdu Sa Tol.[d] Varieties of desirables are granted here, and it extends for some one-hundred leagues in diameter.[140] The branches and leaves reach out to cover a diameter of fifty leagues. The fragrance is carried by the wind so that it reaches some eight leagues. Unlike flowers in the human realms, the fragrance permeates fifty leagues in the opposite direction that the breeze blows.

In front of this tree is the square-shaped precious Ahmo Lika'i flat plateau[141] that extends on each side for fifty leagues. The height is approximately half a league, six, or eighteen [leagues]. [There are flowers blooming everywhere] with perfect shapes and multitudes of colors that number into the hundreds; and when walking through them, they cover up to the knees.

In the midst of this is the throne of Indra, and in front of it are other thrones set out for Vișhṇu[e] and the rest. During the fourth month of summer, Indra and his retinue experience their individual karmic ripening and celebrate and enjoy the desirable objects of the gods. Outside the city to the southwest at a place called Chözang Lha'i Dunsa,[f] all gods congregate to engage in both appropriate and inappropriate behavior. In front of that is a golden throne set out for Indra to teach from, and surrounding it are golden thrones for Vișhṇu and the others as well. The gods of the thirty-third realm gather there, and they contemplate the dharma as well as the purpose of gods and humans. It is said that they then discuss both spiritual and nonspiritual deeds. Although the way the thirty-third realm is arranged is not necessarily pertinent to this explanation, it seems necessary to mention that the so-called desire-god realm[142] extends all the way up to the form realms of the gods. As for both the plateau and the tree—since they specifically belong to the gods of the thirty-third realm, they are described as a matter of course during the explanation that accompanies that god realm.

In other chöd texts, it states that the consciousness is transferred into the

[a] *rnam par rgyal*; Fully Victorious
[b] *shing rta sna tshogs tshal*; Various Carriages
[c] *'dres pa'i tshal*; Mixed Pleasures
[d] *yongs 'du sa rtol*; Piercing the Earth
[e] Khyab Jüg (*khyab 'jug*); All-Pervading One
[f] *chos bzang lha'i 'dun sa*; Excellent Dharma Gathering Place of the Gods

heart of the field of refuge as the sole wrathful mother, Tröma Nagmo, and the body and mind separate. From that, once again, the nature of awareness arises as Vajrayoginī holding a curved vajra blade and skull filled with blood. Cutting open the illusory body, the skin is flayed to become the golden foundation of the earth. Upon that, the torso is piled to become the king of mountains, Meru. The right part of the abdomen including the arm is Pūrvavideha; the left is Jambudvīpa to the south; the left lower body including the extremities is Aparagodanīya to the west; the right lower body with extremities is Uttarakuru to the north. The head is the fully victorious palace; the eyes are the sun and the moon; the ears are the parasol and victory banner; the eight secondary limbs are the subcontinents; all remaining aspects of the body, whatever they may be are visualized as the desirable objects that are said to be the offerings. Nevertheless, that is not necessary to include here.

Here, when reciting "the arrangement of my body"[a] as mentioned before, instantly visualize this and make the offerings. For those who are inclined toward elaborations, then in other texts there are similarities as follows:

> *Phet!* From the central channel of one's body—huge, fatty, and majestic—the purest essence of the bindu joined with awareness, life force, life expectancy, and merit is sent out [of the body] like an archer's arrow, to arise from the basic space of prajñā in the mudrā of method. *Phet phet phet!*
>
> Tröma Nagmo arises as the spontaneous presence of the three kāyas, holding a curved vajra blade and skull filled with blood, while gazing with three eyes into space. Both legs are in the dancing posture; [she] wears bone ornaments and stands in the midst of a blazing fire, sporting a trident, with a squealing pig's head jutting from the crown. With the blade in the right hand, the skin of the corpse is flayed and spread to cover the entire golden foundation of the earth. The spine is the king of mountains, Meru; the limbs are the four continents, and the eight secondary limbs are the eight subcontinents; the ribs are the iron fence; the flesh and fat are the golden ring of mountains; the intestines are the turbulent oceans, and the kidneys are the supreme horse; the liver is the cow of plenty and the spleen is the Ahmo'i plateau; the diaphragm is the dwelling place of the gods; the lungs are the wish-granting tree; the heart is the treasure vase; the chakras are the divine offering goddesses holding the eight substances and the seven royal signs; the head is the fully victorious palace; the eyes are the sun and moon; and the pores are

[a] *lü köd pa* (*lus bkod pa*)

the abundance of gods, nāgas, humans, and the like. This fully endowed arrangement of my body as the maṇḍala is offered to the embodiment of all victors and families, as well as the three-kāya ḍākinīs, Triple Gem, Three Roots, and the dharmapālas. So that self and others may perfect the two accumulations, this offering is made. *Phet!*

It is excellent to visualize and offer in this way.

3.2.1.1.4.1.3 Secret Maṇḍala

Third is the secret maṇḍala offering, as it states in the terma commentary:

> **The ālaya is the golden ground of the earth. Passion-based mental activity is the king of mountains. The eight groups of consciousness are the four continents and the subcontinents. Mental activity is the sun and moon. Secondary states of mind are the glorious qualities of desirable objects. Manifesting and offering this is the secret maṇḍala.**

So, it is taught. The way of identifying the ālaya, the eight states of consciousness, and so forth is as stated in the writings of the omniscient Longchenpa, such as in his *Resting the Mind in Repose*:

> The support of all of that [i.e., the eight states of consciousnesses and so forth] is the neutral basis of all [i.e., ālaya]. Like a mirror, this is nonconceptual and empty by nature—lucid cognition that does not conceptualize objects. As the basis for the arising, this resembles a clear mirror. From that, the cognitive faculties of the five gateways that grasp after objects such as form emerge. Not recognizing this self-nature: like reflections in a mirror, phenomena are pursued; and all cognitive states of dualistic fixation upon objects come into play. Instantly pursuing, whether grasping or not, conceptualizing or not, passion-based cognition will emerge.

Thus, the ālaya is this support for karma, habits, and the rest. From it, the other states of consciousness that emerge are also clearly revealed through analogies mentioned in the commentary upon this [i.e., *Resting the Mind in Repose*] entitled *The Great Chariot*:[a,143]

[a] *shing ta chenpo* (*shing rta chen po*), commentary on *Resting the Mind in Repose*, *sem nyid ngal so* (*sems nyid ngal gso*); Longchen Rabjam

> Now, the distinctions for the ālaya and its gatherings are: the ālaya of various habits, neutral like a mirror; the ālaya of the consciousness, similar to the clarity of the mirror; and the five cognitive faculties, resembling the arising of a reflection. Initially, there is immediate investigation, or the field of perception of the five faculties recognizing something as "that's it". The individual thoughts that then arise are the consciousness of mental events. Following that, when the three—attachment, aversion, and neutrality—arise, those are referred to as passion-based mental events.

The quote continues:

> The consciousness of the basis of all is the aspect of cognition that is clear but does not grasp to any object or subject. The five consciousnesses of the gateways that emerge from that are [first] the visual consciousness that perceives forms, does not develop concepts, and is a cognitive state. In a similar way, the audial [consciousness] hears sound, the olfactory smells scent, the gustatory experiences tastes, the tactile feels sensations; and although being aware of objective phenomena, concepts do not develop as there is only the aspect of cognizance.
>
> The objects of the five gateways either appear or, similar to that aspect, there is a momentary arising; and they are phenomena, as well as the consciousness of mental events. In addition, the aspect of being cognitive is referred to as the consciousness from the perspective of the object, phenomena, and the perception of them.

Thus, it is as taught. The other [faculties] are easier to understand. Aside from appearing individually based on the perspective of dualistic confusion involving both the outer objects and the inner cognition, ultimately, there is a single nature that is not established to externally exist. Concerning the aspect of the object and saying that is referred to as "phenomena"—although many scholars assert that this way of not believing in external existence belongs to the Mind Only School and others, in our tradition it is known that one must believe in the general assertions of the Mahāyāna philosophy. Hence, this is taught according to that.

To expand upon this, the meaning of the last three lines of the verse is as follows:

> Following the initial moment of visual consciousness, the aspect of grasping and fixating upon individually perceived objects and the cognition that determines this all arise in the initial instant [of perception].

> Subsequently—based on the difference of either grasping or not—if engaged, then conceptualization comes into play as passion-based mental events. If that is not the case, then it is just the consciousness of mental events. In that case, the thought "there is a form" will occur in the first moment, and that is the mental event. Given that the instant is fleeting, the definitive determining feature does not occur, so this is nonconceptual. When the object is materialized, it is then referred to as "grasping conceptualization"; and following that, there is the thought of "this and that". That is the passion-based mind that will occur as a continuity of momentary events. Therefore, when the object is definitively determined and grasped at, the aspects of conceptualizing and conceptual grasping are fully established.

Thus, it is. Having revealed this in a general sense, in order to clearly identify the basis that defines it, it is mentioned in *Resting the Mind in Repose*:

> When cognition is nonconceptual and distraction occurs, to not grasp to objective appearances but rather remain single-pointed is the moment of resting in the [experience of] ālaya. Not engaging or grasping toward any lucid appearances is the unmoving pure, lucid consciousness of the basis of all. Due to the objects of the five gateways and dualistic refuting and proving: when the seven gatherings of consciousness conceptualize coarse phenomena, those are designated as the seven states of consciousness.

Thus, as taught in the commentary to that [i.e., *The Great Chariot*], it states:

> Without having any conceptual thought toward objects, the distraction of that stupor is the occasion of the ālaya. When objective appearances are clearly perceived, to be nonconceptual without a single thought is the occasion of the consciousness of the basis of all. At that time, individual objects are lucid; and when their aspects can be perceived, that is the consciousness of the five gateways. Initially, when the mind momentarily arises and grasps with objectification, in the next moment it mingles with the passions of the one analyzing, giving rise to fixation. That is the occasion of passion-based mental events and the consciousness of mental events; hence, these are the seven gatherings.

In the *Bodhisattva Grounds*,[a] it states:

[a] *chang chüb sem pa'i sa* (*byang chub sems dpa'i sa, bodhisattvabhūmi*); Asaṅga

> Nonconceptuality that is not connected to the pursuit of objects is the occasion of the ālaya. Nonconceptuality that is connected to objects is the occasion of the consciousness of the ālaya. The aspect of perceiving individual objects is the occasion of the consciousnesses of the five gateways. The initial conceptualization of an object and the subsequent determination gives rise to grasping and fixating that are the occasions of the consciousness of mental events and passion-based mental events.

So, it is as taught. Here, reference to the coarse perception of the seven gatherings means that is the ability to apprehend objects with clarity from the perspective of the ālaya. On the occasion of passion-based mental events, previously this was described as involving all aspects of the grasping mind. Here, it is said to be the passions mingling with mental events. According to the way of understanding the terminology, the earlier description was general, whereas here it is more specific. Once there is the development of subsequent grasping with conceptualization, then either the mental events mingle with the passions or the possibility for that to occur comes into play. That is why this intent designates them as passion-based mental events.

Nevertheless, if the upadesha oral instructions of the precious Tertön himself are emphasized here, then the ālaya is a neutral stupor within which no object whatsoever is considered and cognition abides nonconceptually, like deep sleep or fainting. From that, by the movement of subtle karmic winds when the aspect of clarity is still barely apparent, that is the occasion of the consciousness of the ālaya, lucid but nonconceptual. To then turn inward, the subtle cognition of the phenomena of a self is passion-based mental events; and from that, the objective appearances of self and others are established. When that increases slightly and cognition engages with objects, then the aspect of fixating upon "mine" is the consciousness of passion-based mental events. When this lucid cognition then emerges externally, that is mental events; and from that, all form, sound, smell, taste, and touch emerge. The cognitive aspects are the consciousnesses of the five gateways. From that, names and meanings are designated, along with forms and the rest. Fixation toward that occurs, and perpetual comprehension is the consciousness of mental events. This summarizes the crucial points of what all of this means. An extensive explanation can be found in the tantra *Self-Occurring Fundamental Nature*,[a] as well as notes taken by the great Tertön's heart disciples based on his oral instructions to them. Keep these points in mind. Although there are many ways this can be analyzed, here I have chosen not to overelaborate aside from identifying the meaning itself.

[a] *ney lük rang chung* (*gnas lugs rang byung*)

In the tantra *Source of Vows*,[a] it states:

> The stainless mental events of various characteristics appear as emanations of all maṇḍalas.

So, it is taught. Although the meaning of Tantra's wisdom intent is vast: here when applied to the maṇḍala, the basis of the appearances of various aspects of outer objects and inner bodies is this innate state of mental events that has never been sullied by the stain of obscuration. This is the aspect of the way the maṇḍala emanates and appears. In the *All-Creating Monarch*, it states:

> The *kyil*,[b] or center, is the unmistaken essence of the meaning. The *khor*[c] is that which surrounds it; so *kyil khor*, or maṇḍala, means that saṃsāra and enlightenment are perfected as exaltation.

Thus, the essence of the meaning refers to the wisdom of self-awareness as the center. From that, the emerging intrinsic nature abides as the play of exaltation's purity and evenness that surrounds. Hence, one must know the way that the spontaneously present array of the maṇḍala is pure as phenomenal existence arising from the ground.

To expand upon this, even all states of impure cognition that arise, including the ālaya, are by nature abiding as innate wisdom itself. That tantra itself states:

> The array of the essentially pure maṇḍala is that all recollections, awareness, and concepts—whatever they may be—are recognized as the meaning of the unborn, all-creating [monarch] itself.

So, all recollections and states of awareness are naturally unborn and said to be the nature of the genuine, great wisdom of the ground, the innate all-creating monarch.

In the tantra *Charnel Ground Partaking of the Aggregates*,[d] it also states:

> This mind's nature is wisdom.

Thus, it states; and this [nature of] the phenomena of saṃsāra and enlightenment is not only just mentioned here but also in the classes of Sūtra as follows:

[a] *dom jung* (*sdom 'byung, saṃvarodaya*)
[b] *dkyil*
[c] *'khor*
[d] *dur tröd püngpo rolpa'i gyü* (*dur khrod phung po rol pa'i rgyud*)

> Various concepts based on virtue such as faith and yearning and non-virtue such as attachment and aversion emerge from the mind. If the mind is realized, that is wisdom; and since there is no need to search for buddha elsewhere, meditate in this state of recognition.

Thus, the ultimate wisdom intent of that source is also stating the same thing.

In order to merely clarify the main wisdom intent with all of these references, the [root] verses read:

> The arrangement of spontaneously present self-appearances is the secret maṇḍala.

Since this refers to that which is extremely secret, it should not be freely spoken to those who have not received unsurpassed Mantra empowerment or to beginners who lack faith. If arranged in verses for recitation then:

> *Phet!* From the great originally pure ground of basic space, the arrangement of the spontaneously present aspect of appearances is unceasing. Upon the golden ground of the all-pervasive ālaya are the passion-based mental events as the king of mountains, Meru. Surrounding that are the eight gatherings in the array of the four principal and subcontinents. Mental events are the sun and moon; secondary events are the glory of all desirables. This purity of phenomenal existence and the great space of evenness are one taste with the mind's nature as the secret maṇḍala that is offered to the field of merit of perfectly pure self-appearances. *Phet phet phet!*

Thus, visualize this while reciting.

Having described these three ways of offering the maṇḍala, it also states in the *Hevajra Tantra*:

> Just as the outer appears, so does the inner.

Thus, it is as taught. The nature of outer and inner [phenomena] is mutually concurrent. Here also, the outer arrangement of the universe and the inner aspect of one's body—as well as secretly pure cognitive awareness, the dynamic strength of the mind—are arranged as the maṇḍala and applied according to their similar aspects and presented as the offerings.

What the commentary is identifying does not necessarily reveal the aspect of pure cognitive awareness. It emphasizes only the impure aspect of the ālaya because the outer mountains, continents, and so forth appear in the impure aspect. Hence, this teaching applies to that. The ultimate key point of all of this is the harmony concerning the dynamic strength of the mind's secret nature and the nature of the interconnectedness of the fully apparent array of outer and inner phenomena based upon that. It is for that reason that the outer aspect is visualized as the maṇḍala of the pure land and offered. The mode of the inner and secret are similarly visualized and offered.

Through this, the perfection of the two accumulations is similar to the simultaneous contributing circumstance. [For instance] within the genuine way of abiding, the array of the dynamic strength of self-awareness is primordially pure as the intrinsic nature of the maṇḍala. That is the root cause. By precisely realizing this and through familiarity with view and meditation, know then that—in the manner of the controlling circumstance—this is the unsurpassed method for actualizing self-appearances as the pure lands.

According to other texts, the order is applied to the maṇḍala of the three kāyas as follow. Outer objective appearances of the trichiliocosm pure realms are the places where the supreme nirmāṇakāya reveals the mode of awakening and appears according to the common perceptions of those to be tamed. Given that is the realm of those to be tamed, it is the nirmāṇakāya maṇḍala. Within the inner vajra body abides the pure wisdom channels through which the winds function to induce the appearances of the sambhogakāya realms. The support for this is the aspect of the body as the sambhogakāya maṇḍala. The clear-light wisdom of one's mind is, at the time of the result, the dharmakāya. That aspect is referred to as the dharmakāya maṇḍala.

> The outer arrangement appears as the realms of the world; the inner appearances are the aspects of one's body; and the secret nature is the mind's nature of awareness as the maṇḍala.
> By offering these, the skillful upadesha for perfecting accumulations occurs.

Thus, these are the verses that summarize the section.

3.2.1.1.4.2 Practicing the Seven-Branch Prayer

This has seven parts:

1 Prostration
2 Offering
3 Confession
4 Rejoicing
5 Prayer that the wheel of dharma be turned
6 Prayer for buddhas to remain in the world
7 Dedication of merit

Second, the seven-branch offering is as follows:

> *Phet!* I prostrate to the three kāyas of all the victorious ones and offer all of my bodies and abundance. All accumulated negativities and obscurations of the three doors are confessed, and all wholly positive virtuous accumulations are the causes for rejoicing. I request the dharma wheel be turned in whatever way is necessary, and the victorious ones are beseeched not to pass beyond sorrow. I fully dedicate the root of virtue to all sentient beings. [May all beings] without exception simultaneously attain the state of enlightenment!

Thus, as these root verses state, saying ***phet*** indicates one must visualize the field of refuge. In the perfectly pure nature of basic space, even all temporary stains to be abandoned are perfectly pure. The nature of the immaculate oceanic qualities is indivisible basic space and awareness as the dharmakāya. According to the perspective of those to be tamed, this nature possesses the five certainties of the rupakāya appearances.

The five certainties are the certainty of the place being Ghanavyūha[a] of the Akaniṣhṭha, the certainty of the kāya [i.e., teacher] as the perfect adornment of the major and minor marks and signs, the certainty of the retinue as the ārya bodhisattvas on the grounds, the certainty of the dharma as the sole doctrine for the great vehicle, and the certainty of time as the permanent continuity of time that always abides without passing beyond sorrow. Until saṃsāra is emptied, benefiting through whatever means are necessary throughout all realms of the world for the purpose of the diverse objects to be tamed is the nirmāṇakāya. These are **the three kāyas** that are **the victorious ones** over the enemy of the two obscurations. With great respect and regard, one **prostrates to** all fully perfected buddhas and their heirs.

One's coveted **body and abundance** that sustain it, as well as **all** pleasing material things whatever they may be, are presented and **offered.** Motivated by passion, no matter how much **negativity** the body, speech, and mind have **accumulated** through **the three doors**, this has created **obstructions** and interrupted the possibility of higher states of rebirth and liberation. **All** of this **is** openly exposed, **confessed**, and purified. **All wholly positive virtuous accumulations** from the perspective of pure motivation and action unmingled with negative karma **are the causes for rejoicing** with intense satisfaction and fulfillment. The buddhas and their heirs of the ten directions are **requested to turn the dharma wheel in whatever way is necessary** to tame beings. Until saṃsāra is empty, **the victorious ones are beseeched to not pass beyond sorrow** but to remain firm. Whether **the root of virtue** accumulated is large or small, **I fully dedicate to**

[a] Tügpo Ködpa (*stug po bkod pa*); Above All of Rich Array

all sentient beings. Through the power of this prayer, **may all beings without exception simultaneously attain the state of enlightenment**. So, it is.

3.2.1.1.4.2.1 Prostration

While **reciting these verses, visualize in the space in front the entire field of refuge, including all gurus, buddhas, and bodhisattvas without** a single **exception. In their presence**, imagine oneself surrounded by the beings of the three realms, including all gods-māras. **Manifesting innumerable emanations of one's body** as many as there exist **atoms** throughout the oceans of realms, imagine they are all **offering prostrations**. Showing respect through the body, their palms touch their three doors; showing respect through speech, they recite melodious praises; and with respect through their minds, they recall the qualities of enlightenment. In this way, they prostrate with single-pointed devotion.

In the *Sūtra of Great Liberation*,[a] it states:

> Just like a lotus bud about to blossom, both hands are brought together at the crown. With bodies as numerous as massing clouds, prostrate to the buddhas of the ten directions.

Thus, it is as taught. Machig said:

> To all those who reveal the wisdom of self-awareness, the gurus, I prostrate. To those who bestow certain siddhis, the meditation deities, I prostrate. To those who have removed the abandonments and attained realization, all buddhas, I prostrate. To the state of quiescence that is free from desire, all categories of the sacred dharma, I prostrate. To those who when offered to are always meaningful, the sangha, I prostrate. To those who certainly remove all obstacles, the dharmapālas, I prostrate. Until awakening is attained, I supplicate to all of you and pray that you grant refuge.

So, it is taught.

From the hearts of the principal ones who are the field of refuge, light radiates and penetrates into all retinue deities. From the hearts of the retinue, light radiates to gather the potency of all buddhas and bodhisattvas of the ten directions. Gathering back, this dissolves into the hearts of the principal ones. From them, light rays of three colors—white, red, and blue—or only white rays stream forth like pouring milk to enter one's crown and all spirit-elementals gathered

[a] *do de tar pa chenpo* (*mdo sde thar pa chen po*)

there. All negative karma, obscurations, habits, causes, and results accumulated through the three doors from beginningless lifetimes are removed as though bathing the body. From the head down to the toes of the feet and from the lower orifices, a thick black film issues forth and descends nine stages below the earth where the māra Yamā or the karmic messengers of death are waiting to receive this as the designated owners of these unpaid karmic debts. Black in color, sporting terrifying forms with extremely wrathful accouterments, their mouths gape open as one thinks that all the filthy blackness enters them. Yamā becomes satisfied, and one feels assured that all karmic debts are repaid.

Think that the bodies of self and others are now completely cleansed, becoming transparent like crystal. Having purified all negativities and obscurations, consider that everyone gains overwhelming faith toward the objects of refuge. It is necessary to prostrate with single-pointed devotion that is free from a distracted mind. These are pointing-out instructions from the speech of Machig Labdrön.

The benefits of prostrating in this way are as the Vinaya states:

> However much one's body covers the ground and however many particles exist in the space below that, all the way down to the golden foundation of the earth, will be how many times the happiness and prosperity of a chakravartin monarch will be attained. Rebirth will also be taken as higher gods or humans. These and other deeds indicate the limitless benefits. It is taught that prostrations serve as the antidote for pride.

3.2.1.1.4.2.2 Offering

This has two parts:

1 Common offerings
2 Uncommon offerings

It is also necessary to possess the three exceptional pure aspects while making offerings: a pure field of refuge, pure intentions, and pure material things.

"A pure field of refuge" means the exceptional field through which merit is accumulated, namely, the Triple Gem. Through the result of making even a meager offering to the Triple Gem, vast amounts of merit will be accrued. "Pure intention" [is the opposite] of engaging in deeds in order to be famous in this life, gain wealth, and recognition, as those are extremely impure motivations. Likewise, to make offerings by wishing to merely attain the happiness of a god or human in the future and to hope only for personal liberation from saṃsāra in order to gain quiescence and well-being are also impure intentions.

Hence, the crucial point necessary to know here is to consider that, while making offerings, one must wish to attain the state of perfect awakening in order to accomplish the welfare of others. To do so, one must cultivate the essence of the path of Mahāyāna, the profound doctrine that severs the māras, by hoping to realize that which has not previously been realized and to ensure that this does not diminish and remains ever-increasing. Based on that, with the object being all phenomena on the path and at the time of the result, this motivation becomes vast and brings about the swift traversal of the grounds. "Pure material things" means that whatever is being offered whether actual or mentally imagined should be the best quality and pleasing to behold.

In an Indian text by Āryadeva, it states:

> Whether actual or imagined, whatever is brought to mind is presented
> as an immeasurable offering to the gurus, who are the Triple Gem.

Thus, it is taught.

Saying "actual" means actual material things, and saying "imagined" means insubstantial, mental projections. Saying "vast" means that, no matter what the offering is, it is presented with great abundance. In the commentary, it is taught to mainly **present offerings of one's body and abundance**. This is because both of them are, at present, our main source of attachment and fixation. In particular, when offering the maṇḍala or whatever offering is made: if one's body is the main offering, then that becomes the special profound feature of severance.

It even states in the *Bodhicharyāvatāra*:

> Like all the victors and their heirs, I will always offer all of my bodies.

Thus, as taught, the offering of one's body is referenced in many places throughout the sūtras and tantras. Here, the two distinctions concerning the way of making offerings, namely, the common and uncommon distinctions, will be discussed in a way that is easy to comprehend.

3.2.1.1.4.2.2.1 Common Offerings

First, the offerings of water for drinking and bathing, flowers, incense, and the like as actual material things offered according to one's abundance constitute being actual offerings. It is necessary that they be from a pure source, clean, and arranged beautifully as the three special features. This advice originates from the oral teachings of the masters.

"A pure source" means other than something that comes about through embezzlement or stealth, through flattery or wrong livelihood, or by telling an unsurpassed lie.[144] If not, then all offering substances would then be from a pure source. Although the source of an offering may be clean, actual offerings that are considered "clean" really indicate not being inferior.

For example, if butter, food, or beverages are old, rancid, polluted, or left over, they are not considered to be clean. Conversely, any offering substance must be the best portion, pleasing, and so forth. Nevertheless, if one lacks possessions or endowments yet has a pure motivation, it is said that anything can be offered, even earth or stones. Offering those things under such circumstances is acceptable because the Triple Gem are the exceptional field for accumulating merit. If offered to them, it is like when in the past some children offered dirt to the enlightened Buddha and later took rebirth as the dharma king Ashoka,[a] his minister, and so forth. Hence, the reason for offering whatever excellent thing is possessed without any avarice is an exceptional method for amassing merit.

"Making beautiful arrangements" applies toward whatever the substance for offering may be. An excellent arrangement applied to water for drinking would be to arrange the water offering bowls correctly so they are not partially filled, too full, in a crooked line, touching, or with water spilled outside of the bowls. "Having bowls that are only partially full" means the water is not filled to the brim. If so, in the future life one's mind stream will not be filled with qualities and rebirth will be with incomplete attributes. "Too full" means the contents are practically flowing over, which indicates that in the future although qualities are present they will not be reliable. How should they [i.e., the water bowls] be filled? Abandoning these two faults, the water should be high enough to just touch below the rim.

"Crooked" means the bowls are not arranged in a straight line; and due to that in the next life, rebirth will be taken as a dishonest person. "Touching" means the bowls are placed too close together with no space between them. This indicates in the future one will be reborn in a state where negative companions are encountered. If there is too much space between them, it means one will be unable to encounter virtuous spiritual guides and the like. The space between them should be the size of a single grain. If the water spills out from the bowls making the table wet, that indicates the fault of losing moral ethics in a future life. So by arranging the bowls free from these faults, it is then taught that rebirth will be taken as the opposite of that; for instance, the mind will be filled with qualities and so forth. These are oral lineage instructions.

Offerings that are mentally imagined are not actual substances but are imagined in the aspect of flowers with lovely pollen hearts, blossoming petals, attractive to behold, made of various gems, and the like. Imagine the incense to be so fragrant that it can permeate the trichiliocosm and the butter lamps made

[a] *chö gyal nya ngen med* (*chos rgyal mya ngan med*); Beyond Sorrow

from precious gems give off light with the capacity to dispel the darkness for the distance of many leagues. There are excellent jeweled palaces that are the dwelling places of lovely divine males and females who sing melodious praises, and stunning gardens like the realms of the gods are both imagined and offered with multitudes of offering substances.

"Offerings possessed by an owner" are found throughout all realms of the world, such as the things each living being possesses like food, clothing, wealth, abodes, and the like. Whatever exists is brought to mind and presented as the offering. "Offerings not possessed by an owner" are the wondrous things naturally existing in all realms, such as the gods. "Not claimed by anyone" means the jeweled mountains, wish-granting trees, rivers, bathing pools, and whatever pleasing things exist that are presented as the offerings.

The "offering of one's body" is as mentioned above. Throughout all lifetimes until now, the most cherished of objects have been all of one's bodies. That is why they must be offered to all victors and their heirs, while the actual offering is of oneself as a servant to the gurus. The "offering of accomplishing practice" means to maintain perfectly pure discipline, as well as diligent study, contemplation, and meditation—these three. In particular, the "unsurpassed offering of practice" is to cultivate compassion toward all living beings by generating the bodhichitta. It is mentioned in the sūtras that upholding the sacred doctrine in these ways is an unsurpassed offering. Given that this greatly pleases the enlightened intent of the victors and their heirs, it surpasses other modes of offering.

The "unsurpassed offering" occurs through the powers of the bodhisattvas Kuntuzangpo, Mañjushrī, and others' treasury-of-space samādhi,[145] so that offering substances become unrivaled by means of abundance and excellence. Offerings such as these are imagined to completely pervade the reaches of space as an inconceivable arrangement brought to mind and presented as offerings.

In the *Precious Lamp Sūtra*,[a] it states:

> Myriad varieties of flowers the size of pitched canopies, arranged like emanating light rays, are presented everywhere and offered to the victorious upholders of immeasurable qualities.

So, incense, garlands, and the like are similarly mentioned, after which the quote continues:

> Parasols studded with varieties of precious jewels, garlands with silken fringe, tassels, and streamers, and garlands of tiny ringing bells that resonate the speech of the victors are held to the crowns of the tathāgatas.

[a] *kon chog ta la'i do* (*dkon mchog ta la'i mdo, ratnolkānāmadhāraṇīmahāyānasūtra*)

> Inconceivable offerings manifesting from the palms of the hands are presented as though offered to each buddha. In this way, these offerings are made to all victors without a single exception, replicating the magical samādhi of the sages.

Thus, it is as taught.

3.2.1.1.4.2.2.2 Uncommon Offerings

Second, the exceptional offering is as Machig taught:

> In the all-pervasive trichiliocosm realms, all forms that appear are delighted in as the supreme enlightened body's mudrā of offering. Bestow the siddhi of the unchanging kāya. In the all-pervasive trichiliocosm realms, all sounds that are heard are delighted in as supreme enlightened speech. Bestow the siddhi of unceasing enlightened speech. In the all-pervasive trichiliocosm realms, all recollections of the mind are delighted in as the mudrā of supreme enlightened mind. Bestow the siddhi of unconfused enlightened mind. In the all-pervasive trichiliocosm realms, all happiness and suffering are delighted in as the nondual mudrā of offering. Bestow both supreme and common siddhis. If happy, then offer the feast of happiness. May benefit and well-being fill the reaches of space. If suffering, then take that upon oneself and may the oceans of suffering in saṃsāra evaporate. May all sentient beings throughout the three realms be endowed with true happiness. *Phet!*

Thus, it is as taught.

Concerning that, in the all-pervasive trichiliocosm realms of the world, all appearances of forms are perfectly pure as the aspect of wisdom, so they appear as the manifestation of kāyas. Since all impure appearances are sealed by that, that is the meaning of mudrā. From that, by greatly pleasing the enlightened minds of the objects being offered to, the meaning of "delighting in" is efficacious. Through this offering, the bestowal of siddhis upon self and others occurs given that the kāyas of the victors never transfer based on impure faults. Apply this understanding to the verses that refer to sound and recollections as well.

In this way, appearances, sounds, and thoughts—these three—arise as the manifestation of enlightened body, speech, and mind. All things that are based on happiness and suffering are equal as the nature of purity. Another way to phrase it is that they [i.e., happiness and sorrow] are indivisible in the manner of emerging as exaltation; the generation stage of self-awareness, clarity, and emptiness; and the realization of the completion stage as evenness.

In particular, whether Sūtra or Tantra, cherishing others more than self is likened to the life tree of the path of Mahāyāna. Therefore, from the perspective of great courage: if there is happiness, then make that the offering of the feast; and if there is sadness, then take that upon oneself. In this way, happiness will fill space, and suffering will be taken upon oneself until the oceans of saṃsāra evaporate. To pray that sentient beings of the three realms may possess happiness is the unsurpassed mudrā offering that pleases all victorious ones.

Concerning this subject, many commentaries on chöd describe the stages for this visualization as follows. All appearances of form become the goddesses of form holding mirrors; all appearances of sound become the goddesses of sound holding *vinas*; likewise apply the rest, such as the goddesses of smell holding incense, the goddesses of taste holding celestial food, the goddesses of touch holding clothing, and the goddesses of phenomena holding sources of dharma. Given that the magical aspects of appearances are perfectly pure, from one's heart all of those goddesses emanate to present their offerings to the objects who receive them. It is taught that one should then feel that they [i.e., the objects] are pleased.

Machig has said:

> The extent of all appearances of form is the goddess Buddha Ḍākinī;[a] the extent of all sound is the goddess Vajra Ḍākinī;[b] the extent of all smell is the goddess Ratna Ḍākinī;[c] the extent of all taste is the goddess Pema Ḍākinī;[d] the extent of all touch is the goddess Karma Ḍākinī.[e] Think that they fill all regions of space countless in number, presenting offerings.

In short, one must know that whatever appears is the manifestation of enlightened body, speech, and mind. Even the five male deities are subsumed within form, sound, and all recollections—including their objects. The way that the five females are subsumed as classes of enlightened body, speech, and mind are that form arises as the nature of enlightened body, sound as enlightened speech, and thought as enlightened mind. Thinking that the extent of all appearances becomes boundless emanations of form goddesses holding mirrors, this cleanses the fixation that all sentient beings have toward form.

[a] Sangye Khandro (*sangs rgyas mkha' 'gro*)
[b] Dorje Khandro (*rdo rje mkha' 'gro*)
[c] Rinchen Khandro (*rin chen mkha' 'gro*)
[d] Pema Khandro (*padma mkha' 'gro*)
[e] Leykyi Khandro (*las kyi mkha' 'gro*)

The bliss of form is then offered to the gurus, who are the Triple Gem. Pleasing the gurus who are the Triple Gem, the siddhi of enlightened form is bestowed; and the physical negativities and obscurations of self and others are purified so that the body experiences ecstasy and has access to the blessing of enlightened body. Imagine that the extent of all sound becomes boundless emanations of the goddesses of sound and that fixation toward sound on the part of all sentient beings is cleansed. The enjoyment of pleasing sounds is offered to the gurus, who are the Triple Gem. Pleasing the gurus of the Triple Gem, the siddhi of enlightened speech is bestowed; and by purifying the obscurations of the speech of self and others, the blessing of enlightened speech enters one's speech. Imagine all recollections emanate in the aspect of boundless goddesses of phenomena who hold sources of dharma, cleansing the incorrect view held by sentient beings. Given that wisdom awareness possesses supreme exaltation, this is offered to the gurus, who are the Triple Gem. Pleasing the gurus of the Triple Gem, the siddhi of enlightened mind is bestowed. By purifying the negativity and obscurations in the minds of self and others, the mind experiences the exaltation of empty clarity and the blessings of enlightened mind enter the mind. Finally, even these goddesses dissolve into oneself, and all happiness and sorrow become one in the expanse of the dharmatā. Recite the aforementioned verses while naturally abiding within spacelike great emptiness that is inherently nonexistent.

Whatever the case may be, the one making offerings, the object being offered to, and the specific offerings all lack true, inherent existence. It is taught that remaining within the nature of emptiness is the offering of the nature as it is, and that is itself an exceptional oral instruction. Saying *phet*, one must think that these visualizations become clear and stable. Such a presentation of offerings serves as an antidote for avarice.

3.2.1.1.4.2.3 Confession

Confession is as follows. By bringing to mind all negative obscurations accumulated from beginningless time, all of this is confessed with the key point of the four remedial powers. The four powers are as mentioned previously. It said that this [confession] functions as the antidote for anger.

3.2.1.1.4.2.4 Rejoicing

Rejoicing refers to feeling a sense of joy and delight concerning all acts of virtue and states of happiness and takes great delight in the happiness and virtue of self and others. By bringing the happiness and joy of others to mind whatever that may be, a sense of joyful delight is aroused. It is said that, if one wants to meditate like this in sessions: then by reviewing the Mahāyāna sūtras and so forth that describe the biographies and deeds of the buddhas and bodhisattvas, one trains until a sense of joy is aroused. This is the antidote for jealousy.

3.2.1.1.4.2.5 Prayer that the Wheel of Dharma Be Turned

Turning the wheel of the dharma is as follows. Previously, when our teacher Lord Buddha was at Magadha Bodhgayā, he tamed the māras at dusk, entered into samādhi at midnight, and in the predawn was fully enlightened as Buddha. He then spoke:

> The ambrosialike dharma that I have discovered is profound, peaceful, unelaborate, uncompounded clear light. Since whomever I reveal this too will not comprehend it, without speaking I shall remain alone in the forest.

Thus, in order to show just how difficult this profound dharma is to realize, for forty-nine days the Buddha remained without turning the dharma wheel. Then, Brahmā approached the Buddha and offered a golden wheel with one-thousand spokes, Indra approached and offered a conch that swirled to the right, and they requested that the dharma wheel be turned.

For us as well, it has not been long since the buddhas who dwell in the trichiliocosm universes achieved awakening. Hence, think that those abiding buddhas who have yet to turn the dharma wheel are being supplicated to turn the wheel and that they accept. Then, actually supplicate the virtuous spiritual guides to teach the dharma and respectfully implore them to depart the sacred instructions. This branch serves as an antidote for delusion and the relinquishment of dharma.

3.2.1.1.4.2.6 Prayer for Buddhas to Remain in the World

The supplication to the [buddhas] to not pass into nirvāṇa is as follows. Previously, when our teacher completed his deeds of actually taming the field of disciples: according to the common perspective of those to tame, he revealed the deed of passing into the state of nirvāṇa. Just as he [i.e., the Buddha] had already extended his life for an additional three months due to the request of the blacksmith's son, Upāsaka Chaṇḍa,[a] we too must supplicate all buddhas who abide in the realms of the world but are about to pass into nirvāṇa not to do so, but rather to remain as long as saṃsāra exists. Consider that this request is accepted. In

[a] *dge bsnyen tsan dhi*, or *tsandhi*

actuality, one should offer longevity ceremonies to the spiritual guides for their long life. This serves as an antidote for wrong view.

3.2.1.1.4.2.7 Dedication of Merit

The prayer to dedicate merit is as follows. It is necessary to dedicate the root of all of one's virtue accumulated throughout the three times to the simultaneous enlightenment of all beings. In the *Intermediate Mother*, it states:

> O Rabjor! The root of these virtuous accumulations must only be dedicated to attain the state of awakening. Do not dedicate this to attain the states of the shrāvakas, pratyekas, or any others.

Thus, and the quote continues:

> Such is the general dedication for all sentient beings. This is not about merely fulfilling personal goals and aims, but rather that one could fall to the states of the shrāvakas and the pratyekas.

Thus, it is as taught. Furthermore, it is also necessary to seal the dedication with both great compassion and the prajñā that realizes emptiness. By dedicating in this way, even the smallest root of virtue will be increased without waste. This also serves as the antidote for doubt.

According to the speech of Machig:

> At the conclusion of the aforementioned verses for prostrations then include: delight in offerings that please the five senses, confess each nonvirtuous negativity, rejoice in the virtue of all beings, request that the dharma wheel be turned, and supplicate the buddhas to remain firm without passing into nirvāṇa. The root of all virtue is then dedicated to all living beings.

Thus, it is taught. Although there are limitless methods for accumulating merit and purifying obscurations, if synthesized, all of them are included in these seven branches. These seven find their source in the actual teachings of the Buddha and the shāstra commentaries upon them, including the many categories of both Sūtra and Tantra, whether extensive or brief. These, too, can be synthesized into just three branches: accumulating merit, purifying obscurations, and dedicating virtue to ensure this will never exhaust and remain ever-increasing. All seven branches are complete in these [three].

Four of the branches—namely, the first, prostrations, the second, fifth, and sixth—belong to the category of rejoicing in the root of others' virtue; so they are methods through which merit is accrued. Confession is the method to purify obscurations. From one perspective, rejoicing involves rejoicing in the root of one's virtues in order to increase virtue; and dedication ensures that virtue will increase without waste.

To synthesize this further, since the other branches accumulate merit and the confession of negativity purifies obscurations, this is subsumed into the twofold category of accumulation and purification. Based on this, the qualities of abandonment and realization will take root in the mind stream. Hence, there is nothing that is not included in the twofold practice of accumulation and purification.

This is mentioned in the *Heap of Jewels Sūtra* where Maitreya makes his request:

> Since it is said that this tradition of the seven branches is a practical vehicle that is easy to engage and internalize, it is cause for attaining the unsurpassed state of buddhahood. That is why one must persist in this with as much enthusiasm as possible.

So, it is.

> The way of practicing the seven branches, such as prostrations and
> the rest, is given here as the upadesha for accumulating merit and
> purifying obscurations.
> As the supreme method for bringing all qualities to the mind stream,
> always maintain familiarity with this.

Thus, these are the verses that summarize the section.[146]

3.2.1.2 Uncommon Specific Preliminaries

This has two parts:

1 Meditation and recitation for the three kāyas
2 Meditation upon guru yoga

Second are the uncommon preliminaries involving **the meditation and recitation for the trikāya** [ḍākinīs] and the meditation upon guru yoga.

3.2.1.2.1 Meditation and Recitation for the Three Kāyas

This has two parts:

1 Actual practice
2 Supporting instructions for the seven-day retreat

The first has two, namely, the actual practice followed by the supporting instructions for the seven-day wandering in fear-invoking environments.

3.2.1.2.1.1 Actual Practice

First, the *All-Creating Monarch* states:

> The essence of all victorious ones is the trikāya . . .

So just as the quote states, since these are the words of the tantra that carry great import, it is acceptable to apply them to any aspect of the ground and result. If applied to the resultant phase, then all victorious ones of the three times without exception are synthesized within the nature of the trikāya. According to this tradition of the great secret vehicle: since all obscuring stains to be purified are fully cleansed at the time of the trikāya of the ground, the nature of the resultant trikāya is fully manifest. That which actualizes this [at the time of the path] are the sacred instructions concerning both the methods of the generation stage and the completion stage of prajñā.

In the *Subsequent Gathering Essence of the Sugatas Tantra*,[a] it states:

> When all buddhas reveal the dharma, it will perfectly abide with the two stages: the stage of generation and that of completion.

So, it is as taught.

To expand upon this, to initially train in the stages of generation and then move on to the stage of completion is to train in a sequential manner congruent with taking the first step and then proceeding to the next. The *Five Stages* states:

> For those who first excellently abide on the stage of generation and wish to practice the stage of completion, the perfected Buddha taught the method that approaches like steps on a staircase.

Thus, it is as taught.

[a] *de shek dü pa chi ma'i gyü* (*bde gshegs 'dus pa phyi ma'i rgyud*)

Here, **the practice of** generating the deity is emphasized first, so that is the origin of **the trikāya meditation-recitation.** Concerning this, Ḍākinī Tröma Nagmo is a deity that tames difficult and unruly beings. In order to do so, since the nirmāṇakāya is capable of revealing whatever kāya is necessary, this is the nature of the nirmāṇakāya of all buddhas. Vajravarāhī resides in the Akaniṣhṭha as the exceedingly pure aspect of self-appearances. Given that she assumes the characteristics of the sambhogakāya, she is the sambhogakāya embodiment of all buddhas.

The dharmakāya is the quintessence of the briefly aforementioned, as well as the absolute nature of all qualities based on the abandonments and realizations, as well as the intrinsic nature of indivisible basic space and awareness. This is not a rupakāya that involves faces, arms, and attributes perceived by others. Rather this is the self-appearing domain of the buddha—the sole, inconceivably abiding, manifest nature of wisdom. Owing to the fact that ordinary objects to be tamed are incapable of precisely realizing this indwelling nature, here this is indicated through signs and symbols in order to enhance understanding. Meditating upon the aspect of Samantabhadrī, Great Mother of Basic Space, should thereby be understood as an important key point to enhance this understanding. This is also referred to in the tantra *Vajra Tent*:

> Through the practice of awakened pride, the nature of buddha will not take long to know.

Thus, it is as taught. Hence, the activity of familiarizing with the sovereign embodiment of all buddhas as the trikāya ḍākinīs with clarity and pride is as follows.

At the moment of saying ***phet*****, instantly as if awakening from a dream**, all confused appearances awaken within their own ground; so all material phenomena vanish into the clear-light basic space of phenomena. Once again, like a rainbow emerging in the sky, **all appearances** of great wisdom self-awareness **arise as the perfect pure land.**

The arrangement is according to what was previously described as the field of refuge. **In the center of this, upon an [eight-petaled] lotus symbolizing nonattachment** to saṃsāra **is a moon** that indicates being unsullied by faults **and a sun seat** indicating freedom from all defects. The corpse seat indicates having blocked the entranceway to saṃsāra. Then in an instant, **self-nature appears as the** awareness kāya of the absolute dharmatā, the **sole mother, Tröma Nagmo, blue-black** in color, indicating the unborn dharmakāya. Her **one face** designates that the dharmatā is the sole bindu, and her three eyes gaze directly and unwaveringly out into space to represent the spontaneously present trikāya. The natural sound of *hung* resounds from her nostrils indicating the spontaneous accomplishment of the two aims. Her mouth is gaping to symbolize the ecstasy of evenness. Her four fangs indicate taming beings through the four immeasurables. Her flashing tongue, like a bolt of lightning, indicates the equal pervasion of saṃsāra and enlightenment. Both ears designate the nonduality of the two truths. Having purified the fifty-eight concepts in their place, her fifty-eight teeth that shine like the moon indicate the perfected qualities of the fifty-eight herukas. Given that the process of birth and death have been uprooted through the method of exaltation, she wields **a vajra blade** into space **in the right hand and holds a skull filled with blood in the left** hand to her heart to indicate delighting in the blood of the three realms within prajñā's basic space of great emptiness. **Both legs** represent nonabiding **in** either extreme of existence or quiescence, and her **dancing posture** reveals her capacity to fulfill the aims of the fortunate ones by placing them in exaltation.

Her upward swirling hair indicates she seals the mind streams of others with great wisdom that has never known confusion and has fully actualized the fundamental nature. The sign of charismatically attracting beings is the remaining hair flowing down freely. The **black pig's head** that **juts from the crown** is **squealing** so loudly that the trichiliocosm shakes, indicating having liberated hope and fear in basic space and awakening beings from the slumber of dimmed awareness. Her wrathful wrinkles and eyebrows are connected, indicating that absolute truth is unborn, unceasing, and unchanging. Her ten pliant fingers symbolize the spontaneous presence of the five wisdoms and the five kāyas. Her ten toes are splendid and lovely to behold, indicating having closed the door to saṃsāra and rendering the five poisons and aggregates pure in their place. The twelve body joints are supple and pliant, indicating that the twelve links of interdependent origination are pure in their place.

Her *bhaga* is expansive to indicate unity with the ground of unchanging exaltation, and her voluptuous breasts indicate caring for her followers. Her **extremely wrathful demeanor** and immensely large kāya symbolize how she delights in the consummate basic space of the sambhogakāya nature of saṃsāra and enlightenment. Having purified the eight gatherings in their place, she moves in the gyrations of dance; having purified the eight objects, she is **adorned with the eight charnel-ground accouterments.** The indication of her consort of exaltation is the trident held at the cleft of her left arm. Having liberated the three times into basic space, the trident sports three tips that indicate the spontaneous presence of wisdom. The sign of the spontaneous presence of the three kāyas are the three stacked skulls adorning the trident. The symbol of the bodhichitta is the handle made from the plantain tree. The sign that all kāyas and pure lands are perfectly complete is the five silken scarves that flow in the breeze. The indication of nondual space and wisdom is that she stands **in the expanse of a blazing wisdom inferno.**

In her heart, within an amulet of the conjoined sun and moon that symbolize nondual upāya and prajñā is the seed syllable of enlightened mind, **a blue-black syllable *hung*,** as though drawn by the tip of a fine hair. That is **encircled by a garland of mantric syllables** in a counterclockwise direction. **From them, light rays radiate to cleanse all illness, demonic forces, negativity, obscurations, and the heap of aggregates, like the sun's rays striking dew. Think that everything is cleansed.**

Upon her crown is the sambhogakāya Vajravarāhī, the self-radiance of the discerning wisdom of exaltation. **Clear red** in color, she **holds a curved vajra blade** in her right hand that severs materialistic conceptualization; **and** in the left hand, she holds a **skull** filled with blood that symbolizes how she delights in saṃsāra and enlightenment as great ecstasy. Her two legs are **upon a lotus and moon seat** in the **dancing** posture generated **within a brilliant expanse of wisdom fire and massing light.**

Above her crown is the Great Mother of Basic Space, the blue-black dharmakāya Samantabhadrī, indicating the very nature of the great wisdom dharmadhātu. Free from the veil and burden of dualistic conceptualization, she is **naked;** and never disturbed by conceptual materializing, she is **seated in the vajra posture.** Having suppressed all duality, her **hands are in the earth-touching gesture;** and she rests in a spherical orb **of five wisdom-light bindus** that represent having transcended the extreme limits of eternalism and nihilism. Because she abides as the nature of wisdom's inner clarity, she is **generated within an expanse of deep and luminous wisdom** light. **In the heart of the dharmakāya sovereign of the family is a white syllable *ah*; and in the sambhogakāya's heart, upon a sun seat the size of a split pea, is a red syllable *bam*;** [both are] **encircled by the garlands of mantric syllables** revolving counterclockwise. **Light rays radiate to cleanse the mind streams of self and all beings.** Meditate that **everyone awakens in the originally pure** kāya **of clear light.**

Focusing on the seed syllable and mantric syllables in the heart of Tröma, **recite *om benzar trodhi*[147] *kali bam ha ri ni sa sarwa pa pam shintam ku ru ye so ha* as many times as possible.** *Om* is the nature of enlightened body, speech, and mind and is the lead syllable for all mantras. *Benzar trodhi kali* is "vajra Tröma Nagmo," so it is the mantric name for Tröma. *Vajra* means to be indestructible, invincible, and so forth, so there will be no interruption or destruction brought on by the confusion of materialistic fixation. Given that this is the nature of the five wisdoms of inseparable empty awareness, it is expressed in this way.

Bam is the syllable of enlightened mind, *ha* is Vajra Ḍākinī, *ri* is Ratna Ḍākinī, *ni* is Pema Ḍākinī, and *sa* is Karma Ḍākinī. Here, although these ḍākinīs do not appear per se, Tröma represents the embodiment of the four families of ḍākinīs. Given that this is the source for the radiation and reabsorption, it is taught in this way. *Sarwa pa pam shintam* and so forth are the syllables for pacifying all negativity and the like. Through this process, one's three doors arise as the aspect of the deities' enlightened body, speech, and mind; so all nonconducive aspects, such as negativity, obscurations, and habits, are cleansed and fully purified. *So ha* means to establish this ground that is the blessing of Tröma's three secrets.

> As the sole wisdom ḍākinī, sovereign of the five families, may these blessings remain stable and firm in the mind stream.

Thus, one supplicates.

Then, from the mantric syllables in the heart of the sovereign of the family, Vajravarāhī, light rays that are the intrinsic nature **of** the five wisdoms radiate as **five colors** imbued with the potency of blessings and the symbol of evenness as **warm**th that **suddenly emerge to dissolve into the heart of oneself as Tröma Nagmo. One** then **becomes a bindu of white light that dissolves up into the heart of the sambhogakāya wisdom ḍākinī. Then as Vajravarāhī, in one's heart from the red *bam* encircled by the mantric syllables, light rays radiate to cleanse and purify all habits, karma, and passions of the three planes of existence.** In doing so, **imagine** that **the three realms become pure lands and everything is the manifestation of deities, mantra, and the nature of phenomena.** Empty appearances are the pure deity, empty sound is the pure mantra, and empty awareness is pure wisdom awareness. Imagine that this is the play of the nature of emptiness as the wisdom nature of the dharmatā.

While reciting ***om benzar wa ra hi*** and so forth,[148] the mantra carries the same meaning as described before. *Benzar wa ra hi* is the name of Vajravarāhī. *Wa ra hi* means to blaze, move, and remain stable. Likewise, wisdom initially blazes, then increases, and finally becomes very stable. Otherwise, from the blazing of the initial dharmakāya wisdom of enlightened mind, the emanation of the rupakāya moves; and from that, there is constant stability, thus revealing the qualities of the sambhogakāya. To reiterate, given this is the nature of all five families of ḍākinīs in a single embodiment, this applies to the seed syllable *bam* and so forth; and the remaining syllables are as described before.

Then, **from the** mantric syllables in the **heart of the family sovereign Samantabhadrī, light rays radiate. Imagine that self and all appearances dissolve into the unelaborate basic space of phenomena. Recite *om benzar wa ra hi bam ha ri ni sa sarwa pa pam shintam ku ru ye so ha* as much as possible.**

After that, **from the heart of the mother, Samantabhadrī, blue-black light rays radiate to dissolve into one's heart as Vajravarāhī** where they dissolve, **transforming one into an orb of red light. This dissolves into the heart of the dharmakāya wisdom ḍākinī.** Then **in the heart of oneself as Samantabhadrī, from a white *ah* encircled by the mantric syllables, light rays radiate, causing**

saṃsāra to collapse within the state of great transcendence; and one becomes the single taste of the wisdom space of all victorious ones. Recite *om benzar sa manta bha dra om*.

This means that indestructible Samantabhadrī is the intrinsic nature of inseparable basic space and wisdom, where all faults are set free as the pristine nature of dharmakāya. This is what is meant by Samantabhadrī. *Om* is the heart essence syllable revealing the nature of the five wisdoms. After **reciting this with the awareness of saṃsāra and enlightenment's** intrinsic nature being **the great expansive pervasion of evenness**: from the garland of mantric syllables in the heart of the mother, Samantabhadrī, light rays radiate; and self and all appearances naturally dissolve in the basic space of phenomena.[149] **Following the root mantra, recite *dharma ka ya sa ma ti siddhi ah ah ah*.**

Thus reciting *dharma ka ya* means the enlightened body of truth. *Sa ma ti* means single-pointed absorption, and *siddhi* is actual attainment. From the point of view of the relative method, the aspect of the dharmakāya buddhas is imagined so that, by the strength of reciting and visualizing the rotation of the mantras, the previously described meaning that saṃsāra and enlightenment never waver from the evenness of the space of the dharmatā is incited while supplicating for the bestowal of the siddhis of nonconceptual supreme samādhi to be conferred.

From the perspective of absolute prajñā, the meaning of resting in the evenness of the absolute three gateways to liberation is where discerning wisdom awareness is actually rendered evident. Those three [entranceways] are indicated by the final recitation of the three *ahs*. Then, while reciting this mantra, it is important to rest in the evenness of the fundamental nature according to one's familiarity with this realization. **Finally, after reciting according to one's capacity, rest within unelaborate awareness** and sustain that as long as possible.

While engaged in this meditation-recitation, practice without allowing the mind to be distracted elsewhere. One's **three doors are inseparably mingled with** the deity's enlightened body, speech, and mind [i.e., **the three vajras**]. **The** sacred **key point is to take the path of the all-pervasive purity of phenomenal existence.**

3.2.1.2.1.2 Supporting Instructions for the Seven-Day Retreat

Second are the oral instructions for the supplementary practice of wandering in fear-invoking environments for seven days. The visualization for the preliminary suppression is not necessary. Among the four ways of proceeding, here the gait of the dancing ḍākinī is used. Once arriving in the fearful place, it is acceptable to then decide whether *Ḍākinīs Laughter*[150] needs to be performed or not.

Then by practicing refuge, bodhichitta, maṇḍala, on through to the seven-branch offering prayer, begin the trikāya meditation-recitation. Visualize the trikāya ḍākinī practice as usual according to the text. Especially now while visualizing oneself as Tröma, to one's right imagine the assemblies of kingly male demonic forces, to the left the assemblies of female demonic forces, behind the nāga and earth demonic forces, and in front the eight classes of the planetary demonic forces and their assemblies. Visualize the sentient beings of the six classes surrounding. While reciting the mantra: from the seed syllable in the heart, boundless light rays radiate; and all gods-māras of phenomenal existence, including all beings of the three realms, become only the kāya of Tröma. Think that all of them are reciting the mantra.

Then from the heart of Vajravarāhī, light rays radiate and strike all sentient beings that became Tröma. Visualizing oneself as Tröma, when the light rays strike, one becomes a white bindu of light that dissolves into the heart of Vajravarāhī. Within the expanse of that kāya of pristine basic space as Tröma, now everyone becomes only the kāya of Varāhī, appearing like stars on the surface of the vast ocean.[151]

Next, according to the text's description for visualization and recitation, remain practicing while reciting each of the three ḍākinīs' mantras as much as required. Then, go to sleep. At midnight, again begin and practice just like before, and repeat this again at predawn. Once returning home, it is not necessary to practice the visualization for the subsequent suppression. This is the activity for accomplishing the welfare of beings through the gods-māras.

> Although ultimately transcending an object to accomplish and the process of doing so, from the relative perspective, these instructions are infallible key points for practice.
> This supreme method for attaining the ground of the three kāyas is the exceptional quintessence of the profound doctrine of the great secret.

Thus, these are the verses that summarize the section.

3.2.1.2.2 Meditation upon Guru Yoga

This has two parts:

1 General meaning
2 Actual meditation

Second, for the meditation on guru yoga, there are two: the general meaning and the actual meditation taken from the terma involving the manner of engaging in the daily practice.

3.2.1.2.2.1 General Meaning

This has five parts:

1 Characteristics of a qualified guru
2 How to rely on a qualified guru
3 Benefits of relying on a qualified guru
4 Faults of developing wrong view
5 Training in pure view

First, it states in the *Gathering of Precious Qualities*:

> A bodhisattva abiding on the ground of a beginner will, through pure intention, enter the path of the buddhas and bodhisattvas. All such excellent students with respect for their masters must always rely upon learned gurus. If one were to ask why, it is because all knowledge comes from this source. It is said that, by relying upon spiritual guides such as those teachers who reveal the prajñāpāramitā and who possess the supreme qualities of the victorious ones, the truth of the Buddha will become apparent.

Thus, bodhisattvas abiding on the ground of a beginner, whoever they may be, will with pure intentions resolve to perfectly awaken for the welfare of others. All excellent students who enter the path that brings supreme awakening and who have respect toward their masters must rely upon gurus with excellent view and conduct, who are able to reveal the wisdom intent of the Mahāyāna. They must always show such learned masters great respect through their three doors. Why? All learned qualities concerning the mode of the great vehicle's path and result come from reliance upon the virtuous spiritual guide. Therefore, they are the guides who will reveal the path of the Mahāyāna, the pāramitā of prajñā. Saying "the truth of the Buddha" refers to qualities, the development of which also depends upon spiritual guides. Hence, this is the speech proclaimed by all fully perfected victors possessing supreme qualities.

Whatever was mentioned as the characteristics of the students and their spiritual guides, the way of relying upon one another and the benefits of doing so were revealed in the quote. Now that quote continues:

> Generosity, discipline, and likewise patience, diligence, concentration, and prajñā as well are fully dedicated to the state of awakening. Those who are beginners must be cautioned to avoid attachment or a feeling of superiority concerning progress on the path of awakening.

Thus, through these words, the way of leading students on the path is clearly revealed. How so? By training in the practice of the six pāramitās such as generosity and by directing students to dedicate those efforts toward attaining the state of perfect awakening, advice is given based on method.

> Concerning the state of awakening that is the so-called ultimate goal to accomplish: directing students to not fixate upon the goal as concrete, such as having form or holding to that as true or superior, means that one must understand that the phenomena subsumed in the state of awakening have no true, inherent existence. This advice is based on prajñā. That is why one is directed to reveal this teaching to beginning students who show interest toward the path of awakening.

Thus, it is taught. When these points are applied to the practice of chöd, they enhance the key points for internalizing practice. Based on previous explanations, this can be understood in more detail.

To give a more informed explanation about how to rely upon the guru, there are five parts, namely, the characteristics of a qualified guru to rely upon, how to rely, the benefits of doing so, the faults that occur by serving incorrectly, and the way to train in pure vision by seeing the guru as an actual enlightened being.

3.2.1.2.2.1.1 Characteristics of a Qualified Guru

First, the general characteristics of a Mahāyāna guru are as the *Ornament of the Classes of Sūtra*[a] tells us:

> Rely upon a teacher who is peaceful, tame, and tranquil, has surpassing qualities and diligence, is rich with transmissions, has fully realized the nature of truth, as well as being skillful through teachings, has loving kindness, and has eliminated all weariness.

Thus, these ten qualities must be possessed. It is taught that, without taming one's mind, there is no way to tame the minds of others; so first teachers must control their own mind streams.

The best method to tame the mind is most certainly through the three precious trainings. By training in discipline, one is able to tame the mind by severing the tendency to pursue misleading objective appearances. By relying upon mindfulness and conscientiousness concerning what to accept and reject in terms of

[a] *do de gyen* (*mdo sde rgyan, mahāyānasūtralaṃkārakārikā*); Maitreya

good and bad, "peaceful" means to be introspective through the training of samādhi that peacefully abides. By relying upon peaceful abiding that renders the mind functional, being "tranquil" means to possess the training of prajñā that comes about through the determination of the correct meaning. Through the exceptional training of prajñā, the nature of the selflessness of phenomena is then realized.

Just possessing the qualities and realizations that come about through these three trainings alone is still not enough. The qualities of scriptural transmission must be possessed, such as having extensively studied the Tripiṭaka and so forth. Although possessing the qualities of scriptural transmission and realization, it is unacceptable to still be less qualified or equal to one's students; hence, qualities must be surpassing. These six qualities belong to the category of personal attainment.

The remaining ones are qualities involving the care of disciples. For that, among the four, "being skilled in teaching" means to be expert in knowing how to guide disciples gradually and deliver comprehension of meaning to the disciples' minds. "Loving kindness" means to have the pure intention to teach dharma, not dependent upon gaining respect or monetary gain and so forth, but out of total concern, love, and compassion. "Diligence" means to take delight in benefiting others. "Having abandoned weariness" means to never feel tired to teach repeatedly and to possess patience concerning the effort it takes to do so.

The characteristics of the guru of Secret Mantra are also mentioned extensively throughout the Vajrayāna teachings. To summarize, it states in *Resting the Mind in Repose*:

> Rely upon a teacher who has empowerment, pure vows, and samaya; has traversed the ocean of tantric meanings and upadesha instructions; has become expert in the approach, accomplishment, and activity sections of practice; has through view, conduct, meditation, and result attained the heat of realization; has great compassion and skillful means; can place disciples on the stage of resultant liberation; and has not lost the cloudlike blessings of the lineage. Rely upon a glorious guru learned and accomplished in these ways.

Thus, it is taught. If this quotation were to be explained as the aforementioned was, then it is as follows. The qualities of realization involve having the personal qualities of empowerment, pure vows, and samaya and the attainment of the extent of heat indicated through realization of the meaning of the nature as it is, including the view, meditation, conduct, and the result.

The qualities of scriptural realization include having transcendental knowledge of the oceanic meanings of the tantras and upadesha instructions. Surpassing qualities involve qualities that surpass the students in terms of mastery over enlightened deeds, such as the approach, accomplishment, and activity phases of deity yoga. Through great loving kindness, joy is taken in benefiting others; and by having abandoned any weariness, skill is involved in leading disciples on the path. Due to that, by granting empowerments to disciples, their minds are brought to maturity; and by engaging in the yogas of the generation and completion stages, there is the potential to bring students all the way to the state of liberation. Those are the qualities of caring for others.

That which is indispensable for accomplishing the purpose of both self and others is to never allow the cloudlike lineage blessings to vanish. In these ways, one must rely upon gurus who possess these qualities of learning and accomplishment. It is also stated in the commentary called *The Great Chariot* where the author quotes from the auto-commentary composed by Master Vimālā called the *Mirrorlike Magical Matrix*[a] the following:

> The guru must have perfectly received the outer and inner empowerments of the maṇḍala; have pure vows and samaya; be learned with the individual meanings of the tantras; be well trained in the approach, accomplishment, and enlightened activities practices; not be deluded concerning the realization of the view; have experience that has merged with meditation; be fully and consistently capable of interlinking various activities with spiritual conduct; and be able to guide disciples with compassion. These are the eight qualities to possess.

Thus, it is taught. My guru taught that, along with these eight, it was also necessary to hold the stainless lineages and possess cloudbanks full of blessings, making nine qualities. Mention of these qualities is solely according to the upadesha tradition of the great regent Maitreya.

In particular, for this tradition of chöd, the guru must have experience in wandering to the one-hundred and eight terrifying charnel grounds, confidence in the view and meditation of fearless conduct, skill in teaching severance, and at least some experience with upadesha instructions. Nevertheless, it states in *Approaching the Ultimate*:[b]

> Due to the power of the degenerate times, gurus have a mixture of both qualities and faults. They are not always devoid of negativity. So through astute examination of whoever does have any surpassing

[a] *gyutrül drawa melong* (*sgyu 'phrul drva ba me long*); Vimālāmitra
[b] *don dam nyen pa* (*don dam bsnyen pa*)

> qualities, then that is a guru that you, Children of the Lineage, may then rely upon.

Having now arrived in the degenerate times, one can no longer find a master who is completely flawless. Given that both faults and qualities are mingled: through careful analysis if some surpassing qualities are discovered, then it is said to be acceptable to rely upon such a master.

3.2.1.2.2.1.2 How to Rely on a Qualified Guru

Second, the manner of reliance has two parts: the characteristics of the disciple who is relying and the manner in which to do so. First, it states in the *Four-Hundred Stanzas*:

> To be straightforward and intelligent are said to be the characteristics of the listener.

Thus, as taught, "being straightforward" means to not have attachment toward one spiritual tradition or aversion toward those of others. If that were not the case, then due to the lack of open-minded knowledge, qualities would not be seen and the purpose of the sublime explanations would remain undiscovered. It is not enough to only be sincere since a student must also have the intelligence to determine the difference between a perfectly correct noble path and incorrect ignoble paths. Even with both of these [i.e., sincerity and intelligence]—if interest is lacking, then the disciple will still remain an unsuitable vessel for dharma. That is why great diligence must be applied in order to pursue their goal. Along with these three, in the commentary [for that text], it states that having respect toward the dharma and teachers, as well as mental focus, are two further qualities to apply to the rest—making five.

In particular it is as stated in the tantra *Garland of Pearls*:[a]

> While identifying an individual as a suitable support, look for someone who recalls impermanence and death, can let go of this life's phenomena, has faith in the master, practices dharma from their heart, has great courage and commitment, is able to remain in frightening places, can take on adverse circumstances, and who thinks only of dharma. Such a fortunate person as this must be shown the profound essence of the meaning.

[a] *mu tig treng wa* (*mu tig phreng ba*)

Thus, that is a description of a suitable student for these dharma instructions. The quote continues:

> Someone who believes things are permanent and fixates, sees and identifies the master's faults, is self-fixated and takes keen interest in the eight worldly concerns, lacks courage and defames the master, cannot stay in retreat or frightening places, is unable to take on the adversity of upheavals, has many nonspiritual concepts, does not regard the dharma, disparages the sangha, is attached to his or her homeland and loved ones, has an unruly mind filled with passionate attachment and aversion, pretends to love dharma and receive teachings only when convenient, pretends that the master does not exist and takes credit for oneself, and does not practice due to sloth are signs of an unfortunate person from whom the profound doctrine of chöd must be completely concealed.

Thus, this reveals what an unsuitable vessel means. In this way, both suitable and unsuitable vessels are described in the *Gathering of Precious Qualities*:

> A noble disciple who respects the master and so forth . . .

The quote continues:

> . . . someone who accompanies negative companions and is easily persuaded by others, like an unfired clay pot that will crack when water is poured into it.

Thus, as taught, the first [reference to the noble disciple] was previously explained. The last two lines refer to someone influenced by negative companions and who takes delight in activities other than dharma. Even if there is a slight inclination toward dharma, they will still be influenced by others; so that means they are unstable and pursue external influences, for example, like an unfired clay pot that shatters once water is poured in. This reveals what an unsuitable vessel for dharma means.

Second, the actual teachings on how to rely are as the *Gathering of Precious Qualities* continues:

> To expand upon that, the learned who have a stable commitment and search for the sacred ground of awakening must initially subdue their pride. Like how a patient must rely upon a doctor when curing an illness, a spiritual guide must be relied upon without wavering.

Thus, as taught, for the purpose of others from the perspective of intensely wishing to attain or discover the ground of fully perfected buddhahood free from delusion concerning what to accept and reject and with intelligence that certainly determines the master's qualities, pride must be subdued. With faith and devotion, the master's kindness is recalled. For example, just as in order to cure an illness one must rely upon a good doctor, one must comply with whatever the master requires. By serving respectfully without wavering from the three doors, it is necessary to rely on the master by even offering material benefit and more.

This way of practicing is mentioned in the *Bodhicharyāvatāra* as follows:

> Train in how to rely upon the guru, as described in the *Biography of Paljung*.[a]

Thus, it is as taught. In *Arranged as a Stalk*, it states:

> In the biography of the child Paljung, it mentions to rely upon a master using nine attitudes. They are [first] an attitude like a wise child, namely, skillfully doing whatever the father requires. Like that here, whatever activity is engaged, always consider the intent of the master and act accordingly. An attitude like a vajra is, by having rejected any unstable tendencies, to be unaffected by negative companions or demonic forces. An attitude like earth means to not feel burdened when carrying out any responsibilities for the master. An attitude like a mountain is to not back down in the face of whatever suffering may be endured. An attitude like a servant is to accept and adopt whatever the master says, without becoming discouraged. An attitude like a slave is to abandon pride and place oneself lower than the master. An attitude like a rope is to serve with joy no matter how heavy the master's command may be. An attitude like a dog is to not get angry even though the master may insult you. For example, even though an owner may beat his dog, rather than running away, the dog will remain loyal to the master. An attitude like a ship means to continue to forge on no matter how demanding the process of serving the master may be.

In the *Ornament of the Classes of Sūtra*, it states:

> Rely upon the master by respecting, making offerings, serving, and practicing.

[a] *pal jung wa yi nam tar* (*dpal 'byung ba yi rnam thar*); biography of Shrī Sambhava

The quote continues:

> One who accomplishes the supporting bodhichitta according to what is taught will fully please the mind [of the guru].

So, respect is shown by setting out his or her cushion, standing up, offering material things such as food and drink, serving such as massaging, cleaning, and so forth. From the point of view of practicing dharma correctly, it is necessary to rely upon a support; and that is the master. The supporting bodhichitta must be accomplished along with whatever teachings have been given. Just as it is taught, through these methods, it is necessary to completely please the master's mind.

The quote continues:

> To gain qualities, one partakes in the opportunity to receive dharma instruction rather than relying upon the master to gain something such as material benefit.

Thus, one who utilizes the opportunity to rely upon the guru does so in order to develop qualities, not to gain material benefit such as wealth.

Furthermore, it states in *Resting the Mind in Repose*:

> Always recall the qualities of the master; and even if faults are noticed, notice them as qualities. Think with heartfelt conviction that any such faults are self-appearing and certainly not from the master, so confess, restore, and apply the antidote. Abandon anything that displeases the master, and try one's best to please in whatever way necessary. Never break the command of the master; and even if the attendants are ignoble, respect them like the master. Do not take the master's attendants and family members as students. Ask [the master] first before giving any dharma instruction, empowerment, and the like.
>
> While in the presence of the master, control one's body, speech, and mind, do not stretch out the legs, sit in āsana, or show one's back. Do not show an angry, disgruntled face. Do not utter silly, inappropriate words, speak falsely, slander, bring up the other's faults, speak unkind or harsh words, or engage in meaningless conversation. Do not covet the master's wealth or harbor ill will. Control every aspect of the ill-intended mind toward even those who live in the master's vicinity.
>
> The deeds of the guru involve myriad miraculous manifestations, so do not judge any contradictions as though they were ordinary. Think that it is unacceptable [to analyze], for those are the enlightened deeds.

> If there are any slight contradictions or faults, discard them as wrong view. Even if the master becomes upset, think it is one's own fault and immediately confess. Meditate that [the master] is upon one's crown and fervently supplicate. By pleasing the master in this way, siddhis will be swiftly attained. When seeing the master, stand up and offer prostrations; when sitting, offer cushions and other necessities. Praising with melodious speech, bring palms together; and when departing, stand and respectfully follow the master out. Always be mindful and careful with veneration and a sense of shy trepidation.
>
> Like a newlywed, stay in the master's presence with the three doors tranquil. Avoid day-dreaming or acting carelessly. Have no bias, pride, or wish for personal gain. Do nothing that is deceptive, based on pretext, artificial, or motivated by attachment to loved ones or aversion toward enemies. If there is abundance, offer this to the guru. Serve through body and speech with heartfelt devotion. Please the master by giving over this life to practice. Even if others speak negatively about one's master, object to that; and if there is no potential to change their attitude, then bring the master's qualities into one's mind. Close off one's ears and just try to benefit that person through compassion, while not befriending or speaking with that person in a welcoming manner any further.

Thus, this was a compilation of teachings on the manner of relying upon the master taken from the tantras, the *Fifty Verses of Guru Devotion*, and other sources.[152] These verses are easy to comprehend except for the following passages.

The text states that in the presence of the master, if one thinks to confer empowerment upon others, then one must request permission to do so from the teacher. If permission is not granted, then one must not continue. Reference to "not displaying a disgruntled face" means to not show an aggressive expression. Taking the vow to "not harbor harmful thoughts toward the master's family, retinue, sponsors, and general field of devotees" means either intending to harm them or actually doing so. Due to an important reason if the master demonstrates extreme behavior that is peaceful, wrathful, or seemingly worldly, one should not think the master's speech and actions are conflicted by thinking, "This is unacceptable." One must not judge this behavior as confused, deluded, or faulty and never even harbor such thoughts. When the master does something that one may disagree with, to then think, "This is completely wrong" or feel surprised that the master would dare to do or say contradictory things and reach the conclusion that the master has faults amounts to wrong view that must be discarded. If the master gives loving attention to another and shows aggression toward yourself, that too should not be seen as the master's fault. What should be discerned? One must think all of this amounts to one's own abundance of shortcomings and carefully examine them while confessing and purifying.

If others point out the faults of the master, one should call them on that, let them know such speech is inappropriate, and try to correct them. If that is not possible, then one should disparage those words as false and focus on the master's qualities. Without listening to such speech, the ears can be covered, while at the same time the person speaking should not be forsaken from one's heart. Consider with compassion how one might be able to benefit them and show them kindness through body and speech while no longer engaging with them in a casual, friendly manner. If not, then being involved with them any further may cause a personal root downfall.

In brief, it states in the *Fifty Verses of Guru Devotion*:

> It is not necessary to mention many things here. Whatever pleases the master must be done. By rejecting anything that is displeasing, try hard to maintain that. Knowing that the vajra holder has said that siddhis depend upon the master, one must completely please the guru through whatever means are required.

Thus, it is not necessary to mention many things; but to synthesize the key point, one must identify whatever pleases the enlightened mind of the master and accomplish that, while rejecting whatever may bring displeasure. By doing so, since all siddhis depend upon and are received through pleasing the master, to know this is to know the speech of the vajra holder himself. With the three doors and all material things, trying one's best to please the vajra master is the meaning of what was quoted.

3.2.1.2.2.1.3 Benefits of Relying on a Qualified Guru

Third, the benefits of relying are as follows. It states in *Resting the Mind in Repose*:

> The victors' and their heirs' of the three times, including all shrāvakas and pratyekas, attainment of the three levels of awakening comes about through connecting with a spiritual guide. In existence, the happiness of higher rebirth is also due to having relied upon a precious master. Hence, one must rely upon a sublime individual.

So, the attainment of the excellent state of the three times for victors and their heirs and, in existence, the attainment of the higher and lower states of resultant happiness as gods and human beings all come about by having relied upon a sublime spiritual guide.

In the *Sūtra Requested by Maitreya*, it states:

> It must be known that whoever is a shrāvaka, pratyeka, or an unsurpassed buddha—those who are fully liberated and see with wisdom awareness—are all the result of having fully relied upon a virtuous spiritual guide. O Maitreya! Not only that, all benefit others have shown and whatever happiness has occurred are entirely due to the root of your virtue. That, too, came from having relied upon a virtuous spiritual master.

Thus, it is taught and in *Arranged as a Stalk*, it states:

> Child of the Family! It is certain that all bodhisattvas who have been fully sustained by virtuous spiritual guides will not fall into the abyss of the lower realms.

Thus, saying "having been sustained by a virtuous guide and not falling into lower realms" means that all karma that is to be experienced as the great suffering of the lower realms will instead ripen in this very lifetime. In terms of that, there will be the actual experience of degrees of suffering endured by the body and mind, as well as experiences in the dream state. Nevertheless, the purification of that karma will occur, and negative karma will be swiftly exhausted. In fact, the benefits are so great that they cannot even compare with the root of virtue accumulated by making offerings to countless buddhas over many eons of time.

In the *Sūtra of Kṣhitigarbha*,[a] it states:

> By relying upon a master—even if one has previously accumulated karma to wander in the lower realms for boundless eons of time—in that life, calamities that harm the body and mind, such as contagious disease, famine, and the like, will be experienced; and through that, all negative karma will be cleansed. At least, even being reproached or insulted[b] [by the master], including nightmares, will cleanse that karma. The root of all virtue accumulated by making offerings, expressing generosity, maintaining vows, and the like in the presence of boundless buddhas cannot compare to one morning's virtue of serving the master. That is why the qualities derived through respecting the master are truly inconceivable.

[a] *sa yi nyingpo'i do* (*sa yi snying po'i mdo*)
[b] *gyed kag* (*brgyad bkag*)

Thus, it is as taught. Saying "reproached or insulted" is an ancient term used here that has many interpretations. Here, it is acceptable to consider that this also includes being scolded or insulted by anyone, not just only the master.

Furthermore, that all virtuous dharma will be brought to mind is also referred to in the *Inconceivable Secret Sūtra:*[a]

> O Sons and Daughters of the Family! All of you must show respect and rely upon masters with great devotion. If you do, then having heard the dharma, your thoughts will turn to virtue and, from that, your actions will too.

Thus, and the quote continues:

> When a bodhisattva relies upon a master, all accumulated qualities will be perfected.

So, it is as taught. Hence, it also states in the *Jataka Tales*:

> There is no one who should distance themselves from a sublime master. In the manner of humility, rely according to virtue. If close to the master, then even the particles of the master's qualities will affect such a disciple without even trying.
>
> Thus, whoever is intelligent will decide not to distance themselves from sublime ones who are virtuous spiritual guides. Rather they will, through respectful humility, rely in a virtuous manner.

Thus, it is. The reason is that, if one is close to a sublime master, then—even without trying—the particles of the master's qualities will be naturally received.

My own master, Venerable Do Ngak Chökyi Gyatso,[b] a name so venerated it is hard to say without reason, has said:

> The root of goodness in this and the future life depends on devotedly relying upon a protective, virtuous spiritual guide and then having the ability to recall their kindness. O Heart Sons, you must please them.

Thus, he gave this loving advice.

[a] *sang wa sam gyi mi khyab pa'i do* (*gsang ba bsam gyis mi khyab pa'i mdo, tathāgatāchintya-guhyanirdeshasūtra*)
[b] *mdo sngaks chos kyi rgy mtsho*

3.2.1.2.2.1.4 Faults of Developing Wrong View

Fourth, the faults of developing wrong view are as follows. The faults of disrespecting or insulting the master are inconceivable. It states in *Vajrapāṇi's Empowerment Conferral Tantra*:

> O Bhagavan! What is the karma of those who show disrespect to their master? The Bhagavan responded, "Do not even mention that, as it frightens the entire world, including the gods. O Vajrapāṇi, I will give you a brief idea of what will happen. Great Hero, carefully pay heed. I have previously described the boundless suffering and so forth, including the inexhaustible hell realms. Those are the places where such perpetrators will have to abide and remain for limitless eons of time. That is why one must never show disrespect to the masters."

Thus, speaking to Vajrapāṇi and mentioning that even the idea of showing disrespect will frighten the realms of the world, [the Bhagavan asks] that this not even be spoken of. Hence, he says he will not give a full explanation, but will say something in order to answer the question being posed. He calls out to Vajrapāṇi asking him to listen carefully. Suffering that is boundless and without any respite must be experienced, such as in the frightening inexhaustible hell realms of Avīchī and so forth as described by the Bhagavan himself. Those are the places where students who disrespect their masters must dwell, and it is said that is where they will take rebirth in their future life.

Well then, just how long will they remain there? The answer is that they must remain for limitless eons of time. That is why disrespecting the master must never happen under any circumstances. These teachings are also stated in the *Fifty Verses of Guru Devotion*:

> If a disciple intentionally disrespects their master, that disparages all of the buddhas as well and will bring permanent suffering. Those who disparage the master will die from disease, leprosy, and demonic-force possession, contagious illness, poisoning, and the like. They will be killed by rulers, fire, poisonous reptiles, floods, ḍākinīs, robbers, and misguided māras and will fall to the hells. Hence, never disturb the minds of the masters. If one becomes overwhelmed by such delusion, then it is certain the fires of hell will burn beneath one. Frightened by the terror of Avīchī and the rest, it is clearly stated that is where these perpetrators will go.

Thus, the first four lines offer a brief explanation. If described extensively, then there are the two aspects of obvious results that can be seen in this life and invisible results that ripen in the future. The verses subsequent to the first refer to the rulers, and reference to being killed by the misguided ones reveals the obvious results in this life. Invisible results are referred to by reference to falling to the hells and so forth. The rest is easy to understand aside from reference to the ḍākinīs, who are sent to inflict epidemics and contagious diseases. The fevers they inflict bring death in one or two days and are considered incurable.

Other illnesses are also included here, and further detail is given in *Resting the Mind in Repose*:

> Some initially engage in a careless fashion, speaking about secret qualities, and later disparaging. Some pretend to be devoted while privately deceptive. Along with that, they disturb the master's retinue. All of them will experience the result of rebirth in Avīchī.

Thus, prior to relying upon the master, it is necessary to carefully examine his or her qualities. Most people fail to do so initially; they are like starving dogs encountering a piece of meat.[153] They carelessly enter the relationship while receiving teachings and other activities. At that time, due to being shallow, they excitingly blurt out about the master's qualities and act as though they are highly devoted. Later, if they see a single flaw, they will quickly find fault and become disillusioned in private. Some will be two-faced: praising when face-to-face with contrived devotion and, since they actually lack devotion, secretly disparaging and deceiving as best they can. They will even become fed up with the master's retinue. Since all of this indicates our present-day conduct, all of us must be extremely mindful.

The great scholar and accomplished master Shantipa[a] composed a treatise called *Crucial Commentary on the Black Enemy*,[b] where it states:

> Once one listens to even a single verse from a teacher, if thereafter that teacher is not esteemed as such, then that individual will be born as a dog one-hundred times over. After that, they will be born as a butcher.

So, this applies not only to the master from whom one has received empowerment conferral and oral instructions, but also to those whom one has taken an interest in and studied under if even just a single verse of dharma. If they, too, are not esteemed appropriately, then that disciple will be born one-hundred

[a] *slob dpon shan ti pa*

[b] *dra nag gi ka drel* (*dgra nag gi dka' 'grel*); Shantipa

successive times as a dog, after which they will arrive in the negative family line of butchers. Furthermore, qualities not previously developed will never mature, and whatever was developed will diminish. It states in the sūtra *The Present Buddhas' Actual Samādhi*:[a]

> If there is the intention to torment the teacher or if there is aggression, it will be impossible to attain any qualities. Even if that person is not recognized as a teacher, the result will be the same.

To expand upon this, if one does not recognize the practitioners of the three vehicles or respect a bhikṣhu who teaches the dharma or the guru, then it is impossible to imagine that the opportunity to receive dharma not previously received will ever occur. Due to lack of devotion, the dharma will diminish.

Thus, a disciple who has received the dharma but harbors ill intent toward their teacher or holds a strong grudge against him or her for no good reason will not attain any qualities. Even though there may be no dharma connection toward a person who practices the three vehicles or bhikṣhu who teaches others the dharma: if some degree of devotion toward them is not cultivated, faults will emerge to become significant.

In the root *Kālachakra Tantra*,[b] it states:

> In the instant that one feels hatred toward the master, the virtue accumulated throughout an eon will be destroyed. The number of eons that virtue was accumulated will indicate the time tremendous suffering in the hell realms will be endured.

Thus, the root of virtue is destroyed. The *Vajra Tent* tells us:

> Whoever completely disparages the master—even if they had accomplished the supreme among tantras and had abandoned sleep and social distractions in order to practice dharma for one-thousand eons—will still only fall to the hell realms and worse.

Thus, even though they would have practiced the supreme methods found in all tantras for attaining siddhi, without accomplishing the tutelary deity, qualities will not develop.

[a] *da tar gyi sangye ngon süm du zhük pa'i ting ngen dzin gyi do* (*da ltar gyi sangs rgyes mngon sum du bzhugs pa'i ting nge 'dzin gyi mdo*)

[b] *dü kyi khorlo gyü* (*dus kyi 'khor lo rgyud, shrīkālachakranāmatantrarāja*); Wheel of Time

In the root tantra *Guhyasamāja*, it states:

> Even sentient beings that have accrued great sin, such as heinous crimes and the like, can still enter the oceanic vajra vehicle and accomplish this supreme vehicle. Yet, if the master is disparaged from one's heart: even if one tries, accomplishments will never occur.

Thus, as taught, the commentary on this explains that concerning the heinous crimes, giving up the dharma, and disparaging the master, the latter is heavier than the former.

The *Fifty Verses of Guru Devotion* states:

> Like destroying a stūpa, if the negativity is so weighty that one should thereafter avoid that person's shadow, [it is] needless to mention their shoes, cushion, mount, and the rest.

Thus, destroying a stūpa is said to be a close heinous crime.[154] Crossing over the master's shadow is similar to that. By feeling trepidation toward that, for sure one will take care not to cross over the [master's] shadow and, needless to say, would also be careful about the master's shoes and so forth.

In the *Magical Manifestation Matrix Tantra* during the first stage of discernment, it states:

> Do not cross over the shadow of the master because it is said that is equal to destroying a stūpa.

Thus, the negativity is equal, and likewise the faults of crossing over the master's cushion and so forth are mentioned in many tantras. The *Magical Manifestation Matrix Tantra* states:

> Those who disparage the vajra master should not be encountered, even in dreams.

Thus, those who disparage their masters from their heart should not be befriended or even met in the dream state. It is also taught that to enjoy their company by socializing together means that siddhis will not be attained. If one does disrespect the master in the dream state, that too must be immediately confessed upon awakening.

In the *Manifestation of the Consummate Retinue*,[a] it states:

[a] *khor chüb rolpa* (*'khor chub rol pa*)

> If one sees the master's faults during a dream, this must be confessed upon awakening. If not [confessed], this too will be cause for falling to Avīchī.

Thus, it is taught. In *Gathering of the Wisdom Intent*,[a] it states:

> Compared to the one-thousand buddhas of the eon, know that the master is precious. Why? All buddhas throughout the eons without exception have relied upon masters. Before there were masters, even the name of the Buddha did not exist.

Thus, the master is a precious individual, as it states in the tantras:

> Having a master means being able to see their qualities, never their faults. If qualities are seen, then siddhis will be attained. If faults are seen, then siddhis will not occur.

Thus, as taught, by specifically recalling the qualities, keep them in mind. If a fault is noticed, think that it is one's own impure perception and never intentionally hold to that.

To expand upon this—given that a true master mostly possesses qualities—if through analysis a subtle fault is noticed, that will create a significant obstacle toward realizing siddhis. Even if the master does have an abundance of faults, one must not see it that way; and if faith can be cultivated from the perspective of their qualities, then that will be the cause for the attainment of siddhis.

3.2.1.2.2.1.5 Training in Pure View

Fifth, training in pure view is as follows:

It states in the *Vajrapāṇi's Empowerment Conferral Tantra*:

> O Vajrapāṇi, Lord of Secrets, how must disciples view their masters? Just as they see the Buddha himself. Hence, the mind of that person will always be virtuous, and they will awaken as a buddha to benefit all beings throughout the worlds.

Thus, this reveals the need for disciples to see their master as buddha. In doing so, the mind of the student will dwell in virtue. Hence, the many benefits are revealed.

[a] *gong dü (dgongs 'dus)*

The glorious *Guhyasamāja* states:

> Bhagavan, how do the buddhas and bodhisattvas see the master who confers the empowerment gathering of secret vajra enlightened body, speech, and mind of all tathāgatas?
>
> Child of the Family, all tathāgatas and bodhisattvas will see the vajra nature. Why? The master is the same as the bodhichitta, and his aspect is inseparable as such.

Thus, the consummation of all tathāgatas' three secrets as the master who confers the glorious *Guhyasamāja* empowerment is seen not only by disciples but also by the tathāgatas and all bodhisattvas as the awakened mind called "the vajra". This is among the names of Vajradhara, and it is taught that they must see the master just like that.

This also applies to empowerment conferrals for other tantras. What was said here about this empowerment also applies to other masters who are teachers of the tantras.

The *Fifty Verses of Guru Devotion* reiterates this:

> The master and the vajra holder should not be seen as different. Thus, the nature of both master and the vajra holder should not be seen as different. Rather, one must see their nature as inseparable.

So, it is said.

In the *Cloud of Jewels Sūtra*,[a] it states:

> Know that, by relying upon a master, virtue will increase and nonvirtue will decrease—whether learned or not, wise or not, pure in ethics or not. Whatever the case, the master must be esteemed as a teacher. Just as one has faith and love for the Buddha, likewise one should feel the same toward the spiritual teacher. Depending upon cultivating respect and service toward all masters, all levels of bodhichitta not yet accumulated will be perfected and passion not yet purified will be cleansed. Thinking in this way, one will feel joy and gratitude with an attitude to happily engage in dharma. Interest in nonvirtuous behavior will wane.

[a] *do de kon chog trin* (*mdo sde dkon mchog sprin*, *ratnameghasūtra*)

Thus, whether the abbot possesses qualities or faults, he or she must be seen as the teacher. In that case, through them, all incomplete accumulations of bodhichitta will be perfected; and by embracing virtue, nonvirtue is no longer an option. It is said that this is the source of attaining qualities.

Concerning this, one should think that the teacher is an actual buddha and not just being imagined as such. Given that the teacher is an actual emanation of all buddhas, it states this in the *Salty River Sūtra*:[a]

> In the time of the five-hundred *dregs*, I will appear in the form of a master. At that time, by trusting that is me, show due respect.

Thus, and in the *Sūtra of the Great Drum*:[b]

> O Ānanda, do not be sad! Ānanda, do not lament! In my future lifetime, I will manifest as the spiritual guide and will benefit both you and many others.

Thus, and in the *Sacred Samādhi Sūtra*,[c] it states:

> Child of the Family, in future lifetimes, I will manifest as spiritual guides who show the path of these samādhis. Hence, spiritual guides are your teachers. Until you attain the heart of awakening, rely upon them and render them respect and service.

So, the fully perfected Buddha himself proclaimed that he would manifest as a spiritual guide to benefit the objects to be tamed. It is said that, even at the time of the path of training, he purified the fault of false speech and that is why he had such a long and slender tongue. It was impossible for the Buddha to have told a lie; and even if one were to think this feasible, that would have to involve a so-called buddha who was not completely faultless.

Well then, although never lying, did he not teach the various explanations concerning conventional and definitive meanings? In general, that is true; however, this cannot be established only according to the conventional. This is because the main subject cannot be faulted and can be proven through quotations and reasoning. If one claims this subject is faulted, then consider the fact that the Buddha has exhausted all shortcomings and perfected all qualities. Still

[a] *chu lung wa tswa chen gyi do* (*chu klung ba tshwa can gyi mdo*)

[b] *nga wo che do* (*rnga bo che mdo, mahābheriharakasūtra*)

[c] *ting ngen dzin dam pa'i do* (*ting nge 'dzin dam pa'i mdo*)

one may think the spiritual guide is not the same. Establishing the logic that the master is not the same as a buddha is from an individual's perspective like ourselves, such as assuming that the masters always appear to have shortcomings. Such reasoning cannot be accepted as correct. If whatever our confused minds see is held to as true, then the selflessness of phenomena will also be held as truly existing. The impure will be held as pure, the impermanent as impermanent; and fixation upon the true existence of cyclic existence from beginningless time until now would have to be the way things actually are.

It is not just only us. Even Ārya Asaṅga who practiced to accomplish Maitreya for twelve years at Riwo Cha Kang[a,155] initially saw only a rotting female dog instead of seeing Maitreya. The novice[b] Tsembupa[c] saw Vajravarāhī as a leper, and Master Buddhajñāna[d] saw Ārya Mañjushrīmitra[e] as a householder wearing a turban made of his dharma robe, plowing the fields, and boiling creatures alive in a pot. Nāropā saw Tilopā boiling fish alive and consuming them, and the two novices from Liyul saw King Songtsen Gampo[f] killing many people and severing their extremities. Zhonnu Norzang[g] saw his teacher as a king torturing others by removing their eyes, vital organs, and limbs as punishment. Metripa saw Shavaripa[h] killing sows. Our teacher [Shākyamuni] was seen by Devadatta and the six heretical teachers as completely faulted. Needless to mention, whatever we see is not authentic.

From one perspective, I think I must have achieved some degree of karmic purification since—more than seeing my master as a rotten female dog—at least when I see my teacher from any direction, including enlightened body and speech, he clearly surpasses the rest of us. Not only that, to find faults with a nirmāṇakāya buddha who has actually emanated here among us would be a sign that my own karma is extremely negative and difficult to tame.

The tamer of our faults can be proven to be a buddha whose compassion surpasses any other. When in the past, among the one-thousand buddhas of the fortunate eon, our teacher generated the bodhichitta, he promised to tame disciples who lived during the time of strife with life expectancies reaching one-hundred years. Then, the Buddha's heirs of the ten directions proclaimed, "You are like a white lotus flower, whereas other bodhisattvas are mere flowers." Praising him,

[a] *ri bo bya rkang, kukkuṭapāda parvata, giri*; Chicken Foot Peak
[b] *getsul* (*dge tsul*)
[c] *tshem bu pa*
[d] Lopon Sangye Yeshe (*slob dpon sangs rgyas ye shes*)
[e] Pakpa Jampal Shenyen (*'phags pa 'jam dpal bshen gnyen*)
[f] *srong btsan sgam po*
[g] *gzhon nu nor bzang*
[h] *me tri pa* and *sha ba ri pa*

they gave him the title Bodhisattva Nying Tob Chenpo.[a] More than the other guides, he was honored for his enlightened deeds and great compassion.

Even in the world, any army capable of conquering the most highly trained enemies must be extremely powerful, and likewise an antidote for a deadly disease must be extremely potent. If disciples have extremely pure perception, then their master will be seen as a sambhogakāya possessing the five certainties. For those who are below that capacity yet have attained the samādhi continuity of the path of accumulation, the master will be seen as a supreme nirmāṇakāya in the pure realms. If that is not the case, when karmic appearances are extremely impure, the teacher will be seen according to our own conduct, for there is no other way through which to tame us. Even when our teacher abides in the Akaniṣhṭha, he or she is residing as the great sambhogakāya buddha. Lacking the fortune to see them in that way, sometimes the master is seen as sick, other times like the story of Devadatta's catapult,[156] or as a body that bleeds when pricked by a sandalwood thorn. Other times, [the Buddha] was seen as someone who passed away at the age of eighty-one and so forth. Hence, he was required to reveal the aspect of a body that suited the capacity of ordinary individuals perceiving it.

Even these days, countless buddhas dwell among us, so it is not the case that a buddha is no longer present. Nevertheless, we are unable to see even the light rays from their kāyas. Furthermore, concerning the many kāyas that are supreme as well as ordinary, the capacity to tame others through various activities is the nature of all buddhas and this distinguishes their remarkable enlightened deeds. In the *Meeting of the Father and Son Sūtra*,[b] it states:

> Some appear in the aspect of Indra and Brahmā, some as māras, in order to fulfill the purpose of all beings. Ordinary ones will be unable to comprehend this. Some behave and appear like females, some as an animal rebirth; and although having no desire, they will appear as though they do. Having no fear but appearing as though fearful, through these and many magical aspects, all beings will be tamed.

Thus, it is as taught. Hence, it is possible to prove the master is a buddha.

Until now, I have given many quotes from the scriptures to prove this. Now, to prove this through reasoning, the master is an actual buddha because he or she reveals enlightened deeds from the perspective of showing us the dharma, which is a deed of an enlightened being. In that way, we are led upon the path of complete omniscience and liberation and set free from the fear of saṃsāra and the lower realms. Even if we were to actually meet the Buddha, there is no better way to benefit beings than showing them the dharma.

[a] *snying stobs chen po*; Great Courage

[b] *yab sey jal wa'i do* (*yab sras mjal ba'i mdo, pitāputrasamāgamanasūtra*)

In the *Chapter on Impermanence*, it states:

> For the sages, negativity cannot be washed by water; their hands cannot dispel the suffering of beings; and their realization cannot be transferred to others. But when it comes to revealing the tranquility of the dharmatā, others will be brought to liberation.

Since it is as taught, the disciples to be tamed by the actual sambhogakāya buddhas were exclusively taught the Mahāyāna doctrine. Previously, our teacher as well turned the dharma wheel of the great secret doctrine for King Indrabhūti.[a] In order to tame others, he taught only the Vinaya and the common Mahāyāna Sūtra doctrines. For some common disciples, he did not even show the Mahāyāna sūtras. On the contrary, our masters give us everything, beginning with refuge as the gateway to the doctrine, all the way up to empowerment conferral, transmissions, and upadesha instructions. This dharma rainfall of whatever is desired that includes the entire teachings of Sūtra and Mantra surpasses even what Buddha has taught in terms of enlightened deeds.

Furthermore, when all buddhas initially cultivated the bodhichitta, we were held as the objects for that cultivation. In particular, during this excellent Eon of Light, in the field of this Sahalokadhātu[b] to be tamed by Buddha Shākyamuni our teacher, he actually revealed the twelve enlightened deeds[157] in the exceptional field of Jambudvīpa. More than that, during the time of the five *dregs*, it is this land of Tibet that was predicted to be a country where the dharma would flourish. Many of us have taken rebirth here, met the dharma, and are disciples of the Buddha. Having attained a unique form through which to practice dharma, possessing faith in dharma, and feeling inspired to accomplish it, the time has now come to tame even the likes of us. Since all of this is true, it is impossible to consider that the buddhas would abandon their own disciples.

The sūtras tell us:

> It is possible that the ocean's sea monsters and their waves could miss their timing; however, it is impossible for the buddhas to miss their timing when it comes to taming disciples.

Thus, it is as taught. There exists no one besides the master who can be said to be an emanation of the buddhas who tames disciples. Hence, one must determine that the master is the actual buddha.

Omniscient Longchenpa has said:

[a] *rgyal po indra bhu ti*

[b] Mijed Kyi Jigten (*mi mjed kyi 'jig rten*); our world system

> This [i.e., the master] is the emanation of the victors, who guides beings to liberation. In the degenerate times, the master appears in this way.

Thus, it is as taught. The master is an actual buddha because buddha abides within his mind stream. For example, it is like how the protector Vajrasādhu[a] enters the body of an oracle.[158] That, too, is the presence of the protector. That they [i.e., masters] abide in this way is also stated in the *Oral Transmission of Mañjushrī*:[b]

> I abide in that body. I accept offerings from other practitioners; and by pleasing me, the karmic obscurations in their mind streams are purified.

Thus, and in the sūtras:

> It is said that whoever utters any positive word that serves as an antidote for the passions will be someone who mentally abides with the wisdom of the buddhas of the three times. Like that, by attaining the higher stage of the path of accumulation and when revealing the dharma as a supreme nirmāṇakāya, that teacher has many exalted qualities, such as samādhi, omniscience, and clairvoyance. Once attaining the first ground called Rab Ga[c] and while revealing the dharma as a sambhogakāya, the face of one-hundred buddhas will be seen in a single instant. There will be the potential to traverse hundreds of realms of the world, to open the doorway to hundreds of dharma categories, and to bring hundreds of beings to fruition. Hence, the qualities are inconceivable.
>
> Once attaining the second ground, all of that is increased by ten. [For a bodhisattva] who then reveals the dharma, that resembles giving food and clothing to those who are already completely endowed with abundance. Compared to that, when the master teaches us, it is like giving food and clothing to those who are extremely poverty stricken and helpless; so the benefits derived are exceedingly significant. Based on that, buddhas appear to those who are the worthy objects to be tamed, not otherwise. Conversely, the masters appear to everyone, so they are exalted.

[a] Damchen Dorje Lekpa (*dam can rdo rje legs pa*)
[b] *jampal zhal lung* (*'jam dpal zhal lung, mañjushrīmukhāgama*); Buddhashrījñāna
[c] *rab dga'*; Extreme Joy

In the *Sūtra of Stainless Space*,[a] it states:

> O Ānanda, all tathāgatas appear to sentient beings with pure karma. The virtuous spiritual guides appear to everyone, teach the dharma, and plant seeds for liberation. Hence, one must cherish the spiritual guides even more than the tathāgatas.

Thus, it is as taught.

For each verse of dharma that our teacher spoke, he underwent hardships, such as having one-thousand iron nails pierced through his body, one-thousand candle wicks burning on his body, giving up his kingdom, wealth, and so forth. Similarly, the bodhisattvas Norzang, Nāropā, Mila, Atisha, and others underwent many hardships for the sake of dharma. For us, although it is not necessary [for our masters] to undergo hardships, nevertheless—like a mother instructing her child—without concealing anything, to joyfully give all sacred instructions is an expression of great kindness.

If perhaps [the masters] did not compassionately care for us, still the other buddhas would not be met; and even the sound of the Triple Gem would not come to our ears. Unable to know anything about virtue and nonvirtue, just how would we be set free from the fears of saṃsāra and the lower realms? Now, as long as we don't lose our mental capacity and are not afraid to try, there is no shortage of methods for awakening in a single lifetime. How amazing is that! From the depth of one's heart, devotion should be cultivated.

The master's kindness surpasses that of the Buddha's deeds, so it is the greatest expression of kindness. Yet due to our delusion and ignorance, we fail to see the qualities of the master, while digging around for faults. By thinking there is no limit to one's heartless endeavors, one brings shame upon oneself by thinking in these ways. By training in pure vision repeatedly like this, one will eventually see the master as buddha; and according to that capacity, blessings similar to that will enter the mind. However many blessings enter the mind stream indicates how deeply the master is seen as a buddha. However, strong devotion and faith will ensure that all positive, excellent qualities without exception will unite with one's mind.

The teacher Tonpa[b] requested Lord Atisha, "Although in Tibet there are practitioners of dharma, there are no exceptional qualities being attained. Why is that?" Atisha replied, "All qualities derived on the path of the Mahāyāna come by relying upon the master. Nevertheless, you Tibetans are unable to see the masters as anything other than ordinary, so how can qualities arise?" Just as he said,

[a] *nam kha drima med pa'i do* (*nam mkha' dri ma med pa'i mdo*)
[b] *ston pa*

since it is extremely crucial to see the master as a buddha, I have taken the time to emphasize this point.

In the *Doha on the Realization of Seven Excellent Points*[a] by Drigung Kyobpa Rinpoche, it states:

> If the sun of devotion does not shine upon the mountain of the master's four kāyas, then the waterfall of blessings will not descend. Hence, endeavor to cultivate the mind of devotion.

Thus, as taught, one is encouraged to strive in the cultivation of devotion. If the faults of the master are still noticed, then confession and restoration must occur. The way of meditating upon the master above the crown and supplicating is as taken from the speech of omniscient Longchenpa as it states:

> Alas, precious guru, I have no hope other than you! Please look upon me with your eyes of compassion. Suppressed by the confusion of ignorance, whatever negativity I have accumulated through the three doors I fully confess. Having gone against the three vows, my mind is stained by these shortcomings. Through your compassion, may this be instantly cleansed. Through the power of my ignorance, I have accumulated nonvirtue; and failing to acknowledge this, I have wandered in saṃsāra from time immemorial. Because of you, Kind Master, now I pray that all nonvirtue be dispelled in an instant.
>
> When you see this ignorant child's faults, if your compassion doesn't well forth now even more than ever, then when will it? Regarding the faults this child has accrued—like a mother caring for and protecting her child—when you first cultivated the bodhichitta on behalf of myself and all beings in the six realms, you promised to benefit us. If that is the case, then why do you not care for me right now? By seeing myself and all confused sentient beings, if you do not hold us with your compassion, then how do you think your miraculous activities to tame disciples will actually bring them benefit?
>
> Although the previous victors are numberless, they abandoned us and departed for liberation. Now the victors of the ten directions have implored you to help us by manifesting as a guru. How can you abandon us now? That would be like deceiving escorts who accompany someone to a place of great terror. Do you really want to deceive us now? When supplicating a precious wish-fulfilling jewel, it fulfills all

[a] *lek dün tok pa'i gur* (*legs bdun rtogs pa'i mgur*); Drigung Kyobpa Rinpoche

desires. You who are so skilled in the methods of great loving kindness, why not look upon me now?

Even cannibals, at the moment that the words of truth are uttered and offerings made, will abandon their previous aggressive feelings. If they can do that, then when we respectfully offer and lament like this to you who are the compassionate parents of beings, why can you not see this confession of faults? Until all of my negativity is cleansed, if I must go on to my next life, I will only burn in the fires of the hells. If you cannot see this, then how can you be a holder of compassion?

Alas! How tragic! Pray, purify all my negativity without a single exception. Instantly look upon me with compassion. Grant me the blessings of empowerment. Bestow common and supreme spiritual attainments. Clear all obstacles of demonic forces and misguided harm-doers. Allow all wishes to be accomplished in this life, and at the moment of death ensure there will be no torment of suffering. Grant freedom from all fears in the bardo and lead me to the place of Akaniṣhṭha.

Thus, offer this supplication prayer during four sessions in the day and night, seven times each. This will purify all broken commitments so that the common and extraordinary siddhis can be swiftly obtained. There is no key point more profound than this for restoring and fulfilling broken commitments.

Thus, one must do as taught. It is best to supplicate in this way on a daily basis; and since the blessings of this supplication are so sublime, I have included it here in its entirety.

3.2.1.2.2.2 Actual Meditation

This has three parts:

1 Visualization from the perspective of the liturgy
2 Explanation through the stages of visualization
3 Upadesha describing the *phowa* practice

Second, the actual way of visualizing as described in the terma has three parts: the visualization from the perspective of the liturgy, an explanation from the perspective of that meaning described through the stages of visualization in prose, and the accompanying upadesha that describes the way to train in the *phowa*[a] practice entitled *Opening the Gateway to Wisdom*.

[a] *'pho ba*; pronounced "*po wa*"

3.2.1.2.2.2.1 Visualization from the Perspective of the Liturgy

First, Lord Götsangpa[a] has said:

> When meditating upon guru yoga, faults will be purified and qualities perfected.

Thus, and it continues:

> Although there are many categories of generation-stage meditation, none of them surpass the meditation upon the guru. Although there are many categories of mantra recitation, none of them surpass supplication to the guru. Although there are many categories of completion-stage meditation, none of them surpass complete surrender to the guru.

Thus, it is as taught. There is no generation- or completion-stage practice that can surpass the meditation upon guru yoga. Likewise, it states in the *Array of Samaya*:[b]

> More than meditating upon the deity with the major and minor marks for one-hundred thousand eons, recalling the guru is supreme. More than reciting a million mantras of the approach and accomplishment cycles, reciting the supplication to the guru just once is sublime. Meditating upon the completion stage for an eon without distraction cannot be compared to holding the guru in mind for an instant, for the latter is two-million times more potent than the former.

Thus, it is as taught. There are limitless qualities derived by recalling and supplicating the master. In particular, this meditation upon guru yoga is a perfectly authentic method through which to attain buddhahood in this lifetime.

The mahāsiddha Tilopā said:

> For those wishing to attain the state of Vajradhara in this lifetime, the ultimate pathway is guru-yoga practice.

Thus, it is as taught. The way of meditating upon this is as stated in the tantra *Ahbhidhana*:[c]

[a] *rje rgod tshang pa*; one of the foremost masters of the Drukpa Kagyü lineage
[b] *dam tsig köd pa* (*dam tshig bkod pa*)
[c] *ah bhi dha na'i gyü* (*a bhi dha na'i rgyud*)

> The master of great kindness is placed in the core of the heart, on the crown of the head, or in the palm of the hand. In doing so, even the blessings of one-thousand buddhas will be held by this individual.

Thus, and similar to that, it also states in the tantra called *Samantabhadra Abiding within Oneself*:[a]

> In the Mahāsandhi tradition of Ati, whoever meditates upon the master of great kindness in the core of their heart, palm of their hand, or crown of the head will hold the qualities of one-thousand buddhas.

Thus, that quote comes from the sacred instructions of the Ati tradition of Mahāsandhi. As mentioned, in reliance upon this tradition, one may meditate upon their kind master in these various places. Generally, it is acceptable to meditate upon the master in the heart, as well as the crown and such. The tantras state:

> The master is the nature of all buddhas and wisdom deities. Supplicate this hero who holds vajra, bell, and embraces a consort.

Thus, as taught, the meditation upon the surpassing deity yoga involves the nature of all buddhas as the hero Vajradhara with consort. In addition, the great Lord of Dharma Tsangpa[b] said:

> Once there is no doubt that the master is buddha, it is enough to meditate only upon the master. If when doing so there is analysis or limitation concerning how one views the master, then by meditating upon the wisdom deity these concepts based on good and bad will not emerge. Hence, meditating upon the deity is symbolic, whereas the master is the actual emanation who tames. It seems to me that is the reason why only meditating upon the master brings greater blessings.

Thus, it is as taught. Whether the way the kāya of the guru appears needs adjusting or not is up to each individual. It is not one sided.

Nevertheless, according to the exceptional upadesha of this system, the way of meditating upon the master has five parts: the way of meditating upon the master in the space in front of oneself as the wisdom deity, invocation of the wisdom beings and dissolution, supplication and offerings from the perspective

[a] *kuntuzangpo rang la ney pa'i gyü* (*kun tu bzang po rang la gnas pa'i rgyud*)
[b] *chö je tsang pa* (*chos rje gtsang pa*)

of invoking the enlightened wisdom intent [of the master], receiving the four empowerments of samādhi that bring the mind to fruition, and finally resting in the evenness of the great fundamental nature of original purity.

First, the terma states:

> **Guru-yoga practice brings the three doors to maturity through empowerment as the play of the three vajras.**

Thus, it is.

The ripening and liberation of one's three doors as the play of the three vajras—the nature of the four kāyas—is the main result of meditating upon the guru-yoga practice. This is mentioned because it reveals the principal meaning of the key points of binding the three doors by receiving the four empowerments of samādhi.

The terma goes on:

> ***Phet!* Perfectly pure self-appearances are the great basic space of phenomena. In the land of exaltation free from transition or change, self-awareness is the wisdom Tröma, an attractive lucid red color. In the right hand is a curved vajra blade and in the left a skull filled with blood. Both legs are in the dancing posture, and she wears bone ornaments, amidst blazing fire. In the space in front in an expanse of rainbow-light bindus is the glorious root guru as the embodiment of the three lineages of masters in the kāya of Vajravarāhī. She holds a curved vajra blade in her right hand and a skull filled with blood in the left. Her legs are in the dancing posture, and she is adorned with the six bone ornaments. A squealing black pig's head juts from her crown. She has a peaceful, radiant smile with youthful charm, and her beauty is enhanced by the major and minor marks. Above her crown is Samantabhadrī in the mudrā of evenness, surrounded by an assembly of buddhas, bodhisattvas, and vidyādharas. Clearly visualize them as distinct as sesame seeds overflowing their pod.**

Thus, it reads.

Saying *phet*, by the strength of materializing self-appearances, all confused phenomena concerning the impure universe and inhabitants fall apart in the space of the nature as it is. The perfectly pure nature of wisdom's manifest self-appearances—the intrinsic nature of the great unelaborate space of phenomena—is the pure land of exaltation with no transition or change based on root causes or contributing circumstances. Visualizing oneself as Tröma, in the space in front of one's crown meditate that the master appears as Vajravarāhī surrounded by an assembly of buddhas, bodhisattvas, and vidyādharas as distinct as sesame seeds overflowing their pod.

Second, the invocation of the wisdom beings and the dissolution begins with the verses that continue on:

> **They radiate light into the space of phenomena to invoke the inseparable manifestations.**

From "*hung* supreme among pure lands . . ." until ". . . *siddhi hung*," from one's heart light rays radiate into the ten directions to invoke the guru and assembly of wisdom deities. Imagine that the samaya beings and the wisdom beings merge indivisibly.

Hung is the syllable of the nature of the vajra that invokes the continuity of enlightened mind. From the **supreme among pure lands, the land of Khachöd, the sublime place of the dharmadhātu, Akaniṣhṭha, the embodiment of all gurus of the three lineages**—wisdom mind, symbolic indication, and the aural lineage of individuals—the **precious guru**, venerable wisdom ḍākinī, **manifests as the** glorious **sovereign of Khachöd.** "In the manner of dance, **come here to bless** the three doors of **your lineage disciples**, unimpeded and instantaneously through your miraculous powers." This is the supplication for the guru to arrive.

The guru having arrived, one then prays, "**Grant blessings to mature and free my mind stream** to become a suitable vessel to practice the paths of generation and completion." Attaining the qualities of freeing oneself of all obscurations, pray to gain the potential to benefit others. "**Care for me inseparably and grant me the liberation** from abiding in either saṃsāra or enlightenment." Liberated from that and without abiding in the limits of existence or quiescence, pray to be effortlessly led to the state of the victorious ones.

Saying *hung* means to grant siddhis to realize the wisdom intent of the five classes of ḍākinīs as the guru, including their heart mantras of five wisdoms [i.e., ***gu ru ha ri ni sa siddhi hung***]. In conclusion, by reciting this, think that one is inseparable with the invocation of deities.

Third is the invocation of enlightened mind through supplication and the seven-branch offering beginning with *phet*. Recite the verses ". . . **buddhas throughout the three times** . . ." until ". . . **attain confidence** . . . ***Phet phet phet.***"

Thus, reciting ***phet*** refreshes the present visualization. "**Glorious**" refers to the limitless qualities of the **embodiment of all buddhas throughout the three times** without exception. The one who gives empowerment, teaches tantras, explains the upadesha, and so forth shows **kindness** that **is impossible to repay.** That is the meaning of "**precious guru**". As the **sovereign of all** families, such as the five buddha families, [the master] is the principal one who confers empowerment for all **maṇḍalas** of deities from the four or six categories of Tantra. That is the meaning of "**vajra holder**".

> With **omniscience** concerning all knowable things and **loving concern** for all beings, you have the **power** to liberate beings from the fears and torment of karma and passions. Hence, **you are a perfect treasure trove of glorious qualities.** You boldly **free all beings throughout existence** from the trepidation of saṃsāra's suffering; to you **who** are a **great hero, I supplicate with devotion by recalling your kindness and qualities. Look upon me with your eyes of compassion.** In order to benefit us, we implore you to approach **from** the **basic space** of the unborn dharmakāya and **turn your** effortless, spontaneous **wisdom mind to gaze upon us. Not just momentarily, but continuously throughout the three times, think of us with your omniscient loving kindness.**
>
> Until now, **I** have cherished **my body and abundance, including the root of virtue.** Now, these **are offered free from attachment or fixation. With intense devotion expressed through all three doors, I rely upon you as my permanent protector** in all lifetimes, the only source of refuge. **I go for refuge** knowing that **you will never deceive me** and that you are the supreme **source of protection.** By **liberating through sight, sound, recollection, and touch, you are the** great **captain guiding those** with a connection to the pure lands. **With devotion** that is irreversible and **free from transition or change in the three times, I prostrate to you and bring to mind** whatever pleasing material things there are in **phenomenal existence** to present **as the offerings.**

Saying "**all faults and downfalls are confessed**"[159] refers to the inadvertent nonvirtues, as well as formal violations of commitments, all of which are confessed. Saying "**rejoice in virtue**" means the virtue accumulated throughout the three times. "**Always**" refers to the victors and their heirs, and saying "**turn the dharma wheel**" means according to the faculties of the objects to be tamed. Saying "**remain forever firm**" means [for the guru to remain] for oceans of eons. Saying "**the oceanic realms of beings**" means dedicating the root of virtue to all of them, so saṃsāra will be **emptied from the depths** like an empty vessel. By supplicating from the heart, not the mouth, to the nature of the root **guru** who is **precious** like a wish-fulfilling jewel, "**I pray to you, hold me with compassion.**"

"**Wisdom ḍākinī**" means the aspect of the three kāyas. "**Grant blessings**" means to bless one's stream of mind. "**Supreme guide of beings**" means [the guru is] like a captain or leader of the blind. "**Grant blessings for a meaningful precious human rebirth**" means to not waste this opportunity that is adorned with the dharma. "**Grant blessings to remember death from the heart**" means to not hold to this life as permanent with attachment; "**grant blessings to be skillful in knowing what to accept and reject**" means to discover confidence in cause and result in order to identify virtue and nonvirtue. "**Grant blessings to feel revulsion with saṃsāra**" means to see the natural condition of the three realms to be the suffering of karmic passions. "**Grant blessings that the mind will long for nothing**" refers to friends, companions, wealth, or whatever.

"**Grant blessings to tame the mind without pretense**" means being without deception, trickery, or hypocrisy toward others. "**Grant blessings that the mind may be steadfastly free from attachment**" means to not have attachment toward anything that creates obstacles for dharma, such as places, companions, and abundance. "**Grant blessings to be at ease without companionship**" pertains to companions that encourage the circumstance of social distraction. "**Grant blessings to be able to remain in fear-invoking environments**" means that, in order to enhance realization, one vows to remain in indeterminate environments. "**Grant blessings to live in retreat, free of activity,**" means to be without distraction concerning this life's food, clothing, and fame. "**Grant blessings to maintain the dignity of dharma unerringly**" means to know the key point of the correct view and meditation. "**Grant blessings that devotion may be steadfast and unchanging**" means to be free of sporadic, inconsistent practice. "**Grant blessings to cultivate undiminishing renunciation**" means to not be suppressed by flattery, praise, fame, and the like. "**Grant blessings to remember inseparability with the guru**" means to know this throughout all situations whether happy, sad, up, or down.

"**Grant blessings to accomplish indestructible siddhi**" means attainment that is unaffected by nonconducive circumstances. "**Grant blessings to attain great confidence with fearlessness**" means having no anxiety toward benefit, harm, hope, fear, or anything that is encountered. "**Grant blessings to realize appearances lack true existence**" means to know that the phenomena of saṃsāra and enlightenment are primordially like magic or dreams. "**Grant blessings to realize the prajñā of selflessness**" refers to determining this result through the prajñā of discerning awareness. "**Grant blessings to unimpededly see there are no reference points**" means to be without concretizing or points of reference. "**Grant blessings to seize the immutable ground free from confusion**" means to realize that, aside from saṃsāra and enlightenment self-appearing, things are not otherwise.

"**Grant blessings to maintain unceasing continuity in practice without distraction**" means achieving mastery in samādhi without meditation throughout the day and night. "**Grant blessings to realize the great perfection without meditation**" refers to the philosophy that transcends effort-based, intellectual meditation. "**By seeing the self-nature of the uncontrived fundamental ground**" means there are no new causes or contributing circumstances since that is the uncompounded primordial state of liberation. "**May I attain confidence with the glorious nature of the four kāyas**" refers to the sovereign of all buddha families, who is the original buddha. Saying "may" means the supplication is being humbly offered from the heart. As for the **three *phets***, the first one invokes the guru's wisdom intent, the second ensures the blessings enter one's mind stream, and the third stabilizes this.

Fourth, receiving the four empowerments of samādhi starts with "*Phet phet phet!* Father Guru, Buddha of the Three Times, . . ." and so forth until ". . . now I realize the spontaneously present vidyādhara. ***Ah la la phet phet phet!***" Thus reciting this, the line that supplicates the **father guru** as the nature and embodiment of all **buddhas of the three times** calls out by saying "you know" and requesting empowerment.

> In order to cleanse and **purify** your fortunate child's four obscurations, **the obscurations of my body and channels**, confer the four empowerments such as the **enlightened body vase empowerment** and so forth so that I may **fully mature. May I attain the potential** for **my body** and so forth **to become** the four kāyas, such as **the nirmāṇakāya**, and to attain the four states of vidyādharahood[160] while planting the seed **of** the **mature vidyādhara**[a] in my mind.

Imagine this is so. Saying ***ah la la*** means the possibility for this to occur is extremely astonishing. The way for visualizing all of this will be taught later on.

To expand upon this now: at the time of the ground, the coarse three doors of body, speech, and mind and all three combined; the subtle channels, winds, and bindus, including all three combined; the extremely subtle aspect of innate channels, winds, and bindus; and the intrinsic nature of those three as the clear-light bodhichitta nature are all abiding within the body. Receiving the vase empowerment and the view that accompanies that is the wisdom of nonconceptual empty appearances. This means that, aside from all phenomena of the outer universe and inhabitants being adventitious, impure phenomena from the perspective of confusion, the intrinsic nature of those appearances abides as the manifestation of the wisdom deity, purity, and evenness. The aspect of emptiness is the intrinsic nature free from elaborations as the meaning of nondual appearances and emptiness. Realizing this is the way of abiding just as it is, and the consummate ground for all of this is the nature of one's mind.

Due to the functioning of karmic winds and so on, the aspect of adventitious conceptualization emerges while, ultimately, abiding as nonconceptual empty appearances. While visualizing the stages of this empowerment, certainty with

[a] *namin rigdzin* (*rnam smin rig 'dzin*)

this meaning should be precisely ascertained. Otherwise, it is crucial to at least bring to mind some degree of understanding based on pointing-out instructions. Through this, obscurations of the body are cleansed, such as having taken lives and the rest.

The basis of the body abides in the channels, so the impure aspect affecting the channels and the functioning of that is the impure body and the like. The potential that is generated from this is the obscuration of channels. To cleanse that and bring one's mind to maturity involves the stages of meditation on the path, and the potential for attaining the result is placed in the stream of mind. Hence, one prays that the body becomes the nirmāṇakāya. This means that the present impure body does not change into a nirmāṇakāya; but rather this body's nature abides within the channels, so the intrinsic nature of the channels is the self-radiance of innate wisdom. This nature of the channels as extremely subtle clear light primordially abides as what is called "the extremely subtle body".

At present, while the stains endure and their functionality is active, this [impure] body appears. When the time comes that—through the swift path of Vajrayāna—the stains including all habits are eliminated and purified, the effect of that will be that the vajrakāyas of the victorious ones will appear. These will appear in harmony with the aspirations of individuals to be tamed, whether high or low. Hence, one prays, "May there be the potential for the ordinary body to mature and become the vajra nirmāṇakāya." That is the meaning.

If applied to the way of proceeding on the path of Mantra according to the four states of vidyādharahood, then this will bring the attainment of the mature vidyādhara. There are different ways to describe the mature vidyādhara. Nevertheless, according to the assertion given by Omniscient Longchenpa: when stable familiarity on the path of the generation and completion stages occurs and by giving rise to the realization of Mantra's path of unification, the mind is then brought to maturity as a wisdom deity. Furthermore, as long as one is still not separate from the karmic body, that is the time of a mature vidyādhara. For the **three "*phets*"**, the first means the mind is inspired by this meaning; the second, that the meaning is realized; and the third assures that the realization is stable and confidence attained.

Similarly, this applies to the speech, or wind, and the mind, or bindus.[161] When pure, the speech fully matures as the vajra sambhogakāya and so forth, so one must know how to apply this. The remaining empowerments, such as the secret, have views that are in the following order: the nonconceptual wisdom of empty clarity, the nonconceptual wisdom of empty bliss, and the nonconceptual wisdom of empty awareness. Concerning this present mind that has become inseparable with the nature of karmic winds: by the power of this sullying factor, the mind has become obscured. Ultimately, mind is exceedingly lucid as the empty nature and abides as the nonconceptual wisdom of empty clarity. When in reliance upon the practice of winds, there is freedom from the obscuring factor of the movements of karmic wind; so the time for the nature of empty clarity to become evident will occur.

Likewise, the great wisdom of empty bliss, like oil that permeates a sesame seed, primordially pervades the nature of one's mind. Aside from having not actualized this at present, the mind's nature abides as the wisdom of empty bliss. Ultimately, all of this is indivisible awareness-emptiness that transcends thought and expression. Abiding as the intrinsic nature of innate wisdom at the time of empowerment, it is necessary to gain certainty with the meaning of this as mentioned before.

In addition to that, the origin of the mind is posited as bindus. That means that, according to this tradition of unsurpassed Mantra, the ultimate support for the mind are the abiding bindus. This refers to the white and red essential fluids and all coarse constituents whose nature is inseparable with the extremely subtle essence of those elements as the clear-light bodhichitta. The bindus appear and abide due to that abiding nature. If there were no innate bindu such as this, then even during the time of being impure, mental concepts could not possibly emerge. Even during the time of being pure, the enlightened mind of the victors that is the wisdom exaltation of the dharmakāya could not possibly emerge. Here, by applying effort in the practice of bindus, the mind arises as the nature of bliss due to that key point. This is an uncommon explanation that belongs to our tradition of the Earlier Translation School. The gist of what this means is not only difficult to comprehend; it is a subject belonging to the section of profound secrecy.

During the fourth empowerment, saying "the glorious expanse of the four kāyas" means the expanse of the subtle three doors, or the ultimate fundamental nature of empty appearances, empty clarity, empty bliss, and the union of these three as the exceptional wisdom of inseparable empty awareness. One prays to become the nature of the inseparable four kāyas as the wisdom vajrakāya.

Here, it is acceptable to apply the nirmāṇakāya and the other three with the enlightened body, speech, and mind of the victorious ones. "Praying to be brought to maturity and liberation" means that, initially, one must mature the possibility to attain this; and then one must liberate within that nature. For the remaining three vidyādharas, given that the realization of the path of seeing must arise in the mind stream, the karmic body is cleansed. Without the influence of karma and passions when one attains a kāya free from birth and death, that is the immortal vidyādhara.[a] When attaining the realization of the path of meditation, that is the mahāmudrā vidyādhara.[b] When the wisdom of buddha is realized

[a] *tsewang rigdzin* (*tshe dbang rig 'dzin*)
[b] *chag gya chenpo'i rigdzin* (*phyag rgya chen po'i rig 'dzin*)

and the welfare of others occurs spontaneously, that is the spontaneously present vidyādhara.[a] All of these are the assertions of Longchenpa.

Through these empowerments, practitioners are rendered suitable vessels for a particular path. Generally, the vase empowerment corresponds to the generation stage while the final three render practitioners suitable for the completion stage. Through the secret empowerment, there is the practice of the completion-stage winds, or striking the key point through the channels and winds by practicing with one's body. Through the prajñā-wisdom empowerment, there is the practice of the bindus, or relying upon the path of mudrā with the body of another.[162] Through the fourth empowerment, one becomes suitable to practice the path of clear-light Mahāmudrā and Atiyoga.

Based on whatever is emphasized, one applies the path of the three inner tantras to the practice of the four empowerments. Through Mahāyoga, in conjunction with the vase empowerment, the path of nondual, empty appearances is primarily revealed. Anuyoga mainly reveals the practice in conjunction with both the secret and prajñā [empowerments]. Concerning that, the secret empowerment's path of nondual, empty clarity is Anuyoga's preliminary practice with one's own body. The prajñā-wisdom empowerment's path of nondual empty bliss is Anuyoga's actual path. Mahāsandhi Atiyoga mainly reveals the fourth empowerment's wisdom of nondual, empty awareness itself. These are the points to be known.

Fifth, resting within the fundamental nature of original purity applies to the verses that begin ". . . the father guru's wisdom mind . . ." until ". . . now . . . purity and evenness. *Ah la la!*" The blessings of the **father guru's wisdom mind [great expanse] dissolve into oneself as blue-black light**, [and] **one delights in the expanse** of the **ground** as the originally pure **fundamental nature of the great perfection.** Actually **awakening in the nature of the ever-youthful vase kāya,** knowing the **purity and evenness of saṃsāra and enlightenment**, one rests in evenness and recites ***ah la la.*** Train in the subsequent confidence of this realization as the dynamic strength of appearances that are the **nonconceptual,**[163] joyful play that arises as a matter of course.

3.2.1.2.2.2.2 Explanation through the Stages of Visualization

Second, the visualization for this is as follows.[164] **Instantly**, by the dynamic play of **the consummate phenomena of the mind, like** the connection between **a magician**, substances, and mantras, all objective appearances such as houses, people, and so on become like the **illusory display** of diverse magical spectacles. Then, when the potential through substance and mantra is exhausted—just like

[a] *lhun drüb rigdzin* (*lhun grub rig 'dzin*)

how that **vanishes** to become nonexistent in the space of the sky—everything vanishes **within the** [**empty**[165]] **nature of the dharmatā,** the **blissful pure land of Khachöd, free from transition and change. One appears as the wisdom ḍākinī,** clear **red** in color, **holding a curved vajra blade in the right hand and a skull filled with blood in the left. Both legs are in the dancing posture** standing **upon a lotus, sun, and** corpse **seat. Naked,** one **wears** a bone necklace, bracelet, earrings, crown wheel, belt, and garland apron as the six **bone ornaments** that symbolize the six pāramitās.[166] One **is adorned with a long necklace made of white lotus flowers** that symbolizes wisdom exaltation that arises from the way the white essence descends. **The three eyes gaze into the basic space of the sky. With the radiance of light and rays emanating** from one's kāya, one **appears yet lacks true, inherent existence and is clear without being held as true, like a water moon or a reflection in a mirror.**[167] **Visualize in this way.**

In the space in front, upon a lotus and sun seat, appears the embodiment of all three lineage masters without exception as the nature of the root guru appearing as the single **mother,** the **sole** source of all the victors, **Vajravarāhī,** clear **red with one face and two arms, holding a curved vajra blade in the right hand and a skull filled with blood in the left. Both legs are in the dancing posture,** [and she] **wears the six bone ornaments and all of the charnel-ground accouterments.** From her crown, a squealing black pig's head juts out; and with the major and minor marks, she is peacefully smiling while **poised in an expanse of blazing** [red-black] **wisdom fire. At her crown is** the **naked Samantabhadrī in the mudrā of evenness, and both legs are in the vajra āsana upon a lotus and moon seat. Surrounding are all the root lineage masters,** the buddhas, bodhisattvas, vidyādharas, and their assemblies. **All of them are facing one and gazing with loving kindness. Meditate that they appear like banks of colorful rainbow** light.

At the center of the guru's **crown is** the syllable that represents the vajra nature of all kāyas of the victors, **a white *om*.** Within the center of **the throat is** the syllable that represents the vajra nature of enlightened speech, **a red *ah*.** In the center of **the heart** parallel with the breasts is the syllable of the vajra nature of enlightened mind, **a blue *hung*.** All three syllables are **ablaze like the light of one-hundred thousand suns. Imagine** she is **a great wisdom treasury of empowerment** and blessings. **With unflagging faith and devotion** as mentioned before, begin the supplication "... buddhas of the three times ..." and so forth. **After single-pointedly supplicating** with "... father guru ..." and so forth, **the visualization for receiving the four empowerments is as follows.**

From the guru's forehead where the white *om* blazes like the full moon, white *om* syllables with rays of light emanate like stars shooting in space. Entering one's body through the crown, all negativities, obscurations, seeds of karma, and habits accumulated through the body are completely purified and

cleansed. The enlightened-body vase empowerment is received. One's body becomes the vajrakāya. Think that the state of nirmāṇakāya is actualized.

From the *ah* in the throat, red *ah* syllables and light rays like lightning bolts shooting in the sky dissolve into one's throat. Cleansing all negativities, obscurations, karmic passions, and habits accumulated through speech, the secret speech empowerment is received. One's speech is blessed as the play of vajra speech. Think that the state of the sambhogakāya is actualized.

From the *hung* in the heart, blue-black *hungs* and light rays radiate like massing clouds in the sky. Dissolving into one's heart, all negativities, obscurations, karmic passions, habits, and the like accumulated through the mind are cleansed. The wisdom-prajñā mind empowerment is received. The mind is blessed as the nature of enlightened mind. Think that the mind realizes the state of the originally pure dharmakāya.

Once again, from the five places of the guru, light rays in five colors emanate. They dissolve into one's five places, completely cleansing all habits and passions that prevent the attainment of liberation. Think that all cognitive obscurations based on fixation upon the three rounds that prevent the state of omniscience are cleansed. The absolute word empowerment is received. All aspects of mind and appearances become the nature of nondual empty awareness. One is blessed to attain the glory of spontaneously perfecting the two purposes. Meditate that the nature of the three kāyas' enlightened body, speech, and mind is inseparable and actualized as the svābhāvikakāya.

Once again, imagine that the nature of the guru's nonconceptual mind as a blue-black bindu of light dissolves into one's heart. The intrinsic nature of the original ground, **the fundamental nature of the dharmatā, just as it is, is actualized.** The aspect of appearances as self-awareness is introduced as basic space and wisdom kāyas and bindus that are primordially, spontaneously present. **One receives the tögal empowerment of the** supreme **dynamic strength of awareness.** The wisdom intent of the self-appearing, unelaborate dharmakāya is manifest. Through the rupakāya's dynamic strength of compassion that appears to others and in harmony with the faculties and aspirations of individual disciples, the wheel of dharma is put into motion; and **the status of becoming a dharma sovereign of the three realms is rendered evident.** Think that **the state of simultaneously perfecting** the qualities of abandonment and realization of **the four vidyādharas** is realized. The fourth empowerment is explained in two ways: as the common word empowerment and the uncommon dynamic strength of awareness empowerment. The first brings maturity in trekchö and the latter in tögal. It is easy to understand that the final verse mentioned in this practice reveals the dynamic strength empowerment.

Then, think that **one becomes a brilliant bindu of red light that dissolves into the heart of the precious guru.** Reciting ***phet*****, think that the guru enters**

the womb of the space of the dharmakāya, free from transition. **Rest freely in the all-pervasive, unborn state of original purity.**

> So that the oceanic assembly of enlightened guides who dwell in the ten directions and three times may tame unruly disciples such as us, they reveal the rupakāya that is coarse and appears to ordinary individuals.
> Such kindness cannot be repaid, even once the end of existence is met.
> Visualizing oneself as the deity and thinking that, in the space in front, the guru appears in the aspect of the special deity, receive the supreme empowerment of samādhi that brings one's mind to maturity.
> Such is the cherished treasure of this profound path.

Thus, these are the verses that summarize the section.

The explanations given here for the three kāya meditation-recitation, as well as the guru yoga, are now complete. These are placed in the category of the preliminaries given that the actual practice involves the instructions for chöd, or severance. Ultimately, these practices are the main practice on the path because this is the exceptional swift path that connects with unsurpassed Secret Mantra. Therefore—once arriving at this juncture—according to this profound doctrine, it is crucial for disciples to become suitable vessels by having their minds brought to maturity through either receiving an extensive or concise Tröma empowerment.

3.2.1.2.2.2.3 Upadesha Describing the Phowa Practice

Third, the auxiliary practice of **phowa, or transference of consciousness, entitled *Opening the Wisdom Gateway*** follows. The text states:

> The path of phowa called *Opening the Wisdom Gateway* is revealed for all future lineage holders. They must achieve the crucial point in practice. If all fortunate ones who wish to traverse the path to liberation lack this training, then when the time [of death] arrives, they will not be liberated.

Thus, it is as taught. It is important to familiarize oneself with this phowa practice right now.

In order to begin the practice, first complete refuge and bodhichitta;[168] and then begin by reciting, "*Phet!* Phenomenal existence is the pure realm of Khachöd." Thus reciting, bring the visualization to mind. Saying *phet* here means that all impure appearances of this existence instantly become the perfect pure land of Khachöd, the unchanging place of exaltation as a self-appearing array.

Just as described during the explanation of the refuge tree, in the center upon a fully blossoming lotus flower and sun seat, self-radiance of the five wisdoms appears in an expanse of five-colored bindus of light. Within that, self-nature appears as Vajrayoginī, green in color, with one face and two arms. One is peaceful with a semi-smiling expression, holding a curved vajra blade in the right hand and skull filled with blood in the left. In the cleft of the left arm is a trident. Both legs are standing as though about to take a step, and one is naked and otherwise adorned with the six bone ornaments. If viewed from without, one is inwardly translucent; if from within, one is outwardly translucent. Being lucid and lacking inherent existence is the outer empty posture of the body.

The inner empty posture of the channels is that, in the center of one's kāya that is straight like a pillar is the upward pathway that leads directly to the upper pure land of Khachöd. This is the supreme wisdom channel, the pure essence of the five faculties as *tsa üma*, or *avadhūti*.[a] It is straight, subtle, lucid, and rich with all characteristics complete. Indicating the three kāyas, it is white on the outside, red on the inside, and blue in between. The upper end at one's crown is wide open like a skylight or the bell of a long horn. The diameter is similar to a medium-sized bamboo shaft. According to what is mentioned in the texts on the profound teachings on chöd, at the secret place *üma* branches into two directions that travel down to the soles of each foot, where it is then blocked. On the right sole is the white bindu representing upāya received from one's father appearing in a clear expanse as a white bindu of light. On the left is the red bindu representing prajñā received from one's mother visualized in a clear expanse as a red bindu of light. Both are the size of the bodhisattva bird's first egg,[169] buoyant and fluttering.

Regarding the chakras in the five places, the green consort Samayatārā[b] rests in the center of the secret chakra that sustains bliss. She has one face and two arms; her right hand is in the mudrā of giving refuge and the left in evenness. At the emanation chakra in the navel is the golden consort Buddha Lochanā,[c] her right hand in the mudrā of supreme generosity and her left in evenness. In the dharma chakra at the heart is the white consort Māmakī,[d] her right hand in the earth-touching gesture and the left in evenness. In the abundance chakra at the throat is the red consort Pāṇḍaravāsinī,[e] with both hands in the mudrā of evenness. In

[a] *rtsa dbu ma, a wa dhu ti*

[b] Damtsig Drolma (*dam tshig sgrol ma*)

[c] Sangye Chenma (*sangs rgyas spyan ma*)

[d] *ma ma' ki*

[e] Gö Karmo (*gos dkar mo*)

the exaltation chakra at the crown is the consort blue Dhātvīshvarī[a] with both hands in the mudrā of teaching the dharma. Otherwise, her hands may also be in the mudrā of supreme awakening. All five consorts are wearing the perfect garments and ornamentation of the sambhogakāya. Their legs are in the posture of the queen, and they rest in the expanse of their own radiance upon lotus and moon seats clearly visualized as empty wisdom kāyas.

Above one's crown about the length of a cubit is the wisdom chakra of the crown aperture, the perfectly pure land of Akaniṣhṭha, an uncreated, self-occurring perfect array that is the primordial nature of kāyas and wisdom. By transferring to this space, it is free from all elaborations, abides in the manner of the three gateways of liberation, and without meditation is naturally actualized and perfectly complete. Since one will have arrived in a state of permanent exaltation, this name merely indicates the pure land but is not to be understood as an autonomous place that actually exists.

The ḍākinīs of the five places and the Akaniṣhṭha pure land are recognized as the destinations. The central channel is recognized as the pathway, and the nature of one's consciousness as a bindu the size of the bodhisattva bird egg is recognized as the traveler. Practice with those as the three recognitions. Then, recite the lineage supplication in the hauntingly beautiful melody while cultivating intense devotion. When transferring, with the first *phet*, the two white and red bindus at the soles of the feet travel upward and unite as one where both legs connect. There, they become a single bindu mixture of white and red. Again reciting a single *phet*, the bindu enters the secret place and mingles with the consort Samayatārā's enlightened mind of exaltation. One achieves mastery over the pure land of Karmaprasiddhi,[b] and [the wisdom of] all-accomplished activity is actualized.

Again reciting a single *phet*, one's consciousness and the consort Samayatārā—inseparable as a green bindu of light—mingles with the heart of Buddha Lochanā in one's navel. Mastery over the pure land Shrīmat[c] is achieved, and the wisdom of evenness is actualized. Again saying *phet*, the bindu as a golden bindu of light mingles inseparably with the heart of Māmakī. Mastery over the pure land of Abhirati[d] is achieved, and mirrorlike wisdom is actualized. Again reciting *phet*, the bindu as an orb of white light mingles inseparably with the mind of Pāṇḍaravāsinī at the throat. Mastery over the pure land of Sukhāvatī is achieved, and

[a] Yingchügma (*dbyings phyug ma*)
[b] Lerab Drubpa (*las rab grub pa*); northern field of Akaniṣhṭha, Accomplished Action
[c] Paldang Denpa (*dpal dang ldan pa*); southern field of Akaniṣhṭha, Endowed with Glory
[d] Ngon Ga (*mngon dga'*); eastern field of Akaniṣhṭha, Manifest Joy

the wisdom of discerning awareness is actualized. Again reciting *phet*, the bindu as an orb of red light mingles inseparably with the heart of Dhātvīshvarī at one's crown. Mastery over the pure land of the Akaniṣhṭha is achieved, and the wisdom of the space of phenomena is actualized. Again reciting *phet*, the bindu as a blue bindu of light mingles with the wisdom chakra at the crown aperture. Mastery over the pure land of Akaniṣhṭha-Ghanavyūha is achieved. Rest in the evenness of actualizing the fundamental nature of the unceasing, spontaneously present wisdom of the original primordial ground. The five consorts gradually become bindus of light that dissolve upward.

Because these instructions were taught to me on two occasions, they are presented here in this way. Nevertheless, according to several recorded oral instructions: as one's consciousness gradually transfers through the hearts of the five consorts, the five consorts themselves remain static. Later, when actually applied [at death], the five consorts rise up on their seats; and one imagines them naked, wearing bone ornaments, holding curved blades and skulls filled with blood. When reciting *phet* for the seventh time, it is said that then one either transfers to the space of unborn original purity or rests in the [unborn] nature of mind. Given that both of these earlier and later oral instructions are authentic, it is acceptable to practice either one.

After repeatedly training in this way by reciting *phet*: from within the baseless expanse of space, awareness arises as Tröma; and the body is given as the feast of offering and generosity. Finally, one rests in the nature of the nonconceptual three rounds. Given that the practice of offering the body as the feast is clear in the terma liturgy, I found it unnecessary to include further commentary here.

Great care must be taken to clearly engage the stages of visualization without mental distraction. Given that this is the swift lineage of exceptional sacred instruction for the extremely profound path of phowa, even those who have practiced this for a short time have witnessed many signs of accomplishment. The terma states:

> All individuals who practice this will be liberated through this profoundly supreme method. If all sons and daughters who regularly practice this are not set free in this lifetime, then this father has deceived his fortunate children.

Thus, just as he spoke, one must have confidence in this point being made by knowing that this perfectly authentic speech is undeceiving.

> Consciousness, bewildered by the impure five poisons, travels through
> the skylike expanse of the pure five consorts.

Transferring to the pure, definitive Akaniṣhṭha is the quintessential pinnacle of the sacred teaching on buddhahood without meditation.
Given that the habituated corporeal body poses a threat to the consciousness traveling upward, this [body] is offered as a feast of the desirables to the field of the four guests.
Hence, this severance of attachment and fixation is supreme among the sacred.

Thus, these are the verses that summarize this section.

Originally all-pervasive, the meaning of the primordial ground is actualized by rendering awareness evident so that the dynamic strength of awareness prajñā will blaze. To the primordially awakened protector of buddhahood anew who severs the four māras in basic space, the hero Dudjom, I bow down. For wanderers like me of the lowest class of existence, the kingdom of the originally pure dharmakāya is introduced as mastered within ourselves. I will forever remember the kindness of this supreme Lord Father who grants me the opportunity to achieve the status of perfect liberation.

3.2.2 How to Cultivate Realization through the Main Practice

This has six parts:

1 Sustaining the ground through the view
2 Maintaining the continuity of practice in fear-provoking environments
3 Supplementary explanation for the generation stage of Tröma
4 Clarifying the passageway of deviations
5 Taking whatever occurs as the path
6 Final conclusion of select upadesha and accomplishing enlightened deeds

Second, the way of cultivating and realizing the actual practice has six sections: [**first**] sustaining the ground through the view of the supreme, kingly vehicle by **determining the self-abiding wisdom maṇḍala**; maintaining the continuity of practice as it applies to the way of wandering in fear-provoking environments with fearless conduct to encounter self-nature through circumstances at the moment they occur; the supplementary explanation for the generation stage of Tröma as the meditation deity, including explanations concerning the visualizations; clarifying the dangerous passageway of deviations; taking whatever occurs as the path, whether illness, happiness, suffering, and the like; and the final conclusion, including the select upadesha and the manner of accomplishing enlightened deeds for the welfare of others.

3.2.2.1 Sustaining the Ground through the View

This has two parts:

1 Stages of practice
2 Actual stages of the view

For the first, there are two: starting with the stages of practice and the actual stages of the view.

3.2.2.1.1 Stages of Practice

First, from the verses that read "... body, speech, and mind ..." until "... takes up the path is called awareness ..." according to the tradition of some Nyingma meditators, one **analyzes** to discover **which among body, speech, and mind is principal.** This allows one **to recognize** and determine that the mind is obviously primary. Then, resting in the natural state **brings restoration.** In order to realize the mind's fundamental nature, one examines to determine whether **the mind has color, shape,** and the rest. Analyzing whether the mind is permanent with true, inherent existence or negated as void, **the limitations of eternalism and nihilism are dispelled, bringing restoration.**

Once again, in order to stabilize the mind's capacity to concentrate by placing the mind in lucid awareness, one abides in the total recall of **mindfulness.** When distracted from that, **the distinctions are encountered and taken as the path.** This process of encountering, abiding, and movement is well known in most upadesha instructions. **Concerning that,** with the mind abiding **single-pointedly** free from concepts: if applied to the stages of the four yogas of mahāmudrā,[170] then all concepts **mingle** within the mind's nature, or vanish there. Occasionally, cognition either engages with **objects** or becomes distracted based on objects so that concepts **arise and increase.** Concerning these projections **from the** self-radiance of the mind's **expanse,** there is no problem posed except for slight **movement. That is called "mindfulness securing stability".** When the gatherings of thoughts vanish, the aspect of **emptiness arising** unceasingly appears. This **lucidity** is referred to as being "single-pointed".

In this way, maintaining the stages of **mindfulness** through familiarity is as though the mind is **settling into emptiness itself.** Following that, sustained mindfulness will naturally be experienced as intrinsically empty in the nature of **wakeful awareness.**[171] Through the strength of this experience, realization of an all-pervasive, **unelaborate** emptiness will dawn. Fixation as well **falls apart within** the experience of single-pointedness, which is what is meant by being "unelaborate". Meditating in this way repeatedly allows **this nature** to **abide**

within inseparable empty appearances so that the meaning is actualized. Given that the aspects of both appearances and emptiness have no separation, they become a single taste. Even fixation upon the experience of emptiness is purified so that the constant presence of abiding there is the meaning of "one taste". With not even the slightest effort applied toward that, there is nothing whatsoever to meditate upon. Without distraction, to naturally settle and remain within this great **innate nature**[172] is the meaning of "nonmeditation".

If applied to the Mahāsandhi tradition, **by entering the path** in this way: once the mind's movements and proliferations vanish in awareness, **it is said that awareness** simply abides in its own nature. To apply this to the four states of mindfulness: it is taught that "single-pointedness" is mindfulness with familiarity, "unelaborate" is mindfulness with emptiness, "one taste" is mindfulness with nondistraction, and "nonmeditation" is mindfulness with mental transcendence.

That explanation is similar to the description of the four Mahāmudrā yogas, so it is applicable here. Furthermore, according to the Kagyü tradition, each of these [yogas] has three aspects: the greater, intermediate, and lesser—totaling nine categories. That can also apply to the stages of the grounds and paths, such as the process of a beginner's traversal of the path, developing the qualities of abandonment and realization, all the way to total perfection. That is its own system and will, therefore, not be elaborated upon here.

Generally, it is said that Mahāmudrā involves both traditions of Sūtra and Mantra. Whatever the case may be, according to the speech of the Lord of the Gelukpa's lineage of aural instruction, Paṇchen Rinpoche Lozang Chökyi Gyaltsen:[a,173]

> Pacification through severance, the Mahāsandhi, teachings based upon the view of the Madhyamaka, and so forth are individual designations; yet if analyzed by those with knowledge in the definitive meaning of the scriptures who comprehend logic and have practical experience, the conclusion that the wisdom intent is similar will be reached.

Thus, even in the life story of the yogi Drügpa Kunlek,[b,174] he says:

> The perfection of all phenomena as a single wisdom intent is Mahāsandhi; focus without direction is the Madhyamaka; pacifying concepts in their place is pacification; directly cutting through whatever arises is severance; the fundamental nature beyond mind is Mahāmudrā—

[a] *pan chen rin po che blo bzang chos kyi rgyal mtshan*
[b] *'brug pa kun legs*

> these and others are the same with the exception of the enumerations of names.

Thus, it is as taught. Know that the wisdom intent of the view of Mahāmudrā, Mahāsandhi, and Madhyamaka—these three—and the key points of their practices arrive at the same pivotal point. Except for training in unbiased pure vision, one should not—through biased perception—be like a blind yak hesitatingly trying to eat grass.

Even Machig Rinpoche tells us:

> The key point of the view concerning my tradition of subjugating the māras through chöd is an instruction that does not contradict Mahāsandhi, Mahāmudrā, or the Madhyamaka—these three.

So, it is as taught.

3.2.2.1.2 Actual Stages of the View

This has four parts:

1 Nonexistence
2 Oneness
3 Openness
4 Spontaneous presence

Second, the actual stages of the view are the four: nonexistence, oneness, openness, and spontaneous presence.[175]

In the *Precious Treasury of the Fundamental Nature*, it states:

> The absolute meaning of the quintessential mind, expanse, and upadesha classes involves nonexistence, openness, spontaneous presence, and oneness.

Thus, and in the *Precious Heap of Jewels Tantra*,[a] it also states:

> The samaya is great spontaneous presence, nonexistence, oneness, and openness.

So, it is as taught. "Samaya" means to know that it is unacceptable to transgress vows. Here, it is also explained that this means it is unacceptable to transgress

[a] *rinchen püng pa'i gyü* (*rin chen spungs pa'i rgyud*)

the view and meditation of Mahāsandhi. In addition, that which is called a "philosophical tenet" is a definition that describes a meaning established through scripture and reasoning that is unacceptable to transgress because it involves an exceptional philosophical tenet of the Mahāsandhi system. It makes no difference which order these [four] are placed in since there is no contradiction. That is why they appear in different orders.

Here, if placed according to the principal terma scripture's assertion of the Great Tertön himself: since it must be known that all phenomena lack inherent existence, nonexistence is explained first. This also depends upon knowing the precise way in which [nonexistence] never departs from the sole nature of basic space, so oneness is second. Given that it is necessary to know that this is not a partial direction but rather the way all phenomena naturally and evenly pervade, saying "this is openness" is an ancient term that actually means evenness. In this way, by determining that all phenomena lack inherent existence, the nature of that meaning is oneness. The intrinsic nature of the way this abides as openness—hence, these three—primarily reveals the way of abiding as original purity from the perspective of emptiness. Through spontaneous presence, the nature of all phenomena of saṃsāra and enlightenment—being not just an empty vacuity but spontaneously present—reveals that presence from the perspective of the natural way that appearances arise.

3.2.2.1.2.1 Nonexistence

This has four parts:

1 Searching for the designated basis of labels
2 Tearing apart permanent fixation with things
3 Collapsing the false cave of hope and fear
4 Attacking the faults of benefit and harm

First, nonexistence is as follows. It states in the *Precious Treasury of the Fundamental Nature*:

> The intrinsic nature of being nonexistent means the emptiness of the nature as it is. Within the great expanse of the enlightened mind equal to space, whatever appears—although occurring—lacks true, inherent existence.

Thus, all appearances without exception equal to space arise from the great expanse of the awakened mind of basic space. In whatever way they do, that is precisely how they are determined to be free of inherent existence.

For this point, there are four parts: searching for the designated basis of labels, tearing apart permanent fixation with things, collapsing the false cave of hope and fear, and attacking the faults of benefit and harm.

3.2.2.1.2.1.1 Searching for the Designated Basis of Labels

For the first, there are two: an introduction and the actual explanation. Initially in the root terma, it states, "Then the fundamental nature . . ." until ". . . clarify the doubt . . ." As stated, the explanation will follow. **Then, having determined the fundamental nature** of all phenomena's precise way of primordially abiding and by **deciding** this is free of inherent existence as the nature of emptiness, **one must then clarify all faults associated with view and meditation** through certainty.

For the second, there are two: searching for the designated basis of an individual name and then determining selflessness, and searching for the designated basis of other labeled phenomena and then determining nonexistence. First, as stated in the root terma, "Head hair and pore hair . . ." until ". . . exist or not?" is as follows. Concerning the so-called "**me**" or "self", one must examine whether that exists as the **head** hair, **body hair**, heart, lungs, and so forth[176] all the way through to the intestines, feces, and urine. Likewise, one must examine **the head and other limbs of the body** by **examining** just how **each one has its own basis for designation. Aside from** their **being** the inherent nature of **nonreferential** emptiness, come to know just how they **actually exist** or **not**.

Second, searching for the designated basis of other labeled phenomena begins with, "Likewise the universe and inhabitants . . ." until ". . . you think this is existent?" and is as follows. **Likewise, if the** support of the **universe and** the living **inhabitants** who are the sentient beings including their **fivefold sensual desires** are carefully **examined, each of these names and their basis of designation** can be found to not exist at all. **If** it was discovered that something was **unchanging, indestructible, and permanently existing as true and real, then your assertion** of inherent existence **is right**; but that cannot be established!

3.2.2.1.2.1.2 Tearing Apart Permanent Fixation with Things

Second, for tearing apart permanent fixation upon things, there are five parts: revealing how the mode of fixating upon things as truly existent is mistaken, revealing how by merely appearing the fault of that which is intrinsically empty is revealed, examining the nature of dreams to cultivate certainty with that, examining the manner of death and transference, and summarizing the key point by revealing how the three times are not extant.

First, beginning with, "Your perception of . . ." until ". . . assertion is right . . ." is as follows. If any phenomenon is established as true, it must be able to stand alone and remain in its original state without changing or relying upon root cause or contributing circumstance. In that case, then **your present perceptions of holding to the elements** earth, water, fire, and wind **as truly existing** cannot possibly hold up, including the **forms that originate from causes** and circumstances associated with these elements. **If those** phenomena **were to possess** seven **unchanging vajra characteristics, then** your **assertion** that they exist **is right.**

Second, where the root text states, ". . . tearing apart and reducing . . ." until ". . . watch to see", is as follows. Nevertheless, **by tearing apart** these actual material things into parts **and reducing** them to dust, **once scattered, does this not change?** Definitely, it will change to become something other than what it originally was. Coarse substance becomes dust; **dust is reduced to particles that become partless** until there is nothing at all that exists. At that time, **watch to see where those** inherently existing material things **have vanished.** Having not existed from the beginning, fixation upon them as having come into existence, ceasing to exist, coming, and going must be identified as mistaken.

Third, where the root terma states ". . . the ten illustrations of magic . . ." until ". . . how can an object be asserted?" is as follows. Given that whatever appears is similar in character to the ten illustrations [of illusion], such as magic, dreams, and the rest—**except for being merely apparent—from the perspective of being empty, nothing at all exists. How can an** existent **object** still **be asserted when no tangible thing exists?** Such an assertion is unacceptable.

Fourth [i.e., examining the manner of death] is as follows. The root terma states, "During daytime appearances of self . . ." until ". . . who will take on those . . .?" **During daytime appearances,** you express "**self**" by saying "mine" **and** those who are otherwise as "**others**". All appearances are **held to as true,** not considered to be false. **If** whatever **you** hold to as true is indeed **right: then during dream appearances while dreaming** about self and others and so forth, the entire world sees that as false; so if while dreaming one can know that phenomena are not true, then it seems **you may be right.** Nevertheless, that is not the case **from the perspective of daytime appearances** since you see them as **truly existing.**

From the perspective of the dream state, if you **believe that dreams are** also **true, then what happens to the** truly existing **daytime phenomena during the dream state?** Even the [daytime] body **must have naturally perished, so where did you dispose of the corpse? During daytime** phenomena, **where has the dream-state environment gone?** From **what causes** and conditions **did the living beings,** the males and females, **in the dream state come from? Where did you hide those bodies** that you have **in dreams,** and how did you make them invisible? **Having discarded this body that originates from** the **causes and circumstances** of parents in this life, **who are the parents and what are the causes and circumstances for the person who goes to their next life?**

Concerning this present body that originates from causes and circumstances that bring about the fear of illness and suffering: once separated from

this body and the bardo is entered, **who will take** on **those experiences** of suffering since this body will already be gone? The key point here is that, if during waking reality appearances are fixated upon as true and during dreams as well, then in both cases how can the difference be discerned as to which is true or false? No one can discern this. Ultimately, aside from the transformation of appearances, this reveals that nothing exists.

Fifth, it states, "Likewise . . . throughout the three times . . ." until ". . . why wouldn't the false cave of confusion just collapse?" **Likewise, the intrinsic nature of** all phenomena without exception **is to occur throughout the three times** and always be free from birth **and** cessation as **the time of evenness.** Although **having never occurred before, the phenomena being experienced** by that mind **as true are held as the time of the past.** Though **having not occurred as yet:** imagining that there will be phenomena occurring, one **anticipates the time of the future occurring** as true; and it is held as the time of the future. Even now just as **nothing truly exists,** these present phenomena originate from **attaching to the tangible aspects of** appearances based on **confused perception.** The phenomena of **the present time have originated** from that. There are no phenomena not included within the three times. **Hence, once** it is **determined** that **objective appearances** without exception merely appear but do not truly exist, **why wouldn't the false cave of confusion just collapse**? It must collapse! By considering just how it is that the dream appearances have occurred, the meaning of this [presentation] will undoubtedly make sense.

3.2.2.1.2.1.3 Collapsing the False Cave of Hope and Fear

This has four parts:

1 How to stop fixating upon Buddha as the object of hope
2 The way to abandon the designation of compulsory fixation
3 Revealing the absolute fundamental nature of buddha
4 Revealing the qualities of realizing and the faults of not realizing

Third, for collapsing the false cave of hope and fear, there are four parts: revealing the general way to identify how to stop fixating upon Buddha as the object of hope, revealing the specific way to abandon the designation of compulsory fixation with tangible knowable things, revealing the absolute fundamental nature of buddha, and revealing the difference between the qualities of realizing that and the faults of not realizing that.

3.2.2.1.2.1.3.1 How to Stop Fixating upon Buddha as the Object of Hope

For the first, it states, "The noble Buddha is the object of hope . . ." until ". . . manifestations also appear." The meaning is as follows.

Concerning **the noble Buddha** who **is the object of hope: if** he is **held to as the aspect of the universe and inhabitants, that cannot be buddha** because there would then be no difference between buddha and the impure universe and inhabitants. Why? **That which is called "buddha" lacks tangible characteristics,** so **to designate** this arrangement of the universe and inhabitants to be a buddha with **characteristics is to lack awareness.** "Buddha" means **having awakened from the shell of ignorance** and **expanded the self-radiance of wisdom.**[177] Hence, **that is the all-pervasive, unbiased open nature of evenness** that merely designates the state of buddha. Vast **emanations from within** twofold, **omniscient** wisdom **knowledge** of the nature as it is and how it appears free from obstruction[178] are merely posited as the rupakāya self-appearing teachers that **appear** like dreams until the duality of objects to be tamed falls apart.

3.2.2.1.2.1.3.2 The Way to Abandon the Designation of Compulsory Fixation

Second, the root terma states, "That [buddha] is also free from faculties . . ." until ". . . aren't those the divinities of the form-god realm?" In this way, **that** perfectly pure buddha **is also free from** the five sense **faculties** and the rest.

Lacking the aspect of a **form** comprised of tangible **substances,** this buddha **involves no characteristics** or aspects of the **universe or inhabitants. Whatever is** acceptably designated as **substantial and tangible is referred to as a "sentient being".** Whatever appears as **the universe and inhabitants** does so from the perspective of **the** dualistic **phenomena** that occur to **sentient beings. How can one see a buddha to be** similar to **a sentient being? If so, what is the mark of supremacy that delineates a difference** from those who are sentient? How can buddha be like that?

If one thinks that buddha means being extremely blissful and happy in a way that surpasses sentient beings and then **if a** buddha **does not exceed** sentient beings **aside from the experience of mere bliss** and happiness, **are you then deciding that** buddha **is** merely **a divinity of the form-god realm? Otherwise, are you** perhaps **claiming** buddha **is** exalted due to being **an immortal? Similarly, you may be claiming that** buddha **is a state of blissful happiness, excellent companionship, environment, attractive form, miraculous abilities,** and the like that are all exalted. **If so,** then **aren't those the** very qualities **of the divinities of the form-god realm**? If that is the case, then [those gods] are all buddhas too.

3.2.2.1.2.1.3.3 Revealing the Absolute Fundamental Nature of Buddha

Third, recognizing the absolute buddha according to this tradition is as follows. The root terma states, "Buddha is not recognized through the dualistic mind . . ." until ". . . abides in the minds of all sentient beings."

This means that, even according to the definitive meaning of the sūtras:

> Buddha should not be seen as a form, with characteristics, as a class distinction, or analyzed as a mental continuum or sound. Having not fallen to the direction of nihilism, buddha cannot be distinguished through mind or consciousness. Whatever is the nature of phenomena is the Bhagavan.

So, it is.

The great omniscient Rongzom[a] said:

> The nature of buddha himself is the perfectly pure space of phenomena, evident through both scriptures and reasoning.

Thus, it is as taught. The perfectly pure original ground of the space of phenomena is referred to as the genuine state of buddha. It must be known that even the ultimate, self-abiding kāyas and wisdoms are the nature of this spontaneous presence.

To expand upon that,[179] this absolute **buddha cannot be indicated through** the **duality** of subject and object. That is **the meaning of** being nonexistent. Likewise, given that **there is no fixation upon "me"**, that is the meaning of being without fixation upon "mine". This nature of the buddha has not originated from the **interdependency** of root causes and contributing circumstances. **This means having transcended** that. Uncultivated through newly accumulated merit, this **transcends the object of accumulation. Free from** the **elaborations** of true existence—**having collapsed the distinction of duality** by **possessing the three gateways to liberation**—since **there are no linear** three **times, directions and limitations** are nonexistent.

This empty nature of basic space is the dharmakāya, the intrinsic nature of self-clarity is the sambhogakāya, and the unceasing gateway for the arising of compassion is the nirmāṇakāya. That their nature abides as the evenness of the nature of phenomena is the svābhāvikakāya.[180] This **means** [**buddha**] is **the epitome of the four kāyas**. Hence, **who can see this as form** and how could that be possible? Since [buddha] is free from birth, death, aging, and decline, buddha is **ever-youthful**. Since the qualities of spontaneous presence are abiding as inner clarity, **buddha is the vase kāya. Who can recognize** that **this has** shape, colors, and **substance**?

All phenomena of **saṃsāra and enlightenment** without exception **are subsumed** within basic space. **How can one see these as** having **outer and inner**

[a] *rong zom pa*

aspects? **Buddha is the meaning of the awakened mind**, the intrinsic nature of clear light as the embodiment of primordial prajñā. **Who can believe** and have faith **that** [buddha] **is the conceptually** oriented **mind?** The **meaning of being unrestricted** is based on not abiding in any direction or time, or being singular or plural. **How can one believe this has** the characteristics of **directions**, time frames, above, below, **radiation, or reabsorption?** The intrinsic nature of **buddha is** unchanging as **the sole bindu.** How **can** this be **explained** as possessing **shape, color,** or other ordinary characteristics? The absolute **buddha** is that which naturally **abides within the minds of all sentient beings** in the manner of the unchanging essence of the sugatas.

3.2.2.1.2.1.3.4 Revealing the Qualities of Realizing and the Faults of Not Realizing

This has two parts:

1 Qualities of realizing the fundamental nature of buddha
2 Arresting compulsory fixation toward objects

For the fourth, the root terma states, "The fundamental nature of sentient beings . . ." until ". . . must not be misunderstood . . ." Therefore, all that appears to **sentient beings is the fundamental nature of** their minds, and that is the essence of the sugatas, **the dharmakāya** nature.

3.2.2.1.2.1.3.4.1 Qualities of Realizing the Fundamental Nature of Buddha

Aside from being this essential nature of basic space, **this is not the field of experience of those** intellectuals whose minds and eyes **are blinded by cataracts** of delusion **and who speculate** based on their own ideas. **Those with the** three **eyes of prajñā** have mastery to **make use of this.** Deluded, **immature ones** will imagine that buddha **transfers from one location to another** in order to **traverse** or that there is an independent **pure land to** actually **arrive** at. **Holding to that as the genuine** kāya and pure land of buddha is mistaken and **will propel** such believers to continue wandering in unsightly, **loathsome places.**

Therefore, revealing basic space to be the state of buddha is an accurate way to identify the **genuine** fundamental nature. Nevertheless, showing that buddhas abide in other directions and times is the mode of the **relative** method. Based on that and **by discerning the** two truths, **those whose prajñā eyes were closed will then open them.** So-called **buddha must not be misunderstood to be** an **autonomous** individual with a mouth, eyes, ears, and the like. This primordial ground of the space of phenomena's essence of the sugatas is called "the definitive genuine buddha". The nature of buddha is unaffected by faults and stains. Although the qualities of kāyas and wisdoms are not established as having substantial characteristics, from the perspective of the way of abiding, there are no phenomena that surpass this.

Given that this entranceway for the arising of the oceanic wisdoms and kāyas that are only within that nature is unceasingly spontaneously present, it is referred to as such. Based on being aware of this or not, the appearances of both saṃsāra and enlightenment dawn. Due to that pure entranceway of interdependency and according to the perspective of those to be tamed, this is like the water moon reflected in a vessel of water and the reason why the inconceivable pure lands and array of the kāyas' major and minor marks, as well as enlightened speech and miraculous activities, appear.

Even the present rupakāya of the buddha and others should not be considered to be completely nonexistent. Aside from being the dynamic strength of the manifestation of basic space, this does not exist otherwise. Nevertheless, this is unlike the way that we fixate upon the array of pure lands and kāyas as independent. Ultimately, the intrinsic nature of buddha transcends the field of experience of sound and conception as the uncompounded nature of spontaneous presence.

It states in the *Uttaratantra*:

> Uncompounded and spontaneously present, this will not be realized through the circumstance of something that is otherwise.

Thus, as taught, this [state of buddha] is the absolute intention being referred to there. In the *Praise to the Names of Mañjushrī*,[a] it states:

> The buddha has no beginning or end; the original buddha is free from root cause.

Thus, as taught, there are many quotations from the sūtras and tantras that prove this point. The great paṇḍit of definitive truth, omniscient King of Dharma, Rongzompa, also asserts the same point.

According to the tradition of the Mahāyāna's Mahāsandhi, the meaning of the fundamental nature is emphasized. Just as it is taught that this is unaffected by the mind sets of the eight lower vehicles, the mode of awakening must be posited from the perspective of how it actually is. That is also the precise wisdom intent of the precious Tertön himself.

[a] *jampal tsen jöd* (*'jam dpal mtshan brjod, mañjushrīnāmasaṃgīti*)

These explanations are difficult to fit within the minds of those who are habituated with materialization; yet, nevertheless, this meaning has been openly explained without compromise. Aside from adding some additional comments, this has not been extensive. Even if it were, this is difficult for anyone to realize unless they have internalized the key points of the guru's upadesha derived from the potential of the wisdom-lineage blessings. Like the lion's roar that naturally frightens all creatures of the wild—by resonating Mahāsandhi's own language, all those of the lower vehicles whose minds are limited are said to be terrified. Given that is the truth, this could have been explained according to the general way of describing the classes of Secret Mantra and the sūtras of the Mahāyāna. For now, this is enough.

3.2.2.1.2.1.3.4.2 Arresting Compulsory Fixation toward Objects

This has three parts:

1 The way of becoming obsessed with compulsory fixation
2 The way this is not truly existent
3 Synthesis of the key points

Second, arresting compulsory fixation toward the objects of [expectation and] disappointment, namely, the classes and dwelling places of sentient beings, has three sections: the way of becoming obsessed with compulsory fixation; the way this is not truly existent, aside from being merely the transformation of self-appearances; and a synthesis of the key points.

3.2.2.1.2.1.3.4.2.1 The Way of Becoming Obsessed with Compulsory Fixation

First, the root terma states, "The objects of disappointment are the three realms . . ." until ". . . as well as stable and everlasting . . ." So as taught, even though **the objects of disappointment appear as the** dwelling **places in the three realms of saṃsāra**, due to **this dense habit** of compulsory fixation **impressed upon** the aspect of clarity that **is the intrinsic nature** of the ground, the "self" or **notion of "I"** appears. Dependent upon that, all **outer objective appearances are established.** Although **these [phenomena] do not exist aside from appearing as something other than the mere transformation of phenomena,** [beings] do not know that is the case. Those phenomena arise due to the ever-increasing **habit of permanent grasping to true existence** by means of being familiar and **stable.** Hence, these concrete appearances seem **everlasting**, or fully whole, as well as solid and static.

3.2.2.1.2.1.3.4.2.2 The Way This Is Not Truly Existent

Second, the root terma states, "Due to that, if one thinks these [phenomena] exist . . ." until ". . . why are they still functioning?" **If one thinks** that **these** objective phenomena that come about **due to** the transformation of self-appearances **exist other than that, then who created the molten lava ground of the hell realms? From where have the denizens of hell and their weapons come from? Likewise, whose children are those who** must take rebirth as pretas to **bear such a pitiful state** of existence **for eons of time, experiencing hunger and thirst with huge stomachs** the size of valleys, **tiny limbs** the size of a split hair of a horse tail, **and mouths** as small as the eye of a needle? **In which direction do the environments** of the hells and so forth, **including their inhabitants, exist: to the east, south, west, north, or in between?** Aside from being phenomena that **appear as truly existing without being analyzed, if examined everything is only false** because this amounts to the deluded phenomena of the negative mind.

The *Bodhicharyāvatāra* states:

> Who created the ground of molten lava? What caused this raging fire?
> This and everything like it are the products of the negative mind.

Thus, the Sage taught.

Based on these reasons, given that **all such phenomenal appearances occur from within** the mere **transformation** of self-appearances, **equally observe them within the state of** being either **nonduality** or undifferentiated. Nonexistent like a dream, self-appearing saṃsāra naturally occurs to oneself; and **aside from that, in** the places of **saṃsāra there is no** continuity concerning the process of **revolving from one realm to another. Except for merely appearing, there is no continuity that goes from one place to another. If this** assertion of **yours** that another place actually exists where many sentient beings **take one rebirth after another and experience suffering:** then even though they go through the torment of heat and cold, **why do beings still not** lose consciousness or **become physically exhausted? Why are their lives** still **strong and** breath **still functioning?** These days, if someone burns their hands or feet even slightly or are exposed to frigid weather for a day or a night, it is possible they may just die.

3.2.2.1.2.1.3.4.2.3 Synthesis of the Key Points

Third, the root terma states, ". . . the confusion of one's mind and appearances . . ." until ". . . it is a key point to not believe." Well then, why does it appear as though suffering occurs in this way?

Habituated with the confusion of one's mind and appearances, the positive, negative, virtuous, and nonvirtuous **karma** and their **results** appear like magic so that the **unmistakable causes for** revolving in the higher and lower realms **of saṃsāra arise without** delay, deceit, or **doubt. This process of joy versus sorrow** [i.e., karma] **is unreliable,**[181] **and it will mature** like dreams that are uncertain. **Aside from that, it is a key point to not believe** in true, inherent existence.

3.2.2.1.2.1.4 Attacking the Faults of Benefit and Harm

This has two parts:

1 The way the gods-māras of this life bring benefit and harm
2 The way virtue and nonvirtue bring benefit and harm in the future life

Fourth, attacking the faults of benefit and harm has two sections: examining the way the gods-māras of this life bring benefit and harm and examining the way virtue and nonvirtue bring benefit and harm in the future life.

3.2.2.1.2.1.4.1 The Way the Gods-Māras of this Life Bring Benefit and Harm

First, the root terma states, "Also given that this is empty . . . " and so forth until ". . . have proclaimed this." So, it is taught. **In addition**, the way that the faults of confusion collapse is referred to in the sūtra *Ornament of the Rich Array*:[a]

> For instance, when awakening from a dream that involved seeing the aggregate of form, forms of attractive males or females are no longer visible. While a nonlucid dream is occurring—although males, females, and the like are seen—upon awakening, there is nothing left to see.

So, it is as taught. **Given** that the objects of benefit and harm and the actual effects from them amount to empty forms that resemble self-appearing dreams, nothing is really established. Even if one thinks that it is: then as previously proven, the nature of these phenomena **is empty** of a twofold self—unchanging, indestructible, and **free from fear.**

If there were, in fact, a **god who grants protection**, just **how would** he **protect** and bring benefit? **How would harm-causing obstructers bring torment? If** self-nature is **empty**, then **who is the object to be harmed by the substantial** māra? **If the** self has **substantial** existence and the māra **is empty** of existence,

[a] *gyen tüg po köd pa'i do* (*rgyan stug po bkod pa'i mdo, ghanavyūhasūtra*)

then how is this [self] **destroyed? How does the formless** māra **threaten** a self **that is embodied in a form?**

If perhaps the māra is established as having **a form,** then **how can** it **kill** a self that is **formless?** There is no way to perform such a killing. Likewise, **how can a god who is immaterial grant protection to** a self **that actually exists? Similarly,** how can a **form-based god** grant protection to a **formless** self? **There is no way** to do this. **A form** god that **cannot protect a form**-based self[182] is just like a man greeting another man in a dream state. **The** way that a **formless** god grants protection to a formless self **is similar. There is no one** god or māra **who delivers happiness or suffering,** nor is there a recipient to **receive** this.

Like dreams, **the experiences of these patterns of confused phenomena are** impressed [upon the mind] as **the product of** undeceiving **positive and negative karmic causes and results.** In these ways, **all** compulsory fixations based on happiness and suffering in the context **of saṃsāra belong to the relative,** whereas the fact that this is naturally nonexistent **and transcends** sorrow **is the absolute. "I, the learned Saraha have proclaimed this!"** The false impressions of **appearances and mind are themselves the relative, and the nature of that** as emptiness **is the absolute. This is also revealed by many other scholars.**

3.2.2.1.2.1.4.2 The Way Virtue and Nonvirtue Bring Benefit and Harm in the Future Life

Second, the root terma states, "Previously accumulated karma and passions . . ." until ". . . how can that be . . . ?" As stated, **previously accumulated karma and passions, the obscuration of habits,** and the rest belong to the category of negativity. The expression of generosity **and the accumulation of** merit and **all virtuous karma,** including the nature of all positive and negative karma, **are** nonexistent as **emptiness. Where are the** results and impressions of **the activities of benefit and harm** acquired through the **objective** body and mind? **Observe** all of **these** karmic **accumulations** and see **where** within the aspect of body and mind they **gather.** From without or within? If it were possible that there were a subject, still **no object** would **exist; so how can that be possible?**

3.2.2.1.2.2 Oneness

This has three parts:

1 Intrinsic nature of oneness
2 How this appears as either freedom or confusion
3 Failing to recognize oneness, falling prey to bondage and deviation

Second, the explanation of the intrinsic nature of oneness is as stated in the *Precious Treasury of the Fundamental Nature*:

> The oneness of awareness is the basis of all phenomena. It is said that, although appearing as many, this never wavers from oneness and reveals that self-occurring wisdom is the sole basis.

So, it is as taught. To reveal that all phenomena solely originate from the basic-space awareness of self-occurring wisdom, there are three sections: a general explanation on the necessity to know the intrinsic nature of oneness; a specific explanation on how, from that, the way this appears as either freedom or confusion; and by failing to recognize this, the way of falling prey to bondage and deviation.

3.2.2.1.2.2.1 Intrinsic Nature of Oneness

For the first, "As taught, all appearances are . . ." until ". . . crucial to gain confidence." **As taught, all appearances are** understood to be **empty by virtue of their own nature. Nevertheless, if** the way all phenomena of saṃsāra and enlightenment never depart from **the way of abiding** in the expanse of the sole, fundamental nature of the primordial ground **is not understood,** genuine **accomplishment will not occur. Hence, it is crucial to recognize** this **and gain confidence** with that.

3.2.2.1.2.2.2 How This Appears as Either Freedom or Confusion

This has two parts:

1 Revealing freedom as the intrinsic nature of the dharmakāya
2 The way confused appearances arise

Second, for the specific explanation concerning how either freedom or confusion occurs from the way that appears, there are two: revealing freedom as the intrinsic nature of the dharmakāya and the way confused appearances arise.

3.2.2.1.2.2.2.1 Revealing Freedom as the Intrinsic Nature of the Dharmakāya

For the first, ". . . the tathāgata of the primordial ground . . ." and so forth until ". . . the great . . ." states that, **when through** great **self-occurring prajñā** the meaning of **the essential nature of the tathāgata of the primordial ground is actualized** as pervasive evenness, **that is the great, lucid depth of the dharma-**

kāya. If posited from the perspective of its nature, no external appearance of its own manifest, dynamic strength exists.

3.2.2.1.2.2.2.2 The Way Confused Appearances Arise

For the second, there are two: a brief explanation based on analogies and an extensive one based on the meaning.

First, the root terma states, "When the dust of dimmed awareness . . ." until ". . . that leads to exhaustion." So, it is taught. **When the dust of** the delusion that fails to know self-nature **penetrates the eyes** of prajñā—like **dust mingling with the eyes**—through the sullying factor of connate **dimmed awareness, the basis of saṃsāra** comes about. Deluded concerning the genuine meaning of the fundamental nature **like the analogy of a blind man trying to travel,** one wanders in saṃsāra; and **that leads to exhaustion.**

Second, the root terma states, "From this self-fixation . . ." and so forth until ". . . asserted to be dual." So, it is. **From this** ignorance, the subtle conceptualization of **self-fixation** emerges. Due to that, the aspect of **the object of bondage arises as the universe, inhabitants, and all desirable phenomena. From** grasping to **"I", this** aggregation **of a body** that exists as the **self has emerged. This body** then **functions as the dwelling place and mental events as the owner. By** the individual functions of **this mind engaging with the five entranceways,** the distinct **consciousnesses,** such as visual and the rest, **emerge. Through the generation of** the **initial self-fixation,** first there is the consciousness that perceives **self and other. Grasping** to form **appears objectively,** and these **external objects are perpetually fixated upon by the subject** who nurtures **this** process—**the fixating mind.** "Hence, **I, Saraha, have proclaimed this!**" To sum this up, **both** previous and subsequent **concepts are asserted to be** the appearances of duality; and from them, all sentient beings become confused.

3.2.2.1.2.2.3 Failing to Recognize Oneness, Falling Prey to Bondage and Deviation

Third, the root terma states, "The emptiness of external appearances . . ." until ". . . look to see how few." So, it is. Not recognizing this process for what it is, deviation occurs based on establishing emptiness as autonomous. That means establishing **the emptiness of external** objective **appearances** as **empty by virtue of their nature** and the empty nature of **the inner mind** that **is empty unto itself. Those who determine** the basis of emptiness **by deviating into autonomy** such that these **two views can be united,** like joining a pillar with a support, will glean only a partial or limited understanding of emptiness. Hence, they **will not be** set **free from the great lasso of dualistic fixation that binds them.**

Once there is this fixation, even the mere thought of emptiness becomes the process of **external objective appearances posited in their own place, and the inner** recognition of **self is posited within itself. Meditation upon emptiness** then **amounts to** a state where **nothing between them** exists, **resembling a drop of water trapped within a block of ice.** This represents the fault of not knowing saṃsāra and enlightenment as a single pervasiveness of the basic space of phenomena. **Look to see how few attain liberation** due to this. Hence, that is the advice.

3.2.2.1.2.3 Openness

Third, openness is as the *Precious Treasury of the Fundamental Nature* states:

> Phenomenal existence and intangible bodhichitta—while never departing from the unelaborate nature—are without limit or center, are free from conception, and abide as the intrinsic nature of great pervasive openness.

So, it is. The fundamental nature of all phenomena is revealed as nonconceptual, free from expression, and without interruption. As evenness, this is all-pervasive openness.

The root terma states, "In this way, all dualistic . . ." and so forth until ". . . not knowing that." So, it is taught. **In this way, all dualistic confused appearances** of the mind have originated from **their** empty **nature** of basic space. **Aside from that,** they are **uncreated by anyone. Uncreated by the nature itself as well,** in the manner of **naturally self-arising** from within, this **self-appearance is pure within its own being. This** pervasive **play is** the **even**ness of liberation and the reason why **this** basic space of the **nature just as it is constitutes being the** intrinsic, **consummate nature of saṃsāra and enlightenment.** Unlike being posited in the category of root cause or contributing circumstance: **abiding within the uncontrived state—since there is no** newly emerging **gathering or dispersal** of events—**this** abiding nature **is primordially incapable of separation.**

3.2.2.1.2.4 Spontaneous Presence

Fourth, spontaneous presence is as stated in the *Precious Treasury of the Fundamental Nature*:

> The intrinsic nature of primordial, spontaneous presence is that no one has created it for this primordially abides. This bodhichitta is the source of everything, like a wish-fulfilling jewel, remaining as the origin of all that comprises saṃsāra and enlightenment.

Thus, it is as taught. Within this basic space of bodhichitta that abides primordially, uncreated by anyone, the manner in which all phenomena—including pure kāyas, wisdoms, and the like—are spontaneously present is revealed.

In the root terma, it states, ". . . awareness and lack of awareness . . ." until ". . . one must gain confidence . . ." So, it is taught. **Based on the distinction between awareness and lack of awareness, buddhas and sentient beings are referred to separately.** Hence, to see that the basis for the origin of all appearances as saṃsāra and enlightenment is primordially **uncreated, fully complete**, or spontaneously present: with **the eyes of prajñā**, one is able to determine that—within great self-abiding, self-occurring wisdom—phenomena are naturally **unborn and unceasing. Free from being either clear or obscured**, within this view there is separation from an object to **meditate** upon and **contrived** intellectual analysis. **This** [meditation] **transcends** all speech, **thought**, and expression as **self-occurring wisdom** that **is determined** within great natural abiding. Once attaining stability in this **original** buddha of spontaneous presence, **one must gain confidence** in knowing how **to personally encounter the indwelling buddha nature.**

Thus, it is taught that, in the practice of chöd, it is extremely crucial to encounter the view of the fundamental nature. In other chöd commentaries, it is mentioned that one must encounter the view of the Great Mother by resting in the meaning of emptiness. That is described as the category of the actual practice.

In Āryadeva's treatise on chöd, it states:

> If the meaning of the nondual pāramitā, free from the limits of virtue, nonvirtue, acceptance, rejection, hope, and fear is not realized, then—although compounded virtue is accrued—there will not be liberation in that life. Hence, not even a particle of any phenomena whether compounded, uncompounded, positive, or negative exists.

Thus, this demonstrates the need for realizing emptiness. The quote continues:

> The meaning of the prajñāpāramitā cannot be sought after elsewhere for it abides within oneself. The meaning of the great, natural clear light does not exist as substance or with characteristics.

Thus, recognize the nature of the way things abide. The quote continues:

> Free from all mental activity, recollections and thoughts are naturally dispelled.

Hence, this demonstrates the manner of meditating, as it goes on:

> Regarding outer, inner, gods, māras, saṃsāra, enlightenment, appearances, emptiness, and the like, the unmistaken, uncontrived wisdom intent of the buddha is free from dual appearances, for instance, like the space of the sky.

Thus, especially on this occasion, it is necessary to know that the objects of hope and fear, such as gods-māras and the rest, are the nonexistent illusion of emptiness. The meaning of the "fundamental nature being like space" is actually realized as either freedom from dual appearances or that which is concurrent with that. Revealed as the ultimate wisdom intent of buddha, the extent of actualizing the fundamental nature is clearly revealed.

Furthermore, in other authentic upadesha on chöd, it is mentioned:

> The genuine nature of phenomena must be actualized.

So, it is taught. The way to internalize this is that—by relying solely upon awareness—one searches for the mind, receives actual teaching involving pointing-out instructions on the mind's nature, and receives verbal teaching to determine the mind and experiential instructions for sustaining the mind's nature, and so forth. It is said that to recognize the mind's own nature, one must encounter this nature oneself.

Although there are these many categories of instructions, this presentation is based on the path of Mahāsandhi; so it is presented in harmony with that, although not in an elaborate way. If more elaboration is desired, one must study the tantra *Self-Occurring Fundamental Nature*. If time allows, I am hoping to elaborate upon this on another occasion. Here, by applying nonexistence, oneness, and so forth to the uncommon tradition of Mahāsandhi, one must review the root text *Precious Treasury of the Fundamental Nature* and commentaries that clearly illuminate the descriptions on the essential meaning of the three categories.[183]

According to the practice of chöd, if this is applied to the tradition of the *Gathering of Precious Qualities*, it states:

> There is no form, feeling, recognition, or mind; there is also not even a particle's worth of consciousness. Not abiding within any phenomena, the nonabiding is utilized. With total freedom, the bodhichitta of all the sugatas will be attained.

Thus, the way that this is nonexistent and such applies to what is revealed within the sūtras. The first two lines reveal how all phenomena are subsumed within the five aggregates, having no true, inherent existence. To say "this does not abide within any phenomena" means that so-called naturally existing appearances do not abide within any phenomena and, as such, are revealed as the sole, intrinsic nature of basic space. Reference to "utilizing the nonabiding without abiding in any phenomena" is the mode of openness. This [openness] has not fallen to the direction of any phenomena, nor does it abide with specific characteristics. Saying "the bodhichitta of all sugatas will be attained" reveals the way that there is the certain potential to attain this, or it indicates that these qualities are spontaneously present.

If extensively explained, the quote also states:

> When there are uncompounded and compounded virtuous and nonvirtuous phenomena thoroughly examined through prajñā, not even a particle's worth exists. In this world, that discovery is counted as the prajñāpāramitā; for just as space abides nowhere, everything is like that.

Thus, that is to search for the basis of designated labels. And the quote continues:

> The intrinsic nature of all phenomena is totally free from permanence. If a bodhisattva sees the prajñāpāramitā, there is no subject that sees nor are there any conceptual phenomena. That is to utilize the supreme prajñāpāramitā.

Thus, if there is true existence, that would not need to depend upon root causes and contributing circumstances because it would be a permanent nature that never changes. That is not the case. The intrinsic nature of phenomena is revealed to be completely pure and lacking any creator. Hence, permanent fixation upon material things is destroyed.

It states:

> Some may be inspired to respectfully adorn the body of a bodhisattva with sandalwood powder, while others may prefer to throw lava on the bodhisattva's head, yet both acts affect the bodhisattva equally. May the mind of equanimity be developed.

In order to develop equanimity in the face of both benefit and harm, one must know that the fault of benefit versus harm is naturally nonexistent. That is the approach that attacks the faults of benefit and harm.

It states:

> A bodhisattva who engages in this conduct will think, "I have no expectation to enlighten according to the Buddha's prediction, nor do I fear

> that there is nothing to attain." That kind of conduct is the practice of the sugatas' prajñā.

So, this reveals there is no hope toward the object, namely, the Buddha's prediction of enlightenment, nor is there disappointment or fear of no protection. This collapses the false cave of hope and fear. It states:

> This reveals the single nature of phenomena.

The quote continues:

> Wherever there is no form or feeling and recognition is nonexistent, there exists no consciousness and also no mind. The one who knows that phenomena are unborn emptiness practices the supreme prajñāpāramitā. Just as the prajñāpāramitā is empty of characteristics, knowing that the characteristics of all phenomena are similar is to fully comprehend that phenomena are empty and lacking characteristics. That conduct becomes the practice of the sugatas' prajñā.

Thus, form and so forth are naturally nonexistent. Phenomena are unborn emptiness, and emptiness itself is free from characteristics. Understanding singularity is oneness.

It states:

> Form is not seen; feeling as well is not. Recognition cannot be seen, and the mind will not be seen either. The consciousness and mental events are what sees the true nature of phenomena. This is spoken by the Tathāgata. When sentient beings verbally express that they see space, whatever space was seen is what should be examined. The Tathāgata revealed that that is how the true nature of phenomena is also seen. Whoever sees in this way has seen the nature of phenomena.

Thus, by seeing the fundamental nature in this way, it is taught that the nature of all phenomena is seen. Phenomena are open like the sky as the quote continues:

> Like a monarch who gathers the wealth of his kingdom without even venturing out to his capital or surrounding districts, a bodhisattva who realizes the nature of phenomena without venturing anywhere gathers all qualities that exist on the ground of buddha.

Thus, through analogy, it can be known that the mode of the nature of phenomena is revealed to be free from going and coming, as well as being the spontaneously present source for the possibility of all qualities to arise.

Mahāsandhi is the pinnacle of all views and the field of experience for those of sharp faculty. Nevertheless, given that it is the upadesha method for directly encountering the fundamental nature, no matter who practices this—whether learned, dull, or neutral—it will always be easy to comprehend. The great omniscient Fifth Dalai Lama[a] has mentioned:

> The tradition of Nāgārjuna that upholds the pinnacle of the Madhyamaka view is difficult for those who lack philosophical training in the scriptures to comprehend. These days, the so-called Mahāmudrā is a mere state of mental abiding and not the actual Mahāmudrā view. Wisdom that emerges from empowerment and the two stages is asserted by authentic scholars to be the Mahāmudrā. Padmasambhava, Vimālāmitra,[b] Berotsana,[c] and others followed the definitive tradition of Mahāsandhi that stems from the Kāma and Terma. Whoever practices this—whether learned, dull, or neutral—will find it easy to implement, extremely meaningful, and magically profound with its secret key points.

For example, although Mipham Gonpo[d,184] was very elderly, Berotsana led him to awakening in that lifetime. There are many astonishing histories of realization and liberation occurring simultaneously from both India and Tibet.

In the tantra *Reverberation of Sound*, it states:

> In the definitive Heart Essence tradition, it matters not whether faculties are sharp or dull.

So, since this reveals how the definitive Heart Essence tradition subsumes the crucial meaning of Mahāsandhi, that is why it states that there is no difference between faculties being sharp or dull.

These days, except for being a method to still the mind, the so-called Mahāmudrā has been rendered inauthentic. Authentic wisdom emerges from empowerment, generation, and completion stages. Although this statement is a well-known criticism of the Kagyüpas, this well-intended advice is directed toward those who do not know the key points and attempt to still the mind by

[a] Lozang Gyatso (*blo bzang rgya mtsho*), 1617-1682

[b] *bi ma la mi tra*, Drimed Shenyen (*dri med bshes gnyen*)

[c] *be ro tsa na*

[d] *mi pham mgon po*

merely accumulating the coming and going of thoughts while believing that is the Mahāmudrā. The honorable Kagyüpa tradition of the great Mahāmudrā is extremely profound in that it includes the practices of channels, bindus, and so forth that can be combined either with the union of connate awareness and the amulet seal[185] or not.

Machig has taught that the tradition of chöd is connected to the practice of the Mahāmudrā. To expand upon that: by striking the key points through the inner condition of channels and bindus and the outer condition of reliance upon the consort, it is taught that this applies to the four seals [i.e., mahāmudrās] that are the stages of descriptions for generating exaltation.

In the aural lineage, it states:

> My tradition of chöd, this great mahāmudrā, is the dawning of the sun of the great vehicle that dispels the darkness of saṃsāra.
>
> To expand upon this, the mahāmudrā is explained as follows. From the onset, all phenomena that comprise the universe and inhabitants lack even a hair's worth of true existence. This inherently empty way of abiding is called "the mahāmudrā of phenomena". For a practitioner who is able to comprehend this by familiarizing with and fully incorporating emptiness, potential with the wheels of technique [i.e., *trülkhor*[a]] involving channels, winds, and bindus is achieved. In reliance upon a genuine consort, exaltation is taken as the path. When the body's vitality is increased through great rapture, this is called "the mahāmudrā of karma". A practitioner on this level will practice in the manner of concealing all qualities, while never separating from the outer samaya substances. That is called "the mahāmudrā of samaya". This exceptional exaltation, blazing as the heat of emptiness free from desire, is called "the mahāmudrā of bliss-emptiness". A practitioner such as this is free from all obscurations of passions, so all appearances arise as empty and free of inherent existence like dreams or magic. That is called "the mahāmudrā of empty clarity".
>
> The mahāmudrā I am presently explaining is as follows. *Chag* [i.e., first syllable of the term] means all objective appearances. *Gya*, or seal, means that these objective appearances ultimately—from their own perspective—lack even a hair tip's worth of true existence. Hence, that is "the mahāmudrā of empty appearances". Some said that both these appearances and their inherent empty nature are united, so that is "the mahāmudrā of theory". When a practitioner realizes the selflessness of

[a] *'khrul 'khor*

> both outer and inner by the strength of the wind-mind entering the central channel within the exceptional experience of unimpeded lucid bliss, the three times of past, present, and future are fully acknowledged. By the magnificence of the increasing light rays of knowing all phenomena, teaching, debating, and composing become effortless. Many beings are tamed through the light rays of these resultant qualities. Possessing this great ability to benefit others is called "the mahāmudrā of chöd". O Fortunate Ones, a profound and crucial point such as this level of chöd is unique from other spiritual traditions.

So, it is taught. When she [i.e., Machig] refers to the chöd that is presently being described, that is mahāmudrā according to Sūtra. The quote continues:

> Some ordinary individuals claim that the characteristic of the existing mind is mere clarity that is both vivid and opaque. If that deluded state of mind is termed "mahāmudrā", then that mahāmudrā would even fail to know that the characteristic of mind is nonexistent. Such a deluded, misdirected spiritual direction cannot be relied upon and must be completely rejected.

So, it is taught.

The Tertön King of Dharma himself has repeatedly mentioned that, without knowing the meaning of emptiness, to just meditate by focusing on ordinary mind does not even approach the direction of the view of Mahāsandhi or lead in the direction of liberation. Hence, both instructions merge here as one.

The quote continues:

> If it is known that all phenomena are the single nature of mind, then the core of all phenomena is identified. My spiritual tradition is this great Madhyamaka. My dharma is also the resultant Mahāsandhi in that the consummation of all that appears as saṃsāra and enlightenment is perfected within the single nature of the mind. Once the manner in which this is perfected as the single nature of mind is understood, then the meaning of all phenomena will be the Mahāsandhi. All disciples must come to know this.

Thus, this illuminates the key points of the three—the Madhyamaka, Mahāmudrā, and Mahāsandhi—merging as one.

These days, aside from some learned Gelukpas who are expert with philosophical tenets, most scholars in that tradition regard the Nyingma's Mahāsandhi tradition as a cult. Regardless of that, when the mahāsiddha of Lhodrag, Leykyi

Dorje,[a,186] made a direct request for teachings from the Lord of the Secrets, he responded by giving him the *Supreme Ambrosial Medicine*[b] text that Leykyi Dorje then entrusted to the second buddha, Tsongkhapa. It is well-known that in that text the meaning of the Mahāsandhi is accurately illuminated, and it was taken as a primary oral instruction. It is said that Vajrapāṇi was Leykyi Dorje's supreme meditation deity, Lobzang Trakpa [i.e., Tsongkhapa] his supreme disciple, and that this response in the form of teaching from Vajrapāṇi was his supreme dharma. The lord [Tsongkhapa] himself said that the speech of the Lord of Secrets [i.e., Vajrapāṇi], *Ambrosia*, had satisfied his mind, and it was as though he had actually arrived in the pure land of Alakāvatī.[c] These are all actual accounts that occurred.

Nevertheless, without analyzing this, many of them [i.e., Gelukpa scholars] have carelessly engaged in the karma of abandoning the dharma.[187] This is like how the maṇḍala of the sun's rays light up the land for all beings, yet the eyes of the owl still remain afflicted by darkness. Alas! Having to suffer karmic consequences, these faults based on dishonesty make me wonder just how this could possibly occur, and my mind becomes heavy with sorrow.

Not only that, when the Lord himself [i.e., Je Tsongkhapa] was residing in Ölkha Gyasog,[d] he had a vision of Ārya Mañjushrī and received a brief teaching on the view. Even within that teaching, it mentions:

> All phenomena of saṃsāra and enlightenment were previously unseen; and having never been seen, they are free from limitations like space. Objective appearances are nonexistent like a flower appearing in the sky. The fixations of the mind have never been discovered by any of the sugatas. Space and awareness are one, uncreated by anyone like a barren woman's son. Any teachings that describe this are the path of the victorious ones.

Thus, as taught, this clearly reveals the crucial points of Mahāsandhi's view and meditation. I will not elaborate upon this any further at this time.

Those who think they are of sharp faculty and pretend to have realized the view actually fall into the category of attachment and aversion. They should try to protect themselves from falling further into the dangerous precipice of negative conduct by coming to know how all doctrines coexist without contradiction. It would be best if they did not ruin or waste the ultimate aspirations of the great master Tsongkhapa.

[a] *las kyi rdo rje*
[b] *düdtsi'i men chog* (*bdud rtsi'i sman mchog*)
[c] Changlo Chan (*lcang lo chan*); Vajrapāṇi's pure land
[d] *'ol kha rgya sog*

Without inherent existence, there is freedom from eternalism; spontaneously present, there is no tendency toward nihilism. This openness does not even abide in the middle. The intrinsic nature of oneness is the nature of all phenomena. Nonexistent and oneness are the fundamental nature of the Madhyamaka. Sealed by openness is the definitive Mahāmudrā. Spontaneous presence itself is the mode of the Mahāsandhi. The genuine key point of their wisdom intent is subsumed here.

> Being nonexistent and free from elaboration is the objective of the view.
> Oneness and openness are the meaning of uncontrived meditation.
> Spontaneous presence is the method for actualizing the result.
> How amazing it is that, in whatever way they are explained, there is no contradiction.

These are the verses that summarize the section.

3.2.2.2 Maintaining the Continuity of Practice in Fear-Provoking Environments

This has six parts:

1 Advice to fully complete the practice in fear-provoking places
2 Recognizing a fear-provoking environment
3 Instructions for arriving upon the key point
4 Mode of diligence applied with the four feasts
5 Samaya incorporated while wandering
6 The way of visualizing the subsequent suppression

Second, in order to encounter self-nature in the face of circumstances, the practice of wandering in fear-provoking environments while engaging in fearless conduct is applied. To sustain the main practice, there are six parts: once embarking, advice on the need to fully complete the practice of wandering in fear-provoking places; recognizing what a fear-provoking environment is; instructions for arriving upon the key point; the mode of diligence applied with the four feasts that present the aggregates as the feasts; the samaya that is incorporated while wandering; and the way of visualizing the subsequent suppression.

3.2.2.2.1 Advice to Fully Complete the Practice in Fear-Provoking Places

First, the root terma states, "In this way, . . . the fundamental nature . . ." until ". . . be reached." So, it is taught. **In this way, those practitioners who have**

encountered the fundamental nature in a qualified way **possess fully endowed karma and** the power of pure **prayers.** When the **circumstances** of the upheavals of gods-māras, magical deceptions, terrifying incidents, and so forth occur: **in order** for the strength of awareness and the **crucial points** of the innate nature to be directly **encountered, one must wander in the fear-provoking locales** and the like in an **indeterminate** manner. In doing so, the practice of chöd is engaged so as **to attack the faults of hope, fear, and** compulsory **fixation with objects.**

It is said:[188]

> The environment is a fear-provoking place, the view is that there are no gods or māras, meditation is without fixation or distraction, and conduct directly confronts things as one taste. The path taken is the offering of the aggregates to be partaken of; the experience is to be free from cherishing and fixation; the aggregates are offered up as flesh and blood; the consideration is to feel happy, to grow sick, and be joyful to die; and the inspiration for practice is suffering and illness. This is the way to meditate.

The meaning of all of this is as follows. Except for being the magical display of one's mind, gods-māras and so forth are not otherwise, which is the meaning of the view that is without gods and māras. Meditating upon the meaning of the fundamental nature without distraction is the point of being free from fixation or distraction. Discarding any expectations for this life, the eight worldly concerns are equalized; and all happiness and suffering in saṃsāra are balanced as the nature of suffering. Cherishing others more than self equalizes self and others. Equalizing all beings as one's parents [and the preceding] are all the aspects of methods for the practice. Equalizing all phenomena as the manifestation of nonexistent emptiness is the aspect of prajñā. All of these involve the purpose of equalizing [as one taste]. Through the strength of this, no matter what unbearable external phenomena come to one, suppressing through the splendor of the antidote is the meaning of directly confronting.

To express the generosity of the aggregates with the bodhichitta of equal taste is the meaning of expressing the generosity of one's aggregates as food to partake of. When giving one's body as food free from cherishing or fixation, one is able to express generosity through the flesh and blood free from hesitation; so illness and death become companions on the path of awakening. Hence, one is happy to fall ill and joyful to die in a natural way. That is the meaning according to the speech of the learned masters. Like this, all conceptual passions will be **self-liberated** in their own place. **May** the king of results, the **supreme state of the heruka** of self-awareness, **be reached** in that very lifetime!

3.2.2.2.2 Recognizing a Fear-Provoking Environment

Second, for recognizing a fear-provoking environment, there are two: the frightening place and, along with that, the categories of remote places. First, in the *Gathering of Precious Qualities*, it states:

> To observe isolated, worldly locales where inhabitants suffer from famine and disease and don the armor of fearlessness free from trepidation, one must remain diligent in pursuing this until the future life is reached. With this in mind, there must not be even a particle's worth of depression or sorrow.

Thus, reference to a "worldly locale" means a place inhabited by frightening spirits, such as māras and demonic forces. In such a place, one must remain without fear, paranoia, or any dependency upon anxiety. "Donning armor" refers to the initial suppression[a] and the suppression that follows. Saying "until the future life" really means as long as saṃsāra exists; but nevertheless, here, that depends upon the context. In this case, that means either a longer or shorter duration of time and pertains to the time of departing for the fear-provoking place, as well as extensively completing the actual practice all the way until the visualization for the later suppression[b] is performed. From the perspective of "diligence" and knowing all aspects of this practice, one must not succumb to a sorrowful, depressed state of mind. Hence, this explains the meaning.

In the *Sampuṭa Tantra*,[c] it states:

> At mountains and lower valleys; on the banks of rivers and in dense forests; in remote places such as these; on the peaks and faces of mountains; in pleasing lotus gardens, pools, and at the shores of the ocean; in the depths of the forests and base of the mountains; in originally pure charnel grounds that the night-dwelling *mamos*[d] call home—completely abandoning all fear or paranoia, an experienced practitioner must meditate there.

So, as taught, most of this is easy to understand. Reference to "an originally pure charnel ground" means that previously, during the earlier evolution of the world,

[a] *nga non* (*snga gnon*)
[b] *chi non* (*phyi gnon*)
[c] *sam bu ti gyü* (*sam bu ti rgyud*) or *sam bu tra, shrīsamputatilaka*
[d] *ma mo*; wrathful female deities

these places came to be known as "the eight charnel grounds". The "home of mamos" refers to any of the places where the classes of ḍākinīs abide.

In Āryadeva's treatise on chöd, it states:

> At glaciers and frightening charnel grounds, towns and cities, caves, and sacred remote places, one must meditate in nonduality.

Thus, it is. Machig has said:

> Places with uncertain shapes and geomancy, that are wrathful, joyful, depressing, and terrifying are all the magical displays of emptiness. In short, one must sleep in the most terrifying place of all.

Thus, to analyze the geomancy of crags and the like, they are varied and uncertain. It is said that a place that brings up a multitude of concepts and emotions, such as joy and depression, is considered to be a fear-provoking environment.

The best of these environments include the great charnel grounds, such as Shītavana[a] and the others. The great sacred grounds are Devīkoṭa, Himādri [i.e., Mt. Kailash],[b,189] and so forth. The great monasteries are Sera, Drepung, and Ganden;[c] the great environments such as the palaces of kings or rulers; and the great mountains like Tang-lha, Magyal,[d] and others. Great rivers are the Gaṅgā and the Machu [i.e., Yellow River].[e] Great lakes are Manasarovar, Kokonor,[f] and others. If unable to go to any of these, go to whatever kind of charnel ground can be found.

[One should practice] on a great plain or at the center of an empty plain; at the banks of rivers and lakes; in forests or under a single standing tree; where three water sources converge; in the midst of a crossroads; on a mountain where haughty local spirits reside; in a rocky mountain cave or at a mountain water spring; at a mountain with peaks that resemble a pitched parasol or victory banner, with mouth and teeth like a conch or a vase, shoulders like a fish, and between what appears to resemble the mouth and claws of a wild animal. In brief, one should think that the strength of the wild animal is present in those places or that the energy of the animals exists there. Doing so, then plant yourself there. Initially, one must feel fear, followed by severing the one who is afraid. Finally,

[a] Silwa Tsal (*bsil ba'i tshal*); Cool Grove

[b] Tsa'ri (*tsa' ri*) and Gangri Tisi or Gangkar Tisi (*gangs ri ti si* or *gangs dkar ti si*), aka Himāvat

[c] *se ra*, *'bras spung*, and *dga' ldan*

[d] *thang lha* and *rma rgyal*

[e] *gang ga'* and *rma chu*

[f] Ma Dröpa and Trishog Gyalmo (*ma dros pa* and *khri shog rgyal mo*)

unable to discover the one who is afraid and the object of fear, departing for a fear-provoking environment will be adventitious. If not, it is acceptable to rely upon a gentle, sacred place in which to practice.

The locale where the gods-māras abide is that yakṣhas and malignant spirits abide at snow mountains; male-female yakṣhas reside in the crags; spirits of the hunt[a] and female māras[b] abide in the glaciers. At the grassy slopes of the hills the ancestral māras[c] abide. At dark and eerie rock formations and canyons, māras abide. At steep cliffs, nāgas and spirits of the chase reside. At mountain boulders, the local earth spirits and the great powerful mountain spirit malicious nāgas[d] reside appearing as turtles, scorpions, spiders, and even yaks.

In north-facing caves, the animal-headed spirits[e] reside. At crags that form a covering of shade, at steep ravines, and in earth holes, the child-inflicting māras, female māras, female vow breaking māras,[f] and others reside. On vast plains in the darkness of night, the great gods-māras abide; and in the daytime, they move to smaller plains. The powerful nonhuman spirits stay in water pools, and the earth spirits hover around the creeks. The nāginīs live at springs; and at the nine source springs, the untouchable nāgas abide. At seven source springs, the ṛṣhi classes of nāgas reside; at five source springs, the noble classes of nāgas; at three source springs, the royal nāgas; and at a single source spring, the ordinary classes of nāgas remain.

At sources of water where the water swirls as a pool without sunlight, nāgas reside. At single-standing trees and at the shores of lakes where there are swamps and standing water, the powerful nonhuman spirits reside. At naturally formed reservoirs that resemble water held in the palm of the hand, the earth lords abide. At great boulders that resemble tigers, snakes, birds, pigs, turtles, and the like, the earth lords and the four classes of powerful nonhuman spirits reside. At rocky jagged mountain peaks that look like tall people standing, at collapsed crags, crags that resemble the face of a monkey, and at narrow passageways with rivers running through them, the spirits of the hunt abide.

At abandoned homesteads, abandoned nomad encampments, and intersections of marketplaces, the male-female preta spirits reside.[g] At charnel grounds, dharma-teaching venues, and places where warriors have been slain in battle, the mamos, lords of death,[h] and the lords of life all reside. At old temples and

[a] *tsen* (*btsan*)
[b] *men* (*sman*)
[c] *ma sang* (*ma sangs*)
[d] *lu nyen* (*klu gnyan*)
[e] *dri tsen* (*gri btsan*)
[f] *te'u rang* (*the'u rang*), *senmo* (*bsen mo*), and *dam simo* (*dam sri mo*)
[g] *drewo dremo* (*gre bo gre mo*)
[h] *shinje* (*gshin rje*)

especially at run-down stūpas or old houses and buildings, the kingly and local custodial spirits[a] reside. Burial grounds and where animals are corralled, empty homes and riverbanks, in front of stūpas, where narrow pathways run, where others have undergone great hardship, and cremation sites as well are all places where many nonhuman spirits congregate.

Not knowing where a frightening or wrathful place is found and if one runs naked: then wherever a sensation of terror wells up under one's skin, that is a suitable place to practice because either a sense of fear or joy will emerge, making that place unlike any other. Then, it is certain that many signs will become apparent, such as indications with trees, water, and the rocks. The originally pure charnel grounds that are the dwelling places of the mamos of the twenty-four sacred grounds are where the wisdom, as well as the worldly, ḍākas and ḍākinīs reside.

In short, it is necessary to remain in charnel grounds, temples, and such places that induce concepts based on fear and panic to the point where one may even pass out. Without that, there is nothing to sever. In the *Profound Meaning of the Essence of Mind*,[b,190] it states:

> At charnel grounds, empty valleys, temples, single-standing trees, abandoned houses, and the like and in places where the mind is filled with fearful anxiety and trepidation is where one must spend the night.

Thus, it is as taught.

Second are the general enumerations concerning the corresponding things to be known about isolated environments. From the teachings of Lord Kaldan Gyatso,[c] it is stated:

> O Solitary Meditators, who hope to wander in isolated places, listen here to this song with a mind of delight. Not being able to decide yourself, it is rare to find a true friend who will encourage you in this way.
>
> If you feel inspired to retreat to a remote mountain—then if you can remain at the upper slopes of a mountain concealed by misty clouds where a glacial cave awaits you, happiness in this and the future lives will ensue. If you feel inspired to retreat to a remote forest—if you rely upon a place such as that in the midst of a densely growing grove of trees, a cool abode awaits you where joyful delight will ensue.

[a] *kor dag pe kar* (*dkor bdag pe kar*)
[b] *zab don tük nying* (*zab don thugs snying*); Drükchen Pema Karpo
[c] *rje skal ldan rgya mthso*; Rekong mahāsiddha from Amdo

> If you feel inspired to retreat to a remote snow mountain—somewhere on the slopes of the whiteness, by relying upon a practice cave where you can remain alone in solitude, then virtuous activities will increase. If you are inspired to retreat to a remote highland plain—in the meadows of brilliantly blooming flowers, a delightful grassy green shelter awaits you. In a place such as that, true natural happiness will prevail.
>
> If you are inspired to retreat to a remote rocky mountain where vultures' nests abound and with natural astonishing caves marking its face—in a place such as that, awareness will awaken. If you are inspired to retreat to a remote crag in the midst of its colored strips and piles of sliding rocks—in a place such as that within a cave where there are no distractions, whatever comes to mind will be yours.
>
> If you are inspired to retreat in a glacier mountain area—below the sheets of shale, a stone structure where a simple beggar stays will await you. In a place such as that, freedom is natural. If you are inspired to enjoy companionship in these remote places—while observing your friends, the birds and animals that abound, in an instant their sounds captivate you with pleasure; for to rely on such friends is a source of great joy. If you are inspired to go to a remote lake, where slapping waves wash its shores and waters create gentle repetitive sounds—in a place such as that, there is constant delight.
>
> If you aspire to partake of the food of isolation—the provisions are the nettles and fruits that grow here and there; when savored, their flavor is most delicious. To rely upon such sustenance, how astonishing indeed! If you aspire to listen to this song of isolation, a song that benefits your stream of mind—then it is always necessary to keep these habits strong; for to rely upon a song such as this is a great marvel itself!

So, it is as taught.

The person departing for these remote locations should train their mind through the practices of the preliminaries, such as the four thoughts that turn the mind. According to this tradition, the potential of visualization with the meditation and recitation practice of the three-kāya [ḍākinīs] is induced; and in reliance upon guru yoga, the blessings will enter the mind stream. Especially, having perfectly received the teachings for the practice of severance, one will have no confusion concerning the descriptions and mode of wandering in fear-provoking places. Once possessing familiarity and realization with the key points of the view and meditation, at least there must then be some degree of experience.

3.2.2.2.3 Instructions for Arriving Upon the Key Point

This has seven parts:

1 Visualization for the initial suppression
2 Motivation and description of how to embark
3 Visualization for the intermediate suppression
4 Signs of upheavals
5 How to recognize the four māras
6 Repetitive stages of upheavals and how to sever them
7 How to induce upheavals

Third, for the instructions that lead to the key points, there are seven sections: the visualization for the initial suppression; the motivation and description of how to embark; the visualization for the intermediate suppression; the stages of the signs of upheavals; accompanying that, how to recognize the four māras; revealing the repetitive stages of upheavals and how to sever them; and the instructions on how to induce upheavals that are not emerging.

First, Machig has said:

> If the initial suppression is lacking, that will be like exposing plans to a ruthless enemy.

So, as taught, **first** if **the visualization for the initial suppression is** not engaged and the enemies comprehend this, the gods-māras will disperse and escape to another location. There will then be no chance for upheavals to occur; and if so, the adventitious circumstances for the practice of chöd will not be present. These are the reasons why the initial suppression is so necessary.

To expand upon that, a beginner is not encouraged to focus solely on **wandering in fear-invoking environments.** Even though they are initially embarking, they should rely upon a place that is pleasing and attractive, suitable to their needs and comfortable to rest and spend the night. The first step in wandering is the initial charnel ground of one's bed, so that is where the yogin is sent to **remain for three days just inside the threshold of the door. Then** one **ventures out**side while still remaining within the fence[191] or **as far as sight allows** [from the retreat place].[192] Then, one should venture out farther to a pleasing, gentle, and auspicious location. If the practitioner has some potential, then he or she should go to a more rugged, displeasing environment. Whatever the case, if the person is unable to enter an actual **fear-provoking locale**, then they should convince themselves that the place where they are **sleeping** is that kind of place and begin the practice of chöd. Alternatively, they could collect dirt, pebbles, and rocks from a fear-provoking place and deposit them under the bed. Having then initiated the practice of chöd, it is taught that upheavals will occur in that place.

When a practitioner does wander in frightening places, at first he or she must request that their house and things be guarded. To do so, exit from the threshold and blow the *kangling*[a,193] three times and say, "O gods-māras of phenomenal existence, gather here now!" Repeating this three times, one thinks that they suddenly amass and are rewarded by a mentally imagined, abundant display of flesh, blood, and desirable things. Call out to them saying, "Gods-māras of phenomenal existence and eight classes of nonhuman spirits, watch over my home, wealth, and possessions. Stand guard until I return, and do not allow these to fall into the hands of the enemies and obstructers. Guard these without allowing them to be lost. Through samaya, I command you to watch over them. If these are lost to enemies, thieves, or criminals, I swear I will reduce all of you into a pile of leprosy-infested flesh piled like a mountain, a swirling and churning ocean of leprosy-infested blood, fat, and widow's hair until you have been fully obliterated." Hence, they are incited to action.

3.2.2.2.3.1 Visualization for the Initial Suppression

Then the actual initial suppression involves two: specifically, being sent to the mountains and other locations and the important general visualization.

First, [the yogi] takes seven steps forward and visualizes as follows. With awareness that the great emptiness of the trichiliocosm universe pervades manifest appearances, [the yogi] knows everything to be the mere aspect of the mind's phenomena. Saṃsāra and enlightenment are not other than the magical manifestation of the mind. Since the gods-māras and sentient beings are the conceptual appearances of one's mind, then all conceptualizations are gathered into this motionless expanse. Thinking one must sustain this nature of the ground free from confusion is the initial suppression to send forth.

Then, **for [embarking to] the mountains, visualize that there is a conjoined meteorite wheel circling to the right and left. This reduces Mt. Meru into dust that is then dispersed, leaving the gods-māras without basis or support. They become terrified and quiver with fear. Then imagine that surrounding them is a canopy enclosure of blazing vajras of fire. Surrounding that is a fence of fire, and encircling that is a chain of dark-colored humans holding weapons. Outside of that is a fence composed of wrathful Tröma ḍākinīs; and outside of that, fences of water and wind encircle. Think there is nowhere to escape, nor is there any way to break out of this.** Another option is that these six fences become linked vajras that fully encircle and that the female-wrathful ḍākinī

[a] *rkang gling*

fence is facing inward. The dark men holding weapons, the black wind, and the vajra water with pounding waves are also there. I heard this second option through oral transmission, so one may choose either preference.

If one is **embarking for crags, then visualize that meteorite arrows descend upon the crags to completely annihilate, reduce to dust, and scatter everything like piles of sand.** Imagine that happens three times. **Think that the gods-māras that reside there are separated from their places, supports, and protection and are forced to take up residence upon the piles of sand. Imagine they are then deposited into the previously visualized enclosure with no place to escape to or means to do so. For the forests, think there are lightning bolts of fire shooting into the forest to incinerate and scatter everything. The gods-māras residing there become helpless, and imagine that they are bound within an enclosure from which they can never break free.**

For the valleys, think that a great rainstorm of stones descends; and all aspects of the earth, ground, rocks, and mountains vanish like salt melting into water. All gods-māras are left behind without place or support. Think that, like before, they are encircled by the six fences with no way to escape. For plains, imagine that a rainstorm of molten lava descends, and the entire ground becomes a blazing bank of fire. All gods-māras are encircled like before and left with no place or support. For lakes and rivers, a blazing fire storm of vajra meteorites descends and turns into molten boiling lava, causing all gods-māras to experience unbearable heat. They are forced out the other side of the mountain, and the fire blazes behind them like an inferno. All gods-māras are reduced to a humble position with no place to stay, encircled by enclosures imagined **just as before.**

For departure to uninhabited houses and towns, sometimes imagine that a rain shower of molten lava descends to burn and destroy everything. Upon the ashes, the gods-māras remain without support like before. For the charnel grounds, imagine that blazing vajra meteorites radiate and descend upon that place like lightning bolts. The earth is destroyed to become like a heap of ash or molten lava. The gods-māras are left without support, and the encircling fences are meditated upon as before.

Second, **the visualization that is of general importance is** as follows. **From the heart of oneself as the wisdom ḍākinī Tröma Nagmo, magnificent light rays radiate to completely fill the empty trichiliocosm world systems. Everything then melts into light, and all gods-māras are pulled inward from the outer perimeter with no means of escape. Arriving at the fear-provoking places, they are forced into black, blazing tents made of meteorite vajras. All of their strength and powers are restricted, and their haughty splendor is subdued. Think that they remain there shivering with fear. This visualization can apply to any of the aforementioned scenarios. Then** as the light gets

dimmer and dimmer, the force of that gathers into the gods-māras. **No matter what direction they try to escape, they are** caught in the expanse of that light, **unable to break free. Visualizing this will become familiar as a matter of course.**[194] **Given that this is the first suppression through splendor involving messengers, it is the visualization called "overcoming through the great command".**

In addition, the concise visualization for wandering is as follows. Think that nine-pronged meteorite vajras blazing with wisdom fire radiate and descend into the fear-provoking place. If it is a mountain, then the mountain is completely destroyed and flattened. If a crag or a house, it is dispersed. If a forest of trees, they are burned beyond recognition. If a plain or a pathway, it collapses and is dispersed. If a lake or a river, it evaporates. After that, meditate that blazing, erect meteorite vajras appear as solid, stable, heavy, and firm. All gods-māras are separated from their places of support and left without protection or guide. Suppressed by the vajra fence surrounding them, they are unable to escape anywhere. Surrounding that is a fire fence, and around that is a fence of razor-sharp black wind. Behind that are dark-colored men forming a human-chain fence so that all of their [i.e., the gods-māras] powers, strengths, and splendor are subdued. Think that they are stuck there, shivering with fear. Thus, as taught that is the general exceptional visualization.

3.2.2.2.3.2 Motivation and Description of How to Embark

Second, for the description of the motivation and the manner of embarking, it states in the *Jataka Tales*:

> Not for competition or hoping for fame, nor for higher rebirth, a lofty position, nor supreme personal exaltation—rather this has been composed to establish the welfare of others.

Thus, as it states, rather than for the purpose of this life such as competing with others, name, fame, and status nor for the happiness of the future life such as higher rebirth, a lofty position, or one's own exaltation such as that of the shrāvakas and pratyekas, the motivation is to attain perfect awakening for the benefit of others.

Without a competitive mind, the wish to become famous, or due to bravery, pride, or the drive to attack the gods-māras and summon them as one's retinue to derive wealth and respect from others, it is taught that one should embark while meditating upon giving up this life's needs through repulsion toward saṃsāra and with faith and respect for the guru and dharma friends. Possessing the awakened mind of love and compassion for all beings, especially the gods-māras, the body is visualized as a corpse, the mind as the one carrying the corpse, and the fear-provoking places as the charnel grounds.

Furthermore, Jetsun Milarepa said:

> I pray to the Lord Guru, grant blessings that this beggar may be sustained in an isolated environment, a place where my relatives cannot hear that I am happy and my enemies cannot hear that I am sad—if I am able to die in such a solitary place, then this yogi's goal will be accomplished.
>
> In a place where friends will never know I have died and siblings will never know I am sick—if I am able to die in such a solitary place, then this yogi's goal will be accomplished.
>
> In a place where the humans will not notice when I die and the vultures will fail to glimpse my rotten corpse—if I am able to die in such a solitary place, then this yogi's goal will be accomplished.
>
> Where the ants suck at my rotten flesh and guts and the worms devour my veins and ligaments—if I am able to die in such a solitary place, then this yogi's goal will be accomplished.
>
> Where footprints at the threshold are no more and the trail of blood inside goes unseen—if I am able to die in such a solitary place, then this yogi's goal will be accomplished.
>
> Where no one will come to claim this corpse and when death arrives there will be no one to wail—if I am able to die in such a solitary place, then this yogi's goal will be accomplished.
>
> Where no one asks of my whereabouts and no place of association can be identified—if I am able to die in such a solitary place, then this yogi's goal will be accomplished.
>
> In an empty remote cave where no humans reside, this beggar offers his prayer for death. May this be accomplished for the welfare of others; and if so, my goals will have been met.

Hence, just as taught, if one holds the definitive motivation to sever all ties to this life, then that is the extent of a superior chöd practitioner. If that is not possible, one must still embark by genuinely aspiring toward that aim.

In order to embark, there are four ways to do so. First, with the confident demeanor of a ḍāka or ḍākinī and holding the vajra pride of oneself as Tröma Nagmo, the yogin imagines that he or she departs in the confident manner of a hero or heroine. Similar to herding goats and sheep in a hail storm, the gods-māras of the environment are powerlessly pursued and summoned in front.

Embarking with the dance of a ḍākinī is that, as far as one can see, one repeatedly imagines that all gods-māras existing there dissolve into one's body. Then embark in the manner of the ḍākinī dance. Embarking like a slithering black snake is to imagine that gods-māras, such as the nāgas, earth spirits, and their environments, are forced to the front of oneself from the right and left sides of the path, like paper carried by the wind. Think that all of them are delivered to the fear-provoking environment. Embark by weaving to the right and left like a slithering snake.

As Machig said:

> The three modes of embarking must be known.

So, it is as taught.

The [fourth] way of embarking with the confidence of the view is as follows. By gazing at all aspects of the path—above, below, and each direction—gods-māras become bound, lose their strength, and are unable to maneuver. Like when one tries to escape in a nightmare, they are trapped and unable to break free. Imagine they are quivering with terror. Embark with the confidence of the view like a haughty snow lion poised on the slopes of a snow mountain. Other modes of embarking exist but have not been included here.

3.2.2.2.3.3 Visualization for the Intermediate Suppression

This has three parts:

1 Activity of suppression
2 The dance
3 Piercing with the *phurba*

Third, the visualization for the intermediate suppression is as follows. Machig has said:

> If the intermediate suppression does not take place, it is like a warrior dropping his weapon.

As taught, for this, there are three: the activity of suppression, the dance, and piercing with the *phurba*.[a]

[a] *phur pa*; pronounced "*pürba*"

3.2.2.2.3.3.1 Activity of Suppression

First,[195] **at the moment one arrives at the fear-provoking place, the embodiment of all gods-māras who dwell in this hair-raising place appears as a huge, foreboding dark man. Visualizing oneself as the wisdom ḍākinī Tröma Nagmo, take him by the right leg and circle him above your head three times. Think that the gods-māras of the three realms gather and dissolve into him. Then striking him on the ground three times, think that his power and strength based on the three poisons is conquered. Throw him out in a sprawled position, and visualize that you manifest upon him as the maṇḍala of Tröma.** Then **perform the *Suppression through Splendor*.**[a]

In other texts, peaceful and wrathful renditions of this are described; but according to this profound cycle of teachings, this is drawn from the two sources called *Lion's Roar*[b] and the *Garland of Blossoming Lotuses*.[c,196] From that, if the pure-vision *Suppression through Splendor* called *Ḍākinīs Laughter* is performed, the key points are subsumed; and it is easy to follow.

Hence, in order to do so, first through the recitation method of the syllable *pha*, all conceptual thought patterns based on the three poisons are gathered. Then, through the recitation syllable of prajñā, *tra*, imagine that everything is dispersed within the space of selflessness. Then recite *phet* [i.e., *pha* and *tra* combined]. These are oral instructions.

Reciting the liturgy[197] "**the trichiliocosm universe**" and so forth, imagine as follows. Other texts apply this to the way of suppressing self, the place, and the gods-māras through splendor. That would be as follows. Reciting "**the trichiliocosm . . .**" until "**. . . are subsumed**" points out the suppression of the place. From "**the self-manifestation of wisdom . . .**" until "**. . . all gods-māras**" points out the suppression of the gods-māras. Saying "**. . . everything disperses into the fundamental nature of selflessness**" indicates the suppression of self.

If described according to the way of visualizing the recitation: then from one's heart as Tröma, the natural strength of dharmadhātu wisdom appears as countless, inconceivable blue-black Buddha Ḍākinīs manifesting in the central direction. By merely striking with the bloody, flayed human skins held in their right hands, all coarse passions in the minds of the gods-māras are destroyed. Their left hands hold human thigh-bone trumpets that, when blown, resound like the roar of a white lioness. With that, all gods-māras that are the self-manifestation of delusion descend from the middle of the sky like falling meteorites. As though hooking fish, they are drawn out from below the earth; and from intermittent

[a] *wang düd zil non* (*dbang sdud zil gnon*)
[b] *senge'i ngo ro* (*senge'i ngo ro*)
[c] *pema gyepa'i chun chang* (*padma rgyas pa'i chun 'phyang*)

space, they are summoned before you like paper blown by the wind. Think that they powerlessly gather and take the oath to accomplish whatever you require of them as they shiver and shake. Then think that they completely dissolve into the previously subjugated dark man under your seat like snowflakes falling on a hot stone.

Likewise, from oneself as Tröma, visualize that countless manifestations of the natural strength of mirrorlike wisdom as white Vajra Ḍākinīs manifest and summon all gods-māras that are the self-manifestation of the passion of anger from the eastern direction of space and so forth. Likewise, from oneself as Tröma, visualize that countless manifestations of the natural strength of evenness wisdom as golden Ratna Ḍākinīs manifest and summon all gods-māras that are the self-manifestation of the passion of pride from the southern direction of space and so forth.

Likewise, from oneself as Tröma, visualize that countless manifestations of the natural strength of discerning wisdom as red Pema Ḍākinīs manifest and summon all gods-māras that are the self-manifestation of the passion of desire from the western direction of space and so forth. From oneself as Tröma, visualize that countless manifestations of the natural strength of all-accomplishing wisdom as green Karma Ḍākinīs manifest and summon all gods-māras that are the self-manifestation of the passion of jealousy from the northern direction of space and so forth.

These ḍākinīs of the five families have smaller forms, and their colors match their family. In their right hands, they hold flayed human skins and, in the left, thigh-bone trumpets. They capture all gods-māras from their individual directions, like falcons pursuing smaller birds, as the gods-māras emerge from intermittent space, like paper blown in the wind. From below the earth, like dirt piles blowing in the wind, they are helplessly snared and summoned as previously mentioned.

Generally, the key points of the *Suppression through Splendor* are mentioned by Machig:

> The activity of suppression is like this. The outer quelling of the gods-māras is when freedom from attachment and fixation occurs. The inner quelling of illness and demonic forces is when freedom from the mind of benefit and harm occurs. The secret quelling of concepts is when freedom from the focal point of good versus bad occurs. The nature-as-it-is quelling of everything is when the mind is severed from its base.

So, it is.

When free from attachment to the body and external material things, the gods-māras will be overcome. When it is understood that the mind as the source of everything has no true existence from its base: like one-hundred rivers converging under a single bridge, everything will then be able to be quelled and overcome. "Overcoming" actually means that the yogin himself or herself is no longer overcome by anything and gains the freedom of personal mastery.

3.2.2.2.3.3.2 The Dance

Second, the dance is as follows.[198] **Having quelled all gods-māras with the activity ḍākinīs,** the **gods-māras dissolve into the negative, dark man under the cushion. Having previously overcome him, think that now a great sun disk suppresses his heart; and it is there that the wisdom ḍākas and ḍākinīs of basic space dance, while one imagines that he moans and groans.**

[The liturgy for the dance follows.] Reciting "***Phet phet phet!*** . . . confidence with vajra sovereignty . . ." until ". . . collapse in the expanse," with the first *phet*, the proliferation of initial concepts is fully severed. With the second, one's nature is recognized; and with the third, the depth of the view is cultivated.

The wisdom nature that actualizes the meaning of great basic space free from limitations is the sovereign of saṃsāra and enlightenment. This is undefeated by material fixation being invincible like a vajra. [Recite,] "**I am the hero who possesses confidence with vajra sovereignty**, victorious over the three realms of existence. I understand that the object **of expectation**, buddha, **and** the object of **disappointment**, saṃsāra, are the equal, single nature of basic space. **Through the fearless conduct of the great, equal taste**, I subdue the pitfall of believing in self by actualizing the great wisdom that realizes selflessness. Through the strength of this fearless conduct, I arise as the embodiment of **the three-kāya maṇḍalas of the victors. From** the **basic space** of phenomena, I **arise** as the dharmakāya Samantabhadrī, the sambhogakāya Vajravarāhī, and the nirmāṇakāya Tröma Nagmo in group formations with individual colors, faces, and arms."

Holding to the **self of** the person and phenomena, **the dualistic view of** an outer, inner, and secret self is **the rudra** that steals the life of liberation. To **conquer** that state is the reason for **the dance.** When inner self-fixation is destroyed, then the outer self-form of that appearing as the confused phenomena of gods-māras is also destroyed. The way of dancing upon self-fixation is as Guru Dharmarakshita[a] said:

> Now the karmic weapons encircle my head; in the manner of wrath, they circle three times above my head. With the gaping mouth of the two truths, the bulging eyes of upāya and prajñā, and the bared fangs of

[a] *dharma rakshi ta*

> the four strengths, I strike at the enemy. Even if a king of Mantra who strikes at the enemy has no freedom from saṃsāra, he will strike upon the head of the enemy of conception, pounding relentlessly, to destroy the hearts of the enemies, obstructers, and death messengers with the sound of *maraya*.
>
> Wandering while wielding karmic weapons, this lord of self-cherishing is an unruly force. Summon this samaya breaker, who brings ruin upon self and others. Wrathful Yamāntaka, summon him now! Strike and pierce the heart of the enemy of self! Beat upon the head of the enemy of conception, and destroy the hearts of the enemies, obstructers, and messengers of death!

So, it is as taught. Again reciting ***phet***, visualize the **guru** as the **embodiment of the Three Roots**—guru, yidam, and ḍākinī—or that the nature is the guru and the aspect appears as the sole mother, Tröma Nagmo. Holding a joined-skull ḍāmaru in the right hand, she lifts this aloft into space where the sound of its beating overcomes the three realms. In her left hand, she rings a lovely small silver bell held high in space, ringing to suppress the three planes of existence. Her two legs are in the dancing posture, and she is adorned with all charnel-ground accouterments. The brilliance of her aura is overwhelming to behold. Visualize that she resides in the expanse of blazing wisdom fire.

While dancing upon the heart of the rudra that is the embodiment of duality, the self-manifestation of [Tröma's] wisdom appears as the blue **Buddha Ḍākinīs of the central direction**, who **turn their wisdom intent toward** the misguided rudra and arrive to the **dance** in order to tame him. Their intertwined fingers indicate that **the great wisdom of basic space** is free from all limitations and directions, and they dance in an eight- or six-faceted configuration in the manner of invocation. By their **dancing** in that way, think that in the minds of **the gods-māras** the coarse passions arising from **delusion are** destroyed, like dry grass **stomped upon** repeatedly until turning into dust.

Without separating from the key point of the visualization and the physical gyrations, face toward the east while reciting the eight verses of vajra laughter with a melodious tune. Then, while saying *chem chem*, pound and jump with the right foot into the center of the configuration in the gesture of dance. Saying ***hung hung***, place the left foot toward the east in the dancing posture. Likewise, saying ***ha ha***, jump with the right foot facing toward the southern direction. Saying ***he he***, place the left foot toward the west. Saying ***ho ho***, jump with the right foot facing to the northern direction. Saying ***phet***, jump upon the palm of the rudra's right hand, facing east, by landing on the left foot. Remain there in the dancing posture.

Once again dancing upon the heart of the rudra of duality, the self-manifestation of wisdom appears as white **Vajra Ḍākinīs of the east**, yellow **Ratna Ḍākinīs of the south**, red **Pema Ḍākinīs of the west**, and green **Karma Ḍākinīs of the north.**[199] All of them dance in the circle of **mirrorlike wisdom.** Similarly, [upon the rudra's] left hand to the south, left leg to the west, right leg to the north, in that order, the **dances of evenness, discerning wisdom**, and **all-accomplishing wisdom** are performed in square, half-moon, and triangular configurations so as to destroy **anger, pride, desire**, and **jealousy.** The visualization of the dancing postures is the same as previously mentioned.

Then, while reciting ***phet***, jump into the center [of the configuration] with the right leg. In the manner of walking, proceed toward the east to **invoke the ḍākinīs of the space of the dharmakāya, the powerful sambhogakāya ḍākinīs** of space activity, and **the wisdom ḍākinīs of the nirmāṇakāya** so as **to tame the demonic nāgas of delusion, the female māras of desire**, and the **kingly demonic forces of hatred.**[200] From the space of phenomena, they all arise as the rupakāya and **dance in the lively gestures of the spontaneously present three kāyas.** Think that they **destroy the three poisons** and eighty-four thousand **passions** that arise [from the three], as well as the cognitive obscurations that give rise to the **gods-māras of confusion** and the coarse and subtle passions in their mind streams. **Imagine that** all mental perceptions of **the** three **realms of saṃsāra collapse in the expanse of the transcendent nature** of phenomena, great emptiness. With the first ***phet***, the three poisons collapse into the expanse of the three kāyas. With the second ***phet***, the five poisons collapse in the expanse of the five wisdoms. With the third ***phet***, the eighty-four thousand passions collapse in the expanse of the eighty-four thousand categories of the doctrine.

3.2.2.2.3.3.3 Piercing with the Phurba

Third, piercing with the phurba is as follows. **Then, the head and extremities of the rudra suppressed under the seat are pierced by the five wisdom phurbas. Think that** [the rudra] **is unable to move or get up**, and apply this to the process of **pitching the tent. Reciting "*Phet phet phet!*** The white crystal female skeleton . . ." until ". . . becomes nonexistent" is as the liturgy states. Saying *phet* reminds one of the wisdom intent of the three kāyas.

From the heart of oneself as Tröma, the self-manifestation of mirrorlike wisdom arises as a **white crystal female skeleton blazing with light.** She **holds a white conch** spherical **phurba**[201] that is the nature of **great compassion** and **pierces** the right hands of **the gods-māras**, who are the embodiment **of fiery hatred.** Think they are staked between crossed vajra mountains of wind. Likewise, **the** self-radiance of evenness wisdom appears as a **golden female skeleton.** Her hands **hold a** four-faceted **great golden phurba**[202] that is the nature **of great**

love and **pierces** the left hands **of the gods-māras**, whose **pride** is as lofty as a mountain. The self-manifestation of discerning wisdom appears as a **copper-colored female skeleton.** She **holds a** half-moon **coral phurba** that is the nature **of great joy, piercing the** left legs of the **gods-māras**, whose **desire** is as **tumultuous** as a river. The self-manifestation of all-accomplishing wisdom appears as a **black-iron female skeleton.** She **holds a** triangular-shaped **turquoise phurba** of **great equanimity, piercing the** right leg of the **gods-māras**, whose **jealousy** is as **turbulent** as the wind. The self-manifestation of the wisdom of basic space appears as a **great female skeleton with bared fangs.** She **holds a** six-faceted **human-bone phurba** of **great bodhichitta, piercing the** joints of the **gods-māras**, whose **deluded ignorance** is as dark as the night.

Again, think that, by **piercing with the phurba of** the self-radiance of **the five wisdoms** into **the head and limbs of the rudra emanation of duality** and embodiment of **ignorance** concerning the fundamental nature of the ground, [the rudra] **loses all power and potential to get up or move at all.** Meditate that, in the center of this rudra's body, one's dwelling place is a celestial palace with all characteristics and attributes fully complete. All ḍākas and ḍākinīs gather there where the desirable objects fall down like rain.

3.2.2.2.3.4 Signs of Upheavals

This has three parts:

1 Extensive explanation
2 Synopsis of the key points
3 Joining this with the biography of the Buddha

Fourth is an explanation of the stages of signs and upheavals that will occur. In the commentary itself, there are somewhat extensive explanations concerning upheavals. The indications of the extent of the successful conclusion [of upheavals] will be briefly mentioned later on. Here, when the upheavals and magical deceptions occur: by diligently applying the visualizations for the four feasts and so forth, the extent of the signs of conclusion will then occur. That is why they are taught in that order. Nevertheless, if taught together, it seems somewhat easier to comprehend. In order to explain this in that way, here there are the stages of the upheavals that are actually mentioned in the commentary itself and the supplementary descriptions of the upheavals taken from other sources.

First, retaining the key points of the visualizations [and] **having pitched the tent, the practitioner lays upon his or her back and visualizes as follows. One's body becomes huge, solid, [and] heavy, the size of a valley. Under that, the gods-māras are suppressed and wailing in despair. Once again, all oath-bound gods-māras of phenomenal existence are summoned, like paper blown in the** wind, so that they powerlessly dissolve into the gods-māras under the bed. Thinking in this way, recite the following, "*Eh eh!* Until this eon collapses or existence is emptied, I will not move from this place. I will not move or stray from here. I will stay here and sleep. *Phet phet phet!*" Thus, reciting [this three times], think that the buddhas, bodhisattvas, gurus, yidams, and ḍākinīs all gather in the sky above in a mass of radiant light. Remain confident within a state of undistracted nonfixation.

From time to time, clarify the visualization and commitment while continuing to remain there. Then, it is certain that, in the best scenario, actual upheavals will occur; in the mediocre case, there will be visions; and at least, in the dreams. These upheavals are both tangible and intangible. The tangible upheavals are based on appearances of things, such as wild animals, yetis, humans, wealth, and the like. The intangible are upheavals from the formless, nonhuman eight classes, such as the gods and māras. Furthermore, earthquakes, houses collapsing, mountains crashing down, rock slides, tsunamis, hail storms, lightning storms, lights, and the occurrence of loud, marching noises from soldiers and various nonhumans will all occur. In dreams, there will be fighting with many people suppressing you, attacking you, and cannibals trying to chase you. Also, one may think that parasites enter the body through the mouth, remain there, and that zombies approach you. In brief, it is possible that a variety of ominous upheavals will occur in indeterminate ways.

Concerning the upheavals for the body, goose bumps will rise up, muscles will quiver, and sharp and subtle pain will be felt, as well as swelling and sudden outbreaks such as rashes. The body will shake and jerk. Speech-based upheavals include lamenting and crying out in despair, erratic sentences, sighing, panting, difficulty breathing, and so forth that will occur in indeterminate ways. Mental upheavals include fear, blank astonishment, loss of confidence in the visualization or meditation, the inability to sit, the wish to escape, and the powerless pursuit of hope and fear, terror, and paranoia. In brief, the mind will become abnormal so that all feelings based on joy, sorrow, hope, and fear are the upheavals. Know that, when all of these dawn simultaneously upon the three doors, that is a great upheaval. Two of these signs indicate an intermediate upheaval; and only one of them, a lesser upheaval.

Second, a supplementary description of the upheavals taken from other sources is as stated in the *Gathering of Precious Qualities*:

> At that time, the māras will be disturbed. [When the practitioner] feels desperate, sad, depressed, and vulnerable, it is then that they will see how strong this bodhisattva's mind really is. In order to frighten

> the practitioner, they will display fire in all directions and send weapons like shooting stars. At that time, this learned one must firm up his intention and hold the view of the supreme prajñāpāramitā throughout the day and night. Then, both body and mind will become free like a bird in the sky. How could it be possible for māras to then pose harm?

Thus, this clearly reveals the upheavals and the signs of their completion.

When one practices the prajñāpāramitā, all māras become disturbed and uncomfortable. The māras think that, through their powers, it is hard to suppress this practitioner; but if [the bodhisattva] weakens through sorrow brought on by them, he or she will then succumb to mental sadness and physical torment. Through this method, the bodhisattva's mind will fill with doubt. In order to encourage this doubt, they [i.e., the gods-māras] will create fire in all directions, send weapons like shooting stars, and display various magical deceptions. These are the upheavals of magical deceptions on the path. When this happens, the learned must maintain a perfectly pure intention, such as great compassion and bodhichitta, by holding the view of the prajñāpāramitā of great emptiness throughout the day and night. This can be understood according to what was previously described in the overview of this text about who qualifies as a chöd practitioner. At that time, both body and mind of the bodhisattva are free like a bird in flight. In dependence upon those magical deceptions, realization is enhanced and the body is freed from the traps of conceptuality, such as illness, demonic-force possession, self-cherishing, and so forth. That indicates the extent of the severance.

All those categories of negative māras, including their hordes of followers, are unable to cause harm, so the pacification of those magical deceptions is the extent of the completion. Furthermore, the source of this information comes from the chapters that discuss māras within the extensive, intermediate, and concise versions of the Great Mother.

In Āryadeva's treatise on chöd, it states:

> When one meditates upon the nondual prajñāpāramitā, it is unbearable for the worldly gods and māras. Hence, they will create various magical deceptions that occur directly, are enticing, and manifest in dreams.

That refers to the upheavals. The quote continues:

> Once severed, the extent of this severance brings separation from fear.

That refers to the extent to of the severance. The quote continues:

> The extent of completion is that the magical deceptions are naturally pacified.

That refers to the extent of the completion.

In the *Profound Meaning of the Essence of Mind*, it states:

> When resting in the meaning of the dharmatā, it is then that the māras will perform various magical deceptions.

Thus, and the unequalled, great Gyaltangpa has said:

> When one's mind is fully immersed in dharma and the key points of virtue are engaged, that is when the outer, inner, and secret upheavals will rise up. Outer upheavals are obvious to the faculties as this includes any magical deceptions of māras. Inner upheavals occur when the body's elements are disturbed, such as any type of illness. Secret upheavals occur to the awareness nature of mind, including elements gathering to bring about wind imbalance in the heart and stirring up states of panic and paranoia.

Thus, it is as taught.

For this, there are three: an extensive explanation, a synopsis of the key points, and joining this with the biography of the Buddha.

3.2.2.2.3.4.1 Extensive Explanation

First, Machig has said:

> O Children, listen here! Upheavals and magical deceptions are not the same; they are distinct. The extent of the completion and the extent of the severance are not the same; they too are dissimilar. First, the signs of an upheaval will come, then the deception, the extent of completion, and the extent of the severance. Without confusing the order, the continuity of this will be definitive.
>
> To expand upon this, these [indications] will occur during both occasions when the practitioner offers the aggregates as the feast and relies upon a fear-provoking environment.
>
> The key points of the practice include both relative and genuine truth. Following the internalization of the upadesha cycle that unites these

two, the fear-provoking environment will be considered to be either pleasing or joyful, or whatever was described about the environment according to that section of the commentary. In either case, one engages in any of the visualizations, such as peaceful, enriching, powerful, wrathful, or extremely wrathful.

With a single-pointed intention to benefit others as the basis for the motivation, the practice of inseparable compassion-emptiness will strike through the samādhi that exorcises with peaceful means and so forth. In doing so, all elementals that abide in the fear-provoking places are thereafter unable to bear the splendor of that practitioner's power of the dharmatā, and they become disturbed. In order to bring obstacles to the practitioner's practice, those elementals will invoke their companions to gather together with them. That will cause the practitioner's body and mind to become uncomfortable and perceptions hazy and unstable. That is referred to as "the initial upheaval".

It is then that the elementals will gather their forces and, in whatever way they are capable of, demonstrate multitudes of magical deceptions. They will cause obstacles to the practitioner's samādhi and bring different types of harm upon him or her. Then, the practitioner will experience various ominous signs in four ways, namely, those that are obvious, in visions, as splendid perceptions, or in dreams. All of those are called "magical deceptions".

Although those elementals have created these magical deceptions: when these no longer affect the practitioner and the elementals become incapable of tolerating the potential of the dharmatā, their own powers will then exhaust. That is the time they will pay allegiance to the practitioner and begin to follow whatever is commanded of them. Accomplishing whatever is asked, they will assist him or her to produce some degree of worldly siddhi based upon needs; and they will take their place in the practitioner's retinue. Then, the practitioner will feel inspired, and there will be various excellent indications that the early signs of qualities are developing. That is called "the extent of the completion".

Furthermore, the elementals' courage will snap and their previous intensity will become tranquil. Their agitated minds will be weak, and they will begin to listen to the practitioner. From that time onward, they will promise to stop harming others, to befriend practitioners, and they themselves will aspire to enter the path of liberation. By persevering in virtuous activities and through the strength of those elementals definitively guarding the direction of virtue, the practitioner will receive certain signs that those elementals will attain awakening on the path to liberation. Then, the practitioner will be able to sever the neurotic mind from the root, such as the arising of various visions, be it positive or negative conceptuality. With the onset of actualizing the perfectly pure view of the meaning of the fundamental nature of selflessness, the truth of the dharmatā, the self-purpose of the dharmakāya will then be accomplished. Once one possesses this fully endowed potential, the purpose of others will be fulfilled in that many sentient beings, including the elementals and their retinues, will be led to the state of liberation. That is called "the extent of the severance".

The order of these four—the upheavals, magical deceptions, extent of the completion, and extent of the severance—is certain to occur as described, without confusion. Nevertheless, there are varied capacities of individuals, such as their degrees of diligence; knowledge as to how to induce visualizations or not; capacity to sustain the visualizations, clarify them, to practice in a balanced way, to discern what to visualize or not, to generally know the methods for inducing the upadesha or not, understand or not; the differences between the peaceful and wrathful; differences based on the circumstance of illness or not; the degree of obscurations; the degree of previous accumulations and purifications; the degree of courage; the difference between faculties being superior, middling, or inferior; and the varieties of different categories. Due to these many distinctions, it is hard to imagine that the stages of upheavals and so forth will always definitively occur in precise order.

Given that these four, such as the upheavals, may occasionally occur out of order, it is then possible that a magical deception could happen before having an upheaval. In addition, without the extent of completion, the extent of the severance could occur. Without any upheavals or the experience of the extent of completion, it is possible that both magical deceptions and the extent of the severance could occur. Once the upheavals and the extent of completion have happened, it is possible that the magical deceptions and extent of severance may not occur at all. Without either upheavals or magical deceptions, both extents of completion and severance could occur; and without the extents of completion or severance, it is possible for only the upheavals and magical deceptions to emerge. Individual upheavals may occur, and the remaining three may not even come at all. It is also the case that all four may occur at once or all together in a single day. For some, this may occur after three, five, seven, eleven, twelve, or twenty-one days; one month; two months; one year; or sixty years. For some, even after an entire lifetime, all four stages will remain incomplete.

If the order of these four is not congruent, that will depend upon the individual as well as the earth spirits and whether they are more prone to being peaceful or wrathful. Nevertheless, when the individual tames his or her mind: as they approach the goal of liberation, they will gain the potential to give up this life and have exceptional faith in my doctrine as well as the potential to internalize the meaning of all phenomena. Becoming expert in the order of all upadesha instructions and by perfectly practicing, it is certain that the aforementioned order for the four upheavals will then occur.

Concerning that, "the extent of severance" means to know that all outer objective appearances are unstable and lack true existence. When one realizes this lack of true existence, all objective appearances will naturally arise as empty reflections. That is the extent of the severance of external objective appearances. By severing inner self-fixation from the root and actualizing the truth of the empty fundamental nature of selflessness, it is known that the subject himself will naturally arise as an empty reflection. To actualize the meaning of nonexistence to be like magic is the inner extent of the severance. To say both object and subject individually appear and lack true, inherent existence and when there is familiarity with that—while knowing that they are inseparably one taste within absolute truth, like a water moon—is the nondual extent of severance. This also occurs when outer and inner are united.

Likewise, through the strength of the practitioner's view of the dharmatā: externally, the unruly minds of the gods-māras of the fear-provoking environment are pacified and tamed. Becoming members of one's retinue, they are led to the path of liberation and placed in the unsurpassed state. Severing the continuity of their rebirth in saṃsāra is "the extent of the severance of the gods-māras of luring in the fear-provoking place". Having severed in their own place all mental elaborations, such as the mind itself and its events that are negative and positive based on the person's inner pride, the meaning of the mind-transcending dharmatā free from all elaborate events is fully actualized.

When one purifies the passion of ignorance—including the five poisons —by the increasing light rays of the five states of wisdom awareness, deluded darkness in the minds of the beings to be tamed will be dispelled. Limitless benefit for the welfare of others will ensue. It is then that all māras will arise as positive, and all obstacles will help to enhance qualities. Negative circumstances will encourage fully endowed desirable qualities to manifest. Like arriving in a land of jewels where no ordinary stones exist, whatever thoughts this practitioner has, whatever they may say, and whatever they do will only be the causes for benefiting others.

Hence, it is necessary to become like a wish-fulfilling jewel that can fulfill the hopes and needs of living beings. That is also said to be "the inner extent of severance for a prideful individual". Also, the objects of pride that are the gods-māras to be tamed have never existed, from primordial time. Their natures are empty. Even the prideful person himself is by nature empty and has primordially never existed. Both are inherently empty. Although within absolute truth, this nature connately abides as an inseparable single taste based on the relative; mere appearances are distinctly apparent, yet never truly exist as they appear. With this in mind, all things can be known as intrinsically undifferentiated, like reflections in a mirror. When one attains mastery with what this means, that is called "the extent of nondual severance". This level of the extent of severance is so hard to achieve, there may not even be one among one-hundred chöd practitioners who do so. For an ordinary chöd practitioner, this will not occur.

At first, it is difficult to even recognize an upheaval. Hence, it is important to emphasize the key points of the methods in practice so as to not be overcome by sloth and distraction, but rather to take mindfulness as one's companion. The magical deceptions and the extent of the completion are such that they will occur to everyone according to their faculties as long as they claim to be a practitioner of chöd. It is difficult for authentic magical deceptions and specific, exceptional extents of completion to even come about. That is why—even with the deceptions—it is necessary to perfect the individual outer, inner, and secret aspects. Once the general common signs do occur, that will be followed by the uncommon signs. It becomes necessary to know and understand the differences between these magical deceptions.

Even for the extent of completion, it is important to identify the inner distinctions of both the common and uncommon aspects. O Fortunate Disciples, understand the characteristics of the upheavals, magical deceptions, extent of completion, and extent of severance in these ways and practice accordingly.

Thus, it is taught.

Here, an upheaval means that, when an upheaval is occurring, that is the beginning of the process of a magical deception; whereas the difference between an upheaval or not is that, when an actual magical deception is occurring, it is no longer an upheaval. Moreover, once an upheaval is occurring, the gods-māras are unable to keep their ground. These two hold the same meaning [i.e., upheaval and magical deception]. Otherwise, the so-called magical deception occurs when the gods-māras display varieties of deceptions, and that is also the process of an upheaval. The so-called upheaval is that this deception incites fear and paranoia in the body and mind of the practitioner. These distinctions are acceptable.

For the extent of the completion, there are two: the common and the uncommon. Many teachings on the first category exist; and among them, Machig has said:

> At dawn, or sunrise, when wearing clean white clothes, flying in space, climbing upward, after death when the body is reduced to a skeleton, or while circumambulating a stūpa, forging a river, building a bridge—are all indications of the purification of negativity as the extent of the completion.

Thus, and the quote continues:

> The burning of a city, the destruction of a mortar and brick building, the exodus of ordained sangha, and so forth are the extent of the completion of all demonic-force possession.

Thus and:

> In supreme vessels such as *kapalas*,[a] the food of ambrosia is offered—human flesh, human brains, and organs—as well as the five types of jewels, horses, elephants, and the like. These offerings are the extent of the completion of the suppression.

And:

> Prostrating, circumambulating, receiving vows, respectfully listening to dharma discourse, offering body and soul, listening to the command, carrying this out, accomplishing enlightened deeds, and receiving

[a] *ka pa la*; skull cup

> offering and praise from the gods and humans are the extent of the completion of attaining the sacred.

So, it is taught. To expand on this, these signs that occur as a result of the purification of negativities, obstructions, and so forth are posited as the extent of the completion. Likewise, the extent of the completion of attaining supreme siddhis is when, in visions or dreams, the following occurs.

The quote continues:

> Although devouring the delicious flesh of a fresh corpse that is vital, healthy, and fatty but still not feeling satisfied; although devouring the warm and bloody brains of a scalped head but still not feeling gratified, being presented with a fresh skull filled with blood and a dry skull with ambrosia of the one-hundred tastes; drinking everything without anything remaining; presenting a jeweled cup or vase while saying "this is the nectar of the gods" and drinking that—saying they are ḍākas and ḍākinīs, some of the ḍākinīs then present the white and red bodhichitta nectar or feces and urine, and it is partaken of without hesitation. Sitting on piled corpses without hesitation; departing for the supreme peak of Mt. Meru; clearly seeing the three continents without impediment; from a naked girl with bulging red eyes adorned with bone ornaments, receiving churning, bubbling red blood in a skull vessel and drinking this down without a moment's hesitation—arresting all concepts, nonconceptual wisdom expands. Through that, all knowable things are realized, and the truth of the dharmatā is directly witnessed. When these signs occur, the extent of the completion of supreme siddhi is indicated.

Thus, it is taught.

When these signs and indications of attaining supreme siddhi occur, they are the extent of completion; and when actually realized, that becomes the extent of the severance. The reason is because it is taught that the extent of the severance indicates the conclusion of the extent of the completion.

> Concerning the uncommon and supreme extent of the completion, there are four: the outer, inner, secret, and nature as it is. It is said that the indications of the outer extent of the completion involve having no trepidation in the face of whatever concepts based on the four māras occur and no matter what is projected. This especially pertains to the gods-māras of phenomenal existence devouring one's head or ripping out one's heart.

So, it is. The quote continues:

> It is said that the inner extent of completion occurs when heart-wind imbalances, mental agitation, and afflictions are pacified or when there is no sad or adverse reaction following praise or insult.

So, it is. And:

> Seeing the guru as a living buddha, compassion welling forth uncontrollably, emptiness dawning without attempting to recall it, confidence in the law of karma—all situations occurring within great wisdom and absolute resultant qualities being achieved are said to be the signs of the supreme extent of the completion. In brief, for all of this, to be without pride is said to be the secret extent of completion.

So, it is. And:

> Upheavals, luring, and the extent of completion—these three—must be known to be the product of one's mind. The mind itself is ineffable and perfectly pure, as everything is the evenness of the dharmakāya. That is the nature-as-it-is extent of the completion.

Thus, it is taught, that is to see the fundamental nature of mind.

To expand upon this, as mentioned previously, the extent of the severance is more exalted than the extent of the completion. Machig clearly illuminates this:

> Some texts describe that these two hold the same meaning and that a single name is randomly used when describing the process. Others will reverse the order of this meaning and hold the extent of completion as supreme. Noticing these descriptions, it seems the distinctions should be analyzed.

As just stated, both the secret and nature-as-it-is extents of completion are similar when actually realized. Based on that, it is never necessary to misinterpret their order. If these two seem differentiated, then—just as it was mentioned that this is the supreme extent of the completion—it is acceptable to say that this emerges from visions.

Machig has mentioned that, when the extent of the severance occurs, the first bhūmi has been attained; yet, nevertheless, it seems that here she is emphasizing what is principal in comparison. Moreover, it is important to note that it is said that the extent of upheavals resembles the extent of completion and the extent of completion also resembles the extent of the upheavals. The quote continues:

> Receiving blood and food from a negative person; donning armor; receiving rock sugar, onions, turnips, salt, spice, sugar, and varieties of undesirable food; and being accompanied by a well-adorned female companion who gives you various provisions out of deception are the signs of the extent of upheavals that are disguised as the extent of the completion instead.

So, and:

> Horned *dzo*[203] and *yak* charging you, wild animals biting, and being pierced by weapons such as knifes and bleeding are all signs of the extent of completion.

Thus, when the extent of completion seems to be the extent of upheavals, it is like that.

Similarly, in Karma Chagmed's cycle of texts known as the *Secret Teaching of Accomplishing Enlightened Mind*[a] in the section that includes a chöd commentary to enhance realization, it states:

> The extent of completion that resembles magical deceptions occurs when one is being struck by others with horns; bitten by fangs; physically wounded; mourning the death of a close relative; experiencing the collapse or burning down of one's house; losing the most valued wealth; losing possessions to enemies; eating poison; eating oneself; being devoured by garuḍas, snakes, or fish without being masticated; one's body scattering like dust particles; devouring one's own heart; or receiving the internal organs of others. These are all the extent of the completion disguised as magical deceptions.
>
> Magical deceptions that resemble the extent of completion occur when one experiences many maidens from various cultures showing respect; diverse yakṣhas wearing black- and blue-colored hats showing you veneration, inviting you somewhere, trying to accompany you, or offering cushions that are blue- or black-colored; oneself wearing blue clothes or black armor; offering black wool cushions; receiving salt, spice, uncooked, and cooked meat; eating garlic and vegetables or

[a] *sang tük drüb sang tri kyi kor bok don chöd tri* (*gsangs thugs sgrub gsang khrid kyi skor bogs 'don gcod khrid*); Karma Chagmed

> wheat; eating a medicinal root that is an antidote against poison or a maroon-colored wild mountain herb [in the autumn] called *mon-bu*; black molasses; wearing new red clothing; and arriving in a garden of red flowers. These are all signs of deceptions.

So, it is taught. Receiving those edibles and the display of respect seem to be similar to signs that indicate the extent of completion, but most signs involving classes of inedible food are actually deceptive signs; and hence, they are upheavals. Being stricken and pierced by weapons are similar to upheavals since they involve harm; however, these are signs of having purified negative obscurations. Losing cherished wealth to the enemy and having one's heart ripped out are signs of losing self-cherishing, so they are the extent of completion.

If it can be determined that someone actually comes to make offerings, then that is the extent of severance. If foods and wealth are involved without being faulted, it is said that the severance was unsuccessful. These signs depend upon the ups and downs of interdependent origination. Although an excellent sign in the dreams may occur: if the mind is uneasy, then the severance was unsuccessful. If in dreams and signs there are mere indications that occur and the mind is still comfortable with that, then it is a sign of severance.

Especially, the key points that are unwavering like a nail are that, if you are unable to examine whether a sign is either good or bad and if then upon personal retrospect it is found that this sign is mingled with pride and elation, attachment toward respect and gain, or that the mind becomes disturbed while devotion and pure view weaken, then those are not signs of the extent of completion. Conversely, when the mind becomes peaceful and tame, faith and pure view increase; compassion, samādhi, and realization are enhanced; and if there is some elation, when the mind is naturally calm and able to contain that with no hope for fame or reputation based on arrogance, those are the signs of the extent of completion. Hence, it is crucial to determine this based upon personal experience.

3.2.2.2.3.4.2 Synopsis of the Key Points

Second, synthesizing the key points is as Machig has said:

> Outer upheavals emerge as the magical deception of māras, inner upheavals emerge as physical illness, and secret upheavals are the strife of the mind.

So, just as taught, know these to be upheavals. When they occur, one should be able to ensure they are unable to cause obstacles and can be pacified through chöd. Furthermore, any indication of undeniable strength indicated by an individual with exceptional experience and realization is the extent of completion. Other indications involve having tamed the minds of the gods-māras so they enter the door of dharma. When exceptional compassion and realization, such as the view of emptiness, are developed, that must be known to be the extent of the severance. In these ways, the extent of completion will be at the moment that the remedial activity reaches completion and harm no longer occurs, whether upheavals or magical deceptions temporarily occur or not. The extent of the severance is that such negative tendencies will no longer rise up, and that process is discontinued. These are the points that must be known.

3.2.2.2.3.4.3 Joining This with the Biography of the Buddha

Third is to apply this subject to the biography of the Buddha. For example, when Prince Dondrub,[a] or Siddhārtha, was attaining fully manifest buddhahood, an army of māras descended upon him. That was an upheaval. His samādhi of love was the severance; and in dependence upon that, the māras were unable to affect him. That was the extent of completion. That the māras then rendered him praise and respectfully took refuge was the meaning of the extent of the severance.

It is similar even on the path of training. Once when the king of the land of Shibi[b,204] achieved courage in his practice of generosity, Indra manifested as a blind sage and begged him for his eyes. That was an upheaval. Without even the slightest hesitation, he gave up his eyes. The mental strength of compassion and fortitude that he expressed was the severance. Not only did this not become the condition for generosity to weaken, by giving his eyes the pāramitā of generosity increased. That was the extent of the completion. That Indra gained his eyesight back was the extent of the severance.

Similarly, these stages apply in other accounts of the Buddha's life as well. These excellent teachings have come from the speech of many learned masters.

3.2.2.2.3.5 How to Recognize the Four Māras

This has two parts:

1 Description of the four māras in a general sense
2 Uncommon tradition of chöd's description of the four

Fifth, as a distinction of this, the way of recognizing the four māras is explained twofold: according to the common texts that describe the four māras in a general sense and the uncommon tradition of chöd's description of the four.

[a] *don grub*
[b] *shi bi*

3.2.2.2.3.5.1 Description of the Four Māras in a General Sense

First, the māras are form, death, passions, and the māra of luring. The māra of form originates from this contaminated habitual form by the power of karma and passions that are present in the mind stream. Second, the māra of death is the aspect of powerlessly losing the continuity of the life essence. Third, the māra of the passions includes all passions, such as the five and three poisons. Fourth, the māra of luring is the god called Kāmadeva,[a] who abides in Paranirmitavashavartin as the lord of the desire realm. That is a generalization of how to recognize the māras.

3.2.2.2.3.5.2 Uncommon Tradition of Chöd's Description of the Four

This has two parts:

1 Four māras described in brief
2 Four māras described extensively

Second, the uncommon four māras are explained both in brief and extensively.

3.2.2.2.3.5.2.1 Four Māras Described in Brief

For the first, they are **the tangible māras, intangible** māras, **the luring māras of pride, and the māras of elation—these four. First, the tangible** māras **are actual existing material things, such as form, sound, smell, taste, and touch,**[205] fire, water, ravines, weapons, poisons, carnivorous animals, and the like. Intangible māras emerge from the various gateways and include the concepts of mental events, and include passions, slander, threats, shame, disgust, the eight worldly concepts, and the magical deceptions of the gods-māras and the rest.

Third, the luring māras of pride are self-fixation, along with the concepts from which positive versus negative thoughts arise that bring hope and fear. Fourth, the māra of elation is when qualities and the potential to benefit others, such as when they are sick or afflicted by demonic forces, are gained in the mind stream. This also includes a self-righteous attitude about having abundance, fame, and reputation. Given that the mind is not at peace, it is elated. Although it is taught that for beginners it is necessary to have some degree of elation and pride that is not the category of the māras, nevertheless here—from the perspective of being sullied by passions—it is acceptable to consider that these states are the objective to abandon. This self-righteousness can be synthesized as the cognitive obscurity

[a] Garab Wangchüg (*dga' rab dbang phyug*); god of desire or love

of subtle dualistic conceptualization. Nevertheless, it is necessary to analyze this further. I will not elaborate any further here.

3.2.2.2.3.5.2.2 Four Māras Described Extensively

This has two parts:

1 Speech of Machig
2 Teachings revealed in the text

Second, for the extensive explanation, there are two: the speech of Machig and whatever teachings are revealed in the main text [i.e., the terma].

3.2.2.2.3.5.2.2.1 Speech of Machig

First, [the disciple] Mügsang of Gangpa[a,206] asked Machig the following question, "What are the distinctions among māras and how are they understood?" She replied:

> Listen, Child, the characteristics of the māras are as follows. Māras with large forms and dark colors and demeanors that incite fear and terror upon sight actually do not exist. A māra is whatever causes hindrances for the accomplishment of liberation. In that case, even loving relatives can be the māras to liberation. In particular, there is no māra greater than afflictive, prideful self-cherishing. Until that is severed, all māras will be waiting with gaping mouths. Hence, it is necessary to be diligent and skilled in the means through which this māra of self-cherishing will be severed. Along with that, it is crucial to cut through the three māras that emerge from pride or self-cherishing. If these four are given names, they are the tangible māras, intangible, māras of elation, and egotistic māras. Thus, the egotistic māra of self-cherishing is the fourth.
>
> To expand upon this, the tangible māra occurs when form is perceived and attachment develops toward attractive forms that are pleasing and aversion develops toward the displeasing. This process similarly affects the ears, nose, tongue, body, and the objects of those faculties when perceived as sound, smell, taste, and touch where there is attachment toward the pleasant and aversion toward the unpleasant. That is called "the māra that sustains attachment and aversion". Having attachment or aversion toward an object of the faculties that actually exists will

[a] *gangs pa rmug sangs*

directly block the faculties and create a condition. Since this brings on the cause of bondage in saṃsāra, such as harming sentient beings, that is called "the māra". This demonic blockage that occurs through actual positive and negative objective appearances is called "the tangible māra". Hence, any attachment or fixation involving positive versus negative is the māra, so all attachment must be abandoned.

Form is empty by virtue of its fundamental nature. O Child, since form itself is inherently nonexistent, naturally meditate upon emptiness free from attachment or aversion toward form. The appearances of form are unable to be obstructed, so do not hold to them as real but rather as merely appearing. By abandoning attachment to these mere appearances, liberate yourself from form, O Child.

Likewise, apply this to sound, smell, taste, and touch in the same way. O Intelligent One, hold this in mind for this is not only the way the tangible māra abides, this is the way of being liberated from the tangible māra. Listen Child, the tangible māra emerges in this way, so hold these points in your mind without distraction.

The so-called intangible māra does not appear directly as an object of the faculties but rather when any type of thought formations arise in the mind, whether good or bad. If that is called the māra: then by holding to terror-based perception, there will be fear. If that is called a god: then by holding to pure perception, there will be enthusiasm that brings about the experience of joy. Holding both concepts of good and bad in this way, those circumstances turn into passions. Passions are not tangible and do not exist objectively. Nevertheless, because they lead to the direction of nonvirtue, they have the potential to bring certain harm and are therefore called "the māra".

To expand upon that, although not actually existing, given that they also do not conspicuously block anything, they are called "the intangible māra". The so-called gods that are good, the māras that are bad, and the mind that holds both positive and negative concepts in this way have not even a hair's worth of existence from beginningless time. Know that this emptiness is baseless from the root. All mental proliferations that emerge from this will never cease, so whatever positive or negative concepts arise will also never cease. Without engaging in that way, do not hold to whatever thoughts emerge by solidifying them with the mind. All recollections and concepts that arise from the natural, luminous great expanse of the mind's nature are, for example, like the ocean that no one is disturbing yet waves constantly emerge. Likewise, the intangible māra will be suppressed when whatever arises in the mind as positive or negative mental concepts is allowed to remain without contrivance. By abandoning the dualistic mind and remaining relaxed with a motionless body and mind, the intangible māra will be liberated in its own place.

O Noble Child, the māra of elation occurs when one is feeling self-righteous and so pleased that tremendous joy and personal satisfaction arises. These causes come from gaining worldly fame, reputation, many disciples, visions of deities; the ability to tame māras and demonic forces through the potential of mantra; the ability to pacify the pain of illness; having exceptional experiences in practice; lucid dreams; clairvoyant tendencies; the strength of bliss and potential within body, speech, and mind; and when gods, māras, and humans are quickly overcome so that they offer you food, wealth, and abundance and show boundless respect and devoted service. The feelings of joy and satisfaction during such experiences increase egotism that then become the obstacle for the path of liberation. Since that is given the name "māra of elation": no matter what or how many qualities may arise, those experiences should not be considered qualities in terms of the indivisible nature of mind and appearances.

O Noble Child, given that the mind of joy and satisfaction and the objects of that mind have not a hair tip's worth of permanent, true existence, know everything to be like magic and dreams. Meditating on all of this to be like magic or dreams and internalizing that, the mind that is invested in all those qualities, including its objects, is allowed to rest evenly within emptiness, free from all elaborations and limitations. In great emptiness free from limitations, meditating that phenomena are like magic and dreams and taking that as the magical or dreamlike path, the magical māra of elation will be severed. In doing so, the dreamlike or magical welfare of benefiting others will occur.

The māra of egotism is the basis for all three māras. Given that they depend upon egotism, it is crucial to sever the root of this pride. To expand upon that, "arrogance" means self-fixation; and because the cause for wandering in saṃsāra as well as the root of all negativity is self-fixation, that is the māra that prevents one from attaining liberation and is why this is called "the māra of egotism" or "self-fixation". Holding to a nonexistent self, the mind becomes polluted by passion; and whatever arises as positive or negative is then conceptually grasped. Fixating upon that as true is called "egotism" or "conceit".

> To expand, the so-called subject and object, or all outer and inner phenomena fixated upon as "me" and "mine", are not established as true. When with the wisdom of self-awareness this is witnessed, the notion of true existence is completely uprooted. It is then that negative and positive concepts are not lost to egotism. How enraptured to be free from the elaborations of the mind of mental events and aspirations, with no designated mind whatsoever! A mind that has lost self-cherishing, how blissful! A mind unable to be disturbed by the circumstance of passions, how utterly empty! Cognition free from outer and inner fixation, how lucid! Awareness that is not attached to anything, how vivid!
>
> Free from the experience of true existence: when the meaning of space-like nonexistence is encountered, the māra of egotism is severed. If this māra is severed, all māras that emerge from that will be severed as well; because once there is a self, there will be a māra. Once there is no self, there will be no māra. When there is no self, there will be no object to sever; so there will be nothing to fear or be wary of.
>
> As the result of achieving liberation from the four māras, wisdom awareness free from limitations such as these increases with all activities. This brief explanation of categories such as the enumerations of the four māras, of how through severance there is liberation in its own place, and the way of attaining the ultimate result are a gift for the fortunate one Gangpa and others. May all noble ones hold this in their minds, embrace this with expedient diligence, and cultivate vast bodhichitta toward others.

Thus, she spoke. Moreover, descriptions concerning māras occurring while practicing on any path are available through other sources, so I will not elaborate further here.

This information concerning the upheavals and the four māras is extremely crucial for practitioners of chöd. Although lengthy to include, the quotes not only maintain their authoritative freshness, but Machig's teachings are extremely clear and brimming with blessings.

3.2.2.2.3.5.2.2.2 Teachings Revealed in the Text

Second, for the teachings revealed in the text [i.e., the terma], there are two sections: the actual way deceptions occur and explanations based upon historical accounts. **First, for the māra of elation, there are two: the tangible and the intangible.** For **the tangible, when others show respect, praise, become** disciples [and] patrons who give great offerings of wealth and valuables and when one becomes their object of devotion and veneration, the actual manifestation of these excellent, enticing forms is the meaning of "tangible". Developing vivid concepts toward this, such as joy, satisfaction, and the like, is the upheaval. To take that as a siddhi or an indication of excellent interdependence, the habit of repeatedly feeling compulsory attachment out of joy, happiness, and satisfaction occurs and is to be overcome. At the moment elation arises—by seeing that to be nonexistent and faulted like dreams and magic—if attachment is cut off like a poison, that is the severance.

The "intangible" occurs without cause or circumstance by thinking one's abode and tent are the best, one's endowments plentiful, race and status superior, relatives and siblings abundant and excellent, and that even oneself is exalted both spiritually and worldly. Developing an attitude of total delight with body, speech, and mind is the upheaval. Repeatedly thinking in that way with fixated attachment: when that becomes solidified, one is then overcome.[207]

Not only that, this can be revealed through other analogies. The circumstances for deception to occur are uncertain. Some are based on wealth; some deceptions are based on food, some on clothing, business and profit, robbers and thieves. Some are deceived by attachment for lovers, some by cheating and trickery, others by parents and relatives. Some are deceived by wealth, others by taming enemies and protecting loved ones. All of these deceptions are certain magical deceptions of the māra of luring.

Who is deceived in this way? Those who are single-pointedly devoted to dharma have no interest in nonvirtuous activity and have trepidation toward that, as well as having renounced saṃsāra through great weariness. When that person is deceived and the sign of being overcome occurs, they are then incapable of turning the mind from the object of attachment for even an instant. The mind itself becomes unlike before, as the thought of karmic causes and results concerning what to accept and reject diminishes. The heart becomes hard like a stone. Renunciation and weariness vanish like mist. They no longer examine their own mind; and even if they do, they knowingly act free from shame and dignity and are impressed by others who conduct themselves like dogs and pigs.

Even though demonic deceptions occur in this way, the mere appearance or emergence of something does not become the deception. However, one must know that, when concepts arise about appearances and once there is attachment to their arising, that is the upheaval. Once attachment becomes fixation, there is deception. To know that all compounded things are impermanent, to have renunciation for saṃsāra, to recognize all phenomena to be like dreams and magic, and to then train with fearless conduct without fixation is the severance. Given that these are extremely difficult to sever, all practitioners must be especially vigilant.[208]

The so-called māra of egotism includes the various concepts that emerge and continuously arise based on either the presence of objects or not. Subsequent to that, the mind is then forced to pursue them. In brief, by the sudden emergence of hope, fear, benefit, harm, equanimity, and the like, the mind stream becomes disturbed; so that is the extent of the upheaval. Fixation on that becomes habitual, and that brings on the deception. The mere emergence [of these concepts] brings the upheaval; and simply uprooting an upheaval is the severance. Upheavals are uncertain and can be conspicuous, in a vision, or in dream. If conspicuous, it will directly appear to the gateway of the faculties, such as the visual and the rest. In the case of a vision, rather than occurring through the gateway of the faculties, this will occur through mental perceptions that are similar to actual objective appearances. If in a dream, then the upheaval will be a dream perception. In all cases, with the arising of various displeasing sights and feelings, compulsory attachment, hope, and fear develop. Eventually, by seeing this as real and relentlessly repeating this, finally many undesirable consequences will manifest, such as rashes, swelling, and parasites issuing forth from the body along with shooting pain, heart-wind, mental depression, and the like.

In brief, many unwanted calamities will befall one; and if it can be determined that they are nonexistent like dreams, then—without refuting or encouraging—allowing them to rest in their own place, they will naturally vanish. When unwanted illness and the rest occur, without trying to apply medicines or potions, think, "I pray that this may multiply some nine times over. I must purify the suffering of all parent sentient beings. Through this experience of mine, may all beings find fulfillment. This is my initial benefit for others." Then shout aloud:

> *Kyi!* May the suffering of all sentient beings, their illness, and everything without remainders mature upon me! I hope for this; I take this on; I will purify and utilize this! Bring it on! Gather here, now!

Thus, saying this, being able to meditate with fulfillment is a profound upadesha for chöd practitioners to directly suppress negative circumstances. Therefore, for whatever concepts arise [except vows and samaya], such as mental discouragement and thoughts based on hope and fear, it is a key point to constantly suppress them.

Concerning earth-spirit illnesses, such as rashes and swelling, [for this approach] one must bring together various methods to induce this illness even further, such as the smell of burned food and remaining too close to an open fire. If one thinks that used clothing or clothing from lepers causes obscuration or if concepts that afflict one arise, then take up those objects and place them directly upon the head. Rub them on the body, and say, "May I contract the disease of impurities!" In the manner of encouraging this, suppress it.[209]

Here the māras of elation and egotism have been emphasized. The explanations of both the tangible and intangible māras from the perspective of their cause are incidental to that. Hence, these are astonishing enumerations concerning the ways to explain all of this. Given that both elation and egotism are difficult to recognize as māras, they have been revealed in this way.

Second is an explanation concerning the way these upheavals occur based on historical accounts. Previously, in one of the great cities in the land of Magadha, there lived a practitioner named Sūryavajra[a] who was so inspired to practice dharma that he ran away from his parents, relatives, and friends in order to do so. The māras of deception noticed him and converged upon him. The tangible māra said that if he created something extremely terrifying, it would overcome him [i.e., Sūryavajra]. The intangible māra said that if he entered Sūryavajra's heart and caused various emotions such as happiness and sorrow to emerge, that would suffice. The māra of pride said that if he caused him to have many unrestrained emotions, that would do the trick.

The māra of luring weighed in as follows, "Although the tangible māra can bring on terror, the practitioner will sever that by applying the pointing-out instructions on the view of selflessness. That will, in turn, enhance his splendor and vitality such that he will never be defeated in that way again. That must not be allowed. Although the intangible māra may enter his heart, it is easy to identify emotions based on joy and sorrow as counterproductive and negative. He will be able to liberate them in basic space that is free from origination and cessation. It is certain that will be to his advantage. Although the māra of pride may stir up concepts: due to knowing the pointing-out instructions for recognizing concepts as the manifestation of awareness, he will accept negative signs as positive and bring bad circumstances to the path. All three of your deceptions entail negative circumstances that are easy for this practitioner to bring to the path and turn to his aid, so there will be no way to defeat him. Instead, if the three of you come to my aid and through my superior, excellent means of deception, it is certain that together we will destroy him!" Saying this, the māra of luring sneered.

Then, through omniscience, the great saint Lūipā[b] came to know of the māras' plans and called to Sūryavajra to warn him by telling him everything.

[a] *su'rya benzar*
[b] *lu'i pa* or *lu hi pa*

Sūryavajra replied, "*Ah!* Prior to knowing of this plan, there was the danger that I could have been overcome; but now that I know, it is certain I could never be controlled by them." Lūipā replied, "Given they are attempting to defeat you in this way, take care to not have attraction or attachment toward anything that is especially appealing." Thus, he gave his advice.

With that, Sūryavajra began intensive practice throughout the day and night in six regular sessions without any distraction. Meanwhile, the māra of luring entered the hearts of several people, including an exquisitely attractive young maiden, and overcame all of them. When Sūryavajra opened his maṇḍala that night, he had a very special dream. His meditation deity appeared to him and told him that on that day he had received siddhi and that, from tomorrow onward, he would receive the common attainment. The deity told him he was now set free from the obstructing force of māras; and also went on to say that a qualified consort would come to visit him and that, if he practiced with her, even without entering into a permanent relationship, certain attainments would occur. At the moment of dreaming this, Sūryavajra was overcome with joy and bliss; and the very next day several youthful people came to pay him a visit and offer food and wealth. This was so satisfying to him that he felt the predictions of the deity were authentic.

Several days later, a lovely young maiden came to pay him a visit with rice and a white silk scarf, requesting pointing-out instructions from him. She stayed to receive the teachings, and he wondered if this was the maiden that the deity predicted he should practice union with. He assumed that she was and, if he practiced with her, it would be easy for him to not get entangled in a deeper relationship with her. They practiced union, and afterward he fell deeply in love with her, so much so that he had a hard time even parting company with her. From that time onward, his heart and mind became so obsessed with her that he could not bear even a moment's separation. The girl continued to visit him regularly so that, then, even the townspeople began to get suspicious that the practitioner they had been honoring was in fact turning his back on the dharma.

Thinking that—although he might become a householder—he would never forsake the dharma, Sūryavajra went again to Lūipā and reported everything that had taken place. Lūipā replied, "You have allowed the māra of luring to enter your mind, and it has worked. This indicates exactly what I was warning you about. Now you must sever your ties with this maiden immediately and once again seize the stronghold of your inner practice. If you fail to sever this now, then you will become so ensnared in the murk of saṃsāra that you will never come to know freedom!"

Hence, Lūipā warned him again; and although his words were of value to Sūryavajra, they fell on deaf ears as he could not bear to sever his ties with the

object of his attachment. He lost all power and control and was reduced to the status of an ordinary individual; and even worse, the townspeople who had once extoled him were now disgusted by him. With anger, they ridiculed him; and even the ruling king decided to punish him so that he no longer possessed even a hair's tip worth of spiritual **intention. Eventually, he lost everything and became the most impoverished man in the region.**

This account is a superb example that advises us about the obstacles of the māras. The commentary [i.e., root terma] describes the way of being deceived by the māra of elation, whereas the way of being deceived by the other māras is only indirectly implied. That is why the categories for the [other māras] are present here. Given that all of this contributes to the cultivation of elation and egotism, it seems acceptable to apply this to be the category of deceptive gods-māras. It is well known that, generally, elation and so forth [are passions] that belong to the category of concepts; yet here they exemplify [the māras]. The intention of this presentation is to understand this just as it was presented.

The commentary [i.e., root terma] mentions glorious Saraha's advice as follows.

> **The supreme Dharmagarbha[a] also fell prey to the obstacles of māras in this way; and when he was almost completely overcome, I** [i.e., Dudjom Lingpa] **pointed out this account to him so he could cut off his attachment and fixation. He then went far away to a secluded place to practice and successfully reversed the path of the māras.**
>
> **For all future lineage holders to use positive circumstances as the path, these accounts must be held in their hearts. It is easy to recognize that the negative circumstances are unwanted; but when it comes to positive situations, since they are associated with desire, they are hard to identify and extremely difficult to bring to the path. Know that finding someone who will not be overcome by this is as rare as a daytime star.**
>
> **During the degenerate times when negative karmic forces are strong, there is no one who is not under the power of māras. That is why holding firm to one's ground, like an injured deer, is a crucial key point to be known. In the self-manifesting absolute great Akaniṣhṭha, out of great compassion for their welfare, I, Sarahapa, give this testament as advice for sentient beings of the degenerate times. This is a special transmission for all with a karmic connection to me. Since this dharma is incomparable, may everyone take this to heart!**

[a] *dharma garbha*

The source of all dharma is the land of India. It is in India where all buddhas are to be born. India is also the place where the Buddha taught the dharma, as well as being the sacred ground where aspirations are fulfilled. Hence, it is a land considered to be more sacred than any place on earth. It is there that, aside from the distinction of being Buddhist versus non-Buddhist, there is no dispute that both categories of buddhadharma, Sūtra and Tantra, were propagated. Given that the Victorious One was skillfully compassionate, he taught according to the faculties of those to be tamed.

Disputing between right and wrong based on an attitude that a single direction is correct will undoubtedly escalate the accumulation of the negative karma that rejects the dharma. That is why, conversely, the learned will without dispute see clearly through their prajñā vision. The dharma is not an object the totally blind will guess about. The doctrine of the Buddha is so profoundly vast, it never falls in a biased direction [and] does not abide as a single extreme; and except for the Buddha himself, there is no individual who can within their mind stream actually fathom the depth of this doctrine.

For instance, a wish-fulfilling jewel bestows only that which is precious; yet it has the capacity to bestow wealth that is only in harmony with what is wished for. Likewise, the nature of all phenomena is only originally pure; yet due to the minds of those to be tamed and the power of truth, their needs will be fulfilled. It is, therefore, a key point to not fixate on any extreme. Holding to extremes or biased tendencies, a person who still claims to understand the wisdom intent of the Buddha is extremely delusional. For example, just imagine how astonishing it would be to see someone cover the sky with their hand! Given that the doctrines of Kāma and Terma will be disputed during the time of the five-hundred *dregs*, I have mentioned these points.

So, it is.

3.2.2.2.3.6 Repetitive Stages of Upheavals and How to Sever Them

Sixth, once again the stages of the upheavals are explained, along with the manner of severing them. During this time of practice, know that various phenomena that are the extent of the upheavals will occur, such as earthquakes, mountain slides, collapsing crags, houses collapsing, dust storms, the earth cracking open, sink holes, rock slides, meteorite showers, falling trees, ceilings collapsing, and so forth. Upheavals with water involve floods, swollen rivers, accidents such as falling into lakes, being carried off by a river, torrential rainfall, hail storms, and flooding tributaries.

Upheavals with fire include sudden fire storms, the body burned by fire, fire sparks issuing from the body, seeing fire infernos, igniting fire, the entire environment being consumed by fire, sparks, and so forth. Upheavals associated with wind include the sound of intense wind, hurricane-force winds, being carried away by wind, sudden tornados, the tent being carried off by the wind, whistling wind, howling wind, and so forth. Upheavals with space include lightning flashing, thunder roaring, sitting on the edge of a cliff or canyon, being shrouded in darkness, and so forth. Upheavals through forms are the phenomena of humans, undomesticated animals, carnivorous animals, domesticated beasts, amphibious creatures, classes of birds, and those who attempt to harm through various movements during the upheaval.

All upheavals based on sound, smell, taste, and touch are called "tangible". Although formless, they still appear to have a form, such as making meaningless noises, engaging in activities, people congregating and going here and there, seeing heads and limbs without bodies and torsos without limbs, seeing various substances such as entrails and organs, parasites trying to harm you, displeasing sights appearing, or receiving food, drink, clothes, and ornaments. Whatever occurs, by rejecting all reactions, such as fear, hope, disappointment, retaliation, beating, striking, utilizing, or joy and sorrow, the upadesha is to allow all of this to fall apart in the empty nature of nonreferential appearances. Why? By seeing one's body incorrectly, striking or harming it with a weapon is the way many have actually lost their lives. Hence, it is a crucial point to abandon various incorrect activities.

If these occur and one is unable to distinguish between the form and the formless, then the consciousness of that upheaval and one's own consciousness should be mingled as a single taste and transferred to the spacelike expanse of Samantabhadrī with twenty-one repetitions of *phet*. If it is formless, it will be impossible for this to not vanish during the repetitions. If it is still apparent, then it is a form upheaval. Finally, one's consciousness rises up from space, and the flesh and blood are presented as the feast.

An upheaval means that initially one's body, speech, and mind are completely shocked. Upon that, if one is able to hold self-confidence that this is nonreferential and unimpeded, then that is the severance. During all times and situations when strong concepts develop, mingle the mind with the object. Seal this with the space of Samantabhadrī by strongly reciting *phet* and resting within nonreferential awareness, and the severance will occur. This is the destruction of all fixations, including the idea of māras, into the dharmatā

that is free from elaborations. Know this to be a key point, and regard it as principal.

Furthermore, the way of severing upheavals is taught by Machig:

> Separate the body and awareness, and mingle awareness with space. Remain in emptiness as much as possible. Practice giving the aggregates as the offering of food.

Thus as taught, whatever outer, inner, or secret upheavals occur, think that any fixation to one's body or possessions has been given as the effigy for the welfare of parent sentient beings. To fulfill the needs of harm-doing gods-māras, there is no reason to be attached to anything; so mingle awareness with space. Separating body and awareness, from the perspective of compassion, give the accumulated flesh and blood of the body as the feast without attachment or fixation. Awareness is without support, so the gods-māras are powerless to do anything. Thinking that, aside from body and mind, no self as the subject of fear exists: by remaining in emptiness, all upheavals will naturally vanish. This practice unifies both upāya and prajñā.

Also, while the gods-māras are sending magical deceptions, recognize the outer gods-māras of objective fear as parents and imagine them with love and compassion. Recognize that illness, suffering, and the like are the results of negative karma, and think that this inspires you to try to purify negative karma and not engage with nonvirtue. In dependence upon that, train in the visualizations for sending and receiving. In order to increase bodhichitta through the method of bodhichitta itself, take what is referred to as "negative circumstances as the path". In dependence upon that: when enhancing the bodhichitta of love and compassion, take what is referred to as "negative tendencies arising as companions".

Outer objective fear of gods-māras, inner subjective fear of the mind's grasping, and the interim actual fear of appearances are perfectly severed through the nonconceptual awareness of the three rounds. Then by the strength of realizing from its own perspective that this state does not exist even slightly, trepidation will be pacified in its place. During the post-evenness of the deluded mind, it is realized that phenomena merely appear and amount to being mere conceptual designations. Not realizing this, beings become more and more accustomed with the manner of wandering in saṃsāra. Gaining certainty in the awareness of that [i.e., experiencing phenomena as conceptual designations] is referred to as "severing the root of the ground of confusion". This is the way of taking negative circumstances as the path with the view of prajñā. Based on that, enhancing the experience of the view is referred to as "nonconducive tendencies arising as companions".

This is mentioned in Āryadeva's treatise on chöd:

> Concerning the superior, middling, and inferior extents of the visions, remain within a state free from recollection and meditate by focusing on that. Reach a determination through investigation and analysis.

Thus, it is taught, and similarly the great Gyaltangpa also said:

> Those with superior minds will sever all upheavals in the space of genuine truth through nonconceptual awareness. The middling will intentionally focus on the upheavals and directly sever them in their nature. All those of inferior minds will examine to see what the upheavals are, who is afraid, and what is the object of fear?

So, it is taught. Those of superior intelligence will allow [upheavals] to rest in their own place with nonconceptual confidence in the view. Those who are middling will intentionally focus on whatever upheaval occurs and then remain in nonconceptual awareness. Those who are inferior will analyze through reasoning; and by determining [that the upheaval] is nonexistent, will sever it. The way of severance is as stated:

> For instance, like a dense forest and a strong man with a sharp axe . . ."

Thus, and the quote continues:

> Concerning all of this, the superior ones will rest in the meaning of nonduality. The middling will focus upon that and meditate, and the inferior will transform the aggregates into the feast. Following that, awareness free from the support of the intellect will be experienced.
>
> Departing for a fear-provoking environment, the body and awareness separate; and the body is offered to the gods-māras who show great abilities. The corpse becomes like a stone, so it is not possible to harm; whereas the mind is immaterial like space. Who can harm that and who will that harm? Thinking in this way, rest within the dharmatā free from hesitation or trepidation. Even if you imagine that your body is taken away by those gods-māras: without wavering from your seat, have no anxiety-based reaction. Whatever concepts arise are the māras, and they have arisen from your mind. Not even a particle of the mind truly exists in terms of its origin, locale, or destination. If set free, this mind does not become a buddha; and even while confused, it is impossible to wander in saṃsāra.

Thus, it is as taught. Reference to nonduality is constantly referred to in this treatise as meditation upon transcendental nonduality. Like that, this means that both objects and subjects rest within the evenness of empty bliss.

To expand on this, it is merely a more elaborate way of explaining the abovementioned quote. The mind that is set free to become buddha and sentient beings that emerge from confusion and the like must be realized to be inherently nonconceptual. The other lines in the quote are easy to comprehend. This [discussion] is extremely congruent with the tradition of Mahāsandhi.

Again, from the speech of Machig:

> By cherishing one's body, speech, or mind with egotistic fixation, untimely death will then occur. If, without attachment, there is freedom from grasping fixation: then even if a billion classes of māras were to emerge, they will be reversed like massing clouds.

So, it is as taught. No matter what upheavals arise, if left alone without acceptance, rejection, hope, fear, establishment, or refutation—including disturbances—it is taught that, since that is the nature of the upheavals, they will liberate in their own place.

Machig has also mentioned:

> No matter what the qualities of the extent of completion may be: without engaging in the pride of fixation, internalize this like dreams and magic. O Child, sever the root of egotism within its nonexistent nature. Listen here, all disciples who are gathered! All upheavals, magical deceptions, and extents of completion are merely mental designations that are primordially nonexistent. In this nature of phenomena that is primordially nonexistent, whatever is accepted and rejected is the māra. Without pursuing objects, the cord of egotism must be cut off. The māra of self-fixation is the great realization of selflessness. Knowing selflessness liberates one from fixation upon self. If this nature is known, then any type of māra—including the object to sever and severance itself—becomes nameless. If the process of egotism is known in the face of the māra of egotism's object and the māra of egotism itself, then the māra will be unable to affect you. When it is determined that the māra is this egotism, then the mere appearance of egotism is similar to a water mirage.
>
> An illusory person cannot harm self or others; the moon is free from the dualistic mind and vision; without rejecting space, clouds themselves arise in space. When everything is self-appearing and self-liberating, it is then impossible to accept and reject with oneself. If so, then where

> are the objects to accept and the objects to reject? Hence, fixation itself is the māra. O Disciples, do not cherish and fixate upon anything! If fixation is liberated, then there is no object to sever or severance itself. That is the supreme path of liberation, as well as the siddhi. The māra of the objects to reject is similar to deities to be accomplished. Saying "similar" is a mere designation since they primordially do not exist. Just as there is no one who can show this: if one's own egotism is known, then that will liberate in its own place. One's own experience of this nature is free from thought or expression. Both objective and subjective duality are severed from the root. Selfless emptiness is free from elaboration and pure like space. All disciples, rest freely within this uncontrived nature of phenomena!

Thus, as taught, to synthesize the key points, it states in the *Gathering of Precious Qualities*:

> It is difficult for the four māras to defeat or distract the learned bodhisattvas who possess the knowledge and power of the four causes. Abiding in emptiness, they [i.e., the bodhisattvas] never give up on sentient beings. Following in accordance with what was taught, they hold the blessing of the tathāgatas.

So, it is. Saying that "they abide in emptiness," as just mentioned above, points out that they know how to understand and remain in emptiness. "Not abandoning any sentient being" means that, through compassion and so forth, they consider others and know how to sever self-cherishing. "Following in accordance with what was taught" means that, just as the bodhisattvas have committed diligence, the practice of severance is not lost. "Holding the blessings of the tathāgatas" means to unflaggingly regard the lineage masters as buddhas so that blessings enter the mind.

3.2.2.2.3.7 How to Induce Upheavals

Seven, the visualization for encouraging upheavals when they are not emerging has two parts: the speech of Machig and the teachings mentioned in the text [i.e., terma].

First Machig said:

> Meditate that you are hoisting a mountain, gulping down the ocean, that the earth and sky reverse, and that the Great Mother destroys environments.

So, as taught, these have four names, namely, holding a mountain on the lap, gulping the ocean, reversal of the earth and sky, and the Great Mother destroying environments.

For the first, with the awareness of oneself as Tröma or whatever deity: wherever demonic forces of the body may dwell, such as on the four continents and the like, summon them through samādhi so they absorb into the mountain. Then one hoists the mountain up into space with both hands; it then drops, and one thinks that the bodies [of the demonic forces] are reduced to dust particles. Rest the mind in the nature of phenomena. It is important to repeat this visualization again and again.

Secondly, meditating on the visualization as before, think that from one's heart either a large garuḍa or many garuḍas emanate out—whatever is easiest—or that the demonic forces absorb into the ocean as before. By drinking all the water without exception, think that it evaporates and that all demonic forces are eliminated without exception. Repeat this many times.

Third is to think that the earth and sky instantly reverse wherever demonic forces exist. With the sky becoming the earth, you as Tröma stand upon the sun, moon, and so forth. With the earth becoming the sky, the peak of the mountains and the heads of the demonic forces are hanging downward. Think that you strike them with your hand emblems, shredding them to pieces so they become like particles. Repeat this again and again.

For the fourth, if the upheavals still do not emerge from these methods, then imagine that from one's heart Tröma emanations like oneself emerge as large as Mt. Meru and as small as particles of dust, boundless in number. Think that wherever the visualization is focused, or just upon the demonic forces, these emanations pierce through everything wherever they go. Practice this as an offering from the hands of the Great Mother, Tröma. By practicing in this way, all outer, inner, and secret upheavals will then emerge.

Second, the explanation from the text [i.e., terma] is as follows. **If no upheavals emerge from the previously described suppression techniques, then meditate upon oneself as Tröma Nagmo the size of Mt. Meru. By devouring Mt. Meru and gulping down the ocean, all the abiding gods-māras are then spread out as one's cushion. Thinking that this repeatedly occurs will induce the upheaval.**

If there is still no upheaval emerging from this, then think that phenomenal existence pervades the entirety of one's appearances and that the abiding gods-māras clearly gather there like images upon a mirror. Then, imagine that all of them are suppressed below one's seat. If there is still no upheaval, then circle the flayed, human skin held in one's right hand above the crown of your head as Tröma. Strike this upon the ground and imagine that all mountain ranges quake, oceans churn, and tidal waves occur. All vegetation is dispersed,

and the abiding gods-māras are exposed to arrive quivering with fear. Blowing the human thigh-bone trumpet held in the left hand three times: with the first sound, all mountains crumble; with the second, the mountains, crags, and all bodies of water scatter, and then evaporate; with the third, the gods-māras gather under your seat as though being forcefully awakened.

If the upheavals still do not come: then, with both hands, place the entire environment and dwelling places of the gods-māras upside down and ignite a vastly deep and blazing molten fire underneath them. Then hold the gods-māras over that as though you are ready to drop them in. Meditate that upon that [fire] appears the palace of Tröma, huge, majestic, and solid and that inside of that are billions of ḍākinīs shouting wrathful sounds of laughter. After that, it is certain there will be an upheaval.

If swirling, ominous hail-storm clouds consume the sky, then upon the crown of self-nature as Tröma imagine the nature of all buddhas to appear as the glorious Orgyen Pema,[a] Tamer of Māras, who is inseparable with the root guru. Dark-red in color, he hoists a meteorite vajra dagger in the right hand with the threatening mudrā. In the left, he holds a skull filled with blood. He rests in the kingly posture upon a thousand-petaled lotus, sun, and moon seat. His orange-colored hair reaches upward to touch the Blazing Fire Mountain pure realm.[b] He has a haughty wrathful expression, and his presence radiates like millions of suns. Within an expansive, dark-red massing wisdom fire, his orange-colored eyebrows and mustache light up golden-red like lightning. He dons a cloak, robe, and bhikṣhu shawl; and his three round eyes are red and bulging as they gaze into the expanse of the three kāyas.

Meditate that the upper aspect of his kāya is filled with the nirmāṇakāya buddhas of this fortunate age; the middle section has the complete maṇḍalas of the four and six lineages of meditation deities; and the lower aspect of his kāya is the spontaneously present maṇḍala of oceanic ḍākas and ḍākinīs. Surrounding are the wisdom and karmic dharmapālas like an assembly as vast as the ocean. From all of them, boundless light rays radiate to invoke the maṇḍalas of the three-kāya victorious ones to dissolve. Then, from all of their kāyas, light rays, firelight, miniature wrathful ones, scorpions, lions, and such boundlessly emanate to hover like clouds in space. Meditate that there are flaming wheels of wisdom fire, palaces ablaze with wrathful deities, radiation and reabsorption of meteorite scorpions, and lions tossing their manes and roaring so loudly it shakes the trichiliocosm. Devouring all elementals of the eight classes, everything is incinerated. Think that all harm-doers of the upper

[a] *o rgyen padma*

[b] *me ri bar wa'i zhing* (*me ri 'bar ba'i zhing*)

dimensions sink into a meteorite triangular vortex within the depths of the great ocean.

Then, between the joined palms of oneself as Tröma Nagmo, imagine a dark-red syllable *hung* blazing within wisdom fire. Imagine all power and strength of the three kāyas of the victorious ones being synthesized to dissolve into this *hung*. While focusing on space and opening the palms, from the single syllable *hung* shooting like a star into the sky, countless syllables emerge. All clouds are prevailed upon by the density of the blazing dark-red *hungs*. Imagine that the potential to annihilate and incinerate all eight classes of harm-doers is attained.

Below the seat, from *bam*, imagine that a oceanic maṇḍala of water appears to be even more frigid than the coldest hell realm. Meditate that all eight classes are suppressed below that water where nothing can possibly penetrate. Recite:

> *Om guru raksha trota buddha dewa dakini bam ha ri ni sa hung phet*
> *ah ya ma du ru tsa sha na maraya jhyo nan phet*

Furthermore, by reciting this initial mantra, for a while remain in the even consummation of saṃsāra and enlightenment; and by doing so, severance will be guaranteed. Practitioners who have definitively realized the genuine nature of the dharmatā will not be affected by any type of fear. Even if those who lack this confidence remain within awareness, it will be impossible for the gods-māras and other types of terror to disturb them. Given that the terror induced by lightning is extremely poignant, vigilance must be applied to the visualizations.

Then, by rejecting all hope, fear, [and] paranoia, including protection reversals, meditations, recitations, and expelling rituals performed for others, it is a quintessential point to freely abide in one taste. Having expectation toward anything is the māra that controls all dimensions of desire, so expectation must be severed. Having disappointment toward anything is the messenger that seduces one toward negative directions, so reject disappointment. Fixating upon any harm-doers just sets up interest toward obstacles. Fixating upon everything as lacking benefit is the profound upadesha for turning negativity into siddhis and ominous signs into prosperity. If illness is meditated upon as well-being and negative circumstances are taken as the path, then for instance—like how initially any spicy substance can be unbearable when applied to the mouth and nose—[gradually] if something is thought to bring about well-being and is necessary, then one will feel it surely does bring happiness; and eventually one will be unable to function without it. Likewise,

when applied here, all negative dimensions will then arise as though beneficial. For example, the Buddha transformed the hordes of perverted māras into ornaments and supports, so the key point is to know that the ornaments and supports are indispensable.

In order to assure the realization of fearless conduct, one must rely upon an isolated charnel ground that is fear-provoking. In order to overcome the god-māra guests who are objects of fear, suppress them with the realization of fearless confidence. Upon the rudra form of confused self-fixation, the ḍākinīs of the five wisdoms dance the suppression and pierce with the dagger of the four immeasurables and bodhichitta, which ensures they [i.e., the gods-māras] are immovable within the space of selflessness.

> The appearances of the mind's confusion are the various magical
> deceptions of external gods-māras, including the concepts that
> hold to that as true.
> By severing with the realization of the extents of completion
> and severance, evenness prevails; and there is victory over the
> obstacles of the four māras.

Thus, these are the verses that summarize the section.

3.2.2.2.4 Mode of Diligence Applied with the Four Feasts

This has five parts:

1 Motivation
2 The black feast
3 The white feast
4 The mixed feast
5 The red feast

Fourth is the offering of the aggregates as the feast that involves practicing the four feasts in five ways as follows. First meditate upon the guru, mingle the mind, and offer one's body to the four classes of guests. In order to purify negativity and obscurations, the black feast is offered; to accumulate merit, the white feast; to engage various visualizations, the stages of the mixed feast; and the red feast is offered to engage the exceptional methods.

3.2.2.2.4.1 Motivation

First, **the basis of confusion for sentient beings who abide in saṃsāra is the establishment of the aggregates that are fixated upon as a "self". That is the**

root cause. The perpetually fixated mind creates the contributing circumstance that brings about confusion.

In the *Moon Lamp Sūtra*,[a] it states:

> The heap of this body, along with life itself is impermanent and powerless, like the illusion of a dream. The immature who become attached to this create extremely unfortunate karma. Those unskillful ones who are controlled by nonvirtue have already mounted Yamā. Such are the ones who will fall to the unbearable realms of hell.

So, it is as taught. To expand upon that, in the *Jataka Tales* concerning the account of giving his [i.e., the Buddha's] body to the tigress, it states:

> This ownerless, impermanent body that lacks essence is full of suffering, is not beneficial, and is always impure. If there is any benefit that this body can afford to others, then it is imprudent to not feel a sense of joy toward that.

Thus, as taught, **in order to annihilate fixation upon this cherished heap of aggregates, the body is presented as the feast** for the celebration.

The motivation is also stated as the quote continues:

> One thinks that, when there is benefit for others, even this body of mine [can be given]. Hence, I must ensure this prayer comes true and that I am approaching the supreme state of awakening. This is not for competition or fame, not for rebirth in higher realms, nor to gain royal status. Not for personal happiness but rather for the welfare of others, I engage in this deed.

Thus, and in the *Jataka* called *Strength of Love*,[b] it states:

> Difficult to obtain and easy to lose, there is no satisfaction or peaceful tranquility. I have no interest in the so-called abundance of saṃsāra. If interest in even the glory of the highest gods is lacking, it is needless to mention having interest in something else. If this were only to bring an end to my own misery, for me that is not enough. Embodied and lacking a guide, forever tormented by the unbearable suffering of illness, if these beings were to have to rely upon me: then through the merit of

[a] *dawa dron ma'i do* (*zla ba sgron ma'i mdo*, *candrapradīpasūtra*)
[b] *jam pa'i tob* (*byams pa'i stobs*)

> this virtue, may all of them attain the state of all-knowing. By taming the enemy of their faults, may I bring all beings out from the ocean of existence where they must endure the turbulent waves of aging, illness, and death.

So, it is as taught. Lacking the attitude of self-purpose and by **resting the mind within the nature free of elaboration**, a perfectly pure intention **is the profound method that severs duality from the root.**

Then, in the space in front, the nature of the root guru appears as Rigdzin Pema Duddul,[a] flesh-colored with an attractive demeanor. Naked, he wears a tiger-skin skirt and a long garland mālā made of three types of skull. In his right hand, he holds a five-pronged vajra that overcomes the three realms; and his left hand holds a meteorite phurba that suppresses the three states of existence. His two feet are in the kingly posture upon a seat of a lotus, sun, and four māras. His hair is flowing freely down his back; his three eyes are gazing into the sky. He has wrathful wrinkles, while showing a smiling expression. His kāya contains the entire maṇḍala of victorious ones. Imagine that he remains in an expanse of blazing fire, wisdom light, and rainbow molecules. He has no inherent existence, yet appears like a rainbow or a water moon. Meditate without holding to true existence, and recognize that he appears objectively like magic or a dream. By just seeing, hearing, recalling, or experiencing him, there is the potential to bless the three doors with the three vajra natures. With intense faith and complete devotion given over to him, pray with a total commitment from one's heart, mind, and soul.

Then, recite ***phet*** and the verses that begin ". . . perfectly pure . . . self-appearances . . ." and so forth until ". . . delight within the wisdom mind . . ." It is as taught.

> **In the perfectly pure, absolute Akaniṣhṭha of self-appearances, the lord guru of perfected kāyas and wisdom is the absolute fully manifest kāya, the intrinsic nature of the great bindu**—indestructible, unchanging nature of the self-occurring wisdom that abides as the ground—**arising as the oceanic treasury of ripening empowerment and liberating instructions.** With ***phet*,** **I invoke your** wisdom intent and supplicate you, perfect **embodiment of the glorious qualities of the four kāyas. By invoking your wisdom mind through intense faith and devotion, I pray, release** or unite **all concepts of the mind and mental events** that are **shrouded** as if encased **in the shell of** deluded **ignorance to delight within the great expanse of the wisdom mind,**

[a] *rig 'dzin padma bdud 'dul*; Vidyādhara Lotus Māra Subduer

> **the** primordial **ground of original purity** that is the self-nature free from elaboration.

Having supplicated in this way, self-awareness[210] **and the guru's enlightened mind of nonconceptual wisdom mingle** inseparably.

One awakens in the wisdom expanse of the three kāyas. Think that the great confidence of exaltation free from transition or change is attained. Mingle with the first *phet*; purify obscurations with the second; and with the third, all four empowerments are perfectly **received. Imagine that the great dynamic strength of the four kāyas**[211] **is attained. Mingling the mind with the guru dispels all illness, demonic forces, negative circumstances, and obstacles. This is the sole, profound key point for bringing forth the common and supreme siddhis.**[212]

Then, by transferring awareness into space, [the practice] **called *Opening the Gateway to the Sky* is as follows.**[213] One recites, "... one's body that is huge, fatty . . ." and so forth until "... the kāya ... arises..."[214] **Thus, while saying this, imagine that—in the middle of one's body that is huge, fatty, oily, and heavy—the central channel appears possessing the four characteristics.**[215] **Empty and clear, it is the dimension of a medium-sized bamboo shaft. The upper tip connects with the crown aperture, and the lower tip is blocked below the navel. Within that, parallel to the heart, is the combined nature of all life essence, longevity, and merit as a five-colored bindu. The size of the bodhisattva's first egg, the bindu is clear, shiny, rich, and vibrant as it shoots upward like the shot arrow of a strong man. Think that this arrives in the upper regions of space. With the first *phet*, awareness transfers to mingle with basic space. With the second, it arises from basic space; and with the third, visualize that it becomes the kāya of Tröma.**[216]

To expand upon that, reference to the mingling of basic space and awareness is not only mingling in space. It is to abide in the meaning of the dharmatā, free from duality, as the empty nature of space. Then, by remaining in all-pervasive spacelike awareness without contriving body and mind, one must engage in this key point of Mahāsandhi's view and meditation. In Āryadeva's treatise on chöd, it states:

> While mingling basic space and awareness, there is natural freedom from material things, characteristics, refutation, and establishment, as well as freedom from holding to reference points. Being free from duality is to remain in the meaning of the dharmatā without contriving body and mind. In this way, wherever empty space pervades, this present awareness also pervades; so one rests in this great, all-encompassing expansive dimension.

So, it is as taught. Then say "... the spontaneously present three kāyas ..." until "... *om ah hung ha ho hri* ..." While reciting this three times, visualize one's body as described, such as one's body being huge, fatty, and so forth.

Concerning this, Machig has said:

> As soon as the breath separates from this corpse and while the warmth is still present, it becomes youthful and full; and the flesh turns smooth and fine. With a vital healthy glow, the corpse is huge, heavy, fatty, and oily while appearing lovely and attractive, large enough to completely fill the realms of the world.

Thus, one should visualize as taught.

To expand upon this,[217] from the space of empty prajñā, the rupakāya of mudrā and method arises as **Tröma Nagmo, holding a curved vajra blade in the right hand.**[218] **By merely pointing it, the skull falls from the corpse and lands upon a tripod of three types of human skulls. With hair intact, the skull expands to become equal to the vast dimensions of the dharmatā. Again, by pointing the curved vajra blade, the body's skin is flayed to cover the golden foundation of the earth. The headless body drops into the skull cup; and the fire and wind below the tripod ignite the stove, heating up the skull. The body melts and begins to boil profusely, while the steam and froth spill out to cover the human-skin base. Think that the edibles become like mountains of flesh; the drinkables are oceans of blood; the chewable substances, like banks piled with bones; the substances to lick, like heaps of melting fat; and the substances to suck, like the marrow, cartilage, and so forth are ever-increasing.**

Furthermore, think that inexhaustible, desirable wealth suitable to the individual guests of saṃsāra and enlightenment appears like an ornamental wheel equal to the reaches of space. Bless this with the mantra. With the first *phet*, the exalted guests as the objects of refuge—namely, the buddhas, dharma, sangha, gurus, meditation deities, and ḍākinīs, the dharmakāya, sambhogakāya, nirmāṇakāya, and so forth; the guests who are the protectors with noble qualities, such as the eight groups of gods, nāgas, and rāhulas,[219] **the ten directional guardians, the nine terrifying ones, the four great kings, the twenty-eight astrological deities, and so forth; and the guests who are objects of compassion, the six classes of beings, such as the hell beings, pretas, animals, gods, asuras, humans, and the like—all hear this. With the second [*phet*], think they depart from their domains; and with the third, they gather to fill all regions of space and earth.**

Once again, with *phet*, think that boundless karmically **emanated ḍākinīs** arrive **to facilitate the feast.**[220] Saying "***phet* to the buddha, dharma** ..." and so forth until "... **spontaneously fulfilled**" means that—by offering an inexhaustible ornamental wheel of clouds of offerings to the exalted guests of refuge—**with the first *phet*, they receive this; with the second, they are satisfied with the flavor of empty bliss; and with the third, think that their enlightened minds of nonconceptual wisdom transfer into oneself.**

Then,[221] saying "... **the twenty-four supreme sacred places** ..." and so forth until "... **be the potential** ...," the outer objects of the twenty-four sacred places, the inner arrangement of the compatible maṇḍala of the vajra aggregates, and the ḍākas and ḍākinīs that abide there are offered the ambrosia of immaculate, empty bliss. They all belong to the category of the guests who are the exalted objects of refuge. **With the first *phet*, the offering is made; with the second, they receive it; and third,[222] their enlightened minds are satisfied with the taste of empty bliss.**

Saying "***phet* the eight classes of gods** ..." until "... **be fulfilled** ...," think that all guests who are the protectors of noble qualities are fulfilled by the fully endowed desirables in harmony with each individual need. **With the first *phet*, the offering is made; with the second, they receive it; and with the third, they are satisfied by immaculate exaltation.**

Saying[223] "... **the hell beings** ..." and so forth until "... **attain buddhahood**" dedicates to all guests, who are the six-realm beings and objects of compassion, whatever objects of desire that they may wish for. **With the first *phet*, they receive this; with the second, they are satisfied; and with the third, imagine that they are set free.**

Again, for all guests who are karmic debtors, demonic forces, and obstructers, the feast of flesh, blood, and so forth is presented as follows. First perform the blessing, and then summon the guests by saying "... **pervade the trichiliocosm** ..." and so forth until "... ***om ah hung ha ho hri*.**" **With the first *phet*, the gods-māras of the eight classes hear this. With the second, they depart [from their realms]; and with the third, they suddenly arrive and gather.**

Call them by chanting "**from the uppermost peak of existence**" and so forth and think that all eight classes, including the gods, yamās, and the like are each given whatever brings them satisfaction according to their desires. Then, they become fulfilled. **With the first *phet*, offer to the mightiest among them; with the second, to the middling; and with the third, to the weakest. Imagine that the final *phet* ensures their fulfillment.**

King Pekar[a] and others are from the kingly class; the female cannibal with the bloody mane and the rest are from the classes of female demons. The demonic nāgas and so forth from the nāga class and the five passions and poisons are present as the other classes of demonic forces. Spirits that wander the towns[b] and

[a] *rgyal po pe dkar*
[b] *dritsen drong gyug* (*gri btsan grong rgyug*)

others are the owners of karmic debts that suddenly appear as gods-māras. Tell them, **"If I am unable to give each of you what is preferred, then it is my fault. If any of you are unable to partake of it, then it is your fault."** Thinking like this, abandon cherishing the body through heroic confidence. **With the first *phet*, imagine that they hear you. With the second *phet*, they are satisfied; and with the third, they are set free.**

Then, the remainders are given by saying "**. . . equal to the reaches of phenomenal existence . . .**" and so forth until "**. . . they are invited.**" Thus, bless and invite the guests saying "**. . . self-created . . .**" and so forth until "**. . . may the empowerment . . . be attained.**" Dedicate the desirable objects to them, such as edibles, medicines, and the like so as to dispel all suffering. **Think that, with the first *phet*, they receive this; with the second, they are satisfied; and with the third, they awaken into immaculate exaltation.**

Once again, to offer dedication in the great, perfectly pure three spheres, continue by saying "***phet* . . . magical nature of phenomena . . .**" until "**. . . ground . . . be attained**"; think of the meaning of these words. Then saying "***phet* . . . mind and mental events . . .**" and so forth until "**. . . free from meeting and parting *ah*,**" **self and all objective appearances dissolve within nondual emptiness. Think that one enters the womb of the original protector of the primordial ground and rest in evenness. This is the sole, profound upadesha to be internalized through practice during all times and situations.**

3.2.2.2.4.2 The Black Feast

Second, **so that** [practitioners can] **purify negativity and obscurations, the black feast** is as follows.[224] Saying "***phet* . . . one's body is fatty . . .**" until "**. . . *ha ho hri*,**" one's body as a heap of aggregates that has originated from the confusion of dualistic ignorance is huge and fatty, equal to the size of Mt. Meru. In the center of this is the central channel with all characteristics complete. The upper tip runs to the crown, and the lower connects below the navel. Parallel to the heart is the nature of inseparable wind and mind as a five-colored bindu, the synthesized pure essence of the five elements. Imagine this to be about the size of an egg. Saying *phet*, it rises up into space; and awareness mingles with basic space.

Once again, the nature of inseparable basic space and awareness appears as the blue-black Tröma wearing the complete accouterments. From the light of her kāya, all negative obscurations of the three-realm sentient beings, including all gods-māras without exception, are gathered in the aspect of black-colored light that dissolves into the corpse. The corpse becomes even larger than before, and this human corpse fills the trichiliocosm. Mesmerizing the minds of the gods-māras who see it, hear of it, taste it, or experience it, think that the corpse is fully endowed with all glorious desirable qualities.

Imagine that, from space, the five syllables descend like rain and transform this [corpse] into wisdom ambrosia that liberates through taste. Then calling the guests is as follows. Saying "**the nāga king of demonic forces . . .**" and so forth until "**. . . come here**," the embodiment of the confusion of desire that abides on earth is the bird-headed demoness. She has webbed feet and hands and holds a butcher's knife in her right hand and a bag of disease in her left. Wearing a fresh human skin as the upper garment, she stands without a mount encircled by boundless female demons that resemble her.

Above her is the embodiment of ferocious aggression as the kingly male demonic force with a snake head. His right hand holds a staff, and his left a begging bowl. He wears the three robes of ordination and a monastic hat. He rides a white lioness and is surrounded by an assembly of kingly spirits, such as sadhus, barbarians, and a retinue of ministers and masculine demonic forces wearing a variety of regalia.

Above them is the embodiment of delusion-based ignorance as the kingly demonic force of the nāgas with a pig's head. His upper body is human, and the lower is a coiled snake. His right hand holds a serpent lasso, and his left a bag of disease. He rides a green-speckled water monster and is surrounded by a countless assembly of delusion-based demon nāgas just like himself.

Above them is the powerful female of saṃsāra and enlightenment in the aspect of the black Remati,[a] whose nature is the queen of basic space. She holds a sword in the right hand, and a skull filled with blood in the left. Her long black, unruly hair flows downward. She squeezes a bag of disease under her armpit and wears a fresh human skin upper garment and a woven yak-hair skirt. Her white incisors are bared, and her turquoise eyebrows twitch. She rides upon a three-eyed, white-muzzled donkey that wears a double-sectioned saddle. The first part is made of the upper jawbone skull of a cannibal, and the back part is made of the lower section of the cannibal's jaw and is draped with a fresh human skin. The donkey also wears snake-skin breast and belly plates. In the front and back of the saddle hang balls of colored yarn, as well as dark- and light-colored pebbles for dice, a ledger, and a bag of disease. Imagine she is surrounded by an inconceivable gathering of females tossing their hair and appearing just like her. Thus, as mentioned in the notes [on chöd], these are the essential ornamentation of the māras that are congruent with the liturgy of the main text [i.e., terma].

Another option is that the sole queen of existence [i.e., Remati] holds a sword and a bag of disease in her right hand and a butcher's knife and lasso in the left. Below her is the demonic force of the nāgas appearing as a charnel-ground, pig-headed one riding a black pig and holding an axe in the right hand and lasso in the left. Below that is the kingly masculine force with a horse head, riding a black

[a] *re ma ti'*

horse, and holding a saw and fresh human head. On the earth is the demoness negative force holding a woven yak-hair flag and a lasso while riding a black bird. I received these explanations given as oral instructions.

Then during the invocation, blow the thigh-bone horn, or say *phet*; and during the first recitation, think that they hear you; the second time, they depart [from their realms]; and at the third, think that they gather like a crowd. This applies to all invocations mentioned either previously or later.

Then, the song of the view that calls from afar is as follows. Saying "**the even taste of saṃsāra and enlightenment** . . ." until ". . . **the great method of generosity**," all mental appearances of impure saṃsāra are actually seen as the equal taste of good and bad, the fundamental nature of original purity free from bias. I, a practitioner with the confidence of fearlessness, have from beginningless time until now cherished this nonexistent self through fixation. These aggregates that have emerged from confusion have brought about meaningless previous lifetimes. Now, in order to perfect great waves of the two accumulations for self and others: just as the previous victors have performed deeds, I, too, will engage in the great method of giving generosity.

This is also mentioned in the *Sūtra Requested by Nyewa Khor*:[a]

> "Generosity" means to give the gift of one's kingdom. "Great generosity" is to give the gift of one's sons and daughters. "Tremendous generosity" is to give the gift of one's body parts, such as the head, legs, eyes, skin, and marrow.[225]

Thus, as taught, tremendous generosity involves this method of giving the body, so one must give the body as a gift. So, it is.

Then, saying ". . . **recipients of generosity, confused by ignorance** . . ." and so forth until ". . . **consume everything** . . .", the gods-māras along with their retinues are the objects of generosity who are overwhelmed by ignorance, as mentioned above. By offering the feast of the human corpse in the charnel ground, think that they [i.e., the gods-māras] partake of this with the sounds of gobbling, consuming, tearing, and ripping, leaving nothing behind. With the first *phet*, this is offered; with the second, they receive it; and with the third, they are satisfied with the taste of empty bliss. Think that merit is perfected and negativities are purified.

Then saying ". . . **accordingly the recipients of generosity** . . ." until ". . . **vanish** . . ." is that, by partaking of this, all gods-māras as the objects of the generosity become like a black heap of coal. The smaller members of the retinue are con-

[a] *nyewa khor gyi zhü pa'i do* (*nye ba 'khor gyis zhus pa'i mdo, āryavinayavinishcayaupāliparipṛcchānāmmahāyānasūtra*)

sumed by the larger, and finally they are all consumed by the three main ones of their categories. The kingly force eats the demoness, the nāga force eats the kingly force, and the earthly kingly force is then eaten by the great black female without masticating. She also eats her entire assembly of servants, and they all vanish in the expanse of the dharmakāya. With the first *phet*, rest in nonconceptual awareness; with the second *phet*, this is actualized; and with the third, through achieving the depth of confidence, liberation occurs. This visualization for eliminating gods-māras just mentioned may be omitted, and also there is no section of offering to the guests who are the remainders.

Then, abiding in the expanse of the view is that, by saying "**self and objective appearances . . .**" until "**. . . rest in the evenness . . .**", self and all objective appearances are like awakening from a dream. Everything gathers into the fundamental nature of the primordial ground of original awareness, the genuine heruka. All gods-māras, buddhas, sentient beings, subjects, objects, and harmdoers and their objects are within this great spontaneous dimension of unbiased original purity, equally pervading as uncontrived self-occurring wisdom just as it is. With the first *phet*, this dynamic strength mingles with the basic space of the nirmāṇakāya. With the second, this radiance attains the confidence of the sambhogakāya; and with the third, think that the wisdom intent of the dharmakāya nature is rendered evident.

Other versions of the black feast are as mentioned in the *Dispelling All Obscurations*[a] version of the black feast from the cycle of the Treasury Expanse of the Spacelike Dharmatā.

The feast of the nectars is that, by saying *phet*, the consciousness is transferred some seven cubits into the upper regions of the sky. There, it becomes a vast mass of light that strikes the earth, transforming it into a skull equal to the trichiliocosm. Then in the upper space, the gurus, Triple Gem, and oceans of victors all reside like massing clouds; and from their kāyas, streams of purifying wisdom nectar descend. Imagining oneself in an ordinary body, at one's crown is a white syllable *ah* of the gods that includes all habits. At the nape of the neck is the yellow syllable *su* of the asuras, including all habits. At the heart is the human syllable, a pale blue *nri*, including all habits; and at the navel is the blue animal syllable *tri* and all habits. At the secret place is the red syllable of the pretas, *dre*, along with the habits; and at the soles of the feet is the hell realm syllable, a black *du*, along with those habits. Then imagine that black liquid descends from them [i.e., the syllables] and that illness descends as blood and pus, demonic forces as insects and parasites, and negative obscurations as dust-colored smoke that fills up the skull cup.

From space, the three syllables descend like pouring rain to transform this

[a] *drib pa kun sel* (*sgrib pa kun sel*)

[substance] into fully endowed wisdom ambrosia that liberates upon taste. Imagine that the nectar is black and swirling as the guests partake of it. It is unnecessary to visualize the guests individually like before. Perform the subsequent feasts by following according to the text [i.e., terma].

3.2.2.2.4.3 The White Feast

Third, in order to accumulate merit, the practice of the white feast is as follows. Saying "***phet*** **... the habit of self-grasping** ..." and so forth until the verses "... **ever-increasing desirable offerings**," as taught, visualize the central energy channel as before in the middle of this magical heap of aggregates that originate from the unyielding habit of self-grasping. In the middle of that channel, vital innate awareness transfers to the great basic space of the ground of original purity. From the space of the dharmatā, the magical manifestation of wisdom emerges as one's nature appearing as a clear white-colored ḍākinī.

From one's kāya, boundless light and rays radiate to purify the negative obscurations and habits of sentient beings. The right hand wields a razor-sharp sword; and by merely pointing this toward the corpse, it is flayed. The left hand holds a banner of wind that blows the flesh and blood into particles, dispersing them in all directions to fill the trichiliocosm. Mingling indistinguishably with the outer appearances of the objective elements, instantly the entire earth becomes mounds of cakes, mountains become heaps of butter, crags become mounds of the three sweets, rivers flow with milk, and lakes overflow with yogurt. Just like the manifestations of the array of the god realm known as Paranirmitavashavartin,[226] all desirable things of phenomenal existence become clouds of white offerings. By the showering rain of the three syllables from basic space, everything is blessed to become wisdom ambrosia that grants liberation upon experience.

Saying "***Eh ma!*** ... **buddha** ..." and so forth until the verses "... **emanates from me** ...", as it teaches concerning buddhas and sentient beings, the universe, inhabitants, and the rest: aside from being the dynamic manifestation of the great wisdom clear-light nature of one's mind, nothing is otherwise. Saying "***phet*** **I, a practitioner of the Madhyamaka** ..." and so forth until "... **actualize** ...", it is taught that in accord with the key points of the views of the Madhyamaka, Mahāmudrā, and Mahāsandhi in that order: by realizing the intrinsic nature of all phenomena as great emptiness, self-grasping is severed. By sealing with the samādhi that realizes the view of the magical nature of all phenomena, everything becomes the dance of offering and expressing generosity. In this way, fixation upon objects is severed. By realizing with naked awareness that everything is perfected within the dharmatā in the manner of the perfectly pure three circles, the great space of purity and evenness is rendered evident.

Then saying "**the ground of the tathāgatas** . . ." and so forth until ". . . **to awaken** . . .", it is taught that the self-radiance of the buddha nature's basic space of the ground is the three supreme ones who are the guests known as "the exalted objects of refuge". The dynamic strength, or array of awareness, on the path appears as the guests known as "the protectors of noble qualities". Saying "**the mind of the three poisons** . . ." and so forth until ". . . **given as the abundant** . . ." is taught from the perspective of the mind's three poisons, and there comes to be the objective field of the three realms of saṃsāra. The dynamic strength of that appears in the form of concepts as the guests, who are known as the classes of obstructing forces and karmic debtors. Each are given that which they are worthy of receiving.

By saying ". . . **outer grasping** . . ." and so forth until ". . . **offerings are partaken of** . . .", it is taught that the gods-māras that emerge from external grasping manifest as the objects that are given varieties of desirable phenomena. The gods-māras that emerge from the confused conceptualization of the inner fixating mind are given the desirables that are nonexistent yet appear. Between these, the gods-māras of interdependent grasping and fixating are given all phenomena that originate from the continuity of confused existence. It is necessary to understand this from the perspective of how this applies to both the manner of generosity and offering according to relative truth and the description of absolute truth's liberation of confusion. Otherwise, it is difficult to comprehend this just through the words alone. For now, I will leave it at that. Then saying ". . . **the objective three realms** . . ." and so forth until ". . . **purity and evenness** ***ah la la***", it is taught for one to remain within the fundamental nature that lacks true existence.

3.2.2.2.4.4 The Mixed Feast

Fourth, the mixed feast is as follows. Saying "***phet*** **in the center of one's body** . . ." and so forth until ". . . ***ha ho hri*** . . .", it is taught to visualize that, in the center of one's body as vast as the earth and sky, upon the joint at the heart center within the central energy channel like a crystal pipe, the nature of one's consciousness as a lucid five-colored bindu possessing all glorious qualities appears.

Like a shooting star, this shoots upward into the sky; and from basic space, one appears as Tröma Nagmo holding a curved vajra blade in the right hand. By merely pointing this at one's abandoned body, one's bodies and endowments from all past lifetimes are gathered to dissolve there. By merely pointing the curved vajra blade, the skin is then flayed to stretch and evenly cover the entire ground of this world. Upon that on the right side, all raw and cooked meat becomes the mountains; broth and fatty oils, as well as the warm blood with steam, become the oceans. To the left, the crags and mountains are made of all the marrow, brains, and cartilage, as well as the fat. In front, the skull descends onto a skull tripod filled with the five types of flesh and the five nectars. Below this, the winds blow, the fire blazes, and the nectars begin to boil. The steam and vapors become the seven outer offerings and the inner five desirables, while the secret medicine, blood, and torma are presented by countless offering goddesses and the sixteen consorts. Moreover, there are pennants, parasols, and victory banners, the eight auspicious signs, and the seven royal symbols as an array of boundless offering substances that fill all regions of space.

The earth as well is divided into portions, whereby to the east there are silver mountains and valleys; to the south, golden mountains and valleys; to the west, copper mountains and valleys; and to the north, the mountains and valleys are made of jewels, uncultured pearls, turquoise, iron, and so forth. In the regions between the mountains and valleys, there are yogurt and milk lakes, butter and cake mountains, and crags of the three sweets that have plateaus surpassing the height of Mt. Meru. The lakes are deeper than the oceans, and their numbers surpass the particles of the sun's motes.

To the perimeter of that, there are varieties of grains, medicines, edibles, gold, silver, copper, iron, household items, clothes made from brocades, silks, cottons, and woven cloth that are not only lovely but soft, thin, and so refined that to touch them brings pleasure. There are various types of armor and varieties of wild animal skins. There are jeweled palaces and ordinary homes, canopies, and tents; earthen and rocky caves; beds, thrones, and cushions; close companions, guardians who protect from fear, retinues, servants, and subjects; wild and domesticated animals, creatures that live in the water, and all classes of nāgas; multi-colored silken and wool balls of yarn; fields of herbs, meadows, gardens; and varieties of birds—all of which are pleasing to behold. All sounds are sweet to the ears, scents are enticing, and tastes are delicious. Imagine everything to be soft to the touch and so forth, as there are no enjoyments or desirable qualities that are left incomplete.

From basic space, the blessings of all the victorious ones' kāyas rain forth as white light rays, their enlightened speech as red light rays, and their enlightened minds as blue-black-colored light rays. Imagine that this transforms everything into the ambrosia of enlightened body, speech, and mind. Saying "***om ah hung ha ho hri*** and **permanent protectors** . . ." until ". . .**be attained** . . .", it is taught that by invoking the guests, from one's heart, countless activity ḍākinīs emanate to invite the exalted guests of refuge, who are offered the desirable offering substances explained immediately above that fill all regions of space. The protectors of noble qualities are offered the three sweets and three white substances and whatever is desired among the vast array of the purest abundance. The guests who are the six classes of beings, the objects of compassion, and the obstructing forces and karmic debtors are given fresh flesh and warm blood, the three sweets and whites, as well as whatever is able to fulfill their needs and desires. Thinking they receive this, recite *phet* until the visualization is stable. Recite *phet* again until there is confidence. Recite *phet* until one is fully satisfied with this.

Having offered this to the higher guests, they are satisfied with the taste of empty bliss; and self and all sentient beings together perfect the accumulation of merit and purify obscurations. Think that they all become awakened. By expressing generosity to the lower guests, they become fully satisfied; and think that, after fulfilling their individual desires, they become awakened. By blessing the remains and offering this to the recipients of the remains, all weak and feeble ones become stronger; the lowly ones gain power; the slow ones gain swift vitality and strength; and the blind, mute, and deaf regain their faculties so they can see, hear, and speak once again. Think that they then possess the faculties of prajñā.

Then saying "... **by this virtue, may all beings** ..." and so forth until ..." **even pervasion** ...", it is taught that by dedicating the virtue, one rests in nonconceptual awareness. This is the mixed feast that corresponds to the external body according to the teachings in the main text [i.e., terma].

Moreover, there are three visualizations that correspond to the way of offering the feasts. They include the visualization of a jeweled mountain, of a wish-fulfilling jewel, and of a wish-granting tree. For the first, one's body instantly becomes like a mountain. The peak is gold, the bottom is silver, and below that there are other precious metals such as copper. The aspects of the white and red elements appear as the light of the sun and moon that shine upon this mountain. Think that the four guests' domain of their six faculties is satisfied with whatever is desired and that they accumulate merit and purify obscurations.

[The second visualization of the wish-fulfilling jewel is missing from the text. Perhaps the visualization given below for the precious mountain can be applied to this missing section for the wish-fulfilling jewel. This needs to be analyzed.[227]]

Third, imagine that one's body becomes a wish-granting tree. The tree's nature is the bodhichitta that appears to be blown by the cooling winds. Through that motion, myriad clouds of desirable offerings equal to space are presented to the domain of the guests' faculties including form, sound, smell, taste, and touch. The minds of all exalted guests are fully satisfied through the taste of empty bliss, and self and others perfect merit and purify obscurations. The lower guests all rejoice and delight in the substances. Think that they attain the state of omniscience.

In addition, the visualization of the jeweled mountain is that one's body becomes a jeweled mountain; and by the light of this, the phenomena of all sentient beings transform. Like awakening from sleep, imagine that all beings awaken from their suffering and achieve the abundance of mastery like the glorious abundance of the kingly gods from the Tuṣhita god realm.[a] I received these teachings as oral instructions.

3.2.2.2.4.5 The Red Feast

Fifth is the offering of the red feast as follows. Saying "***phet*** **. . . the impure elements . . .**" and so forth until ". . . ***ha ho hri*** **. . .** ," it is taught that this magical heap is habituated through karma with the contaminated elements that appear in the aspect of a corporeal body of flesh and blood. In the center of this, as mentioned before, within the path of the central channel, vital cognitive awareness appears as a five-colored bindu. With the first *phet*, this transfers; with the second, awareness mingles with basic space; and with the third, from within that, the kāya of Tröma arises.

In the right hand, she holds a curved vajra blade; and by merely pointing it, this body that fills the trichiliocosm instantly falls to pieces. With the edibles as abundant as mountains of flesh and so forth all the way to oceans of churning marrow, fat, and cartilage, the vaporous steam produces clouds of bounty, such as the five desirable objects. From space, the intrinsic nature of the tathāgatas' bodies, speech, and minds descends like pouring rain in the aspect of the three syllables to bless this corporeal body of flesh and blood. The body becomes immaculate wisdom nectar, the five aspects of enlightened body, speech, mind, qualities, and activities, as well as being fully endowed form, sound, smell, taste, and touch.

Calling the guests is that, from one's heart as the wisdom ḍākinī Tröma Nagmo, light rays boundlessly radiate above, below, and into all directions. From the unchanging nature of the dharmatā, the eleven wisdom ḍākinīs in the manner of the perfect dynamic strength of magical emanation, accompanied by millions of ḍākinīs and an assembly of the gods-māras of phenomenal existence, are all invoked.

Then saying "**wisdom mothers of basic space . . .**" until "**. . . dispel . . . in basic space**", it is taught to visualize the ten ḍākinīs and each of their assemblies that include millions of retinue members, as well as the gods-māras. The nature is the ten principal ones; the dynamic strength is the millions of ḍākinīs; and the radiance is the gods-māras of phenomenal existence.

Conversely, the magical aspect is the wisdom ḍākinī, and the manifestations are the millions of emanations. The play is the gods-māras of phenomenal existence, all of whom are gradually imagined to fill heaven and earth. To expand, all of that becomes the intrinsic nature of empty prajñā, the mother of all victo-

[a] *ga den nam par gyal wa* (*dga' ldan rnam par rgyal ba*)

rious ones. From this empty space of wisdom, myriad emanations are revealed according to how they will tame beings. Hence, they are the dancers of this emanation.

Buddha Ḍākinī of the central direction along with millions of emanations, including the classes of gods-māras of phenomenal existence, all delight in partaking of the corpse of flesh and blood, this heap of illness, demonic force, negative obscurations, and the source of that, the passion of delusion. Fulfilled with the taste of empty bliss, finally the outer dynamic strength as the gods-māras of phenomenal existence dissolves into the millions of ḍākinīs. They dissolve into Buddha Ḍākinī, and she dissolves into the space of phenomena.

Likewise, know that the same sequence applies to Vajra Ḍākinī and her assemblies concerning that which originates from the passion of anger; Ratna Ḍākinī and pride; Pema Ḍākinī and desire; Karma Ḍākinī and jealousy; the ḍākinīs of the intermediate directions and the eighty-four thousand passions; the upper-space ḍākinīs and the three poisons; the lower ḍākinīs and duality; and the flesh-eating ḍākinīs and ignorance. During this offering, with the first *phet*, offer to the principal one; with the second, to the millions in the assemblies; and with the third, to the gods-māras of phenomenal existence. Then saying "**wisdom mothers of the basic space of phenomena** . . ." and so forth until ". . . **awaken within** . . .", it is taught that, by inciting the wisdom intent and supplicating, one must rest within the fundamental nature.

One may also apply this to the pure-vision red feast. There, the central ḍākinī holds a skull and curved blade. The ten intermediate ḍākinīs hold their own emblems in their right hands and skulls filled with blood in the left. Visualizing the ten intermediate ḍākinīs, their assemblies of ḍākinīs, and the gods-māras simultaneously, the feast is presented to them together. With the first *phet*, the stages of giving the feast are presented. Otherwise, with the first *phet*, the feast is offered to the wisdom ḍākinī; then with the second, to the assembly of ḍākinīs; and with the third, to the gods-māras. Finally the stages of dissolution occur simultaneously. Conversely, when the corpse and awareness separate, to give the feast in individual portions is also fine. Either one of these ways is considered equal according to the oral instructions.

For a sick person, once the corpse and awareness separate, offering in portions is best. It is also best to perform individual dissolutions. That is to rotate methods while offering the feast. If the feast is given all at once, then visualize that one's body is huge, fat, and majestic like Mt. Meru. Having transferred the consciousness, then at the moment that this body collapses onto the ground, like sparks from a fire, think that the corpse expands to fill up the trichiliocosm world systems. Call the guests and offer the feast like before.

The meaning of saying "emanations are uncertain" is that—in order to teach dharma—the expressions of kāyas, such as peaceful, wrathful, older, youthful, and so forth, all occur. Their colors are variegated, such as white, yellow, red, green, and blue-black; and the emanation of their ornaments and accouterments is also uncertain. Abiding in the pure lands and being keepers of the charnel grounds, it is said they will do and be whatever is needed to accomplish deeds in harmony with benefiting beings.

The red feast for the fear-provoking environment is that, from the verses of refuge and bodhichitta all the way through the generation of the body, the transference recitation, and the purification and increasing, one imagines that countless corpses fill the entire world. Bless them to become the wisdom nectar that liberates upon taste, and then make the offerings. Think that all the guests delight in this by biting with their mouths and hands and some even use knifes until nothing at all remains. Then imagine that the dissolution occurs.

If this is being performed especially for a sick person, then mingle one's consciousness with the sick person and then transfer. Arising in space as Tröma, the feast is then offered. If one is focusing on an enemy, then imagine that you perform a feast for each of the ten ḍākinīs as they depart for the enemy's locale. Imagine that the enemy and their retinues are partaken of by the gods-māras of phenomenal existence.

> Among these four feasts, the white feast is offered in the early morning, the mixed at noon, the red in the evening, and the black feast during predawn.
> **Applying them** [i.e., the feasts] **to these four times, always maintain diligence in this practice.**
> With the view of emptiness and motivated to benefit beings: by transforming this cherished body into the feast in conjunction with accumulating merit and cleansing obscurations, self-fixation is tamed.
> This way of actualizing the enlightened expanse of the Great Mother is superb.

Thus, these are the verses that summarize the section.

3.2.2.2.5 Samaya Incorporated while Wandering

Fifth is the samaya for the fear-provoking environment. Generally, it states in Āryadeva's treatise on chöd:

> The training of the bodhisattvas is to never abandon one's practice even at the cost of one's life. One must exert oneself in guarding the vows. For killing and so forth—the ten nonvirtues—one must abandon them

> as well as encourage others to do the same. Those who abandon killing must be encouraged and verbally acknowledged. When the ten non-virtues are abandoned, then the six pāramitās are refreshed through personal engagement and influencing others. The six pāramitās must be reinvigorated and verbally acknowledged.

Thus, it is taught. Reference to "reinvigorating" means to express the qualities derived when others have engaged in that way, as well as working to inspire even those who have not engaged in that way. Furthermore, it states:

> Cutting off entanglement with objective appearances that are terrifying and impossible to deal with, as well as food and wealth, and reversing fixation toward retinue and family . . .

Thus, and so forth, these are the words of Machig that refer to all aspects of samaya. Especially, she repeatedly refers to the necessity of engaging carefully with the conduct of body and speech and exerting oneself in the practice of acceptance and rejection. Once receiving the empowerment of Tröma, one must be diligent in guarding all root and branch Mantra samaya more than cherishing one's eyes and heart.

In particular, while wandering in the fear-provoking places at night, one must not make fires, burn candles or any light, not walk barefoot, recite wrathful mantras, meditate, or generate wrathful deities. Feces and urine should be excreted at one location; one must not scream or shout; and shoes should be put under one's pillow, with hats placed under the foot of the bed.[228] **Lay down on the right side and stretch out the thighs and shoulders like a cushion. Keep the palm of the hand open to support the head like a headrest. Abandon any form of entertainment or distraction.**

All of these directives involving the way of communicating with the gods-māras through threatening speech start from "dancing ḍākinīs of the chöd lineage . . ." and so forth until ". . . supreme praise rendered to the mount of the seven horses, samaya *ih thi*." As taught, the meaning of this is given according to explanations found in notes.

After completing the stages of practice for the four great feasts, one must then definitely depart to wander in fear-provoking places some nine times. It is acceptable to do so while still receiving instructions. During that time, one must practice all aspects of the wandering section, such as the initial suppression and the like. Once receiving the chöd commentaries, either stay in retreat for one-hundred days or depart for the one-hundred and eight charnel grounds and wander there. It is acceptable for the one-hundred and eight-day wandering to occur in either fear-provoking places or where water springs emerge. Wandering for just nine days is a way of not forgetting the traditional way of practicing [the wandering].

At first, it is best to stay in retreat in order to accomplish the recitations. Once that is done, one should go to the one-hundred and eight frightful places. For that, it is ideal to then offer a feast in every place or at least to offer one every ten days. Following that, in order to repair any errors, offer one-hundred thousand accumulations with fire pūjā. Other traditions mention that to keep pebbles from those places is acceptable, in that one would then not need to perform the visualization for the subsequent suppression, nor would they wander outside to beg for food and the like. In this tradition, it is better to not keep the pebbles since that is the case. Once performing the subsequent suppression, it is acceptable to go into the homes of others without performing the initial suppression. It is also permitted to give transmissions and so forth to others.

Nevertheless, once arriving at the frightening place, this kind of activity must then conclude. The best would be to remain in each frightening environment until the extent of completion and the upheavals have all occurred. Whatever the case, one should not remain longer than a week [in one place]. By then, if both the extent of completion and the upheavals have not occurred, then suffice it to say that they will not. Without them, if one is practicing just in order to not break any commitments, then it is irrelevant whether the upheavals and extents actually occur or not. In that case, one should stay for a day and then move on. Until the wandering practice to the one-hundred and eight places is complete, it is better to not go to other locations as well. All of this information is based on oral instructions, so I have included it here.

While remaining in the fear-provoking places, **the key point is to try not to escape, supplicate, or find protection no matter how terrifying the phenomena may be. If there is an attempt to escape, then once again return and remain until the severance is successful. If one tries to escape some nine times, then it is considered to be a failure of the practice; so one must refrain from continuing on and no longer return to that place. If one tries to escape eight times and finds success** [in the practice] **by the ninth, that is still fine.**[229]

Following the upheavals, the extents of completion will emerge. Once that occurs, it is no longer acceptable to stay in that same place, so one must move on. The extent of completion includes actual visions, dreams, and experiences whatever the case may be, such as many people prostrating, making offerings, offering wealth and food, taking refuge, listening to orders, taking oaths, praising, and playing many musical instruments. The sun and moon may be rising, flowers blossoming, celebrations occurring, and so forth.

In brief, whatever arises or appears, if the mind feels ecstatically satisfied, realization increases and the body, speech, and mind relax. Then, whatever good or bad signs may come—given that this is the extent of completion—it

indicates that one must transfer locations. Even if good signs arise, the mind will feel a sense of heightened hope and fear, distraction, joy and sorrow, trepidation, and many other reactions that make the body, speech, and mind uncomfortable. Although these experiences may seem to be the extent of the completion, they are actually upheavals. Hence, it is a quintessential key point to know the single taste of whatever occurs, whether good or bad.

The initial extent of completion is indicated when the severed heads, extremities, and hollow and solid organs of others are presented to you; you are given ornaments, wealth, and abundance; you destroy all grass shacks, rocky caves, and frightening locations that you come into contact with; or at evaporated lakes, you are giving energy and well-being to many disadvantaged beings. If these experiences occur, then move the distance of a pebble flung from a slingshot.

The final extent of severance is that all gods-māras will take an oath to join you as retinue and servants. They will offer their hearts to you, many people will be praising you as their crown ornament, you will be enthroned, and many great lamas and leaders will receive empowerment from you and be admitted into your retinue. Donning armor and metal plating, you will be placed on a great throne to become the leader of grand classes of subjects. Accompanying great armies, you will invade and conquer countries [and] will ride and tame dragons, lions, tigers, wild and domesticated yaks, as well as various types of birds. The sun and moon will be spread out as your cushions, and you will take a seat at the peak of the highest mountain of all. You will also gain mastery over many places and countries. Once these signs occur, one should no longer practice at that location. Know that these signs are ominous, much like a mistreated servant turning against his or her persecutor.[230]

3.2.2.2.6 The Way of Visualizing the Subsequent Suppression

Sixth is the way to practice the visualization for the final severance of the subsequent suppression. If one is unable to complete the subsequent suppression, they [i.e., the gods-māras] will pursue you like an owner pursuing the robber of his wealth. Given this is similar:[231] **for the final severance, prepare the backpack; and when it is time to go, replace the cushion where you have been staying with a support of enlightened body, speech, or mind and consecrate that. Recite the verse of auspiciousness and think that the gods-māras are circumambulating and making offerings there. Perform *Giving the Dharma*[a] and then stand up and visualize as follows. Think that one's corporeal body of flesh and blood completely falls apart and becomes mountains of flesh, oceans of blood, and**

[a] *chö kyi chin pa* (*chos kyi sbyin pa*)

steaming vapor of inexhaustible desirable objects, such as marrow, fat, and cartilage. Imagine that the gods-māras of that place then partake of this.[232]

Saying *ha ha hi hi he he ho ho hung hung phet phet*, take seven steps and drop the backpack. Say, "*Ki ki*, hey powerful gods, nāgas, and local lords of this place, listen all of you! Don't allow any gods-māras who were not here before to come to my place. Don't let the gods-māras who abide here get out. I entrust you to do this. Take care of this. I will watch to see just how much power you have. Quickly, quickly!" Saying this, pick up the backpack.

With *phet*, one's awareness becomes the five wisdom ḍākinīs; imagine that they depart for the four directions, including the fifth central direction. Proceeding about as far as you can see, drop the backpack and visualize that you make the boundary marker. This becomes a red-black wisdom garuḍa, ablaze with fire filling heaven and earth. Think that this sets up the boundary between the gods-māras and oneself.

Say, "*Eh eh!* You wisdom garuḍa king, lord of power and strength, listen to me! Powerful gods, nāgas, nonhuman spirits, and powerful mountain protectors—all of you, listen here! Do not send any gods, māras, spirits, or obstructing forces of any type after me. Set the boundaries now. Do not allow your strength and powers to decline. Hurry! Hurry up, with samaya!" Then while imagining that phenomenal existence becomes filled with mountains of flesh and oceans of blood, recite *phet* nine times.

Alternatively, there is a separate visualization for establishing the boundary marker that may be performed. If one is departing for another frightening place from there, begin with the *Suppression through Splendor* as before. If departing for yet another uncertain locale, do so without further elaboration. If one is returning home, imagine that awareness dissolves into the Akaniṣhṭha and shout *phet*. Again, from the heart of Samantabhadrī, white light like a silken thread extends down to enter the roof of one's house. Awareness becomes a white bindu the size of a mustard seed that rolls down the shaft of light to enter one's house. Departing and imagining in these ways are all profound severance techniques that follow the subsequent or final suppression.

Whatever the case, the master Drogon Tsangpa Gyarey[a,233] has said:

> In the citadel of conceptual existence, the zombie of the eight worldly concerns dwells in the frightening charnel grounds. If one aspires to practice the one taste of everything, then practice must occur right there.

[a] *'gro mgon gtsang pa rgya ras*

Thus, as taught, if the practice is successfully carried forth: aside from this, it is unnecessary to achieve severance in another frightening place.

> The exceptional locale is to wander in the fear-provoking charnel grounds.
> The exceptional practice is to cast off the heap of aggregates as the feast.
> The exceptional objects to tame are the gods-māras to care for, and the exceptional point to be known is the realization of selflessness.

These are the verses that summarize the section.

3.2.2.3 Supplementary Explanation for the Generation Stage of Tröma

Third is the supplementary explanation for the generation stage of Tröma as the meditation deity. First, for refuge, the field of refuge includes Samantabhadrī without ornaments, with hands in the mudrā of evenness. To her right is Vajravarāhī standing, while holding a curved blade and skull. To her left is Tröma Nagmo in the dancing posture, holding a curved blade and skull. They are surrounded by an assembly of the three-kāya wisdom ḍākinīs—the dharmakāya, sambhogakāya, and nirmāṇakāya. In front are all sentient beings, including oneself, taking heartfelt refuge and offering their bodies, wealth, and root of all virtue.

Supplicate thinking, "May all of you bless my stream of mind." During the generation of bodhichitta, the field of refuge is invited to bear witness. Imagine that all sentient beings undergoing tremendous suffering are present in front. Aspire to place them all on the ground of unsurpassed awakening. In order to do so, think, "I will actually accomplish the state of the three-kāya wisdom ḍākinīs," and arouse the bodhichitta and offer the seven-branch prayer. All ḍākinīs then dissolve into oneself in the aspect of orbs of white and red light. Think that one's three doors are blessed.

It is unnecessary to meditate on expelling the obstructers or the wheel of protection. During the descent of blessings, from one's heart, light radiates. Through the power of intense devotion, the Triple Gem, Three Kāyas, Three Roots, and all assemblies of deities, including their pure lands, are invoked. All perfectly pure lands dissolve into the environment. The celestial palaces dissolve into the abodes. All deities dissolve into the practitioners, while some dissolve into the accomplishment substances. To bless the offering materials, all phenomena of dualistic existence vanish like a rainbow into the nature of emptiness. Instantly, from that, the self-radiance of clear-light wisdom free from sullying factors arises in the sky like a rainbow. All offering substances fill the upper realms of the buddhas, pleasing them as clouds of Samantabhadra's offerings. Filling the lower realms of sentient beings, visualize that all suffering is fully purified.

During the generation of the deity, all impure appearances of the karmic eon dissipate into basic space. Actualizing the nature of phenomena, the pure appearance of the wisdom deity emerges. The outer support of the universe and the inner movement of sentient beings as the inhabitants, including one's body, elements, and sense sources, all dissolve into the space of the ground, like a magical illusion. Otherwise, like a rainbow vanishing in space, think that one remains in the equal pervasion of the great fundamental nature of emptiness. The dharmatā nature, as it is, is rendered evident as the *samādhi of the nature as it is*.

From within that, to render evident the all-pervasive, all-knowing clear-light wisdom free from sullying factors is to actualize and illuminate all essential qualities of the sugatas. That is the *all-illuminating samādhi*. Then think that the nature of this wisdom appears as the syllable *hung*. Given that is the cause of the support and supporting maṇḍala, it is *the causal samādhi*.[a,234] Light radiates from that *hung*. Think that, then, self-appearances become the absolute Akaniṣhṭha equal to the domain of the space of phenomena. It is mentioned in the oral teachings that, in order to practice the ritual of chöd, this alone will suffice.

If the meditation deity is being emphasized, it is then necessary to visualize the celestial palace. In the midst of that, upon lotus, sun, and moon seats, the syllable *hung* descends from space while radiating light. This light penetrates into the pure lands of the trikāya victors and their heirs. Reabsorbing back, all of their power and blessings are gathered. Once again radiating downward, the suffering of all beings is purified. Gathering all longevity, merit, and glorious abundance, this dissolves into the *hung*.

Then the nature of awareness as *hung* fully transforms into the sole mother, Tröma Nagmo, visualized according to the deity generation in the main text. Within the space of that kāya, all maṇḍalas of the victorious ones are generated like a reflected form within a mirror. From the self-radiance of wisdom's magical play, like the sun and its rays, the assembly of retinue deities are generated. From Tröma, who is like the sun, the self-radiance of the five wisdoms like the sun's light radiates as the five ḍākinīs such as Vajra Ḍākinī and the others, who are like sun rays. From that, their emanations and further emanations with their individual colors manifest, holding curved blades that indicate their family and skull cups filled with blood, while they pose in the dancing posture.

In the four intermediate directions, they are surrounded by their individual retinues, who are similar to them as the ḍākinīs of the self-radiance of the four immeasurable qualities, such as compassion. Their further emanations also

[a] *de zhin nyid kyi ting ngen dzin*, *kuntu nang wa'i ting ngen dzin*, and *gyu'i ting ngen dzin* (*de bzhin nyid kyi ting nge 'dzin*, *kun tu snang ba'i ting nge 'dzin*, and *rgyu'i ting nge 'dzin*)

include the ḍākinīs who are located to the east as the ḍākinī of peaceful activity, white in color, with a snake head, riding a blue iron wolf, and holding a blazing vajra in the right hand that severs duality. To the south is the enriching-activity ḍākinī, golden, with a lion head, riding a golden donkey, and holding emblems as described in the main text.[235] To the west is the power ḍākinī, red in color, with a vulture's head, riding a vulture, holding a copper rod that sucks out the heart blood of perverted ones. For example, this resembles the tip of a drum stick that is slightly curved at the base. To the north is the wrathful karmic ḍākinī, green in color, with a bear head, riding a red jackal. In her left hand, she holds a snake lasso that takes away the breath of beings. Encircled by a vast, inconceivable host of ḍākas and ḍākinīs, who are the owners of the sacred grounds and the charnel grounds, think that they actually appear in their dwelling places like an assembly gathering.

By the splendor of their kāyas and wisdoms, all harm-doing gods-māras, including all sentient beings of the three realms and sponsors—like salt melting in water—mingle with the enlightened mind of great clear light to merge with the great perfection. Just as the sun, its light, and rays of light are the play of a single sun, it is necessary to know that the principal one and the retinue are not other than a single manifestation.

Then, the way of generating the dharmapālas is that, in the eastern direction in a vast and deep ocean of milk, the embodiment of all earth lords, nāgas, and nonhuman spirits appears as the King of Nāgas, Migon Karpo,[a] wearing a white silken turban adorned with the heads of nine snakes. His lower body is a coiled snake; and the five nāgas, five nonhuman spirits, and five earth-lord families are indicated in front by an arrangement of deities that sequentially appear as white, gold, red, and green. Think that they are under one's control and that they embody the subterranean earth lords, nāgas, and nonhuman spirits, with coiled snake lower bodies.

In the southern direction in a nine-tiered iron fortress is Shinje Yamāradza,[b] blue-black in color, extremely terrifying, delighting in flesh, and eager to kill. In his right hand, he holds a hammer for killing; and the rest is according to the main text. Wearing a leopard skin, he rides upon a water buffalo, with legs drawn up. He is surrounded by yamās, such as the horse-headed yamās of anger, the pig-headed yamās of delusion, and the eight classes of gods and cannibals—all anxious to kill, sever, and chop.

In the western direction within a copper palace that has a dazzling peak reaching into the firmament is the red King of Tsen, riding a red horse. He is frightening to behold, brandishing a spear with a banner in the right hand that flashes

[a] *mi mgon dkar po*
[b] *gshin rje ya ma ra dza*

with lightning. In his left hand, he holds a lasso and wears a red robe. At his waist, he sports a bow and arrow, as well as a long sword. His orange-colored hair swirls upward. Within the amulet that he wears around his body are the three-hundred and sixty retinues of tsen held in a hidden manner. A red bird soars above him, red men go before him, and red dogs bring up the rear. Meditate upon him as a single horseman. Without a consort, his swiftness is reduced, for as it states according to worldly proverbs, "The mind of a man is changed by a female, and the obstacle for a woman's life is a strong man." Like that, if he has a consort, then his activity will be swifter. It is taught that his consort is Soglen Marmo,[a] who rides a red horse. Shinje's consort is Tsamuntri,[b] and the nāga king's consort is Zhal Karmo.[c]

To the north, within a red lake of blood with pounding waves and flames of fire that reach to the sky, is the black female Remati. She squeezes a bag of disease under her armpit. Her color and hand emblems are according to the information in the main text. She is surrounded by an army of one-hundred thousand females. All of them are as stated previously. The principal ones represent the nature, and the retinues represent the dynamic strength of the magical manifestation. To distill this to the essence, it is taught that one must know all deities and the entirety of saṃsāra and enlightenment to be mingled as the single taste of great clear light within the expanse of the wisdom intent.

The nature of the retinue of hundreds and thousands of ḍākinīs, the ocean of dharmapālas, and the eight classes of god-cannibals of phenomenal existence is the sole mother, Tröma Nagmo. To expand upon that, believe that their kāyas represent an oceanic maṇḍala of nirmāṇakāyas; their speech, an oceanic maṇḍala of the sambhogakāya; and their minds, an oceanic maṇḍala of the dharmakāya. As an inexhaustible ornamental wheel of the Tathāgata's enlightened body, speech, and mind, even all oceans of maṇḍalas are invoked in the aspect of self-radiant light that dissolves; and this, too, cleanses all suffering within the six realms. Dissolving in the aspect of light, think that saṃsāra and enlightenment become a single taste; and the upper pure buddhas and lower impure saṃsāra, the nature of saṃsāra and enlightenment, as well as the self-strength of this magical manifestation are all established as a single maṇḍala. This is the unsurpassed upadesha.

Even while reciting the invocation verses, invocation occurs in this way from basic space; so there comes to be inseparability with the three vajras of enlightened body, speech, and mind. That is the understanding of stability. To elaborate, although initially invoking [the blessings] from basic space as that is the place

[a] *srog len dmar mo*
[b] *tsa mun tri*
[c] *zhal dkar mo*

they are invited from, ultimately this is spontaneously present from the beginning. One must know that the originally pure nature is the single nature of the dharmatā.

In addition, during homage, to know the primordial, self-awareness nature is unborn, the intrinsic nature is unceasing, and unbiased compassion is the nature of the ḍākinīs is the supreme homage of reverence toward the view. In order to indicate that, one then sequentially emanates enumerable bodies as many as there exist particles, all offering prostrations. While doing so, bringing palms together at the three places pleases the enlightened body, speech, and mind of the victorious ones. Think that the obscurations of one's three doors are purified; and from one's heart as the deity, light radiates and penetrates the one who is prostrating so that his or her longevity, merit, glory, and abundance increase. This, too, is a crucial upadesha.

During offerings, imagine that the three realms self-occur and naturally arise in the aspect of outer, inner, and secret offering substances, such as the outer offerings of the desirables and so forth. Even the five desirables, such as visual objects that appear as form, are self-occurring and naturally arising so that visual consciousness becomes the ornament of awareness. Even all appearances of the five dynamic strengths are, by nature, ornaments of the mind. With this awareness and given that one's mind is the ḍākinī, one will be able to know how clouds of offerings arise as that ornament.

In brief, all objective appearances are vividly known to be the universe that is nonreferential, consummate emptiness as perpetual as space. All phenomena as the abundance of the contents of existence are regarded as pure outer, inner, and secret offering clouds. That is the offering of phenomenal existence arising as the ground. Especially, all material offering substances fall apart in the nature of emptiness and once again, by the force of magically manifest wisdom, arise in the aspect of oceanlike clouds of Samantabhadra's offerings.

The inner mind becomes outer space; the inner pure elements become the coarse, outer elements and such. In the manner of all outer and inner elements being interconnected in unity, delusion is human flesh, anger is ox flesh, pride is horse flesh, desire is peacock flesh, and jealously is dog flesh [i.e., the five types of flesh]. Know that these five nectars that originate from the essence of the unsurpassed substances of empty bliss are by nature unparalleled, empty, blissful wisdom nectar that liberates upon experience. Their aspect is blessed as offering substances according to the liturgy found in the root text [i.e., terma]. In particular, according to the unique practice of chöd, one must imagine the body dissolves into emptiness; and from the space of emptiness, this appears as flesh and blood—the nature of which is wisdom nectar—offered to the assemblies of wisdom ḍākinīs.

For the praise, just as during the homage, the body emanates as countless particles; and bodies dance beautifully while melodiously singing the songs of praise. While recalling the qualities of the subjects, praise is rendered. Having attained all siddhis and powerful blessings of the ten directional victors and their heirs, the objects of praise who are the maṇḍalas of deities and all fixated appearances within saṃsāra and enlightenment, including hope and fear, that render one an unsuitable vessel are purified in the space of the dharmakāya. To gain certainty in knowing that all phenomena of saṃsāra, enlightenment, and the path—these three—are singularly perfected in the expanse of awareness is unsurpassed praise. In truth, there exist no qualities that surpass awareness becoming the aspect of Tröma and all phenomena perfected in her expanse.

During the mantra recitation, one recites *phet* three times, as mentioned previously, since all principal ones and retinue are the magical manifestation of Tröma; so they are all the same nature. Even all mantras are the nature of Tröma Nagmo's deities, as well as the inseparable play that is complete as Tröma. One must know how to remain within this nature.

Since one's nature is the space of the three-kāya ḍākinīs as Tröma, generate this as the nirmāṇakāya. Then in one's heart, within a heart-shaped orb of maroon-colored light like a pitched tent, is the sambhogakāya Vajravarāhī with a pig's head jutting from her crown as she usually appears. In her heart, within an expanse of wisdom light and bindus, appears the naked, unadorned dharmakāya Samantabhadrī. In her heart, upon a split-bean-sized sun seat, is the life essence syllable, a blue-black *hung*, as though drawn with the tip of a hair. Surrounding that are the mantric syllables. Just like light from a candle and rays from the sun, know this to be the self-radiance of wisdom and that all states of deluded obscurity are completely cleansed like lighting a candle in a dark room. Recite the mantra within the confidence of knowing the single taste of the wisdom mind.

In addition, while eating, sleeping, going about, and sitting—basically whenever—even if the visualization of the deities is not clear, it is important to not allow awareness of self as the deity to discontinue. If there is no deity pride, then whatever you try to do will not be accomplished. Until now, we have been subject to the dormant habit of assuming we are human beings; so, henceforth, it is necessary to transform this into the awareness of oneself as the deity.

To expand upon this, there is nothing that exists aside from the nature appearing as the dynamic strength of awareness; hence, it is empty. The intrinsic nature is the aspect of the deity, and compassion means that the entirety of saṃsāra and enlightenment without being liberated is fully perfected as the manifestation of that dynamic energy. Know this meaning, without becoming distracted by other thoughts, words, or allowing the warmth of the cushion to diminish.

While reciting mantra, from the seed syllable in one's heart, light rays radiate; and all potential as the inexhaustible ornamental wheel of the victors' and their heirs' power and blessings of enlightened body, speech, and mind dissolve into the body, speech, and mind of oneself as Tröma. The entire assembly of the three-kāya wisdom ḍākinīs dissolves into oneself. By performing this visualization—similar to that at the time of the invocation—like replenishing the deity's blessings, the potency will increase.

During the accomplishment recitation, the life-essence syllables of saṃsāra and enlightenment transform into *hung*. All mantras are subsumed as *benzar trodhi*. The natures of all deities, awareness, and mantra become inseparable. The heart essence of saṃsāra and enlightenment gathers into the syllable *hung* so that all qualities, powers, and potential mingle with the single life-essence syllable. Then, light radiates from that, so think that the blessings of the victors and their heirs dissolve into one's heart syllable in the aspect of five-colored orbs of light.

During the activity recitation in the early morning, visualize oneself as a white-colored Tröma with light rays radiating from the white garland of mantras. Gathering all blessings of the victors and their heirs in the aspect of white orbs of light, the suffering of all beings in the three realms is dispelled. Like awakening from sleep, they are liberated in the ground of the dharmatā that has never known confusion. Reabsorbing back, all illness, demonic forces, and obstacles are pacified.[236]

Likewise, at noon visualize oneself as golden and engage in enriching activity; in the evening as red, powerful activity; and in the darkness of night as a black-green Tröma. Light rays that emit foul smells and various weapons in the aspects of fire bolts completely destroy all harm-doers. Countless wrathful ones and iron scorpions furiously devour them, and razor-sharp wind storms scatter them everywhere. Heaps of raging fire incinerate them, so think that they are liberated in the great wisdom manifestation of empty bliss. Finally, all appearances of deities gather into the space of clear light. Again, one re-emerges as the wisdom kāya of the deity and so forth for the post-evenness experience.

These explanations were received directly from the mouth of the Great Tertön himself, and I wrote them down as notes. Because this is identical to his speech, the blessings are tremendous; and one can have full confidence in this.

> The magical manifestation of basic space is the phenomena of saṃsāra
> and enlightenment.
> In the maṇḍala of the victorious Mother, the single taste of basic
> space: through total awareness, this maṇḍala of the spontaneously
> present deities of the ground is the supreme method for actual
> realization.

These are the verses that summarize this section.

3.2.2.4 Clarifying the Passageway of Deviations

Fourth is dispelling the passageway of deviations. Machig has told us:

> Trying to accomplish buddhahood in this life but not severing with the view of emptiness while taking the deity as the practice will bring deviation through the reversed circumstance of using chöd for protection-based ceremonies.

Thus, instead of severing fixation by knowing that all self-appearances are empty, some practitioners attempt to clear away and dispel the circumstance of māras and demonic-force possessions for patrons and so forth. Through this, it causes chöd to deviate into a practice of protector ceremonies.[237] The quote continues:

> Without cultivating internal understanding of all phenomena being distinct yet fully perfected and, instead, to individualize the self, māras, and frightening places—these three—[the severance] will turn the deviation into a state of confusion.

Thus, failing to comprehend that, from within a single nature of emptiness, all relative phenomena appear distinctly yet fully perfected like magic and dreams, self and māras are individualized and held as true. This causes severance to deviate into confusion. Failing to seize the vital point, it is as the quote continues:

> With arrogance like an ox, no matter how defiled or contagious the clothes or people may be—although thinking their act of severance is not a deviation—in fact, it is, for instance, like a blind man fighting with a stick.

Thus, not knowing the crucial point, brazen ones like bulls cultivate baseless confidence and courage. Careless about contagion and the like and thinking they are not deviating, the severance falls into senseless [conduct]. And:

> With harmful intentions toward the object, severance is performed. Even though one's illness may be cured, this conduct resembles killing one's own child and eating their flesh.
>
> Thus, by holding to the gods-māras and the like as the harm-doers and imagining that they cause harm, they are severed. Even though illness may be cured, like the image of killing one's child and eating the flesh, this severance deviates to the status of a butcher. Moreover, having meditated upon the fundamental nature: when the signs of potency and blessings emerge, to then wander into towns giving out blessings, boasting of visions, and uttering wrathful mantras is to lose all blessings to the hands of evil forces.

Thus, it is. Meditating upon the meaning of the unborn mother—when the experience of empty appearances dawns—by ignoring karmic results based on virtue and nonvirtue, superiority develops toward the lord guru. Engaging in many senseless deeds with an arrogance that feels there is nothing to lose, the loosely taken vows are lost to the hands of the māras. Therefore, having ill will toward the guru's wealth and such, engaging in various senseless actions, and proclaiming there are no vows or words of honor that will be lost—although holding vows—in truth, through that, negative karma is accrued and the mind lost to the trappings of the māras. Hence, by knowing well the manner of deviating and how the path is lost in these ways, one must never allow this to happen.

It is as Machig cautions:

> These so-called dark directions occur for those who try to engage in chöd. Always wandering in frightening places and towns in the company of dark-sided companions while practicing to beat down the dark māras; [partaking of] a dark abundance of provisions derived from perverted livelihood; [having] mental images that send vile, poisonous thoughts; wearing the skins of dark-colored dogs and the hat of a black bear; blowing an off-colored horn as a human thigh-bone trumpet; shouting the sound of *phet* like a yelping dark-colored dog—don't you think anyone in their right mind would be afraid of such a person?
>
> A practitioner like this brings ruin upon everything, like a poisonous tree, and is an enemy of my doctrine. In the degenerate times, practitioners such as this will fill the face of this earth.

Thus, as she taught, one must fully disengage with all such incorrect conduct.

3.2.2.5 *Taking Whatever Occurs as the Path*

Fifth, taking whatever occurs, such as illness, joy, and sorrow, as the path is as follows. Ngulchu Tokmed Rinpoche[a,238] has said:

> If this magical body of self-fixation falls ill, then let it be so. That will exhaust previously accumulated karma since engagement in myriad spiritual activities is only for the purification of the two obscurations.

[a] *dngul chu thogs med*

> If there is no illness, then let it be so. When the body and mind are well, then virtuous activities will increase. Making this human life meaningful only occurs by engaging in virtue through the three doors.
>
> If there is no wealth or abundance, then let it be so. Then there will be no need to busily try to sustain and protect that. Whatever disturbances or bickering that come about have certainly emerged from fixation upon wealth.
>
> If there is wealth and abundance, then let it be so. That allows one to increase virtuous merit, for whatever happiness of the present or future is certainly the result of merit.
>
> If death comes soon, then let it be so. Having not been overcome by negative circumstances and having befriended the excellent propensities for this juncture, it is certain the unmistaken path will be entered.
>
> If life is long-lived, then let it be so. While growing the crops of experience by not allowing the warmth of the oral instructions to vanish, to rely on this for a long time will bring a mature result. Whatever comes must be taken up with delight.

Thus, it is as taught. Whatever positive or negative things occur must be taken as supports for the practice.

3.2.2.6 Final Conclusion of Select Upadesha and Accomplishing Enlightened Deeds

Sixth, the way of accomplishing enlightened deeds for the welfare of others and the select upadesha that adorn the conclusion is as follows. Āryadeva's treatise on chöd states:

> If—by proceeding with compassion—other living beings are benefited, know that the place of illness, demonic forces, and the illness itself are all empty. Strike the object while meditating on emptiness.

Thus, and Machig has said:

> Performing chöd so as to alleviate recurring calamities, to acquire yogurt,[239] alcohol, protection from hail or lightning storms, animal-based diseases, illness, demonic force, corpses, curses, the final threat, and so forth . . .

Thus, she clearly states the way the upadesha deals with the issue of recurring calamities. Although there are many incidents concerning these cycles called Iron Matrix and so forth[240] that originate with the sublime ones, to synthesize it is as follows.

With the practice of realizing loving compassion and emptiness, the consciousness of the person with recurring calamities is mingled with basic space. Their heap of aggregates is then offered to the guests; and from the perspective of exerting oneself in the instructions on the lineage of chöd in whatever way is necessary, the severance must then occur. There are many important instructions that have been taught, such as Machig's stages of the lightning-bolt visualization and whatever else is found according to the treatises on chöd. Nevertheless, this is an abbreviated version of the wandering practice that I have heard directly through oral instructions.

Sequentially visualize the three-kāya ḍākinīs above the crown of one's head. Meditate that above them appears Padmasambhava and Vajrapāṇi with immense kāyas as large as Mt. Meru. Their heads reach into the Akaniṣhṭha, and their kāyas fill phenomenal existence. Surrounding them like massing clouds, all places are filled with lions, meteorite scorpions, five classes of garuḍas, and various weapons like shooting stars as tumultuous as the wind. Then meditate upon a blazing red *hung* like a fire cloud. In the upper regions of space, all dragons and the eight classes of gods-māras have no chance to move for even an instant. Even if they tried, like dried grass blown by the wind, they are scattered and expelled some three fathoms' distance away. The vastness of lower earth is composed of diamonds, and intermediate space is filled with the gurus, meditation deities, ḍākinīs, and dharmapālas. Then recite *ni na ga dza mun tri ah*.

Next are the random visualizations that have been taken from the main text. **If the gods-māras of the frightening places are powerful and overbearing and the practitioner is weak, upheavals will not occur. If, on the other hand, the practitioner has a high and confident view but the gods-māras are weak, again there will be no upheavals. Whatever the case, upheavals will be drawn out through the profound visualization and conduct of the final threat.**

Place a rope around one's neck; then tie the other side of the rope down to a sacred object of support. Otherwise, toss the end of the rope out to the gods-māras while shouting out loud as follows, "Hey! Gods-māras of phenomenal existence, come gather here immediately!" Reciting this three times, perform the visualization as follows. From all of one's places, boundless light rays radiate, powerlessly summoning all gods-māras in front of one, like fish caught on a hook. Think that they have no chance of escape or place to hide.

With strong confidence, repeat the following aloud, "You powerful and wrathful gods-māras of this place, what I have to ask of you is this. At best,

throw me into the lowest hell realm at this very moment. Second best is to kill me on the spot, or at least torture me so that I am neither dead nor alive. If your ears are not deaf, then listen. If your eyes are not blind, look. If you are not crippled, then come. If you are not dead, be swift; and if you are not a corpse, then get up!" Thus, repeat this three times and then fall asleep.

If you suffer from an incurable disease, then go to an extremely frightening place and burn some of your hair, nails, and dry skin in order to make a strong stench. Saying, "Hey! Powerful, wrathful gods-māras of this place, if your ears are not deaf, then listen. If your eyes are not blind, look. If your arms and legs are not crippled, then come here. If your nose is not blocked, then smell this foul stench. If your mouth is not closed, eat me. If you are not a corpse, then get up. If you are not yet dead, then don't be late. If you have not fainted, then quickly approach!" Repeat these verses three times.

Then say, "I have had this incurable disease for many days and months. No matter what I try, nothing helps me. Even the local inhabitants, as well as my neighbors, are all praying that I will just die. All my relatives and loved ones are saying that it is best for me to die. I, too, feel that, if death were to arrive immediately, nothing would be better than that in all lifetimes. At best, I should be thrown into the lowest hell realm right now. The second best would be if I stopped breathing on the spot; and at the least, I should be slain before sunrise tomorrow." Having said this, take the other end of the rope and tie it to a frightening, dangerous object while shouting *phet* and screaming out *ki*. Then, sleep there for a short period of time.

After this, repeat the appeal by calling out again. No matter what happens—whether good, bad, or terrifying—completely sever any doubt you have about wanting to die. If you receive a sign that night, then perform the white feast in the morning and the mixed feast at noon. In the evening, perform the red feast and the black feast at predawn. To conclude with the final suppression is the traditional course of practice, as well as the ultimate, profound final threat.

When practitioners of this profound path fall ill, they must diligently practice special visualizations during the five times of day. In the early morning, visualize that from the heart of the powerful sovereign of saṃsāra and enlightenment, Samantabhadrī, the white hatred-subduing ḍākinī emanates with the face of a snake. In the afternoon, visualize the yellow pride-subduing ḍākinī with the head of a horse. In the late afternoon or early evening, visualize the red desire-subduing ḍākinī with the head of a vulture; and at midnight, the green jealousy-subduing ḍākinī with the head of a dog. Before dawn, visualize the black delusion-subduing ḍākinī with the head of a pig. Sometimes imagine that meteorite scorpions and other times garuḍas boundlessly emanate to gulp down your specific illness and its source. Imagine that nothing remains.

Once imagining this, repeatedly perform the liturgy known as *Giving the Body*[a] many countless times, after which abide in nonconceptual awareness. It is certain that the illness will then be dispelled.

For a sudden sickness or contagious disease, visualize that your body is a dry skeleton with no flesh at all. Imagine that, from the nine orifices, the smell and steam of poisonous venom, along with fiery vajras, emerge. Think, "My body has no flesh and consists only of bones. There is no basis for illness to occur. What a loss! In order to purify my obscurations and unpaid karmic debts, I pray that a serious illness will befall me." Thinking and hoping in this way will dispel the illness. This is called "the activity of making a heap of flesh and blood into a disease".

Then, imagine that the hair of a dead person and of a living person and the tail of a youthful animal are braided in eight strands to make a slingshot that indicates the spontaneous presence of the five kāyas and the five wisdoms. Just by hurling a stone, imagine that the slingshot has the potential to thrust the dualistic notion of self and appearances, including all gods-māras, into the unelaborate nature of phenomena. Recite the root mantra ten-thousand times and bless the slingshot carried with you. Consider that the curved vajra blade you also carry has all the strength of one-hundred thousand ḍākinīs.

In addition, all practitioners who practice this profound dharma and are threatened by robbers or thieves must first go to an extremely frightening place and call all gods-māras of phenomenal existence just like before. Say, "The enemy has stolen everything, leaving me helpless. Now, I will die of famine or cold. There is no way to avoid death. Therefore, it is best if you send me directly to the hell realms. The second best is to kill me on the spot, and at least you should take my breath before sunrise tomorrow."

Saying this, tie the neck rope to a frightening support and go to sleep. If this method does not bring about the return of your stolen objects, then go to another frightening place and imagine it to be the dwelling place of the enemy. All gods-māras of phenomenal existence converge as red- and black-colored monkeys with their hands linked together, carrying human corpses. They are running and jumping back and forth in the rear of the enemy's house. In addition, make torma replicas of the monkeys, and then call out, "Hey, all you oath-bound gods-māras of phenomenal existence! Right now you must show the enemy how you appear as red-black monkeys with linked hands carrying corpses. If you don't, then kill me right now. If not, then I swear I will destroy this eon." After saying this, go to sleep. If after doing this there are still no signs, offer your body as the red feast. Then recite, "Gods-māras of

[a] *lü chin* (*lus sbyin*)

phenomenal existence, gather here as a great army to wrathfully charge the enemy of aggression. Sending all negative signs such as sudden afflictions upon them, annihilate all enemies without the slightest trace remaining."

Thus, adding this to the feast of each of the ten ḍākinīs, imagine the ḍākinīs from above, below, and all directions assemble to surround the eight classes of gods-māras in phenomenal existence. Visualize this repeatedly. Think that the gods-māras are screaming "Kill, kill! Strike, strike!" Then, go to a mountaintop and destroy the sacred castles of the earth lords. Spread out the windhorse flags under your cushion. Wear your clothes inside out; and without any holding back, call out the following, "Hey lords of the mountains and local spirits! If your eyes are not blind, then look. If your ears are not deaf, listen. If you are not crippled, come. If you are not dead, be swift. If you are not a corpse, get up. The enemy has stolen from me, and I never did anything to him. I owe him no debt. For no reason, he has robbed me. Rather than die from famine, it is better to die right now. The best is for you to throw me into the lowest realm immediately. The second best is to kill me right now. At least, you should kill me before sunrise tomorrow. If not, then kill the enemy without delay; and as quickly as possible, bring me his warm heart." Thus, saying this, go to sleep. Practice the *Suppression through Splendor* repeatedly.

Otherwise, after offering your body as the feast of flesh and blood, meditate that the enemy, his wealth, and all possessions are piled up at the center of your flayed skin. Then recite the *Treasury of Space Mantra*[241] to bless this heap of flesh, blood, and bones. Meditate that the eight classes of gods and cannibals, including all gods-māras of phenomenal existence, gather in multitudes like dust motes in a sunbeam. Shout *phet*, blow the thigh-bone trumpet, and roll the drum while playing the bell to summon the guests. Finally, in the right hand of oneself as Tröma, gather your flayed human skin from the edges inward to bring together your flesh, blood, and the classes of god-cannibals, including the wealth of the enemy. Bind this up with ropes made of snakes and intestines. Swirl the bag over one's head and pound it down so that it lands upon the golden ground. Until the enemies are fully exhausted, think that there is no way for escape or freedom; and then success will be certain.

If you come across the cook stove of the enemies,[242] then imagine that the enemies, their wealth, and retinue are destroyed. Throw the stove downward, and imagine that it falls down into the mouth of black Yamā. This will ensure success. Furthermore, meditate that the remains from the feast and the tormas are the enemies, their wealth, retinue, and so forth. When offering all of this to the mouths of the guests, imagine that the enemies and the rest are partaken of. In all cases, it is crucial to never separate from the vajra pride of self-nature as Tröma Nagmo. It is also important to take care while inter-

changing the words in the verses of the liturgy in conjunction with performing the *Suppression through Splendor*.

In brief, deciding that all phenomena are self-appearing and achieving confidence with this is the best indication of the extent of the severance. When awareness achieves confidence with itself, this does not involve intellect, mental analysis, or pride. If toward consummate saṃsāra and enlightenment one possesses definitive comprehension, experience, and realization—these three—there is no doubt that will indicate the extent of severance from the root.

> Having fully dispelled the mistaken deviations, whatever happiness or suffering occurs is taken as support for the path.
> Having included the crucial visualizations for accomplishing whatever deeds are needed, this sacred lineage of oral instructions is immaculate.

Thus, these are the verses that summarize the section.

3.2.3 Supplementary Advice for Training in the Complete Transmission of the Entrustment

Third, concerning all of the above, auxiliary advice is given as the complete entrustment. The way of giving this sacred transmission to the fortunate disciples as their inheritance is as it states, ". . . **Sovereign of Accomplishment** . . ." until ". . . attain **buddhahood.**" As taught, advice is given on how to avoid the trap of attachment toward loved ones, friends, and those who create the circumstances for obstacles.

Saying " . . . **my future lineage holders** . . ." until ". . . **sole child**", as taught, advice is given on the necessity of reducing future plans from the perspective of holding the key points concerning the four extremes of conducive conduct for practitioners. Saying "**future plans** . . ." until ". . . **fortunate sons and daughters**", as taught, advice is given on how to rely upon the stages of clothing and necessities from the perspective of qualities and indications. Saying "**do not groom the hair** . . ." until ". . . **isolation in the mountains**", as taught, advice is given concerning the seven important abandonments for the path of sublime practitioners. Saying " . . . **signs of accomplishment actually**. . ." until ". . . **path of the sublime ones**", as taught, advice is given on never transgressing the precise instructions that one must train in. This is the supreme auxiliary advice pertaining to the profound path of severing the māras that is the exceptional upadesha that the mahāsiddha Saraha entrusted to his followers through compassion.

4 Results of Accomplishing the Practice

Fourth is the teaching on the results of accomplishing the practice. If this doctrine of the supreme meaning of the Great Mother, the severance of māras, is practiced precisely, then in this life compulsory fixation will be cut off. Liberating illness, demonic forces, and obstacles in their own place, the qualities of experience and realization will suddenly emerge in one's mind stream. The confidence of a practitioner of fearless conduct will be gained. There will be the potential to turn the minds of unruly objects to be tamed toward the dharma and place them in maturity. There will be victory over the hordes of māras that create obstacles for self and others.

Especially, if one familiarizes with the key points of the practice of the supreme vehicle of clear light: even though in the degenerate times this life is short, the wisdom intent of the victorious mother's dharmakāya will be actualized. Becoming inseparable with the original buddha, the glorious supreme Lord Mahāsiddha, enlightenment will occur. [The root terma] states:

> **Since these are the stages of a practitioner's path, those fortunate sons and daughters who precisely rely upon them will be inseparable with me, a buddha. If buddhahood is not achieved in this lifetime, then I have deceived you, fortunate followers.**[243]

Thus, he spoke.

These undeceiving vajra words that reveal the meaning of authentic transmission are, in brief, the source of all that is excellent within existence and the state of quiescence. The *Gathering of Precious Qualities* states:

> Regarding the buddhas, their heirs, the shrāvakas, pratyekas, and all gods, as well as sentient beings, whatever phenomena of happiness exists for them has in all cases originated from the supreme prajñāpāramitā.

Thus, it is so. Concerning this, the quote goes on:

> All beings who wish to acquire supreme qualities, the supremely superb wisdom of the buddhas, and to express the generosity of giving the sublime dharma must rely upon this exalted doctrine.

Thus, these sacred oral instructions that the supreme sugatas have passed on to us must be made meaningful.

With single-pointed conviction, I have clearly illuminated this commentary based on the profound upadesha that holds the blessings of the close lineage. To that end, there should be no doubt that this effort will pacify faults and shortcomings of the degenerate times, propagate and increase the precious doctrine of the victorious ones throughout all directions and times, increase the well-being of all living creatures, and fully illuminate the spontaneously present signs of virtue that indicate the twofold purpose of self and others.

Concluding Aspiration

Whatever transcends words, expressions, concepts, and thoughts is the supreme discerning wisdom of self-awareness. The mother of all the sublime ones, the prajñāpāramitā, is the intrinsic nature free from birth or cessation, like space. The supreme upāya of bodhichitta as the companion is the only seed that gives birth to the victors of the three times. The well-known, sacred dharma that severs the māras is the subsequent bodhisattva training in conduct that eradicates all obscurations.

Having emerged from the source of the sacred nāga spring of the supreme ones, overflowing throughout the golden ground of my mind, this precious treasure of perfectly pure transmissions and reasoning possesses the taste and essence of the eight branches[244] of the profound meaning. Having composed this through the strength of joyful enthusiasm and pure intent, this glory rejuvenates immortal life, maturity, and liberation. Having completed this exposition entitled *An Ambrosia Ocean*, may this be cause for all fortunate ones to celebrate.

The great master treasure revealer, who is the embodiment of all buddhas, gave me permission to compose this through his vajra speech. By the interdependency of his wisdom intent transferring into my heart, this emerged as a treasury of his oceanic blessings. Given that the previous master's sacred instructions, like potent eye medicine, have been gradually and continuously mixed with the lethal speech of attachment and hatred—like once again removing the cataract of deluded bias—even thinking that I could somehow restore that excellent vision of intelligence is itself the play of māras.[245]

The meaning of the wisdom ḍākinī's speech from the distant lineage and close lineages and the heart essence of the supreme mahāsiddha Saraha merge as a single flow in this profound treatise, the core wisdom intent of the three lineages of the vidyādharas. The lineage of māra severance that takes ominous signs as positive involves dealing with māras and demonic forces with unruly aggressive minds. Nevertheless, this compassionate doctrine leads them to the state of awakening through skillful means that is not based on wrathful aggression.

Some think this is practiced in pursuit of gain and respect or used in situations of loss or misfortune—the careless conduct engaged by charlatan vagabonds, who tame māras and perform protection rituals. Lost in the deep ravine of deviation, these ordinary male and female Mantra practitioners of chöd even have the audacity to hold their heads high. Although that is the case, it is still unacceptable for someone like me to judge what is pure or impure. Yet, if compared with the teachings of the wisdom ḍākinī Machig, who would not be able to know the difference?

The evenness of saṃsāra and enlightenment is but a single experience of good and bad. This uncontrived fundamental nature is that to be actualized. By leaving this cherished body behind as the feast, the conduct of the bodhisattvas will be fully perfected. Through realizing emptiness, the root of existence, self-fixation, will be severed; and through great compassion, the cherishing of self will be completely cut through. By familiarizing with deity appearances, ordinary phenomena will be severed; and by seeing the innate truth, dualistic concepts will be cut off. Aside from that, misdirected chöd practitioners will take this as a tool for this life alone, such as beating down māras and making offerings to gods. Any attempt to establish their bondage-based fame, name, gain, and respect is completely against the characteristics of this authentic path.

These vajra words belong to the ancestor of one-hundred mahāsiddhas and are the heart essence of a million ḍākas and ḍākinīs. Through this great offering of words that clearly illuminate this treatise, may the ḍākinīs of the three places perform their joyous dance. Rāhula,[a] along with yamā, tsen, and nāga, tamers of the conceptual three poisons, through wrathful means, including the hordes of hateful enemies, and Remati, who empties phenomenal existence in basic space—you are the four dharmapālas bound by oath to guard and protect this doctrine.

Although I was born with favorable intelligence, overcome by the causes and results of sloth in past lifetimes and addicted to bad habits of distraction and the like, just to write this exposition took a very long time. Nevertheless, due to the persistent request of two Mantra adepts[246] possessing intelligence, diligence, and courage, I lost the freedom to remain in the neutrality of complacency. Cultivating enthusiasm, I was then able to bring this exposition to completion.

From beginningless time, my mind has been overcome by delusion. Hence, by the fault of not knowing, explanations are rendered incorrect. Whatever mistakes may have occurred, I confess them all in the presence of the deities, gurus, and wise and noble ones who act as my witnesses. By this virtue, may the accumulations of merit and wisdom be perfectly accumulated. Completing the qualities on the grounds and paths, may the state of the Victorious Guide be swiftly attained and may the glory of the spontaneously present twofold purpose be achieved.

Having composed this clear exposition on the close lineage of chöd entitled *An Ambrosia Ocean of Sublime Explanations,* the embodiment of all the victori-

[a] Sogdag (*srog bdag*); Master of Life

ous ones, the Great Dharma Tertön, king of incomparable kindness [i.e., Heruka Dudjom Lingpa], enthroned me through proclamation to be the dharma holder of this doctrine. Armored with full permission to compose this, my own disciple, Lama Gendun of Rekong,[a] persistently requested me to write this for a long time. He himself is highly praised and acknowledged as an incarnation of the great yogi Matog[b,247] of supreme hearing, contemplation, and meditation. Later, the Mantra adept and *kilaya* dagger holder, Kunzang Pema Chödzin,[c] and the faithful samaya holder from Dronlung, Dorje Namgyal,[d] sent me a scripture composed by Lord Tanagpa entitled *The Great Determination of Reasoning*[e] along with their request. In addition, the wise one named Sherab[f] offered a silver coin with a white scarf. The Great Tertön's son, himself a rinpoche with a wealth of knowledge and compassion, requested this along with a stainless white scarf.[248] More recently, this was again requested by the supreme one prophesized through vajra speech, the Mantra adept Dorje Namgyal, along with a maṇḍala offering of an ounce of silver. The faithful and learned yogi Kunga[g] offered five silver coins with his request as well.

Based on all of this and by placing the feet of many living enlightened masters upon the crown of my head, knowing the profound crucial points of the ecumenical tenets of the Earlier and Later Translation Schools, I, who was born with the name Pema Lungtok Gyatso, composed this. My scribe was Namgyal, a principal disciple who also made this request.

By this virtue, may the doctrine in general—and specifically the supreme doctrine of the māra-severing chöd lineage—spread and increase throughout all directions.

May virtue prevail! May the virtue of the three times prevail and may all be auspicious!

[a] *re kong bla ma dge 'dun*
[b] Matog Rinchen (*rma thog rin chen*)
[c] *kun bzang padma chos 'dzin*
[d] *rdo rje rnam rgyal*
[e] *tsed ma'i ta chöd chenpo* (*tsad ma'i mtha' dpyod chen po*); Je Tanagpa
[f] *shes rab*
[g] *kun dga'*

Part Two

From the Treasury Expanse of the Spacelike Dharmatā:

As the Innermost Essence of the Secret Mantra Vehicle,
These Pith Instructions on Severing the Hope and
Fear of Materializing Fixation
Are the Upadesha for Encountering the
Fundamental Nature Itself

entitled

The Profound Heart Essence of Saraha

SECOND EDITION

A Terma Revelation of
Heruka Dudjom Lingpa

May all my lineage-holding disciples be blessed and cared for by the glorious Lake-Born Orgyen and Saraha, to gain the freedom to become dharma rulers victorious over the three realms.

Due to the great entanglement with self and objects [i.e., objective self-grasping] having collapsed in its own place, the truth of selflessness is directly realized and seen as the secret space of immediate liberation that wells forth effortlessly. In the vast expanse of the great-bliss *bhaga* of Samantabhadrī's secret enlightened mind, the sacred ground that illuminates the maṇḍala of the unification of *eh wam* manifests as this self-appearing Akaniṣhṭha. The king of the magical manifestation of teacher and retinue appear to the retinue as the dynamic strength of Saraha. Initially, Yeshe Nyima and Sherab Dawa'i Wangpo were empowered to listen so that the gateway to the great treasure trove of the dharmatā expanse was opened; and these great concealed notes called the precious inexhaustible ornamental wheel were given to me, Longdrol Dorje Migyur, as cherished wealth. At that time, the all-encompassing clear-light luminosity self-arose. The radiance of this light, free from effort-based activity and unidentifiable, will be self-emergent for those fortunate disciples who possess meritorious accumulations, aspirations, and karmic convergence, whoever they may be.

Within the limit of the interconnected hands of the garland of subject-object, the innate nature of upāya and prajñā united is impregnated in the womb of the mother and sealed in the expanse of empty bliss. The extent is subsumed or completely contained to be held as the king of the vase. Since the space of great emptiness is a great analogy for the nature of emptiness, this great state of openness will not be determined through the core of a reed of grass.

[illegible] is the source of this.[249]

Kye! Embodiment of all victorious ones and their heirs without exception, you who bring the minds of fortunate disciples to fruition, with the power to liberate saṃsāra in the expanse of enlightenment—Sovereign of All Families, Guru, know me!

> Attaining a precious human life with freedoms and advantages is born from the excellent causes and results of interdependent accumulations and prayers—difficult to acquire again and again, like the *udumwara* flower. May this state of perfect omniscience be swiftly achieved!

To meditate upon this meaning and train one's mind is to consider the nature of the precious human rebirth itself.

First, I would say that, concerning the places of rebirth, there are eight outer and inner states of birth that lack freedom. A hell being suffers such intense extremes of heat and cold that not even a single moment of leisure remains. It goes without saying there is no freedom to engage in dharma practice. A deprived spirit suffers such intense thirst and hunger that, except for the thought of food and drink, all concepts cease, leaving no freedom whatsoever. Due to ignorance, animals are tormented by the suffering of being harnessed and domesticated by others. Lacking the eyes of intelligence that discriminate virtue and nonvirtue, they have no opportunity for freedom. Long-life gods are always intoxicated by the taste of the enjoyment of bliss and joy; so due to this preoccupation, the idea of engaging in dharma practice never occurs to them. By avoiding rebirth in these four places of nonfreedom, the opportunity for freedom and obtaining the human body is cause for meditating with joyful gratitude. Even though a human body may have been acquired: if this does not become a vessel for dharma, there are four further states that lack the opportunity for freedom. These four are as follows.

Those who take rebirth as heretics and barbarians will develop confidence in erroneous views and meditations and will thus turn their backs on the Buddha's doctrine. Those who take rebirth in a land devoid of dharma and during a dark age will not recognize the difference between virtue and nonvirtue; and by disparaging the dharma and followers by disbelieving in even the relative interpretation of cause and result, they will remove themselves from the [direction of] dharma and have no freedom. Those who are mentally impaired—such as having faculties that are dysfunctional or with diminished mental capacity—will lack the intention to engage in dharma and be incapable of comprehending or communicating words and their meanings. Hence, there will be no freedom. Whoever takes rebirth in one of these eight states will lack the freedom to practice the dharma, whereas those who are not born in any of these states will possess the freedom to practice dharma. Hence, that is called "freedom".

In addition, in order to practice dharma, it is necessary for all ten endowments to be complete. The reason is as follows. If a human body is not acquired, then the opportunity to meet with the profound dharma will not occur. Therefore, the endowment of the support of the body must be obtained. Even if a human body is acquired: if birth is not taken in a central land, then there will be no dharma available. Since rebirth is taken in a special environment referred to as "a central land", that is the endowment of the place. If the sense organs and faculties are not intact, this indicates the fault of being an inadequate vessel for receiving dharma. Since these are complete, there is the endowment of being a vessel with all faculties complete. If karma is reversed and the door to dharma is not entered, to be just a human being who is entirely subservient to others is merely the appearance of a meaningless human form that will never encounter dharma. Possessing the karma to practice dharma is the endowment of fortunate karma. Having faith in the sublime doctrine rather than unsuitable negative objects, such as heretics and the like, is the endowment of the wealth of faith. If these five are complete in a human lifetime, then they are referred to as the five personal endowments.

These are the enumerations of the freedoms and endowments. The way to meditate upon what this means is as follows. Since the present human body replete with eighteen freedoms and endowments is the result of previously accumulated excellent virtue, consider that—if this is not made meaningful now—once this previous result of virtue is exhausted, there will not be another opportunity to obtain happiness after that. Thinking in this way, make certain that the three doors engage in virtue! Generally, by taking into consideration and carefully examining the perceptions and feelings of the beings in the six classes, obtaining an excellent physical support complete with all these noble qualities is a crucial point of consideration for bringing the mind to the path of dharma. Then, thinking that each moment of this precious human rebirth is being consumed, meditate upon impermanence as follows:

> The external universe, this world, is impermanent and subject to destruction, creation, and endurance. The inner inhabitants, sentient beings, are subject to birth and death like the comings and goings in a marketplace. The days, months, and years—time itself—are like dancers' gyrations. O Guru, bless me to recall death and impermanence!

Reciting these verses, meditate as follows. Although the external vessel, this universe, seems solid, firm, tangible, and real, eventually—with the forty-nine great fires, the seven great floods, and the one great wind—it will be dispersed to become empty space where nothing whatsoever endures. Carefully consider the homes, countries, farms, and so forth that were once inhabited, including all the men and women of the past who worked so hard taking great care with a strong sense of self, believing that all of their cherished wealth was permanent. Look at what remains as the legacy of their hardships. Use this as the impetus for viewing your own actions, activities, and cherished wealth. All beings who are the inhabitants of existence have vanished in the past and will appear in the future like the coming and going of merchants in a busy marketplace. The measure of the life span of all males and females seen and heard of is utterly uncertain; and since death can occur at any time, one must meditate upon the uncertainty of the time of death. If the duration of this life from the time of birth until the present is truly examined, it seems no longer than dream appearances. Without relaxing into complacency, practice virtue! Meditating with steadfast renunciation and a sense of repulsion is the second crucial point.

Kye! O Child of Fortunate Rebirth, be attentive! Without this crucial point—no matter what dharma one practices—courage, diligence, and forbearance will not endure; so practice will resemble frost in the summer, mist on a mountain peak, or firelight in the darkness. Even I, the grandfather of one-hundred siddhis, rode this great chariot to accomplish the two purposes. There is no doubt that all of the buddhas and bodhisattvas of the three times rode, ride, and will mount this great chariot that crosses over to the citadel of great liberation. Hence, maintain these pointing-out instructions as one's main practice.

> In this dungeon of unbearable misery, hopelessly pathetic, not a moment exists to experience happiness; further-increasing, limitless accumulations of karma continue to intensify. O Guru, grant liberation from this ocean of saṃsāra!

The meditation upon this meaning is as follows. If the suffering of the hell realms is taken into consideration, there are the eight hot hell realms beginning with Black Line and descending to the Avīchī hell. The fire at the conclusion of this kalpa [i.e., age of time] will be seven times more intense than the fire of this world. The fire of the Black Line hell is seven times stronger than that. The fire of the Crushing hell exceeds that by seven times, and accordingly the strength of the fire increases by seven all the way down to the Avīchī hell. Not only does the heat intensify, the misery becomes increasingly unbearable. Thinking about this, these days if a mere spark of fire lands on one's bare skin, it is so unbearable one may scream out in pain. If that is the case, it goes without saying that experiencing such suffering would be intolerable. Deeply consider this and train the mind.

The winds of the eight cold hells are also one-hundred times colder than the frigid winds that will destroy this kalpa. The intensity of the cold is so punishing that it can split a block of gold as though it were an *utpala* flower opening. Given the degree of suffering that must be endured: if one considers the difficulties these days of enduring even a single day of frigid weather and icy wind, needless to mention what it would be like to endure suffering such as this for myriad kalpas. Take this to heart and train the mind.

The second environment in the lower realms is that of the deprived spirits [i.e., pretas] who suffer the torment of hunger and thirst so that their bodies catch on fire. The third realm is the animals, where there is the continual torment of stupidity, delusion, and abuse. In the three higher realms, humans suffer birth, old age, sickness, and death; asuras suffer from constant battle; and devas suffer from death and the inevitable plunge to the lower realms. These fire pits of suffering resemble being trapped in an immense dungeon of darkness where not even a hair's worth of happiness exists that is not tainted by suffering. Considering this, taking it to heart, and training the mind are all crucial points that ensure the path becomes the practice of dharma. Those who train their minds like this and practice the path will be able to establish irreversible stability. Those who fail to train their minds in this way, although having entered the path, will be like a boulder rolling downhill. It will be easy for such individuals to revert back [to saṃsāra] because their mental supports are uncertain and unstable. Given that this is the inspiring force behind all dharma practice, to constantly work on developing disdain in this way alone is the third crucial point.

> The ripening of the results of positive and negative karma are undeceiving. The perpetually fixated mind habituated to joy and sorrow is the subjective agent who experiences causes and results. O Guru, undeceiving Permanent Protector, know me!

Reciting these verses, constantly examine one's mental shortcomings and refrain from negative conduct. The root cause for the unceasing, unbearable suffering in this ocean of the three realms of existence is nonvirtuous karma. Given that is the case, the nonvirtues are as follows. The three that correspond to the body are killing, stealing, and sexual misconduct; the four of speech are lying, slander, harsh speech, and gossip; and the three of mind are craving, ill will, and wrong view. Given that all nonvirtue is spawned from these ten, they are the basis. With those as the foundation, depending upon motivation, the degree of suffering experienced will be major, middling, or minor. Through the karma of hatred, one is thrown into the Avīchī hell. Through the karma of desire, there is [the result of suffering] as a preta. Through the karma of delusion, the animal realm [is produced]. All of this is due to motivation. The power of the result and result in accord with the cause will be determined by the weight of each individual nonvirtue. This will then be in harmony with the intent directed toward either an actual object or an imaginary object. In addition, negative karma can be either certain or uncertain. Certain karma is produced by killing one's parents, spiritual teacher, or an arhat and also by shedding the blood of a buddha based upon negative intentions. Given it is certain that through any of these five acts the perpetrator will fall to the Avīchī hell, this is referred to as certain nonvirtue.

Otherwise, except for the impairment of samaya, the negative results of nonvirtuous deeds are uncertain because they depend upon the extent to which the basis, intention, action, and final result apply. Even if these [four] are all operative: if eventually there is no stain based on craving and becoming, then it is uncertain as to whether that karma accumulated in a single lifetime will have the potential to bring one to such states [i.e., the hell realms]. Hence, it is referred to as uncertain nonvirtue. This type of karma is even easier to cleanse through purification and confession.

Virtue on the other hand is either tainted or untainted. Tainted virtue means virtue that is not sealed by bodhichitta. The best result of such virtue is rebirth in the form realms, mediocre rebirth may occur in the desire-god realms, and the lowest would be as a ruler among humans and the like. Until such virtue is exhausted, the result will be well-being that becomes merit. This is also referred to as being an aspect of merit. Given that untainted virtue is sealed by the motivation of bodhichitta, it is everlasting and continues to increase, making it inexhaustible. The prajñā that realizes selflessness is the simultaneous perfection of the nondual two truths on the grounds and paths. Liberated from the three realms, permanent exaltation is attained, which is referred to as an aspect of liberation. These are the unmistaken upadesha instructions from Sūtra and Tantra that describe the outcome of all actions associated with the acceptance and rejection of positive and negative deeds. Given this is the great chariot that enters the exalted citadel of liberation, it is the fourth crucial point.

> *Phet!* To the primordial ground pure from the beginning, free from direction, Samantabhadrī; the intrinsic nature pure within itself, Khachödma; and all-pervasive compassion evenly pervading as the kāya of the Wrathful Mother, Tröma—I go for refuge to actualize the consummate expanse of this wisdom mind.

Thus, the array of self-appearances instantly transforms into the perfectly complete pure land of Khachöd Dewachen.

In the center of this, imagine that in the space in front of self and all sentient beings appears the sole mother, blue-black Tröma Nagmo, inseparable with the root guru upon a lotus, sun, moon, and corpse seat. She holds a vajra blade in her right hand and skull filled with blood in the left. Her two legs are dancing upon a corpse; her mouth is gaping, tongue rolling, and three eyes are bulging. Her orange hair stands on end to touch the peak of existence, while a squealing black pig's head juts from her crown. Her breasts are voluptuous, her lotus mature, and she wears the eight charnel-ground ornaments while standing in an expanse of wisdom fire and shimmering orbs of light.

Above her crown is the embodiment of all sambhogakāya gurus as red Vajravarāhī. She holds a curved vajra blade and skull filled with blood, while playfully dancing amid a blazing expanse of wisdom fire. Visualize that above her crown appears the nature of the entire maṇḍala of all dharmakāya gurus appearing as the blue-black Samantabhadrī. She is naked and seated in the full-lotus posture upon a lotus and moon seat. Her hands are parallel to her heart in the mudrā of union with emptiness. Envision that she abides within a radiant expanse of blue-black light molecules.

Imagine the sublime masters of the nine lineages surrounding, and that all [objects of refuge] are facing and gazing down upon you with great loving kindness and compassion. In their presence, oneself and all beings go for refuge together with the three doors united while thinking, "From this moment onward, until the heart of enlightenment is realized, I take refuge in you, supplicate you, bow down to you, rely upon you, place all hope in you, and offer my three doors. In all situations, whether high, low, happy, sad, good, or bad, you are all-knowing. Grant blessings that my three doors may become the three vajras." In this way, completely offering oneself is the key point.

Having taken refuge, there are three vows to accept and three to abandon. The three to accept are that, once confidence is placed in the Buddha, one must never disrespect that which represents the Buddha [i.e., any statue] and not even the shadow of an image of the Buddha. Great respect must be rendered. One must never disrespect even a single syllable of the dharma, and respect must be shown. One must not show disrespect to the sangha, including their robes or even their shadows. These are the three to accept. The three to abandon are to not accept heretics, barbarians, or those with power in worldly realms, such as gods, nāgas, earth lords, guardians, kingly forces, or mighty lords of the land, as objects of refuge or homage. One must abandon the intent or action of harming sentient beings and must not befriend negative companions who have corrupt views and conduct, have turned from the dharma, or are themselves heretics. These are the three things to abandon. Immediately implementing the knowledge of what to accept and reject is the fifth crucial point.

> *Phet!* I promise to liberate all beings from the ocean of existence. All sacred supreme objects of refuge, bear witness. Through my training to cultivate the bodhichitta, may I attain the glorious potential to empty the depths of saṃsāra.

In order to cultivate the two levels of bodhichitta—aspirational and practical—for aspirational, from the perspective of the four immeasurable qualities when bodhichitta is cultivated, that is referred to as aspirational bodhichitta. In brief, that means feeling overwhelming compassion for parent sentient beings, who are enduring unbearable misery in the infinite places of saṃsāric existence, and thinking, "I shall separate them from their suffering and place all of them in a state of well-being. From the perspective of evenness, may they all be placed in the state of freedom!" This cultivation of the precious bodhichitta is the aspirational intention.

Then, in order to engage, given that the six pāramitās are the profound method that simultaneously perfects this, one must now apply them. For that, in the space in front, visualize all gurus, buddhas, and bodhisattvas and respectfully pay homage to them. Thinking, "Just as all the buddhas and bodhisattvas of the ten directions and three times have generated the awakened mind and trained in order to liberate all beings from the vast ocean of existence, so too shall I, for the purpose of freeing all beings from the ocean of existence, give rise to the precious awakened mind and engage wholeheartedly in the training." Consider this from the depth of one's heart; and as you recite the verses, take this vow. To practice this six times during the day and night without discouragement is a crucial point for this path of practice.

The advice is to consider that all aspects of virtue whether tainted or not are dedicated to the welfare of all sentient beings free from bias. That is the consummate training. During all times and situations, one must maintain an impartial equal view toward all parent sentient beings and fully abandon harming any of them through the four factors. Maintaining a sense of mindful conscientiousness throughout the three times: if downfalls occur, then confess them and dedicate all merit to the welfare of sentient beings so that it is sealed. Know that the restoration of vows is a crucial point for guarding pure morality.

In addition, there are the two phases of practice for sending and receiving. First, wishing that all of the unbearably painful misery and habits experienced by beings that are in this ocean of saṃsāra may ripen upon oneself and that self alone would have to experience this, imagine all beings are freed from their misery at that very moment. Think that the result of one's happiness and virtue is received by all sentient beings and that they come to possess supreme well-being.

Second, with each exhalation of breath, think that all causes and results of one's happiness and virtue are equally distributed along with one's breath to all beings, dissolving into them. Exhale the breath. While inhaling, imagine that the suffering, negativity, and obscurations of all sentient beings dissolve into oneself and that frees them from all suffering. Train the mind in this way. Continuously emphasizing this practice is the crucial point, and to know that is the sixth crucial point.

> *Phet!* The outer maṇḍala is the external arrangement of the all-pervasive trichiliocosm, the inner glory is the perfectly complete arrangement of one's body, and the self-appearing, spontaneously present array is the secret maṇḍala. In order to amass the accumulation of the two levels of merit, these offerings are made to the victorious ones.

While reciting these verses, the visualization is as follows. With the field of refuge envisioned as explained before, the method for offering the maṇḍala is to contemplate the outer, inner, and secret maṇḍalas. The outer maṇḍala is the outer vessel of the universe, including Mt. Meru, the four continents, as well as the subcontinents, and one-hundred million realms among which are the realms of the gods. Without considering that even as much as an atom's worth belongs to oneself, bring this to mind and present the offering. Then, imagining that the maṇḍala of one's body is complete, present that as the offering. The skin is the golden foundation of the earth; the spine the king of mountains, Mt. Meru; the right arm is the eastern continent Pūrvavideha, Lüpakpo; the right leg, the southern continent Jambudvīpa, Dzambuling; the left leg is the western continent Aparagodnīya, Balangchöd; and the left arm is the northern continent Uttarakuru, Draminyen. The fingers and toes are the subcontinents and their islands.

The ribs are the ring of mountains; the body fat, the golden mountain; the intestines are the great turbulent oceans. The kidneys are the supreme steed; the liver, the wish-granting cow; the spleen, the great plateau of Ahmo Lika'i. The diaphragm is the dwelling place of the gods, the lungs are the wish-granting trees, and the heart is the treasure vase. The chakras are the offering goddesses who hold the eight auspicious emblems, and the seven royal signs are the glorious qualities of gods and humans. The blood and yellow fluids are the rivers and rainfall, the neck is the crystal stūpa, and the throat is the unceasing water source of the Gaṅgā. The head is the palace of perfect victory; the teeth, the uncultivated crops. The nose is Rāhula, and the eyes are the sun and moon. The ears are the formless realms, and the brain is the nectar of the gods. The pores are the wealth and endowments of gods, nāgas, and humans perfectly complete. Imagining and offering this is the inner maṇḍala offering.

The ālaya is the golden ground of the earth. Passion-based mental activity is the king of mountains. The eight groups of consciousness are the four continents and the subcontinents. Mental activity is the sun and moon. Secondary states of mind are the glorious qualities of desirable objects. Manifesting and offering this is the secret maṇḍala.

Next is the accumulation of merit through the seven-branch offering prayer.

> *Phet!* I prostrate to the three kāyas of all the victorious ones and offer all of my bodies and abundance. All accumulated negativities and obscurations of the three doors are confessed, and all wholly positive virtuous accumulations are the causes for rejoicing. I request the dharma wheel be turned in whatever way is necessary, and the victorious ones are beseeched to not pass beyond sorrow. I fully dedicate the root of

virtue to all sentient beings. [May all beings] without exception, simultaneously attain the state of enlightenment!

Thus, reciting these verses, visualize in the space in front the entire field of refuge, including all gurus, buddhas, and bodhisattvas without exception.

In their presence, offer prostrations by manifesting innumerable emanations of one's body, like atoms. Present offerings of one's body and abundance by imagining clouds of outer, inner, and secret offerings free from fixation. With intense remorse for all nonvirtuous accumulations acquired throughout myriad lifetimes, offer confession and the vow to abstain and rejoice in the virtuous deeds and paths of the āryas, including all shrāvakas, pratyekas, and bodhisattvas. In the presence of the ten directional buddhas, imagine infinite emanations of one's bodies, like atoms, offering the golden dharma wheel, the conch that swirls to the right, and the seven precious signs to request the dharma wheel to be turned. Consider this request is granted. Then by single-pointedly supplicating, beseech the buddhas and bodhisattvas of the three times and ten directions not to pass into nirvāṇa until the beings within the oceans of saṃsāra are emptied. Consider this request is granted. By gathering the root of all virtue accumulated throughout the three times, dedicate this completely to the welfare of every living being. From the perspective of the seven branches, this becomes a perfectly pure crucial point for accumulating merit. This completes the eighth section.

Then, the meditation and recitation of the trikāya ḍākinīs is as follows.

> *Phet!* Instantly, as if awakening from a dream, all appearances arise as the perfect pure land. In the center of this, upon an eight-petaled lotus symbolizing nonattachment, is a sun and moon seat. Upon this, self-nature appears as the sole mother, blue-black Tröma Nagmo, with one face and two arms holding a curved vajra blade in the right hand and a skull filled with blood in the left. Both legs are in the dancing posture, and a squealing black pig's head juts from the crown. Adorned with the eight charnel-ground accouterments, she has an extremely wrathful demeanor and stands in the expanse of a blazing wisdom inferno. In her heart, within an amulet of the conjoined sun and moon is a blue-black syllable *hung* encircled by a garland of mantric syllables. From them, light rays radiate to cleanse all illness, demonic-force possession, negativity, obscurations, and the heap of aggregates, like the sun's rays striking dew. Think that everything is cleansed.
>
> Upon her crown is the sambhogakāya Vajravarāhī, clear red, holding a curved vajra blade and skull, while dancing upon a lotus and moon seat, within a brilliant expanse of wisdom fire and massing light. Above her

crown is the great dharmakāya mother of basic space, blue-black Samantabhadrī, naked, seated in the vajra posture with both hands in the earth-touching gesture, generated within an expanse of deep and luminous wisdom-light bindus. In the heart of the dharmakāya sovereign of the family is a white syllable *ah*; and in the sambhogakāya's heart, upon a sun seat the size of a split pea, is a red syllable *bam*. Encircled by the garlands of mantric syllables, light rays radiate to cleanse the mind streams of self and all beings; and everyone awakens in the originally pure kāya of clear light.

Recite the mantra as many times as possible:

Om benzar trodhi kali bam ha ri ni sa sarwa pa pam shintam ku ru ye so ha

Then from the mantric syllables in the heart of the sovereign of the family, Vajravarāhī, warm light rays of five colors suddenly emerge to dissolve into the heart of oneself as Tröma Nagmo. One becomes a bindu of white light that dissolves up into the heart of the sambhogakāya wisdom ḍākinī. Then as Vajravarāhī, in one's heart from a red *bam* encircled by the mantric syllables, light rays radiate to cleanse and purify all habits, karma, and passions of the three planes of existence. Imagine the three realms become pure lands and everything is the manifestation of deities, mantra, and the nature of phenomena.

Om benzar wa ra hi bam ha ri ni sa sarwa pa pam shintam ku ru ye so ha

From the mantra syllables in the heart of the family sovereign Samantabhadrī, light rays radiate. Imagine that self and all appearances dissolve into the unelaborate basic space of phenomena. Recite as much as possible:

Om benzar wa ra hi bam ha ri ni sa sarwa pa pam shintam ku ru ye so ha

From the heart of the mother, Samantabhadrī, blue-black light rays radiate to dissolve into one's heart as Vajravarāhī, transforming one into an orb of red light. This dissolves into the heart of the dharmakāya wisdom ḍākinī. In the heart of oneself as Samantabhadrī, from a white *ah* encircled by the mantric syllables, light rays radiate, causing saṃsāra to collapse within the state of great transcendence; and one becomes the single taste of the wisdom space of the victorious ones. Recite:

Om benzar sa manta bha dra om

Thus, recite this with the awareness of the great expansive pervasion of the evenness of saṃsāra and enlightenment. Following the root mantra, recite:

Dharma ka ya sa ma ti siddhi ah ah ah

Finally, after reciting according to one's capacity, rest within unelaborate awareness.

While engaged in this meditation-recitation, practice without allowing the mind to be distracted elsewhere. Mingle the three doors inseparably with the three vajras. The key point is to take the path of the all-pervasive purity of phenomenal existence. This completes the ninth section.

Guru-yoga practice brings the three doors to maturity through empowerment as the play of the three vajras.

> *Phet!* Perfectly pure self-appearances are the great basic space of phenomena. In the land of exaltation free from transition or change, self-awareness is the wisdom Tröma, an attractive lucid red color. In the right hand is a curved vajra blade and in the left a skull filled with blood. Both legs are in the dancing posture, and she wears bone ornaments, amidst blazing fire. In the space in front in an expanse of rainbow-light bindus is the glorious root guru as the embodiment of the three lineages of masters in the kāya of Vajravarāhī. She holds a curved vajra blade in her right hand and a skull filled with blood in the left. Her legs are in the dancing posture, and she is adorned with the six bone ornaments. A squealing black pig's head juts from her crown. She has a peaceful, radiant smile with youthful charm, and her beauty is enhanced by the major and minor marks. Above her crown is Samantabhadrī in the mudrā of evenness, surrounded by an assembly of buddhas, bodhisattvas, and vidyādharas. Clearly visualize them as distinct as sesame seeds overflowing their pod. They radiate light into the space of phenomena to invoke the inseparable manifestations.
>
> *Hung!* Supreme among pure lands is the land of Khachöd, the sublime place of the dharmadhātu, Akaniṣhṭha. As the embodiment of all gurus of the three lineages, precious guru, who manifests as the sovereign of Khachöd, come here to bless your lineage disciples. Grant blessings to mature and free my mind stream. Care for me inseparably and grant me liberation.
>
> *Gu ru ha ri ni sa siddhi hung*
>
> *Phet!* Glorious embodiment of all buddhas throughout the three times, Precious Guru, whose kindness is impossible to repay, sovereign of all

maṇḍalas, vajra holder, you are a perfect treasure trove of the glorious qualities of omniscience, loving concern, and power. Great hero, who frees all beings throughout existence, with devotion by recalling your kindness and qualities, I supplicate. Look upon me with your eyes of compassion. Turn your wisdom mind from basic space to gaze upon me. Not just momentarily but continuously throughout the three times, think of us with your omniscient loving kindness. I offer my body and abundance, including the root of virtue free from attachment or fixation. With intense devotion expressed through all three doors, I rely upon you as my permanent protector. I go for refuge in you, undeceiving source of protection. You are the captain who leads beings to liberation through sight, sound, recollection, and touch. I prostrate to you with devotion free from transition or change in the three times and bring phenomenal existence to mind as the offering. All faults and shortcomings are confessed, and I rejoice in all virtue. I always beseech you to turn the dharma wheel and to remain forever firm. Pray empty the oceanic realms of beings from the depths! I pray to you, Precious Guru! Hold me with compassion, wisdom ḍākinī!

Grant blessings, supreme guide of beings. Grant blessings for a meaningful precious human rebirth. Grant blessings to remember death from the heart. Grant blessings to be skillful in knowing what to accept and reject. Grant blessings to feel revulsion with saṃsāra. Grant blessings that the mind will long for nothing. Grant blessings to tame the mind without pretense. Grant blessings that the mind may be steadfastly free from attachment. Grant blessings to be at ease without companionship. Grant blessings to be able to remain in fear-invoking environments. Grant blessings to live in retreat, free from activity. Grant blessings to maintain the dignity of dharma unerringly. Grant blessings that devotion may be steadfast and unchanging. Grant blessings to cultivate undiminishing renunciation. Grant blessings to remember inseparability with the guru. Grant blessings to accomplish indestructible siddhi. Grant blessings to attain great confidence with fearlessness. Grant blessings to realize appearances lack true existence. Grant blessings to realize the prajñā of selflessness. Grant blessings to unimpededly see there are no reference points. Grant blessings to seize the immutable ground free from confusion. Grant blessings to maintain unceasing continuity in practice without distraction. Grant blessings to realize the great perfection without meditation. By seeing the self-nature of the uncontrived fundamental ground, may I attain confidence with the glorious nature of the four kāyas. *Phet phet phet!*

> Father Guru, Buddha of the Three Times, purify the obscurations of my body and channels; by fully maturing through the enlightened body vase empowerment, may my body become the nirmāṇakāya. Now I attain the potential of a fully mature vidyādhara. *Ah la la phet phet phet!*
>
> Father Guru, Buddha of the Three Times, purify the obscurations of my speech and winds. By fully maturing through the enlightened speech secret empowerment, may my speech become the sambhogakāya. Now I attain the potential of an immortal vidyādhara. *Ah la la phet phet phet!*
>
> Father Guru, Buddha of the Three Times, purify the obscurations of my mind and bindus. By fully maturing through the enlightened mind prajñā-wisdom empowerment, may my mind become the dharmakāya. Now I attain the potential of the mahāmudrā vidyādhara. *Ah la la phet phet phet!*
>
> Father Guru, Buddha of the Three Times, purify the two obscurations of my habits. By fully maturing through the great absolute word empowerment, may I breathe the breath of the glorious expanse of all four kāyas. Now I attain the potential of the spontaneously present vidyādhara. *Ah la la phet phet phet!*
>
> The great expanse of the father guru's wisdom mind as blue-black light dissolves into oneself. One awakens in the expanse of the fundamental nature of the great perfection and delights in the ground of nonconceptual original purity. Awakening in the nature of the ever-youthful vase kāya, now saṃsāra and enlightenment are purity and evenness. *Ah la la phet phet phet!*

Instantly, the consummate phenomena of the mind vanish like a magician's illusory display within the empty nature of the dharmatā. In the unchanging blissful pure land of Khachöd free from transition and change, one appears as the red wisdom ḍākinī holding a curved vajra blade in the right hand and a skull filled with blood in the left. Both legs are in the dancing posture upon a lotus and sun seat. Naked, she wears bone ornaments and is adorned with a long necklace made of white lotus flowers. The three eyes are gazing into the basic space of the sky. With the radiance of light and rays emanating, she appears yet lacks true, inherent existence and is clear without being held as true, like a water moon, reflection, or a dream. Visualize in this way.

In the space in front, upon a lotus and sun seat, appears the embodiment of all three lineage masters without exception as the nature of the root guru who appears as the sole mother, Vajravarāhī, red with one face and two arms, holding a curved vajra blade in the right hand and a skull filled with blood in the left. Both legs are in the dancing posture, [and she] wears the six bone ornaments and all of the charnel-ground accouterments, while poised in an expanse of blazing red-black wisdom fire. At her crown is the dharmakāya Samantabhadrī, naked, in the mudrā of evenness; and both legs are in the vajra āsana upon a lotus and moon seat. Meditate that all the root lineage masters are surrounding and appear like banks of colorful rainbow light. All of them are facing one and gazing with loving kindness.

Each is marked at the crown with a white *om*, a red *ah* at the throat, and a blue *hung* at the heart. Ablaze like the light of one-hundred thousand suns, imagine they are a great treasury of empowerment and wisdom. With unflagging faith and devotion, single-pointedly supplicate, after which the visualization for receiving the four empowerments is as follows.

From the guru's forehead where the white *om* blazes like the full moon, white *om* syllables with rays of light emanate like stars shooting in space. Entering one's body through the crown, all negativities, obscurations, seeds of karma, and habits accumulated through the body are completely purified and cleansed. The enlightened-body vase empowerment is received. One's body becomes the vajrakāya. Think that the state of nirmāṇakāya is actualized.

From the *ah* in the throat, red *ah* syllables and light rays like lightning bolts shooting in the sky dissolve into one's throat. Cleansing all negativities, obscurations, karmic passions, and habits accumulated through speech, the secret speech empowerment is received. One's speech is blessed as the play of vajra speech. Think that the state of the sambhogakāya is actualized.

From the *hung* in the heart, blue-black *hungs* and light rays radiate like massing clouds in the sky. Dissolving into one's heart, all negativities, obscurations, karmic passions, habits, and the like accumulated through the mind are cleansed. The wisdom-prajñā mind empowerment is received. The mind is blessed as the nature of enlightened mind. Think that the mind realizes the state of the originally pure dharmakāya.

Once again, from the five places of the guru, light rays in five colors emanate. They dissolve into one's five places, completely cleansing all habits and passions that prevent the attainment of liberation. Think that all cognitive obscurations based on fixation upon the three rounds that prevent the state of omniscience are cleansed. The absolute word empowerment is received. All aspects of mind and appearances become the nature of nondual empty awareness. One is blessed to attain the glory of spontaneously perfecting the two purposes. Meditate that the nature of the three kāyas' enlightened body, speech, and mind is inseparable and actualized as the svābhāvikakāya.

Once again, imagine that the nature of the guru's nonconceptual mind as a blue-black bindu of light dissolves into one's heart. The fundamental nature of the dharmatā, just as it is, is actualized. One receives the empowerment of the dynamic strength of awareness. The status of becoming a dharma sovereign of the three realms is rendered evident, and the state of the four vidyādharas is simultaneously perfected.

Then, one becomes a brilliant bindu of red light that dissolves into the heart of the precious guru. Reciting *phet*, [think that the guru] enters the womb of the space of the dharmakāya and rest freely in the all-pervasive, unborn state of original purity.

At this point, the phowa practice called *Opening the Wisdom Gateway* may be inserted. This completes the tenth section.

Then, as for the uncommon cycle of instructions, initially one determines the self-appearing [abiding] wisdom maṇḍala. First is to analyze which among body, speech, and mind is principal. That brings recognition and restoration. Then the limitations of the mind's color, shape, eternalism, and nihilism are dispelled, bringing restoration.

Once again, with mindfulness concerning concepts, the distinctions are encountered and taken as the path. Concerning that, mingling as one, single-pointed, [the mind's] objects arise and increase as movement from the expanse. That is called "mindfulness securing stability". Within emptiness, wakeful awareness arises as lucidity. Mindfulness settles into emptiness itself. Mindfulness falls apart within the unelaborate. To abide within this nature is the innate nature; and by entering the path, that is said to be awareness. Then, having determined the fundamental nature, one must then clarify all faults associated with view and meditation.

Head and body hair are not "me"; flesh and bones are also not "me". Blood and pus are not "me", and teeth and nails are not "me". Intestines, feces, and urine are not "me". Similarly, if the head, legs, arms, and joints are examined, each one has its own basis for designation, so do they actually exist aside from being nonreferential? Likewise, if the universe, inhabitants, the fivefold sensual desires with each of these names and their basis of designation were unchanging, indestructible, and permanently existing as true and real, then your assertion is right. If your present perception of holding to true existence concerning elements and forms that originate from causes actually were to possess unchanging vajra characteristics, then [your] assertion is right. By tearing apart and reducing [them], once scattered, does this not change? [When] dust is reduced to particles that become partless, watch to see where those have vanished. Like the ten illustrations of magic—from the perspective of being empty—except for being merely apparent, nothing at all exists. How can an object be asserted when no tangible thing exists?

During daytime appearances of self and others—if held to as true and you are right—then during dream appearances while dreaming, you may be right.

From the perspective of daytime appearances seen as truly existing and from the perspective of the dream state, if you believe that dreams are true, then what happens to daytime phenomena during the dream state? The [body] must have naturally perished, so where did you dispose of the corpse? During daytime, where has the dream-state environment gone? What causes did the living beings in the dream state come from? Where did [you] hide those bodies in dreams? Having discarded this body that originates from causes and circumstances, who are the parents and what are the causes and circumstances for the person who goes to their next life? Concerning this present body that originates from causes and circumstances that bring about the fear of illness and suffering: when separated from this body, who will take on those experiences?

Likewise, the intrinsic nature [of phenomena] is to occur throughout the three times, and that is the time of evenness. Having never occurred before, the phenomena being experienced as true are held as the time of the past. Having not occurred as yet, [one] anticipates the time of the future occurring. Nothing truly exists [concerning] the aspects of confused perception that attach to the tangible, [so] the present time has originated. Hence, once objective appearances are determined, why wouldn't the false cave of confusion just collapse?

The noble Buddha is the object of hope. If held to as the aspect of the universe and inhabitants that cannot be buddha. That which is called "buddha" lacks tangible characteristics. To designate characteristics is to lack awareness. Having awakened from the shell of ignorance and expanded the self-radiance of wisdom, [buddha or *sangye*] is the all-pervasive, unbiased open nature of evenness. From within omniscient knowledge, emanations appear. That [buddha] is also free from faculties and involves no form, characteristics, substances, universe, or inhabitants. Whatever is substantial and tangible is referred to as a sentient being. The universe and inhabitants [are] the phenomena of sentient beings. How can one see a buddha to be a sentient being? If so, what is the mark of supremacy that delineates a difference? If a [buddha] does not exceed [sentient beings] aside from the experience of mere bliss, are you then deciding that [buddha] is a divinity of the form-god realm? Otherwise, are you claiming [buddha] is an immortal? Similarly, you may be claiming that [buddha] is a state of blissful happiness, excellent companionship, environment, an attractive form, or miraculous abilities. If so, aren't those the [qualities] of the divinities of the form-god realm?

The meaning of buddha cannot be indicated through duality. Buddha means no fixation upon "me" that has transcended interdependency, has transcended the object of accumulation, and is the meaning of being free from elaborations. Buddha means possessing the three gateways to liberation. Buddha means having collapsed the distinction of duality. Buddha means having transcended linear time. With buddha, there are no directions or limitations.

Buddha means the epitome of the four kāyas. Who can see this as form? Buddha is the ever-youthful vase kāya. Who can recognize this as substance? Buddha means saṃsāra and enlightenment are subsumed. How can one see these as outer and inner? Buddha is the meaning of the awakened mind. Who can believe that [buddha] is the conceptual mind? Buddha is the meaning of being unrestricted. How can one believe this has directions, radiation, or reabsorption? Buddha is the sole bindu. Who can explain its shape and color? Buddha abides within the minds of all sentient beings. The fundamental nature of sentient beings is the dharmakāya. Aside from being this essential nature, this is not the field of experience of those who are blinded by cataracts and who speculate. Those with the eyes of prajñā will make use of this. [Like] transferring from one location to another, the immature [think they can] traverse and arrive in the pure land. Holding to that as the genuine will propel [them to arrive in] loathsome places. By discerning the relative and the genuine, those whose prajñā eyes were closed will then open them. Buddha must not be misunderstood to be autonomous.

The objects of disappointment appear as the places in the three realms of saṃsāra. This dense habit is impressed upon the intrinsic nature. From the notion of "I", outer objective appearances are established. These do not exist aside from appearing as something other than the mere transformation of phenomena. [Without knowing that], there is the habit of permanent grasping to true existence as stable and everlasting. Due to that, if one thinks these [phenomena] exist other than that, then who created the molten lava ground of the hell realms? From where have the denizens of hell and their weapons come from? Likewise, whose children are those who can bear such a pitiful state for eons of time experiencing hunger and thirst with huge stomachs [and] tiny limbs and mouths? In which direction do the environments exist, including their inhabitants—to the east, south, west, north, or in between? Without being analyzed, it appears as truly existing; yet if examined, everything is only false.

Based on these reasons, all such phenomenal appearances occur from within transformation and are nondual. Equally observe them within the state of no duality. In saṃsāra, aside from that, there is no revolving from one place to another. Except for merely appearing, there is no continuity that goes from one place to another. If this [assertion] of yours of taking one rebirth after another and experiencing suffering [is true], then why do [beings] not become physically exhausted? Why are their lives strong and still functioning? Habituated with the confusion of one's mind and appearances, the positive and negative results of karma cause saṃsāra. That will unmistakably arise without doubt. This process of joy versus sorrow is unreliable, and it will also mature. Aside from that, it is a key point to not believe [in true existence].

In addition, given this is empty and free from fear, how would a god who grants protection protect? How would harm-causing obstructers bring torment?

If empty, who is the object to be harmed by the substantial? If the substantial is empty, then how is this destroyed? How does the formless threaten that which is embodied in a form? How can the formless be killed by a form? How can a god who is immaterial grant protection to that which actually exists? Similarly, there is no way for a form-based [god to protect] the formless. A form cannot protect a form. The formless is similar. There is no one who delivers or receives happiness or suffering. The experiences of these patterns amount to confused phenomena and are the product of positive and negative karmic causes and results. All of saṃsāra belongs to the relative, and transcending that is the absolute. I, the learned Saraha, have proclaimed this!

Appearance and mind are themselves the relative, and the nature of that is the absolute. This is also revealed by many other scholars. Previously accumulated karma and passions, the obscurations of habits, and the accumulation of all virtuous karma are the nature of emptiness, so where are the activities of objective benefit and harm? Observe where these accumulations gather. No object exists, so how can that be possible?

As taught, all appearances are empty by virtue of their own nature. Nevertheless, if the way of their abiding is not understood, accomplishment will not occur. Hence, it is crucial to recognize this and gain confidence. When the essential nature of the tathāgata of the primordial ground is actualized through self-occurring prajñā, that is the great, lucid depth of the dharmakāya. When the dust of dimmed awareness penetrates the eyes, dust mingling with the eyes is the basis of saṃsāra. Like the analogy of a blind man trying to travel, that leads to exhaustion.

From this, self-fixation is the object of bondage arising as the universe, inhabitants, and all desirable phenomena. From "I", this self of a body has emerged. This body functions as the dwelling place and mental events as the owner. By this mind engaging with the five entranceways, the consciousnesses [emerge]. Through the generation of initial self-fixation, self, other, and objective grasping appears. External objects are perpetually fixated upon by the subject. This is the fixating mind. I, Saraha, have proclaimed this! Both are asserted to be concepts.

The emptiness of external appearances is empty by virtue of their nature, and the inner mind is empty unto itself. Those who determine [emptiness] by deviating into autonomy, [thinking] these two views can be united, will not be free from the great lasso of dualistic fixation that binds them. External objective appearances are posited in their own place, and the inner self is posited within itself. Between them, [one] meditates upon emptiness that amounts to nothing. This resembles a drop of water trapped within a block of ice. Look to see how few attain liberation.

In this way, all dualistic confused appearances are, aside from their nature, uncreated by anyone. Uncreated by the nature itself as well, this play is naturally self-arising self-appearance that is pure and even within its own being. This nature just as it is constitutes being the consummate nature of saṃsāra and enlightenment. Abiding within the uncontrived state, there is no gathering or dispersal since this is primordially incapable of separation.

Based on the distinction between awareness and lack of awareness, buddhas and sentient beings are referred to separately. The eyes of prajñā are uncreated, fully complete, unborn, unceasing, and free from being either clear or obscured. This meditation transcends being contrived or [based upon] thought. Self-occurring wisdom is determined there. One must gain confidence to personally encounter the indwelling original buddha nature.

In this way, those practitioners who have encountered the fundamental nature and who possess fully endowed karma and prayers must wander in fear-provoking, indeterminate locales in order to encounter the crucial point through circumstances to attack the faults of hope, fear, and fixation with objects. May the supreme state of the self-liberated heruka be reached! This completes the eleventh section.

First, for wandering in the fear-invoking environments, remain for three days just inside the threshold of the door. Then venture out as far as sight allows and fall asleep there for the same duration as the aforementioned. Then, the practices for wandering in uncertain fear-invoking locales are as follows. First, the visualization for the initial suppression is that for [embarking to] the mountains, visualize that there is a conjoined meteorite wheel circling to the right and left. This reduces Mt. Meru into dust that is then dispersed, leaving the gods-māras without basis or support. They become terrified and quiver with fear. Then imagine that surrounding them is a canopy enclosure of blazing vajras of fire. Surrounding that is a fence of fire, and encircling that is a chain of dark-colored humans holding weapons. Outside of that is a fence composed of wrathful Tröma ḍākinīs; and outside of that, fences of water and wind encircle. Think there is nowhere to escape, nor is there any way to break out of this.

If embarking for crags, then visualize that meteorite arrows descend upon the crags to completely annihilate, reduce to dust, and scatter everything like piles of sand. Think that the gods-māras that reside there are separated from their places, supports, and protection and are forced to take up residence upon the piles of sand. Imagine they are then deposited into the previously visualized enclosure with no place to escape to or means to do so. For the forests, think there are lightning bolts of fire shooting into the forest to incinerate and scatter everything. The gods-māras residing there become helpless, and imagine that they are bound within an enclosure from which they will never break free.

For valleys, think that a great rainstorm of stones descends; and all aspects of the earth, ground, rocks, and mountains vanish like salt melting into water. All gods-māras are left behind without place or support. Think that, like before, they are encircled by the six fences with no way to escape. For plains, imagine that a rainstorm of molten lava descends, and the entire ground becomes a blazing bank of fire. All gods-māras are encircled like before and left with no place or support. For lakes and rivers, a blazing fire storm of vajra meteorites descends and turns into molten boiling lava, causing all gods-māras to experience unbearable heat. They are forced out the other side of the mountain, and the fire blazes behind them like an inferno. All gods-māras are [imagined] just as before. For departure to uninhabited houses and towns, sometimes imagine that a rain shower of molten lava descends to burn and destroy everything. Upon the ashes, the gods-māras remain without support like before. For the charnel grounds, imagine that blazing vajra meteorites radiate and descend upon that place like lightning bolts. The earth is destroyed to become like a heap of ash or molten lava. The gods-māras are left without support, and the encircling fences are meditated upon as before.

Alternatively, the visualization that is of general importance is that, from the heart of oneself as the wisdom ḍākinī Tröma Nagmo, magnificent light rays radiate to completely fill the empty trichiliocosm world systems. Everything then melts into light, and all gods-māras are pulled inward from the outer perimeter with no means of escape. Arriving at the fear-provoking places, they are forced into black, blazing tents made of meteorite vajras. All of their strength and powers are restricted, and their haughty splendor is subdued. Think that they remain there shivering with fear. This visualization can apply to any of the aforementioned scenarios. Then [the light] gets dimmer and dimmer; and no matter what direction they try to escape, they are unable to break free. Visualizing this will become familiar as a matter of course. Given that this is the first suppression through splendor involving messengers, it is the visualization called "overcoming through the great command". It is a key point to make no mistake concerning the way of practicing while wandering, and secrecy must be strictly enforced during all occasions, such as when moving about and remaining. While wandering, one must not rely upon or make use of any weapons, companions, or rites of protection.

First, the generation of bodhichitta is as follows. Thinking, "I must place all sentient beings, beginning with the gods-māras, in the state of liberation and perfect omniscience," embark. While embarking, the supreme practitioner will recognize that saṃsāra and enlightenment self-appear. Within that view, one embarks by assuming the confident gaze of the dynamic strength of mind's appearances being perfected. Those incapable of this must meditate upon themselves as the wisdom Tröma Nagmo, huge, heavy, and extremely terrifying. Thinking that phenomenal existence is all-pervasively empty like the sky, begin chasing all gods-māras of phenomenal existence into the fear-invoking locale like falcons pursuing birds.

At the moment one arrives at the fear-provoking place, the embodiment of all gods-māras who dwell in this hair-raising place appears as a huge, foreboding dark man. Visualizing oneself as the wisdom ḍākinī Tröma Nagmo, take him by the right leg and circle him above your head three times. Think that the gods-māras of the three realms gather and dissolve into him. Then striking him on the ground three times, think that his power and strength based on the three poisons is conquered. Throw him out in a sprawled position, and visualize that you manifest upon him as the maṇḍala of Tröma. Perform the *Suppression through Splendor*. Having quelled all gods-māras with the boundless activity-emanation ḍākinīs, the gods-māras dissolve into the negative, dark man under the cushion. Having previously overcome him, think that now a great sun disk suppresses his heart; and it is there that the wisdom ḍākas and ḍākinīs of basic space dance, while one imagines that he moans and groans.

> *Phet phet phet!* I am the hero who possesses confidence with vajra sovereignty. Through the fearless conduct of the great, equal taste of expectation and disappointment, the three-kāya maṇḍalas of the victors arise from basic space. The rudra of the dualistic view of self is conquered by the dance.
>
> *Phet!* Guru embodiment of the Three Roots and Buddha Ḍākinīs of the central direction, turn your wisdom intent toward the great wisdom dance of basic space, dancing and stomping on the heads of the gods-māras of delusion with *hung hung ha ha he he ho ho phet.*
>
> Guru embodiment of the Three Roots and Vajra Ḍākinīs of the eastern direction, turn your wisdom intent toward the great wisdom dance that is mirrorlike, dancing and stomping upon the heads of the gods-māras of anger with *hung hung ha ha he he ho ho phet.*
>
> Guru embodiment of the Three Roots and Ratna Ḍākinīs of the southern direction, turn your wisdom intent toward the great wisdom dance of evenness, dancing and stomping upon the heads of the gods-māras of pride with *hung hung ha ha he he ho ho phet.*
>
> Guru embodiment of the Three Roots and Pema Ḍākinīs of the western direction, turn your wisdom intent toward the great wisdom dance of discerning awareness, dancing and stomping upon the heads of the gods-māras of desire with *hung hung ha ha he he ho ho phet.*
>
> Guru embodiment of the Three Roots and Karma Ḍākinīs of the northern direction, turn your wisdom intent toward the great wisdom dance

of all-accomplishing activity, dancing and stomping upon the heads of the gods-māras of jealousy with *hung hung ha ha he he ho ho phet.*

All gathering ḍākinīs of the basic space of dharmakāya are invoked to the dance to tame the demonic nāgas of delusion. The powerful sambhogakāya ḍākinīs and their retinue are invoked to the dance to tame the female māras of desire. The wisdom ḍākinīs of the nirmāṇakāya including their retinue are invoked to the dance to tame the kingly demonic forces of hatred. They dance in the lively gestures of the spontaneously present three kāyas. Destroying the heads of the gods-māras confused by the passions and three poisons, imagine that the realms of saṃsāra collapse in the expanse of the transcendent nature. *Phet phet phet!*

Then, the head and extremities of the rudra suppressed under the seat are pierced by the five wisdom phurbas. Think that [the rudra] is unable to move or get up.

While pitching the tent recite:

Phet phet phet! The white crystal female skeleton blazing with light holds a white conch phurba and pierces the gods-māras of fiery hatred with the phurba of great compassion.

Phet! The golden female skeleton blazing with light holds a golden phurba and pierces the gods-māras of pride with the phurba of great love.

Phet! The copper-colored female skeleton blazing with fire holds a grand coral phurba and pierces the gods-māras of tumultuous desire with the phurba of great joy.

Phet! The fierce black-iron female skeleton holds a turquoise phurba and pierces the gods-māras of turbulent jealousy with the phurba of great equanimity.

Phet! The great female skeleton with bared fangs holds a human-bone phurba and pierces the gods-māras of deluded ignorance with the phurba of great bodhichitta.

Phet! The head and extremities of the rudra emanations of dualistic ignorance are pierced with five wisdom phurbas. [The rudras] lose all power and potential to get up or move at all. *Phet phet phet!*

Having pitched the tent, the practitioner lays upon his or her back and visualizes as follows. One's body becomes huge, solid, [and] heavy, the size of a valley. Under that, the gods-māras are suppressed and wailing in despair. Once again, all oath-bound gods-māras of phenomenal existence are summoned, like paper blown in the wind, so that they powerlessly dissolve into the gods-māras under the bed. Thinking in this way, recite the following:

> *Eh eh!* Until this eon collapses or existence is emptied, I will not move from this place. I will not move or stray from here. I will stay here and sleep. *Phet phet phet!*

Thus, reciting this three times, think that the buddhas, bodhisattvas, gurus, yidams, and ḍākinīs all gather in the sky above in a mass of radiant light. Remain confident within a state of undistracted nonfixation. From time to time, clarify the visualization and commitment while continuing to remain there. Then, it is certain that, in the best scenario, actual upheavals will occur; in the mediocre case, there will be visions; and at least, in the dreams.

These upheavals are both tangible and intangible. The tangible upheavals are based on appearances of things, such as wild animals, yetis, humans, wealth, and the like. The intangible are upheavals from the formless, nonhuman eight classes, such as the gods and māras. Furthermore, earthquakes, houses collapsing, mountains crashing down, rock slides, tsunamis, hail storms, lightning storms, lights, and the occurrence of loud, marching noises from soldiers and various nonhumans will all occur. In dreams, there will be fighting with many people suppressing you, attacking you, and cannibals trying to chase you. Also, one may think that parasites enter the body through the mouth, remain there, and that zombies approach you. In brief, it is possible that a variety of ominous upheavals will occur in indeterminate ways.

Concerning the upheavals for the body, goose bumps will rise up, muscles will quiver, and sharp and subtle pain will be felt, as well as swelling and sudden outbreaks such as rashes. The body will shake and jerk. Speech-based upheavals include lamenting and crying out in despair, erratic sentences, sighing, panting, difficulty breathing, and so forth that will occur in indeterminate ways. Mental upheavals include fear, blank astonishment, loss of confidence in the visualization or meditation, the inability to sit, the wish to escape, and the powerless pursuit of hope and fear, terror, and paranoia. In brief, the mind will become abnormal so that all feelings based on joy, sorrow, hope, and fear are the upheavals. Know that, when all of these dawn simultaneously upon the three doors, that is a great upheaval. Two of these signs indicate an intermediate upheaval; and only one of them, a lesser.

Furthermore, when upheavals occur, they are categorized as the tangible māras, the intangible, the luring māras of pride, and the māras of elation—these four. First, the tangible are outer, actually existing things, such as of form, sound, smell, taste, and touch. At the moment the eyes perceive these things when instantaneous concepts based upon hope, fear, joy, and sorrow emerge, that is the upheaval. If pursued and indulged through the various modes of body and speech, then one is overcome. At the moment the upheaval is upon oneself, if recognized, it will vanish without trace; and that is the severance. The intangible māra does not arise in dependence upon an object. Nevertheless, if fear develops and appearances become confused, then indeterminate perceptions and feelings will surface and a sense of panic will occur concerning all immaterial phenomena. From this initial feeling of panic, paranoia becomes the upheaval. Pursuing this will bring habituated attachment to hope and fear such that one will be overcome. From the time that arises, whatever degree of upheaval manifests—be it great, middling, or weak—at the moment it occurs, one must remember to decide that these are all confused phenomena that lack true existence; and by arriving in that state of confidence, that is the severance.

First, for the māra of elation, there are two: the tangible and the intangible. First, the tangible is when others show respect, praise, become disciples [and] patrons who give great offerings of wealth and valuables, and when one becomes their object of devotion and veneration. The actual manifestation of these excellent, enticing forms is the meaning of "tangible". Developing vivid concepts toward this, such as joy, satisfaction, and the like, is the upheaval. To take that as a siddhi or an indication of excellent interdependence, the habit of repeatedly feeling compulsory attachment out of joy, happiness, and satisfaction is to be overcome. At the moment elation arises—by seeing that to be nonexistent and faulted like dreams and magic—if attachment is then cut off like a poison, that is the severance.

The intangible occurs without cause or circumstance by thinking one's abode and tent are the best, one's endowments plentiful, race and status superior, relatives and siblings abundant and excellent, and that even oneself is exalted both spiritually and worldly. Developing an attitude of total delight with body, speech, and mind is the upheaval. Repeatedly thinking in that way with fixated attachment: when that becomes solidified, one is then overcome.

Concerning this, it is not certain that all of this will occur simultaneously. As revealed through other analogies, the circumstances for deception to occur are uncertain. Some are based on wealth; some deceptions are based on food, some on clothing, business and profit, robbers and thieves. Some are deceived by attachment for lovers, some by cheating and trickery, others by parents and relatives. Some are deceived by wealth, others by taming enemies and protecting loved ones. All of these deceptions are certain magical deceptions of the māra of luring.

Who is deceived in this way? Those who are single-pointedly devoted to dharma have no interest in nonvirtuous activity and have trepidation toward that, as well as having renounced saṃsāra through great weariness. When that person is deceived and the sign of being overcome occurs, they are then incapable of turning their mind from the object of attachment for even an instant. The mind itself becomes unlike before, as the thought of karmic causes and results concerning what to accept and reject diminishes. The heart becomes hard like a stone. Renunciation and weariness vanish like mist. They no longer examine their own mind; and even if they do, they knowingly act free from shame and dignity and are impressed by others who conduct themselves like dogs and pigs.

Even though demonic deceptions occur in this way, the mere appearance or emergence of something does not become the deception. However, one must know that, when concepts arise about appearances and once there is attachment to their arising, that is the upheaval. Once attachment becomes fixation, there is deception. To know that all compounded things are impermanent, to have renunciation for saṃsāra, to recognize all phenomena to be like dreams and magic, and to then train with fearless conduct without fixation is the severance. Given that these are extremely difficult to sever, all practitioners must be especially vigilant.

Previously, in one of the great cities in the land of Magadha, there lived a practitioner named Sūryavajra who was so inspired to practice dharma that he ran away from his parents, relatives, and friends in order to do so. The māras of deception noticed him and converged upon him. The tangible māra said that if he created something extremely terrifying, it would overcome him [i.e., Sūryavajra]. The intangible māra said that if he entered Sūryavajra's heart and caused various emotions such as happiness and sorrow to emerge, that would suffice. The māra of pride said that if he caused him to have many unrestrained emotions, that would do the trick.

The māra of luring weighed in as follows, "Although the tangible māra can bring on terror, the practitioner will sever that by applying the pointing-out instructions on the view of selflessness. That will, in turn, enhance his splendor and vitality such that he will never be defeated in that way again. That must not be allowed. Although the intangible māra may enter his heart, it is easy to identify emotions based on joy and sorrow as counterproductive and negative. He will be able to liberate them in basic space that is free from origination and cessation. It is certain that will be to his advantage. Although the māra of pride may stir up concepts: due to knowing the pointing-out instructions for recognizing concepts as the manifestation of awareness, he will accept negative signs as positive and bring bad circumstances to the path. All three of your deceptions entail negative circumstances that are easy for this practitioner to bring to the path and turn to his aid, so there will be no way to defeat him. Instead, if the three of you come to my aid and through my superior, excellent means of deception, it is certain that together we will destroy him!" Saying this, the māra of luring sneered.

Then, through omniscience, the great saint Lūipā came to know of the māras' plans and called to Sūryavajra to warn him by telling him everything. Sūryavajra replied, "*Ah!* Prior to knowing of this plan, there was the danger that I could have been overcome; but now that I know, it is certain I could never be controlled by them." Lūipā replied, "Given they are attempting to defeat you in this way, take care to not have attraction or attachment toward anything that is especially appealing." Thus, he gave his advice.

With that, Sūryavajra began intensive practice throughout the day and night in six regular sessions without any distraction. Meanwhile, the māra of luring entered the hearts of several people, including an exquisitely attractive young maiden, and overcame all of them. When Sūryavajra opened his maṇḍala that night, he had a very special dream. His meditation deity appeared to him and told him that on that day he had received siddhi and that, from tomorrow onward, he would receive the common attainment. The deity told him he was now set free from the obstructing force of māras; and also went on to say that a qualified consort would come to visit him and that, if he practiced with her, even without entering into a permanent relationship, certain attainments would occur. At the moment of dreaming this, Sūryavajra was overcome with joy and bliss; and the very next day several youthful people came to pay him a visit and offer food and wealth. This was so satisfying to him that he felt the predictions of the deity were authentic.

Several days later, a lovely young maiden came to pay him a visit with rice and a white silk scarf, requesting pointing-out instructions from him. She stayed to receive the teachings, and he wondered if this was the maiden that the deity predicted he should practice union with. He assumed that she was and, if he practiced with her, it would be easy for him to not get entangled in a deeper relationship with her. They practiced union, and afterward he fell deeply in love with her, so much so that he had a hard time even parting company with her. From that time onward, his heart and mind became so obsessed with her that he could not bear even a moment's separation. The girl continued to visit him regularly so that, then, even the townspeople began to get suspicious that the practitioner they had been honoring was in fact turning his back on the dharma.

Thinking that—although he might become a householder—he would never forsake the dharma, Sūryavajra went again to Lūipā and reported everything that had taken place. Lūipā replied, "You have allowed the māra of luring to enter your mind. This indicates exactly what I was warning you about. Now you must sever your ties with this maiden immediately and once again seize the stronghold of your inner practice. If you fail to sever this now, then you will become so ensnared in the murk of saṃsāra that you will never come to know freedom!"

Hence, Lūipā warned him again; and although his words were of value to Sūryavajra, they fell on deaf ears as he could not bear to sever his ties with the object of his attachment. He lost all power and control and was reduced to the status of an ordinary individual; and even worse, the townspeople who had once extoled him were now disgusted by him. With anger, they ridiculed him; and even the ruling king decided to punish him so that he no longer possessed even a hair's tip worth of his previous intention to practice the dharma. Eventually, he lost everything and became the most impoverished man in the region.

The supreme Dharmagarbha also fell prey to the obstacles of māras in this way; and when he was almost completely overcome, I [i.e., Dudjom Lingpa] pointed out this account to him so he could cut off his attachment and fixation. He then went far away to a secluded place to practice and successfully reversed the path of the māras.

For all future lineage holders to use positive circumstances as the path, these accounts must be held in their hearts. It is easy to recognize that the negative circumstances are unwanted; but when it comes to positive situations, since they are associated with desire, they are hard to identify and extremely difficult to bring to the path. Know that finding someone who will not be overcome by this is as rare as the sighting of a daytime star.

During the degenerate times when negative karmic forces are strong, there is no one who is not under the power of māras. That is why holding firm to one's ground, like an injured deer, is a crucial key point to be known. In the self-manifesting absolute great Akaniṣhṭha, out of great compassion for their welfare, I, Sarahapa, give this testament as advice for sentient beings of the degenerate times. This is a special transmission for all with a karmic connection to me. Since this dharma is incomparable, may everyone take this to heart!

The source of all dharma is the land of India. It is in India where all buddhas are to be born. India is also the place where the Buddha taught the dharma, as well as being the sacred ground where aspirations are fulfilled. Hence, it is a land considered to be more sacred than any place on earth. It is there that, aside from the distinction of being Buddhist versus non-Buddhist, there is no dispute that both categories of buddhadharma, Sūtra and Tantra, were propagated. Given that the Victorious One was skillfully compassionate, he taught according to the faculties of those to be tamed.

Disputing between right and wrong based on an attitude that a single direction is correct will undoubtedly escalate the accumulation of the negative karma that rejects the dharma. That is why, conversely, the learned will without dispute see clearly through their prajñā vision. The dharma is not an object the totally blind will guess about. The doctrine of the Buddha is so profoundly vast, it never falls in a biased direction [and] does not abide as a single extreme; and except for the Buddha himself, there is no individual who can within their mind stream actually fathom the depth of this doctrine.

For instance, a wish-fulfilling jewel bestows only that which is precious; yet it has the capacity to bestow wealth that is only in harmony with what is wished for. Likewise, the nature of all phenomena is only originally pure; yet due to the minds of those to be tamed and the power of truth, their needs will be fulfilled. It is, therefore, a key point to not fixate on any extreme. Holding to extremes or biased tendencies, a person who still claims to understand the wisdom intent of the Buddha is extremely delusional. For example, just imagine how astonishing it would be to see someone cover the sky with their hand! Given that the doctrines of Kāma and Terma will be disputed during the time of the five-hundred *dregs*, I have mentioned these points.

The so-called māra of egotism includes the various concepts that emerge and continuously arise based on either the presence of objects or not. Subsequent to that, the mind is then forced to pursue them. In brief, by the sudden emergence of hope, fear, benefit, harm, equanimity, and the like, the mind stream becomes disturbed; so that is the extent of the upheaval. Fixation on that becomes habitual, and that brings on the deception. The mere emergence [of these concepts] brings the upheaval; and simply uprooting an upheaval is the severance. Upheavals are uncertain and can be conspicuous, in a vision, or in dream. If conspicuous, it will directly appear to the gateway of the faculties, such as the visual and the rest. In the case of a vision, rather than occurring through the gateway of the faculties, this will occur through mental perceptions that are similar to actual objective appearances. If in a dream, then the upheaval will be a dream perception. In all cases with the arising of various displeasing sights and feelings, compulsory attachment, hope, and fear develop. Eventually, by seeing this as real and relentlessly repeating this, finally many undesirable consequences will manifest, such as rashes, swelling, and parasites issuing forth from the body along with shooting pain, heart-wind, mental depression, and the like.

In brief, many unwanted calamities will befall one; and if it can be determined that they are nonexistent like dreams, then—without refuting or encouraging—allowing them to rest in their own place, they will naturally vanish. When unwanted illness and the rest occur, without trying to apply medicines or potions, think, "I pray that this may multiply some nine times over. I must purify the suffering of all parent sentient beings. Through this experience of mine, may all beings find fulfillment. This is my initial benefit for others." Then shout aloud:

> *Kyi!* May the suffering of all sentient beings, their illness, and everything without remainders mature upon me! I hope for this; I take this on; I will purify and utilize this! Bring it on! Gather here, now!

Thus, saying this, being able to meditate with fulfillment is a profound upadesha for chöd practitioners to directly suppress negative circumstances. Therefore, any thought based upon hope and fear that thinks something is unacceptable or inappropriate must be directly suppressed again and again.

Concerning earth-spirit illnesses, such as rashes and swelling, [for this approach] one must bring together various methods to induce this illness even further, such as the smell of burned food and remaining too close to an open fire. If one thinks that used clothing or clothing from lepers causes obscuration or if concepts that afflict one arise, then take up those objects and place them directly upon the head. Rub them on the body, and say, "May I contract the disease of impurities!" In the manner of encouraging this, suppress it. Except for vows and samaya, it is a key point to constantly quell whatever concepts arise, such as mental discouragement and thoughts based on hope and fear, with body, speech, and mind. Why? Because this is a profound key method through which severance upon itself occurs.

When practicing this, know that various phenomena that are the extent of the upheavals will occur, such as earthquakes, mountain slides, collapsing crags, houses collapsing, dust storms, the earth cracking open, sink holes, rock slides, meteorite showers, falling trees, ceilings collapsing, and so forth. Upheavals with water involve floods, swollen rivers, accidents such as falling into lakes, being carried off by a river, torrential rainfall, hail storms, and flooding tributaries.

Upheavals with fire include sudden fire storms, the body burned by fire, fire sparks issuing from the body, seeing fire infernos, igniting fire, the entire environment being consumed by fire, sparks, and so forth. Upheavals associated with wind include the sound of intense wind, hurricane-force winds, being carried away by wind, sudden tornados occurring, the tent being carried off by the wind, whistling wind, howling wind, and so forth. Upheavals with space include lightning flashing, thunder roaring, sitting on the edge of a cliff or canyon, being shrouded in darkness, and so forth. Upheavals through forms are the phenomena of humans, undomesticated animals, carnivorous animals, domesticated beasts, amphibious creatures, classes of birds, and those who attempt to harm through various movements during the upheaval.

Otherwise, upheavals will occur by virtue of their presence and movements. All upheavals based on sound, smell, taste, and touch are called "tangible". Although formless, they still appear to have a form, such as making meaningless noises, engaging in activities, people congregating and going here and there, seeing heads and limbs without bodies and torsos without limbs, seeing various substances such as entrails and organs, parasites trying to harm you, displeasing sights appearing, or receiving food, drink, clothes, and ornaments. Whatever occurs, by rejecting all reactions, such as fear, hope, disappointment, retaliation, beating, striking, utilizing, or joy and sorrow, the upadesha is to allow all of this to fall apart in the empty nature of nonreferential appearances. Why? By seeing one's body incorrectly, striking or harming it with a weapon is the way many have actually lost their lives. Hence, it is a crucial point to abandon various incorrect activities.

If these occur and one is unable to distinguish between the form and the formless, then the consciousness of that upheaval and one's own consciousness should be mingled as a single taste and transferred to the spacelike expanse of Samantabhadrī with twenty-one repetitions of *phet*. If it is formless, it will be impossible for this to not vanish during the repetitions. If it is still apparent, then it is a form upheaval. Finally, one's consciousness rises up from space, and the flesh and blood are presented as the feast.

An upheaval means that, initially, one's body, speech, and mind are completely shocked. Upon that, if one is able to hold self-confidence that this is nonreferential and unimpeded, then that is the severance. During all times and situations when strong concepts develop, mingle the mind with the object. Seal this within the space of Samantabhadrī by strongly reciting *phet* and resting within nonreferential awareness, and the severance will occur. This is the destruction of all fixations, including the idea of māras, into the dharmatā that is free from elaborations. Know this to be a key point, and regard it as principal.

If no upheavals emerge from the previously described suppression techniques, then meditate upon oneself as Tröma Nagmo the size of Mt. Meru. By devouring Mt. Meru and gulping down the ocean, all the abiding gods-māras are then spread out as one's cushion. Thinking that this repeatedly occurs will induce the upheaval.

If there is still no upheaval emerging from this, then think that phenomenal existence pervades the entirety of one's appearances and that the abiding gods-māras clearly gather there like images upon a mirror. Then, imagine that all of them are suppressed below one's seat. If there is still no upheaval, then circle the flayed, human skin held in one's right hand above the crown of your head as Tröma. Strike this upon the ground and imagine that all mountain ranges quake, oceans churn, and tidal waves occur. All vegetation is dispersed, and the abiding gods-māras are exposed to arrive quivering with fear. Blowing the human thigh-bone trumpet held in the left hand three times: with the first sound, all mountains crumble; with the second, the mountains, crags, and all bodies of water scatter, and then evaporate; with the third, the gods-māras gather under your seat as though being forcefully awakened.

If the upheavals still do not come: then, with both hands, place the entire environment and dwelling places of the gods-māras upside down and ignite a vastly deep and blazing molten fire underneath them. Then hold the gods-māras over that as though you are ready to drop them in. Meditate that upon that [fire] appears the palace of Tröma, huge, majestic, and solid and that inside of that are billions of ḍākinīs shouting wrathful sounds of laughter. After that, it is certain there will be an upheaval.

If swirling, ominous hail-storm clouds consume the sky, then upon the crown of self-nature as Tröma imagine the nature of all buddhas to appear as the glorious Orgyen Pema, Tamer of Māras, who is inseparable with the root guru. Dark-red in color, he hoists a meteorite vajra dagger in the right hand with the threatening mudrā. In the left, he holds a skull filled with blood. He rests in the kingly posture upon a thousand-petaled lotus, sun, and moon seat. His orange-colored hair reaches upward to touch the Blazing Fire Mountain pure realm. He has a haughty wrathful expression, and his presence radiates like millions of suns. Within an expansive, dark-red massing wisdom fire, his orange-colored eyebrows and mustache light up golden-red like lightning. He dons a cloak, robe, and bhikṣhu shawl; and his three round eyes are red and bulging as they gaze into the expanse of the three kāyas.

Meditate that the upper aspect of his kāya is filled with the nirmāṇakāya buddhas of this fortunate age; the middle section has the complete maṇḍalas of the four and six lineages of meditation deities; and the lower aspect of his kāya is the spontaneously present maṇḍala of oceanic ḍākas and ḍākinīs. Surrounding are the wisdom and karmic dharmapālas like an assembly as vast as the ocean. From all of them, boundless light rays radiate to invoke the maṇḍalas of the three-kāya victorious ones to dissolve. Then, from all of their kāyas, light rays, fire-light, miniature wrathful ones, scorpions, lions, and such boundlessly emanate to hover like clouds in space. Meditate that there are flaming wheels of wisdom fire, palaces ablaze with wrathful deities, radiation and reabsorption of meteorite scorpions, and lions tossing their manes and roaring so loudly it shakes the trichiliocosm. Devouring all elementals of the eight classes, everything is incinerated. Think that all harm-doers of the upper dimensions sink into a meteorite triangular vortex within the depths of the great ocean.

Then, between the joined palms of oneself as Tröma Nagmo, imagine a dark-red syllable *hung* blazing within wisdom fire. Imagine all power and strength of the three kāyas of the victorious ones being synthesized to dissolve into this *hung*. While focusing on space and opening the palms, from the single syllable *hung* shooting like a star into the sky, countless syllables emerge. All clouds are prevailed upon by the density of the blazing dark-red *hungs*. Imagine that the potential to annihilate and incinerate all eight classes of harm-doers is attained.

Below the seat, from *bam*, imagine that a oceanic maṇḍala of water appears to be even more frigid than the coldest hell realm. Meditate that all eight classes are suppressed below that water where nothing can possibly penetrate. Recite:

Om guru raksha trota buddha dewa dakini bam ha ri ni sa hung phet ah ya ma du ru tsa sha na maraya jhyo nan phet

Furthermore, by reciting this initial mantra, for a while remain in the even consummation of saṃsāra and enlightenment; and by doing so, severance will be guaranteed. Practitioners who have definitively realized the genuine nature of the dharmatā will not be affected by any type of fear. Even if those who lack this confidence remain within awareness, it will be impossible for the gods-māras and other types of terror to disturb them. Given that the terror induced by lightning is extremely poignant, vigilance must be applied to the visualizations.

Then, by rejecting all hope, fear, [and] paranoia, including protection reversals, meditations, recitations, and expelling rituals performed for others, it is a quintessential point to freely abide in one taste. Having expectation toward anything is the māra that controls all dimensions of desire, so expectation must be severed. Having disappointment toward anything is the messenger that seduces one toward negative directions, so reject disappointment. Fixating upon any harm-doers just sets up interest toward obstacles. Fixating upon everything as lacking benefit is the profound upadesha for turning negativity into siddhis and ominous signs into prosperity. If illness is meditated upon as well-being and negative circumstances are taken as the path, then for instance—like how initially any spicy substance can be unbearable when applied to the mouth and nose—[gradually] if something is thought to bring about well-being and is necessary, then one will feel it surely does bring happiness; and eventually one will even be unable to function without it. Likewise, when applied here, all negative dimensions will then arise as though beneficial. For example, the Buddha transformed the hordes of perverted māras into ornaments and supports, so the key point is to know that the ornaments and supports are indispensable. This completes the twelfth section.

The basis of confusion for sentient beings who abide in saṃsāra is the establishment of the aggregates that are fixated upon as a "self". That is the root cause. The perpetually fixated mind creates the contributing circumstance that brings about confusion. In order to annihilate fixation upon this cherished heap of aggregates, the body is presented as the feast. Resting the mind within the nature free from elaboration is the profound method that severs duality from the root.

Then, first, in the space in front, the nature of the root guru appears as Rigdzin Pema Duddul, flesh-colored with an attractive demeanor. Naked, he wears a tiger-skin skirt and a long garland mālā made of three types of skull. In his right hand, he holds a five-pronged vajra that overcomes the three realms; and his left hand holds a meteorite phurba that suppresses the three states of existence. His two feet are in the kingly posture upon a seat of a lotus, sun, and four māras. His hair is flowing freely down his back; his three eyes are gazing into the sky. He has wrathful wrinkles, while showing a smiling expression. His kāya contains the entire maṇḍala of victorious ones. Imagine that he remains in an expanse of blazing fire, wisdom light, and rainbow molecules. He has no inherent existence, yet appears like a rainbow or a water moon. Meditate without holding to true existence, and recognize that he appears objectively like magic or a dream. By just seeing, hearing, recalling, or experiencing him, there is the potential to bless the three doors with the three vajra natures. With intense faith and complete devotion given over to him, pray with total commitment from one's heart, mind, and soul.

> *Phet!* In the perfectly pure, absolute Akaniṣhṭha of self-appearances, the lord guru of perfected kāyas and wisdom is the absolute fully manifest kāya, the intrinsic nature of the great bindu, arising as the oceanic treasury of ripening empowerment and liberating instructions.
>
> *Phet!* I invoke you, the embodiment of the glorious qualities of the four kāyas. By invoking your wisdom mind through intense faith and devotion, I pray, release all concepts of the mind and mental events shrouded in the shell of ignorance, to delight within the great expanse of the wisdom mind, the ground of original purity.

Having supplicated in this way, self-awareness and the guru's enlightened mind of nonconceptual wisdom mingle as one taste.

One awakens in the wisdom expanse of the three kāyas. Think that the great confidence of exaltation free from transition or change is attained. Mingle with the first *phet*; purify obscurations with the second *phet*; and with the third *phet*, all four empowerments are received. Imagine that the great dynamic strength of the four kāyas is attained. Mingling the mind with the guru dispels all illness, demonic forces, negative circumstances, and obstacles. This is the sole, profound key point for bringing forth the common and supreme siddhis.

Then, by transferring awareness into space, [the practice] called *Opening the Gateway to the Sky* is as follows.

> In the middle of one's body that is huge, fatty, oily, and heavy, life essence, longevity, and merit mingle with awareness as a clear bindu that shoots upward like the shot arrow of a strong man. From the basic space of prajñā, the kāya of method arises.

Thus, while saying this, imagine that—in the middle of one's body that is huge, fatty, oily, and heavy—the central channel appears possessing the four characteristics. Empty and clear, it is the dimension of a medium-sized bamboo shaft. The upper tip connects with the crown aperture, and the lower tip is blocked below the navel. Within that, parallel to the heart, is the combined nature of all life essence, longevity, and merit as a five-colored bindu. The size of the bodhisattva's first egg, the bindu is clear, shiny, rich, and vibrant as it shoots upward like the shot arrow of a strong man. Think that this arrives in the upper regions of space. With the first *phet*, awareness transfers to mingle with basic space. With the second, it arises from basic space; and with the third, visualize that it becomes the kāya of Tröma.

> *Phet phet phet!* The spontaneously present trikāya, Tröma Nagmo, holds a curved blade and skull in her two hands and gazes into space. Wearing bone ornaments, with both legs in the dancing posture, she stands in a blazing mass of fire while sporting a trident with a squealing pig's head jutting from her crown.

By reciting *phet*, one is aware of the nature of the spontaneously present three kāyas.

> With her right hand, she severs the skull from the body with the curved vajra blade. This naturally descends upon a spontaneously occurring tripod of skulls. The corpse is placed within the skull, where it melts into an ocean of nectar. The froth boils over upon a great human skin that stretches to cover the earth. Mountains of flesh, oceans of blood, riverbanks of bones, and glistening piles of fat appear upon this. The desirables increase like an inexhaustible space treasury.
>
> *Om ah hung ha ho hri* [Repeat this three times.]

The visualization is as follows. Clearly visualize oneself arising as Tröma Nagmo, holding a curved vajra blade in the right hand. By merely pointing it, the skull falls from the corpse and lands upon a tripod of three types of human skulls. With hair intact, the skull expands to become equal to the vast dimensions of the dharmatā. Again, by pointing the curved vajra blade, the body's skin is flayed to cover the golden foundation of the earth. The headless body drops into the skull cup; and the fire and wind below the tripod ignite the stove, heating up the skull. The body melts and begins to boil profusely, while the steam and froth spill out to cover the human-skin base. Think that the edibles become like mountains of flesh; the drinkables are oceans of blood; the chewable substances, like banks piled with bones; the substances to lick, like heaps of melting fat; and the substances to suck, like the marrow, cartilage, and so forth are ever-increasing.

Furthermore, think that inexhaustible, desirable wealth suitable to the individual guests of saṃsāra and enlightenment appears like an ornamental wheel equal to the reaches of space. Bless this with the mantra. With the first *phet*, the exalted guests as the objects of refuge—namely, the buddhas, dharma, sangha, gurus, meditation deities, and ḍākinīs, the dharmakāya, sambhogakāya, nirmāṇakāya, and so forth; the guests who are the protectors with noble qualities, such as the eight groups of gods, nāgas, and rāhulas, the ten directional guardians, the nine terrifying ones, the four great kings, the twenty-eight astrological deities, and so forth; and the guests who are objects of compassion, the six classes of beings, such as the hell beings, pretas, animals, gods, asuras, humans, and the like—all hear this. With the second [*phet*], think they depart from their domains; and with the third, they gather to fill all regions of space and earth.

Once again, reciting *phet*, think that boundless emanation ḍākinīs radiate to distribute the feast:

> *Phet!* To the buddha, dharma, and sangha; the guru, yidam, and ḍākinī; the dharmakāya, sambhogakāya, and nirmāṇakāya; and so forth, all guests of exalted supreme qualities, an unceasing ornamental wheel of offerings is presented. May the accumulations be perfected and the two aims spontaneously fulfilled!

With the first *phet*, they receive this; with the second, they are satisfied with the flavor of empty bliss; and with the third, think that their enlightened minds of nonconceptual wisdom transfer into oneself.

> To the twenty-four supreme sacred places and thirty-two countries; the ten sacred grounds of the heruka and the eight charnel grounds; the city of vajra aggregates and the ḍākas and ḍākinīs that are interconnected, this offering is made. By fully perfecting this fearless conduct, may there be the potential to accomplish the welfare of the gods-māras! *Phet phet phet!*

With the first *phet*, the offering is made; with the second, they receive it; and third, their enlightened minds are satisfied with the taste of empty bliss.

> To the eight gods, the eight nāgas, and the eight great rāhulas; the guardians of the ten directions and four great kings; the twenty-eight constellations and the nine terrifying ones, including all guests who are the protectors with noble qualities, this pure offering of desirable qualities is presented. May the sacred bond with your wisdom minds be fulfilled! *Phet phet phet!*

With the first *phet*, the offering is made; with the second, they receive it; and with the third, they are satisfied by immaculate exaltation.

To the hell beings, pretas, and animals; the humans, gods, demigods, and the like, all beings of the three realms, I dedicate whatever desirable objects are required and wished for. May all find contentment and satisfaction; and through this interdependency, may all attain buddhahood! *Phet phet phet!*

With the first *phet*, they receive this; with the second, they are satisfied; and with the third, imagine that they are set free.

Upon the flayed human skin that stretches to pervade the trichiliocosm are mountains of flesh, oceans of blood, riverbanks of bones, swirling melted marrow, fat, cartilage, and the desirable objects equal to all pervasive space. Through the power of the three syllables, this transforms into nectar; and all guests are instantly invited.

Om ah hung ha ho hri [Repeat this three times.]

Phet phet phet! With the first *phet*, the gods-māras of the eight classes hear this. With the second, they depart [from their realms]; and with the third, they suddenly arrive and gather.

From the uppermost peak of existence to the lowest possible hell realm, oath-bound gods-māras of the eight classes and all gods-māras of phenomenal existence come to this celebratory feast of flesh and blood. Come and fill the sky like stars! Come and cover the firmament like clouds! Come and envelop like wind on the plains! Come quickly without delay or distraction! Gather here to enjoy this everlasting abundance! *Phet phet phet!*

Today, I, the ultimate warrior, have—through the fearless conduct of the equal taste of saṃsāra and enlightenment—arranged my body of self-cherishing as the feast. The father-mother gods-māras are the guests. *Phet phet phet!*

To the gods, yamās, wrathful ḍākinīs, and māras; the cannibals, māras of the crags, yakṣhas, and nāgas; māras of addiction, kingly māras, and rāhulas; to the gods-māras of the eight classes who are bound to the oath—I give whatever objects are required or desired. Completely consume it all without a single leftover! *Phet phet phet!*

With the first *phet*, offer to the mightiest among them; with the second, to the middling; and with the third, to the weakest. Imagine that the final *phet* ensures their fulfillment.

To King Pekar, Penag, and Tsimar with the nine brotherly spirits and to all the masculine māra forces of hatred, I will offer a space treasury of desirable objects. May all find contentment; and becoming completely satisfied, may they encounter their own unconfused nature! *Phet phet phet!*

To the female cannibal with the bloody mane, the great female deprived spirit Jvālamukha, the queen demons with nine relatives and others—to these female māras of attachment, this inexhaustible treasury of desirable objects is dedicated. May all be satisfied and filled with delight! *Phet phet phet!*

To the nāga demon Nāgarādza, the classes of royalty, lords, holy ones, and the class of untouchables—to the earth lords who are the subterranean māras of delusion, this inexhaustible treasury of desirable objects is dedicated. May all attain buddhahood together! *Phet phet phet!*

To the three and five passion-based poisons and the support and supporting gods-māras; to the eighty thousand classes of obstructing forces and the fifteen great māras that afflict children; to the female preta and her five hundred offspring and others, as well as to the ancient gods-māras that still abide—I dedicate whatever is useful as an abundance of desirable objects. Through your total satisfaction and delight, may all attain buddhahood together. May the karmic debts of blood revenge be cleansed! *Phet phet phet!*

To the deer-headed Dritsan, the māras who wander in villages, the māras who cause samaya corruption, miscarriages, and the child-slaying māras; to the māras of opportunity and messengers of death, male and female alike; to the keepers of karmic debts of blood ransom and revenge, including all additional gods-māras, harm-doers, and the entire assembly without exception—I dedicate this space treasury of desirable objects. Without leaving a trace behind, partake of it. Delight in it! Use it in whatever way pleases you! If I am unable to give each of you what is preferred, then it is my fault. This will be my final body through which to express the perfection of transcendental generosity. All karmic debts are now repaid. Depart for the pure land of exaltation and gain the confidence to never return to saṃsāra again! *Phet phet phet!*

While presenting the feast of the body like this, with the first *phet*, imagine that they hear you. With the second *phet*, they are satisfied; and with the third, they are set free.

> Within the skull equal to the reaches of phenomenal existence is a treasure trove of desirable remainders that liberate upon taste. Inexhaustible ornamental wheels of clouds invoke the weak and feeble guests of the remains. *Phet phet phet!*
>
> Tortured by self-created karma, the subservient, powerless, and humble, the blind, crippled, deaf, dumb, and impaired—to all of you without a single exception, these medicines, food, and nectar that dispel all suffering are dedicated as desirable objects for your enjoyment. May you rejoice in the pleasure of this realm of exaltation! May the empowerment of great primordial wisdom be attained! *Phet phet phet!*

Think that, with the first *phet*, they receive this; with the second, they are satisfied; and with the third, they awaken in immaculate exaltation.

Once again, to offer dedication in the great, perfectly pure three spheres, continue:

> *Phet!* Through the samādhi-like magical nature of phenomena and beginningless generosity, as well as the merit of the three times, this is dedicated within the immaculate state free from elaboration or limitation. May this mature as great wisdom and kāyas!
>
> *Phet!* Through the virtue of this fearless conduct that has forsaken self and self-fixation, may all beings that wander in saṃsāra through the six root causes discover the confidence of wisdom's effortless expanse. In doing so, may the ground of a fearless vajra holder be attained!
>
> *Phet!* May all phenomena that appear as the perception of mind and mental events be placed within great all-pervasive wisdom. By entering the womb of radiant unceasing wisdom, all is cleansed in the great primordial ground of the originally pure space of phenomena. Saṃsāra is nonexistent and so is enlightenment, cause and result; purified within the equal taste of joy, sorrow, hope, and fear, basic space and wisdom are free from meeting and parting. *Ah phet phet phet!*

Self and all objective appearances dissolve within nondual emptiness. Think that one enters the womb of the original protector of the primordial ground and rest in evenness. This is the sole, profound upadesha to be internalized through practice during all times and situations.

Then, so that practitioners of chöd who are always engaged in the sacred instructions for practice can purify negativity and obscurations, there is the method of offering the black feast in the predawn.

Phet! From within the central channel of one's huge, heavy, and fatty body, awareness is transferred into space as a pure vital bindu. Nondual basic space and wisdom then appear as Tröma, blue-black, holding a curved vajra blade, wearing bone ornaments and in the dancing posture.

Phet! All suffering based upon the habits of the three realms is gathered as black light to dissolve into the corpse. This human corpse that grows to fill the trichiliocosm becomes like a vast heap of coal that captivates and steals the minds of all gods-māras.

Om ah hung ha ho hri Repeat this three times.

Phet phet phet! The pig-headed nāga king of demonic forces, surrounded by gods-māras and their assemblies who have originated from delusion; the snake-headed king of anger, surrounded by demonic forces, obstructing forces, and elementals who have originated from anger; the bird-headed female māra of desire surrounded by the gods-māras of demonic-force possession and obstructions that originate from desire; the great dark-colored female Remati, sovereign of saṃsāra and enlightenment, surrounded by a million black powerful females tossing their wild hair, gather in the charnel ground for the feast of the corpse. Without delay, come here as the guests! *Phet phet phet!*

I, the fearless practitioner of the even taste of saṃsāra and enlightenment, have from beginningless time cherished this heap of aggregates based on the confusion of a nonexistent self, believed to exist. Today, I give it up through the great method of generosity.

Phet! Gods-māras, recipients of the generosity, confused by ignorance; nāga-māras and all classes of earth lords, confused by delusion; king of hatred and all masculine demonic forces; female māras of desire and all female spirits as well—all of you without a single exception are offered this feast of the human corpse in the charnel ground. Quickly consume it without leaving a trace behind! *Phet phet phet!*

Accordingly, all god-māra recipients of the generosity ravenously devour the feast, becoming indistinguishable with it like a vast heap of coal. The large ones consume the smaller, and the main three eat them all. The king eats the female māra, and the great earth lord eats him [i.e., the king]. Then, great black Remati swallows everything that remains without masticating so all retinues and assemblies simply vanish in the expanse of the dharmakāya. *Phet phet phet!*

Self and objective appearances, as though awakening from a dream, gather as the absolute heruka of primordial awareness. There are no gods, māras, buddhas, or sentient beings; no self, objects, objects who harm, or harm-doers. Within the great, spontaneously vast expanse of nonreferential original purity, rest in the evenness of the uncontrived nature as it is. *Phet phet phet!*

The white feast to be performed at day break is as follows.

Phet! From this magical heap of aggregates derived from the habit of self-grasping, innate awareness transfers to the original ground. Arising as the magical manifestation of wisdom from the basic space of phenomena, self-nature appears as the white Vajrayoginī. Holding a sword in one's right hand, the body is chopped, reducing it to particles. By waving a wind banner in one's left hand, the flesh, blood, and bones are scattered in every direction. This evenly pervades all appearances of external phenomena. Permeated by white, red, and blue light rays, like the emanations from the god realm of Paranirmitavashavartin, phenomenal existence becomes the clouds of the white offering of desirables. This nature is the nectar of empty exaltation that brings liberation upon taste. The three white substances appear as the lakes, mountains, and plains; the three sweets as the rocky crags, the desirable banks of wafting clouds. As a space treasury of glorious qualities that are unsurpassed, the universe and inhabitants become ever-increasing desirable offerings.

Om ah hung Repeat three times.

Phet phet phet [Ring the bell and roll the drum.]

Eh ma! I am a buddha and I am a sentient being. I am the appearance of the universe, inhabitants, and all desirable things. Everything is my magical manifestation. Everything is my interdependent phenomena. Although everything is manifest, it manifests from me. Although everything reabsorbs, it is subsumed within me. *Phet phet phet!*

I, a practitioner of the great Madhyamaka, realize that all phenomena are great emptiness. Celebrating this feast of objects being neither positive nor negative, I engage the fearless conduct of severing self-fixation. *Phet phet phet!*

I, a practitioner of the Mahāmudrā, through samādhi see the magiclike nature of phenomena. Now, through the manifest dance of actually offering and expressing generosity through things, I engage the fearless conduct of severing fixation with material objects. *Phet phet phet!*

I, a practitioner of Mahāsandhi, realize all phenomena to be naked awareness. Now, through the fearless conduct of the perfectly pure three spheres, I will actualize the great basic space of purity and evenness. *Phet phet phet!*

The ground of the tathāgatas is the Triple Gem; the path of manifest awareness is the manifestation of the guests of noble qualities. Ultimately, immaculate exaltation is offered to awaken in the radiant basic space of original purity. *Phet phet phet!*

The mind of three poisons, the three realms as objective saṃsāra, the dynamic strength of conceptual gods-māras, and obstructing forces are ultimately transformed through the nondual play of phenomena and given as the abundant sky treasury of basic space. *Phet phet phet!*

To the gods-māras of outer grasping to objects, various magical emanations of appearances are offered. By purifying the habit of actual attachment to objects, ultimately the unimpeded nonreferential offerings are partaken of. *Phet phet phet!*

To the gods-māras of the inner grasping mind, the appearances of desirables that are nonmanifest are given. Liberated from the habitual entanglement with compulsory attachment to objects, partake of the ultimate offering that is baseless and free from the root. *Phet phet phet!*

To the gods-māras of interdependent clinging and grasping, the magical interdependent phenomena of saṃsāra are given. Through the natural collapse of accepting and rejecting objects, partake of the offering of the all-pervasive ground of original purity. *Phet phet phet!*

The phenomenal appearances of the objective three realms of saṃsāra collapse like a magician's illusory creations. In the space of the queen's three gateways to liberation, now saṃsāra and enlightenment are purity and evenness. *Ah la la phet phet phet!*

The mixed feast practiced in the afternoon is as follows.

Phet! In the center of one's body—youthful and endowed with all glorious qualities—from within the hollow, crystal-pipe channel, one's consciousness is ejected into space like an arrow; and one appears in space as the blue-black Tröma holding a curved vajra blade and skull. By merely pointing the curved blade held in the right hand at the corpse, one's bodies and abundance from all lifetimes gathers there and dissolves. The flayed human skin stretches over the ground and the flesh becomes like mountains, the blood like swirling seas. The skull fills with immaculate wisdom nectar. Upon the vast and sprawling ground of the trichiliocosm appear the three whites, sweets, and sour foods; scents, medicine, grain, and every type of edible. Gold, silver, copper, iron, jewels, and precious things; cloth, silks, soft luxurious fabrics, tents, houses, all places of support; [and] wild, domestic, and aquatic animals, including every variety of bird and so forth appear as an ornamental wheel of inexhaustible desirable objects. The power of the three syllables transforms everything into nectar that liberates upon taste.

Om ah hung ha ho hri [Repeat three times.]

Phet phet phet! Permanent protectors, precious Triple Gem, protectors of noble qualities, guests who guard and uphold virtue, please come without delay as recipients of this offering. Beings of the six classes and the bardos as well, all classes of māras, and obstructers that are owed karmic debts, including the recipients of generosity who are the māras, come without exception to descend upon this like vultures upon flesh. Come here instantly with this invocation. *Phet phet phet!*

I offer this to the objects of refuge, who are the Triple Gem, the Three Roots, and the Three Kāyas. I offer to all guests, who are the protectors of noble qualities. I dedicate this to all beings of the six classes and those who are in the bardo. I dedicate this to those who are karmic debtors, the gods-māras of phenomenal existence, and all who are impoverished, powerless, and weak. Whatever is desired becomes an abundant treasure trove of the desirables manifest and offered as an inexhaustible treasury of space. Satisfying all exalted guests with the taste of empty exaltation, may self and others perfect the two accumulations of merit. *Phet phet phet!*

All lower guests are satisfied with an abundance of joy and well-being. Freed from the confines of their karmic habits, negativities, and obscurations, they come to know the constant glory of fully endowed permanent happiness. May the immutable stronghold of the unchanging vajra nature be attained. *Phet phet phet!*

By this virtue, may all beings awaken the nature just as it is; and together may buddhahood be realized in the ground of original purity. Within the play of inseparable offerings, generosity, and recipients: by entering the womb of the great spontaneously present three kāyas, rest in the even pervasion of the original buddha's wisdom mind. *Phet phet phet!*

The red feast to be performed after dusk is as follows.

> *Phet!* From the impure elements based on the impression of karma, this illusory dwelling place of unclean habits, the vital essence of cognitive awareness gathers in the original ground to once again arise as the wisdom ḍākinī. *Phet phet phet!*
>
> The skin of this impure body stretches to cover the ground. The flesh, blood, and bones become disembodied to transform into mountains of flesh, oceans of blood, and riverbanks of bones spread out everywhere with marrow, fat, gristle, and lymph like a swirling ocean of oil. The bubbling vapor becomes massing clouds of the desirables, and the power of the three syllables transforms them into nectar that liberates through taste.
>
> *Om ah hung ha ho hri* Repeat this three times.

From the heart of oneself as the wisdom ḍākinī Tröma Nagmo, boundless light rays radiate in all directions to invoke the eleven wisdom ḍākinīs from the unchanging nature of phenomena. One-hundred million classes of ḍākinīs in the manner of the dynamic strength of their perfected magical manifestation appear, surrounded by the gods-māras of phenomenal existence.

> *Phet phet phet!* Dancing wisdom mothers of basic space, ḍākinīs of the central Buddha Family with one-hundred million manifestations, surrounded by your retinue of gods-māras of phenomenal existence, come here now and partake of my flesh, bones, and blood. Dispel circumstantial obstacles in basic space.
>
> *Phet phet phet!* Dancing wisdom mothers of basic space, ḍākinīs of the eastern Vajra Family with one-hundred million manifestations, surrounded by your retinue of gods-māras of phenomenal existence, come here now and partake of this flesh, bones, and blood. Dispel circumstantial obstacles in basic space.
>
> *Phet phet phet!* Dancing wisdom mothers of basic space, ḍākinīs of the southern Ratna Family with one-hundred million manifestations, surrounded by your retinue of gods-māras of phenomenal existence, come here now and partake of this flesh, bones, and blood. Dispel circumstantial obstacles in basic space.
>
> *Phet phet phet!* Dancing wisdom mothers of basic space, ḍākinīs of the western Pema Family with one-hundred million manifestations, sur-

rounded by your retinue of gods-māras of phenomenal existence, come here now and partake of this flesh, bones, and blood. Dispel circumstantial obstacles in basic space.

Phet phet phet! Dancing wisdom mothers of basic space, ḍākinīs of the northern Karma Family with one-hundred million manifestations, surrounded by your retinue of gods-māras of phenomenal existence, come here now and partake of this flesh, bones, and blood. Dispel circumstantial obstacles in basic space.

Phet phet phet! Dancing wisdom mothers of basic space, activity ḍākinīs from the upper realm of space with one-hundred million manifestations, surrounded by your retinue of gods-māras of phenomenal existence, come here now and partake of this flesh, bones, and blood. Dispel circumstantial obstacles in basic space.

Phet phet phet! Dancing wisdom mothers of basic space, activity ḍākinīs from the intermediate directions with one-hundred million manifestations, surrounded by your retinue of gods-māras of phenomenal existence, come here now and partake of this flesh, bones, and blood. Dispel circumstantial obstacles in basic space.

Phet phet phet! Dancing wisdom mothers of basic space, activity ḍākinīs of the lower earth with one-hundred million manifestations, surrounded by your retinue of gods-māras of phenomenal existence, come here now and partake of this flesh, bones, and blood. Dispel circumstantial obstacles in the space of phenomena.

Phet phet phet! Dancing wisdom mothers of basic space, intermittent ḍākinīs who are samaya-bound flesh-eaters with one-hundred million manifestations, surrounded by your retinue of gods-māras of phenomenal existence, come here now and partake of this flesh, bones, and blood. Dispel circumstantial obstacles in basic space.

Phet phet phet! Wisdom mother ḍākinīs of basic space, your indeterminate manifestations become anything whatsoever. Mothers, your sole purpose is the welfare of beings. Partake of this feast as the guests to whom I present my flesh, blood, bones, and marrow. Partake of all circumstances such as illness, demonic possession, suffering, causes, and results within unimpeded nonreferential basic space. Entanglements of the confused mind of grasping and fixation collapse within the unelaborate space of phenomena. The habitual cause of objects and the self that creates them are set free within the unborn ground of original purity. The dualistic mind that holds to preferences and limitations is severed in the wisdom mind of the great mother of basic space.

Phet phet phet! Objects devoid of good and bad are the innate nature; root causes devoid of virtue or nonvirtue are the original ground; contributing circumstances devoid of benefit and harm are unimpeded; the mind stream devoid of saṃsāra and enlightenment is the consummate expanse; the path devoid of training or traversing is the great perfection; life without past or future is the time of original purity. Now the original buddha awakens within me. This great realization is beyond meditation, placement, or intellect. Primordially, the space of the queen's three gateways to liberation awakens within this indestructible nature. *Phet phet phet!*

Applying them [i.e., the feasts] to these four times, always maintain diligence in this practice. In particular, while wandering in the fear-provoking places at night, one must not make fires, burn candles or any light, not walk barefoot, recite wrathful mantras, meditate, or generate wrathful deities. Feces and urine should be excreted at one location; one must not scream or shout; and shoes should be put under one's pillow, with hats placed under the foot of the bed. Lay down on the right side and stretch out the thighs and shoulders like a cushion. Keep the palm of the hand open to support the head like a headrest. Abandon any form of entertainment or distraction.

The key point is to try not to escape, supplicate, or find protection no matter how terrifying the phenomena may be. If there is an attempt to escape, then once again return and remain until the severance is successful. If one tries to escape some nine times, then it is considered to be a failure of the practice, in that one must refrain from continuing on and no longer return to that place. If one tries to escape eight times and finds success [in the practice] by the ninth, that is still fine.

Following the upheavals, the extents of completion will emerge. Once that occurs, it is no longer acceptable to stay in that same place, so one must move on. The extent of completion includes actual visions, dreams, and experiences—whatever the case may be—such as many people prostrating, making offerings, offering wealth and food, taking refuge, listening to orders, taking oaths, praising, and playing many musical instruments. The sun and moon may be rising, flowers blossoming, celebrations occurring, and so forth.

In brief, whatever arises or appears, if the mind feels ecstatically satisfied, realization increases and the body, speech, and mind relax. Then, whatever good or bad signs may come—given that this is the extent of completion—it indicates that one must transfer locations. Even if good signs arise, the mind will feel a sense of heightened hope and fear, distraction, joy and sorrow, trepidation, and many other reactions that make the body, speech, and mind uncomfortable. Although these experiences may seem to be the extent of the completion, they are actually upheavals. Hence, it is a quintessential key point to know the single taste of whatever occurs, whether good or bad.

The initial extent of completion is indicated when the severed heads, extremities, and hollow and solid organs of others are presented to you; you are given ornaments, wealth, and abundance; you destroy all grass shacks, rocky caves, and frightening locations that you come into contact with; or at evaporated lakes, you are giving energy and well-being to many disadvantaged beings. If these experiences occur, then move the distance of a pebble flung from a slingshot.

The final extent of severance is that all gods-māras will take an oath to join you as retinue and servants. They will offer their hearts to you, many people will be praising you as their crown ornament, you will be enthroned, and many great lamas and leaders will receive empowerment from you and be admitted into your retinue. Donning armor and metal plating, you will be placed on a great throne to become the leader of grand classes of subjects. Accompanying great armies, you will invade and conquer countries [and] will ride and tame dragons, lions, tigers, wild and domesticated yaks, as well as various types of birds. The sun and moon will be spread out as your cushions, and you will take a seat at the peak of the highest mountain of all. You will also gain mastery over many places and countries. Once these signs occur, one should no longer practice at that location. Know that these signs are ominous, much like a mistreated servant turning against his or her persecutor.

Having gone to another fear-invoking environment, the activity of the final severance is as follows. Prepare the backpack; and when it is time to go, replace the cushion where you have been staying with a support of enlightened body, speech, or mind and consecrate that. Recite the verse of auspiciousness and think that the gods-māras are circumambulating and making offerings there. Perform *Giving the Dharma* and then stand up and visualize as follows. Think that one's corporeal body of flesh and blood completely falls apart and becomes mountains of flesh, oceans of blood, and steaming vapor of inexhaustible desirable objects, such as marrow, fat, and cartilage. Imagine that the gods-māras of that place then partake of this.

Saying *ha ha hi hi he he ho ho hung hung phet phet*, take seven steps and drop the backpack. Say, "*Ki ki*, hey powerful gods, nāgas, and local lords of this place, listen all of you! Don't allow any gods-māras who were not here before to come to my place. Don't let the gods-māras who abide here get out. I entrust you to do this. Take care of this. I will watch to see just how much power you have. Quickly, quickly!" Saying this, pick up the backpack.

With *phet*, one's awareness becomes the five wisdom ḍākinīs; imagine that they depart for the four directions, including the fifth central direction. Proceeding about as far as you can see, drop the backpack and visualize that you make the boundary marker. This becomes a red-black wisdom garuḍa, ablaze with fire filling heaven and earth. Think that this sets up the boundary between the gods-māras and oneself.

Say, "*Eh eh!* You wisdom garuḍa king, lord of power and strength, listen to me! Powerful gods, nāgas, nonhuman spirits, and powerful mountain protectors all of you, listen here! Do not send any gods, māras, spirits, or obstructing forces of any type after me. Set the boundaries now. Do not allow your strength and powers to decline. Hurry! Hurry up, with samaya!" Then, while imagining that phenomenal existence becomes filled with mountains of flesh and oceans of blood, recite *phet* nine times.

If one is departing for another frightening place from there, begin with the *Suppression through Splendor* as before. If departing for yet another uncertain locale, do so without further elaboration. If one is returning home, imagine that awareness dissolves into the Akaniṣhṭha and shout *phet*. Again, from the heart of Samantabhadrī, white light like a silken thread extends down to enter the roof of one's house. Awareness becomes a white bindu the size of a mustard seed that rolls down the shaft of light to enter one's house. Departing and imagining in these ways are all profound severance techniques that follow the subsequent or final suppression.

Next are the random visualizations as follows. If the gods-māras of the frightening places are powerful and overbearing and the practitioner is weak, upheavals will not occur. If, on the other hand, the practitioner has a high and confident view but the gods-māras are feeble, again there will be no upheavals. Whatever the case, upheavals will be drawn out through the profound visualization and conduct of the final threat.

Place a rope around one's neck; then tie the other side of the rope down to a sacred object of support. Otherwise, toss the end of the rope out to the gods-māras while shouting out loud as follows, "Hey! Gods-māras of phenomenal existence, come gather here immediately!" Reciting this three times, perform the visualization as follows. From all of one's places, boundless light rays radiate, powerlessly summoning all gods-māras in front of one, like fish caught on a hook. Think that they have no chance of escape or place to hide.

With strong confidence, repeat the following aloud, "You powerful and wrathful gods-māras of this place, what I have to ask of you is this. At best, throw me into the lowest hell realm at this very moment. Second best is to kill me on the spot, or at least torture me so that I am neither dead nor alive. If your ears are not deaf, then listen. If your eyes are not blind, look. If you are not crippled, then come. If you are not dead, be swift; and if you are not a corpse, then get up!" Thus, repeat this three times and then fall asleep.

If you suffer from an incurable disease, then go to an extremely frightening place and burn some of your hair, nails, and dead skin in order to make a strong stench. Saying, "Hey! Powerful, wrathful gods-māras of this place, if your ears are not deaf, then listen. If your eyes are not blind, look. If your arms and legs are not crippled, then come here. If your nose is not blocked, then smell this foul stench. If your mouth is not closed, eat me. If you are not a corpse, then get up. If you are not yet dead, then don't be late. If you have not fainted, then quickly approach!" Repeat these verses three times.

Then say, "I have had this incurable disease for many days and months. No matter what I try, nothing helps me. Even the local inhabitants, as well as my neighbors, are all praying that I will just die. All my relatives and loved ones are saying that it is best for me to die. I, too, feel that, if death were to arrive immediately, that would be the best gift for all lifetimes. At best, I should be promptly thrown into the lowest hell realm. The second best would be if I stopped breathing on the spot; and at the least, I should be slain before sunrise tomorrow." Having said this, take the other end of the rope and tie it to a frightening, dangerous object while shouting *phet* and screaming out *ki*. Then, sleep there for a short period of time.

After this, repeat the appeal by calling out again. No matter what happens—whether good, bad, or terrifying—completely sever any doubt you have about wanting to die. If you receive a sign that night, then perform the white feast in the morning and the mixed feast at noon. In the evening, perform the red feast and the black feast at predawn. To conclude with the final suppression is the traditional course of practice, as well as the ultimate, profound final threat.

When practitioners of this profound path fall ill, they must diligently practice special visualizations during the five times of the day. In the early morning, visualize that from the heart of the powerful sovereign of saṃsāra and enlightenment, Samantabhadrī, the white hatred-subduing ḍākinī emanates with the face of a snake. In the afternoon, visualize the yellow pride-subduing ḍākinī with the head of a horse. In the late afternoon or early evening, visualize the red desire-subduing ḍākinī with the head of a vulture; and at midnight, the green jealousy-subduing ḍākinī with the head of a dog. Before dawn, visualize the black delusion-subduing ḍākinī with the head of a pig. Sometimes, imagine that meteorite scorpions and other times garuḍas boundlessly emanate to gulp down your specific illness and its source. Imagine that nothing remains. Once imagining this, repeatedly perform the liturgy known as *Giving the Body* many countless times, after which abide in nonconceptual awareness. It is certain that the illness will then be dispelled.

For a sudden sickness or contagious disease, visualize that your body is a dry skeleton with no flesh at all. Imagine that, from the nine orifices, the smell and steam of poisonous venom, along with fiery vajras, emerge. Think, "My body has no flesh and consists only of bones. There is no basis for illness to occur. What a loss! In order to purify my obscurations and unpaid karmic debts, I pray that a serious illness will befall me." Thinking and hoping in this way will dispel the illness. This is called "the activity of making a heap of flesh and blood into a disease".

Then, imagine that the hair of a dead person and of a living person and the tail of a youthful animal are braided into eight strands to make a slingshot that indicates the spontaneous presence of the five kāyas and the five wisdoms. Just by hurling a stone, imagine that the slingshot has the potential to thrust the dualistic notion of self and appearances, including all gods-māras, into the unelaborate nature of phenomena. Recite the root mantra ten thousand times and bless the slingshot carried with you. Consider that the curved vajra blade you also carry has all the strength of one-hundred thousand ḍākinīs.

In addition, all practitioners who practice this profound dharma and are threatened by robbers or thieves must first go to an extremely frightening place and call all gods-māras of phenomenal existence just like before. Say, "The enemy has stolen everything, leaving me helpless. Now I will die of famine or cold. There is no way to avoid death. Therefore, it is best if you send me directly to the hell realms. The second best is to slay me on the spot, and at least you should take my breath before sunrise tomorrow."

Saying this, tie the neck rope to a frightening support and go to sleep. If this method does not bring about the return of your stolen objects, then go to another frightening place and imagine it to be the dwelling place of the enemy. All gods-māras of phenomenal existence converge as red- and black-colored monkeys with their hands linked together, carrying human corpses. They are running and jumping back and forth in the rear of the enemy's house. In addition, make torma replicas of the monkeys, and then call out, "Hey, all you oath-bound gods-māras of phenomenal existence! Right now, you must show the enemy how you appear as red-black monkeys with linked hands carrying corpses. If you don't, then kill me right now. If not, then I swear I will bring down this eon." After saying this, go to sleep. If after doing this there are still no signs, offer your body as the red feast. Then recite, "Gods-māras of phenomenal existence, gather here as a great army to wrathfully charge the enemy of aggression. Sending all negative signs such as sudden afflictions upon them, annihilate all enemies without the slightest trace remaining."

Thus, adding this to the feast of each of the ten ḍākinīs, imagine the ḍākinīs from above, below, and all directions assemble to surround the eight classes of gods-māras in phenomenal existence. Visualize this repeatedly. Think that the gods-māras are screaming "Kill, kill! Strike, strike!" Then, go to a mountaintop and destroy the sacred castles of the earth lords. Spread out the wind-horse flags under your cushion. Wear your clothes inside out; and without any holding back, call out the following, "Hey lords of the mountains and local spirits! If your eyes are not blind, then look. If your ears are not deaf, listen. If you are not crippled, get over here. If you are not dead, be swift. If you are not a corpse, get up. The enemy has stolen from me, and I never did anything to deserve this, nor do I owe any debt. For no reason, he has robbed me. Rather than die from famine, it is better to die right now. The best is for you to throw me into the lowest realm immediately. The second best is to kill me right now. At least, you should kill me before sunrise tomorrow. If not, then kill the enemy without delay; and as quickly as possible, bring me his warm heart." Thus, saying this, go to sleep. Practice the *Suppression through Splendor* repeatedly.

Otherwise, after offering your body as the feast of flesh and blood, meditate that the enemy, his wealth, and all possessions are piled up at the center of your flayed skin. Then recite the *Treasury of Space Mantra* to bless this heap of flesh, blood, and bones. Meditate that the eight classes of gods and cannibals, including all gods-māras of phenomenal existence, gather in multitudes like dust motes in a sunbeam. Shout *phet*, blow the thigh-bone trumpet, and roll the drum while playing the bell to summon the guests. Finally, in the right hand of oneself as Tröma, gather your flayed human skin from the edges inward to bring together your flesh, blood, and the classes of god-cannibals, including the wealth of the enemy. Bind this up with ropes made of snakes and intestines. Swirl the bag over one's head and pound it down so that it lands upon the golden ground. Until the enemies are fully exhausted, think that there is no way for escape or freedom; and success will be certain.

If you come across the cook stove of the enemies, then imagine that the enemies, their wealth, and retinue are destroyed. Throw the stove downward, and imagine that it falls into the mouth of black Yamā. This will ensure success. Furthermore, meditate that the remains from the feast and the tormas are the enemies, his wealth, retinue, and so forth. When offering all of this to the mouths of the guests, imagine that the enemy and the rest are partaken of. In all cases, it is crucial to never separate from the vajra pride of self-nature as Tröma Nagmo. It is also important to take care while interchanging the words in the verses of the liturgy in conjunction with performing the *Suppression through Splendor*.

In brief, deciding that all phenomena are self-appearing and achieving confidence with this is the best indication of the extent of the severance. When awareness achieves confidence with itself, this does not involve intellect, mental analysis, or pride. If toward consummate saṃsāra and enlightenment one possesses definitive comprehension, experience, and realization—these three—there is no doubt that will indicate the extent of severance from the root. This completes the thirteenth section.

I, Saraha, Sovereign of Accomplishment, leave this quintessential nectar of my heart's instructions as a source of refuge for beings of the five-hundred year decline. For those with the karmic fortune to attempt to approach the state of permanent happiness and peace, this gift is their share of the profound attainment of the blessings of the wisdom-mind lineage. Through this, there is no doubt that buddhahood will occur within a single lifetime.

All those with the karmic fortune to be my lineage holders must observe the timelessly endless cycle of past and future lifetimes. Although there is no end in sight: if there were to be a conclusion, that time would have to be now. All accumulations that have occurred until now are as ephemeral as a dream; so whether one decides to continue in saṃsāra or attain enlightenment, it is a personal choice. Those who are capable of enduring great hardships just to put food in their mouths will also be inclined to easily squander the opportunity for accumulating merit that lasts for all lifetimes.

O weak and heartless ones, when the time comes to transfer to the next life, what will you do? O, those who bear the burden of sustaining loved ones and cherished friends, when will the time come for you to repay the karmic debts owed to all beings? While tied to this fire wheel of saṃsāra, do you think you can take your cherished loved ones with you when you depart [this life]? Once the activities of this life are complete, you were hoping to then have a chance to accomplish holy dharma, right? It would be astonishing if Yamā would stop to take the time to wait for you. Watch to see how close relatives with their love, yearning, and advice consume all permanent merit. Since parents and relatives are the māras' handcuffs, the best way to repay their kindness is to decide to attain buddhahood in this life. Otherwise, even the wealth of the trichiliocosm will not be able to protect them. Escape from this dungeon of suffering in order to reach the state of permanent exaltation! The one who accomplishes this ultimate goal is a sole child of mine, Mahāsiddha Saraha.

Spend this lifetime in the practice of perfectly pure virtue. Beg for food and clothing and retreat to inspiring, uninhabited sacred places to practice. Make the time of your death the limit of your dharma practice. Maintain the four boundaries of the conduct of a practitioner and do not be persuaded by anyone. Trust only yourself. Cut off the continuation of endless activities. Curtail expectations about postponing practice until tomorrow or the next day. Rejecting the aim to establish fame first and permanent happiness later will lead you upon the path of a true practitioner. Do not just assume that accomplishment occurs after mere days, months, or years. Given that I have striven for accomplishment with single-pointed conviction, I have discovered the sublime ground of Buddha Vajradhara. I give this to all of you as my loving testament, O Holders of the Lineage. Practice accordingly, Fortunate Sons and Daughters.

Do not groom the hair, but let it be natural like the leaves on a tree. This will protect one from the fear of robbers and thieves and is a sign of the supreme, self-originating unaltered nature. Do not engage in contrived conduct, but rather be natural in whatever you do. Stay fearlessly alone in isolation like a great, haughty snow lion. Do not concoct the nature of mind, for within the unaltered essence lies the expansive dynamic strength of the totality of saṃsāra and enlightenment. Engage in the fearless conduct of the even taste of hope and fear.

Wrap one's hair around a scripture amulet bound at the crown and take all spiritual guides as the Lord of the Family. Wear a white meditation belt across one's chest as a sign of mingling with unceasing clear light. Keep a trident as a sign of the nondual connection with upāya and prajñā. Keep a single-poled pup tent for your abode as a sign of the nature of phenomena free from limits and elaborations. Rely upon a beautiful and excellently shaped ḍāmaru as a sign of the nonduality of the two truths. Keep a lovely bell with a faultless melodious ring as a sign of the awakened mind of the space of phenomena. Rely upon a sharp, well-sounding thigh-bone trumpet as a sign of unobstructed unceasing realization. Keep a well-tanned flayed human skin as a sign of the destruction of the root of confusion. Rely upon a supreme vessel that is a skull with all the fine characteristics as a sign of existence being the play of the dharmakāya. Wear an un-dyed white zen with a border as an upper robe, as a sign of freedom from the fault of habits. Adorn the ears with precious conch-shell earrings as a sign of being a lineage holder. Keep the skin of a wild animal with claws intact as a sign of discerning saṃsāra and enlightenment. A practitioner who owns these thirteen articles must depart for a life of isolation in the mountains.

Until the signs of accomplishment actually manifest, reject intoxicating substances and beverages [and] reject lovers who are deceptive due to attachment. Reject negative, careless, and confused conduct and abandon eating karmic food offerings given out of faith or deceptive means to obtain donations. Abandon fixated habituation to objects of attraction and aversion. Abandon ties to friends and companions and connections with wealth and social engagements. The abandonment of these seven things will bring a practitioner to the path of honor.

Since these are the stages of a practitioner's path, those fortunate sons and daughters who precisely rely upon them will be inseparable with me, a buddha. If buddhahood is not achieved in this lifetime, then I have deceived you, fortunate followers. This great unsurpassed vehicle is the essence of the dharma, surpassing in value the blood of one's own heart.

Entrusted to and expedited through samaya by nāga, yamā, tsen, mamo, rāhula, and others—guard the sons and daughters who keep samaya and uphold the lineage. Eliminate those who corrupt samaya and hold perverted views. Sealed with the severity of samaya and command, sealed by enlightened form, sealed by enlightened speech, and sealed by enlightened mind. Dissolved within the sign of the ḍākinīs.

From the expanse of the clear-light space of dharmakāya, this was revealed from the unchanging vajra crag by the vidyādhara Dorje Drolöd. Based upon the request of Dorje Zangpo, this welling forth of the expanse was decoded from the receptacle of awareness. So that lineage holders may enter the path to liberation, this was put into writing by Rigpa'i Dorje.

May virtue prevail!

Works Cited by Author

Sūtras

Actual Revelation Sūtra, *ngon chung gi do* (*mngon byung gi mdo*)

Ānanda Entering the Womb, *gawo ngal jüg gi do* (*dga' bo mngal 'jug gi mdo*), *garbhāvakrāntisūtra*

Arranged as a Stalk, *dong po köd pa'i do* (*sdong po bkod pa'i mdo*), *gaṇḍavyūhasūtra*

Autobiography of a Female Preta, *yi dak mo'i tok jöd* (*yi dvags mo'i rtogs brjod*)

Biography of Paljung, *pal jung wa yi nam tar* (*dpal 'byung ba yi rnam thar*); biography of Shrī Sambhava

Chapter on the One Truth, *denpa chig po'i le'u do* (*bden pa gcig po'i le'u mdo*), *satyakaparivarasūtra*

Clarification of Transmissions, *lung nam ched* (*lung rnam 'byed*), *vinayavibhaṅga*

Cloud of Jewels Sūtra, *do de kon chog trin* (*mdo sde dkon mchog sprin*), *ratnameghasūtra*

Cultivating the Bodhichitta according to the Mahāyāna, *chang chub tu sem kyed pa tekpa chen-po'i do* (*byang chub tu sems bskyed pa theg pa chen po'i mdo*)

Descent to Laṅkā, *lang kar shek pa* (*lang kar gshegs pa*), *laṅkāvatārasūtra*

Dialogue with Subāhu, *püng zang gi zhü pa'i do* (*dpung bzang gis zhus pa'i mdo*), *subāhuparipṛcchānāmatantra*

Exceptional Extensive Prayers Made by Seven Previous Tathāgatas, *de war shek pa dün gyi ngon gyi monlam gyi khyed par gyey pa'i do* (*bde bar gshegs pa bdun gyi sngon gyi smon lam gyi khyad par rgyas pa'i mdo*), *āryasaptatathāgatapūrvapraṇidhānavisheṣha vistāranāmamahāyānasūtra*

Gathering of Flowers, *metog tsok kyi do* (*me tog tshogs kyi mdo*)

Gathering of Precious Qualities, *yon ten rinpoche düd pa* (*yon tan rin po che sdud pa*), *prajñāpāramitāsañcayagāthā*; verse summary of the *Sūtra of Transcendental Incisive Knowledge*

Gayagori Sūtra, *ga' ya go ri do* (*ga' ya go ri mdo*), *āryagayāshīrṣhahāmamahāyānasūtra*

Heap of Castles, *khang bu tsekpa* (*khang bu brtsegs pa*), *kuṭāgarasūtra*

Heap of Jewels Sūtra, *kon chog tsek pa* (*dkon mchog brtsegs pa*), *ratnakūṭasūtra*

Inconceivable Secret Sūtra, *sang wa sam gyi mi khyab pa'i do* (*gsang ba bsam gyis mi khyab pa'i mdo*), *tathāgatāchintyaguhyanirdeshasūtra*

Intermediate Mother, *yüm bar ma* (*yum bar ma*), *pañchaviṃshatisāhasrikāprajñapāramitā*; intermediate-length *Prajñāpāramitā*

King of Samādhi, *ting dzin gyalpo do* (*ting 'dzin rgyal po mdo*), *samādhirājasūtra*

Meeting of the Father and Son Sūtra, *yab sey jal wa'i do* (*yab sras mjal ba'i mdo*), *pitāputrasamāgamanasūtra*

Moon Lamp Sūtra, *dawa dron ma'i do* (*zla ba sgron ma'i mdo*), *candrapradīpasūtra*

One-Hundred Verses on Karma, *ley gyapa* (*las brgya pa*), *karmashatakusūtra*

Ornament of the Rich Array, *gyen tüg po köd pa'i do* (*rgyan stug po bkod pa'i mdo*), *ghanavyūhasūtra*

Palpoche, *palpoche'i do* (*phal po che'i mdo*), *buddhavataṃsakasūtra*; Sūtra of the Great Bounteousness of the Buddhas

Piṭaka of the Bodhisattvas, *chang chub sem pa'i de nöd kyi do* (*byang chub sems dpa'i sde snod kyi mdo*), *bodhisattvapiṭaka*

Praise for the Worthy, *ngak ö ngak töd* (*bsngags 'os bsngags bstod*)

Praise to the Names of Mañjushrī, *jampal tsen jöd* (*'jam dpal mtshan brjod*), *mañjushrīnāmasaṃgīti*

Prayer for Excellent Conduct, *zangpo chöd pa'i mon lam gyi gyalpo* (*bzang po spyod pa'i smon lam gyi rgyal po*), *bhadracaryāpraṇidhānarāja*

Prayer for Supreme Love, *jampa chog jin gyi mon lam* (*byams pa mchog sbyin gyi smon lam*)

Precious Lamp Sūtra, *kon chog ta la'i do* (*dkon mchog ta la'i mdo*), *ratnolkānāmadhāraṇīmahāyānasūtra*

Sacred Samādhi Sūtra, *ting ngen dzin dam pa'i do* (*ting nge 'dzin dam pa'i mdo*)

Salty River Sūtra, *chu lung wa tswa chen gyi do* (*chu klung ba tshwa can gyi mdo*)

Strength of Love, *jam pa'i tob* (*byams pa'i stobs*)

Sūtra Class Discerning the Pure from the Impure, *do de drang nyik ched pa* (*mdo sde drangs snyigs 'byed pa*)

Sūtra of Advice to the King, *gyalpo la dam pa'i do* (*rgyal po la gdams pa'i mdo*), *rājāvavadaka*

Sūtra of Final Nirvāṇa, *nyang dey kyi do* (*myang 'das kyi mdo*), *āryamahāparinirvāṇasūtra*

Sūtra of Great Liberation, *do de tar pa chenpo* (*mdo sde thar pa chen po*)

Sūtra of Kṣhitigarbha, *sa yi nyingpo'i do* (*sa yi snying po'i mdo*)

Sūtra of Maṇḍala Offering, *kyil khor gyi do* (*dkyil 'khor gyi mdo*)

Sūtra of Manifold Buddhas, *sangye mang ched kyi do* (*sangs rgyas mang byed kyis mdo*)

Sūtra of Sacred Golden Light, *ser öd dam pa'i do* (*gser 'od dam pa'i mdo*), *āryasuvarṇaprabhāsottamasūtrendrarājanāmamahāyānasūtra*

Sūtra of Stainless Space, *nam kha drima med pa'i do* (*nam mkha' dri ma med pa'i mdo*)

Sūtra of the Great Drum, *nga wo che do* (*rnga bo che mdo*), *mahābheriharakasūtra*

Sūtra of the Ten Wheels of Kṣhitigarbha, *sa nying khor lo chupa* (*sa snying 'khor lo bcu pa*); section of the *Sūtra of Kṣhitigarbha*

Sūtra of Transcendental Incisive Knowledge, *sherab kyi pa rol tu chin pa'i do* (*shes rab kyi pha rol tu phyin pa'i mdo*); *prajñāpāramitāsūtra*

Sūtra of Vast Manifestations, *do gya cher rolpa* (*mdo rgya cher rol pa*), *lalitavistarasūtra*

Sūtra on Close Placement of Mindfulness, *do de drenpa nyer zhag* (*mdo sde dran pa nyer bzhag*), *saddharmānusmṛtyupasthāna*

Sūtra Requested by King Bimbisāra, *zük chan nying pö zhü pa'i do* (*gzugs can snying pos zhus pa'i mdo*), *bimbisārapratyudgamananāmamahāyānasūtra*

Sūtra Requested by Maitreya, *jam pey zhü pa'i do* (*byams pas zhus pa'i mdo*), *āryamaitreyaparipṛcchānāmamahāyānasūtra*

Sūtra Requested by Nyewa Khor, *nyewa khor gyi zhü pa'i do* (*nye ba 'khor gyis zhus pa'i mdo*), *āryavinayavinishcayaupāliparipṛcchānāmmahāyānasūtra*

Sūtra Requested by Palchin, *pal chin gyi zhü pa'i do* (*dpal byin gyis zhus pa'i mdo*)

Sūtra Requested by Subāhu, *lag zang kyi zhü pa'i do* (*lag bzang kyis zhus pa'i mdo*), *subāhuparipṛcchāsūtra*

Sūtra Requested by Ugra, *drag shül chen gyi zhü pa'i do* (*drag shul can gyis zhus pa'i mdo*), *ugraparipṛcchāsūtra*

Sūtra that Reveals the Four Dharmas, *chö zhi ten pa'i do* (*chos bzhi bstan pa'i mdo*), *caturdharmanirdesha*
The Present Buddhas' Actual Samādhi, *da tar gyi sangye ngon süm du zhük pa'i ting ngen dzin gyi do* (*da ltar gyi sangs rgyes mngon sum du bzhugs pa'i ting nge 'dzin gyi mdo*)
Thorough Exegesis, *nam shed rigpa* (*rnam bshad rig pa*), *vyākhyāyukti*
Three Heaps, *püngpo süm pa'i do* (*phung po gsum pa mdo*), *āryatriskandhakanāmamahāyānasūtra*
Transmission on Perfectly Correct Truth, *yang dag par den pa'i lung* (*yang dag par ldan pa'i lung*)
Vinaya, *lung zhi* (*lung gzhi*), *caturāgama*

Tantras

Accomplishing Wisdom, *yeshe drubpa* (*ye shes grub pa*)
Accounts from the Gaṇachakra, *tsok kyi tam* (*tshogs kyi gtam*), *saṃbhāraparikathā*
Ahbhidhana, *ah bhi dha na'i gyü* (*a bhi dha na'i rgyud*)
All-Creating Monarch, *kun ched gyalpo* (*kun byed rgyal po*)
All-Illuminating, *kun sal* (*kun gsal*)
Approaching the Ultimate, *don dam nyen pa* (*don dam bsnyen pa*)
Array of Samaya, *dam tsig köd pa* (*dam tshig bkod pa*)
Aspiration for Supreme Conduct, *chog gi chöd pa'i mon lam* (*mchog gi spyod pa'i smon lam*)
Benefits of the Maṇḍala, *mandal gyi pen yon* (*mandal gyi phan yon*)
Chapter on Great Truth, *denpa chenpo'i le'u* (*bden pa chen po'i le'u*)
Charnel Ground Partaking of the Aggregates, *dur tröd püngpo rolpa'i gyü* (*dur khrod phung po rol pa'i rgyud*)
Commentary to the Vajra Essence, *dorje nying drel* (*rdo rje snying 'grel*)
Ḍākinīs' Laughter, *khandro'i ged gyang* (*mkha' 'gro'i bgad rgyangs*)
Dynamic Strength of the Lion, *senge tsal dzok* (*seng ge rtsal rdzogs*)
Essential Ornament, *nyingpo gyen* (*snying po rgyan*)
Excellent Attainment, *cha gyü lek drub* (*bya rgyud legs grub*)
Excellent Golden Garland, *pül chung ser treng* (*phul byung gser phreng*)
Extensive Magical Manifestation, *gyutrül gye pa* (*sgyu 'phrul rgyas pa*)
Garland of Pearls, *mu tig treng wa* (*mu tig phreng ba*)
Gathering of the Wisdom Intent, *gong dü* (*dgongs 'dus*)
Guhyasamāja, *sangwa dü pa* (*gsang ba 'dus pa*), Gathering of Secrets
Guru Magical Manifestation Matrix, *lama gyutrül drawa* (*bla ma sgyu 'phrul drva ba*)
Hevajra Tantra, *kye dorje* (*kye rdo rje*), *hevajratantrarāja*
Kālachakra Tantra, *dü kyi khorlo gyü* (*dus kyi 'khor lo rgyud*), *shrīkālachakranāmatantrarāja*, Wheel of Time
Magical Manifestation Matrix Secret Essence Tantra, *gyutrül sang wa'i nyingpo gyü* (*sgyu 'phrul gsang ba'i snying po rgyud*); Glorious Secret Essence, *pal sangwa'i nyingpo* (*dpal gsang ba'i snying po*), *guhyagarbhatattvavinishcayamahātantra*
Manifestation of the Consummate Retinue, *khor chüb rolpa* (*'khor chub rol pa*)
Precious Heap of Jewels Tantra, *rinchen püng pa'i gyü* (*rin chen spungs pa'i rgyud*)
Reverberation of Sound, *dra tal gyur* (*sgra thal 'gyur*)
Root Tantra of Mañjushrī, *jampal tsa gyü* (*'jam dpal rtsa rgyud*), *mañjushrīmūlatantra*
Samantabhadra Abiding within Oneself, *kuntuzangpo rang la ney pa'i gyü* (*kun tu bzang po rang la gnas pa'i rgyud*)

Sampuṭa Tantra, *sam bu ti gyü* (*sam bu ti rgyud*) or *sam bu tra*, *shrīsaṃpuṭatilaka*
Self-Arising Awareness, *rigpa rang shar* (*rig pa rang shar*)
Self-Occurring Fundamental Nature, *ney lük rang chung* (*gnas lugs rang byung*)
Source of Vows, *dom jung* (*sdom 'byung*), *saṃvarodaya*
Stainless Confession Tantra, *drimed shak gyü* (*dri med bshags rgyud*)
Subsequent Gathering Essence of the Sugatas Tantra, *de shek dü pa chi ma'i gyü* (*bde gshegs' dus pa phyi ma'i rgyud*)
Supreme Ambrosial Medicine, *düdtsi'i men chog* (*bdud rtsi'i sman mchog*)
Supreme Wish-Fulfilling Tantra, *yid zhin chog gi gyü* (*yid bzhin mchog gi rgyud*)
Tantra of the Emergence of Chakrasaṃvara, *gyü dom jung* (*rgyud sdom 'byung*), *shrīmahāsaṃvarodayatantrarāja*
Tantra Revealing the Nature, *de nyid nangwa'i gyü* (*de nyid snang ba'i rgyud*)
Two Segments, *tag pa nyi pa* (*brtag pa gnyis pa*); condensed version of *hevajratantrarāja*
Unwavering Realization, *mi yo wa'i tok pa* (*mi gyo ba'i rtogs pa*)
Vajra Magical Manifestation, *gyutrül dorje* (*sgyu 'phrul rdo rje*)
Vajra Pinnacle, *dorje tsemo* (*rdo rje rtse mo*)
Vajra Tent, *dorje gur* (*rdo rje gur*); instruction tantra of the *Two Segments* (*tag nyi*, *brtag gnyis*)
Vajrapāṇi's Empowerment Conferral Tantra, *lagna dorje wang kur wa'i gyü* (*lag na rdo rje dbang bskur ba'i rgyud*), *vajrapāṇyabhiṣhekamahātantra*
Victorious over the Enemy, *dra ley nam gyal* (*dgra las rnam rgyal*)

Treatises

Advice from a Spiritual Friend, *she tring* (*bshes spring*), *suhṛllekha*; Nāgārjuna
Bazhed Chronicles, or the Assertions of Ba, *ba zhed* (*sba bzhed*); Ba Salnang
Bodhicharyāvatāra, *chang chüb sempa'i chöd pa la jüg pa* (*byang chub sems dpa'i spyod pa la 'jug pa*); Shāntideva
Bodhisattva Grounds, *chang chüb sem pa'i sa* (*byang chub sems dpa'i sa*), *bodhisattvabhūmi*; Asaṅga
Certainty of the Three Vows, *dom süm nam ngey* (*sdom gsum rnam nges*); Ngari Paṇchen Pema Wangyal
Chapter on Impermanence, *mi tag pa'i tsom* (*mi rtag pa'i tshoms*); section of the *Udānavarga* compiled by Dharmatrāta
Collections of Advice, *lab tü* (*bslab btus*), *shikṣāsamuccaya*; Shāntideva
Collections of the Dharma King, *chö gyal ka büm* (*chos rgyal bka' 'bum*); Songtsen Gampo
Commentary on Bodhichitta, *chang chüb sem drel* (*byang chub sems 'grel*), *bodhichittavivaraṇa*; Nāgārjuna
Compendium of Logic, *tsed ma nam drel* (*tshad ma rnam 'grel*), *pramāṇavārttika*; Dharmakīrti
Concise Commentary, *drel chung* (*'grel chung*), Piṇḍārtha (*pinda 'rtha*), *shrīguhyagarbhapiṇḍārthaṭīkā*; Vimālāmitra
Crucial Commentary on the Black Enemy, *dra nag gi ka drel* (*dgra nag gi dka' 'grel*); Shantipa
Doha on the Realization of Seven Excellent Points, *lek dün tok pa'i gur* (*legs bdun rtogs pa'i mgur*); Drigung Kyobpa Rinpoche
Encountering the Three Kāyas, *ku süng tük tred* (*sku gsung thugs phrad*); introduction by Garab Dorje

Entering the Middle Way, *üma la jüg pa* (*dbu ma la 'jug pa*), *madhyamakāvatāra*; Chandrakīrti
Essence of the Middle Way, *üma nyingpo* (*dbu ma snying po*), *madhyamakahṛdaya*; Bhāvaviveka
Fifty Verses of Guru Devotion, *lama nga chu pa* (*bla ma lnga bcu pa*), *gurupañchashikā*; Ashvaghoṣha
Five Stages, *rim nga* (*rim lnga*), *pañchakrama*; Nāgārjuna
Four-Hundred Stanzas, *üma zhi gya pa* (*dbu ma bzhi brgya pa*), *catuḥshataka*; Āryadeva
Garland of Blossoming Lotuses, *pema gyepa'i chun chang* (*padma rgyas pa'i chun 'phyang*); Dudjom Lingpa
Garland of the View, *ta wa'i treng wa* (*lta ba'i phreng ba*); Padmasambhava
Hearing Lineage of Ganden Guru Yoga, *ganden nyen gyü la chöd* (*dge ldan snyan brgyud bla mchod*); Paṇchen Rinpoche Lozang Chögyan
Illuminating Lamp, *drel pa dron sal* (*'grel pa sgron gsal*), *pradīpodyotananāmaṭikā*; Chandrakīrti
Jataka Tales, *kye rab* (*skyes rabs*), *jātakamālā*, *Garland of Rebirths*; Āryashūra
Jewel Garland, *rinchen treng wa* (*rin chen phreng ba*), *ratnāvalī*; Nāgārjuna
Lamp of the Path of Enlightenment, *chang chüb lam dron* (*byang chub lam sgron*), *bodhipathapradīpā*; Atisha
Letter to a Disciple, *lob tring* (*slob spring*); Chandragomin
Lion's Roar, *senge'i nga ro* (*senge'i nga ro*); Dudjom Lingpa
Master Kampala's Maṇḍala Ritual, *lobpon kam pa ley dzad pa'i mandala gyi cho ga* (*slob dpon kam pa las mdzad pa'i man da la gyi cho ga*), *maṇḍalavidhi*; Ratnākarashānti
Mirrorlike Magical Matrix, *gyutrül drawa melong* (*sgyu 'phrul drva ba me long*); Vimālāmitra
Oral Transmission of Mañjushrī, *jampal zhal lung* (*'jam dpal zhal lung*), *mañjushrīmukhāgama*; Buddhashrījñāna
Ornament of Clear Realization, *ngon tok gyen* (*mngon rtogs rgyan*), *abhisamayālaṃkāra*; Maitreya
Ornament of the Classes of Sūtra, *do de gyen* (*mdo sde rgyan*), *mahāyānasūtralaṃkārakārikā*; Maitreya
Pearl Garland, *mu tig treng drel* (*mu tig phreng 'grel*); Vimālāmitra
Praise called One-Hundred and Fifty Verses, *gya nga chu* (*brgya lnga bcu*), *shatapañchāshatkanāmastotra*; Ashvaghoṣha
Praise of the Minor Marks, *pe ched la töd pa* (*dpe byad la bstod pa*)
Praise to the Dharmadhātu, *chö ying töd pa* (*chos dbyings bstod pa*), *dharmadhātustava*; Nāgārjuna
Precious Treasury of the Dharmadhātu, *chöying rinpoche'i dzöd* (*chos dbyings rin po che'i mdzod*); Longchen Rabjam
Precious Treasury of the Fundamental Nature, *ney luk rinpoche'i dzöd* (*gnas lugs rin po che'i mdzod*); Longchen Rabjam
Precious Wish-Fulfilling Treasury, *yid zhin rinpoche'i dzöd* (*yid bzhin rin po che'i mdzod*); Longchen Rabjam
Profound Meaning of the Essence of Mind, *zab don tük nying* (*zab don thugs snying*); Drükchen Pema Karpo
Resting the Mind in Repose, *sem nyid ngal so* (*sems nyid ngal gso*); Longchen Rabjam
Secret Teaching of Accomplishing Enlightened Mind, *sang tük drüb sang tri kyi kor bok don chöd tri* (*gsangs thugs sgrub gsang khrid kyi skor bogs 'don gcod khrid*); Karma Chagmed

Seven-Point Mind Training, *lojong don dun ma* (*blo sbyong don bdun ma*); Atisha

Seventy Meanings on Emptiness, *tong nyid dün chu pa* (*stong nyid bdun cu pa*), *shūnyatāsaptati*; Nāgārjuna

Seventy Verses of Refuge, *kyab dro dün chu pa* (*skyabs 'gro bdun cu pa*), *trisharaṇasaptati*; Chandrakīrti

Speech Bringing an End to the Four Incorrect Views, *chin chi log zhi gog pa'i tam* (*phyin ci log bzhi 'gog pa'i gtam*), *caturviparyayaparihārakathā*; Mātṛceṭa

Sublime Praise, *khyed par pak töd* (*khyad par 'phags bstod*), *visheṣhastava*; Udbhaṭasiddhasvāmin

The Great Chariot, *shing ta chenpo* (*shing rta chen po*); commentary on *Resting the Mind in Repose, sem nyid ngal so* (*sems nyid ngal gso*); Longchen Rabjam

The Great Determination of Reasoning, *tsed ma'i ta chöd chenpo* (*tsad ma'i mtha' dpyod chen po*); Je Tanagpa

The Heart Essence that Dispels the Darkness of Ignorance, *tük chüd marig munsel* (*thugs bcud ma rig mun sel*); Machig Labdron

The Udumwara of Secret Mantra, *sang ngak udumwara* (*gsang sngags u dum ba ra*); Machig Labdron

Treasury of Precious Qualities, *yon ten rinpoche'i dzod* (*yon tan rin po che'i mdzod*); Jigmed Lingpa

Treasury of Transmissions, *lung gi ter dzöd* (*lung gi gter mdzod*); auto-commentary to the *Precious Treasury of the Dharmadhātu, chöying rinpoche'i dzöd* (*chos dbyings rin po che'i mdzod*); Longchen Rabjam

Uttaratantra, *gyü lama* (*rgyud bla ma*); Maitreya

Vase of Instructions, *be'u büm* (*be'u bum*); teachings on the Khadampa tradition's *Stages of the Path* composed by Dolpa Sherab Gyatso

White Lotus, *pedma karpo* (*padma dkar po*); Longchen Rabjam

Wish-Granting Tree, *pag sam tri shing* (*dpag bsam 'khri shing*); Kshemendra

Words that Describe the Eight States of Nonfreedom, *mi khom pa gyed kyi tam* (*mi khom pa brgyad kyi gtam*), *aṣhṭākṣhaṇakathā*; Ashvaghoṣha

Yogāchārabhūmi, *sa de* (*sa sde*), *yogāchārabhūmishāstra*; Asaṅga

Glossary

able to bear suffering, *düg teg pa* (*sdug theg pa*)

able to remain in isolation, *drog gon zin* (*'brog dgon zin*)

actual attainment, *ngö drub* (*dngos grub*), *siddhi*

actual fixation, *ngon zhen* (*mngon zhen*)

actually witnessed, *ngon tong* (*mngon mthong*)

all-pervasive, *kun kyab* (*kun khyab*)

awakened mind, *chang chüb kyi sem* (*byang chub kyi sems*), *bodhichitta*

awareness, *rigpa* (*rig pa*), *vidyā*

awareness holder, *rigdzin* (*rig 'dzin*), *vidyādhara*

baseless from the root, *zhi med tsa dral* (*gzhi med rtsa bral*)

basis of all, *kun zhi* (*kun gzhi*), *ālaya*

black feast, *nag gyed* (*nag 'gyed*)

black spirit, *pe nag* (*pe nag*)

blood debt, *sha khon bu lon* (*sha mkhon bu lon*)

bringing positive circumstances as the path, *zang kyen lam long* (*bzang rkyen lam slong*)

buddha nature, *de shek nyingpo* (*bde gshegs snying po*), *sugatagarbha*

carrying negative circumstances as the companion, *kyen ngen drok khyer* (*rkyen ngan grogs khyer*)

central channel, *kundarma, tsa üma* (*kun 'dar ma, rtsa dbu ma*), *avadhūti*

channels, *tsa* (*rtsa*), *nāḍī*

clear light, *ödsal* (*'od gsal*), *prabhāsvara*

compassion, *tük je* (*thugs rje*), *karuṇā*

completion stage, *dzok rim* (*rdzogs rim*), *sampannakrama*

concealed notes, *gab chang* (*gab byang*)

concentration, *sam ten* (*bsam gtan*), *dhyāna*

concepts, *nam tok* (*rnam rtog*), *vikalpa*

conduct, *chöd pa* (*spyod pa*), *charyā*

confidence with the depth of the view, *ta deng to wa* (*lta gdeng mtho ba*)

confused appearances, *trül nang* (*'khrul snang*)

confusion, delusion, *trül pa* (*'khrul pa*), *bhrānti*

connate, co-emergent, *lhen kye* (*lhan skyes*), *sahaja*

consciousness, *nam she* (*rnam shes*), *vijñāna*

consciousness of the basis of all, *kun zhi'i nam she* (*kun gzhi'i rnam shes*), *ālayavijñāna*

consummate, *kun chüb* (*kun chub*)

continuum, *gyü* (*rgyud*), *tantra*

contributing circumstance, *kyen* (*rkyen*)

conventional meaning, *drang dön* (*drang don*), *neyārtha*

corpse, *bam ro* (*bam ro*)

crossing over with spontaneous presence, *lhun drüb tögal* (*lhun grub thod rgal*)

curved vajra blade, *tri güg* (*gri gug*)

cutting through to original purity, *ka dag trekchö* (*ka dag khregs chod*)

cyclic existence, *khor wa* (*'khor ba*), *saṃsāra*

dairy, meat, and sour foods, *kar, mar, kyur* (*dkar dmar skyur*)

daytime appearances, *nyin nang* (*nyin snang*)

deceived through excellent, pleasing conditions, *zang po dzey chey kyi lu* (*bzang po mdzes byas kyi bslu*)

defeat of heroic splendor, *pa zil chom pa* (*dpa' zil chom pa*)

definitive truth, *nge dön* (*nges don*), *nītārtha*

demon, *düd* (*bdud*), *māra*

deprived spirit, *yidak* (*yi dags*), *preta*

devotion, fervent regard, *mö gü* (*mos gus*)

direct liberation, *tad drol* (*thad grol*)

disciple, those to be tamed, *dül cha* (*gdul bya*)

discover confidence, *deng nyed* (*gdeng rnyed*)

doctrine, teaching, *ten pa* (*bstan pa*), *shāsana*

down to the hell realms, *ma ki nyal kham* (*ma ki dmyal khams*)

dream appearances, *mi nang* (*rmi snang*)

drum used to practice chöd, *chöd dam* (*gcod dam*)

duality, grasping and fixating, *züng dzin* (*gzung 'dzin*), *grahyagrahaka*

emptiness, *tong pa* (*stong pa*), *shūnya*

empty bliss, *de tong* (*bde stong*)

enlightened body, *ku* (*sku*), *kāya*

enlightened mind, *tük* (*thugs*), *chitta*

enlightened speech, *süng* (*gsung*), *vāk*

equal taste, *ro nyom* (*ro snyoms*)

evenness, *nyam pa nyid* (*mnyam pa nyid*)

exaltation, great bliss, *dechen* (*bde chen*), *mahāsukha*

experiential appearances, *nyam nang* (*nyams snang*)

expose the [hidden] faults, *tsang la gol* (*mtsang la rgol*)

extent of the completion, *tsar tsed* (*tshar tshad*)

extent of the severance, *chöd tsed* (*chod tshad*)

faith, *dedpa* (*dad pa*), *shraddhā*

fear-invoking place, *nyen sa* (*gnyan sa*)

fearless, *jigmed* (*'jigs med*)

fearless conduct, *tül zhük* (*brtul zhugs*)

feast offering, *tsok* (*tshogs*), *gaṇachakra*

female evil spirits that eat human flesh, *senmo mi zan* (*bsen mo mi zan*)

five wisdoms, *yeshe nga* (*ye shes lnga*), *pañchajñāna*

fixation upon true existence, *den dzin* (*bden 'dzin*)

fixation with objects, *yul dzin* (*yul 'dzin*)

flayed human skin, *yang zhi* (*gyang gzhi*)

four feasts, *gyed zhi* (*'gyed bzhi*)

four guests, *dron zhi* (*mgron bzhi*)

four immeasurables, *tsed med zhi* (*tshad med bzhi*), *chaturaprameya*

four states of vidyādharahood, *rigdzin zhi* (*rig 'dzin bzhi*): mature awareness holder, *namin rigdzin* (*rnam smin rig 'dzin*); immortal awareness holder, *tsewang rigdzin* (*tshe dbang rig 'dzin*); mahāmudrā awareness holder, *chag gya chenpo'i rigdzin* (*phyag rgya chen po'i rig 'dzin*); and spontaneously present awareness holder, *lhun drüb rigdzin* (*lhun grub rig 'dzin*)

free from meeting and parting, *du dral med pa* (*'du 'bral med pa*)

frightening, terrifying appearances, *jig nang* (*'jigs snang*) frightening environment, *nyen dröd* (*gnyan khrod*)

fundamental nature, *ney lük* (*gnas lugs*)

genuine truth, *dön dam den pa* (*don dam bden pa*), *paramārthasatya*

gesture of dance, *gar tab* (*gar stabs*)

god-cannibals under oath, *ka yi lha sin* (*bka' yi lha srin*)

gods-māras, *lha dre* (*lha 'dre*)

grandfather of one-hundred siddhas, *drüb gya'i me po* (*grub brgya'i mes po*)

grasping fixation, *dzin zhen* (*'dzin zhen*)

ground, *sa, bhūmi*

ground, basis, *zhi* (*gzhi*), *āshraya*

guesswork of the blind, *long wa'i ol tsöd* (*long ba'i 'ol tshod*)

guest of the remains, *lhag dron* (*lhag mgron*)

habit, *bak chak* (*bag chags*), *vāsanā*

happily satisfied, *ga gu* (*dga' mgu*)

hearer, *nyen tö* (*nyan thos*), *shrāvaka*

hope and fear, *re dok* (*re dogs*)

human skin, *zhing pak* (*zhing lpags*)

ignorance, dimmed awareness, *ma rigpa* (*ma rig pa*), *avidyā*

incisive knowledge, *sherab* (*shes rab*), *prajñā*

inexhaustible ornamental wheel, *mi zed gyen khor* (*mi zad rgyan 'khor*)

initial suppression, *nga non* (*snga gnon*)

inseparable, *yer med* (*dbyer med*)

instantly arising, *tol gyi shar wa* (*thol gyis shar ba*)

intangible māras, *tok med kyi düd* (*thogs med kyi bdud*)

intrinsic nature, *rang zhin* (*rang bzhin*), *prakṛti*

kāyas and wisdoms, *ku dang yeshe* (*sku dang ye shes*)

later suppression, *chi non* (*phyi gnon*)

liberated from the bondage of habituation, *ah tey chang drol* (*a 'thas 'phyang grol*)

liberation, deliverance, *dral wa* (*bsgral ba*)

liberation in the expanse, *long drol* (*klong grol*)

magical, *gyu ma* (*sgyu ma*)

magical deception of "mine" [or self], *nga yi chom trül* (*nga yi cho 'phrul*) magician's magical display, *gyu ma'i trül khor* (*sgyu ma'i 'phrul 'khor*)

māras of elation, *ga tröd kyi düd* (*dga' brod kyi bdud*)

māras of luring, *nyem ched kyi düd* (*snyems byed kyi bdud*)

masculine demonic forces, *po don* (*pho gdon*)

material fixation, *ngö zhen* (*dngos zhen*)

means for accomplishment, *drüb tab* (*sgrub thabs*), *sādhana*

meditative equipoise, evenness, *nyam zhak* (*mnyam bzhag*), *samāhita*

meditative stabilization, *ting ngen dzin* (*ting nge 'dzin*), *samādhi*

mental disturbance, *gyü long wa* (*rgyud slong ba*)

mind, *sem* (*sems*), *chitta*

mixed feast, *tra gyed* (*khra 'gyed*)

mountains of flesh, oceans of blood, *sha ri trag tso* (*sha ri khrag mtsho*)

nāga demonic force, *lu don* (*klu gdon*)

naked awareness, *rigpa jen pa* (*rig pa rjen pa*)

narrative context, *leng zhi* (*gleng gzhi*)

nature, *ngo wo* (*ngo bo*), *svabhāva*

nature just as it is, *de kona nyid* (*de kho na nyid*), *tathatā*

nature of phenomena, *chö nyid* (*chos nyid*), *dharmatā*

negative place, *ney ngen* (*gnas ngan*)

object of fear (or disappointment), *dok yul* (*dogs yul*)

object of hope (or expectation), *re yul* (*re yul*)

offering, *chöd pa* (*mchod pa*), *pūjā*

one gone to suchness, *de zhin shek pa* (*de bzhin gshegs pa*), *tathāgata*

one taste, *ro nyam* (*ro mnyam*)

oral pointing-out instruction, advice, *dam ngak* (*gdams ngag*), *avavāda*

original purity, *ka dak* (*ka dag*)

overcome, suppress, *wang düd* (*dbang sdud*)

pacification-severance, *zhi chöd* (*zhi gcod*)

passions, poisons, *nyon mong* (*nyon mongs*), *kleshas*

path of liberation, *drol lam* (*grol lam*), *mokṣhamārga*

path of meditation, *gom lam* (*sgom lam*), *bhāvanāmārga*

path of method, *tab lam* (*thabs lam*), *upāyamārga*

path of seeing, *tong lam* (*mthong lam*), *darshanamārga*

path of unification, *jor lam* (*sbyor lam*), *prayogamārga*

permanently habituated, *ah tey ter züg* (*a 'thas ther zug*)

phenomena, *chö* (*chos*), *dharma*

phenomena appearing to the mind, *sem nang chö* (*sems snang chos*)

pith instruction, *men ngak* (*man ngag*), *upadesha*

powerful females, *wangchukma* (*dbang phyug ma*), *īshvarī*

powerful gods-māras, *lha dre chang che wa* (*lha 'dre byang che ba*)

practice, *naljor* (*rnal 'byor*), *yoga*

principal frightening place, *nyen mig* (*gnyan mig*)

red feast, *mar gyed* (*dmar 'gyed*)

relative truth, *kun dzob den pa* (*kun rdzob bden pa*), *saṃvṛtisatya*

sacred configuration, *kyil khor* (*dkyil 'khor*), *maṇḍala*

sacred recitation, *ngak* (*sngags*), *mantra*

saṃsāra and enlightenment from the perspective of Secret Mantra, saṃsāra and nirvāṇa from the perspective of lower paths, *khor dey* (*'khor 'das*)

seal, symbolic hand gesture, *chag gya* (*phyag rgya*), *mudrā*

self-fixation, *ngar dzin* (*ngar 'dzin*)

self-originating wisdom, self-occurring wisdom, *rang jung yeshe* (*rang byung ye shes*)

sentient being, *sem chen* (*sems can*), *sattva*

severed upon itself, *rang tog tu chöd* (*rang thog tu gcod*)

skull, *bhan töd* (*bhan thod*)

skull cup, *töd por* (*thod phor*), *kapala*

skull filled with blood, *töd trag* (*thod khrag*)

skull of the corpse, *bam kyi töd pa* (*bam kyi thod pa*)

skull vessel, *töd nod* (*thod snod*)

skull with hair attached, *bhan dha chang lo chen* (*bhan dha lcang lo can*)

space of phenomena, basic space, *chö ying* (*chos dbyings*), *dharmadhātu*

spontaneous presence, *lhun drüb* (*lhun grub*), *anābhoga*

stomping upon negative circumstances, *kyen ngen tog dzi* (*rkyen ngan thog rdzis*)

subsequent severance, *je chöd* (*rjes gcod*)

subsequent suppression, *je non* (*rjes gnon*)

suppression through splendor, *wang düd zil non* (*dbang sdud zil gnon*)

suppression through splendor with the messengers, *po nya'i zil non* (*pho nya'i zil gnon*)

tantra, continuum, *gyü* (*rgyud*), *saṃtāna*

taking negativity as positive, *tey ngen yang len* (*ltas ngan gyang len*)

tangible māras, *tok chey kyi düd* (*thogs bcas kyi bdud*)

tent of practitioner, pup tent, *chog pu* (*cog pu*)

thigh-bone trumpet, *kangling* (*rkang gling*)

three gateways to liberation, *nam tar go süm* (*rnam thar sgo gsum*)

three sweets, *ngar süm* (*mngar gsum*)

three whites, *kar süm* (*dkar gsum*)

transcendental perfection, *pa rol tu chin pa* (*pha rol tu phyin pa*), *pāramitā*

tripod of skulls, *töd gyed* (*thod sgyed*)

ultimate, *tar tük* (*mthar thug*)

ultimate truth, *tar tük gi don* (*mthar thug gi don*)

unclear perception [literally, eyes mingled with dust], *mig dul drey pa* (*mig rdul 'dres pa*)

underworld serpent, *lu* (*klu*), *nāga*

unimpeded and nonreferential, *yul med zang tal* (*yul med zang thal*)

unsuitable faith, *ded mi rung wa* (*dad mi rung ba*)

unsurpassed Secret Mantra, *sang ngak la med* (*gsang sngags bla med*)

up to the peak of existence, *ya ki sid tse* (*ya ki srid rtse*)

upheaval, *long tsed* (*slong tshad*)

upheavals through objects, *yul gyi long wa* (*yul gyis slong ba*)

view, *ta wa* (*lta ba*), *dṛshṭi*

vital essence, *tigle* (*thig le*), *bindu*

weak practitioner, *naljorpa chang chung wa* (*rnal 'byor pa byang chung ba*)

white feast, *kar gyed* (*dkar 'gyed*)

white offering, *kar chöd* (*dkar mchod*)

white spirit [King Pehar], *pekar* (*pe dkar*)

will not be determined, *har mi sang* (*har mi sangs*) [Note: This is a translation of the meaning in the context of appearance.]

wind, vital wind, *lung* (*rlung*), *prāna*

wisdom, *yeshe* (*ye shes*), *jñāna*

word of honor, *dam tsig* (*dam tshig*), *samaya*

wrathful female deities, *mamo* (*ma mo*), *mātaraḥ*

wrathful female deities with various animal heads, *tramen* (*phra men*), *pishāchī*

Notes

1. Saraha was one of the eighty great mahāsiddha masters of ancient India who achieved the state of fully enlightened buddhahood in that lifetime and went on to perform countless miracles and reveal signs of supreme accomplishment in order to inspire disciples for countless generations to come. Heruka Dudjom Lingpa is said to be indivisible with Saraha; and in the state of being nondual, the Tertön revealed his treasure revelations.
2. The words in boldface type within the foreword by H.H. Katok Getse Rinpoche delineate the name of the commentary.
3. Upadesha are the esoteric or pith instructions that are passed down orally from master to disciple. In the context of Ati as a vehicle, there are four cycles that are outer, inner, secret, and quintessential. The quintessential is the principal cycle, or genre, within which the upadesha transmissions thrive.
4. Based upon the advice of Dungsey Thinley Norbu Rinpoche, in our translation the term "enlightenment" is used for *'das* rather than nirvāṇa, or the state beyond sorrow, as this teaching is based upon the view of the tradition of unsurpassed Secret Mantra, where enlightenment is the absolute goal, not that of nirvāṇa.
5. Severing the māras is the meaning of "severance", or "chöd", in that all passion-based and cognitive mental afflictions that are the actual māras or demons that obstruct a practitioner's ability to achieve realization must be eliminated. The practice of severance is the method through which to eliminate or sever these habitual patterns.
6. The *yüm chenmo* (*yum chen mo*), or Great Mother, is the great, all-pervasive nature of emptiness, the prajñāpāramitā birthplace of all the enlightened ones.
7. This refers to the lineage of Terma as opposed to the distant lineage of Kāma that originates with the Buddha and spans a time duration of over twenty-five hundred years. In comparison, the Terma lineage of Dudjom Lingpa, which is the inspiration for this treatise, was brought into the world sometime in the later part of the nineteenth century, so roughly only two-hundred years ago. Hence, the term "close" is applicable.
8. The Kāma and Terma lineages form the corpus of dharma that is studied and realized according to the Earlier Translation School of the Nyingma.
9. Āryadeva's text is based upon the meaning of the second turning of the wheel that reveals the meaning of lacking characteristics. The text is explained as the profound pith instructions for understanding chöd called *The Great Composition of Verses* (*tshigs su bcad pa chen po*) by Āryadeva. The four major Indian texts that expound upon chöd are *The Great Composition of Verses* just mentioned, Nāropā's *Secret Severance of Equal Taste* (*ro snyoms gsang gcod*), Padmasambhava's *Severance of Confusion* (*'khrul gcod*), and Padampa's *Pacification-Severance* (*zhi gcod*). This information was taken from the *Collected Works of Padampa Sangye*.
10. Here, "unborn nature" means emptiness.

11. Dudjom Lingpa.
12. Dudjom Dorje was one of the twenty-five disciples of Guru Padmasambhava, and Dudjom Lingpa is a reincarnation of this master.
13. The appearance of the words in boldface type indicates that these are root-terma words found in *The Profound Heart Essence of Saraha* terma of Dudjom Lingpa called *The Upadesha for Encountering the Fundamental Nature Itself*, or Part Two. This extensive commentary by Pema Lungtok Gyatso closely follows that terma and serves to clarify, interpret, and supplement the words of the root terma.
14. The nine vehicles are enumerated as the hearers, *nyen tö kyi tegpa* (*nyan thos kyi theg pa*), shrāvakayāna; solitary realizers, *rang gyalwa'i tegpa* (*rang rgyal ba'i theg pa*), pratyekabuddhayāna; bodhisattvas, *chang chüb sempa tegpa* (*byang chub sems dpa'i theg pa*), bodhisattvayāna; Kriyātantra, *cha wa'i gyü kyi tegpa* (*bya ba'i rgyud kyi theg pa*); Ubhayatantra, *upa'i gyü kyi tegpa* (*upa'i rgyud kyi theg pa*) or Charyātantra, *chöd pa'i gyü tegpa* (*spyod pa'i rgyud kyi theg pa*); Yogatantra, *naljor gyi gyü tegpa* (*rnal 'byor gyi rgyud kyi theg pa*); Mahāyoga, *naljor chenpo'i tegpa* (*rnal 'byor chen po'i theg pa*); Anuyoga, *je su naljor gyi tegpa* (*rjes su rnal 'byor gyi theg pa*); and Mahāsandhi, Atiyoga, *dzogpachenpo shintu naljor gyi tegpa* (*rdzogs pa chen po shin tu rnal 'byor gyi theg pa*).
15. Among substances, the vajra is diamond hard; and its nature is described to epitomize seven qualities: invulnerable, indestructible, authentic, incorruptible, stable, unobstructed, and invincible.
16. "Bindu" is the Sanskrit term for *tigle* (*thig le*), or vital essence, that refers to the sole essence of the mind's nature when used in conjunction with the view of the Great Perfection.
17. The three reasons correspond to three categories of individuals who have varied capacities to comprehend and realize the inner meaning of the teaching contained in the text: superior, middling, and inferior.
18. Most probably present day Pakistan, somewhere close to the Swat Valley.
19. "The Lake-Born One" is an epithet for Guru Padmasambhava, who manifested as a supreme nirmāṇakāya buddha in this world by appearing miraculously from within the pollen heart of a lotus in the middle of Lake Dhanakosha in the land of Oḍḍiyāna, or Orgyen. Readers should refer to *Lives and Liberation of Padmasambhava* published by Dharma Publishing to gain a complete understanding of this enlightened manifestation. Reference here to the fact that he constantly accomplishes the welfare of sentient beings as an immortal vidyādhara means that, when Padmasambhava departed from this world, his wisdom kāya did not decay or vanish; but rather just as he appeared in this realm, he departed like a rainbow in the sky to remain in another world system where he presently resides accomplishing the welfare of beings unceasingly. It is taught that, until the ocean of saṃsāra is empty, he will remain in this wisdom kāya guiding beings to liberation.
20. Shāstras are enlightened commentaries describing the Kāma, or the Buddha's speech. They are composed by highly qualified masters who abide on the bodhisattva grounds. Having realized the nature of phenomena, they are capable of composing teachings that comment upon Buddha's actual speech without adding incorrect, misleading, or self-motivated information. Their commentaries are compiled in what is referred to as the Tengyur.
21. Here, we have put in boldface both the Tibetan name and the English translation so that readers can be sure to see the meaning of the names. This is reference to the two disciples mentioned by name in the terma, namely, Sherab Dawa'i Wangpo and Yeshe Nyima.

22. This is a definition for the term "inexhaustible ornamental wheel". Among Secret Mantra terminology, this specifically refers to the sambhogakāya manifestations.
23. This is a tertön title for Heruka Dudjom Lingpa.
24. A translation of this root text was included in a publication translated by Light of Berotsana entitled *The Guhyagarbha Tantra, Secret Essence Definitive Nature Just As It Is, with commentary by Longchen Rabjam* (Snow Lion Publications, 2011).
25. Shāripu was an incarnation of Dribpa Namsel (*sgrib pa rnam sel*), or Nivāraṇavishkambhin, one of the eight bodhisattvas.
26. This is an epithet for Padmasambhava.
27. Throughout this commentary, the author embeds the root-terma verses when possible. He also occasionally includes the entire quote from the terma before beginning a section, or he will mention the beginning and ending words of the root terma only and then go on to define them in his commentary. Whenever he includes a full quote and does not define them immediately following that, we have decided to boldface the quote as it represents the root verses. If the author does define each word or practically each word, then we do not put the quote in boldface and bold the words only as they appear in the text.
28. *Nam pa kun gyi chog dang den pa'i tong pa nyid* (*rnam pa kun gyi mchog dang ldan pa'i stong pa nyid*) refers to emptiness that is affirming in that it possesses wisdom awareness. This presentation of the meaning of emptiness is unique to Secret Mantra.
29. The "fully manifest resultant buddha" is buddha that appears as rūpakāya to benefit beings.
30. This is a reference to the three lineages through which the tantras are brought into the world of humans: wisdom mind, symbolic indication, and aural transmission. The wisdom-mind lineage originates with the primordial buddha and leads to Vajrasattva. The symbolic-indication lineage comes from Vajrasattva to Vimalamitra and includes the three final testaments that were brought into the human world. The aural-transmission lineage begins with Garab Dorje and extends down through the root masters of the lineages.
31. Atiyoga, or the Mahāsandhi vehicle, involves three general classes: the mind class, the expanse class and the upadesha class. The upadesha class has four inner divisions: the outer, inner, secret, and quintessential secret heart essence. The teachings presented here correspond to the fourth of these four inner divisions.
32. Each section in the commentary will conclude with a *shloka* or verse composed by the author that will poetically sum up the main point of the section.
33. This example corresponds to the intent to care for and engage in deeds for the welfare of others that is like the example of a ferryman who takes the full responsibility to actively bring all passengers safely across the water to the shore of their destination.
34. The four continents are: Pūrvavideha, Lüpakpo (*lus 'phags po*), Elevated Body Height, in the east; Jambudvīpa, Dzambuling (*'dzam bu gling*), Rose-Apple Continent, in the south; Aparagodanīya, Balangchöd (*ba glang spyod*), Bountiful Cow, in the west; and Uttarakuru, Draminyen (*sgra mi snyan*), Ominous Sound, in the north.
35. Also known as Jatsul Dorje, a teacher from the Ja Family of Golog.
36. This identifies the actual meaning of the three gateways to liberation as being without characteristics, without aim, and emptiness.
37. This refers to a text composed by Nāgārjuna that is among the six collections of Madhyamaka.

38. A dhāraṇī is also referred to as a retention mantra or recitation that holds the power of wisdom energy and blessing or sustains the power of the words of truth. These powerful formulas are chanted to avert obstacles, grant profound blessings and virtuous potential, and bring certain benefit based upon altruism. The specific reference here must be to the dhāraṇī of the *Heart Sūtra*, or essence of the prajñāpāramitā, which is the well-known mantra *gate gate para gate para sam gate bodhi so ha*.
39. This points out how easily humans are affected and persuaded by others; hence, there exists the danger of being led in a misguided direction or even just wasting precious time unnecessarily.
40. The seven are the precious wheel, jewel, queen, minister, horse, elephant, and general.
41. The author expresses his confident view that what he has presented here is as complete as it could possibly be. This is followed by a possible rebuttal, so he must make his stand clear and strong to precede that argument.
42. Among the five paths that a practitioner ascends on the journey to awakening as buddha, namely, the path of accumulation, unification, seeing, meditation, and no further learning, this is reference to the second and third paths as just mentioned.
43. The eight categories of phenomena are the omniscient mind, knowledge of the paths, knowledge of the ground, complete unification with all aspects, unification with the peak of training, sequential unification, instantaneous unification, and the resultant dharmakāya.
44. This is reference to the fact that many general practitioners of chöd may be skilled in pūjā, using the instruments, and chanting the melodies but have not received instruction on the profound meaning of the practice.
45. This is reference to relative and absolute bodhichitta.
46. The four feasts will be taught later in this text. They correspond to four periods of time in a day and the energies in the atmosphere and mind that are predominate during those times. They are the black feast practiced in the predawn, the white feast after sunrise, the mixed feast at noon, and the red feast at dusk, in the evening, or darkness of night.
47. A phrase mentioned in this quote—*don kun drub pa* (*don kun grub pa*)—is an epithet for the Buddha and means "accomplish all goals".
48. Those who have turned their backs on the dharma, *gyab kyi chok* (*rgyab kyis phyogs*) is another way of referring to one of the nihilist schools known as the Charvaka School, *gyang phenpa* (*rgyang 'phen pa*), or the Flung Afar.
49. There are four avenues through which birth occurs in the realms of existence: miraculously, through the fusion of heat and moisture, through an egg, or a womb.
50. The four categories of close mindfulness, *drenpa nyer war zhag pa zhi* (*dran pa nyer bar bzhag pa bzhi, catuḥsmṛtyupasthāna*) correspond to the close mindfulness of body, *lü drenpa nyer zhag* (*lus dran pa nyer gzhag, kāyasmṛtyupasthāna*); feelings, *tsor wa drenpa nyer zhag* (*tshor ba dran pa nyer gzhag, vedanāsmṛtyupasthāna*); mental events, *sem drenpa nyer zhag* (*sems dran pa nyer gzhag, citasmṛtyupasthāna*); and phenomena, *chö drenpa nyer zhag* (*chos dran pa nyer gzhag, dharmasmṛtyupasthāna*).
51. Ba Salnang was a contemporary of King Trisong Detsen and abbot of Samye Monastery after Shāntarakṣhita. The *Bazhed Chronicles* contain histories of the reigns of King Trisong Detsen and Mune Tsenpo.
52. This is a literal translation. The actual place was the King's palace, at which time Padmasambhava subdued all the gods-māras and the Khenpo and King gathered together with the Master to decide upon the construction of Samye Monastery. That became the site

known as the Tamarisk Forest of Trakmar, which is actually the palace of King Trisong Detsen.

53. This refers to delineations based upon faculties: the superior, mediocre, and inferior.
54. Geshe Chedkhawa was born in the second Rabjung Year of the Iron Snake, 1101, and died in 1165. Born in the family of yogis, he became a disciple of Milarepa's student Rechungpa under whom he studied the oral instructions of the great yogi Milarepa. Other masters he relied upon include Sharawa, Choyulba, and others; and he became learned in the Tripiṭaka and especially the four principal philosophical tenets. He memorized practically one-hundred volumes of scriptures. In the district of Maldro, one of the eight districts in Lhasa presently known as Maldro Güngkar Dzong (*mal gro gung dkar dzong*), he founded the Chedka Monastery. Taken from the *düng kar tsig dzöd chenmo* (*dung dkar tshig mdzod chen mo*), p. 866, compiled by Dungkar Lobzang Thrinley.
55. This refers to false tertöns.
56. The seventeen classes of the form realm are included within the four levels of concentration. Three belong to the first level, three to the second, three to the third, and eight to the fourth. In ascending order, they are Brahmākāyika, *tsangri* (*tshangs ris*), Province of Brahmā; Brahmāpāriṣhadyā, *tsangpa kunkhor* (*tshangs pa kun 'khor*), Attendants of Brahmā; and Mahābrahmā, *tsangchen* (*tshangs chen*), Great Brahmā; Parīttabha, ödchung (*'od chung*), Little Light; Apramāṇashubha, *tsedmed öd* (*tshad med od*), Immense Light; and Ābhāsvara, ödsal (*'od gsal*) Clear Light; Parīttashubha, *gechung* (*dge chung*), Little Virtue; Apramāṇashubha, *tsadmed ge* (*tshad med dge*), Immense Virtue; and Shubhakṛtsna, *gegyey* (*dge rgyas*), Abundant Virtue; Anabhraka, *trinmed* (*sprin med*), Cloudless; Punyaprasava, *sonam kye* (*bsod nams skyes*), Merit-Born; and Bṛhatphala, *drebuche* (*'bras bu che*), Ample Fruit; Avṛha, *mi chewa* (*mi che ba*), Slightest; Atapa, *mi dungpa* (*mi gdung pa*), Painless; Sudṛsha, *gya nom nangwa* (*gya nom snang ba*), Attractive; Sudarshana, *shintu tong* (*shin tu mthong*), Extreme Insight; and Akaniṣhṭha, *ogmin* (*'og min*), Above All.
57. This is the author's way of saying that the same opportunity will not come around again immediately.
58. These are among the thirty-two sacred places of India.
59. These are heavenly musicians with men's bodies and horses' heads or vice versa.
60. This is a great serpent preta from the class of demons.
61. Ānanda, or Kungawo (*kun dga' bo*), was one of the six original disciples of Buddha Shākyamuni and became his personal servant.
62. This is one of the Four Sectors of Statements from the Vinaya, which are as follows: Clarification of Transmissions, *lung nam ched* (*lung rnam 'byed*); Basis of the Transmissions, *lung zhi* (*lung gzhi*); Request for the Transmissions, *lung zhu wa* (*lung zhu ba*); and Auxiliary Transmissions, *lung tren tsek* (*lung phran tsegs*). They are otherwise referred to as the Extensive Transmission, the Intermediate Transmission, the Perfectly Correct Transmission, and the Transmission that Emerges from Oneness.
63. In ascending order, the six god realms of desire are Caturmahārājakāyika, *gyalchen zhi'i ri* (*rgyal chen bzhi'i ris*), Four Great Kings; Trayatriṃsha, *süm chu tsa süm pa* (*sum cu rtsa gsum pa*), Heaven of the Thirty-Three; Yāma, *tab dral* (*'thabs bral*), Strifeless; Tuṣhita, *ga den* (*dga' ldan*), Realm of Joy; Nirmāṇarata, *trül ga* (*'phrul dga'*), Delighting in Emanation; and Paranirmitashavartin, *zhen trül wang ched* (*gzhan 'phrul dbang byed*), Mastery over Others' Creations.

64. See Endnote 15.
65. This is the *Pterospermum acerifolium*, pericap of a lotus.
66. Another name for the saffron plant also known as *kunkuma*, or *Crocus sativus*.
67. Buddha Maitreya is the fifth buddha of this eon, who will follow the fourth, Buddha Shākyamuni.
68. Möpa Tayey (*mos pa mtha' yas*), or Buddha Boundless Devotion, will emanate as the final buddha of this kalpa. He will be the incarnation of Kyabje Dudjom Rinpoche as proclaimed by himself in his prayer to the successive lifetimes entitled *Crystal Pearls*. Dudjom Rinpoche, Jigdral Yeshe Dorje, 1903-1987, was the undisputed reincarnation of Heruka Dudjom Lingpa.
69. This is not just in reference to the killing of another human being but of any living creature.
70. Among the four that surround Mt. Meru.
71. These are the four great rivers that originate in the high plateaus of Tibet near Mt. Kailash. They are the Brahmaputra, Gaṅgā, Yamunā, and the Indus.
72. Lake Manasarovar is a sacred pilgrimage place in western Tibet near Mt. Kailash. One of its epithets is Anavatapta Lake, the Ever-Cool, because it is the resting place of the nāga king Anavatapta, who never warms up.
73. This is a commentary to Longchen Rabjam's *Precious Treasury of the Wish-Fulfilling Jewel, yid zhin rinpoche'i dzod* (*yid bzhin rin po che'i mdzod*).
74. The author's reference to the fact that life cannot be extended refers to the view that the life expectancy is predetermined by karmic accumulations in previous lifetimes. Due to this, if the living fail to accumulate further merit or virtue that will actually contribute to life expectancy, then the predetermined timing will take precedence.
75. The actual title of this text is *ched du jöd pa'i tsom* (*ched du brjod pa'i tshoms*) in Tibetan and *Udānavarga* in Sanskrit. It is a collection of verses from the Buddhist Canon that was compiled by Dharmatrāta. Within this collection, there is a section called the *Chapter on Impermanence*, or *mi rtag pa'i tshoms*.
76. At the time the author composed this commentary [i.e., the late 1800's], the life expectancy in Golog, Tibet was around sixty-five.
77. These are the three humors of traditional Tibetan medicine based upon the medical scriptures as taught by the Medicine Buddha. Due to habitual tendencies to accumulate nonvirtue motivated by the three poisons, any of the three humors will be affected and become imbalanced as a result. For instance, anger triggers bile to become imbalanced, desire triggers wind, and delusion triggers phlegm. Based upon these principles, all diseases are brought about.
78. In Tibet, the butter was not pasteurized; and since it was usually churned and produced by females with long black hair, it would be common to find random hairs in the butter. Hence, this example was pertinent to the traditional culture since hair is easily extracted from butter.
79. King Bimbisāra was the earliest patron and friend of the Buddha.
80. This is reference to the Zhechen Monastery tülku who was one of the author's root teachers.
81. Although mentioned as Poputo in this text, this master is often times referred to as Geshe Putowa, whose ordination title is Rinchen Sal (*rin chen gsal*). He lived from 1027-1105.
82. Each shāstra begins with the title, homage, and author's commitment to compose. Here,

the point is made that those stages are second in importance to the meditation upon impermanence.

83. When the Buddha taught the Four Noble Truths and specifically the Truth of Suffering, it involved an understanding of these three degrees of suffering that all beings must endure. As the text reminds us, for as long as one remains in saṃsāra, these three degrees of suffering will not be transcended.
84. The other three are going, staying, and sleeping.
85. The five aggregates are form, feeling, recognition, reaction, and consciousness.
86. The four seals are that all compounded phenomena are impermanent, based upon suffering, empty of inherent existence, and selfless.
87. Each bhikṣhu possessed a walking stick or staff and a begging bowl that would be used when they went out begging for alms.
88. This ārya had the capacity to see into the other realms and omnisciently know how the beings were suffering.
89. Kapilavastu is a city-state west of Lumbinī in Nepal.
90. This refers to the ocean, which is where the four great rivers merge.
91. A kind of ancient sea monster that lives in the depths of the subterranean oceans and is depicted on the frescos and temples of Asia.
92. This refers to the four continents that surround Mt. Meru according to the Buddhist cosmological presentation. [See Endnote 34.]
93. This is based on the notion that sentient beings can be found within earth and other metals; so by cooking them down, it is possible to extract valuable substances as well. Hence, beings are tormented in myriad ways for these purposes.
94. This practice of sacrificial offering of flesh and blood is carried out by schools of Hinduism that believe this kind of "red offering" will please the gods and deliver the victim and the ones performing the deed to higher levels of happiness or that this will assist them in whatever they are trying to accomplish.
95. These creatures are nervous when they hear the sound of the dhāraṇī being chanted as they know that it will cause their nonvirtuous ways to cease and that, until that negative karma is fully cleansed, they must suffer the consequences of their karmic deeds.
96. In Tibet since yogurt was a commonly used food, the analogy is given as this resembles the consistency of yogurt when it is thick. Another example is like the thickness of a solid block of butter.
97. This refers to the mortar used to grind the barley, indicating that the fetus becomes more grounded or solid.
98. In Tibet, the main form of burial is the sky burial that takes place at a certain location called a burial ground, where the body is left. Then, the practitioners who perform the rituals of sky burial take care of the process of presenting the body as an offering to vultures, which involves many types of visualizations that transcend the ordinary realm of perception.
99. This means the true nature of reality, namely, emptiness and the magical nature of all appearances that are inseparable with emptiness.
100. These four branches are the armies of horsemen, elephants, charioteers, and infantry.
101. This term *zan tri* (*gzan khri*) indicates the support that a diviner will use in order to induce their visions and prophetic indications. For example, this may be a mirror or crystal.
102. An armory in the asura realm.

103. Indra's capital on the summit of one of the seven mountains of Mt. Meru.
104. Surrounding Mt. Meru, there are seven golden mountains and seven lakes. This is reference to the first of those encircling lakes.
105. Devadatta was brother to Ānanda and cousin to the Buddha.
106. This is the buddha in the realm of the devas. He is also known by other names.
107. The three supports refer to the representations of enlightened body, speech, and mind, namely, statues, scriptures, or dharma books and stūpas or other holy shrines.
108. "Ill-intended tales" refers to misguided stories that inspire people to pursue incorrect, perverted beliefs and directions. The example of heretical literature is given in the commentary itself.
109. This means human-generated nonvirtue that has not been confessed or purified, so it will continue to proliferate until it is remedied.
110. Devadatta was the Buddha's cousin and in the inner circle of disciples. However, he was deceitful and considered himself to be more exalted than the Buddha. His opinion was that he was far more learned than Buddha, so he taught the five trainings to the followers with the attitude that this information was authentic dharma surpassing that of the Buddha. He sought to divide the sangha and was temporarily successful. In fact, later a stūpa was erected to remember the eradication of divisiveness in the sangha caused by Devadatta. This stūpa is one type of the eight stūpas that are built as monuments to commemorate enlightened awareness around the world.
111. "Definitively abiding bodhisattva" refers to an individual who, from the time of becoming a bodhisattva, will establish the marks and signs until fully awakened buddhahood is realized.
112. This term indicates that a particular reference or statement is unacceptable without a direct confrontation or rebuttal.
113. The words of confession in this sūtra are extremely detailed as they make reference to the nonvirtue accumulated throughout the three times and represent a very comprehensive and powerful confessional prayer. There are references to the circumstances that bring about negative accumulations that occur through body, speech, and mind so that these shortcomings can be openly acknowledged, confessed, and purified.
114. These were outstanding disciples of the Buddha.
115. It is possible that this is referring to the tantra *All-Illuminating Bindu*, *tigle kun sal* (*thig le kun gsal*).
116. This is the auto-commentary to the *Treasury of the Dharmadhātu* by Longchen Rabjam.
117. It is traditional for Tibetan authors to occasionally compose poetic verses to accompany their exposition. This is based upon being personally inspired by the pith meanings that are being presented and is a way to also inspire faith in the readers. Poetic verse is a different style of writing known as free-style verse as opposed to the many rules and strict order of a prose presentation.
118. At this point, the author begins to comment on the words that appear in the root terma recitation for the recitation and visualization of the field of refuge.
119. Khachöd Wangmo is another name for Vajravarāhī, the Vajra Sow.
120. This is reference to the historical Buddha as the ultimate symbol of this refuge and the qualities he embodies, but this also refers to the state of buddha that is realized by anyone who is able to actualize this; hence, the source of refuge is both the historical Buddha and the state of buddhahood.

121. The four exceptional qualities that the Buddha embodied are freedom from fear, skillful means, compassion for all beings, and no expectation for personal benefit.
122. This analogy is often used throughout the Buddhist canons to indicate something that is unmistaken and obvious. It seems that this herb must symbolize being unveiled, hence clearly perceived.
123. These are the well-known refuge verses of the Longchen Nyingthig preliminary practice compiled by Vidyādhara Jigmed Lingpa.
124. The triune wisdoms of the ground.
125. By reciting *phet* three times, one brings to mind the teachings given earlier in general and specifically rests in the directive given at this particular juncture, the nonconceptual dharmakāya nature of mind.
126. There are several masters who hold the name Gyaltangpa. We think that this is reference to Gyaltangpa Samten Ödzer (*rgyal thang pa bsam gtan 'od gzer*). He was known to have visions of Machig Labdron, during which time she bestowed chöd transmissions upon him. That then became the chöd tradition of Gyaltangpa. Nevertheless, we are unsure as to when he lived.
127. The four immeasurable qualities are equanimity, compassion, love, and joy.
128. The seven upadeshas are otherwise known as the cause-and-effect precepts spoken by Maitreya to Asaṅga on the subject of bodhichitta. They are to recognize all beings as having been one's mother, to recall their kindness, to repay their kindness, to have love, great compassion, and pure intentions for them, and to generate the bodhichitta.
129. The *Palpoche* refers to the *Jataka Tales'* description of Norzang's life as a bodhisattva in training. Norzang [Skt. Manibhadra] was the name of Buddha in one of his past lifetimes during his training as a bodhisattva.
130. The twofold aim of self of others leads to the goal of accomplishing the dharmakāya as one's personal aim and the rupakāya as the aim to fulfill the needs of others.
131. The author is referring to the fact that he removed the word "therefore" from the quote and also added the word "protector".
132. The full name of this master is Jawa Alak Do-ngak Chökyi Gyaltsen (*'ja' ba ah lags mdo sngags chos kyi rgyal mtshan*). He was one of the author's root gurus.
133. Readers should note that the author did not literally quote the root terma in his own commentary on both refuge and bodhichitta. Of course, the subject being discussed is identical, and his commentary is particularly extensive in the bodhichitta section. Aside from quoting the sending and receiving section that we have put in boldface, there does not seem to be any continuity with the exact words from the terma beyond that.
134. This sentence that appears in boldface here has been taken from the BBPH version of the text since it clearly seems to be omitted from the Bhutanese versions of the commentary.
135. This is one of the Indian mahāsiddhas also known by his Tibetan name, Lopon Jigmed Jungney (*slob dpon 'jigs med 'byung gnas*).
136. This text is one among four kriyāyoga tantras, namely, the *General Kriyā Tantra*, the *General Secret Tantra*, the *Excellent Attainment Tantra*, and the *Tantra of Subsequent Concentration* that were requested by Pünzang.
137. Guardians of Mt. Meru and a type of wealth god or divinity of abundance.
138. These faults also apply to males but are mentioned here in the context of females because of the category of the precious queen.
139. Hairy fish head with beaver teeth.

140. This distance is also mentioned in the *Treasury of All-Pervasive Knowledge, she cha kun khyab dzöd* (*shes bya kun khyab mdzod*) by Kongtrul Yonten Gyatso (*kong sprul yon tan rgya mtsho*), 1813-1899. We are assuming that this is accurate and that the term is spelled incorrectly in the text we are working from. The wish-granting tree seems to extend upward for one-hundred leagues and fifty leagues downward into the earth.
141. The plateau that is in front of this tree is not a single plateau. Each level of the extended plateaus stretch for fifty leagues. Some of the levels rise up one-half of a league, some for six, and some for eighteen leagues. Hundreds of varieties of colorful flowers abound there with superb shapes and patterns.
142. This must be a spelling error in the text, as the term is actually *'chums*, which is an ancient term for desire. This then refers to the desire-realm gods.
143. The commentary *The Great Chariot, shing ta chenpo* (*shing rta chen po*) is a commentary composed by Longchen Rabjam based on his treatise *Resting the Mind in Repose, sem nyid ngal so* (*sems nyid ngal gso*).
144. An "unsurpassed lie" means to lie about one's spiritual accomplishments, such as telling others that one has had visions of deities or that the buddhas have spoken to one in dreams and so forth when this actually never really occurred.
145. This involves the power to imagine that, based upon a single support for the offering, the bodhisattva can increase that to become manifold offerings as immeasurable as the treasury of space, meaning the reaches of space itself, or the inconceivable.
146. Again, most of the verses for the seven branches mentioned in the root terma are not precisely indicated in the commentary.
147. This can also be pronounced according to the Sanskrit, which is *krodhi*. We think that Dudjom Lingpa must have pronounced this as *trodhi*, since the Tibetan pronunciation of *vajra* is *benzar* in this case as well.
148. The entire mantra is mentioned just below.
149. The latter part of this sentence was taken from the modern BPPH version of the text, as it was missing from both Bhutanese versions.
150. *Wang düd zil non* (*dbang sdud zil gnon*), the ḍākinī's laughter that overcomes and suppresses through splendor.
151. All surrounding beings simultaneously dissolve into white bindus of light that dissolve into the heart of Vajravarāhī.
152. Although the quote begins with the words taken from the tantra *Resting the Mind in Repose*, the author has also included words from other quotes as mentioned at the end. It is unclear as to when the first quote ends and the others begin, so all are included as a single quote.
153. The Tibetan term used here literally means "lung" because, culturally, the meat was enjoyed by the humans and other body parts would be tossed out for the dogs.
154. *Nye ba'i* or "close" means that this nonvirtue approaches the weightiness of the original five.
155. Following the parinirvāṇa of Lord Buddha Kāshyapa, his disciples convened to commit themselves to the propagation of the lineage. This is the mountain where they were said to have convened along with Mañjushrī, Maitreya, and oceanic bodhisattvas who all came to this place to generate the bodhichitta. It is said that whatever prayers are made in this place will be effortlessly accomplished. This sacred mountain is located in the present day Yunnan province of southwest China.

156. One time when the Buddha was meditating in a cave at Vulture's Peak called Nodjin Kuwera's Cave, the māra Devadatta and his retinue of five hundred came to disturb him. They tossed a catapult into the cave, and Vajrapāṇi intercepted it; but half of it flew off closer to Buddha's body. Then Nodjin Kuwera tried to grab that; but it exploded in his hands, and a piece then struck Buddha's foot and drew blood. That was when Buddha spoke the well-known verse that, no matter where one resides, there is no place to escape karma, whether in the sky, the ocean, or even in a cave.

157. The twelve deeds are transferring from Tuṣhita, entering the mother's womb, taking birth, proficiency in the arts as a youth, enjoying the pleasures of his queens, becoming a renunciate, practicing asceticism, departing for the heart of enlightenment, vanquishing the māras, attaining fully manifest awakening, turning the wheel of the dharma, and passing into parinirvāṇa.

158. This analogy of the protector entering the body of an oracle is a commonplace occurrence in the Tibetan culture and Vajrayāna context of practice. Certain individuals possess the capacity to receive the divine presence of the wisdom protectors within their body, and they actually enter into trance and are then capable of reciting verses, speaking languages, and even carrying great weight with supernatural powers that they do not possess once the trance concludes. The presence of the protector allows them to bring important teachings and predictions into the human plane immediately, such as with the Nechung Oracle who regularly advises H.H. the Dalai Lama during such ceremonies.

159. At this point, the LN Bhutanese version includes small print for the brief commentary to the root terma words. We suspect these comments are made by someone besides the author, as they appear in a different format to set them apart.

160. The four states of vidyādharahood, *rigdzin zhi* (*rig 'dzin bzhi*) are mature awareness holder, *namin rigdzin* (*rnam smin rig 'dzin*); immortal awareness holder, *tsewang rigdzin* (*tshe dbang rig 'dzin*); mahāmudrā awareness holder, *chag gya chenpo'i rigdzin* (*phyag rgya chen po'i rig 'dzin*); and spontaneously present awareness holder, *lhun drüb rigdzin* (*lhun grub rig 'dzin*).

161. Given that the terma terminology is the same for receiving the four empowerments, the author will not repeat the explanations that he gave just above for this section. Hence, the specific terma terms that delineate the differences in the four stages will not be in boldface.

162. The literal translation "relying upon the body of another" refers to consort practice, or karma mudrā. This practice follows the accomplishment of reliance upon one's own body, at which time the completion-stage practitioner purifies and gains mastery over the channels, winds, bindus, and the fierce-wisdom fire. Once that is accomplished and the appropriate empowerments and transmissions have been received, then the secret consort practice with the body of another can be engaged. This level of practice is always engaged in extreme secrecy and never discussed publically for any reason. These days, there are many extremely misinformed ideas about so-called tantric sex, and that entire genre has no place in this tradition.

163. This term is interchangeable with *gnyis med*, which appears in the terma and means "inseparable" or "nondual". Here, the author uses *dmigs med*, so we are translating this as "nonconceptual".

164. Here, there is a discrepancy between the texts and the terma terms that they contain.

The older version [BQM] of the terma begins this next section by saying *'khor 'das kyis bdus pa'i chos thams cad*, whereas the versions of the terma terms in both newer commentaries [LN and BPPH] read *sems kyi bsdus pa'i chos*. The first phrase means "the consummate phenomena of saṃsāra and enlightenment", and the second means "the consummate phenomena of the mind".

165. The term "empty" (*stong pa*) is missing from the commentary, but appears in the terma.
166. The six bone ornaments are the bone ornament at the crown of the head that symbolizes concentration and Akṣhobhya, the earrings that symbolize patience and Amitābha, the choker that symbolizes generosity and Ratnasambhava, the bracelets and anklets that symbolize discipline and Vairochana, the belt that symbolizes diligence and Amoghasiddhi, and the human ashes and apron on the torso that symbolize prajñā and the Vajra Bearer, or Vajradhara.
167. The author omits the term "dream" (*rmi lam*) that is found in all versions of the terma.
168. Refuge and bodhichitta verses may be taken from the general Tröma liturgy, such as the concise sādhana. It is also acceptable to recite the verses from the preliminaries or the intermediate sādhana. Dungsey Thinley Norbu Rinpoche compiled the phowa practice for the convenience of practitioners and extracted the auxiliary verses from the concise sādhana. The root terma does not include the phowa practice at this juncture.
169. The "egg of a one-time mother" refers to the bodhisattva bird emanation of Tārā and Avalokiteshvara who came from the pure realms into India to lay a single egg. After giving birth, the bird returned to the pure realm. The egg was very colorful with the same qualities as a wish-fulfilling jewel and said to be the size of a robin's egg. This analogy is given since it is so auspicious; yet according to upadesha instruction for the phowa practice, the visualization is meant to be spherical rather than oval like an egg.
170. The four yogas are one-pointedness, *tse chig* (*rtse gcig*); no elaboration, or simplicity, *trö dral* (*spros bral*); one taste, *ro chig* (*ro gcig*); and nonmeditation, *gom med* (*sgom med*).
171. In the terma, the term *shar rig* appears, which does not seem to make any sense. In the commentary, this appears as *shes rig*, or wakeful awareness; so we have used that term instead.
172. Although the terma has the term spelled *rang shes*, the commentary explains this to be *rang gshis*, or innate nature.
173. This is the fourth Paṇchen Rinpoche, 1567-1662.
174. Drügpa Kunlek was born in the eighth Rabjung Year of the Wood Pig, 1455, and died in 1528. He was originally a fully ordained monk; and as his inner realization began to blaze, he gave up all inhibitions and revealed conduct that was free from hope and fear. He was a prolific writer and composed many spiritual hymns and writings, most of which have been lost.
175. These are the four samayas for the view of the Great Perfection.
176. Reference to "not me" is not found in the commentary and can be understood only through the words of the terma itself. In addition, the author does not list the names of all the body parts as they appear in the terma.
177. This literally defines the term *sangye* (*sangs rgyas*) in Tibetan, as *sangs* means to awaken from the shell of ignorance and *rgyas* means to expand the self-radiance of wisdom.
178. These are the twofold omniscient wisdoms, namely, the omniscience of the nature of things as they are [i.e., fundamental nature], *ney lük ji tawa khyen pa'i yeshe* (*gnas lugs ji lta ba mkhyen pa'i ye shes*) and as they appear [according to relative truth] in their multiplicity, *she cha ji nyed pa zik pa'i yeshe* (*shes bya ji snyed pa gzigs pa'i ye shes*).

179. Here the author does not repeat the term "buddha" for each point being made in the terma text.
180. This explanation of the four kāyas is missing from the modern Tibetan version [BPPH] that we are comparing with the Bhutanese version [LN].
181. There is a correction in the commentary, where it reads *ngos mi zin* [i.e., without recognizing] rather than *so mi zin* [i.e., will not be reliable], which is how the terma reads. The meaning of the latter makes this passage more lucid.
182. In the modern version [BPPH] of the terma and commentary, the term *gtan*, or permanent, is included here; whereas, it is not included in the Bhutanese version or the Dudjom Collection of the root terma. So we have opted to omit it. That would simply include the notion that a permanent refuge could not be given.
183. The three classes of mind, expanse, and upadesha.
184. Mipham Gonpo attained the rainbow body after encountering Berotsana and receiving instructions. He was from Kham and was already in his late eighties when he encountered the pointing-out instructions of the Great Perfection.
185. The name of a Mahāmudrā teaching that combines prajñā and upāya like the two parts of an amulet that make a perfect seal is known as *Mahāmudrā's Amulet, chag chen ga'u ma* (*phyag chen ga'u ma*).
186. This was a great Gelukpa master who received the whispered lineage instructions and passed them to his famous disciple Je Tsongkhapa. He lived from 1326-1401 and was also known as Namkha Gyaltsen (*nam mkha' rgyal mtshan*).
187. The karma of abandoning dharma occurs by forsaking or disparaging any lineage of teachings by considering it to be inauthentic or misguided.
188. This quote seems to be taken from the teachings of great chöd practitioners that the author has compiled, but he does not specifically state who actually said this.
189. These are two of the so-called "Three Holy Places of Tibet" associated with the body, speech, and mind aspects of Chakrasaṃvara and Vajravarāhī. The third is Godāvarī, or Labchi (*la phyi*).
190. This is called the *chöd yul zab don tük nying* (*gcod yul zab don thugs snying*) by the fourth Drükchen Pema Karpo who lived from 1527-1592 and went by many titles. At one point in his illustrious life, he became the teacher for the emperor of China.
191. Boundary of the retreat place.
192. Several of the words found in all versions of the root terma are not embedded in any of the commentaries. We have translated them in the root.
193. Thigh-bone trumpet.
194. These are terma words that are not found in any versions of the commentary.
195. Here, there are several verses from the root text that are unable to be identified in the commentary. We begin to boldface the words where we are able to identify them again. This break begins with the root verses the read, "It is a key point . . ." until ". . . into the fear-invoking locale."
196. Both of these texts belong to the revelations of Heruka Dudjom Lingpa. The *Lion's Roar* is from the cycle of pure vision, wisdom matrix revelations called "Lion's Roar, the Suppression of Self-Appearances and Quelling of the Appearances of Others", *dag nang yeshe drawa'i kor ley rang nang wangdud shen nang zilnon senge'i nga ro* (*dag snang ye shes dra ba'i skor las rang snang dbang sdud gshan snang zil gnon senge'i nga ro*). The *Garland of Blossoming Lotuses* belongs to the revelation cycle known as "Treasury Expanse of the Spacelike Dharmatā" and is called the Suppression through Splendor by the Gathering

of Ḍākinīs known as Garland of Blossoming Lotuses, *chö nyid namkha'i long dzöd ley khandro düpa'i wangdud zilnon pema gyepa'i chun chang* (*chos nyid nam mkha'i klong mdzod las mkha 'dro dus pa'i dbang sdud zil gnon padma rgyas pa'i chun 'phyang*).

197. This liturgy is the *Suppression through Splendor, Ḍākinīs Laughter*. Although the entire liturgy is not included here in the commentary, it is a practice that is being performed continuously in this section on wandering; so the author makes reference to it specifically at this juncture.
198. Several words in the root terma are missing from the commentary here.
199. For the remaining four ḍākinīs, the root terma mentions each one in the manner of the liturgy; whereas, the commentary refers only to the differences in names, directions, colors, and passions. Hence, those have been indicated by boldface type, while the other words are generic.
200. Once again, since words in the liturgy are generic, the root terma mentions them all; but the commentary mentions only the changes in the names of the three-kāya ḍākinīs and the demonic forces that each ḍākinī specifically tames.
201. The dagger phurbas that they hold correspond to the directional color of each ḍākinī. They are made of precious substances that are the same color as each family's direction. The shapes mentioned also correspond to the families and refer to the shape of each handle.
202. "Four-faceted" means that there are four ridges that come down to form the point of the dagger. In the commentary, it mentions that this phurba is made of rhinoceros horn. We translate this as a golden phurba since that is the color of the direction, and it seems that there may be a spelling error.
203. Mammal whose sire is a yak and dam is a cow.
204. This was one of the earlier minor kingdoms in India.
205. At this point in the root terma, there is a long paragraph that we are unable to identify in the commentary. It begins with "At the moment the eyes perceive . . ." and extends until ". . . by arriving in that state of confidence, that is the severance."
206. Mügsang was one of Machig's disciples.
207. Here there is a line from the terma missing from the commentary.
208. The order of presentation is switched at this point between the root and the commentary. The root terma begins the historical account of Sūryavajra's deception from the māra of luring at this point, whereas the commentary picks up with the teaching on the māras that follows the story in the root terma. Whatever the case, we have put all sections in boldface; and everything seems to be included within the translation.
209. The order of presentation between the root terma and the commentary is different in this section, yet all boldface words indicate the fact that this is being directly quoted from the root.
210. In the root terma, the term *gzhan*, or other, is included just before *rang*, or self. We have chosen to omit it here since the translation would then read "the awareness of self and others"; and that does not seem to be correct at this point in the visualization. The term *gzhan* is not found in the Bhutanese [LN] version of the commentary.
211. In the root terma, it mentions three kāyas; but since the commentary refers to four and in fact all four have been received, we decided to change that reference in the root terma to four rather than three.
212. This is the guru-yoga practice that usually precedes a feast.
213. The Tröma phowa practice is called *Opening the Gateway to the Sky*, and this visualiza-

tion was set forth earlier in this commentary at the conclusion of the preliminary teachings of the uncommon specific preliminaries. [See 3.2.1.2.2.2.3 Upadesha Describing the Phowa Practice.] Here, this feast offering is the extensive feast that comes at the conclusion of the phowa practice, where one then offers the discarded corpse as the feast for the diverse guests who come to partake of this. This is placed in this section since it is a feast offering, but specifically it belongs to the phowa practice. It may also be performed on its own.

214. Here the visualization is mentioned in brief in the root terma, and then it is elaborated upon; so in a few cases, the boldface words are repeated twice.

215. The four characteristics of the central channel are that it is straight like a bamboo shaft, subtle like the petal of a lotus, rich like the essence of butter or ghee, and clear like the flame of a candle or butter lamp.

216. At this point, there is a paragraph in the root terma that is missing in the commentary. It begins with, "The spontaneously present trikāya . . ." and extends to "The visualization is as follows." It seems that the root terma includes an excerpt of the visualization that is given in a more elaborate scenario just below.

217. The brief version of this visualization mentioned in the root terma is not included here in the commentary.

218. The liturgy phrase "the spontaneously present trikāya" is missing from the commentary.

219. This is one of the eight classes of gods and demons. From the outer point of view, the rāhula spirits manifest as the seven days of the week, including Bitiphatra. The inner rāhulas are the oath-bound protectors such as Drachen Dzin and Kyabjug Chenpo, while the secret aspects are the female categories of oath-bound guardians. Historically, Za or Rāhula was a monk who was bound to the oath to serve the doctrine by Vajrapāṇi, and he is also considered to be a wrathful manifestation of Vajrapāṇi. Rāhula is one of the principal protectors for the Tröma termas.

220. The visualization that is mentioned in the root terma is not included here in the commentary.

221. The visualization that is mentioned in the root terma is not included here in the commentary.

222. The root verses are not included here in the commentary.

223. The root verses are not included here in the commentary.

224. This is not the exact wording as found in the root text, but the meaning is the same.

225. This is not to be taken literally by those who have not fully realized selflessness and have not yet reached the bodhisattva grounds. Occasionally, bodhisattvas will offer body parts when it is necessary for the higher purpose of guiding and liberating beings. Otherwise, this is mentally imagined as a powerful tool to eradicate self-cherishing and fixation upon the body as truly existent.

226. Paranirmitavashavartin, *zhen trül wang ched* (*gzhan 'phrul dbang byed*) is one of the six realms in the desire-god realm where wealth and enjoyments are manifested by others so that whatever is wished for is received.

227. It seems that the visualization for the wish-fulfilling jewel is missing from the body of the text; and the small print, which was inserted by one of the editors for this commentary, indicates that.

228. In the Tibetan culture, this is the opposite of where these objects would be placed. Shoes are considered filthy and never placed close to the head or in a higher place, while hats are always placed close to the head and in a higher location.

229. This is reference to actually giving up in terms of being so frightened and full of concepts that one is no longer able to focus on the point of the practice. Given that this level of practice is entirely dependent upon these kinds of extremely upsetting and adverse circumstances: then without those tests to go through, it is considered that the practitioner is not capable of this level of practice. That is why it is referred to as "a failure".
230. The lists of signs that may occur are all indications of bad things to come. Hence, although they seem enticing, the practitioner must be vigilant and aware and take care to shift locations right away. If a servant is mistreated by his boss or leader and gains a chance for freedom, then it is almost certain that retribution will be on his mind. That is the analogy that fits this scenario since these signs give a certain clue that retribution by the gods-māras will be imminent.
231. Here, the root text states, "Having gone to another fear-invoking environment, . . ." The modern commentary BPPH includes this; whereas, the Bhutanese versions do not.
232. This represents an effort to appease them so they will not pursue the practitioner and cause further obstacles to this final stage of practice.
233. This master was born in the third Rabjung Year of the Iron Snake, 1161, and died in 1211. The reincarnation of Tsangpa Gyarey was Drükpa Pema Karpo.
234. The three samādhis are italicized here to highlight the importance of this sequence. This emergence of appearances as the nature of emptiness, or the basic space of the ground, underscores the fact that all phenomena appear as the illumination of great emptiness. The inseparable unity of emptiness and appearances, or original purity and spontaneous presence, is the root cause for birth as the deity that occurs through the seed syllable, in this case *hung*. Hence, this is how all deities are born. This process purifies ordinary birth and awakens the trikāya wisdom buddha nature as the special feature of generation-stage deity-yoga practice.
235. The ḍākinī in the south holds a hammer and a wish-fulfilling jewel.
236. The four enlightened activities correspond to times of the day: peaceful in the morning, enriching at noon, magnetizing in late afternoon or evening, and terrifying after dark in the night.
237. This means that the practice then becomes merely a method to accomplish worldly concerns and departs from the wisdom aspect that is the pith emphasis for a practice of this level.
238. Ngulchu Tokmed (*dngul chu thogs med*) was born in 1295 and passed in 1369. He was a great bodhisattva and well known for composing the thirty-seven precepts of the bodhisattvas.
239. An important staple in the Tibetan diet.
240. This is reference to the practice of slaying and liberating, which are specific upāya methods used in Secret Mantra practice when necessary to benefit beings through wrathful activity.
241. This mantra and mudrā combination serves the function of multiplying and increasing offerings to become immeasurable like space.
242. This must be taken in the context of the nomadic culture because the stove is a seasonable item that is constructed on the ground of stone and dirt. Later, the cooking place is abandoned. If someone had caused disturbance for a practitioner, they may be considered an enemy. If the wandering practitioner comes across this kind of abandoned stove area that was used by one of their so-called enemies, then the teaching applies to that scenario.

243. This is the last direct quote that we could find. The root terma concludes with the entrustment and commands for samaya to be observed.
244. This refers to the supreme qualities of pristine water that are analogous to this profound meaning. The eight are coolness, sweetness, lightness, softness, cleanliness, freedom from impurities, soothing to the stomach, and soothing to the throat.
245. This is reference to those who disparage the lineage of terma revelations and implies that one of the reasons the author decided to undertake this commentary was to illuminate the greatness of this lineage tradition. He is also making the point that it is presumptuous of him to even assume that he could possibly do that; and if any ego is involved, then that becomes the play of the māras once again.
246. Kunzang Pema Chödzin (*kun bzang padma chos 'dzin*) and Lama Gendun of Rekong (*re kong bla ma dge 'dun*) are the two Mantra adepts mentioned here.
247. Mathog Rinchen was one of the twenty-five disciples.
248. This is reference to one of the eight great sons of Heruka Dudjom Lingpa, Khentrul Dzamling Wangyur (*mkhyen sprul 'dzam gling dbang sgyur*), who was a well-known emanation of the great master Do Khyentse Yeshe Dorje.
249. These are the original terma ḍākinī symbols that the Tertön received to decode and reveal the terma.

Index

About the Authors & Translators

Pema Lungtok Gyatso, or Wangda'e Kyabgon, was born in 1852 in the Golog region of Tibet and was a nonsectarian scholar learned in the philosophical tenets of the schools of Buddhism in their entirety, including all subjects of knowledge. He was a great master of the lineage and a highly realized individual, as well as being a regent of the terma revelations of his father guru, Dudjom Lingpa. He received all empowerments, teachings, and transmissions from the Great Tertön directly, as well as permission to compose this commentary. There are various accounts of the astonishing signs of accomplishment that occurred when he left his body, but the date is unknown.

Dudjom Lingpa (1835-1904) was one of the most prolific tertöns, or treasure revealers, of the nineteenth century from the Golog region of Tibet, who received many termas through profound visionary experiences. Thirteen of his heart disciples attained rainbow body. His enlightened speech, mind, and activity emanations included Kyabje Dudjom Rinpoche, Jigdral Yeshe Dorje, as his immediate enlightened mind incarnation; Tertön Kunzang Nyima as his speech emanation; and Tülku Natsok Rangdrol, his enlightened activity emanation. Kyabje Dudjom Rinpoche traveled to many countries throughout the world where he propagated the dharma, in particular the Nyingma tradition and the new termas of his predecessor as well as his own.

Lama Chönam, Chöying Namgyal, was born in the Golog area of Tibet in 1964. His root teacher, Khenpo Münsel, was a direct disciple of Khenpo Ngagchung and was himself one of the great authentic Mahāsandhi masters of the twentieth century. Lama Chönam spent many years studying and practicing under his guidance. In 1992, Lama Chönam left Tibet and later came to the United States, where he met Thinley Norbu Rinpoche and was fortunate to become his disciple. With Rinpoche's blessings and encouragement, he has been working to translate, teach, and propagate the dharma for nearly twenty years in the United States. In 1999, he established the Light of Berotsana Translation Group and within that context works to translate classical texts of the Tibetan Buddhist literary tradition.

Sangye Khandro has been a student of Buddhism since 1971 and a translator of the Dharma since 1976. She has helped to establish numerous centers in the USA and has served as translator for many prominent masters in all four lineages. Sangye has been the spiritual companion of the Venerable Gyatrul Rinpoche for nearly forty years and has continued to help serve the centers established by her root teacher, Kyabje Dudjom Rinpoche, with whom she studied and practiced for many years. In 1999, Sangye founded the Light of Berotsana Translation Group and continues within that context to translate classical texts of the Tibetan Buddhist literary tradition.

OTHER BOOKS TRANSLATED BY LIGHT OF BEROTSANA

A Garland of Immortal Wish-fulfilling Trees

Generating the Deity

Ancient Wisdom, with B. Alan Wallace

Perfect Conduct, Ascertaining the Three Vows, with Khenpo Gyurme Samdrub

The Fierce Wisdom, Channels, and Winds

The Lives and Liberation of Princess Mandarava

An Ornament of the Great Mother's Wisdom

Heart Essence of Saraha, 1st Edition

Sole Essence of Clear Light

Yeshe Lama

The Epic of Gesar of Ling—Gesar's Magical Birth, Early Years,
and Coronation as King, with Robin Kornman, PhD

The Guhyagarbha Series:

- The Guhyagarbha Tantra & Dispelling Darkness throughout the Ten Directions
- Essence of Clear Light
- Key to the Precious Treasury

ཡི་གེ་ནི་ཤྲུ་ཙྪ་ཧྲུག་པ་འདི། དཔེ་ཆའི་ནང་དུ་བཞག་ན་དཔེ་ཆ་དེ་ཅི་འདྲར་
བགོམས་ཀྱང་ཉེས་པ་མི་འབྱུང་བར་འཇམ་དཔལ་རྩ་རྒྱུད་ལས་གསུངས་སོ།